The Majority Press

EYES TO MY SOUL: The Rise *Or* Decline of a Black FBI Agent.

TYRONE POWERS is an instructor of Criminal Justice and Law Enforcement at Anne Arundel Community College in Arnold, Maryland. He is also a part-time instructor of Criminal Justice and Public Administration at Coppin State College in Baltimore, Maryland. He received his MPA at the University of Cincinnati and his B.Sc. in Criminal Justice at Coppin State College. He is currently a Ph.D. candidate in Sociology/Justice at The American University in Washington, D.C. He was a Maryland State Trooper for three years and a Special Agent with the Federal Bureau of Investigation assigned to Cincinnati, Ohio and Detroit, Michigan for nine years. He currently resides in Baltimore, Maryland.

EYES TO MY SOUL

The Rise *Or* Decline of a Black FBI Agent

Tyrone Powers

THE MAJORITY PRESS
P.O. Box 538
Dover, MA 02030

Library of Congress Cataloging-in-Publication Data

Powers, Tyrone, 1961-
    Eyes to my soul : the rise or decline of a Black FBI agent /
Tyrone Powers.
        p. cm.
    Includes bibliographical references and index.
    ISBN 0-912469-33-1
    l. Powers, Tyrone, 1961- . 2. Afro-Americans--Maryland
-Baltimore--Biography.   3. Baltimore (Md.)--Biography.   4.
Maryland
    State Police--Officials and employees--Biography. 5. United States.
    Federal   Bureau   of   Investigation--Officials   and   employees--
Biography.
    6.   Afro-American   police--Maryland--Biography.   7.   Police--
Maryland-
    -Biography. 8. Racism--United States. 9. United States--Race
    relations. I. Title.
    E185.97.P69A3 1996
    363.2'092--dc20
    [B]   95-47232
                                                                         CIP

First published in 1996

10 9 8 7 6 5 4

The Majority Press, Inc.
P.O. Box 538
Dover, Massachusetts 02030

Printed in the United States of America

EYES TO MY SOUL

The Rise *Or* Decline of a Black FBI Agent

Tyrone Powers

This book is dedicated to the life and death
of my brother, Cornelius Elijah Powers.

...Listen to the silence

Only guard yourself and guard your soul carefully.
Lest you forget the things your eyes saw. And lest
these things depart your heart all the days of your
life. And you shall make them known to your children,
and your children's children.

–Deuteronomy 4:9

And so the formula, the recipe,
for killing Black men emerges:

Imbue them with the American dream; then deny them the fulfillment of that dream. Tantalize them with the faith that things can be changed through application of the Christian gospel; fill them with guilt if they deviate from this gospel and then violently refuse to respond to their attempts at nonviolent protest. Finally, push the Black man to the point where he must violate his own ethical code in order to achieve that which he deems good, worthy and just.

Stir all this well; administer liberal doses in church, in school, in all public media, in every aspect of the Black man's daily life. Repeat as often as needed.

Death—as Malcolm X and Martin Luther King Jr. proved—will follow.

–Louis E. Lomax, To Kill A Black Man

Acknowledgments

The writing of this book was not completed due to my efforts alone. It could not have been accomplished without the dedication, patience, and understanding of many people. Truly, those having the most impact upon my life and my efforts in the writing of this book were women. I suppose that they were tired of seeing their men wasted. To all who assisted, I would like to extend my deepest appreciation. First and foremost, I would like to thank my beautiful wife, Doris. She endured all that I endured during the writing of this book. She was also a constant and sturdy shoulder for me to lean on. She assured me that telling the truth, no matter how painful and no matter the consequences, was always worth the effort.

Thank you, my lovely daughters Tamara and Tyra and my sons Tyrone Jr. and Malcolm, for your patience during the many hours that Dad could not share his time with you. Thanks to my strong mother Ruth Hinnant Powers, my grandmother Sarah Mae Smith, and my wonderful sister Sheila Thompthin. Thanks to my brothers, Frank, Quincy, Cornelius (Neil-Nate), and Warren. Thanks to my mother-in-law, Shirley Temple Day, who passed on during the writing of this book. Her strength to the bitter end allowed me to stand strong against the blatant racism that I encountered in the FBI. Thanks to Dorothy Prude, who, before she passed away, inspired me to work on this book and urged me to finish.

A very special thanks to the people listed below for lending me your ears, advice, and support. Nothing is accomplished without unity.

Ronald Allen; Dr. Tingba Apidta; Dr. Mary Bailey; Edward Blackmon; Lecia Blackmon; Demaris Carter; Bernard Clark; Jeffrey Covington; Connie Crowder; Joyce Day; Constance Deweese; Charles Fowler; Byron Fox; Hattie Francis; Glenn Gest; Henry Glaspie III; Pamela Glaspie; David Grant; Dr. Raymond Ellis; James Harding; Paul Harris; Jean Hinton; John Hollifield; Ben Jefferson; Rhonda Kennedy; Edward Larkin Jr.; Kenneth Moore; Gwendolyn Powers; Jada Powers; Sheila Powers; Gregory Prude; Uvell Reeves; Arlene Robinson; Dwayne Robinson; Samuel Robinson; Gloria Ross; Prince Earl Ross; Gregory

Sanders; Sarah Garret-Sanders; Corrine Shaw; Elijah Shaw; Chris Shivery; Jose Thompson; Wanda Thompson; Carmen Walker; Corrine Walker; Kevin Walker; Paul S. White; Gerald Williams; Martha G. Dunbar Williams; Kathee Williams; Rohan Williamson; Wanda Williamson; Frederick Wilson; Betty Jean Wilson; Royce Winters; Christine Witherspoon; Johnathan "X" (Carrol).

A very extra special thanks to my second mother and mentor, Dr. Elizabeth Gray, to my extraordinary editor, Sheila Thompson, and to my attorney and best friend, James William Morrison, Esquire. He guided me throughout the writing of this book and assisted me in confronting and overcoming the racially motivated persecution that I encountered within the hallowed halls of the Federal Bureau of Investigation.

Table of Contents

Introduction

I spent my youth on the streets of Baltimore City living in what many have defined as a ghetto. I witnessed the senseless murders and the unbridled drug dealing. In fact, on many occasions, I came within seconds of committing one of those senseless murders. I also came close to being a victim. I can say without equivocation that it was self-hate that caused me to come so close to taking the life of another human being. I hated myself; I hated my situation; and I hated those who were in the same position as I. My anger was uncontrolled and misdirected. The schools I attended, for the most part, helped to keep my soul fertile ground for more self-hate. They taught me nothing of the astonishing accomplishments of those like me. As a result, I had little faith in what I could accomplish. My Black history lessons started at slavery. Thus, I believed all that my ancestors had ever done was to work for white people. I was taught that we, as a race, had invented nothing and contributed nothing to "civilization." That many of the teachers who taught me were African American is an indication of how deeply rooted the problem is. I based my seeming inability to do math on the fact that my ancestors, during slavery, had been deprived of education and therefore had been unable to educate generations to come. It was a pitiful excuse, an easy way out. Strangely enough, very few of my teachers refuted the awful myth that I, and others like me, were uneducable.

Before I was too far gone, however, my family awakened me to reality. They forced me to open my inner eyes and take a long, hard, analytical look at my soul and the souls of those like me. They put me on the path to the true history of my people. Once I began to understand what those like me had accomplished, I believed in myself. I re-directed my energies from the deadly

1

streets to the enlightening libraries. I read the works of Frederick Douglass, Dr. W.E.B. DuBois, Booker T. Washington, Marcus Garvey, Kwame Nkrumah, Dr. John Henrik Clarke, Dr. Cheikh Anta Diop, Dr. Yosef ben-Jochannan, Dr. Carter G. Woodson, Dr. Ivan Van Sertima, Dr. John G. Jackson, Ernest Hemingway, William Faulkner, Winston Spencer Churchill, Thomas Jefferson, Abraham Lincoln, Stephen Douglas, John F. Kennedy, Max Hastings, Robert A. Caro, Paul Kennedy, Niccolo Machiavelli, Jean Jacques Rousseau, Adolf Hitler, and many, many others.

Mathematics and science were no longer insurmountable obstacles. I obtained a thirst and zeal for knowledge of every kind and in every field.

The opening of my mind and soul revealed to me what a brutal, unjust world we live in. These lessons were reenforced during my employment with two paramilitary organizations. During my employment with the Maryland State Police, I encountered racism on a daily basis. It didn't matter that I did the same job as the white troopers. I was Black and automatically considered inferior. I was called a "nigger" by the citizens whom I was sworn to protect and by the people for whom and with whom I worked. I witnessed firsthand the racial hatred of the Ku Klux Klan as I guarded their rally.

During my employment with the FBI, I felt the full blow of the racist hammer. I was persecuted for speaking up and defending African American people. I was shunned for complaining about Blacks' being referred to as "niggers." I was chastised for identifying racial problems and for trying to mend the fences of racial understanding. This persecution included surveillance of me and my family and false charges to destroy my character. When I spoke out against the persecution and presented my case to a law firm, I was told by an attorney that I had better find some *white* agents to corroborate my charges, because the judge and the jury would not be inclined to believe me if I had only Black *FBI agents* as witnesses. This statement in itself was ironic. All FBI agents were credible and believable during criminal trials, but if the judge had to choose between believing the sworn testimony of a Black agent and believing that of a white agent, the choice was obvious. The attorney who told me this was on my side. He was just telling me the brutal truth. In fact, he would be proved right when an administrative law judge refused to even hear my case against the FBI.

The Maryland State Police and the FBI taught me other lessons. I learned that the end really did justify the means. I took it upon myself to learn more about the Federal Emergency

Management Agency and the Federal Emergency Preparedness Agency. I studied the Trilateral Commission and the Committee on Foreign Relations. With the help of professors at Coppin State College in Baltimore, Maryland, I studied the international banking system and the intricacies of multinational corporations. The world that I had moved into was much more callous and brutal than the streets of Baltimore. There was so much deception.

This book is based on my life story and the story of my brother, Cornelius Elijah Powers. It is an account of how being an agent with the FBI played a prominent role in my education. That experience may also enlighten some of those who have been asleep.

Certain incidents in this book were relayed to me, while others I witnessed firsthand. Certain names have been changed for obvious reasons. The meetings and conversations took place. This is not just a surface book. It digs deep into the souls of the people involved. Deep into the souls of Black folk. I interviewed the people involved about the specifics of incidents and about the profound feelings they experienced as a result of the incidents. I wanted to take a thorough and sometimes painful look into their souls. I canvassed the neighborhoods of Baltimore to get a gut feeling of what was occurring on the day of my brother's death. This book adequately and accurately reflects those incidents and feelings.

W.E.B. DuBois was convinced that it was impossible to tell a story about Black folk without taking a deep look into their souls. It will probably surprise some that many so-called ghetto dwellers are not as dumb as they are thought, or portrayed, to be. The soulful people of Baltimore are not as unprepared to deal with the future as anticipated. The deception does not always work. I am living proof of that. True education and knowledge lowers the veil. I am sure that those who practice the art of deception understand this. I'm also sure that one of the reasons the education of inner-city youth remains such a low priority—despite the empty rhetoric—is that real education may create more analytical thinkers. It may shift the focus of young African Americans from the streets to the libraries. It may cause them to understand the constitution and its framers. It may destroy the desire to be conspicuous consumers. "Never awaken a sleeping GIANT."

Prologue

"Resist the devil and he will flee from you."
–The Holy Quran

My FBI supervisor approached my desk and looked over my shoulder at the *Cincinnati Enquirer* newspaper article I was reading. I knew exactly where he was positioned. I knew his height, weight, and strength. I read his vulnerabilities. Nate had taught me how to do this. How to get the most out of my soul. How to use its suppressed, hidden powers to protect my very life, its very life. How to cause it to revolve around my brown shell, like a surveillance camera, and assess the threat from my surroundings. I sensed my supervisor's cold, drawn body move up closer behind me. I could visualize the pastel-colored eyes that sat in his sunken sockets, the lifeless, stringy hair. His eyes moved from left to right with my eyes, across the article on the sanctions that had been placed on the South African government for the continuation of its satanic system of apartheid.

I felt the coldness from the depths of his soul as he opened the door to his frozen morgue and began to speak. "I don't understand these sanctions. They're stupid. We are only hurting Americans. I mean, take for instance my wife, how am I going to buy quality diamonds for her if we can't get them from South Africa? Everything else South Africa does to its people is irrelevant to me."

I didn't acknowledge his presence. As far as I was concerned he was just another zombie Klansman being utilized by the true holders of power to cause me to act in a self-destructive manner.

He was one of the cretins, shrouded in government sheets, who had invaded my FBI Academy dormitory room, attempting to bait me into a physical confrontation. I had ignored them, and I could certainly ignore this shadow of a man, this mentally infirm, frail agent-provocateur.

It seemed as if he was on a mission to engage me in a verbal and physical battle, a battle in which I could easily be made to seem the savage aggressor. Who would speak against him? Who would tell the truth? He was shadowboxing with me, waiting for me to throw an undisciplined rabbit punch so that he could justify my disqualification from this historically segregated and sexist arena. Or maybe he was testing me. Seeing if I were willing to make a Faustian deal, as the FBI's selection process had indicated. If not, this was the time to weed out a real Black man who was unwittingly let in through the narrow back door over which hung a sign that read "Negroes Only."

My supervisor continued his volley. "You know, being a racist is not the worst quality a man can have, or the worst thing a man can be. As long as he provides for his family and does his job, it shouldn't matter." I continued to read and to ignore. But now the simmering volcano deep within my agitated soul began to heat up. A mild rumbling from within overtook my calmness.

As the FBI's "defender of racists" continued his diatribe, I felt warm blood rushing over scattered, broken pieces of suppressed anger that had fallen from the neatly organized shelves of my previously orderly soul. Here before me, or rather behind me, was an FBI supervisor trying to draw me into a discussion on the "righteousness" of a racist and the "complications" that his wife faced because of sanctions in South Africa. Here stood a fraction of a man, whose duties included the defending of civil rights, telling me that the right of his wife to wear diamonds was more important than the lives of African people. He was perilously and wantonly poking a dagger into the soul of a Black man, and he knew it.

A cold, steely silence filled the suffocatingly warm room. A few of the other agents, who were seated at their desks, stopped working and provided the supervisor with the smiles and then the laughter that he so desperately craved. The laughter indicated recognition of a frail insecure human being. It indicated support for a being who needed to know that he had the power to do *something*—the power to move people toward some type, any type, of emotion. The laughter echoed throughout his hollow soul and puffed up his bony chest. His smile widened. A few other agents, who I believe did not agree with the warped statements of their superior, presented only dry grins to the speaker.

The supervisor was not yet completely satisfied. He had not moved me. I was not smiling or laughing. I sat there, solid, unmoved, unruffled. Either I was supposed to create a fake grin, show my white teeth, and chuckle like a good ol' negro or I was supposed to get up and scream and holler like a hysterical, distressed nigger. Maybe I would physically strike out at him. He had provided the necessary stimulant. It was the same type of incitement that James Thorton had told me was intentionally being used to goad the inner-city community to react in a certain, predicted manner, thus allowing those in control to justify their own heightened reaction, which in reality was a well-planned, well-thought-out, strategic provocation.

The supervisor was determined to fit me snugly into one of two clearly defined categories: "good nigger" or "malcontent troublemaker." He just needed me to reveal myself. Thoughts and memories of words said reverberated in my mind. Echoes of past conversations made relevant by the current event. "They always know what buttons to push." James said that those in power knew how to cause a riot. Well, James was right. For within my soul there was a riot of emotions. I could feel the heat from the fire. Nonetheless, I refused to succumb to the urgings of my emotions. I would not extinguish the fire, rather I would control it and limit its expansion with a strategically placed fire line.

My refusal to bare my soul to this FBI provocateur caused him much consternation. His thin pink lips straightened across his reddened face. His eyebrows became hunched like the back of an agitated cat. Something was wrong. He had put a worm on the hook but the fish wasn't biting. He would get a reaction. He had to. He decided to attempt the more risky tactic of direct confrontation. This tactic would most assuredly cause him to reveal his white Klan hood; his provocation would be obvious. But it no longer mattered. No witness would testify against him. I had to be classified.

"Mr. Powers, what do you think? Do I have a point?" I hesitated. I knew what I wanted to say and how I wanted to say it. I wanted to say "Fuck you and your wife." I wanted to tell him that any woman that would marry an idiot such as him didn't deserve a diamond or anything else. I wanted to confront him physically. To crush every bone in the coward's racist body. But what would that get me besides dead? His whinnying voice broke into my pleasurable plans of forbidden murder. "Do you agree?"

I scanned the room, stood up, and looked straight into the eyes of my tormentor. "Personally, I want nothing to do with a racist. I have found that most of them are cowards who would never confront the object of their hate one-on-one, face-to-face. They hide away in some dark closet and engage in perverted conversations with their sick, cowardly cohorts. Have you ever known a racist to face a man one-on-one without his friends or a weapon? Secondly, I have to assume that every racist is out to destroy me; therefore, I must make it my goal to be prepared to destroy him. I don't give a damn about what he does for his family. In fact, I don't give a damn about his family because I know he cares nothing about mine."

The room fell completely silent. The smiles and smirks disappeared. I continued, "As for the sanctions against South Africa, I think it's all bullshit. I think the United States is supplying South Africa with everything they ask for when they ask for it. I think the U.S. is still trading with them. I think that if the Blacks in South Africa want freedom, they are going to have to take it and not wait for the effects of sanctions or the benevolence of the rest of the uncaring world. There are too many people more concerned about their wives' having diamonds than about Black folks' lives. Once they realize that in South Africa, they won't expect help from any outside forces. They will either obtain their freedom by force or die trying."

I moved around or through the thin, frail being and out into the silent hallway. I headed nowhere or anywhere, just away from the danger of my anger—the danger of striking out at an insignificant decoy. I had heard enough and so had he. I figured that I would be labeled because I had dared to express the truth. I had dared to look him right in the eyes. I had not remained silent. I had not shuffled and smiled and shown my teeth. I had stood up. I was not supposed to do that; I was supposed to reply in a meek fashion, nodding my head in agreement with whatever he said. To have done so would have meant that I passed the test, that I was okay, that the selection process worked perfectly. I was to have no thoughts except those propagated by my FBI "superiors." I had gone too far. I was reading and thinking on my own and had the nerve to voice my thoughts. I had defied the system. I had not stayed "in my place." From this point forward the FBI would try, in its own words, to "handle the troublemaker."

1

Valley of Death

...Yea, though I walk through the valley of the shadow of death, I will fear no evil: for Thou art with me; thy rod and thy staff comfort me. Thou preparest a table before me in the presence of mine enemies: Thou anointest my head with oil; my cup runneth over. Surely goodness and mercy shall follow me all the days of my life and I will dwell in the house of the Lord forever.

–Psalm 23

As the plane descended from the dark summer sky, I tried to prepare myself for the scene that I was about to encounter. The descent was smooth and uneventful, but my soul was in turbulence and there was nothing I could do to stop the uncomfortable rumbling within me. An oppressive warmth engulfed my inner body, and I felt as if I were sweating internally. I took a deep breath and attempted to scan the airplane to see whether any of the other passengers noticed my discomfort. I couldn't have that. It was important that I kept my feelings hidden. I had learned that exposing my inner feelings was not unlike an army general giving away battle plans—once my feelings were known, my soul would be subjected to all kinds of attacks.

My attempt to scan the plane was futile; I was unable to remove my fixed stare from the lights of the city below. I was hypnotised. My attention and thoughts were drawn to those lights by some powerful magnetic force which I had no ability to resist. I felt as if I were trapped within an awful dream. I felt myself calling out to the other passengers. If only one of them would touch me, then maybe I would be free. But this was no dream. There would be no great escape. The lights were real. Soon I would be under those lights. I would be back in the city of my birth. I felt as though I were returning to the womb of my mother. The city below was a familiar place in which I had resided, yet the return would not be pleasant.

I had left Baltimore feeling as if I had accomplished something, but a more thorough examination revealed that I had actually regressed. I had abandoned those who cared the most about me for a vision that was nothing more than a purposeful illusion. I had left the womb prematurely and was suffering all the ill effects of such an early departure. Now I was coming home, home to a dying brother.

The loud roar of the engines as the jet pulled up to the gate was not enough to drown out the cries of my dying brother. I could hear him. The dinging sound notifying me that I was free to unlock my seat belt and leave could not release me from my paralyzing state of guilt. Unfastening the seat belt could not release me from my thoughts. I stood up and reached into the inner pocket of my dark blue Brooks Brothers suit. I wanted to make sure that I had not lost my FBI credentials. My badge had come to represent me. And every FBI agent knew that the losing of his FBI credentials would result in severe disciplinary action. The threat—and fear—of disciplinary action reenforced to all Special Agents of the FBI that the badge was the men and women who carried it. The agent belonged completely to the FBI. Nothing was more important. To lose your badge was to lose your very soul. I was relieved to find that my credentials were still in my left inner pocket. And then I felt guilty for caring.

I rented a car at the airport and began my journey to the hospital. I drove along the same route I had taken when I had left Baltimore three years earlier. Since my departure, it seemed that my life was in a constant state of reversal. Now, once again, I was returning to a path that I had previously traveled. There was no need to call anyone to let them know I was in town. They all knew that I would be coming home eventually; they just didn't know what it would take to bring me back. Besides, I needed time alone to think. I needed to cry alone. Once I came in contact with people, there could be no more crying. Tears were an unacceptable show of cowardice, an indication of weakness in a world where weaknesses were exploited.

The frantic call from my crying sister Sugar had made me aware that my brother Nate had been rushed to the Greater

Baltimore Medical Center. The call had come hours earlier. I was too many miles away to respond quickly. Too many miles away to be of any assistance, or to offer any words of encouragement. There was no need to rush now. But I was rushing. I felt as if I were running in slow motion. Running in water. Moving toward something or some place that I should have never left.

To ensure that I would not reach the hospital in tears, I decided to stop by the home of Dwayne Robinson. Dwayne was a real good brother, a close friend whom I had grown up with. He had a strong family behind him, and his mom and dad treated me as if I were their natural child. Dwayne and I had attended Southwestern High School together. We had spent our Sunday mornings together at the Christian Community Church of God located on Baltimore Street, listening to, or actually pretending to listen to, the sermons of Reverend Elder C. Green. We had sung in the United Voices youth choir. We had fought together in the mean streets of Baltimore. Thanks to our families, we evolved from fighting to studying. We studied together. He and I became intimately concerned about the plight of Black people and Black youth in particular.

I admired Dwayne and his stand on issues involving Black people. Dwayne was no sellout. He and I had been through some difficult times, times that had tested our friendship. But nothing or no one could divide us. We wouldn't allow it to happen. I believe that Dwayne admired me, though we sometimes disagreed on various topics of discussion. He had tried to talk me out of leaving Baltimore. And he certainly was not in favor of my becoming a Special Agent with the Federal Bureau of Investigation. He felt that there was so much to be done for our people and that we had to play a role—we had to be a part of the solution. I recall him saying that we could not allow our knowledge to go to waste. So many times over the years his words had reverberated in my ears: "...part of the solution. We must be a part of the solution." I knew that brother Dwayne would be there for me.

Dwayne had already received the news about Nate. He was also aware that I would be in town. I slowly pulled up and parked on the street in front of his town house. Dwayne lived on Carriage Court, on the northwest side of Baltimore. Across from his house stood Rock Glen Middle School, which I had attended. I put my hand up to the car window and tried to touch the memories that I had left behind. I took a deep breath and began to get out of the car. As I turned toward Dwayne's house and peered through the cold, driving rain, Dwayne opened his door and, in seemingly slow motion, began to walk toward me. No rush. It was as if he knew that I would be coming for him; as if he somehow knew the exact time of my arrival. He paused for a second and looked around. As he continued his walk, I noticed his wife Bobbie in the lighted doorway behind him. I saw Dwayne; I saw Bobbie—yet I could hear nothing. It was as if I were watching a silent movie.

Bobbie watched Dwayne as if he were a warrior going out to fight some battle in a never-ending war. Dwayne had once said that a Black man in America entered battle every time he walked the streets. He said that every time he left his home he had to prepare for the worst and assume that the enemy was all about him. It was unfortunate, but as Black men in America we had to deal with the cold reality. We had to deal with the results of miseducation. Dwayne believed that the strong young Black warriors that preyed on other Blacks were a deliberate creation of those who wanted to annihilate the Black race. He said the devised division within the Black race and the deliberate destruction of the Black man were two of the most interesting and incredible events in history. He stated that they would make the perfect subject for a doctoral dissertation.

As Dwayne approached, I returned to the car. He never said a word. He pulled the collar of his black raincoat up close around his neck and got into the car. Beads of rainwater raced down his coat. Dwayne never turned my way. I slowly drove away. The image of Bobbie standing in the doorway faded into the night. The sound of rain beating down on the car broke into my once silent world. Dwayne peered out the window into the darkness. He remained silent. I turned on the radio. Miles Davis' "Blue in Green" oozed out of the car speakers. Miles was all we needed. There was nothing to be said.

The drive to the hospital took only a short period of time, or so it seemed. Nothing was really as it seemed anymore. As we exited the car, Dwayne appeared to be in prayer. My praying days were over. I had seen too much misery and experienced too much pain to believe that prayer could do anything for me, especially now. I looked up at the tall building that housed so much pain. The rain poured onto my face. Dwayne and I slowly crossed the parking lot and entered the hospital. I turned and walked toward Nate's room. Despite the fact that I had never been there before, I seemed to know just where to go.

Dwayne and I moved through the phenol-smelling hallways. As we turned a corner and began to walk past a sign designating the Critical Care Unit, a nurse stopped us. Before she could question me, I looked into her eyes and said, "Nate Powers. I mean, Cornelius Elijah Powers." She turned slowly and pointed me to a room at the end of the hall. It seemed as though she had been through this scenario before; only the faces were different. I continued my walk down the hallway. But now it no longer seemed to be a hallway. It seemed different, like a tunnel, maybe a road—a road that seemed to have a steep descent. I felt as if I were taking a long, lonely walk into the valley of the shadow of death.

Dwayne stood with the nurse. He had the feeling that I was going to cry, and he didn't want to see me that way. He, too, believed that feelings were better left covered. I dared not look back until I reached the door to the room. I paused at the door to Room 700, took a deep breath, and finally looked back toward Dwayne. I returned to my silent world. I could read Dwayne's lips, "Stay strong, brother." I entered Room 700.

My eyes immediately became fixed upon Mom. She stood next to the bed that held my brother...and she was crying. Tears easily rolled down her face. I had never seen her cry like this before. I had once seen her weep, but never cry like this. Tears flowed freely. A small amount of mucus trickled from her nose. Her body quivered from head to toe. Her smooth hand was tenderly wrapped around Nate's hand. Nate's hand was motionless. Mom cried and prayed. "Please, God, don't take my boy. He ain't so bad. Hold on, Nate. Hold on." She never looked up at me. I looked at Nate. He wasn't moving. I wanted him to move, even if just a little. I noticed Mom's tears streaming down Nate's arm.

Mom continued to pray. "Please, God, he's too young to die. Give him a chance, Lord. Nate ain't never had a chance. Please, God, save Nate for me. I been good, God. I done all you said to do. Please, somebody help me. Somebody help him. God, please save my baby." Mom's crying was cutting through my soul. Her crying was breaking down my defenses. I couldn't let it happen. I wanted to cover Mom's mouth. I didn't want her to talk about Nate's life or Nate's death or Nate's youth.

Mom's prayer seemed so simple. She was just asking God to save her son. That was all. She wasn't asking Him to save the world. She wasn't asking Him to save the poor starving children of Africa, as she had often done. Tonight she was only asking God to save her son. Save the child that she had carried for nine months. Save the child that had been in this world for only a short period of time. Mom believed that God would do it. It was a simple, uncomplicated request. God would save Nate. He had to save Nate. Nate was just too young to die.

Never too young to die. Why couldn't Mom understand that fact? No one is ever too young for anything. In fact, it was Nate's youth and his attempt to escape his youth—as if his youth were a spider's web and he, an ensnared insect—that caused him so much pain. It was the turmoil of being young and Black that drove him to this bed, in this room, on this day, with all of these tubes sprouting from him. It was his life, his youth, his existence, his color that drove him here to this machine with all its lifeless tubes. This lifeless machine whose job it was to restore life or keep life in Nate's body, or in any body; this manmade machine whose purpose was to save a life, any life, gave no regard to whose life it was trying to preserve. It seemed strange. Only something inanimate had the ability to deal fairly with everyone and anyone it encountered. This machine had not been brainwashed into a superiority or inferiority complex. This machine had not been taught to hate or destroy. This machine did not know about greed. Only a lifeless mechanical device was willing to give a Black man an equal chance at living.

I returned my attention to Nate. I wanted him to call out my name as he had done when we had been home together. I wanted to see him smile and hear him laugh a little. I wanted him to re-create the dance that he had made up when we were younger. I wanted him to get up, grab a broomstick, and mimic the Temptations as he had once done. I wanted him to sing Marvin Gaye's "Trouble Man," which he claimed was a song about him. I wanted him to call out to his family, to all his brothers and his sister. I wanted to hear him call for Mom or Frank or Quincy or Sugar or Warren. A few hours earlier, he had been calling out for Mom. He was calling for Mom while he waited for someone to come and save him from death. He had cried and screamed and yelled for Sugar and Warren. He had reached for Frank's hand and looked for Quincy's face. He had whispered for me as his insides twisted with burning pain. He wanted his family to stop the pain. To stop his blood from boiling. His eyes had been wide open as he searched for one familiar face. Now my brother lay in this chamber of death, with his eyes closed. He could not see or call out to us. He could not feel Mom's hand wipe the blood from around his mouth as it trickled down the side of his face. Nate could feel nothing, yet he was not dead. Maybe he was dying or trying to die, but he was not yet dead.

Mom's body continued to shake. She kneeled down next to Nate. I didn't want to see her pray. I silently screamed for her to get up. I was in that pool of water again. This time I was completely submerged. I was screaming through the water.

Screaming in slow motion. Always in slow motion. Always too late. No one could hear me. Mom couldn't hear me. *Please, Mom, get up. Don't pray. Get up.*

I shifted my eyes away from Mom and Nate and looked around the room. This awful chamber of death seemed so cold...so impersonal. My mind wandered. How many others had come to this room to be rescued or to die? How many moms had cried for their children? How many prayers had gone unanswered? The room was not unlike the rest of the world: it was a place in which to die. And all the crying in the world would not help. Very few people cared about Nate's dying, just as very few cared about his living. This chamber could not care less who was brought into its bowels to die. It didn't care if Nate lived or died, for tomorrow some other Black child would be lying here and waiting for death inside these cold walls. Some other mother would surely be begging for the mercy of a God that she could not see.

My eyes moved from Mom and turned back toward Nate. I guess I had been turning to Nate all my life. I had turned to him for answers to problems I didn't understand. I had tried to understand his actions. I tried to understand why he had failed to utilize the knowledge that he possessed toward some constructive end, why he had put pressure on me to act on his knowledge. I had turned to him for the courage that I could never muster up on my own. Now I turned and moved closer to him as he moved farther away from this world and from me. He would not be able to answer my questions any longer. I would be alone. There was a void in me that only Nate could fill. A part of me that I reserved for him. Now there would be a permanent vacuum. An eternal emptiness.

I reached out and touched Nate's hand—he felt so cold. He looked so cold that I wanted to cover him with a blanket. I wanted to hide his suffering; he would have wanted that. I watched as blood dribbled from his nostrils. I wanted to wipe the blood away but I couldn't move. I couldn't touch my brother's blood. His chest moved slowly up and down, and a thin streak of blood sneaked out from the side of his mouth and made its way down to the white sheets. A small puddle of blood had formed next to his head and instead of soaking into the sheets, it appeared to get larger with each passing moment. Why was no one wiping the blood away? Why was no one cleaning out Nate's mouth? Nate wasn't dead yet. God was coming to save him. God was going to save him for Mom. Mom would always sing about God taking care of us. It wasn't too late. God was coming. Why was Nate here anyway?

I abruptly turned away from Nate. I couldn't cry now. I felt Dwayne watching. I could hear him saying, "Be strong, brother." A nurse appeared in front of me out of nowhere. Maybe she had been there all the time. She stared into my eyes and then quickly turned away. I caught her. She must have been trying to read my soul. I resented it. I swore I heard her sarcastically say, "Special Agent Tyrone Powers, huh." I loosened my tie and unbuttoned the top button on my shirt. I wanted to take my suit off. I didn't want to be dressed for a funeral. Nate was not going to die. I wiped the beaded sweat from my forehead. I felt my pocket for my badge. It was still there. I returned my attention to the nurse. What was she thinking? Was I just another brother to another nameless ghetto child? Did she know what I did for a living? Did she know that I had abandoned my brother to live in a make-believe white world? Did she know that I had abandoned those who desired to be with me to be with those who resented me? She had no business knowing anything about me. She had no business trying to read my soul. She was supposed to be saving my brother. Who gave her the right to open me up?

I wiped more sweat from my face; it just kept coming back. The room had been remarkably cold just moments earlier and now it was unusually hot. I took off my jacket and moved even closer to Nate. *Please, Nate, please move for me. Don't do this to me, brother. Don't leave me here.* I loved Nate and yet, right now, I hated him, too. I hated him for being here and making me feel this way. I hated him for making Mom cry, for putting his family on display. I hated Mom for crying and for not being able to save Nate with her prayers. Mom told us that prayer worked. She promised us that God heard our prayers. She promised us that we could lean on Him. Mom said we all would die one day—but Nate was only twenty-nine.

I wanted Mom to call on God—as I had wanted Sugar to pray to God when Dad attacked her. I always wanted God to show me He existed, to show me He cared about what happened to us. God was always so real to Mom. I wanted God to forgive Nate and to stop punishing him. I wanted God to stop spanking Nate now. Nate had been spanked by God all his life; it was time for all the punishment and pain to end. But not like this. *Please, not like this.*

As I looked at Nate's beautiful brown face, I knew he was not afraid. He would always tell me that he agreed with Kwame Nkrumah's statement that the secret to life was to fear nothing.

He was not afraid of this day. It was not death that he feared. Death would cause him no pain. It was the pain which led to dying that he dreaded. Nate just wanted to get it over with. He wanted everything to happen quickly. No gradualism. No slow motion.

I didn't want to pray. I didn't want Mom to pray. Yet, I longed for understanding. I wanted Mom's God to help me understand why Nate was lying here dying. I needed to understand before it was too late. I wanted to fight the hate that I felt seeping into my body and attaching itself to my soul like a parasite. I was beginning to ache with hatred. I had seen what hate could do. Hate, the most powerful of all the emotions, could cause so much damage, so much destructive anger. Mine enemies could redirect the hate that emanated from me and use it against me. Booker T. Washington once said to never let a man drive you so low that you are made to hate him.

Hate. If I could be made to hate myself, I could be destroyed. I had been taught never to hate anyone or anything. Mom had taught us that hate was a destructive emotion. She told us to love everyone, because God made us all and God could make nothing bad or wrong. I just couldn't believe it anymore. Hate was taking all the love right out of me. Nate lying before me was creating hate.

As I stood watching Nate, I thought of all that he had taught me, all that he had asked of me. I had to turn my anger into something positive. I had to transform my hatred into courage. I was determined to do what Nate had asked of me: I was going to stand up and be a Black man, even if it meant that I would be persecuted. Maybe it was all right to hate if the hatred was channeled and directed at the right thing or the right person. Maybe I could utilize hate toward a constructive end. Maybe. But it was all too much to handle right now. It was too complicated a task for a twisted, confused soul. My hate was still uncontrollable. I hated life and death. I hated people. I hated that nurse who was trying to read my soul. I hated myself for not being able to help Nate.

Sweat rolled down my forehead. I felt for my badge—it wasn't there. I looked around for it. It had fallen to the floor and lay next to a puddle of Nate's blood. I didn't reach to pick it up. I didn't worry about it. I didn't care about the FBI's disciplinary system. Blood seeped from Nate's mouth. Mom continued to cry. "Nate, don't die. Don't leave me. Don't leave us. I've done everything I could to help him, to keep him moving in the right direction, to teach him love and forgiveness, to lead him right, to make him know God, and now when he needs me most, I can do nothing, nothing but watch him try to live. Please, God. Please come by here."

I felt rotten inside. My soul was dying. My spirit was dying. I felt as if I had abandoned Nate, abandoned Mom, abandoned Warren and Sugar; and I knew I had abandoned God. Mom had told us that God had given His only begotten Son to save the world. Now God was taking my brother. I did not wish to sacrifice my brother for this cold and callous world. I wasn't willing to give Nate up for any reason. God was giving me no choice. Mom cried; I watched—and Nate lay dying. He needed rest, I suppose. It had been a long journey traveled in a short period of time. Nate had never had time to take a break; he never had time to rest. I remembered a Bible lesson that I had learned in summer Bible school at the Christian Community Church of God: "To everything there is a season...a time to be born and a time to die." A time to die. Mom prayed, "Set thine house in order, for thou shalt die and not live. Pray, Nate. Pray with me."

2

God Knows

*If you can look into the seeds of time, and say
which grain will grow and which will not, speak
then to me, who neither beg nor fear your favors
nor your hate.*

—*Shakespeare*, Macbeth, I, 3

I remember Mom telling us that God knows everything. She would say that only God knows what will happen to us and exactly when it will happen. God knows the day and time we will be born and He knows the day of our death. God knows what is in our hearts. He knows our intentions. I wish God had told Mom what would happen to her when she met Dad. Maybe if she had known, she would have never dated him. Maybe she would have never married him. Maybe she would have never borne us. But Mom didn't know what would happen; only God knew—and He wasn't telling. I suppose God knew that this child of the so-called ghetto would some day become a Maryland State Trooper and one of the youngest African American FBI agents. God knew that I would speak out against racial injustice within the FBI. God knew that I would speak out against the biased manner in which the FBI handled civil rights investigations. God knew that the FBI would persecute me and try to drive me to insanity for my efforts. I guess God knew a long time ago what would also happen to Nate.

Mom was a beautiful sixteen-year-old girl. She was tall and slender with long black hair. Her skin was light, revealing an interracial union of her blood ancestors. On the day Mom met Dad she was wearing a below-the-knee-length brown dress trimmed with a border of white lace around the hem. A pair of long, slim legs jetted down from under her dress into a set of flat brown shoes that brought a logical but abrupt end to such a lovely creature. She had come to the Wilson, North Carolina bus station

18

to pick up Aunt Pearl and was quite unaware of the events that were about to take place. She didn't know that she was about to meet Dad and things would never be the same. Only God knew.

The Greyhound bus station in Wilson, North Carolina was typical of all bus stations in the South in 1948. It was a small, nondescript building in the middle of a dirt lot. A group of elderly white men sat outside playing a game of checkers and keeping an eye on the "colored folks." The men watched the buses as they arrived and departed. Every time a Black man or woman entered or exited a bus, the old men's concentration on the checker game would be temporarily broken and all eyes would become fixed upon the Black person. A "Whites Only" sign hung over the doorway to the lobby and the old men sat like guards to ensure the message on the sign was enforced. They knew that Blacks were coming home from the war, and they wanted to remind the Blacks that nothing had changed. They wanted to make it clear that the war the Blacks had fought had been for white Americans, not all Americans. The message was clear: it was okay to kill white men in Germany and yellow men in Japan, but it was not okay to be seated next to or eat with white men in the United States. In fact, it would never be okay to kill a white man again in peace or in war, no matter the justification.

Mom and her cousin Betty Jean sat outside at the rear of the station. It was a hot August day, but they really didn't mind being outside. Being outdoors and at the rear of the building kept them out of the intimidating glare of the old men. Mom heard the roar of a bus engine and the screeching of brakes. She and Betty Jean ran to the front and noticed a bus which had just arrived. A heavy-set old white man with sweat dripping from his face turned toward Mom and Betty Jean as they ran toward the bus. The man looked Mom up and down and smiled. Mom noticed him looking and quickly turned away. The man stood up and started walking toward them. A group of white people slowly exited the bus and attempted to shield their eyes from the bright southern sun. Just as the fat white man reached Mom, a Black soldier stepped down from the bus. The white man must have thought the soldier was coming home to Mom, because when he saw the soldier he stopped in his tracks. He looked up at the soldier and walked away. Mom didn't know this soldier yet. She didn't know that he would become her husband. She didn't know of the pain that would follow.

Dad stood there like an African warrior coming home from a battle. His dark ebony skin shone bright in the heat of the summer. His green uniform was neatly ironed and showed no evidence of the long journey that had been taken. His shoes were shined to perfection and he seemed unfazed by the dirt that was blowing across them. His long black fingers were wrapped around the handle of a cream-colored suitcase. He stepped down from the bus and stared at the group of checker players. The players stared back. Mom felt the tension between the group and Dad and moved to dispel it. She spoke to the uniformed stranger in a low trembling voice. Betty Jean looked at Mom in amazement because she knew that they were never to speak to strangers. Dad hesitated in removing his stare from the players, yet he could not ignore Mom's beauty. He smiled and spoke back.

Aunt Pearl stepped down from the bus and Betty Jean hugged her. Mom turned from Dad momentarily and embraced Aunt Pearl. Mom was mesmerized by Dad. Dad was a hero. He had gone off to fight in a war in another land and had returned still a strong man. He was strong enough to stare down a group of white men in the South. Mom was attracted not so much to Dad's handsomeness as to his bravery.

Dad came back from a war. He had conquered fear. He had been shot at and he had returned fire. He had stared Death in the face. Dad didn't mind fighting another battle. He knew that the group of men playing checkers had the same feelings toward him as did Adolf Hitler. He knew they wanted him dead. He knew they wanted all Black people dead, or as slaves. He knew that America and Germany were separated by boundaries, but philosophically they were one. As he stared at the men, he conjured up all the images of slavery. He could see Black men getting whipped and being separated from their wives and children. He could see beautiful Black women being raped and made to perform all kinds of perverted, degrading acts for white men. He could see Black women being made to have babies they never wanted. He could see those beautiful Black babies being torn from their mothers' arms and sold off to be the next generation of slaves. He could see big fat white men staring at young Black teenage girls with lust. He could see the young girls' fathers watching motionless and powerless as their daughters were raped. He could see young Black children being made to curl up around the feet of white men and women to keep them warm at night.

Dad had lost his fear of death. He had joined the army to kill. He wanted to kill white men who did awful things to Black people. It no longer mattered if he were killed in the process, for he felt he was already dead. It was a psychology that whites could not understand. It was a psychology they could not tolerate. If this Black man would not submit, if he would not sell out, then he had to be broken. His instinct to kill had to be harnessed and redirected. If he could not be taught to stop killing, then he had to be positioned where he could only hurt his own. He had to be stripped of any knowledge of his past; his mind and his soul had to be controlled. In fact, it was advantageous that he didn't stop killing, for there might be another war that required the services of uncontrolled killers who did not fear death. At that point they could use Dad and those like him.

Mom moved to Baltimore, Maryland in 1949 to live with her mother, who had moved from North Carolina years earlier. Mom had been reared by her grandmother. Now, like most country farm girls, she wanted a taste of the big-city life. Dad migrated north in search of better employment opportunities that he had heard were available in the North. His parents had also moved to Baltimore years earlier. Dad found a job in the hot and dangerous steel mills of the Bethlehem Steel Company in Dundalk, Maryland. Mom attended school.

Dad and Mom stayed in touch with each other since their meeting in North Carolina. In Baltimore they began a full-blown courtship. Dad treated Mom like an African queen. They enjoyed each other's company and smiled at the mere mention of each other's name. Dad was very protective of Mom. He was afraid that she was too innocent and naive to survive on her own in a racist country such as America. He loved her and vowed to kill anyone who brought harm to her. In 1951 they were married. Mom didn't know at the time that it would be Dad who brought the most harm to her. Only God knew.

3

Family

*The optimist proclaims that we live in the best of
all worlds; and the pessimist fears this is true.*
    –*Branch Cabell,* The Silver Stallion

It wasn't a bad place to live. Baltimore was an average east
coast city with a mixed population of Blacks, whites and Jews.
The inner-city school system was not the best or the worst. As in
most large cities, the best equipped and staffed schools were those
attended by whites. Everyone somewhat accepted the fact that the
city schools were not there to prepare us for college. We were to
be prepared for basic survival. We were to be the blue-collar
workers of America. The field hands. This was the unstated
mission of inner-city public schools.

The city was full of streets with common urban names such as
Washington Boulevard, Harlem Avenue, and Lincoln and
Jefferson Streets. And there was the notorious place of night
dreams and social gatherings: Pennsylvania Avenue. There was
the usual scene of boarded-up houses pasted with outdated posters,
which nobody read, announcing events, which nobody attended—
or, at least, no one admitted his attendance. There seemed to be a
church on every corner and a bar opposite every church. I suppose
the church was to save the souls of those in the bars, or maybe the
bars served as a meeting place for those disillusioned with the
church. Ironically, the churches and the bars were intended to
help the people escape the problems which life in the inner city—
or, for that matter, in the United States—presented. And they both
could be used to keep the people they served from making
progress.

We lived at 2247 W. Baltimore Street. Our home was a two-
story, red brick row house on the west side of town. Three pearly
white steps led up to a brown front door with a mock-brass

knocker on it. There was one large window on the first floor facing a rather wide two-lane street with traffic flowing in both directions. On the second floor there was a frontal bay window with two smaller windows on each side of the bay configuration. The second floor front room belonged to Mom and Dad.

An old door with peeling paint separated Mom and Dad's room from ours. There were six of us. Warren and I slept on bunk beds next to the wall in common with Mom and Dad's room. Quincy and Nate also had bunk beds which were positioned alongside the wall opposite ours. Frank slept on a twin-sized bed which was beside the middle wall in between the set of bunk beds. A single closet against the wall opposite Frank's bed held all of our clothing. Next to the closet there was an old scratched dresser with three drawers which stored our underwear. The room was small but we never complained. In fact, I don't think we realized how diminutive and confining it was until we left home.

A beige-colored door led from our room to a short hallway. Off to the right of the hallway was Sugar's room. At the end of the hallway was the bathroom. The bathroom was small with barely enough space to house the tub, sink, and toilet. The tub rested on four short legs. There was a small window on the back wall of the bathroom and a skylight above the toilet. The walls of the bathroom were beige and always appeared to be sweating as if they, too, were confined.

A stairwell with creaky wooden stairs connected the first and second floors of our home. Those stairs were the pathway to much joy as we crept down them on Christmas eve to get a peek at what Santa had left us. They were also the pathway that brought to our rooms the alluring aroma of Mom's scrumptious Sunday morning breakfasts and her mouth-watering Sunday evening dinners. Mom used the aroma of food to arouse us from our sleep and play and to lure us down the stairwell. Dad never lured us down the stairs. He would call out with a voice that created instant anxiety. Dad turned the pathway of joy into a tunnel of fear which seemed to lead to a dungeon of danger. When Dad called, it was not unlike being called down into hell by the devil.

The back porch of the house was our favorite meeting place. Out of the view of everyone else except those with whom we chose to share it, our porch was a place where we did not have to put on the seemingly mandated fake smiles. We could sit there and talk about the best of times and the worst of times. We could fantasize and imagine without being laughed at and told that our dreams were impossibilities. We could amuse ourselves for hours without being called niggers. All of our close friends would join us on the porch and we would talk and laugh and play out of the critical eyesight of the rest of America. That old porch gave us the feeling of being one big family united on our own little island. We were held together by the commonality of our circumstances: poor, Black, and living in America.

Bay-Bay, Craig, and Michael were brothers from next door. Bay-Bay was the oldest; then there was Michael; and finally, Craig. Chas was a close friend from across the alley. He actually lived on Booth Street, but the back of his house faced the alley and we identified as our turf everything that we could see from the porch. Melvin lived up the street. Nate and Bay-Bay were close, and I believe Bay-Bay had romantic inclinations toward Sugar. Warren and Craig were the best of friends and Chas and I were good friends. When we were on that porch it didn't matter that, as Ralph Ellison observed, we were invisible "simply because others refused to see us." We had somewhat accepted that others considered us invisible. We noticed that drug dealing in our neighborhoods was allowed and even encouraged, with police being paid off. We noticed that murders and rapes in the ghetto were ignored by the politicians. We also noticed that all of our accomplishments in academics and entrepreneurship went unseen. When foreign dignitaries visited America, they seemed never able to see us. It was as if the color of our skin were some technologically, or biologically, advanced type of camouflage that should have been the envy of any army. But on the porch, we viewed our invisibility as an advantage. At times it seemed like our perfect private world. This was our place. However, things would change. As Chinua Achebe stated, "things would fall apart."

We would sit on that porch and talk about getting away from Baltimore Street, about getting out of the ghetto. We would talk about what we were going to do when we became rich and could buy anything and everything we wanted. We wanted everything we saw white people with. They dictated our standards of what was good. We wanted new cars and fancy clothing. We wanted a big house with a big yard. And although the porch gave us so much joy, we wanted to get away from it, away from the row houses across the narrow and dirty alley. The television shows replete with white folks flaunted the wealth of America before us. *They* had everything; we had nothing. The television shows and the commercials reminded us that we were poor. They told us that we were lacking what America was all about. In some of us they created the desire to obtain what the other folks had, by any means necessary.

Nonetheless, we believed that our poverty was only a temporary condition and that things would get better. Our school teachers told us that we would never have all the things the white man had because that just was how it was planned. They never told us who planned it that way. Still, we believed that things would change. We believed that God was going to change things for us if we worked hard and obeyed His commandments. Mom had told us that hard work and constant prayer would change things. We would later find out that it took much more. In time we would begin to believe that God must answer the prayers of white people only. We would question the very existence of a God. And then we would question our questioning.

I remember us sitting on our porch on rainy Saturday afternoons. The rain always seemed to mean bad things were coming. In fact, anytime any fluids flowed in the ghetto, something bad was happening somewhere. We would sit there through the worst thunderstorms and wonder what was going to happen. The loud thunder and sharp lightning had little effect upon us. We would not run or jump or hide. We would stare right into the lightning, challenging it to do whatever damage it thought it could to us. The storms were a warning from God that trouble was rolling in. Sometimes we would tell jokes to ease our fears of the inevitable pain that the storm was bringing to some ghetto family. At other times we would just sit and stare into the pouring rain. Listening to it land as it spoke to us in a language that only we understood. Listening to it beat down on the concrete alley and the dirt yards. Listening to it fall on the paper-tarred roofs. Watching it run down the center of the alley like a mighty stream. A ghetto stream. Occasionally, Warren and I would break the silence by whispering something funny about Bay-Bay and Sugar. We would break into mild laughter for a few moments and then return to our silent world and allow the rain to continue its soliloquy. We were all so young.

Frank was seventeen and the eldest sibling; however, Quincy was the leader. We all looked up to Quincy. He never seemed to fear anything. He was fifteen and appeared to have already mastered fear, mastered everything. He was also very intelligent. His school teachers would praise his academic abilities, although they complained about his lack of discipline. Quincy would play hooky for a week and still get good grades on his tests. Everyone agreed that Quincy was going to be a lawyer or a doctor. Quincy never said much about his future. He was intelligent enough to know that there was another challenge that he had to overcome in order to make it. It was a challenge that white kids very seldom had to face. It was the challenge of surviving the inner-city streets of the ghetto.

The Baltimore City Police Department recruiter came to see Quincy while he was attending Edmonson High School. They were looking for bright young Black men to become police officers and they thought Quincy would be ideal. Quincy felt that he would just be a token. He said that the police just wanted a "nigger" to go arrest some "niggers." He said they used Black officers to infiltrate righteous organizations like the Black Panther Party. Quincy said that when something went wrong and one of the Panthers got shot, the white policemen could always point to the Black policemen to say that the shooting was not a result of prejudice or racism. My brother didn't want to be that token; he didn't want to be the one they pointed to as an example of "fairness." Years later I was to become what Quincy had resisted. I would become the "spook" sitting by the door that Sam Greenlee wrote about.

Quincy could not understand how Blacks could be talked into infiltrating Black organizations that were fighting for *equality*. He said there were traitors inside every Black organization. He would stare at us with those intense eyes and say there was nothing worse than a traitor. Quincy said that he would rather die than sell his soul. He would often say that maybe at some point in the future becoming a police officer, a keeper of the peace, would be a good career. But considering the conditions that Black people were being forced to live under, there could be no peace to keep.

It seemed that Nate was always close to Quincy, both physically and mentally, listening intently to whatever he was saying. Quincy was only two years older than Nate, yet Nate looked up to and admired him. He admired Quincy's bravery, intelligence, and seemingly complete lack of fear. Everyone in the neighborhood knew that Quincy would never run from a fight. Nate wanted that same reputation. He wanted everyone to know that he was Quincy's younger brother and that he would fight anyone to the death, if necessary.

Nate was never really accomplished in school work. None of his teachers tried to help him improve. He was to be just another uneducated Black child. His teachers had no time to give individual attention to any child who was having problems, academic or otherwise. There were too many children to look after, too many children to try to educate. There was to be an acceptable loss rate, and in schools that Blacks attended, there was no ceiling on how high that rate could go.

I think the way Dad treated Nate added to his failure in school. Dad had definably changed for the worst and Nate seemed to be paying the full price of Dad's metamorphosis. Dad would beat Nate for anything. He began beating Nate with his fist when Nate was only nine years old. He would punch Nate and tell him that he would never amount to anything. As we grew older, Dad would compare Nate's grades with mine and laugh at Nate. It was as if Dad were punishing Nate for failure; as if he saw in Nate all that had once happened to him and he wanted to destroy it. When he laughed at Nate, it was as if he were laughing at himself. Nate would not be the only one to suffer from the disfigurement of Dad's soul.

Nate wanted Dad to love him and to see that he was trying. Trying to please Dad. Trying to please Mom and Quincy and the rest of the world. Dad never gave Nate a chance. Nate began to hate Dad and everything about him. He couldn't understand how Mom could lie down and have sex with Dad. That's what it was. It was sex. Pure sex with no emotions. Nate became convinced that Dad was now incapable of any emotion except hate. Nate would say that he wished Dad hadn't made him. He denied that Dad was his father and would tell people he had a different father from the rest of us. Nate would say that his father was dead, that his father died in a war. Nate didn't know how close to the truth his statement was.

Nate would always try to sit next to Quincy on the back porch. He would ask whoever was sitting next to Quincy to scoot over so that he could sit down next to Quincy. He expected whatever Quincy had to say would be profound and worth hearing. He would stare right into Quincy's eyes and nod with every other word that exited Quincy's mouth. To Nate, Quincy was his father as well as his brother. Dad didn't exist.

There was something about Nate. He could be smiling and laughing one minute and the next minute he would be lost in his thoughts. He loved to sit and talk, and he enjoyed talking to Quincy more than any of us. He absorbed all that Quincy said to him. He had this constant need to be talked to and listened to. I believed what he liked most about Quincy was that Quincy was always willing to listen. Even after Nate grew older and moved out on his own, he would call Sugar and Quincy and Frank constantly with nothing really to talk about. Nate just needed to know that someone thought that he was significant enough to be listened to. He wanted to know that despite all Dad had said and done to him, he mattered to someone. He knew Mom loved him, but it was as if he needed acceptance from a male figure. Perhaps from someone closer to his age. Quincy became that male figure. And later Nate began to lean on me.

Once I left Baltimore, Nate would call me long distance and ask me about books that he could read. He didn't like the fact that I had left Baltimore to become an FBI agent. He hated what I was doing. But he felt the need to call and talk with me. It was his way of letting me know that he still loved me and respected the fact that I had attained some goal. He also wanted to make sure that I was still reading, because he believed that the more knowledge I obtained concerning our people, the more inclined I would be to return home where I was needed most. He would tell me that he wanted to go back to and complete high school but didn't feel he was prepared yet. I would tell him about various books and send him some from my personal library. He would call me back and tell me all about the books. He always seemed to be searching for the answer—for some answer that would make sense of everything that was occurring to us and around us. Sometimes he would look at me and say, "This is one fucked-up world."

Sugar was a year older than Nate. She was a regal bronze creature. I can remember looking at her from my position across the porch and thinking how beautiful she was. She was the only girl in the family. I could picture her being a young queen of one of the great African nations. Mom adored and spoiled Sugar. I think Mom wanted another girl, but after having all of us boys, she gave up on having another girl. I always believed that Sugar was smart even though the school would send home letters saying she wasn't. I started to believe that they sent letters home to all the Black children, telling their moms and dads that their children were dumb. When the parents told their children that their teachers said they were dumb, the children started to believe this insidious lie. It let the school system off the hook, but damaged the children forever. I knew Sugar was intelligent. I can still visualize her sitting there on the porch and glancing over toward Bay-Bay. Bay-Bay would glance back and they would somewhat smile. Sugar never really smiled that much, but she smiled a little at Bay-Bay. It was wonderful to see my sister smile if only for a little while. I wish she could have smiled all the time.

Nate was two years my elder and Warren was three years my junior. Warren and I would always find the same corner of the porch. We would sit near the back wall against the house. Our friends Craig and Chas sat near us. Chas and I were the same age and Craig and Warren were the same age. I could sometimes look into Warren's eyes and see how much he admired Nate. He jumped right over me to make that same connection with Nate that Nate had made with Quincy.

I recall Warren and me playing cowboys and Indians and Warren saying, "I want to be an Indian warrior like Nate." It was obvious that Nate had engaged in long talks with Warren. It was also obvious that Warren had listened. I would tell Warren that the Indians didn't have guns and the cowboys did. I would try to explain to him the difficulty the Indians had trying to win against the gun-toting cowboys. I told him that if he watched the television shows, he could see that. Warren would turn and say, "Warriors have heart and courage and they ain't afraid of nobody. They'll fight on, no matter what the odds." Later Warren and I would become the closest of all the brothers. Our thoughts would be at one.

Everyone said Craig was crazy. He would take on anyone big or small. Craig had this belief that he could beat anyone in a fight, and he had a desire to beat everyone. He saw it as a way of getting respect and being identified as someone significant. He enjoyed hearing some of the other boys in the neighborhood talking about how tough he was. Warren didn't fear Craig. In fact, although they were friends, they would often fight. When Craig won, he was happy. But when Warren won, Craig would get a bottle or a stick and chase him. I recall once, when Warren and Craig were about nine years old, they had fought and Warren had convincingly beaten Craig. Craig grabbed a large piece of broken board and chased Warren up and down Baltimore Street. Warren tried to run up the front steps to our house but lost his footing and fell head first into one of the corners of a step. Blood poured from the wound. Craig stood above him, holding the stick and breathing heavily. He dropped the stick and yelled out for help. Mom ran out of the house and found Warren lying on the ground holding his head. Craig stood watching with tears in his eyes. Mom gathered Warren up in her arms and carried him up the street to the emergency room at Bon Secours Hospital. It took twenty-six stitches to close the wound. Craig never apologized to Warren. It was all a part of the game. Craig was preparing himself for what he would have to face growing up Black in America. Survival of the fittest was the test, and the ghetto seemed to be an experiment conducted by those who wanted to verify Darwin's theory.

Black children have to grow up faster and learn quicker. From the time we leave our mother's womb we are compelled to start preparing for the worst. A whole different philosophy has to be learned. Black ghetto children have no time to think about college; they have to think about survival. For us survival meant being tough. Being brave. It meant having no fear of death—and that eventually meant having no fear of killing.

At an early age I tried to channel the aggressiveness of those around me into something positive. I understood that every day would be a battle. But something inside me would not allow those around me to die so young. I started an alley baseball league. It was six teams strong and the teams consisted of one man. That's right, one man. The teams were named after the baseball teams in the old Negro League. I learned about the Negro League teams from a book that was given to me by the librarian at Bentalou Elementary School. I was only eleven years old when I started my league. Warren was the Baltimore Black Sox. Craig was the New York Black Yankees. Chas's nephew, Ronald, was the Birmingham Black Barons. Tony, who lived across the street from us, was the Washington Elite Giants. Melvin was the Washington Homestead Grays. And a boy who lived down the street from us was the Philadelphia Stars.

Our baseball field was the hard concrete alley. I crushed corn flakes cereal boxes to make bases. The ball and bat were plastic. I was the umpire. The rules were simple. The kid on one team pitched the ball to the hitter. If the ball was hit straight down the narrow alley past the pitcher, the hitter ran the bases until the pitcher collected the ball and threw it home to me. Wherever the hitter was at that point was the spot where his imaginary runner would be until the hitter was able to get another hit and bring the runner home. If a ball was hit into one of the yards which lined the narrow alley, the hitter was automatically out. However, if the hitter hit the ball into the fourth yard down the alley from home plate, it was considered a home run. Three outs and the other team came up to bat. The hitters became adept at hitting the ball straight and at guiding it into the fourth yard. We played seven innings. And the games went by rather quickly.

I set up a schedule for games and posted it on the wall of our back porch. Everyone enjoyed the games and occasionally Frank, Quincy, Nate, Bay-Bay, and Chas came out and watched the games. The winner of the league would be given a medal that I purchased from the local drug store with money I earned from allowing the spectators (Frank, Quincy, Nate, Bay-Bay, and Chas) to bet on the inning in which they thought a home run would be hit. It was a quarter per bet and there were usually a number of bets on each inning depending on who the player, I mean, team, was. I also made enough money to have ice cream and cake at an awards ceremony on our porch at the end of the season. It was a good way to pass the time on hot, lazy summer afternoons. And the players, or teams, actually got better at playing and competing in the game of baseball. I was proud of myself for putting my little Negro League together.

As a child growing up, Warren was quiet for the most part. He would smile and laugh with Craig and me; however, although loud in volume, there was even a quietness in his laughter. He would play children's games but they always had a greater meaning for him. He always wanted to play the role of the underdog—an underdog who possessed no fear. Warren wanted the odds stacked against him. He said being the underdog was real to him. I wanted Warren to think about childlike things. I wanted him to play for fun. I did not want him to think about problems, or to think about underdogs and fear. I guess I had been taught to close my eyes to problems and I wanted Warren to do the same. But Warren wanted the truth. He wanted to deal with reality. He wanted to be like Nate.

Frank was such a loving brother. He seemed to feel bad for all of us, and he tried to be a father. Dad resented Frank's trying to be the man of the house. He wasn't the same Dad that Mom had befriended at the bus station in North Carolina. He would beat Frank with his fist for no reason at all. He would deny Frank more food at the dinner table. Frank would ask one of us to pass him some food and Dad would look at Frank and say, "You've had too much already." Frank's eyes would water and Mom would turn to him and her eyes would begin to water. Mom dared not say anything because it would just lead to Frank's getting another beating when she was away. Nate and Quincy would stare at each other for a moment, then return to eating. Warren would stop eating and stare at Dad. I would nudge Warren to disengage his stare. Frank would get up and leave the table. Warren would follow. Sugar would, without being excused, push her chair away and begin to collect the soiled plates. Dad, showing no concern, would reach for a bowl and put more food on his plate.

After dinner all of us siblings would go upstairs to our room and talk. Warren and I would sometimes wrestle on the floor. Frank would sit on his bed with his knees bent up to his chest and rock back and forth. Quincy and Nate would sit and talk about Dad. About hurting Dad. About killing Dad. I wished so, so many times that we could have locked ourselves away in that room and played and talked and rocked. But things would never be that simple.

4

Fatherly Betrayal

...Self-hate finally culminates in pure and direct self-destructive impulses and actions.
–*Karen Horney,* Neurosis and Human Growth

Hate is a strange emotion. It can become so intense that it goes beyond being just a feeling. Hate actually becomes something tangible. It can move through you like a cold breeze, chilling you internally. You can feel it as it racks your body and churns your insides. It slithers over your internal organs, causing them to tighten. And then it forces you to act. It cuts off all logical communication with the brain. It can create strength in a weak man. It can cause a strong man to become weak. It can give courage to a coward and make him do things, or make him believe that he can do things, that he is not otherwise capable of doing. It can make a meek, loving man, become an aggressive killer. Hate can ooze into anyone and everyone. Animals hate; humans hate. Adults hate. Unfortunately, children also can hate.

I don't mean the kind of hate that is caused by one specific event; I'm talking about a hate that is the result of a lifetime of compounded deprivation. Compounded insults. A lifetime of being used and abused. A lifetime of thinking you're being used and abused. A lifetime of hopelessness. A lifetime of being told that your life is hopeless. A lifetime of being told that you can produce nothing and contribute nothing. A lifetime of being lied to about your history and heritage. A lifetime of being chased by police for crimes you never committed. A lifetime of being told that you and all like you are criminals. A lifetime of being told that you can never be a leader. A lifetime of pain which leads to another lifetime of pain and another generation of pain and hate.

Hate can make you not want to get up in the morning. It can make you not want to lie down at night, because you know night leads to morning and you will get up hating. You hate to talk because you have nothing good to talk about, so you lie to yourself and pretend you have something good to talk about. Then you hate yourself for being a pretender and for having to pretend, or for believing that you have to pretend. You hate to walk, because no matter how far you walk you can never get away from the pain that surrounds you physically and engulfs you mentally.

If you allow it, hate will make you despise your future, because you know that no matter how far you advance you are the exception to the rule. You also know why you are that exception. You know that there are so many others like you who will not advance, no matter how talented or prepared they are. So you hate yourself for leaving so many others behind. You hate leaving because you know your soul is still not free even if you somehow convince yourself that your body is. You can never walk away from the rodents that are as common a part of inner-city living as the drug addicts and alcoholics that you step over trying to walk away from hate and what hate has created. As long as there are others left behind, you are locked with them.

Once you have seen it and lived it, you can never walk away or turn away from the young men and young women being wasted away by drugs and alcohol. You can never walk away from the beautiful young Black women who—only a few years from being girls—are selling their bodies for money. You can never walk away from the screaming hungry babies. You can never walk away from the lovely little children who will never have much of a chance to be anything but the next generation of ghetto children, children whose fathers are the drug addicts that you see nodding off into oblivion. You can never walk away from the wasted lives hanging on the corners of the inner-city streets. You can never walk away from the children who are known to you as Nate and Tyrone and Angel and Frank, but who are known to others as those little nigger kids. The children who will lose all hope and who will be chastised for having no faith in America and in a God made in the image of a white man.

So hate is created from this and by this. And hate continues and you continue to hate. You hate the future, for it will produce more hatred. You know that those who try to control the future will purposely produce more ghetto children. They will purposely try to produce more young female children who will become pregnant by the age of fourteen because they believe sex is the only free pleasure in their lives. You hate the drug pushers for selling these children drugs that end up killing them. You hate yourself for hating the drug pushers, although you know that the pushers are actually selling death. Ironically, death is the only freedom that is without pain for these children. And you hate yourself for feeling that way because you know that is exactly how those in control want you to feel and think. Finally, you find that you cannot eat or sleep because you hate that you are breathing and living. You would love to be dead, and yet you would hate to die.

It was this kind of manufactured hate that led Nate to the streets of Baltimore. It was this hate that would entirely possess Warren and cause him to act against the object of his hate. It is this kind of hate that will be with Sugar forever. How sad that the only love we had, for a period in our lives, was the love of hate.

It was another Tuesday night and Mom, as always, had left for church. Tuesday night was prayer service. Sometimes Mom would take us all, but this night she allowed Sugar, Warren, and me to stay home. Mom said that Sugar—who, at the time, was fifteen—was old enough to stay home and take care of us and that we were to obey her. I didn't mind Sugar being in charge because she was always so good to Warren and me. Over their objections, Frank, Quincy, and Nate went with Mom. Mom said they needed prayer. Actually, she believed that we all needed prayer, but they must have done something that week that required some extra prayer. Sugar, Warren, and I had been real good that week. We had figured out that being good was the way to get around Tuesday night church service. Not being forced to attend Tuesday night prayer service made us feel smarter than Frank, Nate, and Quincy. With Mom, there was no use arguing about attending church. Church was important to her. It made her happy and kept her believing in something. She had to know that there were brighter days ahead. She had to believe that there was a reason for our suffering and for the suffering of others. The church, at least, provided answers to some of her questions. And Mom refused to question the answers that she was given.

Dad never went to church. He had attended church for a while during the early years of his marriage to Mom, but he became disillusioned with it all. Dad stopped believing the answers that he was being given by the pastors. I don't think he cared too much about God. Maybe at some point he had cared. Maybe at some point he had faith in people and in God and in good deeds.

Something at some point had changed Dad. Mom would say that we all were born pure; we all were somebody's baby; we all cried in our mother's arms. "No one was born hating and killing and robbing and stealing." Mom said white babies weren't born lynching Black people and calling us niggers. It was taught! Whites were taught that they were better than Blacks simply because of the color of their skin. Arrogance, too, was a learned behavior. Blacks—through miseducation—were taught that they were inferior to whites and that they couldn't amount to anything—at least, not anything good. Mom constantly reminded us that we could be whatever we wanted, if we struggled. And there was no need to fool ourselves; we would have to struggle. For us, things would never be easy in this world. But we were not to wait before we tried to make things better for ourselves.

Mom said that people were changed by things outside the realm of what God had produced. God was not to blame. He did not teach people to hate. Dad was once a good strong Black man. Mom said Dad had believed in God but something had changed him. Something or someone had broken him. Some force that he did not understand had reduced him to only pieces of a man. Mom believed that with the help of God, she could rebuild her man.

Mom would be returning home from church around 10:30 p.m. Warren and I decided to stay up and wait so that we could tease Nate about having to go to church. Sugar went to bed early. She told us that she was not feeling well. She made us go to our room and told us to keep quiet so that Dad would not know we were still awake. Dad was downstairs watching television, or pretending to be watching television. Shortly after Mom left I heard the TV go off. Warren and I had been wrestling, but when the TV went off, we both froze. Warren abruptly hit me with a punch to the face. I was bigger and stronger than he, and Warren used my sudden distraction as an opportunity to gain an advantage in our playful struggle. Nate must have taught him that move. He had never done it before, even when the opportunity had presented itself. Nate must have taught him that even when the odds are against you, there always remained the element of surprise—seize the opportunity! Nate had taught me the same lesson. It was the lesson of Sun Tzu in his book *The Art of War*: "In battle, confrontation is done directly, victory is gained by surprise."

I pushed Warren's head down onto the floor; it made a dull thump. He struggled to get away and yelled, "I'm gon' tell Nate on you, punk. Nate gon' kick your ass." "Shut-up!" I quietly yelled back. "Boy you going to get us in trouble for real."

Warren read my face. He knew something was wrong. He could sense that there might be trouble. He looked up at me and whispered, "Is Dad coming up here?" Warren already knew the answer to his question. He could feel it. I looked into his eyes and I knew that he could feel it. He knew something was wrong and he knew that Dad had to be involved.

I heard Dad as he began to ascend the squeaky stairs. Dad had said that he was going to fix those steps. He said he was going to stop them from making noise. Dad hardly ever did what he said he was going to do, anymore. After coming home from work, he just sat around the house and stared at the television. Every once in a while, he would be in a good mood and laugh with us. As time went on, his good moods came to be few, and his laughter all but ceased. Dad began to undergo a metamorphosis. We just didn't know what to think of him anymore. Mom said Dad was under a lot of pressure. She said he had been through too much and couldn't handle any more. Someone was trying to finish him off. Dad was too Black and too strong and he had to be brought down. Dad didn't realize what was happening to him. He didn't realize that he was being broken like a wild bronco or a defiant slave. Dad was striking out at us to vent his frustrations with a white system which he could not touch. We were afraid that one day he would snap.

As Dad got closer to the top of the stairs, I heard his heavy breathing. He sounded like some kind of beast that could barely make it. I jumped up from the floor and turned the light switch off. The door to our room was closed. I was hoping that Dad would think that we were asleep. I whispered to Warren, "Come on, boy. Get in bed before Dad comes in here and beats our butts."

I reached out in the darkness to grab Warren. He was wet with perspiration and shivering. He began to cry, "Mom said we could stay up until she came home. She said we were good and didn't have to go get no prayers." I snapped back at Warren, "We ain't going to bed for real; we just trying to fool Dad so he don't beat us. Anyway, Mom didn't say we could stay up—Sugar did, and she done went to sleep." I pushed Warren toward the bed. He moved a little and continued to cry. I grabbed him with all the strength I had and threw him onto Frank's bed. I smiled to myself in the dark. For the moment, I was proud that I had so much strength, that I was more powerful than Warren. More powerful than somebody. For now, I had to conceal my joy from Warren. In the end, it was Warren who would prove to be stronger than I.

It was Warren who would find the inner strength to do what I could only imagine.

As Dad reached the top stair and stepped into the hallway, I heard him pause and turn toward our door. He was trying to determine if Warren and I were asleep. Even if we had been asleep, his laborious breathing would have awakened us. Dad was no longer the slender, strong soldier that Mom had immediately fallen in love with at the bus station in Wilson, North Carolina. He was older and softer. He had a stomach that appeared to be swollen. His hair was graying. His voice was weaker. He no longer stood erect. Something had entered into Dad's mind and made him forget that he was a warrior. Something had made him forget how he stared down the white checker players. He seemed no longer cognizant of what had made him confront white men in the South. His raucous breathing sounded as if deep down inside him his soul was suffering, suffering and searching for something that had been lost or taken away. Our dad was gone. What stood in front of the door was something created by means that had nothing to do with the biological process.

Warren continued to shiver. He shivered with anger; I quivered with fear. I feared that Warren would get up and confront Dad. I feared that he had had enough of running and hiding from Dad, that he had had enough of running and hiding from anything and everything. But Warren was not ready to confront Dad yet. It takes hate more time to develop than love. And only the perfect hate can cause you to act against that which has created you.

I wanted Mom to hate Dad for all the times he had taken his fist and punched her in the face. I wanted Mom to hate him for the times he wrestled her to the floor and sat on top of her while blood streamed from her nose. I wanted Mom to hate him for the times he held down Frank with his knee and pounded Frank's head to the floor. I wanted Mom to hate Dad for choking Nate. Hate couldn't grow in Mom. Her soul was too fertile with love. But hate could grow in Warren. And hate had already filled the void within Nate's soul.

Dad turned away from our door and walked toward the doorway to Sugar's room. I felt a cool satisfaction inside for being able to make Dad think that we were asleep. I was proud of my disingenuousness. We had played this game of freeze many times before. Warren and I had played it with Frank, Quincy, and Nate so that we could hear all the grown-up sex talk. But tonight I felt as if we had given our best performance. We were being sneaky and slick. On this night we would be taught a lesson. We would never play freeze again.

Dad opened the door to Sugar's room. Sugar was cuddled up in bed asleep. She had her blankets pulled tight around her. She was so beautiful, so calm and peaceful. A slim ray of light entered her bedroom through the partially open window. A cool breeze kept the thin curtains flapping. Peacefully flapping. Sugar had opened the window slightly to allow some of the clean winter air to circulate around her room. The room was usually hot even in the winter. Dad stood there and stared at Sugar. His chest moved up and down. Sweat beaded on his forehead. He reached up and wiped the sweat away from his face, and stepped inside Sugar's room.

His bare foot slid across the dusty floor. Dad used the thin beam of light to help guide him to Sugar. Dad was being drawn to Sugar. The light was drawing danger to Sugar. Something was drawing Dad to do evil.

Sugar must have felt evil at her back. She must have felt Dad staring. She jumped and sat straight up in the bed and turned toward Dad. She could see him through the darkness. She knew it was her dad, yet her fear did not abate. She pulled the blankets closer to her and lay back down. Dad continued to sweat and stare. Dad wanted Sugar to wake up completely. It was as if it were some sort of plan. The stare, the breathing, the sweating, Sugar jumping up—all part of an evil plan.

Sugar lay with her back toward Dad. Her eyes were wide open. She shivered and sweat began to ease down the side of her face. She grasped the blankets tightly and pulled her body into a close, tight knot. Her trembling was noticeable and she thought about the game of freeze that Warren and I had seemed to always master. She wished that she had played freeze with us. She wished that she had perfected the art of being motionless.

Dad took a step toward Sugar's bed and the floor gave away an annoying squeak. Sugar could feel the heat from Dad's body. She wanted to be left alone. She didn't want Dad near her. She had never been comfortable around him. She was hoping that he would stay away from her. He had never really looked at her the way a father should look at his daughter. His stare made her feel dirty. It was as if he didn't realize that she was his fifteen-year-old daughter. Blood of his blood. Sugar was his creation. He was supposed to love and protect her. He was not supposed to put her in fear. He was not supposed to make her tremble and sweat and cry.

Dad's voice made Sugar's insides shudder. "Sugar, you all right?" She hesitated and thought about pretending she was asleep, but before she knew it she had answered, "Ye–yea–yes, Da-aa-d–Daddy, I'm fine." Dad didn't go away. "You want to come sleep in Daddy's bed till Mommy get home?" Sugar pulled her blanket even closer, "Dad, I–I'm fine. I just want some sleep. I–I mean, I just want to go back to sleep." Dad moved closer. His voice became deeper, "Sugar, it's cold in here, baby, and my room is warm." Sugar whimpered, "No...no...I'm not cold. It's nice and warm in here. It always is, Daddy." Dad must have forgotten that he was sweating. He must have forgotten that Sugar's room was always the hottest. He must have forgotten about Warren and me. He demanded, "Sugar, I want you to get up and go to my bed now." Sugar tried to slide across the bed away from him, "No...nooo...no, Daddy, please leave me alone. I'm okay."

Warren was soaked with sweat. He could hear Dad talking. He knew something wasn't right. He knew Dad wasn't concerned about Sugar. My mind wandered. Everything was happening too fast. I didn't know what to do. I didn't know what to say to Warren. Anything that I said now would be pure gibberish. I thought about getting up and going to the bathroom. I thought that might stop Dad from his evil scheme. I thought about getting to the phone and calling Grandma. I couldn't move. Fear was holding me back. Nate had forewarned me of the paralyzing and detrimental effects of fear. He said that fear was worse than any other emotion. He told us to fear no one but God. Nate said fear was worse than death. Nate had told the truth!

Dad walked to Sugar's bedside and tried to pull the blanket from Sugar's grasp. Sugar pulled back and let out a soft shriek. Dad violently pulled the blanket from Sugar. She quickly slid across the warm white sheets hoping to escape Dad's claws. Dad locked his short stubby fingers around her delicate arm. She struggled violently and then slightly, like a wounded animal that knows it has been hopelessly trapped. Fear had taken some of the resistance out of her. She was succumbing to the hunter. She didn't know exactly what Dad would do to her. She didn't know how far he would go to subdue her. She didn't want to make him angry. She feared that he would hurt Warren and me. She didn't want anyone hurt. But, more importantly, she didn't want to be hurt. She just wanted Dad to go away. She wanted him to go away forever and leave her alone, just leave his only begotten daughter alone.

Dad picked Sugar up, locked her in his arms, and walked out of her room. He carried her like a small baby. Sugar quietly wept.

Dad kicked open the door to our room. He hesitated for a second. I watched his big, burly stature in the doorway. I watched him holding my sister. He slowly walked through our room without once looking toward us. He just didn't care. He had become a cold-blooded beast. Dad walked into his room and laid Sugar on the bed—the bed he shared with his wife. He pushed the door to his room to shut it. The old door squeaked and bounced slowly back from its frame. Dad didn't care. He would not make another attempt at securing it. It didn't matter that it was slightly open. It didn't matter that his two youngest sons were in the room next door. Dad turned on the lamp which sat on a broken-down nightstand at the side of the bed. The dull bulb barely lit the room. He walked over and pulled down the torn shades at the front window. We could hear Sugar whimpering.

I relinquished my grasp on Warren. We both slowly got off the bed and crawled toward Dad's door. We moved without any feeling of fear, yet fear was in us, or, at least, in me. It was as if moving toward the door was the natural thing to do. It seemed natural to move toward danger, to enter into the midst of uncertainty.

There was always danger around us. There was the danger of being shot by the police for no apparent or legal reason. There was the danger of being robbed by the neighborhood junkies. There was the danger of being stabbed by some of the hoods who were trying to prove that they were men. Warren and I were aware of danger and we knew that there was no running away from it; it surrounded us and we had to live within it. So we moved toward danger as if we had been hypnotized. We moved toward it on that horrible day when we saw our friend Snooky get stabbed seven times in the back—by his brother. We all rushed out into the street to watch his blood flow and the last breath of life leave his body. Snooky's brother seemed to be engulfed by the same cancer of the soul that had been eating away at Dad. We moved toward danger when Nate's best friend Cookieman was shot in the back after he had tried to rob the local grocery store. We all ran toward the sound of the gun shot. We stood over Cookieman with no regard for where the bullet had come from. Cookieman died lying there waiting for an ambulance. He was invisible to the rest of the world.

Nate had told us that the willingness to move toward danger and to have danger all around and never once turn back was the reason that Blacks made the best soldiers. He said they were always willing to be in the frontline and confront danger even when it was not in their best interest. He said Blacks were willing to fight for causes that had nothing to do with them. Blacks fought in wars for freedom and came home as slaves. Nate said that we needed to identify the right war to fight. We had to identify our own enemies and stop letting other people tell us who to hate and who to kill. If we kept letting everyone else tell us who to hate and kill, we would end up hating and killing ourselves. We had to stop running toward danger under other people's terms.

Warren and I moved close to Dad's door. We could see inside the room. We were scared. We didn't know what we were scared of, but we knew that something was wrong and evil was about to happen. Mom had told us that when evil was in the air you could feel it. "When you feel the evil coming over you or around you, run and pray to God to come get you." That's what Mom said. But we couldn't move, much less run. I don't think Warren would have run anyway. Nate had told him never to run away—but to stand and fight, even if it meant that he would die. Running away was a coward's way out. Nate said that once a Black man starts running, he will always be running. He said the slaves had run from the South to the North, and there they were still chased. And they kept running and running and not fighting. Nate said that we should be prepared to suffer whatever the consequences of not running—just "don't start running."

Even with Warren at my side, I felt lonely. It was as if he weren't there. As if I were somewhere far, far away by myself. As if I had no brothers and no sister and no mother and no father and no grandmother and no grandfather. I thought back to a song we had listened to in school while we were studying the heroism of Harriet Tubman. The words to the song reverberated in my head:

> Sometimes I feel like a motherless child,
> Sometimes I feel like a motherless child,
> Sometimes I feel like a motherless child
> A long ways from home, a long ways from home;
>
> Sometimes I feel like I'm almost gone,
> Sometimes I feel like I'm almost gone,
> Sometimes I feel like I'm almost gone
> A long ways from home, a long ways from home.

The song had evoked in me a fear of being abandoned and alone. Now I felt as if I were in the middle of a snowstorm naked, barefoot, submerged deep in snow. And, in a matter of seconds, I felt hot as if I were in a desert naked, as if my flesh had been stripped and my soul stood to face a tormentor. I felt lonely and stripped and tormented by the actions of my own father, or whatever had created my father, whatever had made him change. Whatever had made him into this unrecognizable monster.

Hatred seeped into my body. Or maybe hatred was already inside me waiting to escape from some small cell. Waiting to move into my soul. Waiting, like a horse at the starting gate, for some cue to set it free. Waiting to take me over and govern me the rest of my life. Waiting to calcify my emotions. Maybe God had made an exception and said that hatred was okay for Black children to feel. Maybe God felt that hatred was justified in our case. He couldn't expect us to keep on accepting abuse from whoever handed it out. Maybe He had prepared a special place inside us to hold all the hate we needed until the time came to let it all out. I didn't know whether to fight hatred or to accept it. I didn't want hatred to turn me into something evil like Dad, but I wanted to have the courage that came with hatred. I wanted the courage of Nat Turner. Maybe it wasn't hatred that made Dad evil.

Warren was crying. I turned to him and whispered, "Shut up! Dad will kill us." I don't even know whether Dad knew anymore that we were in the house. He was too busy being evil. I don't think he cared that we were alive. To us, Dad was Satan and no one could stop him but God. However, on this night, at this moment, God was not in our house. What did God care about poor Black children? Every picture I saw on the cover of Sunday school books portrayed Jesus as white. So God, the Father, must have been white, too. He was watching over white folk while Black people sang His praises and waited for Him to part the sky and take them up into His white heaven to live with and serve His white son.

Nate said it wasn't true. He said God wasn't white at all. Nate said he would never even try to read one of those Sunday school books with a white Jesus on the cover. He said a book like that could only be full of lies. He said it would have been better if they had not put a picture of Jesus on it at all.

God wouldn't stop Satan tonight. God was in church with Mom, Frank, Quincy, and Nate. God was listening to the choir sing songs of praise to Him. He was satisfied for tonight—yet Satan was in our house having his way with our sister. While Dad raped Mom's daughter in Mom's bed, Mom prayed for Dad's soul to God's son Jesus.

Dad must have produced Sugar through an act of hate. He could never have loved anyone. Despite what Mom had said about Dad changing, what could have been so evil that it changed Dad's love to hate and turned hate into hatred of everything, even that which he had produced? Dad was ready to perform his act of hate again—on the very person he had created. I wondered whether Dad had begotten a daughter just for this purpose; had he planned this all along?

I knew I couldn't stop Dad. I couldn't protect beautiful, lovely Sugar. Warren couldn't stop Dad. Maybe Frank or Quincy could have, but they were not here. I could see Sugar. She was shivering and crying, "Please, Da-a-ddy, leave me alone." Did Sugar know what was about to happen? Maybe she didn't. Maybe she just felt the same evil that Warren and I were feeling. Why didn't she just get up and run away from the evil, as Mom said we should? She could have run right to Warren and me. *It was that fucking fear that was keeping her there.*

Why didn't she pray to God? Maybe she had prayed. Maybe God had answered her, and Mom was on the way home to save her daughter from the evil of her husband. Maybe God had touched Mom in church and told her that something was wrong at home. Mom said that the Holy Ghost was a spirit that moved inside the body. She said it was the spirit of God. Maybe the Holy Ghost had stirred inside Mom and moved her to come home to save her baby girl. Maybe Sugar had been through this before and knew that there was no use running and praying. Maybe she knew that neither God nor anyone else would be coming to save her.

I felt like dying. I felt like running into Dad's room and removing my sister. I was willing to suffer whatever the consequences. Jesus had done it. He was willing to die for people he didn't know—but I was not Jesus. I didn't even know whether I believed in Jesus or God or anybody or anything. I wished for the courage of Malcolm X or Dr. Martin Luther King Jr. I wanted to be able to confront my enemy or Sugar's enemy. I wanted to confront the devil or Satan or whoever caused me pain. I wanted the bravery of Huey Newton. Why couldn't I move? I hated the fear that overwhelmed me, immobilized me.

Warren was trembling. Tears crept down his face. He reached up and grabbed my arm. I could not differentiate his trembling from mine. I didn't know whether Warren was angry or scared. It was all so confusing. I couldn't stand to look into his face. I didn't have the answers that he needed right now. I couldn't explain why his father was doing this to his sister. I couldn't explain why God was not stopping Dad or why Mom was not at home. I couldn't explain to Warren why I was doing nothing but watching this happen. I couldn't explain why we were there. I couldn't answer any of the questions that I knew had to be in Warren's mind. He must have known that I didn't have the answers, because he never asked the questions. I had felt so strong earlier when I had grabbed Warren and thrown him on the bed. I had felt strong when I had held him down on the floor. Now I felt weak and helpless.

I turned my face away from his face, my eyes from his eyes. I looked around our room. The cold wooden floors were dusty. No matter how much we mopped and cleaned the floors, they were always dusty. I moved my feet slightly and heard the floor squeak. Why couldn't Dad hear the floor squeak? Maybe if he heard the floor squeak, he would leave Sugar alone. It was a coward's way out. I wanted a squeaky floor to do what I couldn't or wouldn't do. Nate said fear could be overcome if the will to overcome it was present. He said people feared because it was easier than being brave. It was easier than standing up and speaking out. I prayed for the power to overcome my fear. Praying...praying. Why was I praying?

Sweat rolled down my face. I felt as if I were under a shower of water, or blood. My eyes roamed as I tried to fix my attention on something other than what Dad was doing and was about to do. I tried to ignore Warren kneeling next to me shaking and crying. I tried to ignore Sugar's tears. I was hoping that it was all a bad dream and that it would all go away if I ignored it long enough. I tried to imagine another time and another place. I wanted to leave, yet I was compelled to stay. I stared at the walls that enclosed our room. They made me feel as if I were in a dungeon with no escape possible. I was condemned to watch this horror in this place, at this time, from inside these walls.

The walls were supposed to be white but time had turned them to a dull beige. Time turns things and people into something other than what they really should be or what they really are. I wanted those walls to be white again. I wanted to yell at them and make them turn white. I wanted to be white, rich, and happy like all those white folks on television. Television always showed white people as being happy and Black folks as being sad or scared. Television showed Black people as ignorant, frightened, and courageless fools. Mom told us that we could, and should, be happy. She told us not to pay attention to the images that appeared on TV. She said that they were put there to make us think that we could never do anything right except dance, clown, and run from things that the white man would stand up to and fight. Television reminded us that we couldn't go to the same places as white people. We couldn't eat the same food or wear the same clothing as white folks. Television reminded us that we were ghetto children. It reminded us that we were Black in a nation that had always despised Black people. It conveyed the message that we were a people to be controlled rather than a people in control.

My eyes followed the walls up to where they met the ceiling. The paint on the ceiling had peeled back in some places and scraps hung as if they wanted to fall but were waiting for the right time. Waiting for some cue or event that would make it not worth hanging on any longer. Just like Warren and I were waiting, waiting for something terrible to happen. Just like Nate was waiting, waiting for something or someone to take him out of a world which he felt he never should have been brought into. Waiting for the right cause or the right time. Waiting until nothing could make him believe that it was worth hanging on any longer.

I glanced down at my dingy white sneakers. They were imitation Jack Purcells. Mom said she couldn't afford the real thing, yet she didn't want us to feel too out of place around our friends. She said that what we wore wasn't important to her because she loved us, no matter what. However, she knew that our friends would laugh at us if we didn't wear the right clothing. She said that someone had made us feel that if we wore the right things, all of our other problems would go away. If we spent money on things that we couldn't afford, we would seem more important and less inferior. Clothing took the place of education. If we looked good, who cared if we could read or write? Mom said the people who had created this philosophy profited by selling us clothing that they made us feel we needed. We were caught up in it. Saving wasn't important because no one could see your savings. It was important to show people that you weren't all poor, even if you were poor. It was important to look good, even if you felt bad. Somebody had turned us into fakes and, like my sneakers, fakes never last long.

I watched a cockroach crawl past my feet. It moved as though it was in no hurry; as though it had no fear. I thought about stomping it. I thought about ending its life and making it pay for having no fear. It was mocking me. But I didn't want to hurt or kill anything tonight. I didn't want anyone to be hurt or killed. I didn't want Sugar to be hurt or killed. The roach stopped in the stream of light coming from Dad's room. It acted as though it, too, knew that something awful was happening. I turned away from the roach as Warren tightened his grip on my arm. It was foolish of me to be paying attention to this insect while my sister was being hurt.

I looked into the hallway outside our door. Dad had not even shut the door to our room. What if Mom arrived home and came up the stairs? There would be nothing to block her vision of Dad. Dad just didn't care. Or maybe he was confident that whatever forces had created him would prevent Mom from coming home.

There was a hole in the corner of the hall wall. I could hear mice moving about in it. We had stuffed poison in that hole so many times, yet the mice always survived. Just like us. In spite of the poison that was continuously and intentionally being stuffed into the ghetto, we survived. Someone had tried to kill us in so many ways, yet we were still here. Still fighting for something or searching for something that we should be fighting—looking for the poison stuffer.

For the first time I noticed how dark it was in our room, how dark it was in the hallway. For some reason our bedroom seemed darker tonight. The only light came from Dad's room and it burned my face as if it were a light from hell. Tonight Dad's room was hell, and Sugar was in hell. She had been sentenced to hell without ever having been accused of committing a sin. Judgement Day had come early for her. After tonight, no other day of judgement would be important. After tonight, Sugar's soul could not be saved for God, and all the preaching, proselytizing, and praying in the world would not matter. She would not be able to love or pray anymore. She would be condemned to live in hell all of her life. She would never be able to forgive Dad, so she could not go to heaven. Heaven didn't matter anymore. She was afraid of heaven. Afraid that there would be no one in heaven to protect her.

God was supposed to protect her tonight. Mom said God was everywhere and that God was watching over us. But God could not be in Dad's room tonight. He had to be in church. For if God were here, Dad would be dead in body as well as in spirit. God would not allow Sugar to be hurt. God would hear her pleas. God would hear Warren's cries. God would hear my prayers. Maybe hell was better. In hell, Sugar would not expect help or protection. She would not pray or scream or cry because she would know that no one was coming to save her. She would not be disappointed if Warren, Frank, Quincy, Nate, and I did not come to help her. In hell, she would not be expecting God.

Dad pulled his shirt off and threw it on the floor. He had on a white sleeveless tee shirt that had rolled up over his stomach. He pulled it down and then decided to pull it off. He tossed it toward the door. Warren and I jumped back. Dad never looked our way. His chest was full of curly, graying black hair. His belly glistened in the light as sweat rolled over it. His breathing intensified. He never turned toward the door. I wanted Dad to notice us and stop. I was praying that he would look. I wanted him to feel ashamed, but shame was not in Dad.

He must have somehow justified this act. Somewhere in Dad's life he had been made to feel that it was okay to rape Black women. It didn't matter if they were your wife or sister or daughter. It was only important that he feel that Black women were nothing, that they could be beaten and cursed and raped without any consequences, without any feeling of guilt or remorse. Someone had made him feel that Black women were insignificant, that it was okay to call them "bitches" and "whores." Dad had been broken to the point where he not only believed this but was willing to be a part of this crude lie. I remembered Dad telling us about his childhood in South Carolina. He would tell us how his father disciplined him. His father would punch him and throw him across the floor when he did something wrong. He told us it made him tough. He said he didn't fear pain or punishment. He told us about the Ku Klux Klan and how they were a bunch of cowards. He said he wanted to fight one of them. He wanted a one-on-one fight to see how much of a man a Klansman really was. "They never fight when it's only one of them. They need a whole group with horses, guns, sheets and torches. One of them could never beat one of us. They know it." Dad said he had stared one of them in the face one time. He said he had seen nothing but fear in the Klansman's eyes. The Klansman didn't have the courage to fight. He wanted to catch Dad at home with his family and throw torches from a safe distance. He wanted to ambush Dad on some dark night when Dad wasn't expecting it. But he didn't want to take Dad on one-on-one. Dad said it would have been no contest. He said we were warriors and they were cowards.

Dad said the cowardice that was a part of the Klansmen was now a part of the country. He said whenever the country went to war, they looked for some other country to fight along with it. He said the country was always looking for a coalition. He said that the country could probably win by itself, but it had this Klansman mentality, this coward mentality. In Africa, tribes fought tribes without seeking assistance from other tribes. It was "us against them" and may the best tribe win. Dad told us never to be afraid of a racist or a Klansman. He said they both were full of fear.

Dad had seemed so brave and wise then. So intelligent and prophetic. He had seemed like such a strong man. He was preparing his boys to survive and prosper under a system designed to destroy them. He would never smoke or drink because, he said, it made a man weak and vulnerable. But Dad had taken a steep slide into the very state of enfeeblement that he had protested. I wondered what had made Dad so weak and vulnerable. What had broken this African king? What had brought Dad to this point?

Sugar was crying louder now. There was no doubt that she knew what was about to happen. She was crying out to Warren, crying out to me, crying out to anyone who would help her. She needed someone to stop Dad. She was not ready to capitulate. She still believed. She still prayed. The tears flowed from her eyes in streams. She was gasping for air. Dad ignored her. The tears seemed to form a puddle below her head and then they disappeared into the pillow. I tried to get up and move into Dad's room, but I couldn't. My legs were numb. I reached out to grab my sister's hand, but my arm wouldn't move. I was paralyzed. Nate wouldn't have been paralyzed. Nate would have gone in and attacked Dad. Nate would go into a lion's den and attack a lion. Nate was brave. He was willing to take chances with life and with death. Nate was no coward.

Warren put his head down. He could no longer watch. He wanted to do something. He wanted Nate to come home. He was trying to understand what was happening. He was young. But youth has a separate meaning for ghetto children. He had seen so much in so little time that he was as mature as a grown man in the white world. In fact, he had seen things that others would never witness. That's why they would never be able to really understand him. They would not understand his actions. They would not understand his lack of fear. They would consider it a coldness and callousness not unlike that of an animal. They would never see what he saw or experience what he experienced. All of their psychology and therapy would not be able to explain his actions. They would search through books trying to analyze him and those like him, based on their own perceptions and experiences. They would write novels about him and those like him, guided by their prejudices. Their explanations of his behavior would be taken as truth. One Black person in a novel of a white writer would be viewed as the epitome of the race. They would never truly understand. Or maybe they realized that they did not, and could not, understand—that understanding doesn't really matter.

Dad looked down at Sugar and smiled. His lips appeared to be trembling. I took a closer look at him. His hair was receding, making his face look rounder. There were blotches of black freckles around his eyes. His teeth were yellowed and his lips were chapped. Sugar seemed to be staring at him too, like a lamb waiting to be slaughtered. I wondered if she was trying to make him stop by looking into his eyes; trying to make him see that this was his daughter that he was destroying. Was she trying to get him to have some mercy? She rolled on her side and squeezed her knees up to her chest. Dad walked toward an old brown metal wardrobe that was against the wall. He took a key from his pocket and unlocked the lock that hung from the door. He pulled out a small red tool box and sat it on the floor next to the bed. Sugar trembled and sobbed. She began to rock backward and forward.

Dad walked over to the side of the bed. His dark feet were small but thick. They made the floor creak with each step. Sweat dripped from his forehead onto the floor. He wiped the sweat from his eyes and tried to speak calmly to Sugar. His voice trembled, "Sugar, what...what you crying for, baby? Daddy not gon' hurt you." Sugar responded, "Dad, please leave me alone. Please let me go back to my own bed. I ain't done nothing to nobody. Please, Daddy. Please." Dad reached down and grabbed Sugar's arm. She resisted. He pulled harder using both hands. Sugar's grip relaxed. Dad rolled her onto her back and climbed up on her. He put his knee on her stomach. Sugar cried out. Sweat dripped from him to Sugar. Sugar shook with pain, fear, anger, and hate as she looked at the reprobate above her. She hated having been born. She hated Dad. She hated that she was a girl. She hated that she was poor and Black and living in the ghetto.

Dad removed his knee from Sugar's stomach. He held his hand over her mouth. "Sugar, don't make Daddy hurt you. Keep your mouth shut. Okay, baby?" Tears continued to flow from Sugar's eyes. She nodded her head to let Dad know that she would keep quiet. She didn't want Dad's knee on her stomach again. Dad grabbed her night gown and began to pull it up over her head. Sugar struggled. Dad put his large hand onto her chest and put his weight on her. Sugar took a deep breath and held still. He pulled her gown off and threw it toward the door. Her brown body was naked except for her panties. Dad pushed her head into the pillow and pulled her panties off. Sugar lay still. Dad's eyes canvassed her body. He rubbed her small golden breast. Sugar closed her eyes and grimaced. Dad moved to the end of the bed, reached down, and grabbed his tool box. He opened it and removed a screwdriver. He parted Sugar's legs and tried to insert the handle of the screwdriver into her vagina. She began to kick. Dad straddled her and sat on her stomach. He held her legs apart

and inserted the screwdriver. Sugar screamed. Dad laughed.
Warren cried. I could hear Sugar screaming. I could hear Dad
laughing and always, Sugar's crying. I could hear the common
sound of sirens in the distance. Yet, there was silence. It was a
strange eerie silence. Quiet and cold.

Dad slowly pulled the screwdriver out of Sugar. Her legs
were trembling. He stood up and faced her and unbuckled his
pants. He wiped more sweat from his face. Sugar continued to
cry and shiver. Now her cry was quiet. It was sweet and innocent.
It sounded as if Sugar had given up. As if she had accepted the
fact that whatever was about to happen to her was preordained.
God knows everything. She could not or would not fight Dad.
She felt that what was happening to her had been sanctioned by
God. She could not understand what she had done to deserve this.
Maybe she had committed some evil or sin, and God was
punishing her. She could not and would not fight anymore. Her
eyes were closed and the tears that flowed from them increased.
She thought deeper as her trembling lips muttered her thoughts,
"No...no...God will save me. Mom, you come on home now. You
come home, Mom. Your baby girl needs you." Sugar sobbed
softly as Dad moved closer to the bed, "Mom gonna come home.
Mommy gonna come get me. Nate gonna save me." Dad seemed
to hesitate at the utterance of Nate's name. He stared at Sugar and
advanced.

Dad pulled off his undershorts. He appeared so big and ugly
to me, yet he was my dad. He stood there over my sister with his
penis erect. Sugar's crying and fighting had only increased his
arousal. It was as if he were oblivious of the horrible act he was
committing. He reached down with his large hands and pushed
Sugar's legs apart. She kicked. He slapped her. He yelled in
anger, "I'll kill you, little girl. Don't make Daddy hurt you." It
was the word *kill* that made Warren squeeze my hand tighter. He
wanted to kill someone, kill something, kill Dad. I knew then that
Warren would one day kill. I felt the hatred move from his hand.
It was the kind of hatred that makes men kill. Warren would kill,
and I wouldn't be able to stop him. No one would be able to stop
Warren.

Sugar fell limp. Dad mounted her. I began to cry. Sugar
screamed. I would never forget that scream. Dad put his hand
over her mouth to muffle her scream. Just as the cries and
screams of poor ghetto children had always been muffled. Hidden
away, deep in the ugly side of America, and of the world. Muffled
so that their pain and suffering could be forgotten. So that their
dirty alleys and run-down homes could be shielded from the eyes

of those who wanted to believe that all was well in this country and in this world. But the screams and cries could not be forgotten. They could not be ignored. Deep inside anyone who has ever seen a ghetto or been in a ghetto, that scream exists. Dad could not squelch Sugar's scream. We would never forget that scream. We would never want to.

Sugar wanted to die. She regretted having been born. Why hadn't Mom had an abortion? Mom had told Sugar over and over again that abortion was wrong. She said that it was the taking of a human life and that only God had the authority to decide what was not worthy of living. But why had God decided that Sugar's life was worth living? Why did anyone need to suffer the pain and hurt that made up her life? For even those who fought so adamantly against abortion called her a nigger girl. Is this what they wanted her to live for? Is this what God felt was worth living? Was she to be raped and abused in order to live a life that God felt was worthy of being lived? No, Sugar thought, abortion would have been better. Death before birth would have saved her from this living hell.

Sugar slipped into a deep tunnel of thought. She phased out Dad and the room and the house. She phased out the peeling beige paint hanging from the ceiling and the dull lamp light. She no longer saw the dingy pink wallpaper. She felt no pain. She no longer felt Dad's weight on top of her, or his throbbing penis inside her. She couldn't feel his calloused hand over her mouth. She couldn't feel his sweat dripping on her. She no longer felt the tears rolling down her face. She was numb and blind in a world where it seemed everyone was numb and blind. She felt alone, but it no longer mattered if she was alone. It was too late for Mom and Frank and Quincy and Nate to come home now. It wouldn't matter. She had done what Mom had told her to do when evil came around: she had prayed to God. Maybe God was somewhere else in the world, in some other ghetto. Maybe someone else was being raped.

I could no longer watch. Warren cried louder. It didn't matter. Dad didn't care. Sugar didn't hear him. I grabbed Warren's hand and pulled him up. We ran away from hell and left Sugar. It was too late to save her. We ran from Dad and Sugar. We ran away from prayer and God. Prayer would never be the same. God would no longer be so sacred to me. I had seen and heard too much, and I never saw or heard God walk through our room to stop Dad. I never saw God throw Dad off my sister. I saw Dad rape my sister.

Warren and I ran into the hallway and started to descend the stairs. Dad had cut off the lights. We plunged into the darkness. The stairs no longer squeaked. We reached the bottom stair and ran to the door. We opened the door and entered the cold winter night. We were numb. Although we wore no coats, we could feel no coldness. We couldn't feel pain. The streets were empty except for the trash and stench that were a constant part of ghetto living. We stood there on the sidewalk holding each other's hand. We had just seen the devil, and he was our dad.

The wind blew and dried Warren's tears. We didn't know what to do or where to go. We had just run away from the gates of hell. I turned around. My eyes saw a few people walking the streets. A few minutes earlier, they had not been there. Maybe they had been there all the time and we were too numb and too blind to see them. Maybe we didn't care to see anyone anymore. Where had these people been when my sister was being raped? Why didn't they know what was happening inside? Why didn't they care? Were we just another note in the sad song of the ghetto? Notes to be ignored? Were we invisible even to other ghetto dwellers? Were we only another bad memory that needed to be forgotten? I wondered why God had allowed us, three "good kids," who didn't need prayer on this Tuesday night, to experience hell, while Mom and her "bad kids" were safe in church? Why?

Sugar was in hell being mounted by Dad. Mom was in church with Frank, Quincy, Nate, and God. Warren and I were in the ghetto streets, trying to find someone to tell our story to, trying to find someone to save our sister. There we stood, my brother and I, poor, scared, and angry, standing in the cold, dark streets of Baltimore City. This would not be the last time I would stand on these streets scared, crying, with not a soul to turn to—not even God.

5

Silent Night

All the world's a stage and all the men and women merely players.
—Shakespeare, As You Like It, II, 7

Better a witty fool than a foolish wit.
—Shakespeare, Twelfth Night, I, 5

Christmas 1973. A soft, calm snow fell from the deep, dark-blue winter sky. Multi-hued shadows appeared and then disappeared as the Christmas lights blinked and reflected their colors on the blanket of white snow that covered all of Baltimore. The quietness of the night was broken only by the occasional sounds of a trash can being knocked over by one of the many alley cats and a faint scream coming from some mysterious, unknown place. The police and ambulance sirens had ceased, but only for the moment. The snowflakes could almost be heard coming to rest in their designated locations. Each flake glided with a certain elegance as it took its final place within the winter blanket. Christmas bulbs outlined the windows of almost every house and gave off flashing light at intermittent intervals. Silhouettes of Christmas trees could be seen through thin curtains as each row house stood in anticipation of Christmas day, Christmas joy. A small group of the many urban teenagers sauntered past us. They cursed each other. Laughter from the group indicated that tonight the cursing was all in fun.

Nate and Quincy stood in front of our house talking. I stood in the doorway intently trying to listen in on their conversation. Frank came out of the house and joined the discussion. He made some funny remark and the conversation immediately turned into a fit of laughter. I smiled although I could not hear what they were saying. They turned and walked up the steps and into the house. Nate put his arm around me and pulled me along with them. The luscious smell of Mom's cooking greeted us as we entered the dining room. We gravitated toward the kitchen.

Mom stood over the stove with sweat racing down her smooth brown face. She wiped the sweat away and smiled. "Don't you all dare put your fingers in those bowls." Bowls of scrumptious-looking food sat on the kitchen table and teased us. Warren stood at the end of the table with one of his knees resting on a chair. He was sliding his fingers along the inside of a bowl which had once been full of sweet potato pie filling. He smiled at us as he stuck his finger into his mouth. Frank spoke. "Mom, what about Warren? How come he get to stick his little dirty fingers in that bowl?" Warren flicked his tongue out as Mom answered, "He's the baby of this family. And his fingers aren't dirty. Besides he and Sugar been in this kitchen helping me all night while you boys were outside lollygagging."

Sugar sat at one end of the table stringing green beans. She was a young woman in age, but she had seen so much and experienced so much that her thoughts were like those of a woman advanced in years. Beads of sweat rested on her forehead. It was better that she sweat from the heat of the kitchen than cry. Sugar always seemed to be crying. Dad's attacks had made her feel like Jezebel. But the Christmas joy had brought a smile to her face. Being in the warm, humid kitchen surrounded by her brothers took some of the pain away. She smiled. She enjoyed helping Mom prepare the meal for her brothers. In fact, everyone was in high spirits. It was Christmas Eve.

I slowly strolled into the living room and noticed the presents underneath the tall, green, pine Christmas tree. The tree smelled so fresh and pleasant that it snuffed out the usual scents of the ghetto. There seemed to be more than enough presents for everyone. Somehow we always seemed able to get money for Christmas gifts. Everyone seemed to somehow find the money to buy a Christmas tree and put up Christmas lights. I knew that there were people in Baltimore without gifts, trees, or lights. But in our house, it seemed like nowhere in the world was there a house without a tree. Maybe this is what we wanted to believe. So we believed it. We didn't want to think about the children without trees, without gifts, and without food. A day that should have made us think about everyone seemed to make us forget about everyone. Something was wrong with Christmas. Something had been taken away from it. And even ghetto children were part of this deception.

As I watched the blinking lights on the tree, I thought of the past. I thought of all the previous Christmas Eves. I reminisced about how all of us used to perch on the top stair and peep down the steps into the darkness, trying to see what Santa had brought us. Mom and Dad knew that we were peeking but they refused to disturb us. I could hear them giggling in the darkness of their doorway. It was all a part of the aura of Christmas. We pointed out and identified our gifts as the lights on the Christmas tree blinked on and off. After a while we returned to our beds, our stomachs churning with excitement and anticipation. We tried to go to sleep but the tantalizing smell of Mom's sweet potato pie tormented us. So we engaged in idle conversation. Pleasant conversation.

As I stood watching the tree, Nate walked up next to me and abruptly yanked me from my soothing thoughts by punching my arm. "What you thinking about, boy?" Before I could answer he started to speak. "Christmas makes us just like them, doesn't it? They forget about us. They forget about educating us and giving us jobs or making things so that we can create our own jobs and educate ourselves. They forget about being fair. They forget about feeding our hungry. They forgot about the promise of 'forty acres and a mule.' And when Christmas comes we forget about everything." Nate stared into the tree and continued, "We forget about the murder of Malcolm X and Dr. Martin Luther King Jr. We forget about Brother Fred Hampton and the incident on Monroe Street in Chicago. We forget about the riots that followed Dr. King's death and the purpose for those riots. We forget that the riots didn't accomplish shit. I guess it's good that we forget, 'cause it makes us happy, huh? But, man, I don't want to forget about everything. I don't want to forget about anything. Those Jews are right, you know. Never forget."

Quincy and Frank walked into the room. Nate turned to look at them and then continued his observation, "You know, we Black folk go for anything. We believe in Santa Claus without once asking, What in the hell does Santa Claus have to do with the birth of Jesus Christ? I'm not a big Jesus Christ fan, 'cause he surely ain't done much for us." Frank interrupted, "Nate, man, what you say that for? We got our health and we ain't blind or crippled. We should be thankful."

Nate seemed to be annoyed by Frank's interruption. He responded, "There you go with some of that Sunday morning preacher shit. I'm thankful for my health and that I'm not sick but, man, I have to think about more than just me. Look at this shit out here. Take a look around you, big boy. Look at these fuckin' drug addicts all over the place shooting that bullshit in their arms. Look at you, man—you can't go a day without a reefer cigarette or a drink. And who do you think provides you with that reefer and that drink so that you can escape from reality? You are trying to escape from this bullshit—and yet you feel thankful to be here. Think of how twisted what you're saying is. Be thankful. Yet every time you get a chance, you smoke that shit so you can escape from what you are thankful for. I suppose you should thank God for your ability to afford that shit that helps you escape from the situation that you are thankful to be in. You've even got your wife smoking that shit. It don't make sense."

Frank yelled back, "Nate, you smoke reefer and I know you have tried coke." Nate looked toward me and I stared into his eyes. He turned back to Frank and answered in an agitated voice, "You fuckin' right. And I done killed a few motherfuckers, too. I don't pretend to be a saint. I don't pretend to be anything or anyone, anymore. And I ain't been deceived into believing that if I was good like Mom I'm going to heaven. I don't believe Jesus is going to save me. I know I need to escape this shit and that's why I do some drugs, but I also know that it's going to be here when I get back. Loving Jesus and being thankful ain't going to change that. I ain't the one that you need to be mad with about not believing and not having faith. Do you think the motherfucker who put this Santa Claus shit together believes? Do you think the motherfucker who done duped us into putting a fuckin' tree in the middle of our house in the ghetto, where there ain't even any trees growing outside, believes in Jesus Christ? Do you think the son of a bitch who got us going broke to buy presents to make us forget about our situation is a believer in anything but a fuckin' dollar?"

Nate was sweating now. Mom had heard the yelling and slowly walked into the room. Nate didn't see her behind him; he continued to speak. "That fuckin' tree, those presents, those lights—all that shit is dope, Frank. It's supposed to make you forget about what's really happening. It's supposed to help you escape from the reality that some children are out there starving. All this Christmas shit is cocaine and reefer. And we all are addicted to it, man. We all are trying to escape, whether we know it or not. But I ain't never been so high that I ain't realized that I got to come back and face reality. I know I'm a Black man in a world where being Black automatically makes you the enemy. Ain't none of this Christmas shit gonna make me forget." Warren peered into the living room. His eyes were wet. He had sweet potato mix on his red shirt. He walked in and sat down next to me. Nate turned and saw Mom. She had her hands on her hips. Her eyes looked tired. A tear joined the sweat and trickled down her face. The small toy train made another pass around the base of the tree. I noticed it for the first time. In a moment the train would be hidden behind some of the presents.

I stood up and walked to the window and looked out into the falling snow. Sadness filled the silent room. Dad's car pulled up, spitting snowflakes from the treads of its rear tires, cutting a path through what had been a perfect winter blanket. Dad got out of the car with more presents in his arms. I guess he had forgotten that one year ago he had raped my sister. It didn't matter to him tonight. It was Christmas and we were not supposed to ruin it with thoughts of reality. We were to visualize a calm night with a little white baby lying in a manger and a bright star up above. Dad stumbled up the snow-covered steps. He had a smile on his face as he waved to one of the neighbors and yelled, "Merry Christmas." Nate sat down on the floor and stared into the Christmas tree. Frank backed up and leaned against the wall. Quincy sat next to Warren. Sugar walked over and put her arms around Nate's neck. Mom reached down and turned on the radio. The calm, chilling sounds slowly filtered through the quiet room:

"Silent night, Holy night! All is calm, all is bright...."

6

Revenge

*Any harm you do to a man should be done in such
a way that you need not fear his revenge.*
        –Niccolo Machiavelli, The Prince

The summer of 1975 was not unlike any other summer in the
ghetto. It was hot and miserable. It was the killing fields or what
Master Sun Tzu described as "dying ground." Master Sun Tzu
stated that dying ground is an area where "you will survive if you
fight quickly and perish if you do not." At the beginning of each
summer, bets could be taken and odds given on who would or
would not survive the season. At the end of each school year it
was anyone's guess who would return to the classroom the
following year. The favorite saying of young Black men as they
departed from each other at the end of the day was, "I'll see you
tomorrow eye to eye or I'll meet you at the place that Black men
go when they die." The inner cities of America had been turned
into a battleground. The minds of Black inner-city youth had been
controlled. The miseducation had been successful. The schools
participated in this intentional conspiracy to ensure the failure of
Black youth. As Malcolm X said, "We didn't realize that as soon
as we were made to hate Africa and Africans, we also hated
ourselves. You can't hate the root and not hate the fruit." Another
summer night. Another mother's cry. Marvin Gaye was right:
"far too many mothers crying, far too many brothers dying."
        Timmy and Chas eased past the window and moved slowly to
the other side of the doorway with all the poise of expert burglars.
They didn't make a sound. Nate and Michael stood in the alley
awaiting the appropriate pre-planned signal. It was a signal that
they were acutely familiar with. The setting sun reflected off the

top of a police car that slowly moved down Catherine Street. As the police car passed, the young Black men breathed a sigh of relief. A stream of dirty water trickled down the middle of the rough cement alleyway. A group of four or five children stood frozen at the top of the alley. They had stopped their play in order to watch the two men prepare another deadly urban assault. It was like watching television. Soon a few of the entranced children would make the leap into the position of the men at the alley's end.

The door to the house was open. The summer heat demanded that all doors and windows be left open. James and Carey moved about inside the living room. Their voices could be heard where Timmy and Chas stood. They had no idea what was about to occur. They should have known that on a hot summer night in Baltimore City no one was safe. The heat seemed to bring out a hidden violence and violent attitudes that had accumulated from birth for most of the ghetto dwellers. A violence whose roots were anger. Anger at being denied and confined and thrown the scraps from privileged America. Tonight these attitudes would light the fuse for Nate's revenge.

James and his brother Carey had caught Nate on the way home from the Muslim restaurant at the corner of Baltimore Street and Calverton Road on the west side of Baltimore one night during the winter. They didn't know that he was Quincy's brother. They never would have assaulted him if they had known he was kin to Quincy. They shoved Nate up against a wall and forced their hands into his pockets. He had nothing. They threw him to the ground and stomped him in the stomach. They spit on him. Nate rolled on the cold concrete in agony. They left him there shivering with blood trickling from his mouth. They laughed as they walked away. Nate got to his feet and walked home. He could not fend off his attackers and he had not carried his gun. Not carrying a gun on the mean streets of Baltimore or any major city, for that matter, was a mistake. It was a mistake that Nate would try never to make again. With thoughts of immediate and harsh revenge fresh on his mind, Nate told Quincy and Frank all about the assault as Warren and I listened.

We were older now, and living in the inner city had made us understand that this type of activity could not go unpunished. It would be up to Nate, Frank, and Quincy to get revenge. I was fourteen and still considered too young to participate in the act of revenge. At least, that is what Quincy and Nate had told me. I didn't believe it to be true. I think that they were protecting me from it all. They saw something in Warren and me, and they did not want it tarnished by the dirty, but necessary, business of revenge. They believed that Warren and I had the opportunity to make Mom proud. So they protected us by telling us that they would handle the revenge business for the family. They protected us by telling us that we were too young. We knew it to be a lie because all around us revenge was being sought by those our age and much younger. Nate was only sixteen and he had been in the business of seeking revenge for what seemed like a long time. Time in the inner city was measured in "ghetto-years." A Black man who lived to the age of thirty had lived a long life. Nonetheless, Warren and I accepted their explanation. There was no use arguing.

Revenge was to be meted out to those who deserved it. It was a lesson taught over and over again. It was taught to us in school, if we cared to look deeply into what was being said to us. The United States always took revenge against the countries that attacked it or tried to harm it. Other countries took revenge against the United States for its efforts to dismantle their governments. The Native Americans had tried to take revenge against those who took their land. Everyone all over the world seemed to want to get even, except Black people. And when Black people did take revenge, it was usually against other Black people.

Mom would tell us to turn the other cheek. She would explain to us that it was important to forgive and forget. She said that's what God wanted. Every Sunday morning in church we found the origin of Mom's beliefs. Reverend Elder C. Green would preach about turning the other cheek. "Love thine enemies." He would tell us that revenge was better left up to God and that God had made this request of His people. It's an idea that might work in church. On the street, however, it's the act of an absolute fool.

Reverend Green preached a sermon that shunned revenge. His lessons were full of the turn-the-other-cheek, let-God-take-care-of-it philosophy. Yet, all around us, the world was seeking revenge. We couldn't ignore it unless we were blind and deaf. Quincy told us that the Black man was the only man standing by and waiting on God to do what he was afraid to do. He told us that if anyone ever struck us, we must hit him back. He said that once Black people adopted this philosophy, the world would respect us. He said that once the world respected us, we would no longer need to be violent. It was the threat of violence with the apparent ability to carry it out that would deter others from attacking us. Early on in his life Quincy believed that if a police officer wrongly killed one of our Black brothers, it was up to us to kill that policeman or kill whatever he loved the most. He said that it was time for us to stop being the ones dying and for us to do some vengeful killing for a change. Quincy knew this would lead to more and more bloodshed. "Why not make a statement—we are dying anyway." He said we should at least die like men. Quincy believed deeply in the philosophies of Malcolm X and Niccolo Machiavelli Machiavelli stated: "[M]en ought either to be caressed or destroyed, since they will seek revenge for minor hurts but will not be able to revenge major ones. Any harm you do to a man should be done in such a way that you need not fear his revenge."

Nate had no problem at all with Quincy's philosophy. He had no problem with seeking revenge on those who had wronged him. He, too, believed that we as a people were too meek. He said we were punks to the rest of the world. He said we needed to be warriors again. Nate was convinced that the police were not there to protect us. He said that the courts would never convict a white man for the killing of a Black man. "The killing of a Black man by another Black man is exactly what they want." Nate always talked about "they" and "them."

He was convinced that the condition of the Black man was a plan in which we had been duped into playing a major role. He said if we were ever going to get out of this mess, we would have to do it ourselves. We had to let the world know that we were not to be "fucked with" and that "we were willing to die to stop them from fucking with us." Nate no longer looked to God for anything. He would take care of his own revenge. He would fight his own wars and declare his own enemies. Quincy would keep Nate from accomplishing revenge in a haphazard manner.

Chas was now fourteen. He and I were still close, but he felt better being with Nate and Quincy. He believed that I would never do the things that Nate and Quincy did. I wouldn't do what was necessary. Chas believed that I would never seek revenge. He told me that I had a lot of hatred in me but I had been "taken in by all that Jesus bullshit." He said Nate and Quincy "saw through the bullshit." He said I would probably succeed in the white man's world because I "believed in his Jesus" and I believed that his God was going to save me if I "accepted his bullshit." Chas told me "that Jesus shit has never worked out good for the Black man." He said it kept us where we were. "Only white people prospered under their blond-haired, blue-eyed Jesus." Chas said he believed in Jesus but he didn't believe that "Jesus put out the bullshit that they were saying." Nor did he believe Jesus had blond hair and blue eyes. "Jesus believed in getting revenge. Jesus wasn't no punk. He drowned Pharaoh's army. He killed the

Pharaoh's first born son. He made the walls of Jericho come tumbling down. Jesus got respect." Chas said I would never be at peace until I dealt with the cold, hard facts.

Quincy, Nate, and Chas amazed me. They were so young, yet they had figured out so much. I suppose they had to. They had to search and find reasons for what was happening to us. They knew deep down inside that we were not inferior and that we were made of the same flesh and bone as all men. But something had gone wrong. They knew that if they did not seek and find the truth at an early age, they were doomed. But even the finding of truth did not mean that they would not be doomed. The truth could get you killed and speaking the truth could make a young Black male a target. Quincy, Nate, and Chas were targets. They were seeking the truth. And in some instances they had found the truth. They understood the system of miseducation. Yet, despite their enlightenment, they rejected what the truth revealed to them. They did not act in accordance with their knowledge. They wanted so badly to utilize the knowledge they had obtained, yet they knew that what they had learned could not be easily put into a form that would benefit anyone. Who would listen to these *ghetto children*? They believed that those who knew the truth and could speak it didn't have the guts to say what was really happening. So they continued knowing but not acting on their knowledge.

Michael was different. He was fifteen now. He had become cold and hard. He could kill a man with remarkable coolness. Michael had become a victim of the American dream. Once he realized that the dream was purposely denied Black men, he became a foolish killer. Michael believed that he was being taunted and teased for not fulfilling the dream. Now it no longer mattered. He was willing to kill and steal to get what he desired. Nate had tried to explain to Michael what was really going on around him. Nate tried to explain that the American dream was really a nightmare for Black people. He tried to explain that we need not adopt other people's dreams.

Michael listened to Nate out of respect, but he really didn't hear him. Michael enjoyed the thrill of the fight. He wanted to participate in anything and everything that involved danger. Nate said that "Michael was completely gone. We are all destroyed a little, but not like Michael. I mean Michael is one fucked-up brother." Nate said that Michael had given up on everything positive and that he just wanted to die in some gunfight. Michael didn't want to commit suicide. That was a coward's way out. "Only rich white kids do that kind of crazy shit." Michael wanted it all to end and he wanted it to end quickly. He didn't want to die of cancer in some hospital bed where he would have to depend on white people to supply his every need. He didn't want to die on some battlefield in some foreign country, fighting for something meaningless to him. He knew that one day he would probably die fighting. He knew that the way he died might be termed meaningless by those who did not understand. But if, for once, he could decide what his reason for dying would be, his death would be meaningful, at least to him. He believed that even if he died robbing a store, at least he had been the one to make the decision to rob the store. And the power to make a decision without intervention from anyone, especially anyone white, would be worth whatever the consequences. A decision of his own, even if it ended in death, would mean that he was free, if only for a fleeting moment.

Quincy and Nate tried to explain to Michael that the decision to rob and kill was not a decision made by the Black man. They told him that although it seemed that he had made a choice, the true decision was out of his hands. They explained to him that there were powers, which he didn't understand, pulling the strings and that although these powers could not predict when he would make a certain decision, they knew he would make it. And they knew that the decision would lead to death. "They know it when they sentence us to twelve to thirteen years in inferior schools. They know it when they deny us jobs and loans so that we can't own our own businesses. They know it when they come into our neighborhoods and sell us that swine that is slowly killing us. They know it when they send us cocaine, marijuana, and malt liquor. They know it when they provide us with imported AK-47s with plenty of ammunition. Yeah, brother Michael, they try to play God. Listen to them closely when they say only God knows. Listen to them when they remain silent. Listen to the silence."

James and Carey continued to talk. They didn't notice that darkness had swooped down on the city like a buzzard on its prey. It wasn't important. They didn't care that they had left the door open, and they certainly had forgotten the assault on Nate. They had left the visions of that assault back in the cold streets of winter. They had a short memory. They had forgotten that revenge was important, that revenge meant they could never forget. They had forgotten that revenge could be taken in a day or in a year or in a decade. They had missed the hidden meaning of all those school history lessons: once you wrong someone or some people, always be alert for a payback. They had forgotten the words of Machiavelli: "[A]ny harm you do to a man should be done in such a way that you need not fear his revenge."

James and Carey never noticed Timmy and Chas climb the three white marble steps and enter the dark, fusty hallway. Nate and Michael followed. Dark hallways and dark rooms always seemed to mean ominous things were about to happen. Nate reached into his waistband and removed his .357 magnum. Timmy and Chas had already drawn their guns. Timmy had a forty-five automatic and Chas's weapon was identical to Nate's. Their fingers lightly clutched the triggers as sweat rolled down their faces. Michael removed his thirty-eight revolver from the back of his pants and walked with it along his side. His eyes were big and a smirk remained on his face. They took slow, sure steps as if they had done all this before—the slow walk, the sweating, the smirk, the darkness.

James laughed aloud and startled the foursome. Timmy stopped in place. He turned the gun toward the room where the laughter had come from. Michael smiled and wiped a bead of sweat from his forehead. He seemed to feel no pressure. Either he would kill or be killed. It didn't matter. Someone would die. "We gon' do the motherfuckers tonight." The floor creaked a little. But all the floors in these old, used row houses creaked. It was not enough to alarm anyone. Unless one was prepared for revenge.

Nate jumped ahead of Timmy. He kicked the door open to the room and quickly moved inside. Timmy, Chas, and Michael followed. James fell back from the chair he was seated on. Carey reached into his waist. Nate yelled, "Don't do it, motherfucker." Carey responded, "Goddamn, Nate—don't shoot, man. What the fuck are you doing, man?" Carey was trembling. He moved back to the wall and put his hands in the air. Michael ran over and took the gun out of his waistband. He laughed, "Oh yeah, you gon' get done tonight, motherfucker. You ain't gonna see the sun rise over Baltimore City no mo'." Carey shivered. Chas and Timmy kept their guns pointed at James.

James must have thought it was all a mistake. He scrambled to his feet. Michael turned and spat in his face. James jumped toward Michael. Nate yelled, "Do it if you want, but you'll be one sorry, dead motherfucker." James turned to Timmy. "Timmy, what the fuck is going on?" Timmy didn't respond. James looked toward Chas. "Come on, man, it's me, Chas. Fuck, it's me. Don't do this shit, Chas." He repeated Chas's name as if the calling of the name would indicate some closeness in their spirits; as if the calling of Chas's name would bring up some suppressed memories of friendship. It was not to be. If Chas had remembered that he and James had grown up together, he would not have come here with Nate. If he had remembered the meals that he shared with James at each other's house, he would have stayed home. If he had remembered the jokes that they had laughed at together, he would not have been standing here and pointing his gun at James. Or maybe he did remember it all. Maybe it didn't matter. Maybe he was becoming more like those in power than he wanted to admit. Chas had once said that he wanted to be "as brutal as a white man during slavery."

Quincy had told us that the President and others in power could shake your hand one minute and order your assassination the next minute. He said they could smile in your mother's face in the morning and watch her raped at their command the same night. Friendships didn't matter. Whatever it took to stay on top had to be done and, if necessary, it could be done in the name of God. Killing had been done in the name of God in the One Hundred Year War. It had been done in the name of God in the War of the Roses. And it had been done in the name of God during the Christian Crusades. These were the lessons that were deeply hidden in all the history lessons superficially taught in inner-city schools.

Nate stormed over to James and placed the gun against his temple. "Shut up, motherfucker. Just shut the fuck up or I'll do you right now." James froze. He could tell that Nate was serious. He could see the anger in the sweat that rolled down Nate's face. He could feel death creeping into his body. Somehow he felt that Nate had already shot him. He awaited the pain. He awaited the burning feeling that he knew would come.

James wanted to live, but he felt bad about begging for his life. He had never been afraid of anything. He had to get rid of fear at an early age if he was to survive. He had fought fear and was proud of his fearlessness, yet now he felt fear easing back into him. He felt the tears which he had held back for so many years, which he had suppressed because that's what manhood demanded. Now it no longer mattered. He was about to experience death. And death was to be brought upon him by people he had grown up with. People he had played baseball and basketball with. People he had laughed with. He had sat at their tables and visited their moms and dads. He had spent nights over at their homes. But that was in youth. And for ghetto children, youth is short. Very short.

A cool red mist sprinkled the face of Michael. His smile disappeared. James slumped to the floor. The warm red fluid flowed from his head like lava flowing from the mouth of a volcano. There was no life left in him. The scampering of children's feet could be heard running down the hallway and out onto the marble steps. Nate slowly released the trigger. Carey pushed himself into the corner of the room as tears began to flow freely from his eyes. "Fuck, Nate. Why...why...why you do that, man? Why you go kill him?...him? It don't make no fuckin' sense." Nate stared down at James and looked as if he had done something that he knew was wrong. He turned slightly toward Carey and in a quiet, serene voice said, "Last winter. Remember last winter." The words moved from his mouth in what appeared to be slow motion. Carey trembled, "But...bu–but we didn't know you then, Nate. We didn't know who the fuck you were. We didn't know you were Que's brother. Fu–fuck. Let it go, Nate. Let it *go*!"

Timmy and Chas never moved. They just stared as if they were not involved in the scene. As if it were all an elementary school play and their role was to stand still and observe this particular act.

Michael turned and faced Carey. He smiled and brought his gun straight up in front of him. Carey slid down the wall and put his hands together as if to say a prayer. He started to mumble, "Our Father who ar' in heaven. Thy kingdom come. Thy will be done." His head jerked back twice and he fell silent. Streaks of blood raced down the wall behind him. Michael lowered the smoking gun to his side. He turned toward Nate, who was placing his gun back into his waistband. Timmy and Chas had already started heading toward the door. Michael walked out ahead of Nate. Nate reached the door and turned back. The puddle of blood beneath James's head seemed to be getting larger. It seemed to be moving toward Nate. Nate stepped back. He had marked and tracked Carey and James as though they were fugitives and he, a bounty hunter. He should have been proud of his success. He wasn't. A tear trickled down his face. "It don't make no fuckin' sense."

7

Blues Free

And youth is cruel, and has no remorse and smiles
at situations which it cannot see.
                                    –*T. S. Eliot,* Portrait of a Lady

I guess you could call it a dance. Whatever it was, Warren was doing it and doing it well. He moved with joy and enthusiasm, allowing his arms and hands to cut through the wet and warm summer air. Nate and Chas gleefully laughed at his every motion. Quincy and Frank urged him on by pounding their fist on the wood porch surface and yelling, "Go, Warren! Go, Warren! Go, Warren!" I sat on the stone steps, with Dwayne smiling and me shaking my head in satisfying disbelief. Mom and Sugar stood in the doorway, their faces beaming with a bright, seldom-seen pleasantness. Earlier in the day, we had made a collective decision to get together for a talk. We often had discussions. It was a way of relieving some of the pressures brought upon us by our condition and our color. It was a way of maintaining a little sanity or finding a little sanity in the insane atmosphere that surrounded us. Sometimes our back-porch meetings were pleasant. Often they were not. Decisions had to be made that involved life and death. But today our planned talk had digressed into a party and no one seemed to mind.

Warren and I were growing older. We were now past the cute stage. All of our actions from this point on would be critically judged by our family members and the white experts who considered us specimens to be examined and evaluated for college text books. I was fourteen and Warren was twelve. Getting older in the ghetto did not necessarily denote a change in age. Frank, Quincy, Sugar, and Nate were determined to keep Warren and me on the right track. They were determined to get us out of the ghetto breathing and in one piece. They continuously tried to instill a sense of pride in us; they made us study hard.

Quincy lectured us. "You and Warren have got to be the ones to bring Mom the happiness that she deserve. The rest of us didn't intend to bring Mom trouble but, fuck, we already a part of this fuckin' bullshit system. It's kinda too late for us to turn back now. Sugar a woman. Ain't much a Black woman can do in the ghetto but try to keep from becoming somebody's whore. That's the only way woman get respect down here. Don't be a whore. But you and Warren better not get caught up in this Niggah shit. Don't do no shooting and killing. Don't fuck with these scandalous whores around the 'hood." I started to interrupt but Quincy's words halted me. "I know all the women around here aren't whores. But some of them are caught up in this plan just like us. Somebody might pull them out, but don't let them lead you to your death while they waiting. Some of them will kill your ass quicker than a redneck cop."

Nate listened and nodded as Quincy spoke. After Quincy had finished, Nate spoke. "If y'all get trouble from one of these no 'count motherfuckers around here, just let me know. Ain't no one gonna get away with fucking with my family. Not while I'm alive. I'll die for you all. But I'm gonna take the one who fucks with y'all and with me." Frank stood and stared at Quincy and Nate. He was the oldest. It was his job to defend the family. After Quincy and Nate had finished speaking Frank muttered, "It ain't ever too late, brothers. It ain't too late to change. It ain't too late to get away from this gutter called the ghetto."

It was a hot August day, so we met on the back porch. Mom and Sugar made a large pitcher of strawberry Kool Aid and placed it on a card table, which sat against the painted red brick wall at the rear of the porch. They also placed a bowl of potato chips and some cups on the table. Nate brought out his portable radio and turned it on. The loud music poured into the warm air and rose to the ceiling of the porch in a slow, smooth motion that you could almost see. It paused there a minute, before journeying out into the alleyway. At first Mom docilely protested against the loudness of the music, but then she returned to the doorway to enjoy the scene. It was a rare occasion: everyone smiling and laughing.

Frank was twenty-four years old and married now. He wasn't around as much. Whenever he did come around, Frank had to endure a lot of teasing about getting married to his wife

Gwendolyn at the young age of twenty. Gwendolyn had been nineteen when they married. They had sneaked off to the courthouse in downtown Baltimore without telling anyone. We were notified of their marriage by an announcement in the *Afro-American* newspaper. Frank taped it to the refrigerator and called later that night to make sure that we all had seen it. Dad didn't care. Mom had seemed a little hurt. She would have liked to be at the wedding. After all, Frank was her first born. Quincy and Nate told Frank that they were never going to get married.

Sugar wanted to get married. She would always talk about having a large wedding and inviting a whole lot of people. She said that she would wear a pretty white wedding gown and that her groom would also be dressed in white. She told us that Mom would prepare potato salad, fried and barbecued chicken, spare ribs, and all kinds of cakes and pies, especially sweet potato pie. She promised Warren and me that we would be a part of the wedding. She said that she and her husband were going to buy a big house and move far away from the ghetto. Warren and I were to come visit her as often as we liked. I don't think Sugar ever believed that all those things she wanted would come true. She just wanted to think of pleasant things sometimes. She wanted to escape our harsh reality.

Mom told us never to give up on our dreams. She said that once we gave up we would just be dreamers and that people who just dreamt never did anything to make their dreams real. We had to believe. We had to keep working and hoping. She said all things were possible through God. Mom was a true believer; she always kept the faith. You could see it in her face. She had such a strong, pretty smile that gave us confidence. We felt that with Mom around, things were going to be okay. When we were sick with colds, Mom would sit up all night at our bedsides. She would close her eyes, rub our heads, and hum sweet gospel songs. In the distance we could hear Dad snoring, unaware of our sickness and unaware of Mom's humming. Later, Mom would help me make the decision to become a Special Agent with the FBI. She would also help me make the decision to expose the FBI's unbridled racist attitudes.

Warren was full of sweat when he finished dancing. Nate turned to Chas. "It's your turn now." Chas continued to laugh and said, "I'm not getting out there and making a fool of myself." Nate laughed. "You're already a fool, fool." Mom interrupted, "Nate, I told you never to call anyone a fool. It's in the Bible: Who should ever call someone a fool is in danger of hell's fire." Nate smiled. "I'm sorry, Mom. I know better. The white man got

me like this. Trying to get me to go to hell with him so I can work
on his plantation." Mom shook her head. "The white man ain't
got you like that—the devil got you like that." Nate frowned
quizzically and asked, "What's the difference?" Mom shook her
head.

Sugar took a cool, damp towel and wiped Warren's face. She
kissed his forehead and returned to her previous position behind
the screened door. Mom handed Warren a tall, cool glass of Kool
Aid. Quincy jumped up and began to dance using quick, jerky
motions. There was an air of confidence in his movements. Nate
watched Quincy. He thought there might even be lessons, hidden
from us but obvious to him, in Quincy's movements. The laughter
grew louder. Warren put down his cup and began to dance again.
Dwayne nudged me to get up and dance. I smiled and shook my
head. "Naw, brother." I quietly sang along with the music from
the radio: "Come on and do it, do it, do it till your satisfied; Lord,
I'm ready...."

Frank got up and pulled Sugar from the doorway. He and
Sugar began to dance. Mom laughed. Nate whispered something
to Chas. They leaped from their chairs and ran toward the
doorway. Nate grabbed one of Mom's arms and Chas grabbed the
other. They pulled her onto the porch and tried to force her to
dance. Mom struggled to get away. Sugar blocked the doorway
so that Mom could not get into the house. Mom protested but
continued to laugh. "You children better leave me alone."
Dwayne got up and joined the dancers.

Craig, Michael, and Bay-Bay came out of their house and
stepped up onto our porch. They laughed at the scene and then
joined in on the dancing. Some of our other friends—
Gwendolyn's brother Linwood, Melvin, Chas's aunt Debbie—
who also lived across the alley from us, and Bay-Bay's sister
Jackie joined the crowd on the porch. I looked toward Chas's
house to see whether his sister Angel was coming. I was crazy
about her. I wanted to marry her. I knew she didn't like me, but I
thought that I was in love with her. She was beautiful. Whenever
Sugar talked of a wedding, I thought of Angel. I would send her
love notes and she would rip them up. I still wanted her. I still
loved her—that is, if a fourteen year old really understood love.

I sat there and quietly whispered to myself, "Come on over,
Angel. Please come over." I might have danced if Angel had
come over. I might have been the best dancer of them all. But
Angel wouldn't dance with me. And I haven't danced yet.

Our other neighbors came out of their houses to view this rare
gratifying scene. Some were already in their yards barbecuing ribs

and chicken. The delicious aroma of good barbecued food filled the air. A group of kids played baseball in the alley. Further down the alley another group of kids threw a basketball into a wooden basket that had been attached to a utility pole. Now and then the sound of multiple firecrackers, left over from Fourth-of-July celebrations, could be heard going off in the distance. The popping of the firecrackers caused everyone to pause for a moment. It was a natural and intelligent reaction. I turned back toward the porch and noticed Mom was in a fit of laughter. I felt good inside. It was satisfying to see her happy.

We didn't know where Dad was, and we didn't care. We were happy that he was not on our back porch. He didn't belong there. I turned and looked up toward the bright sun. It was as if I were looking into God's eye. He was watching us. He was watching me watching Mom. I smiled at Him. I could tell He was smiling back. I would look for that smile from God on many future days. I would look for it while the FBI persecuted me. I would wish to be sitting on the back porch on an August day, watching and waiting for Angel. It was a warm summer day in Baltimore City and, for now, all was well.

8

Sweat, Blood, and Tears

Through identification with the aggressor, the subject attempts to magically transform himself from one threatened into the one who threatens; from powerless to powerful; inferior to superior.
    —Amos N. Wilson, Black on Black Violence

Children begin by loving their parents; as they grow older they judge them; sometimes they forgive them.
    —Oscar Wilde, The Picture of Dorian Gray

They say to honor your mother and father. They say to honor your flag and the country for which it stands. But what does honor mean when your country has been reduced to an inner-city ghetto? What is there to honor when the home of the brave is not symbolized by men in uniform marching behind a flag, but is symbolized by young Black men carrying guns to protect themselves against the evils created under the banner of the American flag? What does honor mean when young Black children see young Black men preying on each other for things they believe are worth having? Seeking the fictitious "American dream." What does honor and love of country mean when you are *in* America but not *of* America? When, for the rest of the country, cash-money is the means by which trading and bartering are conducted, but in your neighborhood, food stamps are the norm?

72

What does it mean when the concept of freedom is inconceivable? Freedom of what? Freedom from what? How can you appreciate all that America has to offer when you have never experienced all that America has to offer because of the color of your skin? Warren knew what honor meant. But he didn't put it high on his list of things to remember. The year was 1975 and Warren was fourteen now. He seemed to remember a lot. It was as if he were always remembering, always thinking back to some time or incident which had left an indelible mark on his mind and on his life. Some statement or occurrence which had been branded deep into his very soul. The branding of him by life in the ghetto forced Warren to hide within himself. Warren went into reclusion and began to read all the time. He would no longer fritter away hours of the day playing silly games with Craig and Chas's nephew Ronald. He became interested in how man's soul had deteriorated into its present state. Especially the souls of Black men. He would go to the public library down on Holland Street almost every day to select some books. He also began to bring books home from the school library.

I would often watch Warren as he read. Every once in a while he would slowly raise his head from the book and stare toward the ceiling. He would move his head from side to side and return to his book, murmuring something to himself. It was as if he had found some hidden fact. Something that he had previously been unaware of or something that had been intentionally kept from him. It was as if he had opened some ancient tomb in Egypt and discovered treasure. I watched his facial expressions as he moved through the gamut of emotions: from confusion to surprise, to anger, to satisfaction. The satisfaction of finally knowing. It was as if he were moving through a large maze and every time he found a hall that seemed to lead somewhere, he smiled.

Warren never said much after he witnessed the rape of Sugar. At least, nothing that young men his age usually talked about. He spent his time thinking. He became so much more deep, so much more philosophical. He disappeared within himself. Hibernating from the rest of the world. Just he and his books. Warren was now a bibliophile. After he read, I would watch Warren and could tell that he was curled up somewhere deep in his soul taking a long nap and plotting what to do when his hibernation period was done. He would sometimes play and dance when others were around. But, to paraphrase Smokey Robinson, Warren's smile was only there to fool the public. Warren never really smiled again.

I noticed that Warren and Nate would sometimes stare at each other, but neither would smile. I guess there was very little to smile about. Nothing to be really happy for. Warren would often look at Sugar. Tears would come to his eyes. He thought of her having been raped. He thought of all that she had been through. Sugar still wasn't aware that Warren and I had witnessed her being raped. She would tell me that something was different about Warren. She said something had changed in her little brother. In fact, something had changed in all of us.

Warren seemed to be growing fast. Physically, he was getting bigger and stronger and I dared not wrestle with him anymore. He also seemed to be growing mentally. His reading was having a profound effect on him. Sometimes he would talk to me about the gift of life. I would sit and listen to him intently. I could not believe that the person speaking was my little brother. I was mesmerized by his conversation. He would say how good and important it was to be alive. How the gift of life was the greatest gift God had given mankind. Then in the next breath he would say that we weren't really living. We existed, but we weren't really living—not as God intended. He told me that we were just spirits inside shells. Our eyes were the windows that allowed us to look out at the world. The living, moving spirits inside the shells were the real us and the shells meant nothing. He told me that the spirit had no color, but the shell made some spirits feel that they were superior to others. Although the spirit was more powerful than the shell, the shell could be used to make the spirit feel inferior and once the spirit felt inferior, it was only a matter of time before it would be destroyed.

Warren told me to protect my spirit because the spirit housed the soul and all other significant things. He told me that once this living spirit died, we were dead. Even if our shells continued to move about, we were dead. He said that for a lot of us, the spirit had already been destroyed. The spirit had been destroyed by forces outside the shell. Warren felt that the true crime was that for some of us, the spirit was dead and our shells lived on. Dead spirits in living shells were the root of inner-city crime. Dead spirits were at the root of wars between nations and between Blacks and whites. Urban dead spirits that had been intentionally killed off were at the root of Black-on-Black crime. "Nothing good can come of a dead spirit inside a moving shell. It is like a robot that no one controls. It feels nothing. It has no conscience. It can kill without feeling any remorse. It doesn't know the meaning of remorse. A death sentence means nothing to a dead spirit. You can't kill what is already dead. You can only kill the shell and make it a symbolic killing of the corpse of a spirit."

Warren believed that most people could not really understand the spiritual, although everyone was searching for the true meaning of it all. In Africa Black people were spiritual, until they were introduced to all types of institutionalized religion. He said prior to that, Africans heeded what was deep inside them instead of following a set of rules. They were ruled by their souls and what their God had bestowed upon their souls. Their souls were their "Bill of Rights." Warren was aware that Africa or Africans were the authors of the first written constitution, and he was convinced that the writing of it was only for posterity's sake. The people were guided by their souls and their God.

Warren told me that all Africans could read and write, but what an African could not read or write, his spirit allowed him to feel. Once religion became a script read without feeling, a great many spirits died. Once those spirits no longer felt but denied their spiritualness, they sold their brothers and sisters into slavery. "Blacks are selling other Blacks into slavery today because, over time, their spirits have been destroyed. Blacks are killing other Blacks because the destruction of their spirits has been completed. It no longer matters."

Warren would sit on the side of the bed in the middle of the night and talk to Nate or me. As Warren read more, his nocturnal conversations became more frequent. Nate was proud of how much Warren had learned in such a short period of time. He enjoyed hearing him speak and hoped that he would have an effect on me. Nate said that Warren had surpassed him in awareness of his heritage. Awareness was important. In the words of Buddha, "The path to the deathless is awareness; unawareness, the path of death." It was important that we knew this concept well. It was important that we acted upon it.

I couldn't believe that Warren was so young, yet I knew that in the ghetto you either learned fast or you perished. Maybe the mere fact that I was surprised at what Warren was able to comprehend was an indication of my own brainwashing. This was too much for a Black child to understand or comprehend. This was too much for him to articulate. Only a white, privileged child would be able to understand the inner workings of the soul. Only a white child or a white man or a white professor would be able to put it so eloquently. This is what I had been taught in school. This lesson was ingrained in every ghetto child. Aim, but don't aim too high. Expect, but don't expect the unexpected. And we will constantly remind you of what the expected is.

As Warren spoke, his eyes would be full of tears, but he somehow managed to hold the tears back. Every once in a while, when Nate was not around, a tear would escape and travel the length of his face. He would reach up and roughly wipe it away. It was as if he was angry that a tear would dare to escape. Dare to show how he felt or that he was hurting—that he felt anything at all. He would abruptly turn to me and stare into my eyes as if I had made him bare his soul; as if it were my fault that the tear had escaped. He would hold the stare for a while and then glare back toward the floor. Why should this tear be free to escape? What right did it have to betray him and expose his soul?

We seemed to have our most meaningful conversations in Sugar's bedroom. It seemed the proper place for our conversations. Somehow conversations always find the appropriate room in which to take place. Sugar's room was usually dark. The only glimmer of light entered through the window next to Sugar's bed. The sounds of a dog and a cat fighting could faintly be heard coming from the alley which lay right below the window. A tall lamp pole with a dull light provided some sense of security for those who chose to risk the journey down the alley in the dangerous darkness. As I listened to Warren, I peered out of the window at the boarded-up house which stood next to the house where Chas lived. I got up and walked closer to the window just in time to see some junkie sticking a needle into his shell and nodding off into a deep sleep, or into death. My mind wandered as I thought about how awful it was for my beautiful sister to have to look out of this window and watch death occurring. I thought how awful it was for her to be raped by her father and then return to her room to peer out this window and watch death. Sugar must have thought it was awful too, because every weekend she would go off to Grandma's apartment to stay. Warren and I couldn't blame her. We knew the horrible secret. We were glad that she would not be here for Dad to rape. We also enjoyed sleeping in her bedroom. This was our way of getting back at Dad.

Warren's conversations always seemed to involve the spirit. He wanted to be removed from anything superficial. "Some spirits are still good and it's a shame that they are destroyed. But evil spirits must die. They must be destroyed and their shells must die a physical death. For so long, evil spirits inside of deceptive shells have denied good spirits a chance to grow and develop. They have killed the spirits of ghetto children at birth and then attempted to analyze why the shells of these children could not learn and weren't motivated to work. Why these shells could kill so easily. They plan the killings of the spirits and souls inside of Black shells. Then they call the shell an uncontrollable animal.

These evil spirits, which cause the destruction of souls inside of Black shells, exist inside of God-given shells—and all that God makes is good; therefore, it is difficult to differentiate the bad spirits from the good ones. These evil spirits are masters of deception. They must be destroyed. It's God's will."

Warren believed that somehow the spirit inside Dad's shell had become evil. He felt that Dad was no longer what he had been at one time. Dad had been completely transformed, and there was no way to reverse the process. Mom was right. Something had happened to Dad. Maybe, as Mom said, it wasn't Dad's fault. Maybe the pressures on him were too great. To Warren, it didn't matter anymore. It didn't matter to Warren that Dad had brought him into this world. What mattered was that Dad had raped our sister. Our only sister. He had made her feel worthless and sinful. We had witnessed Dad beating Frank with his fist because he believed Frank had not cleaned the kitchen well enough. We had seen Dad beat Mom and had heard him call her a "whore" and a "bitch." We had seen Dad beat and kick Nate.

Sometimes, Warren would just sit and stare at Dad. It was a haunting stare. Dad would act as if he didn't notice Warren's stare. Dad would try to ignore him. Maybe he knew that Warren had seen him rape Sugar. After Dad noticed Warren watching him, he would just reach over and slap him. Warren would fall to the floor and get back up and begin to stare at Dad again. It was strange. Dad couldn't faze Warren anymore; nothing he did could affect him. Warren knew that Dad's spirit was dead and he would not allow himself to be affected by an evil, dead spirit.

I guess I should have anticipated that Warren would someday confront Dad. I could have determined from Warren's statements that the time was close. But I was blinded by his youthful age of fourteen. Or maybe it was my fear of such a confrontation that contributed to my denial of the forthcoming event. Despite my wishful, fearful denials, the time had come.

It was a cold February evening. Nate and Chas had gone out. I remember seeing them leave. Chas had a pocketful of money and Nate was carrying a bag with some cocaine in it. Nate and Chas were small-time dealers now. They were making money and were the envy of most of the neighborhood youth. I remember walking in on Nate and Chas one day while they were portioning out small amounts of this white substance and putting it into a bag. They were in Sugar's room. I tried to turn and walk out as quickly as I had walked in but Nate grabbed me. "Listen, little brother. I don't ever want to see you messing around with none of this shit here. This is death. If I catch you around some of this, I'll beat your ass." I tried to deny that I knew what it was. "I don't know what that stuff is, Nate. I don't want to know or need to know."

Nate knew that I was lying. It was impossible for any child to grow up in the ghetto and not know what cocaine, marijuana, or heroin was. It was being sold on every street corner. Most of us had witnessed the zombie-like trance that it caused. Many of us had watched as Black and white police officers took payoffs from well-dressed drug dealers. Cocaine poured into the ghetto streets. Cocaine wasn't produced in the ghetto: it was piped in along with alcohol and cigarettes. It was intended to destroy everything and every family in its path. No one could escape seeing it and knowing about it. It was as common as milk to a dairy farmer.

Cocaine, marijuana, and heroin destroyed the revolutionary spirit of many of the ghetto dwellers. It took the fight out of those who should and could fight and those who had fought for civil rights. It made the revolutionaries dependents of a system, dependents of an unseen and unidentified pusher-man. It was chemical warfare. And it had been extremely effective. Columbia and other South American nations produced this anti-Black, anti-revolutionary weapon. These countries were the allies of many in America. When I became an FBI Agent, these truths would become self-evident.

Nate smiled at my lie. "Listen, boy. Don't run that stupid-ass shit by me. I know you know what this shit is. Just stay away from it." I looked past Nate at Chas and watched as he pushed a needle into his arm. He stared at me. I called out his name, "Chas..." He interrupted me. "Don't worry, I got it all under control." I left Sugar's room and ran down the stairs. I ran out onto the back porch. No one was there. The crew from the back porch was gone. Maybe, forever.

Quincy and his friends had gone to the Two-Spot bar, located down the street from our house. Mom had gone to church for choir practice. Sugar was spending another night at Grandma's house. I guess Frank was home with his wife Gwendolyn, or Peaches as we called her. It was Saturday night and Warren and I sat in the living room watching television with Dad. Dad noticed Warren staring at him. He was a little hesitant to slap Warren anymore, since Warren was growing. Dad had no fear of me. I wanted to ease the tension, so I nudged Warren and asked him to go outside with me. He ignored me at first but then got up, put his coat on, and walked toward the front door. Dad's eyes followed him as if they were Warren's shadow.

Warren and I stood silently on the steps watching the cars go by. We saw the cars but we couldn't hear them. We were in the midst of silence. It was as if we were encased in some invisible clear shield that surrounded us and kept the rest of the world at bay. His voice broke into our silence. "Fuck Dad. I hate that punk motherfucker. He better never strike me again, 'cause if he does I'll kill him. I swear I'll kill him." I looked into Warren's eyes. I saw hatred. He continued, "That motherfucker raped my sister. She'll be fucked up the rest of her life 'cause of him." Tears began to flow down his face. "That asshole should be dead and you know it." I was not surprised by his outburst. In fact, I expected it. He had already said these things to me. Our souls had communicated. I responded, "What good would that do, Warren? I mean, you'll go to jail if you kill him. Mom would be all fucked up over that and you would have done nothing but kill the shell of a spirit that is already dead. God will take care of him in due time." Warren sat down on the steps and rested his head on his knees. He wiped tears from his face. "Where is God? Damn, I want there to be a God. I want there to be someone here to help. There has to be something else to all of this. There has to be someone or something to take care of motherfuckers like Dad."

I watched Warren as he rocked back and forth. Despite all he had done to figure it all out, he remained confused. I wanted to reach out to him. I wanted to grab him and tell him that it was going to be okay. Mom always told us that everything would be okay. She always told us to hang in there. She told us that God was on our side. Whenever she noticed us staring deep into empty space, she would hug us and say it's going to be all right. I don't know if she ever really meant it. It didn't matter. Mom was our God. She was the representative that God had sent to tell us to hang in there. She was the only sign of God that we ever saw or, at least, recognized.

I knew better than to touch Warren. I knew better than to put my arms around him. That would be a sure sign of weakness and he was already feeling bad enough for baring his soul. Warren had failed to follow Nate's instructions. He was baring his soul right there on the front steps. Nate told us never, ever bare our souls. Never let anyone but family inside our shells. Nonetheless, Warren sat on the front steps crying. I didn't know how to react. I didn't know what to do.

Warren stared into the city lights. His tears began to dry. Sweat beads appeared on his forehead. He stopped rocking. The all-too-common sounds of sirens could be heard in the distance. My attention was diverted by a drunkard who stumbled out of the bar across the street from us. The drunkard was nearly hit by a car. Our invisible shield was gone now. It was as if the curtain had been lifted on some large stage and the audience lay before us. We had to fix our faces and prepare for the next scene. I blamed the drunkard. Warren never broke his stare. Something in those lights had captured his attention. Or maybe it didn't matter what he was looking at. I sat down next to him. He never turned my way. Finally, he got up and walked into the house. I followed.

Dad looked up from the television. Warren slowly walked by him and sat down at the dining room table. Dad's voice made my insides tremble. "Warren, get me a glass of milk." Warren didn't move. He had removed his coat and I noticed that his entire shirt was wet with perspiration. I moved toward the table and took a seat next to him. I could feel the tension. I wanted to volunteer to get the milk but I knew that Warren would have never forgiven me if I had. I knew that he wanted a confrontation with Dad. He wanted to repay Dad for raping Sugar and beating Mom. He wanted to confront him for punching Frank and kicking Nate. It was better that he confronted Dad. Nate would have just shot him, and Dad knew it. He was now aware that Nate carried a gun.

It was not a time for me to stand in between Warren and Dad. I would help Warren, but I would not try to change the course of this inevitable battle. Strangely, I was now willing to allow Warren to confront Dad over a glass of milk, when previously I had restrained him while Dad raped Sugar. I didn't understand it. It made no sense. I always seemed to have restraint at the wrong time. Never understanding when to move and when to hold back. Never understanding when to act and upon whom to act. I was to learn later that these were important lessons that those in power had practiced over and over again. They were to be practiced against me. I was being prepared for my future.

Dad must have thought that Warren had just not heard him. He wanted to believe that Warren hadn't heard him. Now Dad wanted the coward's way out. I smiled at the thought of it. He repeated his demand in a louder tone. "Warren, get me a glass of milk." Warren continued to sit still. Sweat moved down his face. I looked deep into his eyes and saw boiling blood coursing through the pathways of his soul. It was one of the three fluids that were most common to Black people in America: sweat, blood, and tears—usually in that order. Sweat and blood and tears were common to Black people the world over. I was convinced that unless things changed in the world, Blacks would one day rise up and with tears in their eyes and sweat on their bodies draw the blood from those who had wronged them.

Dad turned around in his chair. He faced Warren. "What the fuck is wrong with you, boy? Get me some milk." I wondered how Warren thought he could defy Dad without getting beaten badly. Sure, Warren was growing and he was now strong and muscular like an African warrior. But Dad was much bigger than Warren and, although he was not in good shape, he was certainly much stronger. Nate would tell us that strength was in the heart. He said that a true warrior was more heart than muscle. Right now, Warren must have the biggest heart in the world, yet I would have traded it for more muscle.

Warren clenched the table. Dad stood up and moved toward him. Dad began to remove his belt from his pants. Warren didn't turn to face him. Dad must have thought that we were still young kids. He thought that the mere sight of him removing his belt would cause Warren to respond. Dad was not unlike the modern slavemaster who still expected every Black man to drop to his knees at the sight of his symbolic whip. I turned to confront Dad. As I opened my mouth, the buckle of Dad's belt landed on my forehead. Blood trickled down my nose. I fell to the floor. Warren jumped over me but it was too late. The belt crashed down across his back. He was no match for Dad. Dad pushed him to the floor, held him down, and administered a slavemaster's whipping. I lay and watched. Once again, helpless—unable to stop what was left of my dad from destroying another one of my siblings.

I wanted Nate to walk through the door and kill this beast that had once been my dad. I wanted someone to kill this thing that this society had created. I tried to escape, to climb the wooden stairs and run to my room. I felt the leather whip land on my back. I went limp. Dad was breathing hard and sweating. He looked as if he wanted to kill me. This was his way of striking back at those who had broken him, those who had emasculated him. He was beating me for those white checker players at the bus station. He was beating me for all the times he had been called nigger. All the hate that was inside him was being expended on me. He was destroying a part of him and I could hear the laughter of those who had waited for this.

They had built a soldier to fight in wars overseas. He had come home ready to fight them, but he had been made to fight and destroy himself; to rape and beat his own flesh and blood; to brutalize the woman who had borne his children. The process was complete. I could hear the laughter and see the faces of those responsible all about Dad. I could feel their evil spirits. It was a Greek tragedy. It was not Dad who was beating me. It was they. I no longer wanted to kill Dad. I loved him. It was those evil faces around him that I wanted to kill.

I put my hands up to shield Dad's blows. My vision was blurred by tears. Dad couldn't hear me. "I–I love you, Daddy." He continued to strike out at me. It was as if he were possessed. He was looking through me at something behind me, at something or someone or some time in his past. His eyes were focused on something that I couldn't see. He couldn't see Warren coming up behind him. I don't think it mattered. Just as it hadn't mattered when we watched him rape Sugar. He had that same look. I thought I saw Warren moving closer to Dad, moving close to hold Dad or to help me. The beating ceased. A calm silence blanketed the room. I sighed deeply.

None of us had control over this scene. This script, this play was written by someone else. We were just actors, expendable actors. We were puppets on an invisible string. The creator, the director or producer of this show was a genius, or maybe a fool. They had prepared us perfectly. Making sure that we would meet at this place in this scenario. They had prepared Dad to destroy himself and his family. It was just as it should have been. Nonetheless, I was glad that the director yelled "Cut." Sweat and blood and tears.

9

Uphold the Laws

*"Yes. There are some good policemen and some
bad policemen. Usually we get the bad ones."*
    —Malcolm X, By Any Means Necessary

*If a man is called to be a streetsweeper, he should
sweep streets even as Michelangelo painted, or
Beethoven composed music, or Shakespeare wrote
poetry. He should sweep streets so well that all
the hosts of heaven and earth will pause to say,
here lived a great streetsweeper who did his job
well.*

    —Martin Luther King Jr.

Uphold the laws of the State of Maryland. That's what I was
about to swear to do. Another pledge of allegiance to America.
This time I would pledge to sacrifice my life to defend the laws
created by the elected leaders. From the midst of the streets of
Baltimore; from the midst of crime and lawlessness; from drug-
infested avenues, trash-strewn boulevards and junkie-plagued
alleyways; from the witnessing of murder and mayhem, I had
arrived here, at this place, at this time. Unbelievable.
Unthinkable.

All five feet eleven inches of me stood stonily vertical.
Nothing on my body moved, at least nothing that was visible to
the adoring audience. My heart pounded wildly, causing my white
sleeveless tee shirt to move with each rebellious pulsating beat.
Rebellious—because I wanted to be calm and show no emotions,

83

as Nate and Warren had trained me. I wanted to be cool. I didn't want this ceremony to affect me any more than my stint of ghetto living. My heart had long before stopped pounding wildly to the bloody scenes of my urban hell. Luckily, the rapid pumping of my undisciplined heart was hidden by my severely starched beige shirt. I stood outside myself to view this specimen that was me. I wanted to take a look at what one of my elementary school teachers had called "nothing but another worthless ghetto child."

My official Maryland State Police uniform was clean and crisp, just as they had told us it had to be at all times. I was a fully disciplined Trooper. Although hidden by my brown dress jacket, the patch bearing the yellow, black, and white emblem of the Maryland State Police on my left shirt sleeve was creased perfectly. My black leather Sam Browne belt was meticulously buffed and polished. It was positioned perfectly and made a flawless trek from its starting position on the back of my gun belt, up and across my back from right to left, over my left shoulder, across my chest diagonally and down to my holster which rested on my right side. A well-cleaned and oiled .357 magnum rested in my heavily polished black holster. The brass badge that hung on the lapel of my class-A uniform glistened in the bright lights that lit the gymnasium which had been converted into an auditorium for this special event. The class-A uniform was for special occasions only. It was not the regular duty attire of Maryland State Troopers. For me and the other Trooper candidates standing alongside me, December 17, 1982 was a very significant day and it certainly qualified as a special occasion.

I had shaven off my mustache as required and my hair was cut short in compliance with agency specifications. I stood there amongst thirty-nine other candidates who were about to become Maryland's finest. I stared straight ahead, as I had been instructed to do, and attempted to pay attention to the words of the superintendent of the Maryland State Police. He was informing us of the proud history of the department. "You, ladies and gentlemen, are about to take a solemn step into a proud and distinguished organization that has sought to judicially enforce the laws of the state without regard to race, creed, or religion." *Bullshit*. I silently contested the lie of equal and judicious law enforcement. I knew better. I had witnessed the brutal and unjust beatings that young Black men received at the hands of their uniformed "protectors."

As the superintendent continued his tympany, my mind wandered. I was twenty-one years old now and still could not concentrate on any one thing but for a short period of time. It was difficult to think and concentrate on only one thing or event while living in the ghetto. As time went on, I found myself losing my concentration more frequently. Wandering to other places and other things. Sometimes I took my body with me; at other times I was a free-floating spirit. My journeys away from reality were not planned. I had no map that would lead me to a set, preconceived destination. There were no boundaries that I had to stay within. Mind-wandering imagination was true and pure freedom. Not freedom with liberty. The frequency of my daydreaming or night dreaming increased as I witnessed more brutality within my preset borders. I unintentionally, or maybe intentionally, drifted from what had become the constant but necessary ugly thoughts of day-to-day survival in a war zone.

I tilted my head back slightly, but not noticeably, and looked into the bright lights which hung overhead. The lights seemed to be a thing of beauty. They diverted me from the constant thoughts I had been having lately of my most improbable journey from the mean streets of the ghetto to the Maryland State Police Academy. I thought of how wonderful it would have been if we had had bright lights in the public schools in Baltimore. What if our auditoriums at Bentalou Elementary School, Gwyn Falls Park Middle School, Rock Glen Middle School and Southwestern High School had looked like this? Why couldn't our halls have been clean and our floors shined? Instead, the hallways and classrooms in the inner-city schools were fusty and dimly lit. Inside the classrooms were scratched and scarred chalk boards that could no longer accept or maintain the markings of broken chalk. The auditoriums were old and the dull floors gave away annoying squeaks. The windows were always full of dirt and smut. Beyond the dirty glass windows stood boarded-up houses, railroad tracks, and burnt-out stores. The boarded houses and burnt-out stores were remnants and reminders of futile riots and callous city administrators.

These dreadful inner-city classrooms caused young, preoccupied minds to roam. I noticed that other students were seldom paying attention. They were thinking of their next meal or where and when they were going to sleep. Some were thinking of drug-addicted parents. I watched as they looked through the windows at the dilapidated houses. It was impossible for us to concentrate on the lessons that were being hurled—with little concern for accurately hitting the targets—by our dry-as-dust teachers. Many of the students didn't care about the homework assignments. They were young, innocent children who had too many other worries and concerns. Too many real-life, adult problems of greater urgency. Who could concentrate on what Dick and Jane were doing under these circumstances? Who gave a damn about a dog named Spot?

I would sit there watching the other students as they watched me. My only escape was my "manchild" imagination. I imagined that I was somewhere else. Imagined that I was up in the sky flying freely over and away from the boarded-up houses. I was flying away from the railroad tracks, flying over and passing police cars and ambulances with blurring sirens. Freely flying and smiling and looking around at pleasant places. Then, I imagined that all the students from my classes, all the so-called ghetto children were flying with me. They, too, were smiling—smiling and happy about their extrication from the ghetto. We were all heading some place, any place—just away from the ghetto; away from the taunts and name-calling; away from being looked down on, abused, and brushed aside as insignificant imps.

Maybe we were flying back to Africa to be with our families who were also making this joyous odyssey. Not the Africa that the Europeans have created. Not an Africa of war and hate and atomic weapons. Not an Africa of colonization. We would travel to the Africa that was there before the brutal, immoral invasions. The Africa that was there before the Muslims and the Christians came to save "heathen" souls. Maybe we were going to sit on the banks of the Nile River, with a warm spiritual breeze blowing through us or over us, and talk among ourselves. Maybe we would have an old and wise, or young and wise, professor standing before us teaching mathematics and science. I mean really teaching us. Maybe another professor would stand up and instruct us in our true history. He or she would tell us about all the great civilizations that we had created. In fact, the professor would tell us that we had been civilized before any other race of people. We had built roads and temples before others even knew what they were. We were the builders of the pyramids, not the destroyers that the world has now identified us as. We had created buildings from rubble—we had not turned buildings into ruins.

The professor would tell us about the wisdom of the Moors of Spain. He would tell us of their cleanliness and how it was the Moors who taught others how to bathe. We would learn how the Moors organized and structured a society. How they had built beautiful cities. How others had learned from them and then expelled them. This point would explain what had happened to Blacks in America. Blacks had labored in the fields of America for years without compensation and in the end, after America had become a great nation, Blacks were treated and looked upon as worthless parasites and were excluded from reaping the benefits of their torturous labors. Used, abused, and discarded.

There would be other professors to tell us about the proper foods to eat. They wouldn't mention Spam or macaroni and powdered cheese. They wouldn't mention pigs' feet, pork sausage, spare ribs, and bacon. They wouldn't mention hot dogs or the intestines (chitterlings or chitlins) of the dirtiest of all beasts, the hog. They would tell us how our ancestors lived long lives and remained strong without the use of any drugs. They would tell us how Africa had been practically free of any diseases before the invaders from the north came.

We would be taught religion. Not some religion given to us by those who had enslaved us. Not a religion taught by invaders. We would learn how foolish it was for us to adopt the religion of those who intended to conquer us. We wouldn't be subjected to pictures of a blue-eyed, long-haired Jesus. We wouldn't see a white Mary holding a white baby while others knelt before them. We would be made to see how ignorant and arrogant it was for one race, any race, to assume that Jesus and God looked like them in the face of biblical descriptions which were in direct contradiction to this assumption and those pictures.

The professors would point out that the movies we watched in America, such as *The Ten Commandments*, had not one Black person in it despite the fact that the events which the movie depicted took place in Black Africa. He would point out that according to that movie, Egypt was populated entirely by whites. The professors would point this out as an indication of just how bold others have been in their attempt to deceive us into believing that we, as a race of people, had played no part in history, not even in African history. If you have no history, you have no roots. If you have no roots, you are dead. Mother nature teaches us that every day. We were being treated as weeds that had to be pulled up from the roots to stop their growth in the midst of the beautiful and much desired green grass.

We would learn about a divine being who created us all in His image. We would learn to do what was right because our soul told us it was right. We wouldn't need the pope—who, in our time, had never been anything but white—telling us that he maintains the closest relationship with God. We would all maintain a close relationship with God and would not look for an interpreter of God's word. And then it wouldn't matter where we traveled in the world or where we lived, because we would all know the truth. The truth would let us know what we were capable of achieving. The truth would unify us with our God. This unification of God and His people would keep us strong and keep us from killing one another, because we would know that to kill each other would be like killing off a piece of God. And we would know that we could not possibly live without God.

Africa is where my imagination took me. That was my destination. But I was not flying. My sojourn was but a fantasy. In reality, I was sitting in a suffocating inner-city classroom where all the lessons were different from those I imagined, different from those I would receive on the Nile. The sound of a slow, uninteresting voice, which belonged to a dull, uninteresting teacher, who stood at the front of a dreary, uninteresting classroom, made me discern my reality. The sight of other children nodding off and thinking about problems they shouldn't have to think about made me realize that I was not in Africa. The view of the boarded-up houses let me know that I had not flown away from anything. I felt no warm breeze. This was not the Nile.

The superintendent of the Maryland State Police spoke in a loud, confident voice. He spoke of the loyalty that the job demanded, the love of country, and the love of the state of Maryland—all of which the badge represented. "Although the badges on your lapels are brass, once they are pinned on, they turn into gold. In fact, the badges are more valuable than gold because of what they symbolize. The badges on your lapels symbolize good. They symbolize the good that is deep down inside of all Troopers. It is the good that the gold badge represents that will help you stand up against all of your adversaries." We were the good guys. We wore the white hats. God was on our side.

I never understood the relationship between gold and good. Mom would say that if we were good we would, one day, walk in heaven on streets of gold. Why would I want to walk on gold? Why would Mom need to walk on gold? She was not a mammonist. God was not a mammonist. I had seen nothing but evil come from gold. I had seen men kill each other over gold. I had read about nations that went to war over it. Many of the forty-niners gave up all they owned to travel west in search of gold. Most of them ended up destitute. Somehow, despite it all, gold was seen as good. Somehow people were made to believe that if they wore gold around their necks, around their fingers, around their wrists, or put it on their teeth or on their lapels, they were worth more. Gold fed their egos. My mind was in motion again. Rapidly moving from one thought to another. Trying to forget what I was doing. Trying to forget the words of my brothers. Why did I care about the hypocrisy of gold? I was searching for understanding. Still trying to understand my trek from the ghetto. Still trying to understand why I wanted to be a police officer. Why I wanted anything. More thoughts, moving at illegal speeds through my mind.

It was always strange to me how we were wanting things and wearing things that we didn't understand. I couldn't comprehend how we could be so easily made to like or dislike something or someone without ever analyzing the reasons for our likes or dislikes. It was as if we were drones or subjects of some massive psychological experiment. This urge for gold—the urge to walk on it, wear it, steal it, fight and die for it—was incomprehensible to me.

Yet, I knew that there was plenty of gold in Africa and, at one point, it belonged to people who looked just like me. I understood that, at one point, all the rich minerals of Africa belonged to us. Everywhere we walked, we walked on gold. Maybe that's what Mom was saying. Maybe that's what the Bible was saying. Maybe, one day, we would again walk on the mineral-rich soils of Africa. Maybe that was our heaven and our streets of gold. Maybe that explained Black people's fixation with gold. Our subconscious, our souls were trying to tell us something. We just didn't read it correctly. The streets of gold were in Africa. We were confused. I was confused. I had to slow the thoughts. Make them obey the process. This was not the time for introspection, or was it?

I bolted from my solitary excursus and returned my attention to the speaker and his audience. For the first time, I noticed the people who had come to view this spectacle. I saw the proud, smiling faces of the other candidates' family members. I carefully scanned the crowd for my family. I found Mom first. She stood there smiling in her white-collared deep-blue dress that she had purchased for the occasion. Her tightly curled jet black hair shone in the lights and indicated a recent perm. She was proud. Maybe prouder than any other parent present. Proud that her son had escaped the misery of the ghetto. Mom felt that she was able to get one son out of Egypt. She believed that at least one of her sons would escape the Pharaoh's wrath.

Grandma stood with Mom. She was a tall lady with short gray hair and smooth honey-brown skin. She was smiling and rocking to some gospel song that was only audible to her. Her head was tilted back as she looked toward the ceiling. I expected her to raise her hand and wave it as she so often did in church when she was thanking the Lord for something. She looked as if she were trying to look past the gymnasium lights and up into heaven. Her gray hair appeared to be short strands of icicles under the bright lights. Her skin gave little indication of her age. I knew she was thinking of God. I knew she was thanking God for allowing her to see this day. She was so happy to be standing next to her daughter and watching her grandson. She was happy and thankful. God did answer prayers.

Grandma knew what we had been through. She knew how Dad had treated us. Sugar had told her the horrifying details of her rape. Grandma had decided not to tell Mom. She said that as strong as Mom seemed to be, she would not be able to handle the news about the rape of her baby girl. She believed that Mom would probably kill herself and that we would be left to live with Dad. Grandma had kept trying to talk Mom into leaving Dad without telling her about the rape of Sugar. She was happy when Mom finally left. She was sorry that it had to come to the point of a physical confrontation between sons and father. She never wanted that. It was against her Christian training. It was against all that she had learned growing up in North Carolina. It was against all that she had taught us. But the confrontation did not surprise Grandma—she expected it to happen. She thought it would be Quincy and Dad confronting each other. In fact, she believed that Quincy would kill Dad. But today, all of that was behind her. She was happy now because Mom was happy. Mom was her only child, and Grandma loved seeing her happy. She looked toward Mom and smiled.

Frank stood next to Grandma. Frank was about six feet three inches tall and weighed two hundred sixty pounds. He had a solid, quiet look on his face. His skin was a shiny black. Frank was proud of his little brother. He was proud that I had made it through six months of training that was intended to weed me out. I had withstood the constant yelling and the grueling physical training. I had hung in there while Sergeant Jeppid had tried to intimidate me into quitting; while he had tried to "break" me.

Sergeant Jeppid was a tall man with blonde hair. He looked as if he could have been one of Hitler's Nazi soldiers. I was sure that he hated me. I was sure he hated every Black man. He would intentionally give me low marks on tests on which I knew I had performed substantially higher. After my test papers had been returned, I would compare them with those of the white candidates. Even they would agree that I had been cheated. They told me the scores didn't matter as long as I hung in there and graduated. The sergeant wanted to make sure that I would never feel that I was as good as the white candidates. He couldn't and wouldn't allow me to compete on equal ground. Who was I to come up out of the ghetto and compete with white candidates that had never seen the ghetto? He wanted to make sure that this "smart-ass nigger" knew where he belonged. He wanted to remind me to "stay in my place." Sergeant Jeppid wanted it understood that I should never challenge him or those like him because he always would have the upper hand. There would always be a way to get me. I was to advance only as far as he would allow me. He was designated to teach me that lesson. Most of the tests that other instructors gave were multiple choice. Sergeant Jeppid's tests were not. He gave essay examinations. He wanted to have the last say. It would be his decision, his interpretation of what was right or wrong. He would be in control. He taught Technical Writing and he was the lone judge of what was technically correct.

Corporal Zachary was a short, muscular Black man with an extraordinary sense of humor. He was also a strong disciplinarian. He taught a variety of classes and everyone respected him and enjoyed his lectures. He believed, more than anything, that it was important for us to learn our lessons well. Before and after class he was strict, but during class he was completely open. It was important to him that we were good policemen. He had seen too many bad ones and now that he had something to do with the making of good police officers, he was determined to make a difference.

I remember Corporal Zachary getting us up at two in the morning to run a mile or two and do push-ups. He was tough. I recall his message to me after one of his classes. He called me to the side. "I've been watching your test scores. You're doing a hell of a job. Your scores are at the top of the class. In fact, last week your average was the highest in the class. So you think you're smart." I responded as Mom had told me, "Yes sir, I do. I believe that I'm at least as intelligent as anyone else in this class." He patted me on my back and smiled, "I think you're smart too, boy. Are you smart enough to know that it ain't always smart to be the smartest in this type of organization?" I looked at him quizzically, "Sir, I don't quite understand. Are you saying I should not do my best?" He shook his head, "No, I'm not saying that. In fact, we didn't have this conversation. You think about it, boy. It'll come to you. I want you to finish this training. We need you in this organization. Your probation period is one year. After that, they can't touch you. There is a time and season for everything. These people don't like to be challenged by our kind. An intelligent Black man scares a whole lot of white folks. A Black man with intelligence, who stands up and says he's a Black man with intelligence, usually dies young." Corporal Zachary winked his eye and lowered his voice, "Read Sun Tzu's *The Art of War*. Dismissed."

Corporal Zachary turned and walked down the hallway. I stood there deep in my thoughts, engulfed in a cloud of confusion. I was to work hard and to study hard. I was to strive to be the best I could at whatever I attempted. And then I was to appear not so smart. From that point on, I didn't try to score as high as before. I knew the answers but I was careful to get a few wrong. I would employ this tactic in later academic situations where it was not a good idea to be "too intelligent." Corporal Zachary was giving me an early lesson in the power of strategic deception.

Next to Frank stood my beautiful wife, Doris. I had taken her as my wife when I was only nineteen. Doris was twenty-six. Our wedding date was etched in my mind: June 20, 1981. I remember my friends telling me that I was too young to get married. They told me that I should "play the field." They said that I was too young to make such a commitment. This myth that an African male was too young to make a commitment was part of the brainwashing. Black men had to make commitments. We had to be committed to achieving freedom. We had to be committed to avoiding alcohol and drugs. We had to be committed to rearing our children and uplifting our communities. And the earlier we became committed, the better.

We needed to start educating our youth on commitment the day they left the womb of their Nubian mothers. We needed to get them committed to education and respect for their Black sisters. This I'm-too-young-for-commitment, I-just-want-to-party philosophy had helped lead to a high school drop-out rate of over fifty percent in most African American communities in America. The lack of will to become committed to the pursuit of freedom had helped lead to generation after generation of "welfare families." This fear of commitment had to be erased or it would eventually erase us. What I was hearing from my friends was fear of commitment of any type. I was committed to marrying Doris. I was convinced beyond a shadow of a doubt that she was the woman for me. She was the woman who would help me grow. She was a woman who was committed to having a strong Black man and not just any Black male. We were committed to building a strong Black family that would have a positive impact on the world.

I didn't need to "play the field." I had learned too much to want to play with the emotions of a Black woman. The emotions of Black women had been played with by everyone else and I did not desire to perpetuate this cruel joke. I would not allow myself to be used as another tool in their destruction. I knew that the destruction of the Black woman would mean the destruction of the Black race. It was not unbelievable to me that an entire race could be wiped out. The so-called Indians were a glaring historical example of what one race could do to another over a period of time. No land, no rights, no pride, no people!

I knew that I loved Doris and I knew that I had too much to do. Life for a Black man is just too short. When a Black man finds that Black woman who is willing to work and fight with him, there is no time to waste. I had matured through education. I understood that it was important for me to respect and to love my woman. I had learned that women-chasing had never been a part of the history of Africans. This degrading conduct, like many others, had entered at a later time.

My study of history had taught me that civilization for Blacks was not progressing but actually regressing. We were doing things now to our women that we would have never thought of in the past. Doris was my *lady* and I, her *man*. She was my wife and I needed her, just as she needed me. We needed each other. I knew I could depend on her. And she knew that I would be there to love and respect her and to protect her from all who tried to do her harm. She knew that I was willing to give my life in her defense. I would destroy all who tried to destroy her.

Doris was a beautiful, mature woman. Her life had not been much different from mine. Her father had been broken into pieces of a man, just as my father had. He, like the so-called Indians, had succumbed to the trickery and destructive effects of "fire water." During one of his drinking binges he shot her mother in the head, leaving her permanently partially blind in the right eye. Her mother somehow survived the shooting. And, like so many other strong Black women, she had managed to rear all five of her children alone. Her emotions had been damaged by a broken man but her children had to be reared nevertheless.

I met Doris when I was eighteen. I was working as a custodian at Maryland General Hospital in Baltimore. Doris was working there as a dietary aide. One year later we were married. She had been by my side during the time I had been in training at the Maryland State Police Academy in Pikesville, Maryland. She had listened to my stories concerning the State Police Academy, and she was now standing there watching the results of our perseverance. She wasn't smiling like Mom and Grandma, because she remembered what we had been through. She knew that I had often thought of quitting. She had kept me going! The job didn't matter. It was the principle. Doris said, "Don't let them break you!" She told me to remember that my father and her father had been broken. It was important for me to be strong. She told me that they could never legitimately flunk me out, so they wanted me to quit. They would provide the atmosphere and the tools for my downfall. Then they would sit back and watch and hope that I would assist in their scheme. That was the way it had always been done to people of color.

Doris' mother, Shirley Temple Day, stood directly behind her. She was a lovely, light-complexioned woman who was always well dressed. She didn't show the battle scars of the emotional war she had been unwillingly engaged in for years. She was proud of her daughter and son-in-law. She had hoped Doris would marry someone who was at least trying to do something positive. She had hoped Doris could find a Black man who was not yet in pieces. She thought my becoming a Maryland State Trooper was a step in the right direction. She had told Doris that she was apprehensive about my going into law enforcement, yet she understood that I had to do what was in my heart. She was happy that Doris would no longer be required to live in the ghetto. The Maryland State Police would be her way out of that urban hell. Her daughter and son-in-law would be respected. They were no longer just ghetto children. She was hoping things would be different for Doris and me.

A few rows back behind Doris stood Dad. Somehow Warren and I had survived the overseer's beating administered by Dad. Right after that incident, Mom packed us up and we moved to the Park Heights area of Baltimore City. Mom finally purchased a house at 4461 Old Frederick Road in the Edmonson Village section of Baltimore City. She and Grandma would live there until Warren was drafted into the National Football League, at which time he purchased Mom another house. Grandma moved in with us at our residence in Park Heights.

I would never be able to forgive Dad. Yet, I would not shun him completely. It was not that I didn't hold him responsible for his actions. It was that I knew other forces had helped create what he had become. I had hoped that somehow he could be stronger. I had hoped that he could resist those forces a little longer. But he couldn't or, at least, he didn't. All I knew was I despised him for it. Strangely enough, I also admired him. This American system had ridden him long and hard. He had put up a good fight against incredible odds. And in the end he had been broken. I admired his willingness to fight when so many others refused. Yet, I despised his failure to win his soul. Now he was broken. He was now only pieces of a man.

I invited Dad because I refused to allow his tormentors to have the satisfaction of alienating and destroying him completely. Yes, he had been shattered, but they had not yet disposed of the pieces. I knew that if Dad—who had created me—were destroyed, a part of me would also be destroyed. Not all of me, because I was determined not to end up like Dad. I'm sure Dad was determined not to end up like his father. I wanted him to come to my graduation. I wanted him to be there standing tall and proud. Proud of what I had become, or what he thought I had become. Proud to know that all of him had not been destroyed. I wanted him to know that I was his creation. And as long as part of him lived in me, he still lived. I wanted him to know that I knew that some of what he did had nothing to do with what he really wanted to do. I wanted Dad to know that I understood the plan to break him, to destroy him. I understood how the plan was created and how it was supposed to work. I could never put Dad back together and neither could all the king's horses and all the king's men. But I understood that he had not merely had a great fall. I knew he had been pushed and I was not going to allow the pieces of him to be swept under a rug.

The superintendent asked us to raise our right hand. We were about to take our oath of office. I visualized the faces of Nate and Quincy. I remembered the conversation we had had the night before in the basement of Mom's house. I blocked out the superintendent's voice so that I could give myself completely to my thoughts of that meeting.

Initially, both Quincy and Nate had been quiet. They sat with their heads hung low. Nate spoke first. "Damn, what do you want me to do, congratulate you on becoming 'the man'? Well, I don't know if I can do that, brother." He got up and paced back and forth across the basement floor. "I'm happy that you are doing what you want to do, but it goes against everything I believe in, everything we believe in. I mean, ever since we can remember, cops have been beating and cracking our heads for no reason at all. Now you're going to be one of them. I don't doubt that you'll be a good cop, if there is such a thing, but what the fuck do you hope to accomplish?"

Nate stared at me as if he were waiting for an answer. Yet, I knew he really didn't want a response. He had the floor and I was only part of his audience. He was talking to Quincy. He was talking to Frank, Warren, and Sugar. Although they were not yet in the basement, he could feel their presence.

Nate was talking to himself. As he spoke to me, Nate was trying to analyze what he was saying. He was trying to analyze my decision. Trying to figure out my thought process. He continued, "I don't imagine that you will be cracking brothers over the head. I don't believe that you will lose your consciousness and try to show off for the white cops. But damn, everyone will still see you as one of them. They'll see you as the enemy. That might not matter to most Black cops who see nothing but a good salary and a pension, but I'm sure it'll matter to you. How are you going to deal with that? How are you going to deal with being called an Uncle Tom? How are you going to deal with being called a traitor?"

My eyes followed Nate as he crossed the room. I knew he would respond this way. He had never really said much during the time I was in training. I think he wanted me to flunk out or quit. Then he could say "I told you so." Maybe he thought that I would come to my senses and realize there were other things I could do. He was hoping I would come to the realization that there were other things I should be doing. It was difficult for him to conceive his brother working for "the man." I understood that. I felt what he felt.

For Nate, and a lot of other Blacks, the word *police* meant trouble. Police were the identified enemy. Police assigned to the inner city saw their job as the keeper of the zoo animals. They were the barrier between the inner-city jungle and the civilized, white suburbs. Blacks had been identified as the most vicious beasts in the jungle. They had to be caught and tamed. Put into the zoo to be watched. They had to be made to call on the keepers or the keepers' bosses for food and housing. They had to be kept in a tranquilized state of being and in a state of not knowing. Ignorance had to be maintained. An educated group of Blacks meant trouble. A group of Blacks who just wanted to party and holler and dance and take drugs was perfect. Tranquilize them with superfluous entertainment.

The keepers were always prepared to shoot in case the beasts decided to wake up from their tranquilized state. They were always making bigger and stronger cages to keep in the biggest and strongest of the beasts. They were always going to their bosses saying, "We need new laws to keep the beasts from procreating. We need to convince them to have abortions. Not abstain. No, they have to keep screwing. Especially the young teenagers. It keeps them occupied. It keeps them from the libraries. But we cannot allow them to multiply."

The bosses of the keepers convinced their bosses that the keepers needed new weapons to handle these beasts. The keepers convinced their bosses that they needed to take away any weapons that these beasts might possess. The bosses were told by their bosses that to take away all the weapons from all the beasts meant weapons might have to be taken from those who were not viewed as beasts. The bosses told the bosses of the keepers that a better strategy was to teach the beasts to utilize their weapons against each other. Teach the beasts to hate themselves. Teach them that their lives are meaningless. Give them the jungle as the arena to do their killing of each other and exploit them in their own arena. The keepers smiled. All was well.

Nate and Quincy believed cops were vicious. They believed they could not be reasoned with. The decision had already been made that all Blacks were targets. Some could be tamed, given positions with the keepers, and used against their own kind. Others would be used against their own kind in their untamed state. Both the tamed and the untamed ones would accomplish the same goal—the psychological and physical destruction of their own kind. Nate said that to the police, a Black man was a nigger, no matter where he stood or what he accomplished. There was no such thing as a good Black. The whole theory of the keepers and the beasts was taught in police academies across the country and around the world.

Nate sat down on the couch and said, "Man, you're intelligent. Why can't you be a teacher so you can teach these little Black children who are hungering for knowledge? I know you can give them some hope. It's too late for me. I've got the intelligence and I know what message I should be delivering. But they've already identified me as the enemy; therefore, they're never going to let me get near a school. You are still in a position to get on the inside. You are still in a position to stop the miseducation of the next generation. You've been prepared for this reality. I just know that you have. I can feel it."

I was older now and would not just sit and let Nate speak, as I had done when we were younger. I spoke up. "Nate, I don't understand it at all. You preach to me about helping the kids, yet you sell that shit. And you and I both know that cocaine has death written all over it. We know that cocaine means death to all these kids you're asking me to go preach to or teach. I know that you have killed. And the victims of the killings were people who look like us as well as those would-be students of mine. Compared to what you have done, and are still doing, what kind of harm am I doing to my people by my being a cop? What the fuck kind of death and destruction am I going to cause?"

I was breathing heavily now. I couldn't believe that I was talking this way to Nate. He stood up and walked toward me a few steps and stopped. His voice became louder. "Don't compare yourself with me. Don't think about what I'm doing. Fuck me. Think about what you are doing and what you could be doing. Don't compare yourself with anyone else. Just do what you know is right. If you start comparing yourself with others, you will become a follower and not a leader. You will beat some brother down because some other Black cop has done the same. It's okay to look at great men like Marcus Garvey, Paul Robeson, W.E.B. DuBois, Booker T. Washington, Elijah Muhammad and Malcolm X and try to follow in their footsteps—but don't even compare yourself with them. You are not in some contest to see who can be the greatest Black man in history. Although that's what others would have you to do. Don't compete with me. Don't base what you do on what I've done."

I tried to respond. I tried to locate and identify an appropriate response somewhere within my brain passageways. Something poetic that would mesmerize my audience and win them over. The words got stuck in the dark corridor between my brain and my voice box. The words were paralyzed, afraid that they would not be adequate. My thought process was halted by this cowardly backup in the corridors. I felt as if I had lost the ability to talk. My mouth became dry. I refocused on Nate. He seemed to have come closer to me. Yet I had not seen him move. I couldn't see past his strong well-chiseled face. I couldn't see past his stare or his stance.

Nate's lips began to move. "Yeah, we need Black cops. I mean real Black policemen who are not just trying to impress the white boys so that they can move up in the organization. We need brothers who don't just want to talk about how they kicked some young or old Black man in the ass. Yeah, I know cops have to kick ass to survive sometimes. But we don't need brothers who have to prove their capabilities or worthiness by kicking other brothers in the ass. Anyway, you ain't no cop, man. You got the knowledge that can't be distributed through the Miranda warnings. You need a classroom full of young Black warriors. You need to be teaching them how to be strong young men."

Quincy's eyes moved from Nate to me. He listened closely to both of us. The stair creaked. Frank walked down the stairs and noted the scene. He slowly walked over next to Quincy and sat down. Warren walked in from the door at the back of the basement. He was coming in from football practice and was still dressed in his football uniform. He was now a star defensive end for the Edmonson High School Redskins. His coach said he seemed to play with anger all the time. Warren had fire in him.

Warren's jersey was white with bold red numbers. His white pants were covered with dirt and mud. His red and white socks had rolled down around his ankles. He dropped his helmet on the floor and leaned against the wall. Nate's voice got lower. "You see, brother, what I do no longer matters. I'm already dead. I'm just hanging on. Yeah, I know what's happening, but I can't feel anymore. The streets that I walk day and night are my world. These motherfuckers that I kill are just like me. They are just the living dead. Crazed, dangerous zombies. I'm just getting them out of the way for people like you and all those kids who are willing to follow you. We're the zombies in that movie *Dawn of the Dead* and the *Night of the Living Dead.* But we just didn't die, man. We were murdered, and you know that. Don't let them kill any more of our young warriors."

I felt a chill come over my body. Nate had just stood there and told me that he was already dead. He said that the hearse with his body in it was moving by me and that it was up to me to prevent the movement of any more hearses. Warren knew exactly what Nate was talking about. He had explained it all to me many times from the edge of Sugar's bed. He had explained it to Nate, Quincy, and Frank. He sat there calmly taking in the entire scene. Nate wasn't revealing anything new to Warren.

Although Warren had explained it all to me, it still was a mild shock. It was a shock that Nate was one of those dead spirits. It was frightening that Nate was waiting for the inevitable and that he expected me to go out and try to help save someone. He expected me to try to make up for his irreclaimable life. I had heard Dr. Martin Luther King Jr. say that no one was free until everyone was free. I had heard him say that everyone had a role to play and that if an individual did not play his role, he didn't deserve to live. Nate was trying to keep my spirit alive. He was trying to make me deserve my life.

Quincy's voice broke the silence. "Can you kill a man?" I was startled by his question. "What?" He forcefully repeated the question, "Can you kill a man?" I resented the question. He seemed to be calling me weak. "Of course I can kill someone if I have to." He stared at me and responded, "It ain't so easy killing a man. It takes more strength than you think. And it will even be harder for you because you have this deep moral conscience. You don't really want to kill, even if it's your enemy. You're not alone in that. Why do you think that so many brothers are dying at the white man's hand in South Africa? Brothers don't want to kill. They want to negotiate with people who wouldn't hesitate to exterminate them. They want to make deals with people who only respect power. Power that comes from a willingness to be ruthless when deemed necessary. It seems that the only time brothers get courage to kill is when the white man places them in uniforms and points the way. Or when they are shooting some other brother and, even then, the way is being pointed, whether they know it or not."

I couldn't figure out exactly what Quincy was trying to say. I didn't know where his argument was heading. Nate was talking about being dead and now Quincy was talking about killing. I spoke up again. "Why did you kill the brothers you have killed, Quincy?" He responded without hesitation, as if he had been asked the same question a thousand times. "That's what's fucked up. I really don't know if I've ever killed anyone. But if I did, I suppose that at the time I felt it was necessary. I guess I thought that I had to prove something to somebody. I had to prove that I was somebody. And being 'crazy Quincy' was at least better than being a nobody. It ain't so much the killing I hate. Somebody's got to do some killing at some time. It's the people who are getting killed that bothers me. I didn't kill the people who were hurting me the most. In fact, for the longest time, I couldn't even identify who was hurting me. Believe it or not, I'm the real meaning of reincarnation. I'm the dead spirit that knowledge returned to life. I can't even remember what I did and who I done it to. It don't really matter anymore. I know that I could kill if I had to." He turned to Nate and Warren and winked his eye. Warren smiled. Nate just stared at the wall.

Quincy stood silent for the moment and then continued, "What if you have to kill another Black man? Can you do that? After all the knowledge you've acquired about why brothers are doing what they are doing, could you still pull the trigger on a brother?" I answered, "Yeah, Quincy. I could kill a brother if he was about to kill me or kill someone close to me. If I don't kill him, then he'll lay me out without a second thought and I won't have the opportunity to impart this little bit of knowledge that I have."

Quincy snapped back, "Fuck that. I'm not talking about killing to defend your life. Can you kill a motherfucker just because he has taken some of the white man's property?" I tried to answer but he cut me off. "I don't think you can. That's why you didn't join the army or any other military branch. You knew that you wouldn't be fighting for anyone's freedom and especially not yours. You knew that you would be dying for land but not land for you and those who look like you. You knew that you would be nothing more than a hired killer with the goal of defending someone else's property and doing someone else's dying. And you couldn't handle that because you knew that all that fighting-for-the-country, patriotic shit was just that, bullshit. You weren't willing to be some dumb foot soldier being brainwashed into doing whatever someone else told you would be in your best interest. You didn't want your God-given ability to reason and think and to make choices taken away from you. You wanted to be able to declare your own enemies. You wanted the ability to decide who to kill and what to kill and why to kill it."

Quincy was digging deep into my soul. He had read me well and he knew it. I couldn't hide my disdain for people who didn't think. People who acted on the instructions of others without thinking through their actions. Without figuring out that they would have to live with the actions that they took the rest of their lives. If I was going to have to live with the mental and psychological consequences of what I did, I was going to be the one to make the decisions. I was not a mindless robot.

Quincy wasn't finished. He wasn't ready to let me respond. I wasn't ready to respond. "So now, maybe you kill to protect some property. It don't matter whether it is out of this country or in this country, it's someone else's property. It don't belong to you or people who look like you; it doesn't belong to anyone in the family. And you're willing to kill and die for it. Tomorrow you're going to stand up and take an oath that you don't really believe in. And you know the man is going to hold you to that promise 'cause they always holding us to promises while they break them all the time. Just like when the army says once you're in, you're in and if you try to leave, we'll put you in jail. You are going to swear to be loyal to something and someone who ain't never been loyal to you or your kind."

Quincy sighed and wiped the sweat from his forehead. "I'm proud that you have enough smarts to do what they do, compete in their world. I'm proud that you've stayed out of trouble. And I know somebody's got to do it. We need brothers on the inside. Good brothers. But you ain't the one, brother. You ain't the one."

Frank looked at me through sorrowful eyes. He knew of the turmoil that I was going through. He could see the struggle occurring deep within my soul. He knew I was hurting. He didn't know how to help me. Quincy was right. Why should his brother shed blood for something that meant nothing to him or his people? No other race or group of people would do it. Frank recalled how the news anchor people debated America's involvement in foreign wars based on American interests. What interests did his little brother have in defending someone else's property? What purpose did it serve? What if I put some bad guys away. As long as there is racism and prejudice, there is always going to be more "bad guys" on the streets. What if his brother dies for nothing. The state police would just get another token brother to take his place. There would still be bad guys around.

Frank thought back to the movie *The Godfather*. He remembered one of the brothers saying that you give your life only for family; you fight only for family. Nothing else mattered. He wondered why I had not given my life to keep Dad from raping Sugar; yet, now, here I stood willing to wear a gun and defend the properties and lives of others. Quincy was right.

I wanted Frank to say something. I wanted him to put up some defense for me even if he didn't really mean it. But I knew a defense would not be forthcoming. I glanced toward Warren. He wasn't going to say anything either. We had had many conversations about the police. At this point in his life, Warren didn't have anything good to say about the police. Accepting the police as something other than evil was difficult for young African American men. It would have to be an evolutionary process. A process that allowed them to see something other than the daily brutality and corruption. I tried to convince Warren that the police protected some of us. I asked him to imagine a city or a state without policemen. But Warren had seen the police beat brothers into submission. He had seen and heard them yell out "nigger" too many times. He had seen them shoot down brothers and laugh at their handiwork. Deep inside he knew that there might have been some good cops out there, but he hadn't seen any during his short lifetime—not in his neighborhood. At this moment he could only view the police from his vantage point—from where he lived and from what he had experienced. Warren would eventually evolve, but not tonight. Tonight he was trying to deal with the idea of his brother being a cop. He would now have to find strength to love at least one cop. He hated me for making him love a cop.

Warren had told me that he couldn't come to my graduation. He said it had nothing to do with what he felt for me. He just couldn't sit in the halls of an institution that had been a constant problem in every Black person's life. It would be hypocritical for him to attend. He had stopped fooling himself. At this point in his young life he believed that the only way a Black man would ever be able to ensure his safety was to buy a gun. Life in

America demanded that each Black person have a gun, and have the ability to use it if it became necessary. He said that the government wanted us to be self-sufficient in everything except self-defense. They wanted us to depend on them to protect our families. He couldn't understand how we were willing to leave the defense of our very lives to the very people who had done nothing but try to kill us.

I knew that they all were waiting to hear something from me. I had answered their questions, but it was still up to me to give them my reasons for applying in the first place. It was up to me to deny that I was selling out. I had to let them know that I was still Black and that I was not afraid of standing up and saying that I am Black. I understood my intended task. I, too, had seen so many Black men back down from white men for fear of losing their jobs. I, too, had witnessed the shattering of strong men who had once stood for something. I had seen men deny their race simply because they felt that if they identified with being Black, whites would think that they were racists. I knew that being Black in color was a lot easier than being Black in thought and actions. I was aware that it was easier to shut up or sing the praises of all white men than to criticize some of them. It would be easier to turn my back on backward schools with backward teachers. I was being given the opportunity to live with "good white folks." I was being given the opportunity to shun being Black and all that it stood for. My brothers wanted to know if I would take that opportunity, as had so many before me. They wanted to know whether I would pursue the American dream at the expense of African people, at the expense of losing my soul.

I walked over and leaned on the wall on which a poster of Malcolm X hung. The words began to move from somewhere deep inside, up toward my mouth. My voice trembled. "I'm not selling out. I know I'm a Black man and I'm damn proud of it. This job can't and won't change that. They've already tried that in the academy. They've tried to break me and make me think that I was of inferior intellect. They've tried to make me and every other Black person in the class feel that we weren't qualified. In fact, they got rid of a few Blacks because they could not play the game or stand the pressure of the game any longer. Quincy, you, Nate, and Frank have taught me a lot. I haven't forgotten what you've told me and I never, never will."

I noticed that their eyes were fixed upon me. They were staring and nothing was going to distract them. They needed to know that whatever I said was sincere. I continued, "My mind will always stay mine. Nothing they do, no way of living will ever take that away from me. I'm not sure why I'm doing this. Maybe something is leading me down this path for a reason that is not obvious to me at the present. I'm a little confused. But I've got to try it. I've got to give it a shot. Maybe I'll learn something. Maybe if I'm at some arrest scene, some brother won't get beaten down or shot. Maybe I'll put more effort into an investigation that would just sit there because the victims are Black. I promise I won't be sucked into being one of those Black cops who enjoy kicking a brother's ass. I'll never try to impress the white man or anyone else by killing off some brother. I know what I'm going to confront. I think I know the consequences of my actions. If I can't handle it, I'll walk away."

I could see disappointment in their eyes. Disappointment was no longer a feeling; it was a tangible object that sat on my brothers' faces like a man on a ledge of a high-rise building preparing to jump. Nate had been sitting up. He sat back in the chair without breaking his stare. Quincy got up and moved toward the stairs. Frank looked at Quincy and then got up. Warren looked down at his helmet, picked it up, and began running his fingers over the red, slightly elevated stripe that ran through the center of the white helmet. He glanced up from the helmet, got up, and walked over to me. We stared at each other for a few seconds and then he hugged me. His voice trembled as mine had earlier. "I love you, brother." Quincy and Frank walked across the room and hugged Warren and me. Nate stood up and walked toward the stairs. We all turned to look at him. He stood silent for a second, then ascended the stairs until he was out of our sight. He was followed by Quincy, Warren, and Frank. I slid down the wall and sat on the floor. Silence. The words on the Malcolm X poster read, "A Man Who Will Not Stand For Something Will Fall For Anything." *Listen to the silence.*

I could not hold my hand steady. I didn't want the other candidates to see my hand trembling. I didn't want them to know that I was unsure about what I was doing, uncertain about why I was here. I had to keep them out of my soul. Out of my life. My hands perspired. It was as if my hands were crying. I wanted to wipe them dry, yet I didn't want to move. I didn't want to draw attention to what I was going through. I tried to focus on whatever it was the superintendent was saying. I knew from rehearsal that I would soon be requested to repeat his words. I would have to make a promise that I would be required to keep. I looked down the row of uniforms until I found Carla Robeson's shiny round brown face. She was the only Black female in the class. Things had been made real difficult for her. Her eyes met mine. We both must have been thinking the same thing. It was as if we were getting married and taking wedding vows. Vows we weren't sure of. I saw the trembling of her hand. I saw the questions briskly moving about in her soul like frantic fish in an aquarium. For a while, we couldn't turn from each other. For the moment, we were dealing with the most important decision of our lives and nothing else mattered.

I heard the mumbling of voices and realized that the oath had begun. I waited for Carla's full lips to move. Like a child, I wanted her to go first. I wanted always to be able to say she said it first. I wanted to cop out and say she started it. It was an eerie feeling. Like two gun fighters waiting for the other to go for his gun. Our lips began to move simultaneously. I still think that Carla went first.

Carla and I were standing there with our lips moving, yet not believing in what we were saying, not knowing what we were saying or why we were saying it. I slowly turned from my female counterpart to the superintendent. I began to mumble the oath. The other candidates stood with their chests out mellifluously reciting the oath. It was obvious that they had studied it and recited it in front of the mirrors in their dorm rooms. They had not made a surreptitious escape on graduation eve to have a meeting in the basement of an inner-city home with a group of brothers. Carla and I stood hoping and praying that we were doing the right thing. One year after the ceremony, Carla Robeson quit. She came to the conclusion that it was all a lie, which she was unwilling to live. She became active in the African American community. I couldn't quit. Not yet. I had something to prove. I was going to make a difference to somebody. Maybe I was too much like Nate to quit. Knowing, yet not doing.

10

Betrayed

Cause division among them.
   —Master Sun Tzu, The Art of War

The next best is to attack alliances.
   —Master Sun Tzu, The Art of War

It took only one firm kick to shatter the old, worn wood door. Splinters floated down out of the frosty winter air in what appeared to be slow motion. Chas vaulted from the living room chair and sprinted toward the stairwell, keeping his head low to avoid incoming rounds. Nita covered her eyes and instinctively rolled off the couch onto the scuffed, dusty hardwood living room floor. Her elbow struck the coffee table, causing the cocaine that was on it to become a puff of thin, white smoke.

Chas started up the stairs. The sound of a booming burst of gunfire from behind stopped him in his tracks. Chas knew he hadn't been hit; yet he twisted and fell on his back, getting even lower and rolling from left to right to avoid being an easy target. He had been combat-trained in the streets of the ghetto. His movements were perfectly timed. He tried to remain calm but it was an impossible task. This was instant combat. His insides churned with indecision and the foreboding of the imminent, inevitable pain that the hot steel would cause as it made its entry into his shell. Sweat rolled down his forehead. He was breathing heavily. *Survival—I must survive.* He took a quick glance toward the area in which he had last seen Nita. He briefly spotted her.

Nita cupped her hands over her light brown eyes as if in prayer. She hoped that whatever was occurring was a bad dream, a horrible 3-D nightmare. She rolled back and forth in the small, narrow trench between the coffee table and the dingy beige sofa. Tears raced down her cheeks and dripped like a faucet badly in need of a washer onto her neck. Her lips quivered. Her knees were pulled up toward her chest and repeatedly banged against the table and sofa as she unconsciously moved violently from side to side. She screamed, "Oh, my God! No. No. Please, no."

Tank and Cliff quickly entered through the shattered, jagged wood door—what was left of it—crouched in combat positions. Tank bolted over to Chas and put the barrel of the sawed-off .12-gauge shotgun against Chas's head. "You die today, punk motherfucker." The barrel of the gun was still hot from the rounds Tank had fired through the now partially fragmented door. Chas had made a strategic mistake. Tank had fired without actually seeing his target. If Chas had continued up the stairs, he could have retrieved his prized AK-47 and sprayed the hell out of the foolish intruders.

Tank turned to Cliff. "Shut that screaming bitch up." Cliff moved across the room to Nita. He cautiously scanned the area surrounding Nita for a weapon. He knew that she would not hesitate to kill for her man. He figured that Chas would have a gun on or near his person. It was one of the rules of inner-city survival: *Never be without your gun.* No gun. Another strategic mistake by Chas.

Cliff knew what his immediate goal was. He had to make Nita fear him. He had to keep her from acting or reacting. Fear would do that. The key was to push her into and then keep her buried in a constant state of bottomless fear. Lloyd Douglas was right: "If a man harbors any sort of fear, it percolates through all his thinking, damages his personality, makes him landlord to a ghost." Fear would paralyze Nita and free Tank and Cliff to concentrate on their dangerous and dauntless victim, Chas.

Cliff was trembling. He squeezed the gun tighter. "You want me to do her?" Tank responded, "Naw, don't do the bitch yet. Just make her shut the fuck up." Cliff grabbed Nita by her fried dark brown hair and put the barrel of the nine millimeter in her ear. "Shut up, bitch, else I'm going to do you. I'm gonna fuckin' do you right now."

Chas made a subtle movement in the direction of Nita. Tank slammed the butt of the shotgun into Chas's chest, causing him to fall backwards. Chas grabbed his chest and spat out blood. "You son of a bitch. Fuck you." Tank pulled the shotgun up high and then blasted another hard blow in Chas's chest. Chas's chest accepted the butt of the gun and seemed to surround it. Chas grunted and turned away, trying to snatch the pain from the cavity he was sure the gun had left in his chest. Tank swung the barrel of the weapon across Chas's face, causing a gash on his jaw which immediately released penned-up blood. Tank smiled. "Naw, fuck you, pretty boy." Chas fell back against the stairwell. His vision was bleared. His head felt as if someone had a belt around it and was constantly pulling it tighter and tighter and tighter. He had to escape before his head exploded. Before he exploded. The only wrong move was to do nothing. *To die like a fuckin' coward.*

Chas glanced toward the shattered front door through his watery eyes. The broken door seemed to be moving. Getting smaller then larger. Getting closer then farther away. Turning. Chas thought about making a run for it, making a great escape. Either he would make it or Tank would shoot him in the back with the shotgun. *Fuck it. Whatever is going to happen will be over with quickly.* That's what was important. It all had to happen quickly. It was as if his life had been a constant barrage of quick decision-making. Always trying to get through that imaginary door that led out of the ghetto. Always taking a chance on running for the nearest exit without knowing what was on the other side. Choosing curtain number one or two or three. *Whatever it is, it's got to be better. It can't be no fuckin' worse.* Always making impulsive, bold decisions that could make or break him. Making decisions that could lead to instant death. This time, the obstacle to overcome was Tank, a tall, chubby, deep dark brother with a fat round face and yellow, rotten teeth. Prior to this moment, the barrier had been Chas's color and his perceived unwillingness to "put it aside" for the pursuit of the illusive American dream.

Chas had become another dead spirit inside a living shell. Or maybe his spirit was not dead, but it certainly was dying. Or as the brothers used to say, borrowing the phrase from the musical group War, Chas was "slipping into darkness." After several frustrating attempts at fighting his addiction to reckless street life, he accepted his status as a roughneck. He no longer strove for positive goals. The goals of his "oppressors" became his goals. Get rich and stay rich, "by any means necessary." That's how the game is played. If that meant killing people, then so be it. If it entailed killing off your own race to attain your adopted goals, then that was okay, too. In fact, it was the preferred avenue to riches—if you were Black. Preferred by those who were in positions of power. Preferred by many white Americans. Not all white Americans. But the white Americans who were to blame knew who they were. The words *white American* have a different ring in the ears of the guilty.

As long as Blacks killed off other Blacks in order to obtain that which had been deemed good by the whites who controlled Madison Avenue, all was well. After all, this is a capitalistic society and capitalism must survive at all cost. *The end justifies the means.* Dope brings money. Money brings power and prestige. And money allows one to become part of "mainstream" America. Or so it was thought.

A little part of Chas's spirit had been kept alive by the knowledge that he had obtained. There were always a few ghetto sages around who imparted knowledge to those who could sit still long enough to hear it. And that knowledge was causing anguish deep inside Chas. A little knowledge can make a man know that his actions are wrong. Knowledge can keep a man's soul from resting. It can keep him from having the peace that he knows he doesn't deserve. Those who wish to destroy a man's spirit must first keep him from obtaining knowledge. They must distract him from reading and researching by providing a constant barrage of meaningless, mindless entertainment. And if that entertainment attempts to sneak in and deliver a little *positive*, non-destructive knowledge, then it must be criticized as being barbaric and worthless. Thereafter it must be distorted and diluted. Such as jazz was. And such is the plan for the future of *positive* rap music. The key is to insert so much bad into the good that the entire music genre is labeled "bad" or "evil."

Chas had acquired knowledge at an early age. He had obtained it from Nate and Quincy. He had obtained it from his mother and his grandmother. Knowledge doesn't dissipate. It wants to be retained and used. In fact, Dante stated that knowledge isn't knowledge unless it is retained. But a Black man with knowledge of self is sought out and attacked. Once knowledge detects melanin, it finds a warm and fertile hiding place deep within the soul. And once hidden, it tries not to be detected. It is available when called upon, but it often disguises itself. Knowledge realizes that it has an enemy. That enemy will try to weed it out and destroy it as if it were a cancerous cell. When knowledge feels the soul dying, it fights back. An internal alarm is sounded and it twists and turns and torments the very insides of its possessor. That's what was causing the pain inside Chas and Nate. Knowledge was crying out. It was making its last stand.

Chas was aware of his Blackness. He knew that the way he was living was wrong. He knew his lifestyle was a detriment to his people. He knew that the cocaine he sold was not unlike the selling of death. Chas was a ball of contradiction. A ball of confusion. It would have been better had he not had the knowledge of his Blackness. His knowledge and his inability or unwillingness to act on that knowledge in a positive way made him crazy. He was never able to understand his actions. It was as if he was driven by an unseen force that was much stronger than his will power. He knew deep down inside that, in reality, he was weak against an enemy that he could not see. An enemy that he could not touch. An enemy that he could not destroy. He hated his weakness. He felt conquered by his stealthy foe. Chas had not prepared himself to deal with this type of adversary. The meager amount of knowledge that Chas had acquired did not provide enough firepower to repel the surreptitious assaults of his unseen antagonist.

I remember sitting with Chas on the steps at the rear of Chas's house on a hot summer day. We drank Pepsi-cola and laughed about my undaunted interest in his sister Angel. We watched a cat paw at a rat hole trying to extract his dinner. Chas pondered the state of affairs of the Black race. He sounded as if he were much older than fifteen. Or maybe he just sounded older because wisdom, at one point, had been associated with old age. He continued to stare into the alley as he began to speak. "You know, there's something keeping us here in this rat hole. Something— some force—that most of us don't understand. Oh, we think we understand it. We think we understand when we see the redneck, confederate flag-waving idiot in front of us. But that idiot doesn't have any power. He's just a tool. There's a greater force behind all this shit."

Beads of sweat gathered on Chas's forehead, waiting to make the journey down his face en masse. I turned toward him and watched controlled anger take its reserved seat just within his eyes. Anger sat there like a patron in box seats at an opera. It waited quietly, silently, and intensely. Chas stared straight ahead and continued to speak in an agitated voice. "The loud-mouth racist is a tool. He has been put before us as the enemy. You see, we need something or someone tangible that we can vent our energies and emotions at. And it's not hard to hate him because of his ignorance." I interrupted Chas's deep and poignant observation. "Are you saying that this redneck is not our enemy?" Chas responded, "No, I'm not saying that. I'm just saying that he's not worth our time. He's a diversion. We'll deal with him one day, but dealing with him now takes our focus away from those who are really controlling this shit."

I turned toward the gray alley. The cat had stopped pawing. It just sat there and stared into the hole. Chas, like so many others, was convinced that there was a plan to keep people of color the world over out of power. He had told me that the reading of history made the plan evident. He told me to look back at what Africa had been and what it had become after the invasion from the north. He told me to look at what so-called America had been and look at what happened to the Native Americans after the arrival of the descendants of those same invaders. He wanted me to look at the hundreds of millions of people who had died or, rather, had been killed in the name of civilization. "Yes," said Chas, "there is a plan. And that plan will some day leave the Black man in the same position as the Native Americans."

Chas was not alone in his beliefs. Nate had explained the same things to Warren and me. Maybe through their many discussions, he and Chas had come up with the theory together. They were like brothers. Nate told us to think of the whole thing as a football game. He said that the players on the team were to be considered the front-line racists that we dealt with on a day-to-day basis. They were the defense and the offense and more times than not they were led by a white quarterback. The quarterback kept the front-line players motivated. The players did the work in the trenches. They called us "niggers" and lynched us. They advanced the ball up and down the field and, on the face of it, seemed to be the ones who were keeping us from advancing the ball. If something went wrong, they were to take the blame. They were to be heckled and called names.

Nate said that on the sidelines were the assistant coaches and the head coach. They were less visible than the players, but they held part of the overall plan in their hands. They held the game plan. The coaches were even allowed to change the plan to some close variation of the master plan as long as the same results were netted. After the players were through being criticized and heckled, the coaches stood next in line. Nate said if things were not going right, if Blacks were advancing and becoming educated, then the game plan was faulty. The team was losing, so they might need a new coach. Coaches could be replaced. Players had to be replaced as soon as they were too old to keep on winning, too old to keep on fighting and putting down the "opposing" team. Sometimes, if the player had done an exceptionally good job while he was on the front line, he was trained and prepared to become a coach.

Nate believed that the owners really controlled everything, but they were hardly ever visible. They were the guys in the

American Express commercials, the people who could never be identified by the public. They were the keepers of the master plan. The owners decided how things were going to happen. They decided on which coaches were going to be hired and fired. They decided which players were not contributing to the ultimate goal of victory and therefore had to be replaced. The owners would watch the players and the coaches from a distance to identify which players were doing their job well. Most of the time, it was obvious who was getting the job done. Almost always, the players were kept removed from the owners. The owners really didn't want to be associated with the players. Every once in a while an owner would allow a player to be seen with him, but this was rare and could be detrimental to the plan. So it was avoided.

I turned toward Chas. The beads of sweat had started their united journey. Chas had stopped talking and was staring at the cat. The cat turned toward us, moved away from the hole, and sauntered down the alley, occasionally looking back at us as if we had caused him to give up; as if we had somehow made him feel guilty for keeping the rat in a hole. The rat was now free. But it still hesitated to exit its hole. The cat was gone but the effect of its presence earlier was keeping the rat from enjoying its freedom. Maybe the rat knew that it would never be completely free. Maybe it knew that it was the cat's nature to come back and keep the rat in a constant state of fearful hell.

Chas wanted to get through the shattered door. But he didn't want to leave Nita. He was hoping that he could get outside and find the fearless trio of Nate, Quincy, and Michael. He figured that they would be armed, as usual, and prepared to deal with Cliff and Tank. He knew that Tank and Nate had never been good friends. Chas knew that Nate would not hesitate to end Tank's existence.

Chas even wished that I would come by. He knew that I was now a Maryland State Trooper and had been so for about a year. I often drove down Baltimore Street and spoke to my friends, angering my co-workers, both Blacks and whites, who couldn't understand how I could maintain my associations with such disreputable individuals. They believed that it was the manifest destiny of the ghetto dwellers to live in poverty and to never achieve anything of significance. I was an oddity. An exception to the rule of eminent failure.

Chas contested the assertions made by his friends that I frequented the neighborhood on mere reconnaissance missions for "the man." "Fuck y'all. T-man is a conscious motherfucker. He ain't a puppet." Now Chas needed my help. He wanted me to respond to his silent call for help. He knew that I always carried my gun. He knew that I had been well trained in how to use it. How to remain calm in the face of an adversary. He was sure that I could take out both Tank and Cliff. They weren't trained. They were nervous and anxious. They would falter in the face of a government-trained trigger-man, especially one who had grown up on the cold, cruel streets of Baltimore.

Chas knew that Tank was not really a killer. He had read him. He had examined his soul many times by looking into his eyes. In fact, Tank was actually afraid to kill. Nate and Chas believed that Tank couldn't and wouldn't destroy a man under any circumstances. He wouldn't kill to defend his own life or the lives of family members. Chas tried to understand what or who had given Tank nerve enough to stand up to him. How had the previous dearth of courage in Tank's soul been metamorphosed? What had possessed Tank to attack him and Nita in their own home? What had given him this kind of bravery?

Cliff was different. He was a truculent monster who could and would kill at anytime. He didn't need a good reason. He could be made to kill for money. A life meant nothing to him. He had once shot a man to death for stepping on his foot. Nonetheless, he had been an underling to Chas and Nate. He had been trying to impress Chas for the longest time. In fact, Cliff liked and admired Chas. Now he was in Chas's house trying to take away all that Chas possessed. Chas hoped that Cliff's affinity with him would keep Cliff from killing him. But it didn't sound like it.

Cliff liked Nita too, but now in his confused state of mind, he was calling her a bitch. He was threatening to kill her for merely crying. Chas had observed the ferocious manner in which Cliff had grabbed Nita by the hair. He had noticed how Cliff was trembling, and he noticed that Cliff had his sweaty, quivering finger on the trigger of the gun. Chas recognized Cliff's condition. Cliff was in the killing state of mind. And Chas and Nita were in the kill zone. If a move was to be made, it had to be made swiftly in the direction of Tank. Tank was the weaker of the two. Tank was a cowardly idiot.

Nonetheless, Tank was the kind of Black man the military loved to recruit. Deep inside, he had a desire to be hard and ruthless. Living in the ghetto had made him know that these were desirable traits, but he didn't know how to attain them. Tank wanted an enemy. Someone or something that could bring out the repressed anger in him. The problem was he didn't know who that enemy should be. He was waiting for someone like Chas or Nate or Uncle Sam to tell him who to "waste." He thought there was some type of magic to it. Some God-given formula that gave some men the ability to kill—the ability to do what was deemed necessary without the cumbersome remorse. Maybe he was right. The military was looking for men who had the desire to kill. But more importantly, the military was looking for people who wouldn't think about who they were killing or why they were killing them. They needed people they could control. People who wouldn't ask questions. Men who wouldn't think or reason at all. "Just kill and kill and kill whenever ordered to do so."

Brothers like Tank were easy prey for military recruiters. A little bit of money. A little respect. And maybe the building of that badly needed, rare ghetto commodity, self-esteem. It mattered not what the self-esteem was built upon. After being beaten down, used, abused, and told that you amounted to nothing for so long, it just didn't matter. The army, marines, and navy would, and could, turn these deficient Black men into trained killers. Of course, they wouldn't be called trained killers, but that's what they would be. And for this new label and the perceived respect that went along with it, they were willing to sell their souls. They were willing to give up their freedom and die for a cause, anybody's cause, or any cause that their so-called leaders or overseers came up with. These ghetto mercenaries were willing to stop thinking on their own. They were willing to have all their days and nights planned. They were willing to imitate their great grandparents and get down on their hands and knees to scrub floors. Willing to be yelled at. Willing to be called names that they would never tolerate from another Black man or woman.

Nate believed this, too, was part of the plan. He said the government provided the only means by which young brothers thought they could get respect. They made Black men feel that killing is bad unless they let the government tell them who to kill. He said that to him, death was death and killing was killing. "If any killing was going to be done, it will not be a white man telling me to do it."

Nate believed the government purposely prepared Blacks to be killers. They broke us down and said, "Come to us. Put on these uniforms if you want to be rebuilt. If you want to have a feeling of pride. If you want to be somebody, don't kill to defend your children and your wife; don't fight to protect your mom and dad and your brother and sister. In fact, leave all of them behind to fend for themselves. Come fight who we tell you to fight. Come kill people who have never assaulted or insulted your family. Come kill people who have never called you a nigger or denied you a job or an education. Come fight them on the basis that they might do to you what I'm doing to you already if you don't do it to them first. Forget about the lynchings, the rapes. That's all history. Remember, your God said to be forgiving. Forgive and forget."

Tank shouted down at Chas, "I want all your fuckin' money and all your dope." Chas studied Tank closely. He could tell that Tank's heart was not into what he was doing. He knew that Tank was trying to be something that he just couldn't be. Tank was trying to do something that he wasn't capable of doing. "Ain't no money here, Tank. I ain't sold no dope today. My dope man ain't brought it by yet. What the fuck are you doing? Are you high off some bad shit?" Tank forced the shotgun into Chas's chest, "You lying, motherfucker. Nate told me that this was the day you had all your money and dope. He told me to hit you today and I know Nate ain't wrong. You and him are partners. He should know. Stop fucking with me, Chas."

Cliff was rocking back and forth. His body shook and his hands trembled. He yelled from across the room, "Yeah, motherfucker, you better stop bullshitting us or somebody gon' die real soon. I'm dying to squeeze one off into this bitch of yours." Chas tried to remain calm, but it was obvious that he was shocked by what Tank had said. He hadn't even heard Cliff. His eyes were fixed on Tank. Chas stuttered, "Na–Na–Nate sent you to hit me."

Nita turned toward Chas. She was crying but no sound came from her mouth. Tears flowed over her smooth brown skin. She was finding it hard to believe what she had just heard. Chas and Nate were close friends. They had put their money together to get started in the cocaine business. It was their escape route out of the ghetto. They had always split the profits evenly. Never any hint of cheating each other. Never any dissension or division. They knew each other's parents and were close to each other's family. Nate had killed for and killed with Chas. And Chas had killed for Nate. Chas had been there for Nate when Nate needed him. They had laughed together. Played together. There would be no civil war or, rather, uncivil war between these warriors. Nothing was to separate them.

Nita wondered what could be so strong that Nate would turn against Chas. What evil force had found its way into this perfect male union? What could make Nate want Chas dead? They were like brothers. It didn't make any sense.

Nonetheless, Chas knew that Tank was telling the truth. Tank hadn't the nerve to come after him unless he was pushed by someone strong, unless he was acting as a mercenary, a remote-controlled soldier. Chas and Nate had discussed how a Black soldier couldn't kill a man of color unless he was pushed by someone or something stronger than himself, or pushed by someone he had been made to believe was superior. Someone he had been made to fear. No doubt about it, Tank feared Nate. He never wanted to be around Nate. He was afraid that Nate would detect his weaknesses and expose them in front of everyone. Nate could push Tank to kill Chas. Tank was telling the truth. Nate wanted Chas eliminated. *Damn.* Slipping into darkness...

Tank was angered by what he had told Chas. He had wanted Chas to believe that this was his own idea, his own initiative. Tank wanted Chas to believe that he was not impotent. He didn't want to give Nate the credit for pushing him. This was to be his initiation into the realm of ghetto respect. He could hear the voices of the ghetto grapevine: "Tank took out Chas and his lady. Tank took Chas's shit, then slaughtered the motherfucker on his own territory." He thought that he had fucked up again. But this time it wouldn't matter. No one would know because he was going to kill Chas and Nita and then he was going to go back and kill Nate. That would complete the cycle. He could then be the man he always wanted to be, or thought he wanted to be—"the baddest, meanest motherfucker around." The Nathan Bedford Forrest of the ghetto's civil war. The killing of Chas, Nita, and Nate would help him ascend the steps to the ghetto's oval office. Only Cliff would know that it was all a facade, and if need be, he would kill Cliff.

Although Tank did not have the courage of Chas and Nate, he was not completely dissimilar from them. He, too, was confused. He, too, had the mindset to kill off other Black men, even if they were close friends of his. His spirit was also dead. Something external to him had destroyed everything internal, and he couldn't figure it out. He couldn't identify this AIDS-like malady. So it no longer mattered what it was. Tank believed that a lack of courage was the only barrier which separated him from Nate, Chas, Quincy, and Michael. He wanted to transcend that barricade, to knock it down and free his repressed soul. Free it so that it could become fully identical with the souls of his idolized nemeses. He didn't have the knowledge that all the others—except Michael—had. But it didn't really matter because in the end they all reacted the same way to the same hidden stimulus. They all killed. In fact, if he could kill at will, then he would not be very different from the rest of the world. If he could be ruthless and act without remorse, then he could almost be considered normal.

People were killing other people all over the world. The reasons for killing were insignificant. Most of the time the justifications given were insanely false. Killers in a uniform were revered as masters of strategy. They were celebrated because of their ability to accurately kill other men, women, and children without remorse. It was strange how "Christians" could line streets and cheer young men who had just returned from killing other *human beings*. The only thing that separated the uniformed killers from the killers on the streets of the ghetto was that the controllers of the uniformed killers came up with rationalizations that the gullible, preoccupied public was more than willing to accept. In fact, they made the public accept them by hiding behind the flag the true motivations for the mass killings. The flag was a very significant part of the scheme. Appeal to patriotism. The world stood by and watched as presidents ordered assassinations. Leaders of countries were ordering the bombing and killing of millions of people under the banner of justified war. It was, nonetheless, killing. Whether it was on a battlefield or on the streets of a ghetto, death meant the cessation of life. Everyone was killing for whatever reason he could conjure up, or maybe for no reason at all. Why should Tank have thought of killing as something evil? It was all around him. He needed only to find a reason or a rationalization.

Chas's mind wandered. He tried to understand why Nate wanted him dead. They had been such good friends for so long. They were probably still living because they had watched out for each other. He couldn't think of anything that he had done to Nate. He knew that reasons for killing could be trivial. What was a minor infraction to one man might be a major violation to another.

Nate and Chas had been together the prior night. They had gotten high and played cards. They had laughed together. Nate had teased Nita about getting fat. Chas wondered if all the time Nate had been plotting his demise. He asked himself if Nate had been sitting there waiting for the right opportunity to take him, for whatever reason he had come up with. Had he said something to Nate to make Nate think that he was trying to kill him? He couldn't figure it all out. But he had figured out for certain that it was Nate who had sent Tank and Cliff.

Chas searched his mind until he stumbled upon a reason, a justification for Nate's possible action. He remembered that he had told Nate about a new connection he had made with some cocaine distributors from Miami. He had told Nate that the cocaine would be coming in the next day and that he had already gotten the money together to pay for it. He said that Nate could pay him back his portion of the cocaine after they had sold some of it. Nate had asked Chas if it was okay that he meet the connection. Chas told him that the connection was paranoid and would only meet with him and that he would let Nate know what went on in the meeting. Nate got upset and said, "Look, man, you and I work as a team. We always meet our connections together. If the motherfuckers can't understand that, then fuck them. We can't let them break us up." Chas responded, "Nate, this is big, man. This could be our way out. We might be able to stop fucking with this small-time bullshit and really start making some money. I don't give a fuck about these assholes. I won't let them mess with our thang. Don't you trust me?" Chas laughed. Nate smiled a little.

Trust was an awkward subject. It was difficult for anyone in the drug business to trust anyone. It was difficult for a Black man in America to trust anyone. Paranoia was an asset to Black people. Nate and Quincy felt that it was trust that had put Black people in the position that they were in. They believed that Black people had put their faith in white people and had expected them to do the right thing. Nate said that our major crime was having too much faith and trust in others. No one was going to make it better for us but ourselves. No one but us was going to solve our problems. "No one else gives a damn."

Nate said that others wanted us to leave the solving of our problems up to them. They wanted this so that they could maintain control of us. They wanted to keep us depending on them, even though they acted as if we were a burden. Nate said that it was reverse psychology. They were only acting as if they were pushing us away. In reality they wanted to keep us right under their noses. He said welfare was not for our welfare but for white folks' mental welfare. Nate said they, white folks, mentally fared well by keeping us dependent upon them. Welfare allowed the government to look in on us from time to time, to see who we were sleeping with, to see where we were working or if we were working. Welfare was a legal form of wiretapping, surveillance, and eavesdropping.

It was all psychological. And it worked well. We begged them to come into our homes. Into our lives. They acted as if they were reluctant to be there and were only coming because we asked. They would even call us names and say we were lazy. But they never pushed too hard to get us off welfare. They never produced jobs so that we could work. They never provided better education. They even made welfare pay higher than most jobs that they considered us qualified for. We really believed them. We trusted them. We had faith that what they said was what they meant. They continued to breast-feed grown Black people. Keeping us close. Watching over us like the plantation's taskmaster. Welfare was the cheapest surveillance system known to mankind. It had been tested and proven. Nate said trust got us here. We trusted too many people. No, Nate didn't want anything to do with trust.

Quincy had told us that we should trust only family. He said that he had been lied to so much during his life that he hardly had faith in anything or anyone anymore. He would tell us that he still believed in God. He said that he had studied the history of Black folks and that he didn't think we could have made it to this point without something or someone more powerful than we watching over us. We had not been as brutal as others, yet we were still here. He said that sometimes, amidst all the confusion in life, it was hard to believe that there was a God in control. It was hard to believe that anyone or anything was in charge. He told us that at times he just wanted to give up and go to the other side to see if there was anything there. But he knew that would merely be capitulating to the evil forces on this side of Dr. Martin Luther King's mountain.

Nate didn't trust Chas. He liked him. Even enjoyed being with him. But he didn't trust him. He couldn't. Mistrust was imbedded in him. Especially mistrust of his own people. Trust meant a certain amount of unity. A certain amount of cohesion. That was not in the plan. In the back of his mind, he wondered if Chas was making more money than he had revealed. He had allowed Chas to keep the books. To divide the money. But they had always travelled together to pick up the cocaine. Now Chas was changing the plan. He was adding more instability to Nate's already unstable, unpredictable life. Nate resented this, but he could not let Chas see his resentment. He could not bare his soul. Nate wouldn't wait for Chas to burn him. But neither would he argue with him anymore. An argument might make Chas careful. It would make him leery. Nate was not at all sure that Chas would not kill him in order to make more money. Money made people do strange things.

"Get the fuckin' drugs, Chas. Don't bullshit me, man." Tank was trembling badly. He didn't want to kill Chas without first getting the money and the drugs. He didn't want to stay around after killing Chas and Nita, to search the house. He knew that Chas had a lot of friends in the neighborhood and that, right after they heard shots, they would come running to help him. He couldn't figure out why they had not come already. Why hadn't they come after the first shot that he had fired through the door? The thought made him turn toward the door. He looked out into the angry-gray, snowy evening. For the first time he noticed how the snow flurries tried to get into the house, unknowingly bringing an end to their very existence. Could that be what he was doing? The thought sent a chilling cold down his spine. His spine felt like a long icicle. He thought he saw someone approaching. He whispered to Cliff, "Drop her, man, and check out who that is outside. These motherfuckers aren't going anywhere but to hell."

Cliff dropped Nita to the floor. She cried out. Cliff kicked her in the side, "Shut up, bitch!" Nita tried to silence her cry. Cliff moved out through the shattered door. He stepped over broken wood and walked down the white marble steps which led up to the red brick row house. Tank noticed that Cliff was no longer in sight. He was sweating. He heard Nita crying a little louder and pointed the shotgun in her direction, "You better be quiet, Nita. I ain't shitting, I'll do you and Chas."

Chas could sense Tank's nervousness. For the first time Tank had called Nita by her name. He was allowing his heart to get in the way of the job that he intended to do—the job he was sent to do. Now was his chance to take advantage of Tank's weakness. He had to seize the time. It was one-on-one and Chas was the stronger of the two. Cliff would be back soon, so the challenge would have to be swift and decisive.

Chas didn't give any thought to the fact that Tank had a shotgun. It all happened so quickly. Chas rolled and rammed his shoulder into the back of Tank's legs. Tank immediately fell to the floor. Chas jumped onto his back and put his forearm under Tank's chin. He pulled back against Tank's throat with all the strength he had left. His life depended on it. He yelled to Nita, "Get the fuckin' gun, goddammit." Nita jumped to her feet. Dizziness overtook her and she fell back to her knees. She never stopped moving toward Tank and Chas. Tank was losing consciousness.

Nita grabbed the gun and fell backwards. Chas released his hold on Tank and quickly crawled over him to Nita. He grabbed the shotgun just as Cliff was reentering the house. Chas fired the gun. Cliff abruptly jerked backwards and down as if someone had hit him with a solid steel baseball bat. He landed in the vestibule. Blood covered the shattered pieces of wood. Chas turned to Tank, "You fuck-up. You fucked with the wrong motherfucker." Tank pleaded for his life, "I'm sorry, man. I wasn't going to kill you. I ain't no killer, Chas. I was just trying to do what Nate told me to do. He told me to bring him the money and the dope. If I did, I could have half. I would be his right-hand man. He told me to kill Nita and tell you that was from him.   He a–a–a ruthless motherfucker, Chas. You know that. He told me that he and I would be partners. Please, Chas, don't do me. I'll do anything you want, man. I'll do Nate for you! I'll go back and kill that lowlife motherfucker. He got my partner Cliff killed. Goddamn, Cliff. Get up, man. I'm sorry, Cliff. I'll kill that motherfucker!"

11

Hillside Blues

It is clear that thought is not free if the profession of certain opinions make it impossible to earn a living.

—Bertrand Russell, Scepital Essays

The society we live in is not actually what it tries to represent itself as to the rest of the world.
—Malcolm X, By Any Means Necessary

A warm summer breeze moved across my face. I watched the darkness as it calmly oozed across the heavens like a slow incoming tide, bringing a subtle end to another hot, muggy day. The sky was a combination of dark shades of blue and burnt orange. There were no clouds. The sun skirmished with the moon for the lead role on the lovely, God-created stage. The bright flowers began to disappear under a slowly encroaching blanket of night. They did not resist. They reached for the blanket and pulled it over them as if protecting themselves from the coldness of a winter evening. I could smell the pleasant odor of freshly cut grass. It was a beautiful night.

I tossed the barrel of the Remington .12-gauge shotgun over my right shoulder and stared down the hill into the group of men assembled below. I could barely hear them. It was early in the evening. I sought solace in the quietness. I knew that later my peace would be interrupted by their awful, arrogant chants. Later, I would seek solitude. I would try to hibernate within myself—within the walls of my soul—and await the end of the brutal storm of ignorance and intolerance. I sought to shield myself from the onslaught of verbal attacks on my people. Not out of fear. I tried to safeguard myself from reacting violently, yet justifiably, to a provocative, powerful stimulus.

The sound of James Thorton's deep, raspy voice diverted my attention away from the faceless assembly. "What do you think, Mr. Policeman?" I never turned to him. He didn't really want my opinion. He was about to slip into his favorite role as my personal pundit. I replied anyway, "I think this is fucked up. In fact, partner, I think this is the most fucked-up thing I've ever had to do in my entire life." James laughed. "Yeah, it's pretty fucked up, but before it's all over, we'll probably do some other fucked-up things." I slowly shook my head from side to side. "I hope not, James. I hope this is as bad as it gets."

James Thorton had become a close friend. He was one of the few Black troopers assigned to the Frederick, Maryland Barrack of the Maryland State Police. I had been dispatched to Frederick immediately after graduating from the Maryland State Police Academy. Upon my arrival, James took me under his wing. I had been trained on how state troopers were supposed to function in the field and in the academy. James taught me how things were actually done. He taught me valuable lessons.

I recall James leaning against his yellow patrol car one evening after our 3 to 11 p.m. shift. He had loosened his tie and unbuttoned the top button on his shirt. His straw Stetson hat was next to me on the hood of my car. I sat on the hood with a Pepsi in my hand inspecting the starry Frederick sky. I had been assigned to Frederick for six months and was no longer required to have another trooper ride with me as a training officer. James sensed my satisfaction with becoming a full-fledged, stand-alone trooper. "How you like it so far, T-man?" I continued my inspection. "I like it just fine, James. Everyone has been real good to me. Trooper Hewitt taught me a great deal over the past six months. He's a sharp trooper." James smiled. "Yeah, he ain't bad for a redneck." I laughed, "What makes you think he's a redneck? James shook his head. "Oh, I can tell a redneck son of a bitch from a mile away. He's a redneck all right."

James took a deep breath and sighed heavily. "I've been meaning to talk to you, T-man. Lend me your ear for a second and listen well 'cause I'm not going to repeat this to you, and I'll deny it if you ever turn into, or turn out to be, a house nigger and start running around telling everybody I fed you this knowledge. Understand, this is between you and me." I nodded in agreement and tried to anticipate what James would say. I was anxious for his words and at that moment would have agreed to any stipulation he attached to them. James looked me straight in my eyes. He was a dark-chocolate brother with serious eyes and a clever smile that seemed to hold secrets. He wore gold-rimmed glasses. His shoulders were slightly slumped as if he were carrying a load, a heavy load. He was about to lighten it.

He waited for me to finish my inspection of the heavens. I tried not to show my eagerness, for fear that he would change his mind and save his treasured secret. James spoke. "I need you to look at me. Look me right in my eyes like a man is supposed to. I hope this makes sense to you. If it doesn't, write it down on your mental tablet and study it tonight and tomorrow and the next night until you can pass it on to some other brother who chooses to become a new centurion."

I stared into James's eyes. He began to speak. "You're going to get along fine with most of the other troopers. But don't ever forget that the Maryland State Police is no different from any other American institution. You are going to encounter racism in its ugliest form. Don't think for one microsecond that the wearing of the same uniform as the white troopers will exempt you from the cold, cruel disease of racism. Most of the people we work with are racist or have racist tendencies. Fuck that—if they have racist tendencies, they are racist. We don't have time to delineate the different degrees of racism."

James was intense. His forehead became wrinkled. His dark brown eyes locked in on their target like heat-seeking missiles. He was trying to connect with my soul. There was no room for error. His lips moved with precision. There could be no wasted words. "You can talk with them and laugh with them, but don't you ever count them as your friends. They accommodate us because they are forced to, but if they had a choice they would rather be handcuffing you instead of helping you handcuff someone else."

I had quietly become a student of James's. Even before this discourse, I had watched him and considered him a *mensch*. He seemed wise and his lessons, although brief, always hit home. I could hear Nate and Quincy in his voice. James continued, "Never get yourself into a situation where your life is dependent upon a back-up. Things haven't changed to the point that a Black man can trust his life and future to a white man. That's an unfortunate fact that you can't afford to overlook. Especially out here. Many of these white troopers were born and reared here in Frederick, Maryland and have never worked with anyone Black. They know nothing about you except what they have been told by their parents, friends, and the media. To them you are a nigger in a uniform. You are not their equal and no matter what you do they will never respect your abilities and intelligence. They've been informed since youth that they are better than you. They've been told that you are a savage who can never really be tamed. They are not going to risk their lives to save a savage. Would you? Don't answer—just remember what I'm saying."

James's words came rapidly as if they were being fired from an internal Gatling gun. Nonetheless, I understood every syllable. I absorbed every hot round. The words were hard, fast, and pointed. No verbal word mongering. These were the facts as he saw them. They had been gleaned from empirical data. I could accept or reject them. I could call him paranoid. It was up to me. But James was going to deliver his soulful barrage, no matter what. He was compelled by an oath to himself to deliver his observations and experiences to another brother, another Black man. I was his chosen recipient.

I stared into James's eyes as he had demanded. I listened. James spoke. "As a Black police officer you must apply the rule of self-reliance. Especially when it involves the defense of your very life. White men are not willing to die for Black men. They never have been! And never will be. You've got to remember that nothing on this job is worth dying for. Fuck that oath. Fuck some patriotic allegiance. Crispus Attucks was a fool. If you get killed, the police department will go on as if you never existed. This ain't one big family like they told you in the academy. And if it were a family, you can be sure that we are stepchildren. We are the 'black' sheep. Despite the so-called camaraderie, we are isolated and expendable."

No doubt about it, James was sincere. I could see the sincerity in his eyes. Maybe that's why he wanted me to look into his eyes. He knew that I had become adept at detecting phoniness. James was worried about me. Worried because I was young and Black and in an organization—in a world—that saw that combination as a threat. He was worried that I would be gobbled up and destroyed by "the system." He was worried that I would become just another milquetoast Black man with a position, on a mission to attain personal prosperity by compromising or abandoning his Blackness. James warned me to separate my private life from the job. "Never allow the two to merge in any form. While at work, never talk about what's going on at home. If you decide to discuss what occurred on the job at home, well, that's up to you. But never vice versa. Never allow those whom you work with to have access to your soul. Never allow them to see that they are bothering you. Never allow them to know your breaking point until you reach it."

James must have thought that he was causing me discomfort, that his warnings were making me afraid. "I'm not trying to make you paranoid. However, I have seen Black men and white men, for that matter, completely destroyed by exposing their weak points. By exposing their souls." James told me that he enjoyed police work, but at times he had trouble determining who was trying to do him the most harm. He said that we Black police officers could easily be lured to sleep. We could forget who we were and whence we came. We could become so busy trying to protect the public that we might forget about protecting ourselves. Our forgetfulness could be a fatal mistake.

James was the kind of policeman that I wanted to become. He was the kind of policeman that I had tried to describe to Nate and Quincy. Although his job and the money that went along with it allowed him to move out of the physical ghetto, James knew that a metaphysical ghetto shrouded him at all times. No matter how much a Black man dressed up or what kind of uniform he put on, the aura of the ghetto surrounded him. This was how many white Americans saw Black men. It didn't matter what job they had or how well they spoke the King's English, they were still of the ghetto. In fact, if a Black man became "successful," he was hailed as a "ghetto child" who had managed to beat the odds. But who had made the odds against him so high in the first place?

James told me that those in power tried to take away the Blackness of men who joined their white organizations, and usually they succeeded. America was not color blind. Saying that racism did not exist would never make it go away. Over a period of time, I found James to be right. During arrests, I heard Black police officers call other Blacks "niggers." I heard them refer to other Blacks as "those people." They were trying to escape the aura of the ghetto, trying to disavow a label that they did not truly understand. They could not understand that in America *ghetto* was synonymous with *Black* and unless they could escape being Black, they could never escape being part of that vast, mystical mental landscape called the ghetto. They could not understand that the term *ghetto* had nothing to do with where they lived.

James knew where he had come from and he didn't want to escape his Blackness. He didn't care how they labeled him or what they said about him. It didn't matter if they labeled him a "ghetto child." He was sure of who he was. He was sure of his abilities. He knew that he had came from a line of spiritual warriors. A line of deeply spiritual people. He knew that he was the child of royal blood, a descendant of African kings and queens. Nothing or no one could take away what he was or what he believed in. The job of policeman was just that, a job. They could take away his job but not his Blackness. They could never steal his soul. Once a man knows who he is, it is difficult to destroy him. *Know thyself.*

Now James was trying to help me protect my soul. James wasn't aware that I already knew all the things he was telling me. He was taking a chance, assuming that I would not go back and tell the other troopers that he was a racist. He knew that in the eyes of many, being proud of being Black meant that he was a racist. Defending his soul against a people who had tried to destroy his mother and father meant that he was a racist. Trying to give other younger Blacks a sense of pride meant that he was a racist. He was aware that more information got into the hands of racists through the mouths of Blacks than by any other source. And he knew that once they had the information, the racists could, and would, twist it and distort it even more so that he would be identified as the problem. They would try to put him on the defensive end of the debate, despite the fact that all the evidence was in his favor. James knew the possible consequences of his actions. Yet, he was willing to take a chance. It was a risk that I never would have taken. It was a risk that I had been warned against taking.

I told Nate and Warren about James. They were happy that I had met a conscious brother in the police department. They hoped that if I were to get into a dangerous situation and needed assistance that James would be there for me. But Nate continued to remind me not to let my guard down. He said that I still needed to keep my private life private. He said I still needed to protect my soul—even from those who appeared to be my friends. Warren told me that there were so many of us that had been bamboozled and brainwashed that I had to be careful. The brainwashing started early in life and had historically been proven extremely effective. Warren said that if I began to trust someone, I would be vulnerable. He said it was a shame that we, as a race, were so easily turned against each other, but it was a fact that could not be ignored. Almost everyone could be bought. Everyone had a price and James was no exception.

Nate believed that police work was causing a change in me. He thought that I was beginning to have too much faith in others, that I was looking for someone to put my faith in, when there was no one worthy of it. The necessary immune system which he, Quincy, Frank, and Warren had helped to build was being threatened. He said if I wanted to have faith in someone, make it God. Nate wasn't very religious, but he thought talking to God meant only God would hear me. And, if there were no God, I would be talking only to myself. Either way, my secrets would be well kept.

I wanted to trust James. I wanted to know that I was not just surrounded by camouflaged hostile forces. I wanted James to be like a brother to me and he seemed to be that and more. I respected his age and his experience. I respected the fact that he had chosen the same profession as I, yet he had not lost his consciousness. James gave me hope. He was my "I told you so" person. I figured that he had gone through the same decision-making process I had. I wondered if he had taken part in a conversation in some basement in the inner city.

I thought of how awful it was that I was required to be so self-protective, that I was required to handle my soul as if it were some fragile piece of china. It was stressful. I understood why conscious Black men and women suffered from high blood pressure. We labored under a feeling of being boxed in—as if we were already stuffed into a coffin. Buried alive. The watchfulness that was required of me made me feel that I was not free. Yet, if I were not watchful, I would be enslaved. How could I be enslaved if I were not free in the first place? Why was it worth it to me to defend myself against my enemies if they already had me locked away in a psychological prison? I, not unlike a turtle, was armored by a hard shell that kept others out. Yet, that same shell kept me imprisoned.

James's voice shattered my thoughts. "They're all sick. The whole fuckin' bunch of them. And I guess we're sicker 'cause we're standing up here watching this bullshit." He seemed to be losing the control that I admired in him. He seemed to have forgotten the lecture he had given me earlier. Anger was erupting from deep inside his soul. I had seen it happen many times before. I was powerless in quelling his anger. I, too, was angry. But I was young and learning. This was not supposed to be happening to my mentor.

I took a deep breath and tried to heave open my interior anger-chest. I responded to James. "No, James, we ain't just watching, we're protecting these assholes." He kneeled down and began to slowly pull strands of grass out of the warm earth. He took his hat off, wiped his forehead, and began to speak. "I ain't protecting these assholes. I'm just up here making money. If someone wants to shoot these motherfuckers, you think I'm going to get in the way? I ain't that fucking stupid. And I'll tell you what, if you jump in front of one of these motherfuckers to protect them, I'll shoot you dead in the ass." I looked down at James and laughed. "If I jump in front of one of these assholes, I'll shoot myself in the ass." He smiled and said, "Naw, let me do it. You probably would miss, you no-shooting, half-blind motherfucker." We both laughed.

A group of white troopers had congregated a short distance from where James and I were standing. A few of them had shotguns slung over their shoulders. They were laughing about something. They seemed to be enjoying their assignment. Most of them lived in the area, so I was sure they were familiar with at least some of the men who had gathered in the valley below. Even on that hill, our worlds were separated. James and I stood in one area talking, while the white troopers gathered in another area. All on the same God-made hill, wearing the same uniforms, doing the same job, after participating in the same training, which required us to pass the same test. Yet, we were separated by ideas and cultures and skin color. Their thoughts would surely be different from ours. Their conversation was no doubt on a different subject. They were home. We were foreigners.

Trooper Anthony Kagen slowly ambled over to where James and I were standing. He held his head low. We didn't turn to acknowledge his presence. He began to speak in a low, hesitant voice. "I know how you guys feel about this." His words were curious. How could a white man know how two Black men felt? He couldn't have known the anger that was engulfing our souls like rampaging fire. He couldn't have realized the stored-up anger and the pain that had been branded into the very flesh of our being. James and I retained the heat of anger as if we were cast iron pot-belly stoves and listened to Anthony. "I just want you all to know that I don't agree with this bullshit, neither. I ain't one of them and I don't think like them. I don't teach my kids to hate people just 'cause they're Black. I hope you guys don't think all of us are like these craven idiots. I hope you don't hate all of us because of this." He took his hat off. "I can't say that I would blame you for feeling angry. I don't think that I could even be up here if I were you."

Anthony Kagen paused and took a deep breath. James sneaked into the silent gap, "Just doing our job, Tony. Just doing our job." Tony Kagen stood there for a second or two and then walked away. He did not join the group of white troopers. He walked to the front of the hill and stood alone. He peered down at the men below and slowly shook his head.

Anthony Kagen seemed different. He didn't like being with the other troopers. He was either alone or in the company of James and me. After work, he would go straight home to his kids. He had told me that nothing was more important than his kids. He said they were so young and innocent that they didn't hate anyone and hardly knew what the word *hate* meant. He said he knew that, at some point, all of that would change. At some point, they would have to make a decision concerning how they wanted to live their lives and whom they wanted to associate with. Anthony knew that his children would be pushed toward the hating of Black people. It was the American way. Racial hatred was a significant piece in the very fabric of America. It was difficult to resist. There was always this competitiveness, this urge for one group of people to feel that they were superior to another group. The media assisted by consistently doing negative stories about people of color. And positive stories about white people. Madison Avenue assisted by ensuring that advertisements concentrated on white people—unless, of course, they were advertisements for tobacco or alcohol or gym shoes. Anthony Kagen's children would have the superiority complex forced directly into their systems like saline from an intravenous bottle.

Anthony seemed embarrassed by the event taking place in the valley. He reminded me of the nurse at Frederick County Hospital Emergency Room. Trooper Rick Stollemyer and I had arrested a man at a local bar for disorderly conduct. The man was drunk and had picked a fight with another patron. Trooper Stollemyer and several other troopers subdued the man. During the struggle, the man had incurred some minor abrasions. We took him to Frederick County Hospital. Once in the emergency room, the man began to call me a "nigger." He screamed, "Nigger, get away from me. I ain't afraid of no niggers. I'll take on every nigger in the world." He turned to Trooper Stollemyer and said, "You are white like me. Help get this nigger away from me."

Trooper Stollemyer turned to me and said, "Don't let him get to you. He's just drunk." Everyone else in the emergency room—doctors, nurses, and patients—stopped what they were doing and listened to the man's screaming. Everyone, except me, in the emergency room was white. The man continued his babbling tirade, "Nigger, get away from me. You fuckin' ugly, chicken-shit nigger. I'm gonna kick your black ass. Let me at that nigger.

Bring him over here. Hey you. You! Hey white man, white cop, fetch me that there darkie."

My insides boiled. I could actually feel my internal organs blistering in a seething river of blood. I wanted to draw my weapon and push the bigot from existence. But something was holding me back. Something was saving me for another day, another time, another mission, a more important confrontation. It wasn't fear. The cold and cowardly fingers of fear could no longer restrain me. I was growing. Maturing. I could have silenced the idiot forever. But that's all he was—a degenerate cretin. A diversion from the real problem. He was merely the manifestation of deep-seated racism. Yeah, he needed to be exterminated, just as an annoying fly had to be. But just like the fly, he was one of many. He was not worth my tossing my life away. Had I harmed one hair on that Anglo-Saxon's head, the other troopers would have filled me with holes.

After the drunkard had calmed down, a delicate white nurse walked up to me. I immediately scanned her eyes, and saw sincerity. She spoke in a low, soft voice that mildly soothed my scaring soul. "How do you handle being called out of your name like that?" I didn't answer. I didn't have an answer. I couldn't figure out what gave me the fortitude to take such abuse. A tear trickled down her pinkish face. She hugged me and said, "I'm sorry. I'm deeply sorry." The nurse seemed genuinely hurt. It was as if she felt the pain that I was feeling. But how could she?

I later found out that the drunkard was a very wealthy and prominent man in Frederick, Maryland. About a month after the incident he wrote me a long letter begging my apology and asking my forgiveness. He thanked me for my patience and restraint. He stated that he remembered very little about the incident and indicated that his activities of that day had been relayed to him by others. He sent a copy of the letter to my supervisors. The feeble apology meant little to me. I knew he had meant every word he had said in his drunken state. Alcohol had given him courage.

I didn't know what to make of Anthony. He seemed so sincere and genuine. Yet, I didn't want to trust him. He seemed to understand, yet I wondered if it was all a plan to enter my soul, and then destroy me like cancer. If he were trying to ruin me, I wouldn't have been surprised. Nate had warned me; I was prepared. In fact, Anthony would not have been very different from most people. I expected him to be deceptive, for I knew that deception was a powerful tool. Anthony lived amongst the men at the bottom of the hill. They were his neighbors and my enemies. I was confused at a time when I shouldn't have been. All I had to do was remember what Nate and Quincy had told me: "Trust no one."

The sun finally gave way to the moon as darkness set in. The sounds of rambunctious crickets echoed over the hill. The Frederick nights usually brought on a calmness in me, but tonight my soul stirred with more anxiety than I had ever felt on the turbulent streets of Baltimore. It was difficult for me to stand there and witness the events at the bottom of the hill. It would have been difficult for any Black man. I wanted to walk off that hill. It didn't matter where I went. I wanted to walk into the darkness and disappear. I wanted to be back on the streets of Baltimore City with my brothers. I wanted to see well-lit city streets with lots of people just hanging out on the corner singing the deeply complex yet simple songs of the late, great recording artist Marvin Gaye. I wanted to hear car horns blowing and police and ambulance sirens wailing. I wanted to hear children playing and moms yelling to their children to stop running. I wanted to hear the sweet sounds of The Temptations and The Supremes pouring from loud car radio speakers. I wanted to smell the odors that emanated from the corner sub shops and the Muslim seafood restaurants. All of these noises and smells would have been much more calming than the quietness of this hill on this night.

A ball of fire bellowed upward and lit up the summer sky. James and I once again focused our attention on the group of men dressed in white sheets at the bottom of the hill. James tapped me on the shoulder and pointed to a group of children who were encircled by the men. The children were also dressed in white sheets. As the fire died down, we noticed a huge cross burning in the middle of the circle. Some of the other troopers moved to the front of the hill. They stood there and watched the cross burn as if it were fire works on the Fourth of July. A few other troopers entered their cars and drove off to guard the perimeter. The troopers at the front of the hill began to talk in hushed tones. Every once in a while, they would erupt into a fit of laughter. James and I failed to see the humor in it all.

The day before the rally, a member of the Jewish Defense League had allegedly driven by and shot at the house of the grand wizard of the Ku Klux Klan. The state police barrack commander had anticipated more trouble, so he assigned a contingent of troopers to guard the Klan during their rally. The rally was held on a large privately owned farm. James and I were working the evening shift and were assigned to the rally. When we were first advised of our assignment, we thought it was some crude joke that was being played on us by Sergeant Stoney. We knew that the sergeant didn't care much for Black people, and I was certain that he hated me.

I thought of an incident which had occurred shortly after my arrival at the Frederick, Maryland barrack in 1982. A Black motorist came into the lobby of the barrack and asked if he could wait there, out of the cold, until someone arrived to pick him up. The motorist stated that his car had broken down on a nearby road. He had contacted a relative to come and pick him up. The Black motorist was well groomed and continuously addressed Sergeant Stoney as "sir." Sergeant Stoney told the Black motorist that he could remain in the lobby until his relatives arrived if he kept quiet and "acted like a white man." The motorist looked perplexed. He meekly thanked Sergeant Stoney and took a seat in the lobby. James and I happened to be standing in the area. I immediately questioned Sergeant Stoney about his comments to the Black motorist. He smiled and made some excuse that was unapologetic and inadequate. He seemed to resent my questioning him. He was a sergeant and I was just a trooper; he was white and I was Black. What right did I have to question him? I never saw the sergeant stripes on his shoulder—I was confronting the man. And nothing about him engendered fear in me.

James and I soon found out that our assignment was not a joke. As we exited the rear door of the barrack and headed toward our patrol cars, I told James that I couldn't guard the Klan and that I was going to quit. "This is the ultimate insult to us. These motherfuckers have the gall to ask us to guard a fuckin' cowardly organization that has lynched our ancestors and is still lynching and shooting Blacks from a safe distance. No way, man. I ain't going to sell out like this. This job isn't worth it."

James slowed his walk and looked as if he was thinking deeply. He had been a teacher in the Baltimore Public School system prior to becoming a trooper. He was familiar with the history of the Klan through his many hours of reading and studying. He had also heard his parents speak of the brutal and spineless acts of the Klan. He knew the type of gutless destruction that they had committed against so many Blacks. He was familiar with their burning of houses and gang-lynchings. I wondered how he could handle this assignment without getting bitterly angry. How could he even pretend that he was going to go through with it?

James abruptly grabbed my shoulder and spun me around so that I faced him. "Listen and listen good. Don't you think this shit bothers me? Don't you think I would like to grab Sergeant Stoney, or whoever the motherfucker was who assigned us to this

shit, by the neck and choke the fuck out of them? I know what's
going on. I know the game. I hate a redneck son of a bitch, but I
refuse to let the motherfuckers make me quit. It ain't going to be
that easy. *And* you better not let them make you quit! You smile
in their ugly-ass, treacherous faces just like they smile in yours.
You laugh with them just like they laugh with you. It's all a game
of deception! *And* I've learned to play it as well as they have. As
long as I know what they're doing, then they can't make me quit.
They can't affect my life. They don't even matter. Quitting is like
getting your ass whipped. If you walk away, they win. If you
stay, believe it or not, you win. That ain't easy to see because it's
caught up in this deception shit. *But* what you have to keep
constantly telling yourself daily is that it's all a fuckin' game and
this assignment is simply them putting on a full-court press. I can
handle the pressure and keep smiling, can you? Or are you ready
to commit a costly turnover?"

James was breathing heavily. I could see that he was speaking
from the heart. He was exposing a little of his soul, and he was
doing it to keep me from surrendering. I didn't know what to say.
I knew he was waiting for a response. Everyone seemed to want a
response from me and, as time went on, I became more and more
capable of replying. I was learning. The events of my life were
making me understand things that I had never thought of, things
that had been foreign to me.

I turned from James and continued my walk toward the patrol
car. James walked with me. I reached the car, put the key in the
door and opened it. James stopped at the door to my car. I looked
at James and said, "Man, you have to understand that this shit is
new to me. I'm twenty-two years old and it seems that I've been
introduced to every side of life. I've lived down on those fuckin'
ghetto streets and now I'm up here in Klan country. You know,
James, that kind of transition can tend to fuck a young brother up."
James smiled slightly. I continued. "I don't understand it all,
James. I mean, I know what's going on. Believe me, my brothers
have taught me enough shit that I could answer Marvin Gaye
when he asks that question, 'Yeah, what's going on?' I just don't
understand the need for white folks to constantly keep us down. I
know it ain't all white folk, but the ones in power have developed
the ability to influence the ones who are not. So, no matter who
they are or what they are doing, white folks feel that they are more
than a Black man. I know it goes back a long ways. Thomas
Jefferson, that prejudiced, rotten-ass motherfucker, started it when
he said that we were only three-fifths of a man. I understand all
that. So I guess it's been white against Black since the beginning

of time, or, at least, since the beginning of the Europeans' invasion of Africa. *And* I suppose that's the way it'll always be. Elitist white people against people of color. I guess that's where all these games that they come up with come from. And I know you're right, James—they try to make us quit. If I didn't have you here now to stop me, I'd probably be unemployed and heading home. But there ain't too many brothers like you left, so I'm glad you're here."

James took his glasses off and wiped sweat, or tears, from his eyes. He put his head down. He looked back up at me and said, "Don't get sentimental on me, motherfucker." I answered, "I ain't getting sentimental. Sensitivity is not one of my strong points anymore. Sometimes I just feel like lashing out at something or someone. My brothers told me that's just the reaction my enemies want from me. But eventually that's what Black people in this country are going to do. Everyone has a breaking point. I'm just surprised that we ain't there already. Now you tell me not to quit. It ain't easy living in two worlds. It ain't easy being a Black man and doing what is considered a white man's job."

I smiled a little and raised my voice. "Now I've got to go up here and protect the Ku Klux Klan from the Anti-Defamation League or the Jewish Defense League or whomever. Ain't this a bitch. They're really fucking with our heads. Black men protecting white men from Jewish men. It's that old military shit again. Black men fighting and killing for everything and everyone but Black people. I'm all fucked up now. Mercy, mercy me, things aren't what they used to be." James spoke up, "Yes they are, brother. Things are what they used to be. And that's the problem. We need a change."

James put his glasses back on. He was smiling now. Some tension seemed to have been eased. His broad shoulders no longer appeared hunched over. We both understood each other better. We both had learned something. I wondered how many other Black officers believed as we did. How many other officers had such twisted feelings deep in their divided souls? How many other officers were confused? I wanted to believe that there were others like us. But I wasn't sure. I knew that although many white policemen wore blue, they knew underneath they were white. But when many Black officers put on blue, they were blue to the bone. They became engulfed in the police mentality. They became obsessed by the perceived power of being a law enforcement officer. This was the only power they had ever known. It shored up their insecure egos and made them a little bit better than their blueless Black brethren. They were more dedicated than anyone else to "maintaining order." The history of the police department became their history. They wanted to read police novels as opposed to Black history books or books by Blacks. They wanted their sons and daughters to become police officers. Nonetheless, I still wanted to believe that, somewhere, two other Black police officers were having a conversation like James and me. We entered our cars and drove off to the dreaded hill.

I took the shotgun off my shoulder and moved toward the edge of the hill. James followed close behind me as if he were afraid that I was going to do something crazy. I wasn't. Black smoke mushroomed into the dark sky. The group of white-clad men and boys moved closer to the burning cross. The smell of the smoke made me think of the burning of stores that occurred after the assassination of the Reverend Dr. Martin Luther King Jr. I thought of all the anger and broken dreams that were the result of Dr. King's death. It seemed that fire and smoke always followed anger. Blacks were angry with whites for killing a peaceful man who had fought for what little hope they had left. Now a group of ignorant whites were burning a cross to signify to Blacks that their hopes were still in ashes and would never be realized in America. Not in "the land of the free."

They had assassinated Dr. King and now they were assassinating all the hopes that he had brought about, or so they thought. They were assassinating any hopes that the race problem could be resolved without more anger and without more fire and smoke. Mom had said that God would destroy the world with fire next time. We seemed to be moving toward this destruction by fire with laser-like speed.

I couldn't hear everything the leader of the rally was saying. Every once in a while he would scream "nigger" and "Jew" at the top of his voice. Somehow the Klan had mustered up the same amount of hate for both groups. I couldn't understand it. I knew that both Jews and Blacks had been victims of a holocaust. The Jews had suffered a great loss at the hands of the white supremacist Hitler. Blacks had suffered the loss of at least one hundred million people during the Middle Passage and slavery at the hands of whites. Many more Blacks had died at the hands of whites through random shootings, lynchings, and assassinations. Millions of Blacks had also been systematically killed in the Congo, with the assistance of the United States. Blacks were still suffering from racism, miseducation, and poverty. I couldn't understand why Blacks and Jews had been lumped into the same group or category. I thought perhaps it was because they had both suffered a holocaust.

For the Jews the holocaust was over. They now ruled their own country, with the assistance of the United States. Blacks still had nothing. America was not willing to aid Blacks as it had aided Jews. For many Blacks in America, there was no difference between whites and Jews.

Most Blacks understood that Israel was giving aid to South Africa when that African country was under the system of apartheid. This made it abundantly clear that there was no alliance between Blacks and Jews. It caused Blacks to conclude that there was nothing that Israel was doing that was any different from what any other oppressive regime was doing against people of color. Israel was helping the white South Africans commit the same horrific crimes against Black South Africans as Adolf Hitler committed against the Jews. The Jews in America were not speaking out against the support and comradeship that the Israelis enjoyed with the Nazis in South Africa. Yet, at the same time, Israel, with the overt and covert support of the United States, was still hunting down those few living Nazis who had committed the tortures and murders of Jews prior to and during World War II. The Jews had been victims of a holocaust and now they were aiding the South African government in committing a holocaust against Blacks. They were hunting German criminals and, at the same time, aiding white South African criminals. While the Jewish community in America was chastising the Reverend Jesse Jackson about a remark and having Jackson renounce and denounce Minister Louis Farrakhan, no one was requiring Israel to stop its embarrassing relationship with the brutal regime in South Africa. Conspirators in the same game. Blacks realized, even if the Ku Klux Klan didn't, that there was no *true* alliance with Jews and never had been.

I looked toward James and could see the reflection of the blazing fire in his glasses. He looked down at his watch and then toward me. "Let's get the fuck out of here." James had had enough. He was reaching his breaking point. He yelled out to Anthony, "Anthony, you all secure this area. We're going to go down to the highway so we can be there when they start pulling out."

Anthony yelled back, "Go ahead, James, we got it covered." James turned and walked toward his patrol car. I put the shotgun barrel back on my shoulder and slowly backed away from the horrible scene. It had been a learning experience. Now I better understood the extent of my bitterness toward America. I had been told about the Klan by my mother and grandmother. I had been told of the night riders, the rapes, the burnings. But there was nothing like feeling the fire for myself. Now I understood what Warren meant when he said every Black man in America should own a gun. This is what we were dealing with—we had to protect ourselves. No one else would do it!

Our patrol cars were parked far down on the other side of the hill. It was pitch dark. Time seemed to have passed by very quickly. It was 11 p.m. already. Our feet made a sweeping sound through the high grass. James reached his car and pounded the hood with his fist. "Goddamn. These motherfuckers—when is it all going to end? Why does one human being feel he's better than another?" I opened the door to my car and put the shotgun in the rack. I tossed my hat on the back seat and walked over to James.

I began to speak. "You know, James, I used to have hope that things were going to change. But I don't think they will now. We've just got to make it without expecting change from anyone else. It doesn't matter if they don't change. It doesn't matter if they yell 'nigger' until hell freezes over. As long as they don't get in our way. If they do, then we have to do what we have to do. But we've got to stop expecting them to change because it just ain't going to happen. It ain't all of them, James. We ain't fighting the whole white race. There are certainly some good white folk out there who are just as perplexed by this division and hatred as we are. *But* there sure aren't enough of them. There sure are a lot of them who participate in the persecution and oppression of our kind. *And* it don't matter whether they're called Jews, Irishmen, Russians or whatever—we have to treat all racists and conspirators with racists just like they treat us. We have to deal with them the way they deal with us. And right now, James, we're getting a raw deal. So as Gil Scott-Heron said, 'It's time to start spreading those goddamn blues around.'"

12

Blue Gardenia University

Philosophers have long conceded, however, that every man has two educations: that which is given to him, and the other that which he gives himself. Of the two kinds the latter is by far more desirable.
—Carter G. Woodson, Mis-Education of the Negro

I am an invisible man....I am a man of substance, of flesh and bone, fiber and liquids—and I might even be said to possess a mind. I am invisible, understand, simply because people refuse to see me.

—Ralph Ellison, Invisible Man

Forgive your enemies, but never forget their names.

—John F. Kennedy

A hot summer day in 1985. You could actually see the heat seep from the pores of the black pavement and rise ominously up toward its original source. The sweltering sun beamed down suffocating heat-rays on the defenseless inhabitants of its captive city. Groups of Black men with white towels around their necks stood around on street corners, conversing and wiping what

139

seemed to be annoying and unending streams of sweat from their faces.

An assortment of cars passed through the neighborhoods of Baltimore, with windows down and music blaring from their radio speakers. Portable radios that sounded more like miniature jukeboxes littered the white marble steps which led to the almost identical row houses along the 2400 block of West Baltimore Street. More music emanated from the corner bars like The Club 2300, Two Spot Bar and Lounge, and The Blue Gardenia Bar and Lounge. The doors to the bars had been tied open to entice customers in for cold drinks and soothing soulful sounds. Young boys tossed dirty white baseballs off boarded-up doorways to long-ago abandoned houses. Pretty little girls with beautiful brown skin intensely jumped rope and sang "Little Sally Walker" as if in defiance of the oppressive heat.

A group of bare-backed Black men sat on the steps leading to the Blue Gardenia Lounge and Cut Rate Liquor Store at the corner of Baltimore Street and Calverton Road. Sweat rolled over their bodies, causing them to shine like waxed figures. The men grimaced in obvious discomfort from the pain inflicted upon them by the blistering sun. This assembly of Black men, like most Black men quartered in the so-called ghetto, were known only by their first names. They demanded that they be called solely by their first names or a nickname. Maybe it was some subconscious recognition of Malcolm X's stance against the utilization of slave names. Maybe it was an act of defiance directed toward the white men who had enslaved their ancestors, taken away their names, raped their female ancestors, and given these Black male descendants the masters' last names.

Stanley was twenty-two. He was a light-complexioned, slender brother with tan eyes and reddish-brown hair. He wiped sweat away from his eyes with a Magic Johnson tee shirt that he had been wearing earlier. He looked up into the sky as if he were trying to get a closer look at the bright orange object that was causing him such discomfort. He looked back toward the group of stony-faced young men who were arbitrarily seated around him and began to expatiate, as was common at these impromptu gatherings. "The mayor should come down here and talk to us about the problems of ghetto living. But he won't do that. He'll go hire some white folks to look into why we niggers are doing so bad. Or maybe he'll go out and ask some of those turncoat middle-class 'negroes' who don't know shit unless the white man tell them they know it. You know, the kind of brothers and sisters who don't feel that they are qualified to do anything positive unless white folks' institutions give them some paper saying they're certified in some field of study."

Gas stood up and sauntered toward the front of the steps. Something Stanley said had aroused him and he had decided that he was to be the next speaker. No one had designated him as such, but everyone just knew that it was time for Gas to speak. Gas was a dark, heavyset brother who always had a mean look on his face. He glanced down Baltimore Street into the traffic and then turned back to Stanley. He took a deep breath and smiled. "You know goddamn well the mayor ain't coming down here and ask you niggers nothing. Not a fucking thing. You keep thinking you count. You keep thinking that somebody gives a fuck about what happens to you. No one cares! That's why they go ask those white people and those so-called middle-class niggers about us. Those fake motherfuckers don't want the truth. Better yet, they probably know the truth and want to make sure the rest of the sleeping brothers never find out what's really happening. Sleepwalkers—that's what we are. Just like Ralph Ellison said in that book Mrs. Marshall gave us, *Invisible Man*.

"They know that most of you niggers will believe anything they tell you. Just say a white man said it and you all will nod your heads in agreement. Start quoting them and shit like that. Ain't that right? Better yet, put it on the evening news and have one of those old, wrinkled rich assholes say it. That way it's really official 'cause they wouldn't lie to you on television. Ain't no need to write lies in the newspapers 'cause you shiftless-ass niggers never read. In fact, half of you can't read and they know that because they taught you, or didn't teach you."

Gas paused and took another deep breath. The men waited for him to continue. Gas was pumping knowledge—and he wasn't pulling any punches. The brothers realized that Gas was intelligent. They had watched him read the newspapers after he got off work every day. Sitting there on the white marble steps of inner-city Baltimore assiduously trying to understand the world around him. The events of his life had calcified his soul. But that was okay. In fact, there was an advantage to being callous. The world that surrounded him was cold and hard. If he was to survive it, he had to shun all thoughts of the angelic nature of the human race. He had to face the indisputable fact that, for the most part, man had become evil.

The entire human race wasn't brutal. Gas knew that. He watched from his bedroom window as the churchgoers strolled up and down Baltimore Street on Sunday mornings on their way to or from Reverend Elder C. Green's church on the hill. He watched them smiling and laughing and giving thanks to God for their many blessings. He had read stories in his newspapers about Mother Teresa and other kind and docile souls. He knew these people would feed the hungry or clothe the poor. He knew they didn't hold malice toward anything or anyone. He knew it was difficult for them to practice violence or even self-defense. But they were in the minority. If he was going to survive, especially as a targeted Black man, he had to emulate those in power.

Gas stared into the eyes of his students. They had better pay attention. He scanned the different faces until he locked in on Sheldon's eyes. Then he continued, "Yeah, and they realize that there are a few conscious brothers out here and they know how to deal with them. They know that a few of us can read and will read on occasion. They know that a few of us have a vague idea as to what they are up to. But there are only a few of us. So all they have to do is break us or discredit us like they have been trying to do to Minister Farrakhan for years. Minister Farrakhan preaches to make brothers conscious. He tells you and I to do for ourselves, to get their education, but to remember it's *their* education. He says to use what they teach you and what you learn on your own to advance yourself, but more importantly, use it to advance your race, your people."

Stanley stepped away from Gas and leaned on the wall. He put his shirt around his neck and eyed Gas carefully. Gas glared at him and continued, "Minister Farrakhan doesn't preach that save-your-own-soul-so-you-can-walk-streets-of-gold bullshit! You see, they hate the Minister for what he says and the fact that they know he means serious business. They don't care about what he believes. You can believe any fuckin' thing you want to as long as you don't open your mouth and tell the masses. They realize he's no Baptist minister or Catholic priest telling us to wait until we all get to heaven for our day of independence."

Sweat rolled down Gas's hairy chest and over his round stomach. He was breathing heavily. He wasn't ready to stop talking. He knew he had his audience captivated, and he knew it was important that his message get delivered in its entirety. He did not have in front of him an auditorium full of people, but maybe he could tell one brother and that brother would tell another brother and so on. "Each one teach one." Maybe that was the best approach, because it seemed that every time Blacks planned mass meetings in order to get a positive message out, the gathering was infiltrated by perfidious traitors who did all they could to sabotage the meeting, dilute the message, and cause disunity.

Gas looked over his small attentive audience and continued, "Every day they tell us to get off welfare. They tell us to be independent of the government, to build our own. They say some of the same things that Minister Farrakhan and others say, but they don't mean it. I agree that we need to build our own. Fuck welfare! We just ask that they don't block the door when we make our move. So we don't need the mayor down here smiling in our faces. We know where he is coming from. We understand his motives and his source of power. And trust me, he fears the fact that someday we might really start building our own. Then, we might figure out that we don't need to buy this bullshit brand name stuff that they sell us. We might stop buying high-priced sneakers and overpriced cars. We might stop drinking beer and other shit that makes us less alert. We might stop eating bad food that results in us being in the kind of shape that I'm in. We might even save our money and spend it in the Black community. That's some scary shit, isn't it?"

No one wanted Gas to end his provocative tirade. He was making so much sense. Giving salient lessons that had never been given before. Saying things that had been purposely concealed from his audience. This wasn't the reclusive, temperate Gas who was prone to falling into a morose mental state. Gas was delivering his message with serious zeal and it was obvious that he was making an impact on his intended targets.

Gas didn't want to stop lecturing. He knew that he might not have another chance. Every weekend the group of men gathered on the steps of the Blue Gardenia. Sometimes the group was larger. At every session of this ghetto think tank, some brother delivered a message to the other brothers. But each week the faces could be different. One or more of the members would be incarcerated before the next gathering. Someone would surely be killed before next week, or before the day came to an end. Gas wanted to take full advantage of his opportunity to reach those present. He knew that in the ghetto, opportunities to do anything came few and far in between. *Seize the moment.*

Gas looked toward the gaps of white marble in between the men. He lowered his voice to a deep, dry baritone. "Just nameless faces—that's all we are. Just a group or a gang of expendable Black men. Slavery in its original form is over. There isn't any wars going on right now. They don't need us. They look right past us. They think we don't know shit. They wouldn't even believe that we could sit here and discuss survival or advancement. They don't think that we can intelligently discuss abortions or the drug problem. You see, to them, me, you, and all these Black motherfuckers up and down this street are just a bunch of drug-taking, alcohol-drinking, pussy-starved, thieving, ignorant, uneducated *niggers*.

"That's what they think of us. That's what they've been taught and are being taught in their schools. And they teach us that they are the opposite of all that they say we are. They teach us that God is white and Jesus is white and that all good things are white. The sad part about it is that most of us buy that shit. That's why you want that white Mayor Shaffer to come down here. You want that high white man to listen to a lowly nigger. Then you can feel big. Hell, he might even take a picture with you. But to him, it would be like going to the zoo and taking a picture with any other motherfucking gorilla."

Gas wiped more sweat from his wide face. Stanley inconspicuously eased into an empty spot on the steps. Timmy sat on the steps staring into Gas. He was holding a brown bag which contained a quart of beer. Timmy was a tall, frail, dark brother with sunken eyes. His skin was pulled tight, allowing no lines to show on his face. It was difficult to tell if he was smiling or frowning. He enjoyed this natural ability to deceive others.

Timmy drank too much. He would rather drink beer than eat. He had been extremely intelligent in elementary school and on several occasions teachers recommended that he be allowed to skip a grade. By the time he reached middle school, his grades had dropped off drastically. He began to cut class and hang in the hallways. Finally, he dropped out and resorted to life in the streets. He would sleep most of the morning, then get up and beg or steal to get money for alcohol or drugs. At the age of twenty-five, Timmy had given up on life. Whenever he spoke, it was evident that although he had given up on book knowledge and life itself, there was still something there—some residue of self-worth that had been mistakenly left in him by those who had intended to take everything positive out of him. It was as if he knew so much and yet so little.

Timmy probably could have told the mayor why there were so many problems in the inner city. He probably could have explained to him why Black kids don't make it under the current school system. He could have explained why he resorted to alcohol and drugs. He could have articulated what needed to be done to avoid the downfall of other young people. But no one was asking Timmy or others like him what to do. No one wanted to sit down with this shirtless group of Black men and listen to their thoughts. The mayor wanted to know what the problem was by asking people who had never experienced inner-city living or who were not living in the ghetto now. He wanted to ask people who had never walked through the halls of one of those institutes of miseducation called schools. Timmy was convinced that the mayor already knew what the problem was.

Timmy finished another swig of beer and wiped the excess from his mouth. He spoke slowly. "I don't know what the fuck the mayor will do or won't do. And you know, it really doesn't matter. All this shit is bigger than Mayor William Donald Shaffer anyway. He's just a pawn in the game. But you can't talk like that 'cause people will say you crazy. When you are Black and you know more than you are supposed to know, people will call you crazy and a troublemaker. Sometimes it's harder on you when you figure it all out and you look around and see that the rest of your people haven't figured it out yet. That kind of shit can drive you to drink."

Timmy took another deep swig of beer. "Ah, this is some good shit. No, the mayor ain't going to ever do a damn thing for us. You don't have to tell me that, Gas. The police aren't going to do shit; congressmen aren't going to do shit; churches aren't going to do shit; and until we do something for ourselves, God or Allah or Jehovah isn't going to do shit."

Sheldon was sitting there with his arms folded on his knees. He admired the group of men he was with and felt honored just to be allowed to sit and listen to them. He was nineteen and the youngest of the group. Sheldon had finished high school but he believed that sitting with the group of indomitable men did more to strengthen him than any class he had ever taken. School was important, but he needed to know what to do with all he had learned. Now he was getting ideas about doing for himself, about starting a business. He was learning that he had to do more than sit on the steps and drink beer. He was learning that he could not just sit and wait on the mayor because the mayor may never come. And even if he did come, the mayor wouldn't listen to him. He was learning that being conscious was important. And being conscious and letting others know you were conscious could cause problems, even death.

Despite what most people thought, there were lessons to be learned in the ghetto. There were teachers in the ghetto with no college degrees but whose lessons were more poignant than any lecture given by a university professor from any of the so-called institutions of higher learning. The steps of the Blue Gardenia were the lecture halls and laboratories of the ghetto. Stanley, Gas, and Timmy were the professors and the ghetto itself was the institute of higher learning for Sheldon and many like him. The

penalty for failing these classes was not an *F*. The penalty was a
D—for death, physical, emotional, and mental death! And just
like in the American school system, brothers were receiving *D*'s at
an alarming rate.

An eerie warm breeze blew over the group of men just as a
Baltimore Mass Transit Administration #20 bus pulled to a stop in
front of them. Nate stepped from the bus. He smiled at the group.
Nate, for some time now, had been slowly losing his hair. To
conceal this fact, he shaved his head bald. The sight of his bright
bald head brought smiles and laughter whenever he approached
friends. The men on the steps were always glad to see Nate. He
was one of the brightest ghetto pundits. He was a formidable
Black man. He was strong. And everyone the world over
respected strength. Nate, Stanley, Gas, and Timmy were all
comrades. Nate was familiar with Sheldon through Sheldon's
brother, Cookieman. Cookieman was dead. He was one of the
tragedies of the ghetto.

Cookieman had once been one of the shirtless men on the
steps. He had heard some of the same speeches and had not
understood the messages, or maybe he had understood the
messages and ignored them like so many others. Maybe he felt
powerless to act on the knowledge he had acquired because there
were so many forces against him and so few brothers willing to
work with him. A barrage of bullets from a store owner's gun had
ended Cookieman's life on a cold November evening in 1984.
Sheldon was the brother of another dead, nameless ghetto dweller.

Gas spoke to Nate first. "What's up, you bald-head
motherfucker?" Nate smiled and responded, "You've got the best
hand, you big, fat, McDonald's hamburger-eating, sloppy
motherfucker." Timmy spoke up. "Why do all of you brothers
use that word *motherfucker* so much? I bet you all don't even
know the history of it and how it relates to your slave mentality."
Nate looked at Timmy and said, "No, we don't know the history
of it, and the only reason you can come up with it is because
you're drunk. I guess the answer is in that beer bottle. Let me
have a swig and I'll be able to tell you the history of it in a
minute." Timmy shook his head and responded, "Nah, brother,
there ain't any history in this bottle. Except maybe the history of
how the white man gets rich selling us this shit. And I'm not
drunk. I was just trying to enlighten a couple of ignorant brothers,
and I catch hell for that."

Nate brushed off the bottom white marble step to avoid getting
his neatly pressed blue jeans dirty. He sat down. Nate was always
dressed meticulously. Today, along with his jeans, he was

wearing a short-sleeved white shirt and a pair of white sandal-like shoes. He pulled a small, clean white cloth from his back pocket and wiped his head. "It's hotter than one of Gas's women out here. You all should get your heads shaved like mine. It's a lot cooler with a bald head. You motherfuckers still wearing those Angela Davis afros. I know the movement is still alive but, damn, you all don't have to keep that look. Next thing you know you'll be wearing big, gold peace symbols around your neck." Gas responded, "What the fuck do you know about the movement? Your punk-ass brother is out there arresting Black men for the white man and you going to come down here and talk about a fuckin' revolution. Maybe if that motherfucker had an Angela Davis afro, he would remember who the fuck he was. Give that motherfucker a peace sign and tell him to come home."

Nate was in an awkward position. I was his brother and his natural instinct was to defend me. Yet, he believed Gas was right. He thought again about the conversation in the basement. He wondered why I couldn't see it. Why couldn't I understand that I was embarrassing him? Why couldn't I see that I was selling out? My arguments had not altered his feelings and he knew that they would be even less effective on Gas. Still, he felt compelled to respond, obliged to save the name of his flesh and blood; he was in fact his brother's keeper. Nate sighed silently and then let the reluctant words drop from his lips. "My brother is just looking at that police shit as a job."

Nate was right. Gas wasn't buying it. He snapped back, "We all got jobs, Nate. I get up every morning and try to pull Timmy's ass out of bed. Then I get on that bus, go down to that construction site. I bust those bricks so we can eat and sleep and maybe, one day, build something. We know it ain't the best we can do, but we ain't going out and running down brothers. We bust bricks, your brother busts us. Plus, Nate, by anybody's standards your brother is intelligent. Why can't he teach? Why can't he come down here and help us build something? He ain't like some of those bourgeois niggers who are scared to walk the streets in the ghetto. He ain't afraid of his own people. I've seen him down here fighting and demanding respect just like the rest of us. I've talked to him. He has sat right here on these steps with us. I know all of us are somewhat confused. We know better but we don't do better. But I can't understand your brother. He knows so much. He knows more than you give him credit for. Money doesn't drive him like it drives most of us. He ain't happy. He don't have a sellout mentality, and yet he's selling out. And you know it."

Nate sighed heavily. He hated that his brother was being called a sellout. The words cut through him like a sharp machete. A sellout was the worst thing anyone could be. He would rather have his brother be a murderer. In fact, Nate believed that a sellout was a serial murderer, whose actions affected the whole race. A sellout would defend all that was wrong, for his own personal advancement. Nate couldn't understand how a man could sell out and put himself in a position of condemnation by his own family. Especially, just to please others who didn't "give a fuck about him."

Nate knew that one of the main reasons that Blacks never seemed to be able to move forward was that the Black community was infested with treacherous sellouts. Men and women willing to tell everything for a favorable place in the white world. Men and women willing to sell their souls, and betray others, just so they could have enough money to buy a new television. Or some crack cocaine. He couldn't understand why every Black man seemed to be willing to do anything to get that "white seal of approval." Nate had always said if the police caught him doing wrong, he would just do his prison time. He said he was not going to tell the police anything about any other brother. He would pay the price for his actions. He would not sell out.

Gas could tell that Nate was bothered by his comments. He had said enough. He could tell by Nate's reaction that Nate agreed with him. He would not press him to admit it. He earnestly wanted Nate to bring his brother home before it was too late. The group of men fell hauntingly silent. Sheldon noticed a white car slowly moving up the street. It pulled to the curb opposite them. The tinted window slowly slid down. Chas stuck his head out. Gas yelled out, "What's up, shorty?"

Nate attempted a smile. His heart beat rapidly. Chas was still alive. He watched Chas's every move. What had gone wrong? Tank and Cliff were supposed to have killed him. But they had failed to do the job. For a moment, Nate was relieved. After all, Chas was his friend and partner. It was good to see him still in an upright position. It was wrong to have ordered his death in the first place. Nate's feelings of relief were short-lived. Chas was an immediate threat to Nate's very existence.

Nate didn't know whether Tank and Cliff had gone to assassinate Chas and Chas had not been at home or whether Chas had killed the both of them and was now coming after him. He instinctively reached into his waistband to touch his gun. He forgot that in a strategic move to avoid being arrested by the police, he had stuffed his gun into Sugar's pocketbook earlier in the day. He had forgotten and left it. The empty waistband brought about an instant anxiety attack.

Chas noticed Nate's subtle movement. He reached down for the fully loaded, nickel-plated .357 magnum that was on the passenger seat next to him. He saw Nate remove his hand from his waistband. He couldn't imagine that Nate would be without his gun. He knew Nate was an excellent shot and was determined not to allow him to get an advantage.

Chas knew Nate well. He knew that despite Nate's feelings on the advancement of the Black man, Nate was a killer. He knew that Nate would kill another Black man if he felt the least bit threatened. Chas recalled that Nate had once told him that all men were killers at heart. He said that it was just a matter of when they were pushed to kill. He said killing was difficult but natural. Nate said that animals have no malice toward each other but they will kill one another. Survival of the fittest. He said that all humans were animals, but humans, unlike most other animals, had the ability to act based on reason.

Nate had preached that the white man had treated Black men like lower primates since the time he had brought us to this country in chains and that it had been necessary for us to sharpen our killer instinct, based on our need to defend ourselves. He said that the white man had always acted as if he was an untrained animal. White men had gone around the world, killing and conquering country after country. They had killed off the so-called American Indians and taken their land. They had killed off the so-called Africans and stolen their land. Nate said that the white man killed and conquered. It was the conquering that allowed him to justify the killing he had done and would continue to do in the name of justice or whatever other reason he could conjure up. He said Blacks were now killing without conquering. Blacks were killing each other and nothing could be achieved by killing someone who has already been conquered. It was like slaughtering sheep.

Timmy and Stanley spoke to Chas. Finally, Nate yelled out, "What's up, partner?" Chas nodded his head at the group of men. He yelled to Nate, "Hey Nate, let me speak to you a second." Nate stood up and slowly walked to Chas's car. He knew he could be walking into death, but he was without his gun and Chas could kill him even if he remained seated on the steps. He definitely wasn't going to run.

Nate approached the car and kneeled down. He peered into the window past Chas and noticed the gun lying on the passenger seat. Chas noticed Nate looking and spoke up. "I got that in here 'cause some motherfuckers tried to hit me this morning." Nate tried to look surprised. Chas continued, "Don't worry, brother, I got the motherfuckers, but I don't know if they had some friends who may be still trying to do me."

Nate spoke. "What the fuck they try to hit you for, Chas?" Chas responded, "I think the son of a bitches was trying to rob me of our dope and money. That's our dope, Nate—yours and mine. You better be careful, Nate. The motherfucker who sent them after me might send someone after you just because he knows that we are partners. You know how that goes. Someone always have to pay the price. You know the rules. Don't you, Nate?"

Nate and Chas stared into each other's eyes. They were trying to look into each other's soul, trying to read each other. Chas thought again about everything he and Nate had been through. They had always been so comfortable talking with each other. Now it was all different. Now he was thinking of ending Nate's life. It was awkward. He would never hear Nate's voice again. Chas knew that in killing Nate he would be setting up a confrontation with Frank and Quincy. Even if they understood his motivations, they would have to react. Nate was their brother.

Chas wanted to exculpate Nate from the attempt on his life. He thought of Mom. She was Nate's mother, but he, too, had known her as nothing other than "Mom." He thought of the pain and grief he would bring to her. He remembered the back-porch conversations and dances. He remembered the meals she had prepared for him as he sat with Nate at our table and ate. He thought of all the nights he had spent at our house. He thought of the basketball and football games we had played together. He thought of the cold winters when we all had gathered in our basement or his basement to listen to the music of The Jackson Five, The Temptations, The O'Jays, James Brown, Marvin Gaye, and others. He remembered the cold, snowy Christmas mornings when we had gathered to compare gifts. He could see visions of the past in Nate's eyes and in Nate's soul.

Nate believed that it would only be a matter of minutes before Chas would reach for the gun and send fiery balls of hot lead through his skin. He knew that he had tried to end Chas's life. He had already made up his mind that he would not run. Chas would have to look him in the face and shoot him. He would make Chas confront their friendship. He would make him go through the difficult task of killing someone who was like a brother. He had no doubt that Chas could do it.

As Nate stood there and looked into Chas's soul, he again wished that he had not ordered his death. He couldn't understand

what had brought him to do it. He wished that Chas had killed
Tank and Cliff before they had gotten the opportunity to tell Chas
who had sent them. Chas was his friend and although he did not
like the way Chas was handling their business, he knew Chas was
the best business partner he could have. Nate was sorry that it had
all come to this. But it was too late for that shit. He understood
what Chas had to do and he understood why. If Chas knew that
Nate had tried to kill him and didn't in turn try to kill Nate, Nate
would lose respect for him. The rules of the game had to be
played out. It was Chas's move.

Chas had made up his mind. Nate had to die. He had to be
killed right there in public. Right on Baltimore Street where he
had grown up. Others had to learn that Chas would tolerate no
"bullshit." They had to know that no one was exempt from
revenge. He reached for the gun. Nate never moved. Chas
opened the glove compartment and put the gun inside. Nate
breathed a sigh of relief. Chas stammered as he spoke. "I–I'm
going to get the fuck out of here, Nate. Be careful and be cool,
brother. I love you."

Nate couldn't respond. He couldn't believe what was
happening. Chas was becoming soft. He was letting him off the
hook. He had told Chas that whenever he had identified a man as
his enemy and had him down, never let him up again, for he will
come back and destroy you. Nate had told Chas that this is why it
is necessary for whites to keep Blacks down. He wondered if
Chas had forgotten that lesson. He thought maybe Chas had made
an exception in his case. There could be no exceptions to this rule.

Nate backed away from the car and wiped sweat from his
forehead with his little white towel. He turned to the steps where
the men had been sitting and noticed that they were gone. He
figured that they all had gone into the bar to replenish their supply
of cold beer. He would give them money for his share of beer
when they returned. He walked to the steps, brushed off a spot,
sat down and stared toward the hot sun.

The sound of screeching tires instantaneously brought Nate's
attention back to Baltimore Street. He reached into his waist band.
"Damn." A black car pulled to a sudden stop in front of the steps.
Tank sprang from the car and ran toward Nate. He had a baseball
bat in his hand. Nate stood up to confront him. He had no fear of
Tank. He would take the bat and beat the fuck out of the
incompetent coward.

Nate never saw Cliff's brother, Richard, jump from the
driver's seat of the car and come around him. Richard grabbed
Nate around the neck and struck him aside the head with the barrel

of his .45 automatic pistol. Nate's knees buckled. Blood trickled from a gash that had been made by the impact of the gun. He struggled to free himself. Richard screamed in his ear, "Hold still, motherfucker, or I'll kill you." Nate reached up to pull Richard's arm from around his neck. "Kill me then, motherfucker. You so goddamn bad, shoot me, motherfucker." Nate hit Richard in the face with a few wild punches. Tank yelled out, "Don't do him right here in the fuckin' street. Everybody's watching. Drag his ass to the back of the store." Nate continued to struggle and yell. "Fuck you, Tank. You punk bitch. Motherfucker, if you couldn't kill Chas, I know you can't kill me. You chicken-hearted bitch."

Tank backed away from Nate and raised the bat. Nate turned away from Tank. He took a quick glimpse up the street and noticed Chas's white car. Chas was peering down the street. The vision of Chas was quickly blurred by blood. Nate felt a hard thump and then dizziness. Tank raised the bat and came down on Nate's head again—more blood. Richard released his hold on Nate and ran back toward the car. Nate fell to the ground. Tank took another swing at Nate's slumping body but missed. He dropped the bat and jumped into the car. Richard sped away. Nate's white shirt was covered with blood. Blood seeped from the corner of his mouth. He pulled himself up onto the white steps and looked back in the direction in which he had previously observed Chas's car. It was gone. "Son of a bitch, should have killed me. Punks, all of them. Ain't none of them got the guts to do the job right."

Nate could hear the all-too-familiar sound of an ambulance siren in the distance. This time it was coming for him. Moving at ghetto speed. Blood bubbled up and dribbled over his split quivering lip. He looked up into the hot tormenting sun. "Fuck them. Fuck all of them pa...pu...punk-ass niggers. They shouldn't have fucked with me." He looked down at the red blood that flowed over the white marble steps of the Blue Gardenia where the group of shirtless men had been seated earlier. He looked for the men. He was alone. No one was left. Nothing was left but him and his dripping blood.

13

Unity

All your strength is in union, all your danger is in discord.

—Henry W. Longfellow, Hiawatha

The true worth of a race must be measured by the character of its women.

—Mary McLeod Bethune

Streaks of cool sweat raced down my back, finding a resting place at the top of my brown buttocks. The silence of the usually quiet room was broken by the sounds of so-called lovemaking. Doris pulled me close to her as if her intention was to make us one in body. It was our time, our place away from the rest of the cold, cruel world. It was how God had intended it. One woman and one man united in spirit. Uniting their bodies. It was neither an act of raw sex nor an act of lovemaking. Our love had been made a long time before we had ever undressed before each other. Our souls had formed a deep, secure bond before our lips had ever touched. We both had decided we wanted more than sex. More than superficial friendship. We had to have more.

Doris was, and is, a sincere, extremely intelligent Black woman. Before ever meeting me she had done her studying, and she demanded the same of me, her man. I was proud of her awareness. In fact, it was her knowledge that like a giant omnipotent magnet drew me to her. A wise woman is more attractive than any beauty contest participant. I immediately discerned the profound beauty within Doris.

Doris was aware of her rich heritage. She was aware of the greatness of the Black women who had gone before her. She was also aware of the horrifying degradation Black women had suffered under the brutal system of slavery in America. She often spoke about the fortitude that had been required of Black women before, during, and after slavery. It was difficult to imagine these proud, strong women having their children torn from their arms by white men, to be sold off like meaningless cattle. Children never to be seen again. It was difficult to conceive of anyone or any group of people being as ruthless as the white man had been in America. But Doris knew that it had happened. And she was determined to never ever forget.

On many cold winter evenings Doris and I would cuddle together in the living room of our modest two-bedroom apartment in Reisterstown, Maryland. We would dim the lights and sit on the carpeted floor. Leaning against our blue sofa, heads laid back, eyes closed, we would listen to the soothing sounds of Miles Davis and glide down a snug tunnel of mental tranquility. In the midst of our euphoric escape, Doris would slip into a blue state of dissatisfaction. I tried to ignore her, hoping that she would leave me in the tunnel, enveloped in peacefulness. But it was impossible. She spoke softly. "You know, they used to rape us at will. That old slavemaster would sneak away from his warm bed, from his woman and enter the slave quarters to have his way with us."

Doris didn't open her eyes. Miles Davis didn't stop blowing. In fact, he seemed to play a little harder. "That slavemaster didn't care that the woman he was degrading was somebody's daughter. Somebody's innocent baby girl. He didn't care that she was someone's wife or mother. He didn't care that the young woman he was raping had feelings and emotions. It must have been difficult for the husbands and fathers of those women to be forced to stand by and watch their wives or daughters being sexually abused by the slavemaster. They had to stand there and watch this brute shove his manhood in and out of the women they loved. And the women—the women cried and prayed to God for mercy. Those poor Black men stood powerless, knowing that any action they took would lead to the certain death of them and their women."

I would turn to Doris and put my arms around her. I could feel the coolness of her body. I could feel her shivering as the chambers of her soul stirred with memories, stirred with the voices of her ancestors as they screamed "Never forget!" Doris put her head on my warm chest and continued. "The children, baby. The young African women who were raped at the age of twelve and thirteen. The brothers of the young women, standing and staring and watching as their beautiful young sisters were destroyed. Standing there in some dusty and dirty dark room, with the flickering light from a kerosene lamp revealing their tears. The pleading whimpers of the young women as the brute of a slavemaster pushed in and out of their womanhood, each time taking a little part of the women permanently away. Mothers, fathers, sisters, brothers—all being destroyed by the same acts, night after night, after night. No, I will never forget. We must never forget."

Doris said that it was important that Black people were cognizant of every gory detail of the whole ordeal of slavery. We had to strip it naked. Examine every single crack and crevice. Every hidden story had to be told. We had to visit the slave cabins that remained. We had to listen to the walls and rocks on the plantations. The more Blacks understood about the cruelty inflicted on their people, the better they would understand the cruelty still being inflicted upon Black people today. The more we understood about the so-called founders and "great men" of this country, the less we would be inclined to worship them. The more we understood that George Washington, Thomas Jefferson, James Madison and the like, participated in and perpetuated this cruel system, the less likely we would hold these slaveowners up as heroes. The more we understood about what had happened, what had been done to us, the more we would prepare to ensure that it *never* happened again.

Doris was not one who wanted slavery remembered simply so that African Americans could one day seek futile revenge. Revenge was not the motive behind her desire for African Americans to study history. She would often remind me of what James Baldwin had stated: "I oppose any attempt that Negroes may make to do to others what has been done to them....I know the spiritual wasteland to which that road leads...whoever debases others is debasing himself."

I could see the torment of those suffering Black women in Doris' face. I could hear their screams for help in her trembling voice. This pain was on the face and in the voice of every Black woman the world over. It had been passed down from generation to generation. It was time for some of that suffering to end. The Black man had to stop standing by, watching his women suffer. Black men could no longer watch Black women being raped both physically and mentally. They could no longer watch their women being stripped of their self-esteem. The Black man could no longer watch as his children were being torn from the arms of their mothers by murder, drugs, alcohol, and appallingly awful schools. The Black man had to stand up beside his woman and fight. He could no longer afford to stand by and watch and cry.

Doris believed that strong Black women could help Black men get back on track. She believed that a Black woman need not accept or reject completely a broken man. She said that a strong woman could rekindle the dying fire in the soul of a Black man. She believed that by helping to rebuild the Black man the Black woman was helping to build a brighter future for her children. The rebuilding of broken Black men was the rebuilding of Black women and Black children. The building and rebuilding of children would lead Black people back to the greatness that was once theirs before the greatest holocaust in the history of the world—the diabolic enslavement of the Black race.

I kissed Doris' tender lips as our bodies moved together in African rhythm. We stared into each other's eyes, feeling the warmth of our love move between us from somewhere deep. From some unseen chamber that anatomists had not yet discovered. We had no reason to turn away from each other, no reason to close our eyes. There was no shame in what we were doing—this joining of souls was divine!

Doris moved her hand over my chest and down my back in a smooth, steady motion as if she were surveying her man, making sure that he was still physically whole. She had already taken care to make sure he was spiritually whole. She had kept her man going when he had wanted to quit. She had kept me from selling out and becoming like the Walter Williamses and Thomas Sowells of the world. She had emphasized to me that I had to go back and help others. She had told me over and over and over again that I had to be a part of the solution. There it was again: *a part of the solution.*

Doris was always there making sure I kept up the fight. She would not allow her man to be broken. A broken man would mean a broken family. Every Black family that was broken made the race weaker and those whose intent was to destroy it stronger. She had no doubt that there was an evil force which had as its sole intent the destruction of the Black race. There was much *prima facie* evidence. Why else would a people who are from the continent richest in minerals be living in such abject poverty? Why would the people of Africa be reduced to being foreigners in their own land? Reduced to depending on handouts from the descendants of those who invaded Africa and took the best areas of the continent for themselves. Why else would every war the United States had fought since World War II be fought against people of color? Why else would the government participate in a heinous experiment at Tuskegee Institute, using four hundred *Black* men to test the effects of *untreated* syphilis?

Doris could point to all kinds of concrete examples that indicated there were those who wanted to rid the earth of Black people. The United States had already committed genocide once. She said the Native Americans should be a glaring example to all nonbelievers of what would and could occur if we did not stay vigilant. "The issue is no longer whether there is a plan or not. The important thing is that Blacks be prepared to repel those forces and their devious plan, by any means necessary." Doris wanted to make sure that her man was physically and mentally prepared to deal with those forces. He was not to look at the obstacles before him and quit. "You must overcome every obstacle, every hurdle and succeed despite it all. And then you must, as Harriet Tubman has taught us, go back and lead others."

I slowly moved my fingers across her forehead and wiped a thin layer of sweat away. I pressed harder against her soft brown body. She continued to pull me to her as she moved her hands up and down my back. We were now one in body. Her very being, her essence was a part of me, and mine, a part of her. We both knew that we would forever be a part of each other. Divorce or separation was not in our vocabulary. We had found each other and had helped to build each other. There could never be a parting. We had to fight all our battles together. Her enemies were my enemies. My secrets were her secrets. We would let no one divide us, as we knew they would try.

Doris had warned me that we had to be careful. "Others will try to destroy what we have. Those who come to part us will not be easily identifiable. Deception is a powerful weapon used by many. But it can, nonetheless, be detected if we seek it out. We can unveil it. We have to unveil it. Our very union depends on our ability to see past the facade. Those who come to destroy us could be dressed in the garments of friendship. In fact, they could be family members who have not yet learned the strength and power of unity or who have been programmed subliminally to break down that which is strong and good."

Doris understood that those who were in support of the annihilation of the Black race recognized that in order for us to fall, the Black man and Black woman had to be divided and put at war with each other. The would-be destroyers promoted and encouraged dissension by rewarding the Black men and Black women who criticized each other in public, for white people's education and amusement. She said we had always been paid best when we were willing to exploit and make fools of each other. She said whenever we became serious and addressed serious issues, we were denied access to the public and dismissed as "troublemakers."

Doris was, and is, a quiet, beautiful Nubian queen. She would always greet everyone with a smile and was ever polite. She told me that knowledge need not make a person arrogant. The gaining of *true* knowledge meant that you knew who you were dealing with and what their intentions were. Knowledge enabled you to read behind the false smiles and feigned laughter. It didn't require that you turn your back or be rude to anyone. You could talk face-to-face with a Klansman and not strike out at him, yet you were prepared to do what you had to do should he or she attempt to harm you. In fact, you were more prepared to act than anyone could ever imagine. But there was no need to brag or boast about it.

Doris convinced me that I needed to control my anger. I was not to rid myself of anger completely, because it was a perfectly normal emotion for a Black person in America or anywhere else in the world, for that matter. But that anger needed to be channeled into something positive. It needed to be packaged and organized so that when it was vented it would have maximum effect. She said there would come a time when it was needed. But it had to be a controlled anger.

Doris also said that Blacks had to learn to utilize the powerful tool of deception. She said that the Ku Klux Klan was not the organization that Blacks had to fear. Although a flagrantly murderous white supremacist group, the Klan was a smoke screen—a deception. The groups that met quietly behind closed doors at secret places were the groups we needed to identify and be wary of. The people who spoke the most about equal rights and fairness were the people who needed to be watched closely. The people who remained silent could be the deadliest of all. She reminded me that Malcolm X's body guard, Gene Roberts, was, in fact, a silent traitor.

Doris believed that the powerful tool of deception had caused the so-called Indians to "lose" America. She said the Indians' generosity and help enabled the Pilgrims to enjoy a so-called "Thanksgiving." The Pilgrims "thanked" the Indians by deceiving and ultimately slaughtering them. The Indians taught the white man how to plant seed for the growing of food so that the white man and his children would not go hungry; they taught the Pilgrims how to hunt and cook. In return, the white man made the Indians landless and powerless by way of deception.

Doris spoke, in our quiet times, of how America had been built by the slave labor of the Black man. The Black man and woman planted the seed and harvested the land. The Black man and woman built and cleaned the master's house. The Black man helped to fight Great Britain during the Revolutionary War. She said that during the Reconstruction period the Black man had to do all the work of rebuilding a country since the white man had not done any labor for a long time. The Black man had to teach the white man how to build houses and how to prepare the fields for crop growing. After all the Black man had done to build and rebuild America, he found himself landless and powerless.

Doris said that although there had been physical violence against the Black man, it was deception and the lack of an ability to see through the deception that had ultimately led to the state of affairs which people of color around the world found themselves in. She stated that a prime example of this type of deception which ultimately leads to destruction is identified in Chinua Achebe's book *Things Fall Apart*.

We separated our still-pulsating bodies and rested our heads on the wood headboard. I ran the back of my hand gently over her face. I kissed her lips once again and pulled her to me. She was almost too good to be true. But I realized that at one point in our history all of our women had been like her. They had been kind and loving and knowledgeable. I knew that just as I lay there and admired her beauty and strength, there had been a time when all African men admired the beauty and strength of their women. I knew there had been a time when African men could not fathom calling their women out of their names, when all Black men respected and defended their women, even if it meant death. I knew that there had been a time when Black men understood that the Black woman was the mother of our creation and that without her we would have no future generations. I thought of the powers that had taken all of this away. The powers that had Black men raping their own women. The powers that had the Black man fighting his woman as if she were his enemy, that had Black men calling Black women all kinds of degrading names and pumping all kinds of destructive chemicals into their bodies. The more I thought about it the angrier I became. "Not now," Doris said. "Not now."

I kissed my Black queen on her forehead, got out of bed, and walked to the bathroom to shower. Doris got up and pulled my

Maryland State Police uniform from the closet. She hung it on the door knob and sat on the bed. She stared at it. She knew that once I put on that uniform, I would become a target for every hater of the law, Black or white. Deep inside she hated the police for all the pain they had caused, and were causing, Black people. She kept trying to convince herself that things had changed. She knew that not all whites hated Blacks and that not all police officers were bad. She was convinced that there were some whites who were for justice and equality. But she had also seen the raw brutality of the police. She had witnessed the name-calling and the harassment.

Black police officers on the force were a positive step. Maybe they would have a better understanding of what was going on in the ghetto. Maybe they would understand that Black men were lashing out at the world for legitimate reasons and were not just behaving recklessly or illogically. Maybe this understanding would lead to a different approach for handling "violators of the law." But Doris also realized that so many Black police officers had forgotten where they had come from and had no sense of justice anymore. They had been transformed into what others wanted them to be and reacted the way others wanted them to react. They had become nothing more than puppets on a string. They would do anything and everything to get promoted. She also understood that the selection and hiring process was set up to identify the malleable Black man.

The type of Black men and women who fit the recruitment guidelines had to be willing to forget whatever they had been told about justice and accept a new, unwritten definition of justice. There was never to be equal justice under the law. Justice was to be blind—blind to equality and fairness. And it would never be color blind.

I finished my shower and walked from the bathroom. Doris watched me with a look of approval. She was proud of her Black man. She was proud of the way my body looked. She had told me to go to the gym and work out, to eat the right foods, and to stay in shape. She said that I must be both physically and mentally prepared to deal with my enemies. She said that it was the ancient Egyptians who had come up with the concept of a sound body and a sound mind. The concept had been stolen by the Greeks. She said a strong body would give me confidence, but it would mean nothing without a strong mind. She told me to listen to lectures on African history by Dr. Yosef ben-Jochannan, Dr. Cheikh Anta Diop, Dr. Ivan Van Sertima, Haki Madhubuti, and others. She told me to play their tapes while I worked out in the gym. She told me to keep a small tape recorder nearby so that I could record my thoughts and any questions that came to my mind as I worked out. The answers to the questions could be researched later.

It was Doris who had told me to build a library of books in our home. Books contained knowledge. Knowledge was a good investment. She and I would go to the public library together and conduct research. She told me that I needed to get high on knowledge and that I shouldn't drink or smoke. It was her urging which led me to the point where I despised alcohol and drugs. I wanted no part of anything that altered my conscious state. I wanted nothing in my system that made me less alert or less prepared to deal with what was going on around me. I didn't need any man-made chemical to make me laugh or smile. Doris was my happiness. Being with her brought a smile to my face. I had the best of all worlds in her. She was loving, knowledgeable, and strong. She had a sincere interest in all I did.

I began to dress. As I put on the shirt to my uniform I could see some of the pride in Doris' eyes fade. It was all too contradictory: her strong African warrior covering up his beautiful brown body with the uniform of those who had done so much harm to his people. She saw some of the power in her man being dissipated. It was like Superman putting on a suit of kryptonite. Yet, in the donning of the uniform, she saw strength. The strength to stand up to all those who had hoped a Black man would never wear such a uniform; all those who wished that a Black man would never be allowed to carry a gun, unless it was to be used against a declared enemy of those in power.

I continued to dress and then walked over to Doris. I knelt down before her and quietly spoke. "Don't worry, baby. Nothing has changed. No way of life is going to change me. Nothing or no one is going to use me against my people. I'm still the man you helped build. I'm still whole." She kissed my lips and said, "You be careful out there, and remember some of the people who hate you the most are wearing the same uniform. Some of the people you arrest are doing what they think they have to do to survive. The people who wear the same uniform and try to hurt you are doing what they have to do to make sure you don't survive."

I stared into her eyes and ran my hand through her hair. I could tell that she was worried that one night I would not return to our apartment. She was afraid that my blood would be needlessly spilled on some road in Frederick County, Maryland. She had once told me that sooner or later we all would die. She said that how we lived our lives was extremely important. She said that if we had to die, it was important that we did it for some cause we believed in. She said that Malcolm X and Dr. Martin Luther King Jr. had not died in vain. Dying on a road in Frederick, Maryland in the uniform of the Maryland State Police would be dying in vain. There was such a thing as death with honor, and it had nothing to do with dying on a battlefield while trying to kill someone else's enemy.

I stood up and walked down the hallway leading to the door. The phone rang. Doris hesitated, answering it as if she knew that it was bad news. She seemed to always know when something bad was about to happen. I slowly turned toward her. I could see her lips moving but could hear nothing. Silence. Painful silence. I detected that something had gone wrong. Doris slowly hung up the phone and turned toward me. She sighed deeply. The words seemed to reach me hours after they had left her lips. I saw the words moving down the hallway, coming toward me like a runaway train that could not be stopped. I braced myself. When they finally reached my ears I felt numb. I wanted to return to the shower; return to our bed; return to our peacefulness. Doris' quiet, soft voice betrayed the harsh message that she was sending me: "Chas ordered Nate's death. Nate is in the hospital fighting for his life."

14

Sleepwalking

There are few things in the world as dangerous as sleepwalkers.

—Ralph Ellison, Invisible Man

A cool rain fell from the moody dark gray sky. Only a few hours earlier it had been sunny and almost unbearably hot. A sudden thunderstorm broke the summer heat's unmerciful strangle hold on the city's besieged inhabitants. I should have peered out our bedroom window. The incoming storm was a sign of impending trouble. I should have been able to discern it before Sugar and Doris' conversation concerning Nate's condition. My back-porch memories should have activated an internal alarm deep within my soul. A storm always means trouble.

Doris and I slowly began our tristful walk to the car to start our journey to Bon Secours Hospital. Unfortunately, it was not an uncommon trip. I had taken the same trip with Mom when someone had tried to kill Quincy by running over him with a car one warm summer night in 1970. I had taken the same trip when Frank had been shot in the chest after a battle with some of Quincy's adversaries. Now it was Nate's turn. I believed that Nate would pull through just as Quincy and Frank had. They were all strong. I wondered what I would do when it became my turn. My turn would surely come. Confronting death was part of the scheme of ghetto life. And despite my position, I knew that sooner or later I would have to confront the inescapable ghetto demon. The only question was, Would I survive the dreaded confrontation?

I wondered what would become of Doris, my daughter Tamara, and my son Tyrone Jr. should something happen to me, should I not be able to defeat the demon. I knew Doris was

163

strong, but the world was merciless. I didn't want her to have to confront this brutal, chaotic world and live her life alone. And she had often told me that without me she would be alone. I didn't want Tamara and Tyrone Jr. to be compelled to grow up without their father's guidance and protection. I could deal with my own death—I wasn't afraid of dying anymore. I just did not want to leave my family unprotected.

I wanted to be in the trenches with them, scouting and awaiting the advance of their enemies, our enemies. I had already made up my mind that I would kill anyone who tried to harm either my wife or my children. I would not wait for the law to punish the perpetrators. It was my duty to defend my family. It was my indubitable obligation to protect that which I had brought into this world. To perform my African orthodox duties as a husband and father, I was willing to suffer whatever the consequences of my actions. I would be less than a man if I asked someone else to protect, and possibly die for, that which I was not willing to protect or die for.

Nate had once told me that if something ever happened to me, he would provide for and protect my family just as if it were his very own. He said that unity of the family was important and that a wife or child of mine should never be left to face the world alone. He would not allow his fallen brother's family to be taken care of by the white man. That would be the ultimate insult. He said if we kept the family strong, we would be okay, no matter what. If we let the family fall, we all were doomed.

I thought of Nate's words as Doris and I drove over the wet streets of Baltimore City.   His voice seemed to merge mellifluously with the swishing sound the tires made as they cut their path through the thin layer of water that rested on the road. I rolled down the window and let some of the heavenly wetness land on my face. It awakened me and reminded me of where I was heading.

Damn. I knew what Nate would say when I reached him. I didn't want to reach him. I mean, I wanted to see him, but I didn't want to hear him. He would test me. He wouldn't mean it, but he would test me nonetheless. He would ask me to be his avenger. He would ask me to hunt down Chas and destroy him.

The feud would never end until either Chas or Nate was dead. Neither would capitulate. It wasn't in their blood. They had adopted and completely ingested the American edict "win at all cost." Death and killing were simply by-products of "success," "making it." That was what they had learned from watching the United States deal with countries around the world—especially

Third World countries. *Win at all cost.* That was the South's attitude in the Civil War as thousands of lives were lost, brother pitted against brother, father against son, in the name of freedom—the freedom to keep other people, Black people, in bondage. The goal need not be noble. *Just win, baby.*

In fact, the battle, now in full swing, between Nate and Chas was an inner-city civil war story with all the tragic contradictions of the American Civil War.   Brothers savagely murdering brothers. Nate and Chas were like brothers, soul mates. Two friends who had grown up together. Practically united since birth. They had eaten together, played together, fought together, and laughed together. Their families were united. They had made a sacred vow to die for each other. Now it didn't matter any more. Their friendship had become a passing memory. Now they were bitterly determined to end each other's existence. To lay each other to rest—permanently.

Chas and I from this day forward would be enemies. It was not my choice; it had to be this way. It was one of the many unwritten laws of ghetto survival. We had once talked about getting out of the ghetto and making it through law school. We had talked about helping our people fight and survive under a system of so-called justice, a judicial system that was stacked against them. Those plans were long gone! They were lost early on in the ruins of this devastating civil war.

Furthermore, Chas was on one side of the law and I was on the other. I was a cop. He was a drug dealer and a killer. He had tried to eliminate my brother from the category of the living. Nate would try to convince me that Chas had to die. It was my brotherly duty to assist in the revenge upon an act of aggression against our family. I was to be my brother's keeper. There was no doubt in Nate's mind that Frank and Quincy would help him seek revenge—it was the natural thing to do. Even Chas expected Frank and Quincy to retaliate. He would keep a watchful eye out for them. He would look out for a sneak attack by Warren. Chas didn't know what to expect of me. I was a ghetto enigma. Chas had prepared himself for the consequences of his actions.   If necessary, he would kill our entire family—that was the rule of engagement. And we all were cognizant of this rule of war.

I pulled off the unforgiving streets of Baltimore and into the parking lot nearest the emergency room entrance at Bon Secours Hospital. The hospital was like a Red Cross haven in a war zone. Helicopters flying overhead. Ambulances delivering wounded casualties. Doctors moving from one tangled mess of brown human flesh to another.

Doris and I got out of the car, joined hands and briskly walked through the heavy rain into the emergency room. Doris held my hand tightly. She could feel that I did not want her to be with me when I initially confronted Nate. She understood. She always understood without my having to say a word. She sat down in the waiting room. I turned to her for a second and then walked past the guard into the restricted patient area. My state police uniform gave me rights of passage. Without it, I would have been stopped and questioned as if I were in South Africa. A Black man was always questioned about why he was where he was, unless he wore something that identified him as acceptable to white men. The uniform was an identification badge. A mark of approval. It signified a kind of submittal.

I stopped at the nurses' station and asked for my brother Nate. The nurse, who resembled the delicate nurse from Frederick County Hospital, hesitated. Something was wrong. Why would this Black man wearing this patriotic uniform be associated with the contumacious "Negro" in patient stall number seven? What did they have in common besides the color of their skin? The nurse spoke in a low whispered voice. "He's going to be fine." She smiled as if she were proud that she had spared me embarrassment by not speaking loudly and notifying others that my brother was the ghetto child who had been nearly beaten to death with a baseball bat. "He needed fifty stitches to close his head wounds but he has suffered no internal injuries. The doctor will see him again in a few minutes. You can go on in now if you would like."

It was just as I had suspected. Nate had defeated the "demon" again. As I walked toward the stall the nurse stopped me. I turned and looked into her eyes. "Officers of the Baltimore City Police Department came to talk to your brother. Y'all are brothers, right?" She asked as if she were hoping I would denounce Nate. I nodded my head. "Your brother wouldn't say a darn thing to them. He wouldn't even tell them who beat him. Maybe you can get something out of him. If you do, let me know and I'll call 'our friends' over at the P.D. They said they sure would like to catch the beast who did this." I created the perfect smile and handed it to her. I was getting better at the game of deception. "Thank you. If he gives me some information, I'll be sure to *run* right over and let you know."

I turned and slowly walked toward the curtained barrier which surrounded Nate and separated him from me. I noticed that the nurse was still standing nearby and staring at my back. I could feel her. She was studying me. Trying to figure me out. Trying to decipher the obvious pretension of the words I had left with her. I let her fade from my mind's eye. I had to. She was inconsequential to the Augean task that literally lay before me in stall number seven.

I pulled the curtain back and penetrated the barrier that separated Nate and me. I stepped in. Once inside, I turned and closed the curtain. I was closing out the rest of the world, if only for a little while. Nate was sitting up in bed. I thoroughly inspected my brother. I noticed that his head and face were badly bruised. His left eye was almost swollen shut. A small bead of pus stood in the corner of his right eye. Strings of black stitches criss-crossed his cleanly shaven head. His white hospital gown was soaked with blood. On the floor, next to the bed, was a basket of bloody clothing.

Nate stared straight ahead. He didn't want to look at me. He didn't want me to see him in this state of agony. I hesitated, then slowly moved closer to him, expecting him to lash out at Chas at any moment. I figured him to be engulfed in thoughts myopically concentrated on revenge. I was surprised by his equanimity. He slowly turned his head toward me. I watched his eyes move up and down as he surveyed my uniform. I awaited his barrage, which I was not so sure would come anymore.

Nate spoke calmly. "He got me, brother. But he should have killed me. He didn't learn his lessons very well." I tried to relay a feeling of tranquility and confidence to Nate that mirrored his perceived state of calmness, by saying something, saying anything. My trembling voice betrayed the lie. "Was it Chas?" Nate glared at me as if I were guilty of some obvious sin. He answered in a low, deliberate tone. "Yeah, it was your boy Chas. But he didn't have the guts to do it himself. He sent punk-ass Tank to do what he didn't have the guts to do. I gave him the opportunity to take me out. I stood there naked with no gun and punk-ass Chas couldn't pick up his gun and do me."

I waited for Nate to pause. I continued with my moronic questions, although inside I knew this was not the proper time. I also knew my questions were irrelevant to what Nate was sure to ask of me. I was stalling. Hoping that Mom or another visitor would come in before Nate reached the point of his request. "Why, Nate? Why did Chas do this to you?"

Nate's face turned solid, as if he had looked upon the face of Medusa. His air of calm seemed to be leaving him. I was provoking him to anger by my questions. Or maybe I was provoking him by standing there in the uniform of the law and he had sworn never to talk to cops. It was a solemn pledge that he and many others like him had taken. The cops didn't worry. They took it as a challenge. It was a challenge to break down that wall of obdurateness and make the big, bad, tough ghetto child talk, cry, and finally plead for help. Cry uncle. If the cop could break through the barrier and get to the ghetto child, he would be the center of esteemed attention in the squad room. Nate was confused. He was trying to discern if he was talking to his brother or just another cop. The cop would get no answers.

Nate took a deep breath and said, "What the fuck does it matter as to why Chas did this to me? Why should you care about that? Chas did this to your brother so you should be out hunting the son of a bitch right now." I responded, "Nate, I'm a cop. I can't just go and hunt him down and kill the man. I can't even arrest him. Baltimore City is out of my jurisdiction. The Baltimore City cops will find him." Nate yelled back, "Fuck the police! Nigger, you done lost your fuckin' mind. They making you out to be another pussy-ass sellout. Don't tell me that you can't hunt down the motherfucker who just tried to kill your brother. You went out of your motherfucking jurisdiction when you left the ghetto. I don't want the white man to seek revenge for me. What the fuck would I look like asking my natural enemy to seek revenge for me. I refuse to put on their uniform and fight their enemies in the name of the American way. I'll be fair about this shit and won't ask them to fight my enemies. Nah, fuck the police."

I had anticipated Nate's wanting revenge. I also knew that he wouldn't seek it through the police. I had anticipated his anger. I had hoped that I could somehow find the right things to say to defuse my brother's fury. But I was saying all the wrong things. Nate was becoming angrier. My presence had not calmed him. In fact, I was throwing another match on what had appeared earlier to be a smoldering fire. His brother standing before him in uniform infuriated him. I listened to him, still trying to mentally formulate some suitable reply. It was difficult for me to refute what he was saying. For years, the police had stood by as Black people were killed by white people. Even as I stood there in uniform, it was difficult for me to conceive of going to the police and asking for assistance. And I was a policeman!

Nate reached up to run his hand over his head. But he stopped. Instead, he balled his long, thick fingers into a tightly clenched fist and pounded the bed. He lowered his voice. "I guess I should be angry with myself more than with Chas. I know the rules of the street. I should have had my shit with me. I left myself wide open. I slipped. I know that a Black man should not be caught without a gun in this country or, for that matter, anyplace in this fuckin' world. The gun is the only thing left that everybody understands. It's the interpreter that allows universal communication. Ever since the white man invaded Africa, the Black man has been required to have a gun. We didn't understand that fact when they first came to Africa bearing gifts. However, we learned and, then, we forgot! And when we forgot, we lost our freedom. When a man loses his freedom he is dead. I forgot my gun. Maybe God was punishing me for forgetting. Maybe he's punishing all Black people."

Nate appeared to be in a deep state of impenetrable thought. It was as if he were reflecting on all he had said to me, reflecting on all that had happened to him on this day or any other day of his tumultuous life. He got like that sometimes. He would say something to Warren, Quincy, and me and then he would ponder what he had said. He would search himself for the episode in his life when he had first received the lesson that he was now dispensing to his captive audience.

I waited for Nate to complete the examination of his memory banks. I waited for him to return from his laconic expedition into the depths of his soul. He didn't seem to know that I was still there, still close to his bedside, aching to reach out to him, aching to help heal both his physical and mental wounds. It was as if I had never pulled the curtain back. As if I were still outside in the waiting area with Doris or driving down the wet road under the daunting, gloomy gray sky. I felt as if I were far away, looking at Nate through the eyes of my soul. This was my opportunity. From my perceived distance Nate didn't look so intimidating. He seemed approachable. My questions no longer seemed inappropriate. "Nate, why would Chas try to hit you?" Nate ignored me. I was ready to fire at him, from my imagined safe distance, with my most powerful long-range ammunition. "What good does it do for every Black man in the world to carry a gun if we're just going to use them on each other? What good does it do for you to have a gun if you are just going to kill off your friends? The invasion and confiscation of Africa should have taught us that we need unity and that we need as many brothers as we can find to fight the invaders. Who's going to be left to keep the descendants of those invaders from eliminating all of us if we keep killing each other off? Who's going to be here to protect your daughters and my daughter and son? I don't know what started this shit with Chas, and you probably won't ever tell me because you don't think it's important. And you're probably right, it isn't important. It certainly isn't important enough for you to kill each other over.

"Just as you said earlier, it doesn't really matter what the basis is of the feud you and Chas are submerged in. What matters is that all this killing shit ends. There's nothing worth this kind of division. Unity brings power, and those invaders that you so often speak of don't understand anything but power. For them, money is just a means to an end. Power is the end. For us, unity is the means to power. Over thirty million unified Black people fighting for our fair share of this country that we helped build means power. Millions of unified, organized Black people the world over means power."

I continued. I couldn't allow Nate to intrude on my thoughts and words now. "Black people, like you and Chas, fighting and killing each other over shit you don't own and don't control isn't power. Selling shit to the race that is intended to kill off the race doesn't equal power. And carrying a gun to protect shit that is really owned and controlled by someone else doesn't mean power. Yeah, I stand here in this uniform a powerless Black man, and you lay there on that bed a powerless Black man whose been assaulted by another powerless Black man. It shouldn't be this way. It doesn't have to be this way. If we come together and start using our God-given senses, then we are not so powerless. If we defeat this divide-and-conquer thing, we are not so powerless."

Nate ran his hand across his forehead. He laid his head against the pillow which had been propped up behind him earlier by the nurse. He spoke slowly. "I hear you, brother, but where do you stand, Brother Powers? I mean, are you going to help us powerless 'niggers' get our shit together? Are you going to help these young brothers coming up get their shit together? Or, are you going to just keep giving speeches?

"You see, these young brothers can't hear speeches from the state police barracks in Frederick, Maryland; they don't really want to hear speeches coming from some milquetoast brother in that uniform. Young brothers don't see a brother in a uniform as a success. They've had too much trouble with motherfuckers wearing uniforms. Why don't you come back and get yourself a classroom and teach brothers some of that heavy shit you are laying on me? Why don't you come down to the cement hallways of hell, called streets, in Baltimore? Why don't you take it to the streets, where the people who need to hear it can hear it?

"It ain't always going to be easy. A lot of these young brothers and sisters aren't going to listen to you, no matter what. *But* a lot more will listen to you in the classroom and on the streets than will listen to you as you parade around in that clown suit and play 'Officer Friendly.' Oh yeah, it's a clown suit, and just like a clown suit it's hiding the real you. It makes people accept you and smile at you but they never really see what's underneath. I know what's in the suit. I know what's under the make-up. So, Brother Powers—not Officer Powers or Trooper Powers—Brother Powers, what are you going to do? What are you going to do about our absence of power? Where do you stand or what do you stand for, or do you stand at all, Brother Powers? I hear you talking and it all sounds real, real good, *but* where do you really stand, Brother Powers?"

The words *Brother Powers* rolled over and over in my head like a huge, rough boulder. They bounced off the sides of my cranium, causing a tremendous headache. I would continue to get these headaches and they would get progressively worse as time passed. I didn't know what Nate was trying to do. He was mixing the unity embedded in the word *brother* with my Irish slave name *Powers*. The two words, the two names equaled the contradiction in my soul.

Nate paused and allowed his words to find a vulnerable spot in my soul to settle into. He turned and stared at the curtain. His anger dissipated, to be recreated at another place, at another time. He spoke in a calm tone. "You just don't understand all this shit, do you? You can't understand that what Chas and I do, and are doing, is normal. It doesn't have to be right, *but* it's how this country is. It's how the world is. Deep inside I know that I shouldn't be trying to kill Chas. He knows that he shouldn't be trying to kill me. But we do it anyway. Just like the government knew it was wrong to order the assassinations of John F. Kennedy, Malcolm X, Dr. Martin Luther King Jr., Fred Hampton, and so many others. Just like they knew it was wrong to try to destroy Paul Robeson."

Nate leaned forward and said, "You see, you and I know the truth. Oh, you don't want to admit it. All of your life you've been the one trying to deny that white folks hate us. Everything in your life is somehow connected to white folks' oppression of us, but you don't want to see it. You want to believe that we all are judged by the 'content of our character.'

"There was a time a long, long time ago that I wanted to believe that too. In fact, I couldn't understand how the color of my skin made so much of a difference. Hell, I got two eyes, two ears, a nose, a mouth, hands, arms, feet and everything else like white folks—why they gotta call me a nigger? But no matter how I tried to figure it all out and make some sense of it, I couldn't. So now I understand that shit don't have to make sense. Some things just are. Chas and I trying to kill each other—well, I guess I could argue that it makes sense but maybe it doesn't. And just like white folks' keeping Black folks down—it doesn't have to make sense. It just happens. So I got to defend myself, just like us Black folks got to defend ourselves from white folk.

"You better wake up, Brother Powers. If you keep running around trying to find the good in everybody, you gonna get hurt real bad. The more you do, in search of fairness, the more you are going to be persecuted. The more you try to love white folk, the more they gonna denounce you. And when you get in trouble, look around and see how many good white folks gonna be standing up for Brother Powers. Watch them treat you like a Jew in Germany. I may not be around to see it. But one day when you trying to do the right thing, they're gonna come for you. And watch who will be standing with you when they surround you." Nate whispered, "Nobody, Brother Powers, nobody but family."

I opened my mouth to speak but Nate interrupted, "Oh yeah, about Chas and me. The powerless killing the powerless, as you put it. We're very normal people for this day and time. Destruction is the norm. Nobody gives a fuck about nothing. Killing or assassinating, depending on who's doing the killing, has become the norm. That's the lesson that these young brothers are getting. These young brothers coming up don't know their history. They just know the present. And the present screams out that it's okay to destroy. I'm caught up in it. I'm addicted. I'm a sleepwalker. But you're not. Not yet."

Nate was sinking deeper and deeper into his inner self. He was descending the ladder that led to the basement of his soul. The place where he had candid discussions with himself. He was reaching for the mason jars of stored knowledge that sat on the basement shelves. Whenever he grabbed one he immediately opened it and dispensed the information to me. There was no order to his poignant tirade. It didn't matter. He did the best he could to make it relevant to our conversation. For he believed that even if his lessons were delivered in a desultory manner, they nonetheless had to be delivered. He didn't know how long he had to live. The demon seemed to be gaining on him. Before he died he wanted to empty the shelves.

Mom pulled the curtain back. I watched her tired eyes as they scanned her wounded son. She was getting older and the strain of seeing her boys in hospital beds was taking its toll on her. I saw her lips move and knew that she was thanking God that Nate was still alive. So much strength in one woman. God must have been with her, holding her up and driving her on. I wanted her strength. Unknown to me at the time, in the coming days and years I would borrow some of her strength to survive under the persecution of the number one law enforcement agency in the world.

Mom stared at Nate. A tear moved slowly down the side of her face. She walked over to Nate and hugged him. In the midst of her hug, Quincy and Frank walked in. They looked toward me and nodded. I stood up to leave. The curtained barrier was now open. But there was still a thin wall between Nate, me, and the rest of the world. Mom moved aside. Nate looked toward me. "Don't become a sleepwalker, Brother Powers. See you tomorrow eye to eye or at the place Black folks go when they die. Peace, brother. Peace."

15

Granddaddy Shaw

Those having torches will pass them on to others.
–Plato, The Republic

What happens to a dream deferred?   Does it dry
up like a raisin in the sun?
–Langston Hughes, "A Dream Deferred"

Elijah Shaw was his name, but all we ever called him was Granddaddy Shaw. As Warren and I pulled up in front of his red-brick three-story house on W. Lexington Street in Baltimore, we found him seated in his usual chair. He gave us a warm, wide smile as I pulled the car to the curb and parked. It was obvious that he was very happy to see us. His round brown face and receding gray hair conjured up pleasant memories each time we saw him. His eyes told stories that his mouth never spoke of, and Warren and I had been reading from them for a long time. Warren and I stepped from the car and immediately put our hands up to shade our eyes from the sizzling August sun.

As we moved closer to him, Granddaddy broke into mild laughter. "Warren, you're getting bigger every time I see you. When are you going to stop growing?" Warren smiled and winked his eye. "I have to keep growing, Granddaddy." Granddaddy responded, "That's right, boy, keep growing and keep learning. I can tell you've been paying attention to me a little bit."

Granddaddy was a tall, round man with a strong, gleaming smile. His frown was as menacing as his smile was pleasant, but he seldom displayed it to us. His hair was graying at a rapid pace and in some areas it had disappeared completely. He was sixty-seven years old now. He had been born and reared in North Carolina and migrated north during the late forties, early fifties with other Blacks in search of work. He and Grandma had separated and he had remarried and had three other children, besides Mom, once arriving in Baltimore. He worked at several odd jobs and finally saved enough money to purchase a building and open a restaurant. Granddaddy had developed his cooking skills while watching his mother prepare meals in North Carolina. The name of his very popular restaurant was simply Shaw's.

Shaw's was initially a seafood restaurant and was located at 202 N. Mount Street in Baltimore City. As business grew, Granddaddy moved Shaw's to 205 N. Gilmore Street, and finally, to Route 198 in Largo, Maryland. Granddaddy changed the name of his restaurant to Shaw's Seafood and finally to Shaw's Barbecue. Granddaddy made the best pork barbecue in town! The restaurant stayed packed with Black people from all over. But then came integration.

Blacks began to beg to sit and eat next to white people. Once Blacks won the integration war, they were so proud of their right to buy at white folk's stores that they spent every cent they had in white restaurants, simply because white people were there. Once the right was gained to eat with white folks, Blacks abandoned Black restaurants and businesses. They wanted to be seen eating at white establishments with white people. It was the popular thing to do. It didn't matter whether the food was good or bad. White folks were there. Thus the downfall of Black economics.

Black entrepreneurs, like Granddaddy, watched as their customers dwindled. At the same time, business in the white restaurants that were willing to abide by the law and serve Blacks (even if only at the back of the restaurant or through the back door) increased. Money fought its way upstream from Blacks to whites in the same odd fashion salmon fight against the natural flow of water. That practice did not work in reverse. Whites did not frequent Black stores or restaurants. Black businesses began to close. The number of Black entrepreneurs steadily declined. Integration was quickly turning Blacks from producers or owners into consumers. And the law of economics prevailed. To paraphrase the great poet and musician Gil Scott-Heron, when producers name the tune, consumers have to dance. And dance Black people did.

White-owned stores in Black communities charged higher prices than the stores in white communities. Once there were few restaurants or stores owned by Blacks, Blacks had no choice but to pay the higher prices. Integration had actually increased profits for white entrepreneurs and decreased profits and ownership for Black entrepreneurs. Blacks were put back in the position of going to whites and begging for jobs and credit. Back to the plantation. Or, rather, the plantation was now the inner-city Black neighborhoods. Shaw's became one of the many victims of integration.

Granddaddy sold his business and put away what money he had made for him and Grandma to live off. At the age of sixty Granddaddy was diagnosed as having cancer in his leg. The cancer began to spread and Granddaddy's health deteriorated quickly. His condition slowed him down physically but not mentally or emotionally. Whenever we visited him his spirits seemed to be high. He hardly ever talked about his illness. He didn't want us to feel sorry for him. His wife, Cora Shaw, took good care of him and made sure that he had whatever he needed. We admired her strength.

Warren and I sat down on the white marble steps that made Baltimore famous—that is, the steps and the row houses. Granddaddy sat in a chair next to the steps. His dark maple cane leaned against the black railing along the steps. Granddaddy reached over and grabbed my knee. I felt his power. "How have you been doing, young man?" I responded, "I'm doing fine, Granddaddy, just fine." He smiled. "Good. I'm glad everything is going well. I'm proud of you, boy. I'm sorry I couldn't make it to that police graduation you had a while back, but you know Granddad don't feel so good sometimes. I know your mom and dad were real proud. You hang in there, you hear?" I nodded my head and said, "Yes, sir. I've got to hang in there."

Granddad turned toward Warren. "How are things going down there at school?" Warren responded, "Things are going fine, Granddaddy. My studies are going well and I'm terrorizing them on the football field." Granddaddy laughed. "I imagine you are. As big as you are, I imagine you're raising all kinds of ruckus. I get a chance to watch you on television every now and then. I've seen you knocking those boys down. I just sit and talk to myself. I just say, there's my grandson."

Granddad ran his hand over his head and turned to look up the street. "Your mother called me and told me about Nate. Damn boy just won't listen. He comes down here all the time and sits right there where you two are sitting now. I talk to him and try to point him in the right direction, but it's like he doesn't even hear me. He's sort of like me and my brothers when we were young. That boy has got a lot of Shaw blood in him. I love that boy—I just wish I could get to him before it's too late. I got two dead brothers who just wouldn't listen. I know you boys have tried to talk to him. I know it isn't your fault. Just don't give up on him. Keep talking to him even if he don't seem to be listening. Something has to sink in sooner or later. Don't ever give up on him." Warren and I nodded in agreement.

Granddaddy smiled. "Speaking of Nate, you know that boy came down here the other day and asked if he could have my old diamond ring. He told me that I didn't need it 'cause I wasn't going to live that much longer anyway. Then he laughed. That boy is really something." Granddaddy, Warren, and I laughed.

I stared across the street at the row houses as I listened to Granddaddy. A small group of little girls jumped rope. A group of little boys played tag. Up the street from them stood three teenage boys smoking marijuana and holding a forty-ounce bottle of beer in a brown paper bag. Ten o'clock in the morning and they were already getting high. Already wasting another day. A few years earlier, they had been one of the group of boys playing tag. Now they had moved on to other things. I wondered whether the group of young boys playing tag would soon take the short journey up the street; would they soon be wasted?

Granddaddy watched me as I watched the young boys. He turned and yelled at the young boys, "Hey Sammy, get away from those kids with that stuff." One of the boys turned toward Granddaddy. "Okay, Mr. Shaw, we're moving right now." Everyone in the neighborhood knew Granddaddy. They even protected him from would-be robbers. He would constantly try to talk to them. He would try to get them to change their ways. He would listen to what they had to say, listen to their reasons for doing what they were doing—and then he would try to direct them toward the Nation of Islam.

I don't think Granddaddy believed in everything that the Honorable Elijah Muhammad and the Nation of Islam were teaching. Granddaddy was now a Christian Baptist minister and sometimes preached in Christian churches around Baltimore. He was well respected. He studied the Bible. However, he had often told me that the Nation of Islam had done more for young Black

men in the last thirty years than Christianity in America had done
in four hundred years. Granddaddy said that the Honorable Elijah
Muhammad had taken brothers who were down and out, and
cleaned them up. He said that the Nation had gotten them off
drugs and into books. He often spoke of what the Nation had done
for Malcolm X. He would tell me that no matter what happened
between Malcolm X and the Nation, it was important to remember
that what Malcolm became was in large part due to the influence
of the Honorable Elijah Muhammad. He said that I must never
forget that, just as I must not forget that Elijah Muhammad's
philosophy concerning Black self-reliance was a result of the
philosophies of the Honorable Marcus Garvey, Booker T.
Washington, and others. Malcolm did not reinvent the wheel. He
just pulled these philosophies together into one powerful force and
rolled with it. Malcolm delivered these philosophies with amazing
effect. Granddad said that the Minister Louis Farrakhan was now
doing the same thing and having the same forceful effect. And,
unfortunately, Farrakhan had also inherited some of Malcolm's
enemies.

Granddaddy wanted to get all of those young boys and girls
into something positive. He had directed Jonathan to the Nation
of Islam. Jonathan was another one of Granddaddy's
grandchildren. He had lived with Granddaddy since he was very
young. Granddaddy believed that the Nation was the best choice
in order to keep Jonathan on the right track. He was right. The
Nation had taught Jonathan so much at such a young age. He
began reading and studying Black history. He began to get better
grades in school. He wanted nothing to do with drugs or alcohol
and he adamantly opposed the abuse of the Black woman. He also
began to prepare himself to do many things well so that eventually
he could be self-reliant.

Granddaddy believed that Black people had to shun those
things that did them no good. The future of our race was at stake.
If Christianity failed, then he would try the Nation; if for some
reason Islam failed, then he would try something else. The
method mattered not. Results, at this point, were all that was
important. The Nation had been the best vehicle thus far. Some
of the Black Christian churches in America didn't even allow
brothers in unless they were dressed in a certain fashion. The
white Christian churches, for the most part, didn't allow Blacks in
period! In the Catholic Church Blacks were disregarded
altogether. The leader of the Catholic Church was the pope. He
was considered the closest man to God. The pope had never been
any color but white, at least as far back as most Blacks and whites

remembered. This suggested that Blacks could never be that close to God under the Catholic system. A visit to the Vatican in search of a Black face would be a revealing experience for Black Catholics. Further, the Catholic Church had sanctioned slavery.

The Nation of Islam went into prisons and earnestly made an attempt to rebuild broken brothers. The Nation went out into the streets of the inner city, looking and searching for brothers to clean up. The Nation didn't preach a wait-until-you-get-to-heaven philosophy. As Malcolm X said, the Nation wanted freedom now for Black people throughout the world and instructed Black people to get that freedom, "by any means necessary."

Granddaddy turned to Warren. "I guess you are hungry." Warren smiled. "Naw, Granddaddy, I'm not hungry. I really don't eat that much." Granddaddy laughed. "I try to convince people of that, too. You keep forgetting that I was a young man at one point in my life. Granddaddy ain't always been old and I was a pretty big youngster, too." Warren was laughing now. "I'm not lying, Granddaddy." I interrupted, "He's lying, Granddaddy; that's why he can't say it with a straight face." Warren playfully punched my arm.

Grandma Cora came to the door. She didn't know what we were laughing about but she was just happy to see us happy. She was happy that two generations were sitting there on those steps enjoying each other. We weren't fighting about who was right or who was wrong. We weren't arguing about what was right with the old generation and wrong with the young generation or vice versa. We weren't drinking alcohol. We were talking and listening and laughing and trying to understand each other, trying to understand what was going on around us and trying to make a difference.

Grandma looked down at us, "Now, don't you boys run off nowhere. I've got some fish on the stove." Warren looked up and said, "Grandma, we don't need anything. We just wanted to stop by and talk to Granddaddy a little while. You know we need his knowledge and insight to survive in this dungeon that we've been thrown into." Grandma was not having it. "Listen, Warren, don't you start no trouble. You all are going to eat this fish I'm frying." Granddaddy laughed heartily. "Don't argue with them, Cora. Warren know he ain't going nowhere as long as there's food around." Grandma walked back inside to the kitchen.

Granddaddy noticed a group of brown girls round the corner. One of them said hello to him in a soft, innocent voice. He spoke back. He watched them as they walked away. Tears formed in his eyes. "Damn shame—fourteen years old when she became strung out on that stuff. Walking up and down these streets from ten in the morning till late at night, prostituting. Sleeping with any man who will give her money to buy dope. I've seen all kinds of men pick her up—old men, young men, Black men and white men; it don't matter, as long as they got money. I've tried to talk to her. She sits and listens and sometimes cries. But, the next day, she's right back at it again.

"I hear those men calling her all kinds of names. Talking about what they've done to her. They are killing that girl. She ain't but seventeen and they ruining her and her future. Ruining our future. You see, in that little baby girl is a little part of us. And if we can't care about her, if we can't feel for her, then that means that we're all dead and just waiting for someone to throw some dirt on us. I ain't ready for that yet. And I hope you boys ain't neither."

Warren reached over and put one of his arms around Granddaddy. "No, Granddaddy, we ain't ready for that dirt. We have been listening to you and learning from you too long to be ready for that dirt. We don't like to see our little sisters suffering like that and we are going to try to do something to save every one of them we can." Warren looked toward me. "Ain't that right, brother?" I nodded my head in agreement. I was glad he didn't say "Brother Powers." I watched a tiny tear trickle down from Granddaddy's eye.

Granddaddy broke the temporary silence. "Well, boys, I think that fish is calling us." The smell of the fried fish surrounded us. Warren smiled. "Well, Granddaddy, I think since Grandma went through all of that trouble of preparing that fish, the least we can do is eat a piece or two, or three." Granddaddy laughed. Warren helped Granddaddy up from his chair and handed him his cane. Granddaddy started up the steps. I held the door for him and Warren. They entered the house. I turned and looked down the street.

The young Black girl who had passed us stood on the corner, waving at passing cars. A car with an older white man in it pulled to the curb. The man rolled the window down and said something to the seventeen-year-old "woman-child." She smiled and nodded her head. She opened the door to the car and began to get in. She turned and saw me on the steps, staring at her with the eyes of my soul. Tears trickled down my face. Tears trickled down her tortured soul.

16

Lessons

They saw themselves as others had seen them. They had been formed by the images made of them by those who had the deepest necessity to despise them.
    —*James Baldwin,* Notes of a Native Son

Negroes have been terrorized to the extent that they are afraid even to discuss political matters publicly.
    —*Carter G. Woodson,* Mis-Education of the Negro

Nate smiled as he looked at me from his seat in the last row at the rear of the auditorium. Each row of seats was slightly elevated above the row immediately in front of it so that the people in the rear could have a clear view of the activities occurring up front. Nate sat alone. My heart began to beat rapidly when I saw the outline of his round face and bald head in the darkness. I filled in his features one at a time until I was able to discern that he was smiling. I was happy, yet apprehensive. I very much wanted him to approve of me. I needed his blessings. With a nod of my head I acknowledged his uncommon smile and continued to speak to the reticent students.

The students listened attentively and intently to my words. I had to keep them captivated. I had to take full advantage of the vital, yet rare, opportunity I had been given. I felt like a surgeon in the midst of a major operation in which life and death hung in the balance. My words had to be used like precision surgical instruments. They had to be true to form. They had to extricate the cancer of destruction that had been implanted deep within the souls of inner-city youth, especially Black youth.

No doubt about it, my audience was at risk of death—extinction—and thus all Blacks were at risk. Very few realized the magnitude of the problem. It was incumbent upon those who were aware, and who cared, to devote their lives to the preservation of those in jeopardy. No excuses would suffice. Nothing was more important than saving the lives of young people. As a result of my ingression into the realm of knowledge, I initiated a program entitled Operation Drug-Out. The intent of the program was to go into inner-city schools and speak with the students in regard to the plague of drugs and murders killing off Black youth—Black people, at astronomical rates. I, along with others, was convinced that the government had little interest in stopping the killings or the flow of drugs into the inner city. I would come to believe this more adamantly once I was assigned to the drug squad in the Cincinnati division of the FBI.

Prior to starting Operation Drug-Out, I had joined an organization called The Young Democrats of Baltimore City. It didn't matter what the organization called itself, I was just interested in finding a group of people who were concerned about the appalling condition of Black people within American society. A group who was interested in saving the youth. The Young Democrats provided the means to that end.

Talmadge Branch was the president of the organization. He was a dark-complexioned, handsome, stately brother with a great deal of political know-how. I learned a lot about politics from him. He had been taught by his employer and mentor, United States Congressman Parren J. Mitchell. Talmadge was Congressman Mitchell's congressional assistant. Donna Harris was Talmadge's secretary. She was also the Director of the Ways and Means committee of the Young Democrats.

Donna Harris was an intelligent, beautiful, light-complexioned Black woman with a great deal of energy and dedication. Talmadge had made a wise choice in making her his personal aide and secretary. She was an enormous asset to the Young Democrats and a loyal confidante to Talmadge in a time when Blacks had to be increasingly aware that there were Judases all around. Donna truly believed that the Young Democrats could have a positive effect on the abject condition of inner-city Black youth, and she also felt that it would be an excellent vehicle for creating and training new, strong Black leaders who wouldn't sell out for a slice of the American pie. Donna believed that the Black community throughout the world was overflowing with traitorous "leaders." She would assist the Young Democrats in finding devoted and steadfast Black men who couldn't be bought. Not an easy task.

I had joined the organization because it was full of young, positive, energetic Black people. I believed that it was important to become a part of a serious unified group; there would be power in numbers. I hated all the infighting and backstabbing that I witnessed once I joined. I understood that infighting was historically a part of politics; however, Black people could not afford to follow the historical policies of white "leaders." Despite my consternation, I decided to continue with the organization and try to create some positive programs for the youth of Baltimore.

I was still employed with the Maryland State Police and was quickly finding out that I would be able to do very little to help Black people from within that organization. The most I could possibly do was to keep some brothers from being beaten down by redneck officers—not an easy task. Despite Nate's pleading, I was not ready to leave the state police. My mind constantly traced the words in Ralph Ellison's book *Invisible Man*, "keep the nigger running." I was no nigger and they certainly didn't possess the power to make me run.

As my level of consciousness grew, so did my depression. However, instead of sitting down and doing nothing, I sought out ways to get involved in positive programs. United States Congressman Parren J. Mitchell had initiated a program in Baltimore City to stop the Black-on-Black killings. I enjoyed sitting in his office and in his living room and listening to him speak. I absorbed his lessons as the earth soaks up the rain. He said the killings were playing into the hands of those who wished us all dead. He was depressed about the way the youth seemed to have adopted a self-destructive attitude. He told me that the Black youth didn't create the attitude or philosophy of "kill thyself"— they merely adopted it. He was convinced that he knew who the creator of this genocidal philosophy was. He told us that this state of coercive genocide being perpetrated against Blacks in America violated international law.

Congressman Mitchell's depression, like mine, didn't cause him to just submerge himself in apathy. It energized him to act and to get others to act. "We have got to attack the problem now or it will get worse. We have got to attack the problem now or we will fear leaving our homes because of the threat of brutal violence from our own kind. We have got to attack the problem before the National Guard is called in and we are made squatters in our own South African-style shantytowns." Congressman Mitchell brimmed with the same type of controlled anger that Doris had spoken of. He urged us to get involved. Dwayne, a member of the Young Democrats, and I took him up on the offer by creating Operation Drug-Out.

Talmadge and Donna were excited when we told them about the program. They promised their full backing and the backing of the Young Democrats. Congressman Mitchell was also extremely delighted. No one was more pleased than Nate. I told Nate that I was going into the schools to reach out to the Black youth. I told him that I was not going in as a police officer and I was not going to play "Officer Friendly." I was going in as a Black man talking to other young Black men and women about a serious subject.

I had not expected Nate to show up on this day, although I had informed him that I would be speaking at Southwestern High School in Baltimore, Maryland. I chose this school because it was the school from which I had graduated in 1979. I knew what lessons were being taught within its walls. I knew what the students were missing. I was twenty-two years old now and returning to a place that I believed needed me. Nothing could keep me from making this speech, talking to these students. Not even the unusually cold November air that greeted me as I left home that morning. Unknown to me, nothing was going to stop Nate from hearing me speak.

I had told Nate that I had paid attention to all of his lessons and that I was prepared to impart that knowledge to the youth. I explained to him that I still couldn't understand how he had so much knowledge at his disposal, yet he seemed to act against that very knowledge. He just stared into my eyes and said, "I'm already gone, brother. I'm like the drug addict that knows better but doesn't do any better. The addict can tell you never to use drugs, but he can't stop himself. They came for me, brother, and they got me. I just don't want them to get you."

The auditorium walls closed in on me and seemed to bring all the students face-to-face with me. I studied their individual African features and spoke. "It is not your nature to kill each other off. You are trapped in a game and you don't understand the rules. You have got to read the rules or you are doomed. You have got to stop being broken down and broken up. You have got to escape the trap by means of the underground railroad of knowledge. You must remember the mighty words of Marcus Mosiah Garvey: 'Up my mighty people, you can accomplish what you will.'"

I told them of their greatness and of all that they could accomplish if they stepped from under the brainwashing machine. I explained to them that many of their public school teachers didn't care whether they passed or failed because some of the teachers were also brainwashed. I told them to do research on their own, to study the self-help philosophies of Marcus Garvey, Booker T. Washington, W.E.B. DuBois, Malcolm X, Louis Farrakhan, and others. I explained to them that they should not fear listening to and studying the philosophies of those whom the media told them were not worth studying. I explained to them that studying the wrong so-called leaders was one of the many reasons Blacks found themselves in their present condition. I reminded them that no Black man had ever directed white men with regard to whom they should study and believe in. They didn't ask us to help them choose the pope, so why should we seek to gain their approval of who we studied, listened to, and learned from.

The students' eyes were fixed upon me. They followed my every movement. I was telling them things that they had not, and would not, hear in the classroom. I knew the lessons I was delivering were necessary for their self-esteem. If I could build up their self-esteem, they would know that they were capable of accomplishing anything. They would begin to believe that no math problem was too difficult; no science problem, unsolvable. They would understand that their lives were worth living. They would learn that education, not indoctrination, was worth having.

I knew that they had only been taught about slave owners like George Washington and Thomas Jefferson. I knew that they would never be given a true understanding of Frederick Douglass, W.E.B. DuBois, Harriet Tubman, Malcolm X, the Hon. Elijah Muhammad, Marcus Garvey, Martin Luther King Jr., Dr. Carter G. Woodson, and other great Black men and women. I was convinced that an understanding of the philosophies of great African Americans would create unity and a thirst for more knowledge, in some of them.

The thirst for knowledge would lead to Black youth studying the great civilizations of the many African nations. This would lead to the knowledge that Black people did for themselves before the invasion of Africa by Europeans. The students would begin to understand that there were many great civilizations that did not necessitate billions of dollars being spent on weapons of mass destruction. They would understand that violence was necessary for self-defense but it was stupid to kill off one's own army. I was trying to spark in the students an interest that I hoped would cause them to examine the situation they were in and move them to turn things around.

I felt good about the speech I was giving. This was my own speech, in my own words. The first speech I had given for

Operation Drug-Out had been a pretense. *CBS Evening News* had come to cover it and everyone wanted a plug on the national news. I had advised the students about notifying the police should they see a classmate with a gun. I had paraded before them with red, white, and blue cards with the number *911* on them. I knew that the students would have a negative reaction to anything involving the police because they saw the police as protectors of property for white folks. They saw the police as part of the problem and they would never respond to a speech that called upon them to assist the police. I was making Operation Drug-Out into another program that would be controlled by those outside the program whose motivations were not sincere, and that just wouldn't work.

Dwayne and I had a conference after the first speech. He told me that I had not reached the students, but had satisfied the media. He said that I was trying to make the students have faith in the police instead of having faith in themselves. I wasn't being real and the young brothers and sisters were adept at detecting hypocrites. The students were living in crime-ridden neighborhoods. They were living in broken homes with broken parents. They were stepping over dead drug addicts in trash-filled alleyways. They were sharing living quarters with rats and roaches. Now I was trying to convince them that the police were on their side. How in the hell could any American governmental body be on their side and still allow them to live in these atrocious conditions? It was like trying to convince Jews in Germany that the Nazi concentration camp guards were there for their protection. The bitter feelings held by the youth toward the police were stronger than many realized.

I agreed with Dwayne. I told him I felt like a preacher who had just told his congregation to leave everything to God, to suffer peacefully, to wait on God and the opening of the heavens. I told him that I felt I had done more harm than good. I promised him that I would never give that speech again, no matter who came to hear it and no matter what national news station came to cover it. I had to take a stand on the dangerous side of telling the awful truth, no matter who was present and what the consequences. Other members of the Young Democrats were happy with the first speech. They believed that it would bring the Young Democrats political notoriety and that the mayor and others would now come to assist us. They suggested that I give more credit to Mayor Kurt Schmoke for efforts in fighting Black-on-Black violence. Dwayne and I listened to their suggestions. We knew what was happening. We were losing control of the program. The goal that we had set was being lost for a measure of political recognition and expediency for the Young Democrats.

Talmadge said nothing initially. He understood what we were trying to do, but he was also cognizant of the need for political clout in order to get things done. "We've got to network. We've got to face the reality that no matter how noble our goals, there are people who will stop us in our tracks unless we include them. We can't be naive, yet we can't sell out. You brothers go ahead and tell the truth. I'll try to take some of the heat for you. But depending on how much truth you reveal, there might be a point when changes have to be made in your delivery."

I explained to Talmadge how important our goal was. I told him that Dwayne and I would not sell our souls. If changes needed to be made that compelled us to capitulate to forces, statements, and circumstances we didn't agree with, we would resign. In the end, we had to live with ourselves. I had to live with Frank, Quincy, Sugar, Nate, Warren, Doris, Mom, and Granddaddy Shaw.

I looked to my right and noticed that Talmadge, Dwayne, and Donna had their eyes firmly fixed upon me. Talmadge was nodding his head in agreement. Dwayne and Donna smiled slightly. Nate looked down on me as if he were looking down from heaven. He was proud of his brother. He felt that part of him was in me and that all the knowledge he had gained and shoved into me had not been lost; his studies were paying dividends at last. He looked over the group of students to see that they were listening. He glared back at me and nodded.

I finished the speech and took a deep breath. The students remained silent. They watched me as I walked toward my seat and sat down. I hoped that I had been successful. I wanted to tell my surgical assistants to close the wound and allow the patient to heal. We had done a fine job. But my success couldn't be that easily measured. It would take years and more sincere surgeons doing more delicate surgeries with well-honed, well-prepared instruments before any victories could be claimed. Dwayne put an assuring hand on my shoulder. I had done well. Donna guided me to my seat with her soul. I felt her satisfaction. Talmadge shook my hand, moved toward the front of the students, and began to close out the session. I watched as a few of the students kept their eyes on me. They were searching my being for any signs of hypocrisy or deception. There were none. I turned around to look up at my brother. His was the blessing I sought the most. His seat was empty.

17

Up From Slavery

Education is our passport to the future, for tomorrow belongs to the people who prepare for it today.

—*Malcolm X*, Malcolm X Speaks

At the bottom of education, at the bottom of politics, even at the bottom of religion, there must be for our race economic independence.

—*Booker T. Washington*, Up From Slavery

Things were moving along fine for me now. I was active in the Baltimore community, trying to do my part to create something positive for the inner-city youth and for my people in general. Trying to be a part of the solution. I kept my position with the Maryland State Police, though it was taking time away from my more important urban community endeavors, so that I could feed my family. The state police was teaching me things that I could and would use for the remainder of my life. I opened up my intellectual pores and absorbed every single lesson, negative or positive. I stored everything in a special place within me, for retrieval at the appropriate time.

I had become a bibliophile and was reading everything I could get my hands on. The more I read, the more I came to understand the magnitude of the problem which confronted the world's people of color. It was definitely an international problem and it had to be analyzed in that context. At the same time, it was necessary for every Black person to actively do his part, wherever he happened to be. Taking what we had learned and applying it to our situation was a major deficiency of the Black community and so-called Black leadership. We, or at least our "leaders," always analyzed, discussed, and understood the reasons for our deplorable condition, but we did not apply what we knew. We were good at rhetoric, but when it came to actually getting out and making changes, we failed miserably. If we were to accomplish the upliftment of the Black race, and thus the human race, this would have to change. We all had to become active. It was time for more physical action and less verbal reaction.

Everyone had to do something because those who were in a position of power seemed to care nothing about those who were powerless, especially if the powerless were people of color—and that was almost always the case. In the United States, it was obvious that no one was truly concerned about the so-called ghetto dwellers. My reading and analyses also gave me a better understanding of what had brought Nate and Quincy to their present states of mind.

I was beginning to better understand the violence, the drugs, and the hatred in which the ghetto was mired. There were so many people stuck in the same situation, with so little progress being made. It was becoming clear to me that very few people truly intended to rectify the problem; very few people intended to do anything. The educational institutions were doing nothing to educate the youth, and I was certain now that education was the key to advancement. The schools needed to emphasize the importance of history. If the students studied history, they would come to know the importance of science and mathematics. They would also come to understand that there was a need to know how to use their hands as well as their heads. Booker T. Washington was right when he stated, "No race can prosper till it learns that there is as much dignity in tilling a field as in writing a poem."

A more thorough and truthful look at history would reveal to the students that the ancient Egyptians wrote books and built, with their own hands, libraries. The students would come to understand that in order to be self-reliant, they would have to learn to build their own houses and repair their own cars. This was the type of education that was neglected, or intentionally omitted, in inner-city schools.

I was more determined than ever to make myself a significant part of the changes that had to take place in order to keep generation after generation of Black people from becoming doomed. The horrible scenes of the ghetto began to gnaw at the nerves of my soul more than ever before. I knew that in order to help, I had to continue to learn, continue to seek understanding. I had to become even more aware of how the system functioned. If I understood how it functioned, I would be better able to utilize it for my purposes. And my purposes were in unison with those of my people.

There were others like me who were already in the system and had an intimate understanding of it. But they did nothing to help their brothers and sisters on the outside. They just looked down on them through the mirrored windows of downtown skyscrapers. These brothers and sisters were concerned only for themselves. In fact, they would criticize, rather than educate, other members of their race who had not learned to use the system. They had a fear that if they helped their own kind, they would lose their privileged positions. They didn't understand that their positions would never be secure until their entire race was secure. They didn't understand that if they retained their positions through their ability to distance themselves from others who looked like them, then it was not a position worth having!

My position with the Maryland State Police allowed me to "move up" to what someone interested in the division of the masses had labeled the "middle class." The division was false but it had been as much a psychological success as the division of the races. It had caused one group of Blacks to distance themselves from another group of Blacks at a time when only unity could overcome the problems facing the entire race. It was an old trick, which continued to have the desired results.

My venture into the so-called middle class enabled me to understand how deep this division is. Even the middle class had been divided into smaller sub-divisions. Part of the Black middle class believed that they were success stories, brainwashed to feel they had achieved on their own. This I-did-it-all-by-myself philosophy allowed them to deny their intricate connection with the rest of the Black community. They felt that they were only indebted to themselves and, of course, to the white folks for whom they worked. This facade of non-indebtedness allowed these African Americans to care nothing about those left behind in poverty. They couldn't understand or didn't want to think about the fact that the majority of people who were left behind looked just like them and had the same aspirations and dreams as they. They didn't understand that a great deal of those left behind were there because of the color of their skin. Or maybe they did understand this. Maybe they were determined to do nothing or say nothing that would cause those in control to toss them back with the rest of their lot. Maybe they realized how fragile a floor they stood on, and they refused to take any actions which could cause it to collapse.

These sometimes blind-by-choice middle-class African Americans refused to see themselves as Africans. Although the people they worked with would readily admit that they were Irish Americans or Italian Americans, these Blacks had been taken in by the media and Hollywood image of Africa as a place of savages—and they did not want to be associated with such a land. They wanted to deny outwardly that their ancestors came from Africa; yet, despite the brainwashing, deep down inside their souls they knew the truth. They turned their heads from the starving brothers and sisters who looked just like them. They turned their heads away from the drugs and senseless violence of the inner-city neighborhoods, from which they had temporarily escaped. They turned their heads away from the intentionally ill-equipped schools that Blacks were forced to attend. They refused to be true to themselves. The truth of the matter was that they were only a few pay checks removed from the ghetto. Although they turned their heads away, the anguished cries of their ancestors tormented their souls.

These middle-class Blacks plugged their ears when anyone spoke of Marcus Garvey or W.E.B. DuBois. They shielded their children's ears from the lessons of Malcolm X and Louis Farrakhan and even Dr. Martin Luther King Jr. They put pictures of a white Jesus on their walls and purchased dolls bearing white faces for their children. I once challenged one of these Black middle-class "Americans" to visit the residences of some of his white peers and note the pictures on their walls to see if any remotely resembled him. I requested that he note the dolls that his white peers' young offspring played with to see if any of these dolls remotely resembled him.

These middle-class Blacks bought only books by whites and about whites, which they wanted their children to read and to identify with. They refused to read one of the greatest books of all time, *Up From Slavery* by Booker T. Washington. They refused to read books by Dr. Yosef ben-Jochannan, Dr. Cheikh Anta Diop, Dr. John Henrik Clarke, Dr. Ivan Van Sertima, the Reverend Albert B. Cleage Jr., Langston Hughes, Toni Morrison, Maya Angelou, and other great African authors. They did the best they could to emulate the white folks around them. They tried to walk like them and talk like them. They tried to dress like them and live near them. They sought out the schools that white folks' children attended, and made sure their children attended the same schools. They tried to deny their Blackness in every way and at every turn. They wanted the world to know they had "arrived." All the while their white peers laughed at such a display of buffoonery.

There were other middle-class Blacks who knew that the success they had achieved would never be complete until all Blacks were free from poverty and racism. They understood that their partial success was the result of not only their hard work and sweat, but the hard work and sweat of people like Frederick Douglass, Paul Robeson, Dr. Martin Luther King Jr., Harriet Tubman, Mary McLeod Bethune, and Miss Jane Pittman. They understood that many of the people who had gone before them had risked their careers and their lives. They realized that, not unlike Jesus, many had in fact sacrificed their lives so that other generations of Blacks would not have to suffer as much. These middle-class Blacks did not wish to erase their memories of little Black children being bitten by vicious attack dogs and crushed under the power of streams of water fired from hoses. They realized that those little children were an integral part of the success of which these middle-class Blacks were now a part. These Blacks understood who they were, and they knew that despite the fact that they had worked and studied as hard as anyone else to obtain their positions, they were still viewed as inferior. This did not stop them from pushing on and trying to learn more and attain more. But they realized that they had to go back and help others. If not, all of what they had accomplished would mean very little.

This group of middle-class Blacks was proud of its heritage. They did not seek to deny themselves or their history. They realized that the term *middle class* was not sufficient to separate them from others who were suffering. They understood that whenever the Ku Klux Klan lynched a Black man, it had nothing to do with his class. They understood that during World War II, the Japanese *citizens* of the United States weren't locked in concentration camps because of class or social standing. They understood that Adolf Hitler never tortured and killed Jewish people because of the Jews' class. These middle-class Blacks understood that when the white man went into Africa seeking slaves for America, he did not ask for only poor, lower-class Africans. They understood that the one-hundred million Blacks who died on the slave ships during the voyage to the "New World" did not die because of what class they belonged to. This middle class vividly remembered the Middle Passage. They knew that if America ever decided to lock away Blacks, there would be no exemptions for the so-called Black middle class.

It was obvious to me that this division was calculated and planned. One group had to be kept ignorant and greedy. In fact, it would have been best if all Blacks in America were made to ignore the facts of racism; it would have been better if all Blacks were made ignorant of their history prior to their arrival on the shores of America. It would have been better if all Blacks could be bought and silenced at the cheap price of a job in someone else's company. It would have been better if all Blacks were willing to criticize their race for a high-profile job in government. It would have been better if there were more Walter Williamses and Thomas Sowells to make white people feel comfortable about their treatment of Black people. But not all Blacks could be bought. Everyone did not have a price. Thanks to the efforts of some sincere Black leaders, and some sincere white people, there would always be a group of conscious individuals. This was an accepted fact by those in power, so they concluded that it was important to divide one group from the other and keep them at odds. This was not a difficult task. In fact, it was one of the principles expressed by Niccolo Machiavelli in his famous 1537 treatise, *The Prince.*

Imbue a man with the American dream and then threaten to take it away. If he does not think as you think or act as you want him to act and if he is not strong, he will immediately become like an obedient dog. Give him toys and trinkets to play with. And, thereafter, demand that he sell his soul in order to keep them. To keep his new-found pleasures, he will gift-wrap his soul and hand it to you. Provide him with all or most of what you have taught him to believe that he needs to be comfortable, and he will cut his brother's throat to keep it. Do this with a group of people, point out that there is another group who wishes to take all of this away from them for the sake of unity and advancement, and you have accomplished the ultimate psychological and physical division.

The more I understood about the American system, the more I wanted to learn. I wanted the truth. I wanted to know the real history of America and to deeply understand the role Blacks had played. I knew that despite what I had already learned, there was so much more that I needed to know. I wanted to know how the theories of economics and of science applied to the Black community worldwide. I wanted to get an even better understanding of world politics. I wanted to get a deeper understanding of the criminal justice theories and then compare them with what I knew to be true from my experiences. I wanted to know how to counteract the miseducation that had been put in place, and that was doing so much damage, in our communities.

In my quest for knowledge, I decided to attend college and pursue a bachelor's degree. I had no illusion that a college education would supply me with all the answers I sought. I was also aware that it could in fact be harmful if I didn't use my education in the proper manner. Education can be a dangerous thing in the hands of an idiot. However, I needed to penetrate the system, just as a doctor cuts and enters a body in order to extricate cancer. If a physician doesn't get inside, there is nothing, or very little, he can do to rid the body of the ailment. Although the doctor's entry doesn't guarantee success, the lack of entry will undoubtedly guarantee failure.

A college education would allow me access to places that otherwise would be closed to me. A college degree would be another stamp of approval, my mark. It was my belief that a traditionally Black college could give me a different perspective. I believed that the lessons at such an institution would be more meaningful and more truthful! I had read about the extraordinary accomplishments Booker T. Washington had achieved by educating Blacks at Tuskegee Institute in Alabama. He had taught them several different trades along with their studies. His goal was to make them self-reliant. In order for Blacks to be self-reliant, they had to be proficient at everything—from the growing of their own food to the building of the houses in which they lived. They not only needed to know how to stack bricks, but, more importantly, they needed to know how to make bricks. They needed to know how to set up a budget to run a household, a city, a state, and a nation. This is what the often-misunderstood Booker T. Washington was advocating. He was advocating what Marcus Garvey stated and what Malcolm X would say many years later: "Up, up you mighty race, you can accomplish what you will," and you must achieve it "by any means necessary."

I decided to go to a local college so that I could continue to work for the Maryland State Police and continue to be a positive factor in the local Black community. I chose Coppin State College in Baltimore, Maryland. My choice of Coppin State College was made for several reasons. Coppin was a predominantly Black college which was nestled comfortably in the middle of Baltimore City on North Avenue. It was surrounded by row houses with white marble steps, an area that many considered to be a ghetto. Coppin stood as a beacon of knowledge and hope in the midst of humble surroundings. Right in the middle of hopelessness, Coppin stood as the key to the progress that W.E.B. DuBois and Marcus Garvey had so often spoken of. Right in the grasp of the community was a conclave of enlightenment. It was a passageway to freedom. I had to be there. I not only wanted to receive an education from Coppin, but I was determined to return to Coppin as a professor some day.

Coppin State College drew my attention for other reasons. It was named after the great educator Fanny Muriel Jackson Coppin. Fanny Muriel Jackson Coppin was born Fanny Muriel Jackson in 1837. She was born into slavery in Washington, D.C. Fanny Coppin's aunt, Sarah Orr Clark, bought Coppin's freedom for $125.00. Sarah Clark also helped to pay for Fanny Coppin's education at Rhode Island State Normal School. Fanny Coppin attended Oberlin College in Ohio. She was the second Black woman to receive a degree from Oberlin College. After graduating from Oberlin, Coppin formed a class for freedmen fleeing from the South after the Civil War. She taught them reading and mathematics. After this experience with teaching, Fanny Coppin decided teaching was the most worthwhile way to serve her people. In 1865, Fanny Coppin went to Philadelphia to teach at the Institute for Colored Youth. Her classes were in high demand and she was later promoted to principal. Fanny Coppin became aware of the young Blacks' need for industrial training. She enlarged the curriculum at the Philadelphia Institute for Colored Youth to include industrial education. In 1900 Fanny Muriel Jackson Coppin joined her husband, Reverend Levi J. Coppin, who was by then a Bishop, in Africa. Fanny Muriel Coppin died in 1913.

Fanny Coppin was an inspiration to me. Born into the brutal institution of slavery, she overcame this man-made obstacle to become a great educator. Now I had the opportunity to attend the school that was named after her. Additionally, Coppin State College was in the best location for what I intended to do with my life. All these factors made it a natural choice for me. However, I was about to get a lesson at Coppin that I had not expected. I would learn that the education in a Black college may not be any different from the indoctrination at a white college if that college is, in the end, controlled by uncaring whites and their middle-class Black surrogates, whose intention was to miseducate Black people and keep them in "their place."

I had never given thought to the fact that although Coppin State College was considered a Black college or a college whose students were predominantly Black, it was a college owned by the State of Maryland. The State of Maryland controlled the purse strings. The college was governed and certified through the State of Maryland. The professors were paid by the State of Maryland. The governor of the State of Maryland was a white man. He had attended a white college that had taught some of the same twisted historical lessons to which I had been exposed while in a predominately Black school system in Baltimore. It was my belief that it was not the governor's intent or in his best interest to make Coppin State College a first-rate college. He would never be willing to give Coppin the required supplies or pay for the best possible scholars to educate Black students. People in power will never educate powerless people for fear that the powerless may take their place.

I was to find out early, and often, that many of the professors at Coppin were just going through the motions. And a number of Coppin's students were just trying to graduate. The goal was not education but, rather, getting a diploma. I saw students cheating on tests while professors watched or simply turned a blind eye. They had no interest in truly educating these Black students. I witnessed professors with no lesson plans or direction. Some of them had no goals and passed students for merely showing up! It was like high school all over again. I became disillusioned. I missed a number of classes. Professors didn't even miss me.

When certain students complained to the administrators about the lack of instruction and about the miseducation that was taking place, they were sent back to the classrooms. Administratively, no action was taken to make the professors more responsible. The miseducation was consistent with what many of the more dedicated and sincere students believed was the goal of the nation. Just as I was making my mind up to attend another college, I enrolled in Dr. Raymond Ellis' class.

Dr. Raymond Ellis was an arrogant professor. His manners made him the gossip of many conversations concerning his sexual preference. I never cared about his orientation, sexual or otherwise, but I loved his teaching style. He was the Chairman of the Department of Criminal Justice, and he was demanding. He required students to do a great deal of reading and writing. He gave research assignments that required students to go off campus to law libraries and onto other campuses for information that could only be found there. He was teaching us that the answers we sought were sometimes not right before us. We would have to search for those not-so-obvious, sometimes purposely hidden, facts that would, in the end, reward our efforts.

Dr. Ellis required that all theories of criminal justice be analyzed from all angles. He would not allow his students to be "yes men" or "yes women" based solely on the fact that the writer of the researched material was a noted scholar. He said we all had the ability to theorize if we were willing to do the research to make our theories viable. He would disagree with our explanations of different theories, causing us to defend them and to better analyze the data. He taught us to take nothing at face value. He demanded that we look deep into what was said. He made us look for another meaning. He told us to attempt to identify the basis for any theory or statement which was put before us. He said what went unsaid was sometimes more important than what was articulated. Dr. Raymond Ellis said the news and information we read in periodicals and watched on television were a prime example of raw data that could hardly ever be taken at face value.

Dr. Ellis convinced me to major in Criminal Justice. He was also responsible for my remaining at Coppin State College. There were a few students who hated him. Those students believed that he demanded too much of them. Those students had a different agenda. They weren't in college for an education. They had already been conditioned for failure and they wanted further indoctrination. They had been prepared to seek a diploma. A diploma that ultimately would mean nothing. Simply an insult to the term *higher education*. Dr. Ellis was not prepared to give up on these students. He tried to undo what had been intentionally done to them; he tried to untie the knots in their brains. He would not allow a group of young people to go to waste. He saw it as his duty to reach down into these students and pull out what he knew had been intentionally suppressed. He knew why they were willing to accept mediocrity and failure. But he refused to allow it to happen—even if the students hated him for it. Dr. Ellis was a true educator, not just another state-paid miseducator.

I was sure that the programmed-for-failure students would not receive this kind of dedication and understanding in a predominantly white college. The professors at the white institutions would fail to understand the background of the students. They would fail to understand the effects of being Black in America. They would know very little of the brainwashing and miseducation that had occurred during the thirteen years prior to the students' arrival at their institutions. This is where the importance of attending a Black college came in. There would always be a few Dr. Raymond Ellises there. The lessons would be no easier. The skills would be taught with no less intensity. There would be understanding, and there would be no giving up on any student for any reason.

With guidance from Dr. Ellis, I concentrated on classes in political science and economics. My economics classes would later assist me in gaining admittance to the University of

Cincinnati, where I would earn a master's degree. At Coppin, Dr. Ellis advised me to enroll in writing and public speaking classes to advance my communication skills. He also convinced me to take several classes in logic and philosophy. He pointed me in the direction of Dr. William Carroll.

Dr. Carroll was a white professor who was dedicated to the education of his students—irrespective of their color. He taught philosophy and he enhanced my ability to break down and analyze information. He enjoyed talking with me; we often sat in his office on campus and talked about my future plans. He suggested that I go to law school; however, once he determined that I had little interest in law school, he suggested that I become a teacher. Dr. Carroll taught me to research different religious philosophies. He told me to note the impact that these philosophies had had on different groups of people. Dr. Carroll was suspicious of religion. He knew how it had been utilized as a mind control device.

I learned a great deal about Christianity and how it had been distorted and perverted to make Black people subservient to their slavemasters. I learned how someone else's interpretation of God and religion had been brought into Africa. I read books such as *The Gospel of Christian Atheism* by Thomas Altizer, *The Bankruptcy of Religion* by Joseph McCabe, *The History of Christianity* by Edward Gibbon, and *Before The Mayflower* by Lerone Bennett Jr.

I learned that the Catholic popes had ordained and sanctioned the slave trade. In 1411 A.D. Portuguese slave traders presented the first slaves to the pope, who deemed Africans to be soulless individuals. The pope sanctioned slavery as a means of bringing salvation to a "soulless people." In 1444 Henry the Navigator ordered his ships to explore the coast of Africa. According to Lerone Bennett Jr. in his astounding book *Before The Mayflower*, when Henry's men came upon the first large group of Africans, they began shouting out "St. James" and "St. George," and attacked the Africans, tracking and killing all they could. They captured seventy of the Africans and sailed home, where they "baptized" the captives and enslaved them.

I read books that revealed the role religion had played in the conquest of people of color, such as *The African Origin of Civilization* by Cheikh Anta Diop, *Cultural Genocide in the Black & African Studies Curriculum* by Yosef ben-Jochannan, and *Pontiff* by Gordon Thomas and Max Morgan-Witts. I learned that the Muslims were the first to enslave the Black people of Africa and that they had brutally massacred millions of Blacks in the name of their religion. They were followed by Christians who did the same thing. I read Chancellor Williams' book, *The Destruction of Black Civilization*, in which he states, "Christians and Moslems added a new dimension to the ancient institution [slavery], capturing and enslaving one another for religious reasons." Williams further wrote that "for several decades before the European trade, Moslem merchants dragged dark captives across the hot Sahara sands."

I learned of how Judaism had been distorted and utilized for Israel's justification of the taking of land and the merciless murder of thousands of Arab men, women, and children. I found out that some of those who professed to practice Judaism were participating in the mass holocaust of Black people in South Africa. I was beginning to understand how godless religion had become. Religion for most groups now was simply a means and justification for control of other groups of people. My studies revealed to me that this new, twisted meaning of religion had evolved over thousands of years.

In Political Science, I had the privilege of having Dr. Richard Bright as my professor. Dr. Bright was also white. He always maintained a smile on his face as he took us through the different theories of political science. He taught us the different systems of government around the world. He taught me a great deal about the power structure, and I began to understand that a great deal of power was maintained outside the seats of government in the multinational corporations and international banks. Bankers such as those who ran Chase Manhattan, Citibank, Manufacturers Hanover, and Bank of America wielded unbelievable power and control over the government. Multinational corporations such as International Business Machines (IBM), Dow Chemical, and others also had enormous say in the policies enunciated by the government. I learned that wars were fought based on monetary issues and often had nothing to do with national security or patriotism. I began to have a better understanding of what Ernest Hemingway meant when he wrote in *Notes on The Next War*: "they wrote in the old days that it is sweet and fitting to die for one's country. But in modern war there is nothing sweet nor fitting in your dying. You will die like a dog for no good reason."

Dr. Bright suggested that I read as much as I could on the history of all people. He said that some of the answers I sought would be hidden away in some other people's history. He said my reading would allow me to understand why certain groups acted in certain ways. He said that no one was reinventing the wheel—those who had practiced deceit throughout history were still practicing it; those who had robbed and raped and murdered in the name of self-preservation were still doing it. He was sure that if I understood the past, I could almost predict the future. There were other professors who were influential in my awakening. Dr. Elizabeth Gray, Dr. Lynn Jones, and Dr. James Avery, all of whom were professors in the Criminal Justice Department, helped me to get a better grasp on the intricacies and the true workings of the criminal justice system. After my graduation from Coppin, Dr. Gray, Dr. Jones, and Dr. Avery monitored my progress. Dr. Alice Grant taught me the importance of improving my writing abilities. Others taught me the importance of economics and science. I learned about great Black scientists like Daniel Hale Williams, George Washington Carver, Ernest Everett Just, Percy Lavon Julian, Charles Richard Drew, and Jane Cooke Wright from professors in the Science Department. The knowledge of these great Black scientists made laboratory experiments more significant and appealing.

I suppose that some of the lessons that I was taught would have been the same in a predominantly white institution. I don't believe they would have had the same impact or would have been taught with the same sense of urgency. They would have been wrapped in a flag and handed to me as if there were no other possibilities. In fact, that was how it had been all my life. All through elementary school and high school, I had been taught that God was on my side because I was an American. I never analyzed the fact that America had dropped atomic bombs on millions of children during World War II. I hadn't even been made aware of the American atrocities in the Congo. But I was aware of the death and destruction ordered by our leaders in the Viet Nam and Korean Wars. Killing in God's name.

I had never tried to figure out how God would support such acts. I had never tried to figure out how God could bless a nation that had infected a race of people, the Native Americans, with the smallpox disease. I had never tried to analyze how God could bless a nation that had enslaved a whole race of people and justified it, even under a constitution which said *All men are created Equal.* The few conscious professors at Coppin State College were making me analyze what professors like Nate and Quincy had been telling me all along. They were loosening that knot in my brain, which had been tightly tied by others.

While in college, I never had time to participate in sports. I studied before and after work. I was learning inside an institution for the first time in my life. Now everything was starting to come together. I was reaching back, grabbing knowledge and experiences, and putting them under a microscope for a more thorough examination. I was starting to feel something stir deep in my soul. Just as Warren said I would. It was not that I had not felt anything before—I had. I could not help feeling something, after all the talks with family, after all the scenes of ghetto life. Somehow the information that I had received seemed to be forming into one big beautiful quilt of knowledge. I was feeling warm inside as I covered myself with it.

I continued my association with the Young Democrats of Baltimore City. However, I was beginning to understand that political party affiliation would never solve the problems confronting Blacks. In fact, I began to believe that it was just another divide-and-conquer strategem. In the end, it didn't matter whether you were Republican or Democrat. It mattered that you were Black. That was how both major political parties in America identified and dealt with us. It was never either party's intention to ensure that the Black race was afforded human rights. We were to be used as a campaign issue. We were not people. We were objectified and used to determine which candidate could be the fairest if he so desired. As Ralph Ellison said in his book *Invisible Man*, we were invisible people until we were needed to serve someone's or some group's purposes. It was important that Blacks understood this fact: No one—no group or political party— would free us. As James Oppenheim had written in his book *The Slave*, "Free men set themselves free."

It was difficult to voice this to others around me. They were afraid that if they criticized the political parties because of a racial issue, they would be labeled racists or accused of using their color as a cop-out. They didn't want to dig too deep for the truth. If they didn't know, they couldn't be held responsible for their actions. I told them not to be concerned with labels. I explained to them that whether they wanted to admit it or not, they were already labeled "niggers." I stated that as long as they knew they were speaking the truth, it mattered not what others thought. I was convinced that Howard Thurman was right when he stated, "He who fears is literally delivered to destruction." I reminded those around me of Marcus Garvey's statement, "Men who are in earnest are not afraid of consequences."

I explained—to those who believed that their newly learned knowledge might be a curse—that knowledge, properly used, could have only positive effects. This new-found knowledge would only make us work harder. I told them that they were going to attend school and learn science, math, and English; they were going to be engineers and farmers and doctors; they were going to thoroughly learn the law. They were going to learn philosophy, psychology, and history. I stated they were going to know how to build a car or build a ship or fly a plane. I told them that it was necessary for them to learn how to manufacture weapons and use them. A man had to know how to defend his life, his family, his people.

All of these lessons were to be part of their learning, part of their recognizing and stating that they were in a world that was hostile to Black people—simply because they were Black! Self-knowledge and the identification of the source of a problem did not make them cop-outs, just as the identification of cancer by a doctor did not make the doctor a cop-out. It was what was done after the problem was identified that was important. I told them that we could never eradicate our color as radiation eradicates cancer, though a great many of us have tried; nor do the majority of us have any desire to. We at least had to be bold enough to point out that things were done to us because of the color of our skin.

I began to read the Bible. This reading was accomplished with the purpose of gaining a better understanding of what those who wrote it were trying to say. It seemed from the beginning that God, Allah, Jehovah or Whoever, was trying to say "Don't sell your soul to the devil." Don't be like Eve in the Garden of Eden. Don't be like Peter, Judas, Pharaoh or so many others. The lesson was: stand up for what you believe in, even if you are the only one standing, even if you are persecuted.

Coppin State College taught me a great deal about how the world worked. I earned a Bachelor of Science degree in Criminal Justice and graduated with honors in 1985. I had also earned my certification as an auto-mechanic from Lincoln Technical Institute on Wilkens Avenue in Baltimore, Maryland. I had attended Lincoln Technical Institute to supplement my academic training with industrial training, as Fanny Muriel Jackson Coppin and, before her, Booker T. Washington had suggested. I understood that we, as Blacks, had to do many things well. Dr. Ellis and Dr. Bright had taught me that I had so much more learning to do. But as I walked out of Coppin State College, I felt freer. I thought of Ralph Ellison's statement, "When I discover who I am, I'll be free." I had a better understanding of the statement, "You shall know the truth, and the truth shall make you free."

18

Runaway Slave

Because I always feel like running, not away
Because there's no such place,
Because if there was I would have found it by now.
Because it's easier to run; easier than staying and
finding out you're the only one who didn't run.
—Gil Scott-Heron, The Oldest Reason in the World

Craig and Terrance noticed the white police car moving ominously and slowly behind them like a stalker waiting to pounce on its tormented prey. They could recognize the headlights cutting through the moist darkness. By necessity, it was one of the sights that they had learned to quickly identify. They could distinguish police car headlights from all other cars. The police was the omnipresent enemy. They listened to the slow roll of the tires over the gritty macadamized street. From this they were able to determine the speed of the vehicle. They awaited its sudden move toward them. They awaited the sound of screeching tires and the thump of a transmission being abruptly thrown into the park mode.

Craig and Terrance had a small amount of cocaine in their pockets, but there was no way the police could have known that fact. This was just another "shake down." Another "we're in charge, nigger" thing. They walked a little faster and the police car moved closer. Craig turned his head slightly and used his peripheral vision to glance at the occupants in the car. He saw four heads but could not make out faces. It didn't matter; they were cops and that alone meant there would be trouble. He wondered why there would be four cops in one car. Maybe they were looking for someone and he fit the description. He always fitted the description according to the "keepers."

At any time, a Black man—especially a young Black man— could be stopped and searched or arrested by the police for fitting the description of another Black man who had allegedly committed a crime. It was all legal. Being Black in America made one a suspicious-looking character. It was a part of America's not-so-hidden apartheid system—the system that so many whites denied existed. The system that kept Black people— whether they were doctors, lawyers, teachers, congressmen, judges, senators, scientists, actors, athletes, authors, or *FBI agents*—leery of the "keepers"—the police. The United States of America (U.S.A.), the Union of South Africa (U.S.A.) and the Union of Soviet Socialist Republics (U.S.S.R.), as suggested by their initials, were all the same to many Blacks, especially in regard to their dealings with people of color.

Craig knew that if the police stopped him, he would be forced onto Baltimore's hard, cold concrete and cuffed so tightly that there would be little blood circulation left in his wrists. He would be roughed up and called a nigger. It didn't matter whether the arresting cop was white or Black, Craig still would be called a nigger.

It was not uncommon for Black police officers to try to impress their white counterparts, to try to show their co-workers that, "although I look like them, I'm not like them; I hate them as much as you do." The Black cop felt compelled by his "privileged" position to demonstrate to his counterparts, and to the white society in general, that he was part of the team. He was just another one of the "boys in blue." He wanted to fit snugly into his new life style. He wanted to be accepted and considered loyal. He wanted to forget his ancestral ties, his bond to the African American community. A smile and a nod from his white co-workers made him feel warm inside—finally accepted by those who he felt despised him before he draped himself in his protective blue garment.

I witnessed this type of search for acceptance in many of the Black officers with whom I worked. Nate was right to an extent that I was half embarrassed to admit. When a Black man was killed at the hand of a Black cop, it was the same as being killed by a white cop. The same type of mentality was involved—the inclination to accept the slavemaster-inspired belief in the inferiority of the Black man and to beat or kill an "animal" whose life really didn't matter. Beating down or killing another Black earned the Black cop his sought-after, begrudged partial stamp of approval from his white counterparts.

Craig took short, careful steps as he considered his alternatives. He thought about stopping so that the cops could see that he was not the person they were looking for. He quickly pushed that thought from his mind. He would certainly fit the description. The cops would only think that he was being a "smart ass." They would assume that he was challenging them. Despite his denials of guilt, they would search him.

Craig searched his mind for reasons for this stalking. He relived his day. He wondered where Melvin and Mark had gone. He and Terrance had argued with Mark over some money that was owed to them for drugs. Craig took the money from Mark, and he and Terrance had left Mark and Melvin standing on the corner. He figured that maybe Mark and Melvin had told the police that he had drugs on him. *Naw.* That was another thought that he was able to quickly force from his mind. No one would go to the cops and tell them about a drug deal gone bad. Besides, Mark also had drugs in his pocket.

Craig knew that Mark didn't want to be labeled a snitch. Sooner or later all snitches were dealt with, and not necessarily by the person they snitched on. To run to "the man" to have him solve your problems or deal with your enemies was the ultimate cop-out. This perverted notion of self-reliance had been instilled in Craig and Terrance and those like them. If only they would seek rightful self-reliance in all their actions. The foundations were there waiting to be built upon, waiting for the right leaders or teachers. All was not lost in the ghetto. The seeds were planted and waiting for proper cultivation.

Craig came to the conclusion that he would have to run. He would make a break. He whispered to Terrance, "When we come to the next alley, you break left and I'll break right." Terrance nodded his head in agreement. They both had been thinking the same thing at the same time. Their minds intersected at a place called survival. It was a location they had visited before. In fact, it was the most important location in their daily lives. They knew running from the cops could be risky. They could be justifiably shot in their backs. Who would care besides their families? And who was willing to listen to the complaints of ghetto dwellers? Running would be better than the alternative. Neither wanted to be locked up; neither was in the mood to be roughed up.

The cops moved closer. Craig looked up into the cold, dark January sky and took a deep breath. White steam exited his mouth and dissipated into the cold air. Terrance removed his hands from his jacket pockets and scanned the ground for ice spots. He wanted nothing to foil his escape. He breathed deeply and whispered to Craig, "There's an alley coming up on your right. You go down the alley; I'm gonna take off across the street and jump Mr. Gardener's fence. Don't let those motherfuckers catch you, man. Ain't that many people out here, so if they ain't got no witnesses they might try to do you." Craig responded, "Them fat-belly, doughnut-eating, sloppy motherfuckers aren't gonna catch me."

The cops noticed Terrance when he removed his hands from his pockets. The young cop on the passenger side tensed. The driver, who was older and fatter, said, "Young blood, here is your chance, 'cause these little niggers are going to try to run." Mark leaned forward from his position in the back seat of the squad car. His voice trembled. "Off–officer, can we get out...? 'Cause I don't want them to see us." The young officer turned around in his seat and asked, "Are you sure these are the two guys who robbed you?" Mark nodded his head yes. The young officer picked up the microphone to the car radio and called in to advise the station that they were about to arrest two suspects for robbery. A crackling voice leaped out of the radio and repeated what the young cop had said. The officer responded, "Ten-four." The crackling voice inside the radio advised any car in the area to respond to "assist in the arrest of two Black male subjects for robbery."

Mark had not gotten a reply to his question. He started to ask the officer again, "Off–officer..." The fat cop interrupted him. "No, you two stay put in the car so that you can positively identify these assholes. You wanted us to catch them and now all of a sudden you're scared. If you ain't lying to us, these bastards are going to be in jail anyway." Mark responded, "But officer, you know they gonna make bail." The fat cop turned around in his seat. "That's your fuckin' problem, jungle bunny." He turned back around and took a deep breath, as if just his turning had been a major effort. "All right, young blood, let's do it."

The young cop's hands began to tremble. He had not been out of the academy that long. His partner had told him about patrolling the ghetto. He had told him about the Blacks and how they all were animals and needed to be tamed. His fat partner told him that Blacks were like broncos: "If you ride them long and hard enough, they'll submit. We are the broncobusters." Prior to becoming a cop, the young officer had never visited the ghetto. He had managed to avoid contact with Blacks outside the ghetto.

The most he saw of them was on television, perhaps on the evening news. He had heard nothing positive. Now he was here in the jungle, dealing with people that he had been taught all his life were savages. It didn't matter that they were doctors, lawyers, politicians or even cops—they were all "nigger savages."

Craig's heart raced as he saw the red and blue lights come on. He continued to walk. The plan was to run at the alley and he was going to stick with the plan. He whispered to Terrance, "Don't run yet. If they get out, then we'll run. If they don't, just keep going to the alley." The squad car raced up alongside Craig and Terrance and screeched to a halt. Terrance panicked and took off across the street. Craig ran toward the alley. The young officer gave chase to Craig. The other officer chased Terrance. Mark turned to Melvin. "Let's get the fuck out of here. Move slowly so the other cops won't think we're running from them." Mark and Melvin exited the squad car and disappeared into one of the dark ghetto streets.

Terrance leaped Mr. Gardener's fence and took off across the open field. The fat officer stopped at the fence and tried to yell, "Stop or I'll shoot you, you motherfucker." His voice was barely audible as he tried to talk through deep breaths. He turned and walked back to the squad car and requested a K-9 unit and a helicopter. More squad cars pulled up to the scene. The fat cop yelled something and pointed in the direction in which Craig had run. The fat officer sat on the seat of the car, with his legs hanging out the side. Sweat rolled over his round face. He murmured to himself, "Fucking niggers...these fuckin' niggers gonna cause me to have a heart attack." He never noticed that his two victims were gone. It didn't matter. Someone had to pay for making him run. It had become a "slave chase."

Craig turned the corner of the alley and took off with lightning speed. The young officer followed with his gun drawn. A group of other officers ran into the alley with guns drawn. Craig could hear them in the distance. He was sure that they would not be able to catch him. Their faint calls were drowned out by the sounds of barking dogs. He jumped over a junkie who had nodded out and was leaning against a wall. The officers continued their pursuit. Craig remembered the old abandoned house at the end of the alley. He decided to make it to the house, run through it and out onto the streets on the other side. He could then run down Baltimore Street and into the home of one of his friends. He smiled as he thought of the success he was having. It was not the first time he had run from the police. He, and many others like him, had to learn the skills of running away from the police. They had learned that the police saw them as prey to be hunted. The police were the modern "slave catchers," hunting "runaway slaves."

Craig could see the abandoned house, so he began to slow down to a jog. The race was won. His *Nike*-clad foot landed on a beer bottle and slid from under him. He screamed out in agony, "Damn...fuck." His ankle collapsed. His body landed on the cold, rocky concrete. A piece of glass slit the palm of his hand. His blood flowed easily into the half-frozen water that trickled down the middle of the alley like a slow-moving stream.

Craig's trembling hand reached for his throbbing swollen ankle. He knew he had made a mistake. He should have kept on running. Slowing down had made him fall. He never should have stopped, until he reached his goal. Slowing down could be a fatal mistake. The Black men on the steps at the Blue Gardenia had talked about that. They had said that a Black man could take nothing for granted; he could never let his guard down. A Black man had to keep running toward his goal, his destination. He had to run a marathon as if it were a forty-yard dash. There could never be a slow jog, not even in old age. There was always someone waiting for him to slow down or to become comfortable or to believe that he had made it.

Craig's mind wandered. He saw Warren lying on the ground against the white marble steps after he had chased him up the street. He saw the blood dripping from the steps as he called out for help. He saw Chas, Angel, Quincy, Frank, Sugar, his brothers Bay-Bay and Michael, and me sitting on the back porch in a driving rain storm on a gray day. He smiled to himself as he remembered the Little Negro League and the one-man teams. The pain from his ankle brought him back to the situation at hand.

Craig looked down at the broken beer bottle. He thought of how Malcolm X and Minister Louis Farrakhan had said drinking had helped in the demise of the Black race. He thought it ironic that a beer bottle had stopped his run toward freedom. He tried to move and felt an excruciating pain in his ankle. It didn't matter; it couldn't matter. He had to keep running through the pain. He stood up and started to move. He thought of the slaves and how they had to keep running to freedom, through the dark and dangerous woods. He felt as if he were one of them and that the slavemaster or the patrollers with their hound dogs were chasing him.

Craig tried to run—it was impossible. He walked slowly, gingerly dragging his damaged ankle as if it were shackled. He could hear footsteps quickly coming up behind him. They were cop feet. Cop shoes. He thought he was in the woods in the South in 1860. He saw the trees and the stars and the moon. He could smell the water from the swamps. He heard the sounds of barking dogs and horse hooves. He turned to see a group of night riders, patrollers, policemen aiming guns at him. Everything went silent as small flashes of fire were discharged toward him. His ankle collapsed for the final time.

19

The Recruiter

*I speak truth, not so much as I would, but as much
as I dare; and I dare a little more as I grow older.*
            —*Michel Montaigue,* Essays, III

When I discover who I am, I'll be free.
            —*Ralph Ellison,* Invisible Man

The reward of suffering is experience.

            —*Aeschylus*

I stared across the table at James Thorton as he spoke in a low,
raspy voice. I listened to him and studied his dark facial features.
He had surprised me with this topic of conversation. It had
jumped out at me like a mugger in a dark alley. I had not
anticipated it. I was not prepared. Maybe that was James's plan.
He knew that had I known what his subject of discussion would be
beforehand, I might not have come to his table. I might have
denied him the opportunity to say what he believed he had to say
to me. He had captured me like a skilled hunter snares his prey,
and he was proud of it. I would have to listen now. I would have
to respond to his questions. This was a dead-end alley, and James
and his topic stood between me and the only exit.
    James stared back across the table at his trapped victim and
slowly repeated the question, though he was certain that I had
heard it the first time, "What do you think about joining the FBI?"

The words hovered there between us for a second and then completed their journey to my ears. I didn't know what to say or how to respond. It wasn't a complicated question. But I had never thought of joining the FBI. Or maybe I had when I was younger and just couldn't remember it at this moment. Maybe I had thought about it when I joined the Maryland State Police. Maybe I had pushed it from my mind because I had become familiar with the FBI and its history of adversarial relationships with people of color. No matter, I didn't have an answer for James. Not now. "I don't know, James. I've never given it much thought." James smiled. "Maybe you should. Maybe it's time for you to make a change in your life."

There it was again. Someone else was telling me to make a change in my life. As if I had not accomplished enough. Once again someone was expecting more from me. Nate and Quincy expected more from me than becoming "the man." I had listened to them and had listened to my soul. I had responded with Operation Drug-Out. Still, they wanted me to get out of the policing business and become a teacher and mentor for young Black men. Now it was James sitting across from me asking me to move on. Asking me to make a change for the better.

James had already submitted his letter of resignation to the Maryland State Police. He had applied and passed all the required tests for the position of Special Agent with the Federal Bureau of Investigation. He would be leaving for Quantico, Virginia for his training in a matter of days. I had congratulated him on his success, but there had been no talk of my going with him. He had waited patiently for the right time to approach me. Now he was concealing his request to make it seem like an uncomplicated question about my plans for the future. No matter how he phrased the question, I knew that he was really asking me to join him. He didn't care what my thoughts were.

I needed time to think before answering James. I could tell that James didn't intend to give me that time. Like the mugger, he wanted everything I had right now. And he had brought the proper weapons to extract his booty. His timing was impeccable. He had invited me over to his place after we had got off work. We had worked a 12 midnight to 8 a.m. shift. He had said that he had something important that he needed to talk with me about and that it couldn't wait.

I didn't mind stopping by his home. He knew I wouldn't. We lived in the same apartment complex in Reisterstown, Maryland. I figured that my wife and my daughter were asleep and that my coming in would only interrupt their dreams. Besides, James and I were good friends and it sounded as if he had a problem. If he needed help, I wanted to be there for him. We had been through a lot together as we dealt with the racist attitudes of the Maryland State Police. But now I knew that he had not invited me over to discuss a problem of his. He wanted to discuss my future. He wanted to convince me that it was time to make a change.

James got up and walked into the kitchen. He took two cups out of the cabinet and poured hot black coffee into them. He glanced out the kitchen window into the early morning sun. "How much sugar and cream do you want in your coffee, or do you like it black?" I looked into the kitchen and smiled. "You just assume that I want my coffee integrated." He smiled back. "I asked you if you wanted it black, you Uncle Tom motherfucker." We both laughed. He brought the coffee to the table and slid my cup in front of me. He walked back into the kitchen and got the sugar and cream. He brought them back and put them on the table. "Now when I turn my back, you can go ahead and integrate it."

James sat down and leaned forward. He began to sip his coffee. I took the spoon off the table and put a little cream and sugar in my cup. James spoke. "You know the state police has nothing else to offer you. You're just wasting your time and talents here. We work for a bunch of rednecks who don't want us around. This is a racist organization, plain and simple. There isn't any other way to state it. They ain't never going to do right by us. All those changes that they are promising to make are never going to happen. They don't give a damn about the law suits. I'm tired of fighting them and I think you should be, too." He sat his cup down and turned toward the kitchen. "It's time for both of us to make a move. I definitely want you to come with me. I wouldn't feel good about leaving you here in this hellhole."

I tasted my coffee and set the cup on the table. I stared past James and out the kitchen window. "I just don't know if I'm ready to make a move yet, James. I think we have done some good here. And all of the people we work with are not racists. Some of them are pretty straight, like Corporal Gerstner and Sergeant Mobley." James turned around and interrupted me, "Yeah, but for every Sergeant Mobley and Corporal Gerstner there is a Sergeant Stoney. Remember his words to that stranded Black citizen who came into the barracks. Remember him telling that brother that if he acted like a 'white man,' he could stay in the lobby until help came. And trust me, partner, if we act like white men, we can stay in this organization forever. But that's not in us. We're not willing to act like white men because we're not white men. Maybe we had been a little more willing at some point. *But* both of us are changing. I can see it in you. You've got the look of a reborn man."

Prior to becoming a Maryland State Trooper, James had been a teacher in the Baltimore City Public School system. He would often tell me of the inferior equipment that he had to work with and the lack of needed materials. He told me of children who were more concerned about where their next meal would come from than about what their next lesson would be. He spoke of the low pay and high turn over rate amongst teachers which led to the children's not having any consistency in their education. He said that sometimes what a child had learned in the prior year was not built upon, but only repeated the next year. This redundancy resulted in increased boredom and a lack of challenge. Sooner or later the few children who had managed to stay attentive, despite their problems outside school, lost interest.

James was convinced that the education of inner-city Black children was not a priority of the government. He said that unless Blacks took control of the education of their children and demanded that adequate funding be provided, we, as a race, were in for a dim future. James became frustrated and left the school system. Now he was frustrated with the state police. He didn't understand that it was not just the school system or the state police that was the problem. It was all of America. It was the attitude of people like J. Edgar Hoover who deemed Blacks mentally inferior. It was the attitude of the "founding fathers" who designated Black people three-fifths human. There could be no running away from it all. Sooner or later, there would be no place else to run and then he would be forced to stand and fight. He would be forced to try to make a change. And as Booker T. Washington said, he would be forced to "cast down [his] bucket where [he is]."

James would often come over and visit Doris and me. He enjoyed playing with Tamara. We worked the same shifts, so more times than not we were off on the same days. On the days we worked we usually left home and returned home at the same time. He knew how close Doris and I were with the rest of our family. James knew that convincing me to join the FBI would not be an easy task. He would have to convince us to uproot and move across the country. He would have to ask us to give up the physical closeness with our families. James believed that he was the only person who could convince Doris and me to make a move. He believed that he would be the only one to even try. The FBI did very little "serious" recruitment targeting African Americans.

James and I often had conversations as we sat in our patrol cars in Frederick, Maryland. We discussed how the Black family had been intentionally uprooted and separated. In South Africa they were separated by law. In America the separation was intentionally and effectively established by custom. In Africa, prior to our enslavement by Europeans, we had moved about as tribes and developed communities wherein everyone was held responsible for the training of all the children in the community. There was no such thing as a single parent-headed family because the man next door was just as responsible for the proper upbringing of his neighbor's son as was his neighbor. Something had torn away at the very fabric of that unity. Someone felt it was better that Blacks were disunited and pitted against one another. Neighbor against neighbor; friend against friend; Black Christian against Black Muslim; brother against brother. Whatever the plan, it was working. James knew how I felt about the unity of family. He would somehow have to convince me that my move would not play into the hands of this plan of division.

I could tell that our conversation on this morning would be a long one. I could tell that James had much more to say. I unclipped my tie and unbuckled my gun belt and removed it. I placed it on the floor next to me, sighed, and waited for James to continue. He didn't disappoint me. "You can just sit here and rot away with the state police until retirement, if that's what you want to do. But I'm sure that you have more drive than that. Otherwise, you wouldn't have pursued your bachelor's degree. Or you wouldn't be doing all of that reading. You are twenty-three years old. That means that you'll sit around here with these red-necked sons of bitches for the next twenty-five or so years. Just think about it."

As I listened to James, I thought of our prior conversations about the state police. James said that the Maryland State Police wore their stigma of racism as a prized medal, just as the New Jersey State Police wore their Nazi-style uniforms as a symbol of racial supremacy. James wanted out and he wanted me to get out with him. He wanted us to move on to what he believed would be "bigger and better" things. He would not sit and wait for the department to change.

He said that no matter how hard we tried, we could never change the state police. There were too few conscious brothers on the force to make a change. He knew I had hoped to do my part to mend the relationship between the police department and the African American community. He knew I intended to let the African American community know that they could get proper police response and help. I had told James that we were the only hope in building some form of trust between Blacks in Frederick County and the department. A white police officer, no matter how noble his intentions, wouldn't have a chance because of the historically justified ill will the African American community felt toward the police. Now James was trying to convince me that I was not selling out on that idea, that I was not giving up or copping out. He was trying to convince me that I could continue my efforts on a larger scale in the FBI.

Although it was obvious that James had prepared a sound argument in order to influence my decision, he now seemed to be reaching for words and ideas which he believed would have the most potent impact. He knew me well and would leave no stone unturned. My decision was important to him. He continued, "I know that it's going to be difficult for you and Doris to up and move away from your families, but sometimes in life you have to make a move to better yourself. Sometimes you just have to take a chance. I mean, I don't see how you can go wrong. What the fuck are you losing? You've worked hard for your bachelor's degree. You worked at night and went to school during the day. Your degree don't mean shit here and never will. You see, bachelor's degree, master's degree, doctoral degree aside, a 'nigger' is a 'nigger' to a redneck and nobody believes that more strongly than the Maryland State Police!"

James believed justifiably that some of the state troopers we worked with were current card-carrying members of the Ku Klux Klan. He and I had never forgotten the night on the hill when we guarded the Klan rally. He had told me that there probably were as many Klansmen on the hill with us as were down in the rally. He continued, "You know they'll never do the right thing when it comes to you. Sure, you've played the game and you've never really displayed any obvious disagreement with the system. But they are scared of an educated hard-working Black man. They've seen how hard you've worked to become educated and although they'll never admit it, they would rather you just stay put and not try to better yourself. They are afraid that if you keep driving forward, you'll be their boss one day. Can you imagine Sergeant Stoney saying 'Yes sir' to you? Shit, he would rather be strapped to a tree, butt naked, and whipped with a bullwhip."

I imagined Sergeant Stoney with his hands and feet tied around a big tree and being whipped like so many Blacks had been during the cruel days of physical slavery. *Never forget.* James paused for a minute and took a sip of coffee. It was as if he needed some time to assess the effect his argument was having on me. Or maybe he, too, was thinking of the bullwhip days.

At any rate, I was not ready to respond. And I don't think he was ready for me to say anything; not yet. He put the coffee cup back on the table and leaned toward me. "I know I don't have to tell you most of this. You're a conscious young Black man and you realize what an educated 'negro' means to these rednecks. An educated negro means trouble, unless they can control him. And I think they already know that they can't control you. At least, not in the way that they want to. They may never say anything, but they know that you've started Operation Drug-Out down in Baltimore. They've seen you on the news. Trust me, my friend, they know every move you make and every step you take. And they got it fixed in their minds that any move upwards for you means trouble for them. You have to be silenced. You're a brother who sees it as one of his goals in life to help other brothers and sisters. You're a troublemaker. So fuck them—get out."

I took a sip of coffee and leaned back in my chair. I had thought of perhaps expanding Operation Drug-Out into a full-time campaign against Black-on-Black violence and drug abuse. I had thought of getting some help from the Baltimore City mayor's office and requesting help from other organizations and individuals that had a sincere concern about what was happening in the Black community. The Honorable Congressman Parren Mitchell had put some ideas before me about what direction to pursue. Initially, I had been hesitant to contact the mayor's office because I believed that I would lose control of the program. I believed that it would just become more window dressing for politicians, and that the true goals would be lost in the rhetoric. I had witnessed so many programs, which were started with the best of intentions, go bad. These programs deteriorated because those running them forgot all about their initial goals.

I also knew that the Maryland State Police was aware of my actions. I had been featured on radio talk shows in Baltimore City and in Frederick, Maryland. I had spoken at many of the schools in Frederick and had been requested by some teachers to expand the program to the Frederick area. The Baltimore City Police Department had vowed to help me in any way it could. My efforts were no secret, nor did I want them to be. James was telling me that my efforts could be seen as a threat to some people. He told me the fact that I had been denied leave on several occasions, despite the fact that more than adequate manpower was available and that Congressman Mitchell had requested my presence at an event, was an indication that someone somewhere within the

Maryland State Police was afraid of my actions. I was determined not to let this stop me.

The problem of Black-on-Black violence was escalating. Drug abuse in the Black community was way out of control. On top of these problems was stacked the AIDS epidemic, which most African Americans were convinced was another Tuskegee experiment. Something had to be done by everyone and I believed that I was taking a step in the right direction with the establishment of Operation Drug-Out. Now James had me contemplating leaving all of this behind.

I rested my arms on the table. A thousand thoughts were darting through my mind. I wanted to latch on to one of them. I wanted to take one thought at a time and break it down. But before I had time to examine a single thought, it was displaced by another thought moving through like a bumper car at an amusement park. Once again, my life was becoming more complicated than I had anticipated. Once again, this "ghetto child" was being asked to make a major decision. I wondered if I would ever be able to just sit back and relax. Would I be able to say the hell with the rest of the world, put on a Brooks Brothers suit, and attend parties or "socials" on Friday evenings. I immediately pushed that thought from my mind.

I didn't want to just sit back and relax like so many others were doing. You see, knowledge does that to you. Once a man knows, it is difficult for him not to act. But as long as he stays in a cloud of ignorance, he can rest. I had figured that this effect that knowledge had on men is what made an educated and conscious Black man such a threat to the status quo. Once a man knew what was happening and what had happened to him and his people, he would be compelled to act in one way or another. He could either sell his soul—and with it the knowledge that he had obtained—to those in power, or he could begin to fight for what was right and just for his people. Too many brothers and sisters had been willing to sell their souls. I just couldn't do it. I knew that there was too much to be done. I could not get the picture of the suffering ghetto children out of my head.

I couldn't shake the vision of African kings becoming African American drug addicts. I couldn't break loose from the image of our beautiful black, brown, and bronze African queens becoming African American prostitutes. No amount of money or comfort or prestige could make me forget my people. Nothing could make me forget about the battle of which I had to be a part. I understood the fall we had taken. I knew that the blame was not all ours, but the solution would have to be. There was no need for me to sit back and write editorials criticizing Black men and women, as so many of our "successful" brothers were inclined to do. It was time for solutions. I had to keep striving and should I forget or lose focus, I need only look into the eyes of my daughter and know that if all the conscious brothers and sisters stepped away from the battle, my daughter could become one of those African American drug-addicted prostitutes. In reality, there was no distinctively drawn line. There was no "us and them." Truth and knowledge would not allow me to be still. As Emerson had written, "God offers to every mind its choice between truth and repose. Take which you please—you can never have both."

I decided to slow down the motion of my undisciplined thoughts by interrupting them with the audible sound of me speaking to James. I watched James as he sat and watched me, thoughts moving about in my mind. He refused to interrupt the activity. I had to say something. "James, what about everything I've started to build here? What about my family and friends?"

James took a deep breath as if he were surprised and relieved that these were the strongest questions I could come up with to counter his proposition. "You're making an upward move—your family and friends can't help but be happy for you. Besides, you're not moving out of the country, you're only moving across it. You've got the opportunity to play in the major leagues, and you're thinking about staying in the minors because you may get homesick at some point in the future." I interrupted, "I'm thinking about staying in the Negro league."

James ignored my comment and continued, "It just don't make any sense. Listen, I feel like a big brother to you and I'm interested in your future. I'm interested in the future of Doris and Tamara and any other children you might be thinking of having. As I said before, the Maryland State Police don't have a fuckin' thing to offer you. The FBI offers you more money, a better chance for advancement, and more prestige. Plus..." I interrupted James again, "What does all that shit mean, James? I mean, what am I advancing to and in whose eyes am I going to be prestigious? All that shit just isn't as important anymore. I can't deal with that looking-out-for-me attitude. It doesn't get you anywhere. Then again, it gets you into old age thinking that your life has been in vain. Then you sit back and look at your people and the tears roll. You look at your daughters and sons, your brothers' daughters and sons, or your friends' daughters and sons, and the tears just roll. And then, all that money and prestige don't mean a damn thing."

James was ready with a reply. He would not even attempt to answer all my questions or respond to all my statements. But he was ready with a general reply. James was maneuvering around my questions with all the dexterity of an experienced politician. His voice trembled slightly. "Those little Black kids are going to look up to you as an FBI agent. You're going to be able to get them to listen simply because their brains have been all twisted up into believing that the FBI is some God-ordained organization. As fucked up as that is, we have to get these kids to listen 'by any means necessary.' This society has it so that most of our own kids won't listen to us unless they believe that the white man has given us his stamp of approval. Only a few well-educated children will listen to you as a Black man without that stamp."

I rubbed my eyes and lowered my head to stare down at a spot on the table. I just needed another focal point besides the eyes to James's soul. His eyes conveyed an honesty and truthfulness that I didn't want to accept. I interrupted him. "That's not true, James. You don't have confidence in your own people. Look at the thousands of kids that listen to Minister Farrakhan. Look at all those young brothers that followed Malcolm X and the Honorable Elijah Muhammad. Look at the young people who paid attention to Dr. Martin Luther King Jr. and Booker T. Washington. What about the extraordinary number of followers of Marcus Garvey, W.E.B. DuBois, Paul Robeson, Medgar Evers, Mary McLeod Bethune, Harriet Tubman, and many others. No...no, James, the young people will listen if they know you are sincere. They'll never pay attention to the Walter Williamses and the Thomas Sowells 'cause they know they aren't sincere. They can tell when a brother has been bought and paid for. You don't give us enough credit."

James wasn't about to accept my analysis of him. He spoke up. "Naw...naw, that's not true. Don't tell me that I don't have faith in my people. You know me better than that. I know we have young brothers and sisters out there that are going to listen and learn. I know that our young people have listened to and followed all those great leaders that you mentioned and many more who you haven't mentioned. But you are talking about thousands of young people, when I'm talking about a race that has at least thirty million people in this country alone. I still say that the white man has done an excellent job of convincing most of that thirty million that what he says is true. He has convinced them that a person or an institution is not worthy of attention unless he stamps and sanctions it. Look around and pay attention to who we go to when we need a lawyer or a doctor or an accountant! Who do our Black athletes go to when they are searching for an agent to represent them? We look for that stamp.

And trust me, the FBI has been stamped or, in fact, does the stamping."

I responded, although I knew that I was digressing. "So I guess that means that the white man approves of our churches, because we don't seek out white churches. We don't look for that stamp of approval when we go to worship at the churches in the 'hood, or are you saying that even our churches have earned their stripes, I mean stamp. I just..." James jumped right in before I could finish the thought as if he had anticipated my impromptu digression. "You damn right the white man has given our churches the stamp of approval. And I would too if I were him.

"If I knew that you were getting your religious lessons from a book that I wrote, or at the very least, edited; if I knew that the Sunday school books that I provided you had people on them who looked like me and not you; if I knew that you were telling your people to turn the other cheek when I smacked them and to wait on God to get revenge; if I knew that you were telling your people to wait until they go marching in somewhere as a saint before they get theirs, then you're damn right, I would sanction your churches. I would also make sure that you could get in and out of them safely every Sunday. That's one time that you would not have to worry about adequate police protection.

"I would give the preacher all kinds of good citizen awards and praise him every time I got the chance. I would name him the head of my committees to improve the city or county. I would make sure the media covered all the major church events. I would even stop in every once in a while to give the congregation a speech. Kinda pep talk-like. I wouldn't allow anyone up in my— I mean your—pulpit—like Vernon Johns or Minister Louis Farrakhan. In fact, I would label Farrakhan, and those who listened to him, a racist and maybe, if I really wanted to destroy him in the public's eye, I might even call him an anti-Semite. That always does the job. That's the trump card. I would make your other leaders denounce Farrakhan and Malcolm X and Dr. Ben and Dr. Tony Martin. And trust me, by the time I've finished getting next to your leaders, they'll denounce *God*, if I told them to. Yeah, you damn right I would sanction your churches. You've got to read your history, brother. Even some of the slavemasters and owners read to their slaves from the Bible and made sure they attended church. Hell, they even baptized their slaves."

James leaned back in his chair and took a deep breath. His talk with me had gone further than he had anticipated. I could tell that he was enjoying it. I was making him dig deep inside, causing him to come up with knowledge that he did not think would be necessary to retrieve, at least at this time. Yet, he seemed to enjoy going into the depths of his soul and pulling out his feelings. He seemed to relish calling up his history lessons. He smiled and spoke again. "Think of it this way, brother: you get the opportunity to shake up a whole lot of those racist white folk. Can you imagine knocking on the door of some white folk's house in the South, or in the North, for that matter, and flashing that FBI badge. They'll probably drop dead. They just ain't used to seeing us carrying that badge. They're used to seeing their own people with that badge, carrying us. You're going to make that faggot redneck son-of-a-bitch J. Edgar Hoover, roll over in his grave."

I shook my head and laughed. James had me seriously considering applying. He was a good friend and I didn't think he would lead me astray. I knew he was a conscious brother who would not ask me to join something that he perceived as being a complete sellout. But I had other people to think about. Doris and Mom would stand behind me in whatever I chose to do. Tamara was too young to know or care. Frank would give me his tacit approval. Quincy and Warren would no doubt try to talk me out of it. They wanted me out of law enforcement altogether. They believed that I would be better as a teacher. To them, a move into the FBI would be a move deeper into the lions' den.

I knew that Nate would be adamantly opposed to my joining the FBI. He believed that he was finally getting through to me. He believed that it would not be long before I moved from law enforcement into teaching, and finally lead young brothers and sisters into something positive and progressive. Baltimore needed that. Nate told me that he had been so proud when he heard me give my speech to the young brothers and sisters at Southwestern High School in Baltimore. He said the students paid attention. "If only someone like you would have come into the schools I attended and said those things. If only some other young brothers and sisters who had found some of the answers would have come to where we lived and shared those facts and stories and reasons with me and those like me. Not write them in newspapers and magazines, but come to where we live, come to our urban plantation like Nat Turner did. Come here and stand face to face, eye to eye and say, 'Brother, you're traveling wrong. Here's the path. Here's the route and this is why you should take it.' Eye to eye. Eye to soul."

I began to feel closer to my brother Nate. I still couldn't understand why he used and sold drugs. Yet, I admired his faith in me and his knowledge. He was adamant that I should never use drugs or drink alcohol. He begged me to stay off the streets of the west side of Baltimore. He told me to use him as an example of what not to become. He called me every day just to say hello, just to stay in touch with my soul. He left message after message in the voice mail system deep within me and they all said the same thing: "Be a part of the solution, brother. Don't allow your life to be in vain." I knew that if I told him that I was going into the FBI and that I would have to move away from my family and friends, he would be deeply hurt. I knew that he would think that I, once again, was abandoning some divine purpose that I had somehow been chosen to carry out. I knew that somehow I would be adding a nail to the coffin that he felt was being built and readied for him daily.

I remembered Nate's anger when he found out that I had taken his gun and gone to kill Gi-Gi. Gi-Gi and I both had attended Southwestern High School. We both were in the tenth grade at the time of our meaningless fight. We both had fallen in love with the same girl, Gloria Smith. I called him out of class one day. I wanted to end his relationship with Gloria. Somehow I had come to the idiotic conclusion that by physically damaging him I could end his infatuation with "my girl." As soon as he exited the classroom, I threw a punch toward his head. He was prepared. He ducked and grabbed me at the waist. I managed to throw him to the floor and land on top of him. We both threw a few well-intended but futile punches at each other. We were pulled apart by my English teacher, Mr. James Harrison.

Mr. Harrison was a large, bulky white man. He was approximately 6'6" and weighed over 300 pounds. Nothing or no one seemed to frighten him. None of his students gave him any trouble, and he seemed to enjoy his job more than any of the other teachers. He had a great deal of confidence in my academic abilities and would often compliment me on my writing skills. He said that I had the ability to take my raw thoughts and put them on paper in an effective format. He said that I didn't get too creative—which he believed took something away from the bare, honest feelings, especially in nonfiction writings—and that my writings were succinct.

Mr. Harrison took a personal interest in my academic development and required that I read the poetry of Robert Frost, Langston Hughes, and many of the other great poets. He required that I read the classics by Mark Twain and the books of Ernest Hemingway. He said that it was a must that I read Ralph Ellison's *Invisible Man*. He introduced me to the library of James Baldwin and suggested I read Richard Wright. He required that I write a term paper on the assassination of Dr. Martin Luther King Jr. And he was so proud of me when I received the highest grade on the city-wide English proficiency examinations. On the day of the fight with Gi-Gi, Mr. Harrison dragged me down the hall to his classroom. He closed the door and moved in close to my face. He stared into the eyes of my soul like no white person had ever done. I stared back into his eyes and saw for the first time genuine concern and sincerity in the soul of a white man. Maybe concern and sincerity had been in the eyes of other whites, but they never gave me the opportunity to see it. White people always seemed to look down on or look away from the African American children whom they addressed.

In a low but stern tone Mr. Harrison lectured me. "What the hell are you doing? You are throwing it all away. Stay away from this type of bullshit. Gi-Gi is an idiot who is going nowhere unless someone pulls his coattails quickly. You, on the other hand, have a bright future, if you don't fuckin' throw it away like so many of these other students. This is one white man who gives a damn about you and these other students. That's why I stay here at this school. That's why I tolerate no bullshit in my classes. I'm not running away. America just doesn't realize what a positive, powerful force an educated population of African Americans can be. They don't realize how the world would be in awe of this country if it stopped degrading the people who built its foundation. But I do. And, Mr. Tyrone Powers, one day you're going to help me show America a thing or two about the power of its African American inhabitants."

Mr. Harrison snatched a piece of paper off his desk and pushed it toward me. "When you get angry, pick up a pen and put your feelings on paper. It's a great deal more profitable and it just might keep you and some of your peers alive. It might keep a lot of Americans alive."

I was suspended from school for the fight with Gi-Gi. Chas and Dwayne kept coming to me and telling me that Gi-Gi was saying that as soon as he got the opportunity, he was going to kill me. I waited until late the next evening to seek my revenge. I was old enough now, or so I thought. After Nate left the house, I took one of his revolvers from the wardrobe in the basement. It was a blue steel Smith and Wesson .38. I loaded it and called Chas. "I gonna do Gi-Gi tonight, can you go with me?" "Yeah, I'll go with you. I told you you should have done his punk ass that same day. You can't let a motherfucker get away with that kind of shit."

I asked my mother if I could borrow her beige 1978 Impala. She agreed and told me to be careful. I drove to the west side and picked up Chas, Tony, Sammey, and Moe. We drove down to the

200 block of West Carey Street. I spotted Gi-Gi and pulled over to the curb. Gi-Gi and two of his friends walked up to the car. Gi-Gi stuck his head in. "What's up. You want to do it over again?" I had the revolver between my legs. I had my hand wrapped tightly around the handle with my index finger gently on the trigger. All I had to do was raise it and fire and Gi-Gi would be another statistic. So would I. I left the car in drive so that I could immediately pull off after the fatal shots.

Tony was in the back seat on the passenger side of the car, with a stainless steel .45 automatic pistol between his legs. He would wait for me to fire first, then he would riddle Gi-Gi's falling body with more bullets. Never leave the job half done. Never allow the enemy to be able to come back and seek revenge. *Wage total and absolute war.* I could feel the beads of sweat forming on my forehead and hands. My soul began to stir. Blood rushed down the walls of the chamber which held my soul. Mom's contorted face moved up from my inner chamber into my eyes. I could see Nate, Quincy, and Frank. I could see Sugar and Warren. Gi-Gi became unimportant background scenery. He was the insignificant tree at the rear of the stage in a child's elementary school play. He faded into some other dimension. His voice drifted away into some deep isolated space. His words were senseless garble. "Why don't you get out of the car? Fuck your boys. This is between you and me." Chas spoke up. "Do him. Do the son of a bitch now, and let's get out of here."

Gi-Gi realized what was going on. He began to tremble. He slowly stepped back from the car. No more words came from his mouth. I stared into his eyes. They watered. "Fuck it, let's go." Chas yelled out, "Do the son of a bitch or he gonna do you as soon as he get the chance. You know the rules, Tye." I turned away from Gi-Gi and pressed down on the accelerator. Mom's Impala jerked up Saratoga Street toward Chas's house. I could barely hear Chas. "What the fuck you do that for? What the fuck you let that sissy nigger live for?" I was letting myself live. Gi-Gi would have killed me with his death.

When Nate found out what had occurred, he was livid. He told Chas that he should have never responded to my call or, at the very least, he should have gotten in touch with him. "If Tye wanted the motherfucker dead, I would have killed the fucker for him. I don't want him caught up in this nonsense. I'm the assassin in this family. We only need one. Tye's heart ain't in this shit, anyway. He ain't the killin' type." Chas agreed. Nate approached me in the basement. "Why you want to get yourself in all kinds of trouble? Are you trying to kill Mom? She's got so much hope for you and Warren. She says God promised her that he was gonna see that you two stay straight. Now you want to go and break God's promise to her. Don't you do that shit no more, you understand?" I responded, "Nate, I felt like I had to get revenge. And really he didn't do anything to me. Just being stupid, I guess. I don't think I could have shot him anyway." Nate stared at me. "Yeah, Tye, but Chas and Tony could have. And you would have been in trouble with them. It ain't always what *you* do." I ran my hand slowly over my face. "Yeah, you're right, brother. I guess God kept his promise to Mom tonight."

I believed that Nate saw in me all that he should have been or could have become. He had the street knowledge, I had the book knowledge. He was somehow trying to get inside me. Trying to merge the street knowledge with the book knowledge. He was trying to put the two together to create something or someone that would keep other children living in the ghetto from abandoning their hopes, goals, and dreams, as he had abandoned his. He was trying to create a person that could stand up and fight off all the evils that he believed had been purposely put in place to destroy Black people. He was trying to create a person that could not be corrupted by all the toys and trinkets and money that would be put before him. He was trying to create a Malcolm X and a Martin Luther King all in one. He was trying to merge Marcus Garvey and W.E.B. DuBois. He was trying to do this with his blood— with me.

I knew that I would have to confront Nate concerning any decision I made to join the FBI. He would want me to explain my reasons for making such a backwards, contradictory move. He would want to know why I was ignoring all of his hard-earned advice, why I was stepping away from the path that he had so painfully laid for me. He had been the scout. He went out front first and saw what was ahead and then came back to warn me of the impending dangers. Not the dangers for me alone, but the dangers that all Black children would face. The traps and hurdles that we would have to negotiate. It was my responsibility to let the children of Baltimore know about the dangerous road ahead. I was to let them know about the enemy who was hidden in the brush, ready to pounce upon them like a beast seeking prey.

I hoped that Nate would give me an opportunity to explain my intended move. I hoped that he would understand that I was not running away. I was going to learn and experience more so that I would have more to tell the youth of Baltimore when I returned. Nate had to understand that. *He just had to.* I needed James to load my mental gun, to provide me with the ammunition to counter Nate's anticipated verbal attack. I needed James to help me prepare my explanation, to make it stronger. I needed him to give me more convincing reasons, more arguments in preparation for my imminent conversation with Nate. I needed something that would help me make Frank, Quincy, and Warren understand. I needed something that would make Sugar, Dwayne, and Talmadge understand. I needed reasons and explanations so that Congressman Mitchell would understand. I needed to justify a move to the FBI, to myself.

I took another sip of coffee and leaned back in my chair. I was preparing another line of questioning for James. He waited eagerly for the proper time to begin his rebuttal and inquisition. I spoke up. "Why would the FBI hire me? You and I both know that J. Edgar Hoover was a no good, redneck, son of a bitch. He hated Black folk and although he is dead and hopefully in hell, the FBI still belongs to him. Half of the motherfuckers that are still there believe everything he said and stood for. These Hoover surrogates are still determined to keep brothers out. That's why there are ten thousand agents and only four hundred of them are Black. So what makes you think they're just going to accept this intransigent Black man into their exclusive white man's club?"

James was poised and ready. Like a soldier hidden in the jungles of Viet Nam, he eased from his state of restraint into a position to verbally fire back. "They'll let you in for the same reasons they let me in. You and I are qualified! It's not just that we are intelligent enough to pass those bullshit tests that are supposed to keep us out. You see, we have been accepted into the 'all right niggers club' which is in the vestibule of this exclusive white man's club. We have been in police work for at least three years and we haven't caused any trouble. We haven't protested against the racist promotion policies. We haven't said anything about those racist jokes that they tell all the time. In fact, we've laughed at those jokes. It didn't matter whether their jokes involved Jews or Polish people or Chinese or whomever, we both knew that whenever they could—as soon as we weren't around— they would substitute the word *nigger*.

"And we stood right there and laughed with those redneck bastards. So they took that to mean that we were with them. They took our acquiescence to their vulgar jokes to mean that we understood our inferior positions and were willing to accept them. We knew what they thought of us. *But* we played the game. We went along with the team. So, when the FBI comes asking about us in their background investigation, they're going to tell them that we were team players. We wore the seal of approval. We will make good 'house niggers.' They'll give you Operation Drug-Out and the little protest remarks you make every now and then. They'll figure that was, or is, just an aberration. That's just a little emotional steam you have to let off every now and then. You know, just like an iron: you let the steam out and then you complete the task of ironing your clothes—no harm done. You can and will be brought around. You can be controlled."

James was making me uncomfortable. I was glad that Nate wasn't here to hear this. James continued, "To them, we are just two Uncle Tom-ass negroes trying to get accepted into the white man's world. They know that you and I don't belong to the Black Troopers Association, or they will know. And they like that. They really believe that we fall for that you're-lucky-to-be-an-American bullshit. They think that, like so many other Blacks, we don't know our history. They don't know that we know that our ancestors did the physical labor to build this fuckin' country and that in reality they're more lucky than us to be here! They don't know that we know that we were brought over here chained up to each other, four hundred or more at a time. And that those of us who got sick from rolling over in our own urine and defecation were thrown overboard to the sharks! They don't know that we know that our beautiful Black sisters were taken for the use and abuse of the crew, that they were forced into acts of sodomy and oral sex. Yeah, we're real fuckin' lucky. They think that we still believe that we were immigrants like the Irish."

I began to perspire. James was confusing me. Earlier, he had said that the state police knew that they couldn't control me in the manner that they wanted. Now he was telling me that although they wouldn't allow me to advance, I had at least played the game well enough to be admitted into a part of "the club." It was painful to hear that I had been playing the role of an Uncle Tom. I knew that there were a few Black professionals out there who would have been happy about their acceptance into this club. It was more important for me to be accepted by my own people. Just as the Jews felt that they were Jewish first and American second! Just as the Italians believed that they were Italians first and Americans second!

I knew that being a man of color meant that I had to be careful of wanting to be with or be accepted by my people. The Japanese were thrown in concentration camps right here in America ostensibly for not denouncing their people during World War II. If ethnicity or color was not the reason, why were the Germans and Italians not placed in concentration camps?

I would not denounce my color or kinship to be accepted by anyone. I would accept the consequences of being Black and proud. Maybe I hadn't accepted my color. Maybe I was fighting it like the so-called conservative negroes. Maybe I was trying to live two lives. Trying to stay Black and be white.

I thought of the times when I had stood as a Maryland State Trooper and listened to racist jokes from my fellow white troopers. Suddenly, I felt like a traitor. James was right. I hated him for bringing all of this to my attention. I sat there and began to hate the Maryland State Police. They had been a part of the problem. A part of my problem. It was with them that I had started to sell my soul. I knew what James had said was absolutely true. I had acted as if I enjoyed those degrading jokes, while visions of my enslaved ancestors were manifested in my head. I had since stopped participating in these degrading sessions. But that did not ease the pain.

I felt as if I had betrayed my whole family. I could see Nate's eyes burning into the walls of my soul. I felt the presence of Quincy, Frank, and Warren standing around me, closing in on me, pushing against me and mumbling "Sellout. Sellout." They all had solemn faces as they stared down at me and tormented me with the brutal and painful truth.

I thought further back to my days in the Maryland State Police Academy. I remembered Eric May. He was one of my classmates. He was much more mature than I and had already been a police officer with the Baltimore City Police Department prior to joining state police. He was extremely intelligent and always quiet unless called upon to respond to a particular question. He very seldom smiled.

Eric grabbed me out of the corridor one day and forcefully pushed me into an empty room. He slammed the door behind us. Eric moved real close to my face. "Why are you playing the role of the dumb nigger? Why are you trying to entertain 'Mr. Charley,' boy? You're not a clown. This isn't a circus. A lot of Black people have worked real hard and died young in order to keep us from having to shuffle about and smile in the white man's face. You don't have to dance around anymore. You're not a dog, so you don't need to do pleasing tricks in order to get a dog biscuit thrown your way. Stand upright and be a man. Stop slumping your shoulders. Be a man."

I told Eric about my conversation with Corporal Zachary. Eric said that I had misunderstood Zachary. Zachary had not intended for me to become a clown. Eric moved even closer and said, "There ain't but a few of us here and before this class is over with, they'll be even fewer of us. You'll probably be one of the ones left here when it's all over. Don't make a fool out of those who have worked hard so you could be here. Don't embarrass us."

I pulled myself out of my thoughts and rubbed my eyes. James was waiting for some sign that I had had enough of the state police and was now willing to try something else. My mind was caught in between a decision to join the FBI and the comments that James had made about our playing the game. James was right. Why hadn't I listened to Eric? Why didn't I listen to Quincy, Nate, and Frank that day in the basement? James was telling me that I had not kept my promise to my brothers. He was saying that I had broken that promise in order to be accepted by the state police. Now he was saying that although the state police had accepted me, they never respected me.

They didn't respect me because I was not willing to stand up and point out their wrongs. They stood back and watched me shuffle about. The selection process had worked well. James was offering me a way to save face and move on. He was telling me that there were broken promises lying all around me and that I needed to step away from them and begin to build anew. For some reason, James saw the FBI as my savior. That part puzzled me.

James got up from the table and walked down the hallway which led to his bedroom. I continued to sip my coffee. I thought of the changes I had gone through and wondered if I was forgetting about those who needed me the most. I didn't want to be another one of those middle-class 'negroes' who made it and then condemned every other Black for not following their crooked path. I believed that I had worked hard not to change, against a system whose intent was to transform me. Now I was finding out that I had done nothing at all, or, at the very least, had not done enough.

Like so many others I had been sucked up into that vacuum of delusions. I, too, was thinking that I was no longer seen as a nigger by those who had come up with that term in the first place. I should have known better. Being a police officer was not supposed to send my conscious mind into a state of stupor. In fact, I was supposed to enlighten and make things better for those with whom I came in contact. I had tried. I thought that Operation Drug-Out was proof of my efforts. Now James had me searching my inner self and questioning my progress.

I had not drunk coffee before becoming a cop. Now I was drinking coffee. No change seemed insignificant anymore.

Everything I did seemed to indicate a change for the worse. I questioned where I lived and why I lived there. I questioned the motive behind the car that I bought, the clothing I wore, the friends I had made. I thought of Chas, Craig, Bay-Bay, and Michael. Where were they all? I needed to see them. To talk with them. I thought of the back porch and the rain. I thought of Angel. I thought of Corporal Zachary and Eric May. I thought of Sergeant Stoney.

James returned to the table and placed an FBI preliminary application-for-employment form before me. He told me to fill it out. I never looked up. I had more questions for James. I wasn't ready to fill it out yet. I began my vacillating line of questioning again. "Do you think all white folks in the state police are racist?" James sat down and took a deep breath. "No, I don't think they all hate us. It's difficult to say, with any certainty, that anyone or any one group is for or against someone or some group. There are those who would say that all white folk are against all Black folk, if not consciously then sub-consciously. And, I'll tell you what, if you look back at history, and I'm talking recent history, you would almost have to say that they have a legitimate point. But I don't believe that is true.

"It's those few ignorant loud-mouthed whites that get the other whites all riled up and thinking Black folk are just heathens. Maybe it ain't even them. Maybe somebody else is behind the scenes, trying to make sure the races stay divided. Trying to keep us at each other's throats for their own purposes. A unified group of human beings is likely to ask a lot of questions about how this world is run. They're likely to question world hunger and a whole lot of other things that will get you labeled as a liberal. But with us divided and so busy fighting each other, we don't have time to find the divider."

I settled back to hear what James had to say. He seemed to be taking the discussion deeper despite the fact that he had laid the application before me as an indication that his talking was done. I thought he would cut off any further questions, but he continued, "If you just take a ride through the streets of Baltimore, it appears that not one white person gives a fuck about one Black person. I don't mean that they should do everything for us, but the reality of the matter is that they have all the power and all the money. Not only are they not doing things for us, they seem to be working real hard to do everything against us. It is as if they want us to know that they are our natural adversaries. And that we must cry 'Uncle' or be an Uncle Tom to get anything from them."

James was speaking as if he were angry. He was jumping backwards and forwards, moving his thoughts from one side to the other, trying to analyze as he spoke. It was as if he were remembering some painful event. Most Black people in America had experienced a painful event involving white people. That event was always lurking somewhere in the soul, waiting to come forward on the right cue. The right code word. Most Blacks tried to put those events to rest. They tried to forget about what had been done to them or their love ones. But sooner or later they were forced to bring it back to the surface. No matter how many good white people they met, sooner or later they were forced to deal with the bad ones. And when that happened, all those stored-away events came back. James was remembering.

He continued, "And it ain't just Baltimore. Every large city in America seems to be the same. Or, for that matter, every city and every rural area in this fuckin' world. But we shouldn't be surprised by this lack of effort on the part of white folk. We just need to recognize it like the Jews have. The Jews realize that wherever they go and whatever they do, they must stick together. It doesn't matter if they all live within the same country. They all share something deep inside that holds them together. We, as African Americans, also have a common bond deep inside, *but* we fail to grab on to it. We are too busy being traitors and backstabbers. The Jews don't necessarily have to hate you to destroy you. But they will destroy you if they see you as a threat to them. And ain't a fuckin' thing wrong with that philosophy. In fact, we need to adopt the same philosophy. That's what Marcus Garvey tried to tell us. He was saying that we, as a race, could deal with anyone as long as they had no bad intentions toward us. Once we find that someone or some group has bad intentions toward us, then we need to segregate and unite from within to deal with those who have to be dealt with. As the Honorable Elijah Muhammad and Malcolm X had said, this is not racial hatred—it's common sense. In fact, it's the only thing to do."

James wiped sweat from his brow and sighed. At first, it had seemed as if he were enjoying our conversation. As if he enjoyed revealing to a friend his true feelings without the fear of being labeled. But now it seemed so painful. I had had many prior conversations with James. He rarely became this emotional. That was one of the qualities that both Dwayne and James possessed. They could discuss issues and provide me with knowledge without becoming outwardly angry. That's why I hated that James had left the teaching profession. His knowledge and his method of providing it to others were so effective. He was saying some of the same things that Dwayne had said to me. That Frank, Quincy, and Nate had said to me. That Warren had said to me. But I never tired of hearing them.

I was about to interrupt so that James could free himself from the painful thoughts that engulfed him, when he began to speak again. "You know, they truly believe that it doesn't make sense for them to help us or to just give us a chance. They feel like they gave the Japanese a chance and that they will be regretting it forevermore. We just have to take control of our communities and do for ourselves. We have to be everywhere and learn everything so that we can prepare to govern ourselves. And when we build our own, we're gonna need cops. Just think of it, I'll be chief and you can be my assistant."

James laughed heartily and leaned back in his chair. He stared into the ceiling as if he were trying to recapture some lost thoughts. "But it ain't all white folk, brother. It just so happens that the white folks who are determined to fuck us are the ones who are in power. Maybe power makes them fear us. Maybe it's the fear of losing power to us or to anyone. I'm not one who has a lot of faith in the big conspiracy theory. I've lived fairly well all of my life. Well, at least as well as a Black man can expect to live in America. But I know that there's something bigger than mere lack of will that's holding the Black man back. I also know that there's a God who ain't gonna let it always be this way. I ain't got it all figured out yet. I don't think anyone has."

The more I thought about it and listened to James, the more I realized that he didn't think that the FBI would be without racism. He was too intelligent for that. He knew that the FBI was a part of America. He didn't figure that all white folk who worked for the Department of Justice would actually be seeking justice for everyone regardless of skin color. That was too unrealistic, and there was no doubt that James was a realist. He knew that for now we had to continue to live and work in a racist society, while at the same time try to figure out a way to get from under the racist yoke that weighed so heavily upon us. Staying away from the FBI would not help our cause. Running scared from racism would not make it go away. The FBI needed a brother like James. James was saying that they needed a brother like me, too.

I took a good look at the application for the first time and removed a pen from my shirt pocket. I laughed to myself, as it seemed that I believed that the mere filling out of the form would give me the job. I was that sure of myself. I knew that I was intelligent enough, and James had assured me that I knew how to play the game. In spite of our living conditions, Mom had instilled a sense of confidence in us: "You all can accomplish anything with hard work and faith in yourself and God. You must believe in yourselves. You must believe in God."

Frank had also kept us confident of our abilities. He had told us that being Black in America was like being in a prize fight that never ended. We had to keep ducking and dodging the punches, and we had to throw a few punches back every once in a while. We could never quit and we always had to be looking out for that surprise blow that was intended to knock us out quickly. We had to keep our eyes on the prize.

Frank said we would have good rounds and bad rounds. If we stayed in the fight to the bitter end, we would win. He said that when it was time for us to climb through the ropes and step down from the ring, we had to go right to the gym and start training the next generation of fighters. Frank said that sooner or later our opponent would get the message that we were never going to give up. He said that whenever I decided to do something, I had to have confidence in myself. I had to know that I could win the fight.

Frank would often tell me that under fair circumstances, I had the ability to be president of the United States of America. He then was quick to remind me that there would never be any fair circumstances in America. He didn't need to tell me that. I was no dreamer. And I did not have a great deal of faith in some of the racist "leaders" of America. Besides, I had no ambition to be president and didn't view it as a job that required much intelligence. I figured that the strongest quality the president of the United States needed was the ability to be ruthless.

The president had to be a tyrant, constantly trying to garner more power; trying to expand and build a larger empire; trying to control people. He needed to be good at lying so that he could convince others that he genuinely cared for them. The President had to mimic Machiavelli's prince. He had to master the theory of self-preservation and convince everyone that all his actions were for the good of the many. He had to be able to start wars and destroy entire groups of people under the pretense of this theory.

A president of the United States of America had utilized this theory to destroy two entire cities full of people of color during World War II. Adolf Hitler had utilized this theory to justify his policy on Jews. Israel was now using this theory to bomb and kill Arabs at will. Britain was using this theory in Northern Ireland. The Soviet Union, North Korea, and many other Communist-block nations were using this theory to justify their repressive policies. The pope had utilized this theory of self-preservation *in the name of God*, in the religious wars throughout history, and in the justification of slavery. No, I didn't care to be president. At least, not the kind of president that I had read about in my world and United States history books.

James came into focus again. He must have noticed that I was deep in thought. He had done his job thus far. He had me, pen in hand, leaning over the application. He was determined not to lose me. In a low, calm voice, he began to speak again. "Listen, man, you really don't want to stay with the state police. Remember that riot training they put us through? Remember how we had to drive that baton into the gut of the crowd and, if necessary, into the gut of the person we would be trying to push back?"

I slowly nodded my head in agreement, while trying to anticipate where James was going with his argument. He continued, "What are you going to do when they send you down into Baltimore City to control the brothers? What are you going to do when you have to jab that baton into the gut of Craig, Chas, Dwayne or any of your other friends? What are you going to do when they send you into a prison to beat some brothers for protesting their being treated like slaves? And you and I both know who they gonna send into the city or to the jail. Who do you think they are going to send to provide security when there is some massive Klan rally in Frederick or Baltimore? Remember who they sent to that damned Ku Klux Klan rally? Remember the sick feeling you got standing up on that fuckin' hill? Protecting the Klan!"

James had me remembering a time that I wanted to forget. He had me thinking about things that I had prayed to God would never come about. "You and I both know that sooner or later the brothers are going to get fed up with the way they're being treated. Then they're going to turn all those guns that they've been using to kill each other with on the men who are oppressing them. Even Thomas Jefferson suggested that this might be necessary at some point. They're gonna head to the suburbs and all hell is going to break loose. But more important than you and I knowing this is the fact that the motherfuckers in power know this, too. They know that a man can only take so much abuse. They know what drove Nat Turner to his rage and they know that once he reached his breaking point, no one identified as the enemy was safe.

"In fact, at times, I think they are trying to push the brothers to this point. They continuously do small things to provoke a reaction from the Black community. For example, the police in some American cities will beat some brother close to death. They won't kill him because they want him to be well enough to relay the details of the beating to the rest of Black America.

"There will be some miscarriage of 'justice' in some court in America where the judge or jury refuses to convict a white person for the obvious violation of some Black person's rights. Another incident to get the Black man's blood boiling. To get him to scream and riot and protest. All these separate, but well-planned, incidents are thrown into a mixing bowl and stirred. Then, Black people react to their persecution with justified violence. White folks respond to Black folks' anger by buying weapons and preparing to shoot any walking man of color. More ingredients thrown into the mixing bowl.

"The recipe is being completed as planned. Everything is put in, in exact and specific measurements. Not too much of anything. A well-planned pinch here and another equally well-analyzed pinch there. Then the results of the recipe are put into the oven to bake. Usually in the heat of the summer. As this yeast-ridden cake rises and explodes, the cook—the government—comes to the rescue, urged on by those Blacks and whites who can't understand the reaction and violence of the Black 'heathens.' Bring in the National Guard. Initiate the McCarran Act. Concentration camps for Black people. The icing on the cake."

James smiled solemnly. "That's why the state police have those small compact urban tanks behind the Waterloo barracks. You see, they're going to be ready to deal with the 'niggas' next time. Oh, and they know there's going to be a next time because the wheels are in motion. The oven is being preheated, readied for the volatile cake. They're gonna be ready to use helicopters and gas and whatever it takes to exterminate us like they did the so-called Indians. Or they gonna put us in concentration camps like they did the Japanese. Far-fetched? Ask the Japanese. Far-fetched? Ask the Native Americans. Far-fetched? Ask the Jews. Never forget the McCarran Act."

I thought about what James was saying. I remembered Dr. Raymond Ellis explaining the McCarran Act to our Introduction to Criminal Justice class at Coppin State College. Dr. Ellis stated that the McCarran Act was initially the Mundt-Nixon Bill. The bill had been sponsored by Senators Karl Mundt of South Dakota, Joseph McCarthy of Wisconsin, James Eastland of Mississippi, and Pat McCarran of Nevada. Congressmen Richard M. Nixon of California, Francis Walter of Pennsylvania, and Harold Velde of Illinois had also sponsored the bill. The bill was passed in 1950 and required the override of President Truman's veto. Title II of the bill authorized the President of the United States to declare an "internal security emergency" in such events as declarations of war or "insurrection" at home which is influenced by a "foreign enemy." According to Samuel F. Yette in his award-winning book, *The Choice*, "Included in such insurrections would be civil rights disturbances, peace demonstrations, or any other disruption which the President alone might interpret as a qualifying emergency."

Samuel Yette further explains that "under such an emergency, the President may implement the provisions of Title II, which would authorize the Attorney General of the United States, without charges or warrants, to arrest and detain in such places of detention as may be provided by him...all persons as to whom there is a reasonable ground to believe that such person 'probably' will engage in or 'probably' will conspire with others to engage in acts of espionage and sabotage." Yette states that "although President Lyndon B. Johnson did not invoke Title II during the 1960's, virtually all such uprisings as those in Los Angeles, Newark, Detroit, and scores of other cities could have been construed as qualifying emergencies."

James interrupted my thoughts. He probably had been talking all along. I could only hear Dr. Ellis. James continued, "If you stay here, brother, you're gonna be a part of that machine when it rolls. You know that some brothers will enjoy being part of that machine. I've seen a picture in the *Washington Post* of a Black cop holding down a brother with a baton for protesting against a Klan rally. Can you believe that shit? Oh yeah, there are some full-blown house niggers out there. But you ain't one of them. You've got to think beyond today. You have to ask yourself what would you do if called upon?"

I faded back into my thoughts. James knew that he was touching on a familiar issue. We had had discussions on the subject before. We both had received the basic riot training at the Maryland State Police Academy. We both had been assigned to the riot-control team at the Frederick barracks. We both had noticed the small compact tanks behind some of the barracks. We noticed how some of the training was geared toward an urban setting. We had participated in some of those training exercises. We knew what it would all come down to one day.

We had taken the tours through the prisons so that we would know the layout in the event of insurrection. While walking through the courtyard at one prison, James pointed up to the gun tower and said, "That's where the power is. The man who stands there and looks over all of us is in control. He could kill you or me or any of us at any second. Big brother with a big gun. That's where Black people have got to get to—in the gun tower."

The ring of the phone brought me back from the journey down memory lane. "Every incident must be stored for retrieval at a later date. Every event in your life is a learning experience. Every place you travel is a classroom. You must pay attention. You must be alert." That's what Dr. Raymond Ellis had told our class. He was right.

I looked down at the application as James got up to answer the phone. Somehow I had already completed it. I noticed James smiling. I heard him talking to Doris. He called me to the phone. I smiled as I thought of going home to breakfast with my family. Doris' words wiped my smile away and chilled my soul. "Craig is dead."

20

Down And Out

Am I my brother's keeper?

—Genesis, IV, 9

We must all learn to live together as Brothers. Or we will all perish together as fools.

—*Martin Luther King Jr.*

Nate crouched down low and squeezed into the tight corner. He held the .45 semi-automatic pistol steady. His long bronze index finger rested tenuously on the trigger. Like a trained police officer, he brought the gun up to eye level and slowly, carefully scanned the room. The gun moved in concert with his dark brown eyes. The wall seemed to press against his back and ribs, limiting his movement. He felt trapped, cornered like some wild beast. His gun gave him a fighting chance against whoever had come for him.

Nate took a deep breath and continued his painstaking, constricted movements. He had to quickly identify where the shots had come from and for whom they were intended. Tiny bubbles of sweat rolled down his face. He stopped the slow scanning motion and steadied his hands. He closed his index finger tighter around the trigger. He pushed backwards to give himself more leverage should he have to fire. He realized that his back was not on a wall but up against a cigarette machine. The metal selection knobs irritated him, but he dared not move forward. He had to be less of a target than his would-be assassins.

Nate blocked out the loud music that continued to emanate from the jukebox in the Club 2300 Bar and Lounge. The jukebox had ignored the popping sound of gunfire and continued with its task. In many instances the people who lived near Club 2300 had to do the same thing. They had to keep going. They had to keep living and working and caring for their families. The children had to keep playing. The city was slowly becoming a war zone, where the firing of artillery was a seemingly normal sound.

Nate squinted his eyes and tried to see through the dense blue haze of cigarette smoke that seemed to dance with the music upward toward the high ceiling. He looked for the bartender and the other people who, moments earlier, had been seated on the stools, cursing, smoking cigarettes, drinking alcohol, and listening to the cool sounds of Motown. The gunshots had silenced the laughter and replaced the cool sounds with the heat of hot lead. The popping sound had caused cigarettes and drinks to become separated from their owners, as all lay glued to the dusty floor.

Nate didn't know where everyone had gone. He only understood the reason for their disappearance. Ducking, running, and disappearing were the only right things to do when shots were fired. The sounds of gunfire in the streets of the ghetto were not unlike the air raid sirens during World War II. Everyone had to get down or get out. No one could afford to sit and try to figure out the bullets' final destination or for whom they were intended. That really didn't matter. Parents had trained their children to get down low and to lie flat; to melt into the floor or the concrete; to stay prone until the popping sounds had ceased and the screaming began.

Nate had been through it many times before. He had been in the "valley of death." He and every other ghetto child. Nate had conditioned himself to believe that every gun in the world was aimed at him and that he had to duck whenever one was fired. He had to be prepared to identify the source of the violence and fire back. He had adopted the age-old self-preservation rule of "shoot first and ask questions later." This rule kept him alive. And he told Warren and me to adopt the same philosophy. He said that it would keep us alive. "Identify your enemies; identify their methods; understand their thoughts, motions, and strategies; and be prepared to counter their attack. Be prepared to retaliate. Be prepared to fire back with maximum force."

Nate knew that one day he would not be able to duck the bullet that came his way. One day the bullet would find its mark.

But until that day came, he would keep ducking and firing back. He would not be easy prey for anyone. When it was his time to die, he would go out fighting. And that was how he wanted us to go out. He didn't want us to be caught sleeping. He wanted Warren and me to look out for that gun that would someday be aimed at us. He said that we were in more danger than he because we were so unsuspecting, or, at least, I was. Nate believed that Warren was now awake and alert. He thought that I was still too trusting. I still had too much faith in others. Maybe he was right.

"We can't be trusting anymore of anyone. We have always had to look out for the enemy. And some of the enemy have always looked just like us. There are a lot of traitors in our race. But now we even got to be more careful. After those riots during the sixties, white folks saw we were too active. Too strong. Too goal-oriented. Too revolutionary. So they had to tranquilize us a little by increasing the flow of drugs and alcohol into our communities. They had to put us in slow motion. Cocaine makes you paranoid.

"With cocaine in our community, we became less trustful of each other. We see everyone in our community as the enemy. And you kill the enemy that is closest to you. The cocaine-induced paranoia makes it feel as if the world is closing in on us. So we strike out. Swinging wildly at whatever or whoever is around us. Ain't no more brotherhood. You can't be brothers with your enemy, no matter what color he is. You've got to get him before he gets you. So we kill each other off because we are in close proximity to each other. We're in close quarters with the 'new' enemy that came into being after the sixties upheavals. Everyone in the 'hood becomes a potential victim. Drugs, forced into our community, put husband against wife, and brother against brother and sister. No more sacred ties. No limits on who you fight or kill to feed your powerful addiction.

"You see, my brothers, someone figured out the worst war mankind can fight is a civil war. A civil war is always the bloodiest of all wars. Someone read the history of the American Civil War and saw how brother was willing to kill brother and father willing to kill son. After those sixties riots, someone or some group decided to initiate a civil war in the Black community. There is nothing more destructive than a civil war. Drugs and alcohol helped this civil war get started. Drugs and alcohol and bullshit schools with teachers full of shit are keeping this civil war going. Drugs and alcohol are keeping brothers in a constant daze, on a constant high. Too high to fight back against the real root of their problems. Too dazed to identify the true enemy. Too high to study history. Now everyone in urban America is a potential victim. Everyone must be prepared to fight back against their drug-induced, alcohol-influenced, brainwashed enemy. You, my brothers, must be ready."

Nate said that the only reason he wasn't dead yet was because those who wanted to kill him feared the revenge that would be brought upon them by Quincy or Frank, and now, even Warren. Nate believed that if your enemies or your so-called friends believed that you would strike back, they would be hesitant to take action against you. "That's what keep countries from going to war. It ain't 'cause they civil. They respect the power of their enemy. They know that the enemy is willing and capable of engaging in a bitter battle until the end. Until ain't nobody left standing. And if there is someone left standing, they don't have any fight left in them." Nate vowed to someday kill Chas for what he had done to him.

"Chas have to pay. Allowing a man to do harm to you and then turning your back and walking away is a sure sign of weakness. This kind of show of weakness will be paid for over and over again. Others who identify such a weakness in a man will take advantage of it. This is the kind of weakness that the white man has identified in the Black man. They are sure that no matter what they do to us, we will eventually forgive and forget. Unfortunately, the white man has all too often been right."

Nate was adamant that Chas's actions could not go unpunished. Friendships were built upon respect. No one could respect a man who would not defend himself and those close to him. No one could respect a man that did not take a stand. No one could respect a coward.

Nate's warnings reminded me of a novel I once read by an author whose name I cannot remember. The name of the novel was *With A Vengeance*. It was the story of a man whose daughter was tied to a tree and burned to death by a group of her friends. The man waited patiently until all of the friends had grown up and had children of their own. Then he stalked their children, finding them, tying them to a tree and burning them one by one. It had taken years of patience in order for him to extract his revenge. But he could not, and would not, allow the wrongful actions of the so-called friends of his daughter to go unpunished. The fear of revenge had kept Nate alive. But now someone was coming for him. Someone had forced him into a crouched position in this corner awaiting the burning sensation of twisted hot lead. Someone no longer feared Nate's vengeance.

As the smoke began to clear, Nate could see people starting to unglue themselves from the floor. The bartender reappeared and picked up the phone to call the police. Nate slowly stood up and lowered his gun. He looked around for Gas, Stanley, and Timmy. They all had come to the bar together, and he wanted to make sure none of them had been hit. Gas moved from behind the bar, with gun in hand. He looked toward Nate and gave a smile of relief. He thought for sure that Chas had come back to finish Nate. Gas was glad that wasn't the case. He liked both Chas and Nate. He didn't know how he would react if he had observed Chas standing over Nate pumping bullets into him. He didn't know, under those circumstances, if he could shoot Chas. He was glad that on this day he was not forced to make that dreaded decision.

Someone unplugged the jukebox, bringing an abrupt stop to the mellow sounds of the Isley Brothers' song "Let Me Down Easy." Nate and Gas moved toward the front door. A loud scream stopped them in their tracks. They both reached into their waistbands. The screaming continued, indicating that the immediate danger had passed. Shootings were done quickly. Danger usually came and left, all in a matter of seconds. Someone was screaming at the results of the gunfire. Nate pushed through the crowd and opened the door. A cold breeze blew past him. He looked down toward the pavement and realized that he had stepped into a puddle of dark red blood.

Timmy was lying flat on his back on the cold concrete. His eyes were closed and his thin brown eye lids seemed peacefully relaxed. Blood bubbled and trickled down from his mouth. A thin streak of blood rolled around his neck. An older woman with gray hair and deep worry lines etched across her forehead knelt down next to him and tried to stem the blood which flowed from his stomach. Timmy never moved. Gas pushed his way through the crowd. He looked down at Timmy and then scanned the crowd. He turned to Nate. "Who did this? Damn, why did they do this to Timmy?"

Nate continued to look down at Timmy's lifeless body. He stepped back, out of the puddle of blood. He slowly shook his head. "It doesn't matter. Timmy's dead. Craig's dead. Everybody around us is dying. All our fuckin' friends are going to the 2300 Club in hell. This shit ain't right. It ain't worth it. Soon it's gonna be you and me and a whole lot of other motherfuckers around here. Ain't no use in us crying over Timmy. Ain't no use of us worrying about death. This is what it's all about. This is our life." Nate paused and pointed down toward Timmy. "That's our destination, and nobody gives a fuck."

The all too familiar sounds of sirens could be heard cutting through the cold wind. A woman ran from her house, crying and carrying a blanket. She dropped to her knees next to Timmy. "Keep him warm. Keep my little baby boy warm." She hugged Timmy and pulled him close to her. His blood covered the blanket. She kissed him tenderly. Her voice trembled. "I know it hurts, baby, but it's gonna be all right. It ain't gonna hurt much longer."

Nate looked up from his dying friend and focused his eyes on Chas, who was standing across from him. Chas's eyes seemed to sit deep within their sockets. He seemed to be aging quickly, losing skin, receding to nothing but the skeleton which held him together. The battlefield of the ghetto was taking its toll on him. Watching for Nate, waiting for a bullet to pierce his heart and end his existence was getting to Chas. It was as if death was creeping over his body—desiring to engulf him, yet enjoying the slow torturous process. How much death could he take?

Chas glanced across at Nate and shook his head. He spoke in a low trembling voice. "It wasn't me, Nate. I didn't have anything to do with this one. Timmy never did nothing to me. It's time for this killing shit to end. It's time for us to get back on track. You ain't the enemy, Nate. I ain't the enemy, either." Nate didn't respond. He turned and touched Gas on the shoulder. They walked through the morbid crowd as police cars and an ambulance arrived.

Nate and Gas walked slowly down Baltimore Street past the steps of the Blue Gardenia Lounge. They left blood-stained shoe prints on the concrete. The prints seemed to move with them. It was as if Timmy was walking with them. As if he was walking behind them, trying to tap them on their shoulders. Trying to warn them of their future. Warning them to change, to end the senseless civil war, and to get back to the real fight. It was as if Timmy's spirit was now moving freely down the streets of Baltimore City with his soulless friends. His friends whose souls were being destroyed by an existence they were forced to live. Timmy was saying, "Don't believe them. It doesn't have to be this way. It doesn't have to end this way."

Gas stopped and looked back as if he heard Timmy's foot steps. He thought he could hear Timmy's voice. "Once we start killing each other, it's all over." He thought he heard Timmy preaching about the Black man and the white man and the world. He thought he heard Timmy say nobody cared about Black folk. He thought he saw Timmy throw down his beer bottle. He saw the bottle break into a thousand pieces. The pieces were covered with blood, which flowed over the sidewalks of Baltimore and rolled into the gutters. Seeping deeper into the city. Heading for other corners, other homes, and other lives.

Tears escaped from Gas's eyes. He thought of the men who had met so often on the steps of the Blue Gardenia. Sheldon was in jail for robbery. Tank had been shot and killed by Stanley during one of their drunken stupors. Now Timmy lay dead on the cold concrete only a few feet away from the Blue Gardenia Lounge. The steps of the Blue Gardenia would never be the same. Or maybe they awaited a new group of shirtless scholars.

No one would remember the speeches that Timmy gave, except for the brothers who had been there to hear them. There would be no movies about Timmy's life. There would be no white man declaring a holiday for this strong but confused teacher. There would be no twenty-one-gun salute for this casualty of war. Blacks just didn't honor their heroes, unless whites said it was okay. Unless whites gave them the criteria for what a hero was or should be. After this cold February day, very few people would know that Timmy ever existed. Another name on a chart in the Baltimore City morgue. That would sum up Timmy's life.

Gas turned to look for Nate. Nate kept walking, never stopping to look at the white marble steps that had held his blood after Chas's attack. Never trying to hear the faint voice of Timmy. Nate faded into the cold, gray ghetto streets of Baltimore City.

21

A Gathering of Young Men

There ain't no man can avoid being born average.
But there ain't no reason a man got to be common.
—Satchel Paige

No man or woman born, coward or brave, can
shun his destiny.
—Homer, Iliad, VI

The chilly air of another Baltimore November forced its way into the house through the partially opened door. A few leaves, which had managed to evade the rakes of Autumn, attempted to become parasites by attaching themselves to their invisible host and enter the house through the same narrow path. Sugar unwittingly foiled their plan by closing the door and blocking their entry, at least for now. At the appropriate time they would make another attempt to escape the cold streets of Edmonson Village.

Quincy and his wife Sheila walked in rubbing their hands together in an attempt to get warm quickly. Quincy turned and gave Sugar a huge warm hug. "I sure can get warm quick in the midst of all of this fat." Sugar laughed and took a playful swing at

Quincy as he started toward the delectable odors that emanated from Mom's cozy kitchen.

Mom leaned back from the hot white stove and peered down the hallway. She smiled as the distinguished chiseled features of Quincy's smiling face came into focus. Quincy hugged Mom tightly and kissed her on the cheek. "What's up, young lady? Getting those vittles together, huh lady?" Mom smiled. "Yeah, I'm cooking. Now, get out of my kitchen and keep your hands out of the pots."

Mom's internal smile was much larger than the one she presented to Quincy. She was happy. Her family was together, alive and united, smiling and laughing. Her grandchildren were present. This was a moment to be cherished. A moment and a gathering that had become rare since her children began to live on their own. Mom was beginning to get that uneasy feeling that creeps into the souls of parents when they feel they are no longer needed. When they feel their work is done. Mom was approaching that period in a mother's life when she wonders whether she has done enough for her children. Mom had done more than enough. *Thank God.*

Peaches and Betty Jean helped clear and set the dining room table for dinner. Tamara and her cousins raced through the house, playing a game of tag. Their simple and innocent laughter brought joy to the hearts of everyone. The smell of fried chicken and sweet potatoes hovered in the warm, genial air. Mom smiled at her grandchildren. She smiled at Sugar and Betty Jean and Peaches as they raised their noses to take in the aroma of the homemade buttermilk biscuits.

Sugar flopped into a plastic-covered, cushioned living room chair and laughed at the sound it made as the air escaped. Doris, Peaches, Betty Jean, Christine, Sheila, and Grandma joined Sugar in her fit of laughter. Mom came into the room, shaking her head and smiling at the gathering of cheerful women. "That's a lot of weight you putting in that chair, baby girl." "Mom, I got it all honest. I got it all from you and Grandma." Grandma shook her head. "I ain't never had those big butts like your mother and you, Sugar. You girls got some heavy hips. And Sugar, you such a young woman. You gained that weight after you married Bay-Bay. What he doing to you, child? Fattening you up so ain't nobody else going to look at you?" The women broke into a fit of hearty and uncontrollable laughter.

Frank walked down the stairs into the basement where Quincy, Bay-Bay, Warren, Dwayne, Howard, Nate, and I were seated watching a football game between the Washington

Redskins and the Dallas Cowboys. Warren had come home from the University of Maryland for a few hours. He had to get back before 10:00 p.m. curfew. He was now a starter on the football team, and all the experts believed that he would end up in the National Football League.

Howard lived next door to Mom. He was a good friend of the family and was always available to help Mom with repairs around the house. Whenever we gathered together as a family, Howard was there with us. Mom said that he reminded her of how the neighbors down South had been. Everyone helping everyone. Everyone's success or failure woven together into one warm, comforting quilt.

Frank had somehow managed to sneak a plate of macaroni and cheese without Mom noticing. Nate noticed him first. "Look at Frank, y'all. He sho-nuff done stole some food already." We broke out in laughter. Frank responded, "You damn right. If the good Lord put it here, I'm gonna eat it. You bony, slave look-alike motherfuckers can sit around with no meat on your bones trying to be pretty boys all you want. But I ain't trying to prove nothing through hunger. I ain't dieting and I ain't fasting. Mama said Jesus done took care of the fasting part, so I don't have to. Besides, I already got me a good and plump wife. As long as I keep her as fat as I am, I ain't got nothing to worry about."

The laughter continued until Frank brought it to a halt by turning toward me and remarking, "So you're an FBI agent now, little brother." I immediately turned and looked into Nate's cold dark eyes. The laughter ceased. I didn't want it to. I answered Frank quickly, hoping that he would let it go at that. "No, I'm not an agent yet. I've got to get through all of that tough training at Quantico."

The room fell silent, except for the annoying voice of some obnoxious television commentator. Dwayne got up and turned him off. He returned to his seat and awaited something more from me. I had never given him an explanation for my joining the FBI. Except for Doris and Mom, I had not given anyone an explanation. This group of young African men wanted an explanation and they wanted it now. Dwayne had questions that could wait no longer. I saw them rolling upwards from his soul, causing his throat to quiver. "Why are you leaving, brother? Why are you going to the FBI?" I had anticipated this session. I knew when I descended the steps into our little meeting space that I would be required to answer a barrage of questions. I knew that once again our basement would become an interrogation room. And my interrogators were experts. There would be no escape and there would be verbal penalties for evasive, ambiguous answers.

Deep inside I was happy that this was occurring. Happy that I was being forced to further analyze a decision that would affect the remainder of my life in one way or another. I was fortunate to have a group of conscious, knowledgeable brothers who would not allow me to falter. Fortunate that I was not alone in some room, staring into some mirror, examining myself without the aid of others. This was an old-time meeting of the village elders. Everyone in that basement, no matter how young, had aged immensely under the burden of being a Black man in America. With age came knowledge. And these brothers had opened up their minds and welcomed all the knowledge that they could find. They had blended that knowledge with street survival skills and what Grandmother called mother-wit.

Nonetheless, I was reluctant to stand before these strong warriors and submit myself to their scrutiny. Although I had thought about my move into the hallowed halls of the FBI, I was still unprepared to answer all the questions and concerns of my brothers. After much reflection, I didn't have all the answers to my own set of perplexing questions concerning the move. And if I couldn't answer myself or satisfy my soul, how could I expect to effectively respond to these elders? I had made the decision to join the FBI, and now, armed or not, I had to go forward and justify my tenuous decision.

I sighed deeply and let it fly from my mouth. It wasn't a reply that was properly prepared in the depths of my soul. I thought, *The brothers will see through it.* And then I answered, "It's a career move, brother. I'll get paid more and I'll have the opportunity to learn a hell of a lot. Just think, no one else from the 'hood has made such a move. I'm moving into new territory. I'm moving into an organization that we couldn't get into twenty or thirty years ago. There's no denying that it's a good job with a lot of prestige."

I knew that I wasn't making much sense. I knew the brothers would recognize it for the nonsense that it was. I was giving the standard "bullshit" answer. Everyone in the room knew that I was not money-hungry and they were sure that I didn't give a damn about prestige. I was acting as if I were in a police interview session and had to say what the interviewers wanted to hear. But this was not an interview room and the brothers at this conference weren't interested in hearing any "bullshit" answers. It wouldn't work here. These brothers were serious and knew me well.

Although all that I had said had an element of truth, I knew that my response would never suffice. Not coming from me.

I had to make the reason for my move more relevant to what I knew was on the minds of the young men assembled before me. I reached into my memory bank and retrieved some of what James had left me. "I think that I can make a difference. Black children will see me and know that they, too, can become FBI agents. And we need more of us in the FBI. Somebody has to keep them honest."

I winked at Dwayne. He didn't smile. He didn't move. He stared into my eyes, trying to read me. Trying to let me know that I was not fooling him at all. I turned from him. "I'm just taking advantage of what civil rights leaders like Dr. Martin Luther King Jr. have worked so hard for."

Quincy had been completely quiet. He, too, had watched my movements. He had looked into my soul. He spoke up for the first time since he entered the basement after leaving Mom's kitchen. "You're not the one. This law enforcement shit is just not for you. You're a teacher. Can't you see what you did with Operation Drug-Out? You had people listening to you. Those young Black high-school kids looked up to you. You've already done your share for law enforcement. You've been a cop for almost four years now. Let some other brother represent us in the FBI. You're needed here with these kids. Your career is here on some college campus or in some high school or elementary school classroom."

Quincy sat back on the sofa. He had said all that he would say. He figured that he had done enough talking. He had discussed the same issues with me when I joined the Maryland State Police Department. There was no need for him to keep pounding the same arguments into me, over and over again. I would have to understand what he was saying on my own. I would have to latch on to his lessons, independent of any more verbal urging from him.

Warren spoke up. "Do you know who killed Dr. Martin Luther King Jr. and Malcolm X? No matter what they tell you, I know you know the truth. J. Edgar Hoover and that fuckin' FBI have made a career out of setting up and killing Black leaders. The FBI devised all kinds of divide-and-conquer techniques to destroy the Black Panther Party. Where are Eldridge Cleaver, Huey Newton, and Bobby Seale? Who killed Fred Hampton? The FBI infiltrated and controlled the NAACP and the Southern Christian Leadership Conference. They have pit Black organization against Black organization and brother against brother. They tried to whitemail King by sending his wife tapes of what they said were sexual encounters. Can't you see how devious that is?

"J. Edgar Hoover was a piece of shit who didn't deserve to live. The FBI still belongs to that asshole. Even in death, he runs it. I can't for the life of me understand why you would want to be a part of that organization. The truth is supposed to set you free. You know the truth but, yet, you keep running deeper into slavery. You keep living a lie."

Frank stopped eating. He looked toward me as if he wanted to help me find a way out of this conversation. He had started it with an innocent enough question. It really didn't matter. Had he not started it, one of the other brothers would have. They were prepared for this meeting. They had some things that could not be left unsaid. They had so many questions that needed answers. I would have to respond. I knew that this day and time would come, when James talked me into filling out the application. I knew that it would come, when Doris told me that my family would never understand. I knew that it was coming, when Mom said that she was having a going-away dinner for me and was inviting everyone. There was no way that Frank or anyone else could get me out of this conference.

I responded to Warren, "All that shit that the FBI did was in the past. I mean, if we just stop participating in all the organizations in this country that have treated us like shit, we couldn't exist. Historically, no one throughout the world has given a fuck about African people. I know that. Even those who pretended that they cared have just used us as a buffer or an instrument to achieve their goals.

"The communists never gave a fuck about Black people and the way we were treated. We just meant numbers for their bullshit organizations. They just tried to use us. The Jews never gave a fuck about African people. Yeah, they understood what we were going through because they had been through something similar, although not as brutal, during World War II. So they sympathized with the situation, not necessarily the people who were in it. They had been chased into ghettos a long time before the African slave trade. I know a little about their history.

"The Jews learned from their experiences. They learned what evil men are willing and capable of doing to other men and women. And they learned 'Race First,' to borrow the expression that Tony Martin so aptly used for the title of his book. Their main concern was for their people, and we were merely a buffer or barrier for their protection. We could deflect some of the heat for them. Hell, we must remember that some of them participated in the enslavement of African people. They bought and sold us just like other white folks. What I'm saying is that if we distanced ourselves from every group of people or every organization that has done us wrong in the past, we couldn't function anywhere, because everyone has used us and abused us for their purposes."

Nate leaned forward as if he was pleased that I had done some studying. He could tell that I was doing some thinking for myself—an indication that I had not been totally brainwashed. I was loosening the shackles on my mind. I was giving him a glimmer of hope that one day I would completely remove the chain and ball from my mind. I could see that he was reliving the speech at Southwestern High School. He was hearing it again and enjoying it as if for the first time.

Warren was not finished yet. He continued, "Do you really believe that all that shit is over? Don't you think they would take the opportunity to kill another Black leader, or at least set him or her up to be killed? Don't you think they would fear another strong, uncompromising Black leader like Elijah Muhammad, Paul Robeson, Malcolm X or Marcus Garvey? Don't you think they've got all kinds of files on Minister Louis Farrakhan, Dr. Ben, and others?

"Things haven't changed that much, brother. And as soon as you think that they have, you're in trouble. That's the problem with Black people today. We're running around and smiling as if the world is all fine, and we are not serious enough to deal with what's happening. Give us a dance floor or a football or basketball, and nothing else matters. If you can't see how all that shit that you say is in the past is still going on, then you are just wasting your time reading."

I turned away from Warren and looked down at the red- and black-tiled floor. The room seemed warm and muggy, although it was usually cold. The walls closed in on me, and the brothers seemed to move in closer to me. I could feel their heartbeats against the walls of my soul. The blood rushed through my body. The thumping of my heart, like African drum beats, merged with the pleasant sounds of my daughter's and her cousins' feet thumping on the floor above. It was as if I were in hell, hearing the sounds of angels in heaven—there seemed to be so much happiness above me. I wanted Mom to call us to dinner. I wanted this conversation to end. But it was not to be. Not yet.

Dwayne interrupted my thoughts. He was like a brother and I knew that sooner or later he would have his say just like everyone else. His initial questions were only the appetizer. "Just what do you expect to accomplish for your people by joining the FBI? I mean, are they going to teach you how to build a business in the Black community? Are they going to allow you to come back and speak to our people about the true source of and purpose for drugs in our communities? Are they going to let you control the hiring process so you can give more brothers a chance? *Or* are they going to take another educated 'negro' out of circulation? Don't misunderstand me, Black man, I believe that we need Black folk in law enforcement. But not you, brother. Your place is here in Baltimore."

Dwayne stood up and paced back and forth in front of me, staring down at the floor as he moved. Suddenly he stopped directly in front of me and stared into my eyes. "And don't feed me that shit about all that shit the FBI did to Black folks being in the past. I know you know better than that. I know, just as Warren said, that you know the truth. We have had too many conversations for you to come down here today and try to pull the wool over my eyes. You insult all of our intelligence when you talk like that. You are talking down to us just like the white man does. You are telling us that we are too ignorant to know better and that you are too fuckin' dumb to know better. You are calling us 'niggers' in a way that is supposed to be not so obvious to us.

"That's what the white man does every day on his news programs and in his newspapers. He says things to us that we are supposed to be too dumb to know is a lie. He insults our intelligence when he says that we are the only ones committing crimes. It's just a nineteen-eighties way of calling us niggers. And now our own brother comes down here and feeds us bullshit. Our own brother insults us like we are uneducated slaves. Well, we aren't. So you might as well come clean."

I turned to Nate. I thought that he would have spoken by now. His silence scared me. I turned back toward Dwayne. "I don't mean to insult your intelligence, brother. And I know that none of you are niggers. I understand what you are saying. But I want you to know that my joining the FBI does not signify and should not signify that I'm turning my back on my people. I'll never do that. I'll never sell out. I'm not going to stop helping my people, no matter what job I get or where I go.

"For four years now I've been in law enforcement and have tried to do the best job I could. I've also maintained my community ties. I've been out here talking to the youth. I've been fighting racism in the state police and everywhere else it has reared its head. I want to try the FBI. It is something that I want to do and if I don't, I'll never be satisfied with my life. There's some unknown force gnawing at my insides and pointing me in the direction of the FBI. I don't know what it is or why it's there. But I have got to deal with it.

"No matter what the FBI has done in the past, or, for that matter, is doing now, they are still considered the number one law enforcement agency in the world. If law enforcement is my chosen field, and for now it is, then I must work for the best in that field. I must learn my trade from those who are considered the best. I must know I'm the best at whatever I do. That's what Mom taught us. Always strive to be the best."

Dwayne interrupted, "But what does it all mean if you only prove that you are the number one Uncle Tom?" I responded, "I'll never be an Uncle Tom and you know that, Dwayne. You can cut that stupid shit short right now. I'll never turn and run, and I'll always point out racism, no matter where it is. If the FBI would ever ask me to do something that I believed was to the detriment of my people, I would refuse—no matter what the consequences."

Dwayne sat down on the couch and leaned back. He ran his dark brown hands over his face. He seemed to be exhausted. Deep inside, he knew that I wasn't a sellout. He was certain that I was proud of my race and that I would not forsake it for a better job or more money, nor for a promotion, nor for any reason. We had sat on his parents' front steps late into the warm summer nights and discussed this very issue.

Dwayne and I had sworn that no matter where life took us, we would never betray our people. Never become sellouts. He admired how the Italians stuck together and would put their lives on the line for family. He said we had to relay that message to our people and especially to our youth. I could tell that he was upset about my leaving. I understood why he was willing to call me an Uncle Tom or any other name that he felt would make me re-think my decision. We were partners—and he believed that together we could do a lot to help our people. Feeling he would be alone, Dwayne was determined to make me stay.

Howard tried to break through some of the thick tension that surrounded us like a dense fog. He could see the agony and confusion in my face. He made an innocuous comment about Frank's fat stomach. No one laughed. The room was full of serious African men dealing with a serious issue. I wondered if other African Americans, especially African American men, had been fortunate enough to have a group like this sit down with them at decision time to engage in a council of African elders. It seemed painful, but it was necessary. History showed us that unless we gave an issue serious thought, mistakes were likely to be made.

I remembered reading about how the elders in each African community assembled before decisions involving the community were made. There could be no doubt that the decision I was about to make would influence my entire family. Every decision that any Black man or Black woman made anywhere in the world influenced the whole race, even if the decision maker was not conscious of this effect.

Every time a Black drug addict stuck a needle in his arm, the entire African race was affected. Every time a Black shot another Black, the race was affected. Every time a Black woman had an abortion, the race was affected. Every time a Black man beat his wife, the race was affected. Any time a Black woman was raped, the race was affected. Every time a Black child was uneducated or miseducated, the race was affected. Every time a Black man or woman sold out in order to get some political appointment, obtain some job, or be able to sell some book, the race was affected. That was what Black people had to understand. That was what the brothers in the basement were trying to make me understand.

When you are in the midst of a war for your very survival, no move is insignificant. When you are in a battle, you need to strategically place your soldiers in the positions in which they can be most effective. As Master Sun Tzu stated in his profound book, *The Art of War*, "forces are to be structured strategically, based on what is advantageous." Black people were at war, whether they knew it or not. Dwayne and the brothers were trying to keep me from making a strategic error.

The brothers were trying to make me understand that my life as an individual meant very little. I had to base my decision or decisions on what I would mean to generations yet to come. I had to have the dedication of Dr. Martin Luther King Jr. and Malcolm X. I had to have the sense of purpose of Marcus Garvey and Booker T. Washington. I had to be willing to make the sacrifices that Harriet Tubman and Mary McCleod Bethune had made. I had to stand up and be a man like Louis Farrakhan and point out injustices without worrying about how I would be labeled by society. I had to understand that when I stood up for America, I would be considered a patriot, but when I stood up and spoke out against the oppression that people of color suffered, I would be considered a trouble-making radical.

Standing up, as a Black man, meant possibly losing a job or a career. Standing up, as a Black man, could mean losing your life. The brothers were trying to make me understand that neglecting my duties to my people meant the loss of my soul. And a Black man whose soul was lost was already dead.

Nate stood up and walked toward the stairs. The room was silent. He looked back at me and began to speak. "I don't know what else to say to you, brother. I've told you that you belong here with your family and with your people. I've told you that your future should be in education. I'm not against you advancing yourself in life. *But* what does it all mean, if you are someday director of the FBI and your people are still living in poverty? What does it mean, if African people the world over and, more specifically, in the 'hood are being divided and conquered? What does it mean, when your young brothers and sisters are still being miseducated by a system that you know is rotten and is kept rotten intentionally? You're a Bible man. Remember 'For what does it profit a man to gain the world but lose his soul'?

"Can't you understand that this world is trying to destroy Black people? And if you think it can't happen and that I'm just paranoid, take a look at the so-called Indians. Take a look at how easy it was for America to wipe off the face of the earth millions of Native Americans and then sit down to dinner and give thanks to God for it. You can't save the world. Gil Scott-Heron is right—there is no such thing as a superman. But we all got to do our part, Brother Powers.

"Take a look around you and see what the infant mortality rate is for Black people in Detroit, Chicago, New York, and right here in Baltimore. Take a look at which race is most affected by AIDS. Take a look at what the white man has done on the continent of Africa. Take a look at how they treat the Haitians and how they blame every new disease that comes about on them or on other African people.

"Take a look at how they've twisted the minds of little Black children, having them waiting for a white Santa Claus to bring them toys on Christmas day. Look at how they have us sitting down to celebrate Thanksgiving, a day when we all didn't have a damn thing to be thankful for. Take a look at the U.S. Senate and the White House and tell me how many Black people you see there. Take a look at how they continuously vote billions of dollars to Israel while Israel turns around and provides aid to Nazi South Africa."

I had heard before all of what Nate was saying. I knew most of it to be true. It was as if he forgot that I had grown up with him, that I had walked past the junkies and the alcoholics. I had witnessed the murders and the rapes. I had sat through those "bullshit" classes and listened to lectures on how great rednecks like Thomas Jefferson and George Washington were. I had heard the "bullshit" about how John Kennedy and Lyndon Johnson liked Black folk. I had read through history books that made no mention of Black Egypt and Ethiopia. I had noticed how Egyptian philosophy had been credited to the Greeks. And I, too, was hurt and embarrassed when I saw African American brothers and sisters marching across college campuses under Greek letters, because I knew that the sororities and fraternities to which they belonged should have been named after the true creators of philosophy, the Egyptians. Whoever heard of a Black Greek? I had noticed how the history teachers never mentioned the Moors' contributions to Spain. Nate was talking to me as if I had not studied the truth.

Nate turned to head up the stairs, then stopped again and said, "You see, brother, nobody is ever going to give a fuck about us but us. We have to have guns to defend ourselves. Only a fool would allow a group of people who have done what the white man has done to us to be responsible for his defense. We have to control our communities and schools. The hell with integration. It doesn't work. White people just don't like us, and we shouldn't be trying to make them like us. To hell with them. We have to educate our people so that they can stop fucking up our kids with those false history lessons. We have to teach them math and science. We have to make sure they can read and write.

"That's where you come in. We need you more than them. Trust me, they'll find another 'nigger' to do the job. It's getting harder and harder for us to find a conscious brother who our people will listen to. I don't think they'll listen to me. I've done too much wrong and that forgiveness shit only works in church. They definitely won't listen to me there. But people will listen to you. I feel that deep inside. Don't abandon us. Not now. Don't let any more of our brothers and sisters end up like me. Please."

Nate walked up the stairs. I looked around the room, expecting to hear someone else speak up. No one spoke a word. Dead silence. Nate's voice startled me. "Mom said y'all come on and eat." This was the signal I had been waiting for ever since this gathering of strong young African men had begun. I got up and walked up the stairs. The African men followed.

22

The Decision Maker

Everywhere in Africa, I have noticed that no greater affront can be offered a Negro than insulting his mother.
— *W.E.B. DuBois,* Darkwater

...but none have I known more sweetly feminine, more unswervingly loyal, more desperately earnest, and more instinctively pure in body and soul than the daughters of my Black mothers.
— *W.E.B. DuBois,* Darkwater

The final decision would be made based on her advice. You see, she was our mom and she loved all of us, no matter what we did. She even loved Dad. Dad had brutally beat Mom on several occasions and had called her all kinds of vulgar names. But deeply etched in Mom's mind were the memories of the strong African American man that Dad had been when she had first met him. She still believed that deep down inside, Dad was a moral man. There was a solid layer of good lying dormant beneath all that calcified man-made evil.

Mom believed in the power of God, just as the slaves had as they toiled in the suffocating heat of hot southern summers. Not only could He reach down into Dad and remove all evil, but God could reverse the years of damage done to Dad's soul. With constant prayer by Mom to the merciful God of the slaves, Dad could recover; God would put him back together. Considering that Dad was an utterly broken man, it would take a miracle to rebuild him. Mom said that God worked miracles. God would make him the strong Black man that she had met at the bus station. God would make Dad a loving and caring father. God could, in Dad, rebuild what man had torn down.

Mom didn't want Dad to change for her. They were divorced and she knew that they would never again be together as husband and wife. It had taken much effort for her to leave him. She believed that leaving Dad was an act of surrendering to all those forces that had conspired to destroy him. But in the end she had no choice. It was obvious that Quincy and Nate were coming dangerously close to a brutal, and probably fatal, confrontation with Dad. She did not want to witness the manifestation of the ultimate result of the divide-and-conquer scheme. Yet, even after leaving Dad, Mom had not given up faith that Dad would be made whole again some day.

Mom hoped that Dad could be made whole for us. No matter what, he was our father. Mom wanted him to be someone for us to look up to. She wanted Dad to show all his sons how to be strong Black men. How to fight those who opposed and oppressed us. In fact, she wanted him to lead the fight against our common enemy. He was to teach us how to survive in a system that was hell-bent on destroying us.

Mom was proud of the knowledge that we had obtained. She smiled as she watched us reading books and discussing our plight. But she believed that there was something missing. Dad was that missing link in the family chain. Mom hoped that he would someday take his proper place within the family, before the chain was weakened beyond repair.

Mom didn't know that Dad had raped Sugar or that Warren and I had witnessed this unforgivable act. She didn't know that my siblings and I had completely given up on Dad. We believed that Dad had irrevocably lost his soul. He was now only a shell of a man. We were intelligent enough to understand what had happened: Dad had fallen into a trap that had been set for all African American men. And he could not be restored. It was too late. We would never again go to him for help with critical decisions, though we would listen to him if he wanted to talk.

After all, he was a victim and all victims have something to say, something to offer. We could learn lessons from his mistakes. Maybe we could identify some of the hidden traps, and possibly avoid them.

Mom would be our decision maker. We had made that determination long before her divorce in 1977. She was the one I went to before Doris and I were married. She was the one I went to for advice before joining first the Maryland State Police and later the FBI. Mom never demanded that we follow her advice. We knew that Mom would never lead us in the wrong direction. She would be honest because that was the only way she knew how to be. She would pray to God for answers and then share those answers with us.

Mom knew that Nate was using drugs and she often tried to dissuade him from such consumption. It hurt her that she could not convince him to stop. Her boy was being destroyed right before her eyes. He was disintegrating back into the dust from which, Mom believed, all men had come. He was being taken away from her by a powerful substance that neither God nor the awesome power of love seemed to be able to overcome. This man-made substance ran through Nate's veins and caused him, at times, not to know his own mother. Man had created a substance that could destroy love, and someone had given this ticket to sure destruction to her boy.

Mom would have horrible dreams about Nate. I would quietly come into the house sometimes and find her immersed in tears. She wouldn't notice me standing, watching, listening. I would hear her question herself, question her worth as a mom. I would hear her contemplate Nate's future. She was so sure that Nate was going to die of an overdose if he didn't stop abusing drugs. She would sit there in the darkness, holding his baby picture and a box of tissue, wiping tears away from her eyes. I would listen as she pleaded to God for answers, through the tears. "What happened, God? What did I do wrong? Where did I go wrong? What happened to my little happy baby boy?"

Mom was suffering, and trying to hide it from the world. She saw her strong brown boys struggling to survive and become men. She saw her boys, to whom she had given so much love and guidance, slowly going astray, taking the wrong road and disappearing into a wilderness thick with danger. She was reaching for them, calling to them, yet they kept moving farther away. She was stuck—unable to move with them and too weak to pull them back.

The Powers boys were moving into the valley of the shadow of death. Frank, Quincy, and Nate carried guns for defense against what Warren called *ghetto zombies* and *Nazi cops*. Mom's boys weren't zombies yet, and even if they were, God could bring them back to life. Mom said since God had brought dry bones to life through Ezekiel of the Bible, He could surely summon the same winds that brought breath and life to dry grave bones to save or revive the children of the ghetto. She said that we all should put our lives in the strong and capable hands of God Almighty. God would protect us. A gun wasn't necessary. Nate said that he would rather have a gun in *his* strong and capable hands.

Mom's eyes had seen so much that I often wondered how much more she could stand. I was happy that she had God to lean on; otherwise, she might have ended up like the mother of Malcolm X—in a psychiatric hospital. Mom had watched as her eldest son Frank was shot in front of our house on Baltimore Street. She had never forgotten that scene. The force of the bullet threw Frank onto the steps behind him. Mom grabbed him and, with the help of a neighbor, carried him up the street to Bon Secours Hospital. Dad had been there too and had witnessed this personal holocaust. But when Frank was shot, Dad went into shock and was unable to move. He sat on the steps with his head in his hands, crying. Frank survived the shooting but they were never able to remove all the fragments of the bullet from his chest. Mom believed that her prayers had saved Frank.

It was Mom who had to sit and answer the questions put to her by the Baltimore City police officers when they were looking for Nate in regard to an armed robbery. They were hunting down her son for a robbery which he swore to her he hadn't committed. They questioned her as if she were a liar. Mom had no idea where Nate had gone. Nate would never put her in the position of knowing. But the cops didn't believe her. They questioned this brave, faithful woman as if she were a common criminal. They watched her break down and cry, yet they refused to end their merciless questioning. She wasn't their mom. She was just another mother of another ghetto child.

The police would drive by or sit outside the house in marked patrol cars as if they were expecting Nate to show up. I think they knew he wasn't coming. Nate didn't live with Mom. Moreover, he knew that the police would be looking for him there. The police were trying to make Mom look bad in the eyes of her neighbors. Why else would they do a "discreet" surveillance in a marked unit in broad daylight? At night, Mom would just sit in the darkness of our living room, staring out the window at the police car, crying and praying. Mom, too, became a victim of the justice system.

It was Mom who sat in a Baltimore courtroom with Nate as he became a victim of a criminal justice system that presumed all Black men guilty of whatever crime they were accused of committing. It was her eyes that witnessed Nate being carried off to jail in shackles. She sat there in the courtroom after everyone else had departed and cried. Dad had not come to the trial.

Mom prayed for Sugar and Bay-Bay. She prayed that Bay-Bay would not lose his senses, as had Sugar's first husband. Her first husband, Robert, had burned holes in her back with cigarettes and beat Sugar unmercifully. Sugar hid the scars because she was afraid to tell Frank, Quincy, and Nate about the beatings. She knew they would kill Robert. Frank eventually found out when he unexpectedly stopped by Sugar's apartment and noticed marks on her face and tears in her soft brown eyes. He then took a television set and put Robert's head through the screen. As Robert sat on the floor, with his head in the television set, Frank kicked him into unconsciousness with a pair of Bethlehem Steel-issued steel-toed boots. Robert got the message and he and Sugar divorced.

Mom prayed that I would not be shot while out on patrol as a Maryland State Trooper. She worried about me constantly. She prayed that I would be treated fairly by those whom I worked for and with. She prayed that I would be able to overcome the high hurdle of racism and bigotry, which she knew I would confront as an African American.

Mom worried about Warren. She prayed that he would not be severely injured on the football field. She prayed that he would get the best education he could, because she knew they would discard him when his body was broken down by the tortures of the game and no longer useful. She prayed for Peaches and Sheila and Doris. It seemed that most of the time, Mom was either praying or crying. Maybe every once in a while she would manage to smile. Every once in a while, we were able to make her laugh.

Mom was not naive. She had experienced racism firsthand as a nurse's aide at Maryland General Hospital, where she had worked for over twenty years. Some of the people Mom worked for had worked her harder than they had worked the white employees. She had seen Black patients treated badly and put on a separate floor away from white people. She had watched as some white nurses refused to minister to Black patients. At one time, Blacks at Maryland General Hospital had to be washed in separate tubs, which had been painted black. Treated as if they had some dreaded disease, Blacks were quarantined because of the color of their skin.

Many of the white nurses refused to deal with Black patients at all. Mom had walked the halls of the hospital while white doctors and nurses stared at her as if she were some type of wild animal. They had talked down to her and yelled commands at her. She could feel the racism all around her. She was smothered by it. She had heard the white nurses having conversations about "niggers."

Through it all, Mom prayed. And eventually things did get better. Later, some of the white nurses who worked with Mom befriended her and were more than helpful. Mom was aware that all her children would have to go through the same gantlet of racism that she had passed through. She told us not to become racists as we defended ourselves against racism and never to give up the fight. It would not be easy but it was necessary that we confront and overcome racism.

I sat in front of her, looking into her tired deep brown eyes and listening as she gave me her tacit approval to join the FBI. "I hate that you have to move away from home, away from Baltimore. But I certainly understand your reasons for leaving. God knows I ain't going to stop you when God starts stirring your soul to go in a certain direction. You got to do what your heart leads you to do."

Mom smiled silently, as if there was a bigger smile hidden beneath the one she displayed to me. "Kinda hard to believe that my son going to be an FBI agent. I wouldn't have thought it when you were younger. Not 'cause I don't think you're capable. I know you are and you better know you are. I've drummed that confidence into your brain since you were a little brown baby. I just ain't never heard you talk of such a thing as becoming an FBI agent when you were younger. I guess it's 'cause everyone always telling little Black kids what they can't be, they afraid to say what they want to be. Shame."

Mom leaned back in the old but sturdy high-backed chair and stared off into the heavens. She was looking through and beyond the ceiling above her. "The FBI will be a good learning experience for you. Oh, I know how your brothers feel. They all done come to me and asked that I make you stay. They say that you don't need to learn about those racists in the FBI."

Mom leaned forward and looked into my eyes. "Let me say something right here and now. All white folk ain't bad. Some folks want you to feel that way. And many of the folks who want you to feel that way are white. They just trying to keep God's people apart. You see, God don't care nothing about no skin color. He just want the righteous to come together to fight off evil. Somebody somewhere don't want to see that. So they gonna try to make all Black people hate all white people and all white people hate all Black people. Once that happens, can't no righteousness get done. But don't you fall for that trap. You've got to judge people by the content of their character, just like Martin Luther King Jr. said: 'content of their character.'"

Mom took my hand and held it tight. "Now, having said that, let me say this: Don't be no fool. There are going to be some white folk that try to keep an educated Black man down. And you are educated and intelligent. Plus, you know a little about what the devious white folk are up to. So they gonna come for you. They gonna call you all kinds of names to make you submit. But don't you dare back down when you right. I ain't taught none of my children to be afraid of nothing or no one but God.

"I don't care what they say or try to do to you. If you are right, then you stand and fight to the bitter end. They respect you when you stand and fight. No one on this here earth respects a coward or a sellout. And I ain't reared no cowards. Oh, they gonna act like they like you if you don't stand for what you believe in. They gonna give you big-time jobs and give you big-time praises. They gonna pat you on the back and call you their man. But they ain't gonna respect nobody with their backs hunched over and their eyes always looking toward the floor. Stand with your back straight and be a man."

Mom wanted me to be careful. She warned me that all those who say that they are for me are not. She said that I would be a rarity in the FBI and that some people would resent my being there. Mom told me to "stay myself." She said that I should not change and become something different because of my environment. I was not to sell my soul, as others had done and were continuing to do—that was too high of a price to pay and "no job was that important."

She said that I should never deny my heritage even when those around me were criticizing my people. There was a reason for what had happened to the Black race in America. There was a reason for the destruction and killing that was going on in our neighborhoods. Mom understood it and so did I. But others didn't, or acted as if they didn't. And those were the ones who were going to try to make me attack my heritage and lineage.

Mom leaned back in her chair again and rested her hands on her lap. I continued to stare into her soul. She began to speak again. "Once others see that you don't agree with their conversations or theories, they gonna say you don't fit the law enforcement profile. They gonna make you an outcast and label you a 'troublemaker,' just like they did with Dr. King and Paul Robeson. Once they notice that you don't laugh at their ethnic jokes or their jokes about women, you will be identified as a radical. Once you take a stand—and you will—and say that you are proud of being an African American, you will become a target. Once you are a target, you will be considered a security risk. Through it all, you must keep your soul intact. You must stay mentally stable and not allow them to cause you any undue stress."

I knew Mom was speaking truth. I was absorbing her words, as a sponge absorbs water. If I couldn't or didn't handle the stress that was sure to come, I would be putting myself in grave danger every time I went out on the streets to do my job. I knew this from my employment with the Maryland State Police. If I did not stay alert, I would be easy prey for those I pursued in the line of duty.

Mom was convinced that after joining the FBI, I would come to understand that my place was back in Baltimore with my family. I would come to understand that I was needed in the classrooms of Baltimore's inner-city schools. She believed that I would understand that prestige and money meant very little if I lost my soul. She was not against the FBI, but she felt that I could be put to better use in another field or in the fields of Baltimore City with the unharvested and vulnerable crop of young African men and women. Even with her inner beliefs, Mom refused to stop me from pursuing my dreams and desires. There were worse choices that I could make. She prayed that God would lead me in the right direction. Mom is a strong woman.

23

The FBI National Academy

Anyone who does not have knowledge of self is considered a victim of either amnesia or unconsciousness and is not very competent.
—Elijah Muhammad, Message to the Black Man

The FBI is J. Edgar Hoover, and I think we can rest assured that it always will be.
—Joseph McCarthy

December 1, 1985. I suppose that just like every other new student, I was in awe when I entered the Federal Bureau of Investigation Academy in Quantico, Virginia. Its location was only about a two-and-a-half-hour drive south of Baltimore, but for me it seemed as if I were traveling to another world, another universe. The FBI was that world-renowned, secret and powerful organization that every other law enforcement agency envied. It was the organization that conjured up visions of "Big Brother," as described in George Orwell's book *1984*. It was the organization that was both feared and hated by the African American community. I was heading there. Driving to this place that I had heard and read so much about.

The location of the FBI Academy did nothing to dispel its reputation of secrecy and power. It was hidden away in a forest, nestled neatly in the midst of the United States Marine Corps Base. As one exited Interstate 95 and drove the long and narrow

265

road to the FBI Academy, one was likely to see U.S. Marines personnel driving jeeps and tanks. One could hear the harrowing sounds of small-arms fire and munitions explosions. One could inhale the odor of burnt gunpowder. Toward the end of the stretch of winding road, stood the FBI Academy—strong, straight, stern, and serene. It seemed undisturbed by all the commotion going on around it, resolutely calm and unchanged.

I parked my 1983 blue Chevrolet Cavalier in the large parking lot, retrieved my suitcases from the trunk, and headed toward the seemingly infinitely tall flag poles, with their enormous waving flags, which stood in front of the FBI Training Academy administration building. When I entered the U-shaped driveway, I put my suitcases down and stared up at the building that stood before me. I took a deep breath and ran my hand over my head, as I had often seen Granddad and Nate do.

The sun shone brightly above the academy as if it were the North Star that I had learned so much about at Sunday school. Through squinted eyes I took it all in: the rippling flags, the academy campus, the tall dormitory buildings, the full parking lot. I smiled as I thought of the irony of my journey from the ghetto to the "sacrosanct" grounds of the FBI. I thought of the cold mean streets of Baltimore. I thought of the back porch and the little back-alley Negro League. I was proud of myself. Proud that I had done what many did not believe I could do. I had made an improbable journey. As Robert Frost stated in his poem "The Road Not Taken," I had certainly taken "the road less traveled by." What difference it would make, remained to be seen. I picked up my suitcases and packed my thoughts of Baltimore away in a small compartment of my glowing soul.

As I entered the lobby of the FBI administration building, I felt as if I had entered into the annals of history. I probably was making too much of the experience, attaching too much significance to my arrival at the academy, but my emotions were out of control. For I would be on the elite list of men who had served as FBI agents.

I looked around the lobby as if I were in some foreign land. Yet, strangely enough, I felt as if I belonged here, at this time in my life. I inhaled the atmosphere of the historic site that was to be my home for the next three months. My eyes moved slowly in their sockets, taking in all that was about me. A few other candidates stood around next to their luggage. They had the same look of pleasure and awe on their faces.

I moved toward the receptionist without consciously taking a step in her direction. It was as if I were a character in a Spike Lee movie—moving forward as though walking, yet standing perfectly still.   I nervously uttered my name to her smiling face.   An overwhelming feeling of anxiety and excitement engulfed my body.   I didn't see all of her.   I didn't hear the words, "Just one moment, please," uttered from her thin red lips.   My attention on her pleasant smile was diverted by the movement of her slim white finger down the list of neatly typed names.   Her finger nails were perfectly manicured.   Her hair seemed to be combed perfectly. Her dress appeared to fit perfectly.

I shifted my attention and slowly looked about.   I wanted to take in the rest of the room.   I was determined not to miss a thing. I wanted to drink in and savor this special moment in my life.   I looked down at the gleaming bright floor; it appeared to have been perfectly waxed.   The pictures in the lobby were hung perfectly. The brass letters *FBI* on the wall behind the desk were perfectly affixed to the rich deep-brown wood panels and polished to a perfect shine.   All of this perfection seemed to relay the message that the FBI was a perfect organization, and that it demanded perfection from all those who entered its academy doors.   No imperfection or corruption of this image would be tolerated.

The receptionist returned her index finger to the top of the page and began to slowly repeat the downward motion, examining each name closely as if it were a signature and she, a graphologist. She hesitated, and without looking up, shook her head ever so slightly and continued down the list.   I thought for a moment that something had gone dreadfully wrong.   I thought that maybe some reproving FBI bureaucrat had rewritten the original list and omitted my name.   Maybe the agents who had conducted my background investigation had taken a second look.   Maybe they had located something in my past and decided I should not be a Special Agent. Maybe James was wrong. Maybe I had not passed all the cryptic tests and therefore had not been accepted into this exclusive club.

Finally, the lady with the thin lips and fingers looked up and smiled a perfect smile.   "Welcome to the FBI Academy!"   I smiled back and the warm, stirring glow returned to my anxious soul. The beautiful friendly receptionist informed me of the room to which I had been assigned.   She gently handed me a name tag inscribed with the words *FBI Academy Student*.   She pointed in the direction of my assigned dormitory room and gave me specific instructions on how to reach it.   I picked up my luggage and slowly walked through the glass hallways, which had been affectionately named gerbil tubes.   I would be housed in this building for the next sixteen weeks.

I lugged my suitcases up a flight of stairs, through a corridor, and into an area where a group of people sat watching a big-screened television set. On the wall behind them was a large picture of a stony-faced, heroic-looking J. Edgar Hoover. No doubt about it, I was in his house now. This was his FBI. Even in death his presence could be felt roaming the halls, watching over the empire that he built. His picture was there to make sure that all who entered the academy understood that J. Edgar Hoover was still the owner of this property.

As I stood staring at the picture of Hoover, I thought of all the trouble that he and his FBI had caused Black people. I thought of his comments about Dr. Martin Luther King Jr. How Hoover had called King a "notorious liar." How he had had Dr. King followed. How his own sexual perversions had led Hoover to try to tape King's so-called sexual encounters. How he was hell-bent and determined, in his own words, to "neutralize" Dr. King.

It was J. Edgar Hoover and his suited henchmen who planned to disunite and ultimately divided the Black Panther Party. It was Hoover who orchestrated the murder of a young and energetic Fred Hampton. I thought of the infiltration of Black organizations by the FBI. I thought of the disinformation campaigns directed at Black leaders and especially at the feared "Black Messiah," Malcolm X.

I thought of the phone taps and phone traps. The counterfeit letters written by FBI handwriting specialists and sent out to various Black leaders, with the forged signatures of other Black leaders—to create a climate ripe for internal strife and murder. Hoover would forever be associated with the FBI. The FBI would forever be identified with J. Edgar Hoover. Now that I was becoming an FBI agent, Mr. Hoover would be associated with me.

I sighed deeply, walked to the elevator, and took it to the fifth floor. I stared straight ahead, never looking up at the lighted floor indicator. The elevator made several stops. People got on and off. I looked past them out into nothingness. My mind had latched on to the unpleasant thought that I was now an underling of the infamous J. Edgar Hoover. I couldn't free myself of this disturbing notion.

When the elevator reached the fifth floor, I instinctively exited. Still deep in my thoughts, I walked slowly, like a zombie, down the hallway toward my room. I noticed other new students smiling and greeting each other, introducing themselves to their elite colleagues. My mind was still with my new, historical associate, J. Edgar Hoover. I was in no mood for smiling.

The students in the hallway were to be the people with whom I would live for almost four months. I would come to know them well. They would come to know who they thought I was. I entered my room and met my roommate, James Chambers. He was frail, white, and bespectacled. He seemed friendly enough. He did not give me the look of shock that I had initially encountered with some of my white co-workers at the Maryland State Police. He smiled, shook my hand firmly, and offered me whatever side of the room I wanted. I chose the bed next to the door.

After settling in and unpacking, we went to dinner in the academy cafeteria. To enter the cafeteria we had to push through a turnstile where we were observed by one of the cafeteria personnel whose job was to ensure that we wore our FBI student badges. We were able to choose from a variety of dishes, which had been prepared by employees of the Marriott Corporation, the company which had secured the contract for service provision at the academy. After choosing and receiving our food, we walked down a narrow aisle, out into the rather large cafeteria. Flags from every state in the United States of America had been framed and hung on the four wood-paneled walls surrounding the room.

My roommate and I sat at one of the many tables and surveyed our surroundings. I noticed that several of the students, who were sitting and eating, wore Black uniforms with the initials *DEA* on their shirts. I was aware that the Drug Enforcement Administration (DEA) now trained its candidates at the FBI Academy. I was to learn in the weeks to come that the DEA and the FBI did not have a very cordial relationship. Some of our FBI instructors would criticize the DEA, while some of our guest DEA instructors took pleasure in criticizing what they perceived as the less than active work of the FBI. The *criminals* benefited from this petty, egotistical law enforcement rivalry.

The DEA students and instructors resented the fact that they had to train in the FBI's house. It made them feel subordinate to the FBI. Further, DEA student rules were different. DEA students were treated like military recruits. They had to be made responsible and molded into agents. They were required to stand up and shout out their names before answering questions in class. And they were not considered agents until their training was completed.

On the other hand, FBI classes, which were sometimes right next to or across the hall from DEA classrooms, were operated like those on college campuses. FBI agent candidates became sworn FBI agents on their first day of class. The position was theirs to lose. The students were told to relax. There was no need to stand to answer questions. There were no uniforms. The instructors were considered co-workers, who were to give as much respect to the students as they demanded of the students. The only important thing was that the students learn their lessons well. Disciplined students were selected during the thorough background investigation and it was a waste of time and energy for the instructors to play military commanders. The differences were obvious. Too obvious, to the DEA administrators and instructors.

It was difficult for the DEA to communicate to its students that they were the best, when they were continuously treated like rowdy children who needed to be constantly inspected and corrected. After all, these were grown men and women, many of whom had held responsible jobs before joining the Drug Enforcement Administration. Some of them had been exceptional police officers. To have other law enforcement officers, many with less experience, yelling in their faces was demeaning to say the least. On top of this, their FBI law enforcement associates across the hall were being treated differently. In fact, many of the FBI instructors who taught in DEA classes suggested that it was difficult to teach in an atmosphere of fear. Students were not likely to ask many questions to which they needed answers. Who wanted to demean himself by standing up and yelling out his name? That kind of performance was for young soldiers in the military.

After eating dinner, I and fellow FBI agent candidates were directed to a classroom, where we met our class counselor, John Finnegan, a short round man who wore glasses. He seemed proud and enthusiastic about being a Special Agent in the FBI and was genuinely excited about having the opportunity to welcome his new, young, bright co-workers. He wasn't what I expected, though. He did not fit the slim, trim, neat image of an FBI agent. He didn't look anything like Efrem Zimbalist Jr.

Special Agent Finnegan's clean white shirt was a little wrinkled and his pants were pulled up too high over his round stomach. His tie was neatly centered and his black wing-tip shoes were polished to a bright shine. His stringy hair was jet black and thinning, especially in the middle. His face was fat and round. He had normal-sized hands, but they looked as if they were swollen. Despite his somewhat unagent-like look, he spoke with confidence and authority as he explained to us what we would experience during our weeks of training.

Special Agent Finnegan explained the testing process. He stated that if we failed one test, we would be given one make-up test and that if we failed the make-up test, we would be dismissed from the FBI Academy. We would be given a physical fitness test after six weeks of training. If we failed the fitness test, we would be dismissed. The gym was available for our use at all times. We would have physical fitness classes, but it was up to us to put in the extra work necessary for our successful completion of the program. No one would be standing over us. We had to have self-discipline.

Agent Finnegan explained the procedures for attending classes and studying. He would be there to help us if we encountered any problems or if a situation arose at home that demanded our immediate attention. He told us that we would be sworn in as Special Agents of the Federal Bureau of Investigation the next morning and at that time we would meet our other class counselors. He also said that he had confidence in the FBI selection process and that therefore he was sure that we all would complete the rigorous training and have long fruitful careers with the Federal Bureau of Investigation.

There was no doubt in my mind that I would have no problem with the academic and physical fitness parts of the training. I had mentally prepared myself. Mom had instilled in me the confidence that I could conquer all if I earnestly and honestly applied myself to the task at hand. I knew I was physically fit. I wasn't in the best possible physical shape, but I certainly surpassed the meager standards set for passing the FBI fitness test.

I worried a little that Operation Drug-Out would come back to haunt me. Someone might determine that I was not as malleable as I should be. I was concerned because Operation Drug-Out indicated that I cared about the upliftment of my people. It denoted a consciousness, which spelled trouble for those who wanted to maintain the status quo.

I had prime examples of what Stepin Fetchiting could do for ambitious self-serving "negroes." I had witnessed what it had done for Walter Williams and Thomas Sowell. In my opinion, they had become popular by attacking their own people. They were given the title of "responsible Blacks" or negroes for their willingness to sell out. They had mastered the art of demagoguery, while making their critics out to be demagogues. Because of their oral and written tympanies, they were viewed as well-read intellectuals. They merely had been well trained by their smiling benefactors in the art of defending the status quo. I could not and would not follow in their footsteps. I wondered what would happen to my career once the FBI found that I was not just another negro sycophant. I was to find out soon enough.

I scanned the room and noticed that there was a total of only six African Americans in this class of forty students. As I looked around I thought of the complaints from some in the white community about affirmative action programs. I was convinced that affirmative action was a policy that had never really been implemented. It was there to be argued about and pointed to by whites as a system of unfairness, of reverse discrimination. Affirmative action was an instrument of diversion and division. I hadn't seen the results of affirmative action in the Maryland State Police. There were no African American barrack commanders and very few African Americans held supervisory positions. And there certainly were qualified African American troopers who merited promotion to these protected positions.

Affirmative action was a delusion. Everyone looked at the title of the program and its stated purpose without looking deeply and critically to discern whether it indeed had been implemented or had had any tangible effects. Dr. Raymond Ellis had instructed me to look below the surface, behind the screen; to read between the lines. I was sure there were a few cases that could have been cited and attributed to affirmative action to appease the liberal masses, but I was also convinced that these examples were few and far between and only for show. Affirmative action had not created an African American Superintendent for the Maryland State Police and it had not created an African American Director of the FBI or the CIA, though there were African American candidates who had paid their dues and were more than qualified to handle these "hallowed" positions. If, unknown to me, affirmative action were in effect, it was a very weak policy and its effect negligible. African Americans need qualified people in positions of *real* power—not just as docile underlings. Looking around my classroom I discerned that this affirmative action policy couldn't even put ten African American or Hispanic agents in a class of forty. No, there was no such thing as affirmative action. African Americans had to realize that affirmative action was nothing more than an illusion. African Americans had to stop arguing about, reaching for, and trying to hold on to something that never really existed—and thereby not let those in power off the hook.

The next day, Monday December 2, 1985, the members of FBI New Agent Class Number 86-1 were officially sworn in as Special Agents of the Federal Bureau of Investigation. As we raised our hands and took the oath, I looked at the proud faces of the students around me. I felt proud, too. I had accomplished what other African Americans in the past could only dream about. I was a part of Dr. Martin Luther King's dream. I believed that he would have been proud of me and the other African Americans, though we were now a part of the very organization that had viciously persecuted him. I hoped that things had changed and that the FBI would never persecute another African American or, for that matter, anyone else again. I hoped that I could make a difference.

After we were sworn in, John Finnegan spoke briefly about the proud history of the FBI. I felt as if I were back in elementary school, learning about the "greatness" of the *slave-catcher* Christopher Columbus and the *slave-owning* "founding fathers" George Washington and Thomas Jefferson. I listened without hearing. It was an art that I had perfected. I had to, in order to protect myself from the deluge of lies that had inundated me since the beginning of my "formal education." One thing that Special Agent John Finnegan said stuck with me and would become of utmost importance later in my FBI career. He warned us against joining the FBI Agents Association. Finnegan did not believe that the Agents Association added anything positive to the FBI. In fact, he thought it was a distraction. Later I and other African American Special Agents of the FBI would wholeheartedly agree.

After Special Agent Finnegan completed his brief informational speech, he introduced us to our other counselors, Special Agent Edward Sulzbach and Special Agent James Carter, both of whom worked under him. Edward Sulzbach was a tall, stout white man with white hair and a bright, friendly, confident smile. He was dressed neatly in what I was coming to believe was an FBI-issued uniform: a white shirt and brown wing tip shoes. He introduced himself, provided us with information on his career in the FBI, and told us a few jokes to settle us down. He, too, seemed proud to be an FBI agent and a class counselor.

Special Agent James Carter was a slim, muscular Black man, who told no jokes. He was stony-faced as he explained his role as counselor. He said that he wanted all of us to become good agents and that he was going to stay on top of us so that we gave our best effort. I admired Carter right from the beginning. He stood up there, strong and proud, and told us what he expected of us. He did not "shuffle and jive." It seemed that whenever Black people got up to talk in front of white people they had to show their bright white teeth. They had to smile and shuffle and laugh—even when nothing was funny. James Carter didn't do that. He felt no need to. He knew who he was and what he was capable of. He had been a sergeant on the St. Louis, Missouri Police Department and had earned the respect of those who worked for him. He had worked undercover for the FBI on drug cases throughout the Midwest and had been extremely effective. He had been strong and confident amid danger. He had been resolute and self-assured when he went back to school and earned his master's degree. He was now working full time and pursuing a doctorate. He had no reason to shuffle. I smiled inside.

The following day, we started classes. As I expected, none of the classes were that difficult. We learned the intricacies of white-collar crime, which, if it had occurred in my neighborhood, would have been classified as pure and simple theft. The violator would have been labeled a criminal and a thief for the rest of his life. The amounts of money stolen by white-collar criminals were astronomical, yet the penalties were lenient. More times than not, once the violator was identified, contact was made with the white-collar criminal's attorney and the attorney brought in his client unhandcuffed. I sat there and thought of all the Black men in my neighborhood who had been wrestled to the ground and handcuffed for taking a candy bar or a radio or some cheap jewelry. Their lawyers weren't contacted to "present" them before the proper authorities and they were sometimes given harsher sentences than the attorney-escorted white-collar criminals. Being a white-collar criminal seemed to be the better choice if one desired a life of crime.

It became clear that "white collar" denoted something about the offender's skin color. Something that entitled him or her not to be labeled a thief, no matter what the amount of the theft. White-collar crimes and public corruption seemed to mean that the offender was an intelligent criminal who deserved a second chance. With one white-collar violation, thousands of victims could be robbed, with the violator reaping immense fruits for his efforts. The consequences, if caught, were minimal. This minimal punishment was reserved for white-collar or simply *white* offenders. I was not the only one who noticed this disparity in the justice system. One of my white instructors suggested to me, in a conversation after class, that it was obvious that the penalties were lighter in white-collar crime violations because most of the offenders were white. He then sternly advised me to just enforce the laws as they were written. "You are not a civil rights leader. Your name ain't Thurgood Marshall. Stop thinking so damn much." Special Agents of the FBI were not to question the "obvious" disparities.

In the days and weeks that followed we studied other violations like kidnapping, interstate theft, drug distribution, bank robbery, unlawful flight to avoid prosecution or confinement, and intelligence matters or spy-catching. We learned the correct procedures for identifying and processing evidence. We were taught the proper manner in which to prepare well-written reports. We learned the internal operations of the federal court system. We were taught proper interview and interrogation techniques and methods for identifying when someone was being deceptive. Our program also comprised several weeks of legal training, which included mock court testimony and proper witness stand mannerisms. We were taught when, where, how, and under what circumstances we could conduct a search or make an arrest. We were taught that FBI policy never allowed us to make an arrest in a misdemeanor case. The FBI just didn't do that. At least, not until the case of Mayor Marion Barry of Washington, D.C.

If a suspect committed a misdemeanor which violated federal law, we were to contact the United States Attorney for that district and he or she would evaluate the evidence and the severity of the violation. The United States Attorney would then decide if the case was worthy of prosecution. If the misdemeanor violation was deemed worthy of prosecution the defendant would be summoned in. Usually he was allowed to come in voluntarily with his attorney. That is the way it was done in the ABSCAM case. The difference was that the ABSCAM violators committed felonies. They should have been, or could have been, arrested on the spot and escorted out in handcuffs, with the press standing nearby.

ABSCAM was an FBI sting operation which began in 1978. Approximately 31 public officials were named as targets, including United States Senator Harrison Williams and six members of the United States House of Representatives. During the ABSCAM investigation undercover FBI agents posed as representatives of an Arab sheik. Thus the name ABSCAM was derived from the words *Arab* and *scam*. The undercover agents offered public officials bribes of up to $100,000 in return for political favors. In the ABSCAM investigation, as in the Marion Barry investigation, the FBI used hidden cameras and other listening devices to record the corrupt activity. Some public officials were recorded actually taking money from the undercover agent who posed as the sheik. As a result of the investigation seven members of Congress were convicted. However, none were immediately handcuffed and paraded before the press after being caught on camera. The congressmen were "presented" before the court on felony charges. Mayor Barry was handcuffed and pushed before the bright lights of cameras on a misdemeanor charge.

Mayor Marion Barry was charged with a misdemeanor. According to FBI policy, he should have been summoned in. In fact, many agents, both Black and white, questioned the FBI's involvement in a case entailing such a minuscule amount of drugs. An agent assigned to the Washington D.C. FBI field office informed me that Mayor Marion Barry was investigated by the Public Corruption Squad. However, Marion Barry was never charged with any of the violations that the Public Corruption Squad handles. I thought it amazing that this point was not emphasized when Marion Barry was arrested. Not for the sake of Marion Barry—he shouldn't have been using drugs. Considering his stellar record during the Civil Rights Movement and his pro-Black reputation—which, contrary to statements by detractors in and outside the African American community, does not automatically mean anti-white—Mayor Marion Barry should have known the effect that his drug use would have on the youth of Washington, D.C. and America, not to mention, on himself. He was one of my heroes, and a hero to those who knew his history.

Further, Mayor Barry should have understood that those he had taken a stand against during the sixties and seventies had not forgotten about his participation in the "radical" movement for change. They never forget. They wait patiently and watch constantly for the mistake that will allow them to get even. Mayor Barry should have recognized that his stance during the Civil Rights Movement meant that he would have to be forever vigilant. His only option, otherwise, was to capitulate as James Howard Meredith had done.

James Meredith was the first Black to integrate the all-white University of Mississippi. His bold move in September 1962 started a series of riots that resulted in one hundred and seventy-five injuries, two hundred and twelve arrests, and two deaths. During the summer of 1966 Meredith walked 225 miles through Mississippi to soothe the fears of Blacks and inspire them to get out and vote. He suggested that if he could walk through Mississippi unarmed, Blacks had nothing to fear. Meredith was shot before he reached the Mississippi-Tennessee state line. He was a strong and brave hero of the Civil Rights Movement.

In 1988 Senator Jesse Helms contacted James Meredith and offered him a job. According to John E. Bradley in an article in the December 1992 edition of *Esquire* magazine, the job offer from Helms came after Meredith wrote a letter to each member of the U.S. congressional delegation and to each of the U.S.

governors stating, "If God sees fit to allow me longevity and good health, I will be in the future the most important Black Leader in America and the World. We need to know each other." Jesse Helms and Senator Patrick Moynihan responded to the letter. Helms, who had once said that Meredith was hand-picked to become the showpiece of forced integration, paid Meredith $30,000 a year.

After leaving the employ of Helms, Meredith went to Louisiana and spent a day with the former Klan member David Duke. According to Bradley, Meredith suggested to the Duke camp that he run as a vice-presidential candidate during Duke's run for the Republican presidential nomination. Duke's campaign staff reportedly found the suggestion intriguing. Meredith stated that he genuinely believed that Duke understood a lot of things. In a period of twenty-five years James Meredith had gone from civil rights hero to supporter of a Klansman. Other African Americans who were willing to sell their souls knew the story of James Meredith well. Some would suggest that with a few minor changes it could be the story of Clarence Thomas. Marion Barry had not taken this path. He would not be afforded the free reign that was allowed those like Meredith.

Mayor Barry's case was handled unconventionally. It was not handled in accordance with FBI policy or at least FBI policy as it had been explained to me at the academy. It was my belief that by not dealing with the unique manner in which this case was handled, the door was left wide open for it to happen again. Someone had to ask the questions. Someone had to make the FBI and every other law enforcement agency understand that the African American community was not going to be treated like a stepchild. We were not ignorant of the way things are "supposed" to be done. We would not stand for arbitrary justice or injustice. It was not a matter of defending Marion Barry. There were deeper implications. We had to demand that things were done right. Frederick Douglass was right: "power concedes nothing without demand."

I cut out of one of the Washington newspapers the picture of Marion Barry being carried off in handcuffs by an FBI agent, and carried it around with me. He was a fallen civil rights leader. Maybe it was his own fault. But J. Edgar Hoover's FBI was determined not to miss out on being involved in Marion Barry's demise, even if it was against the rules. *Another one bites the dust.* J. Edgar Hoover was smiling beneath the six feet of dirt; his plan was being carried on by his heirs.

What I had lived through and witnessed first hand was different from what I was now being told about law enforcement. I was sure now that there were separate law enforcement systems for whites and African Americans. It was one thing to read what African American authors and historians had written about the injustice of the justice system, and quite another thing to have first-hand knowledge of it. I wasn't reading it; Tyrone Powers was living it. I was in the big house, seeing and hearing the hypocrisy. I didn't need to conduct interviews; I was learning about the law enforcement system that dealt with whites. This system was meticulous in staying within the guidelines of the Constitution and the Bill of Rights. All searches were to be conducted in a strict and legal manner. Making an arrest under probable cause rules was considered a last resort. The agent was to prepare an affidavit and seek an arrest warrant in all instances in which there was time. The initiation of investigations had to be based on reliable information rather than on mere suspicion. The agent was to investigate the alleged crime, gather evidence, and present it in an unbiased manner to the United States Attorney. It was then solely up to the United States Attorney to decide whether a particular case was to be prosecuted.

I had never witnessed this kind of law enforcement in the African American community. I had witnessed broken-down doors, illegal searches, and improper arrests. The people I grew up with were investigated on less than mere suspicion. And when "justice prevailed" and mere suspicion was used as a justification for an investigation, that suspicion was based on the color of a suspect's skin. No one could tell me any differently. It was not something I had read in a sociology book or a left-wing magazine. I lived through the brutality of Nazi-style policing on the streets of Baltimore City. I had lived through the police intimidation as a young African American. I had been called a "little nigger" by white police officers patrolling my neighborhood. Without a doubt, the standards and rules of justice were different in the African American community.

I noticed the same clear dichotomy between what I was taught and what I had witnessed while I was a student at the Maryland State Police Academy. But the ultimate realization of the hypocrisy was yet to come. Six years later my coworkers—FBI agents—would force their way into the residence of my ailing mother and sister. They would surround the house with agents and police officers allegedly in search of my deceased brother—to whom the FBI had sent a funeral wreath two years earlier. This was a warning to me for committing the taboo of being a Special

Agent and speaking up against the injustices within Hoover's house. I had no choice but to speak out and voice my concerns. I was a man long before the title Special Agent was affixed to my slave name.

In describing the federal constitutional system of government that was used to deal with the white population, the FBI instructors were protecting the FBI from allegations of institutional racism. Advising the new agents of how they should operate in general allowed the FBI, or the Bureau, as it was known by agents, to state that any racist practices participated in by individual agents were against FBI policy. If racist actions became public knowledge, the FBI, in true Machiavellian style, would offer up as "sacrificial lambs" the violating agents who complained about the racism, and then continue business as usual. The agents would be silenced. This unstated policy became increasingly clear during the investigation of the racist harassment perpetrated by white Special Agents against Special Agent Donald Rochon, a Black colleague whom I will discuss later.

Along with our lessons concerning FBI investigations, we were also lectured on the proper conduct for Special Agents on and off duty. We were drilled on our responsibility to keep our investigations private. Dissemination of information was to be done only with the authorization of proper FBI authorities. We were not to talk to our families about ongoing investigations. If any of the single agents decided to get married, it was their responsibility to notify the FBI so that their prospective mates could be investigated. Married agents' spouses had already undergone thorough background investigations. Divorces and separations had to be reported immediately. According to FBI policy, any violations of law, including traffic tickets, were to be reported to supervisors.

One of the most important duties of all Special Agents was the procuring and operating of "confidential sources," or informants. In reality, confidential sources and informants were one and the same. *Confidential source* sounded better for court purposes and public consumption. Both confidential sources and informants give to the FBI information that the FBI would not be privy to without their infiltration or position within the targeted organization or community. A slight difference is that confidential sources, in some instances, may be contacted only when information is needed about an organization of which they are a part. An informant is contacted periodically to identify any new information that he or she might have developed on any crime—federal, state, or local.

The FBI wanted informants everywhere. In fact, most "successful" investigations are the result of the work of informants or, as street agents call them, "snitches." Informants are a must. Information is power and informants supply that power. J. Edgar Hoover had utilized informants to obtain information on the private lives of almost everyone he came into contact with— friends and foes alike. He utilized this information to secure his position as Director of the FBI. He also utilized this information to destroy the lives and careers of other American citizens. Through the use of informants, J. Edgar Hoover obtained a great many of his secrets, which he loved. It was Hoover who said, "There is something addicting about a secret."

It was not easy for Special Agents of the FBI to circulate in various communities or organizations, so informants were needed. Since they were part of the community, informants were accepted and trusted, to an extent, by those with whom they came in daily contact.   The informants were asked by agents to obtain information on illegal activities and on those suspected of committing illegal acts.   Sometimes, however, these informants reported on actions that were completely legal. Thus, the FBI was able to monitor the movements, the operations, and the thoughts of ordinary law-abiding citizens whose positions on varied subjects may have differed from those of the FBI or from those controlling the FBI. This became evident in the CISPES case.

The FBI reverted to its days under J. Edgar Hoover, with its investigation of the Washington, D.C.-based Committee in Solidarity with the People of El Salvador (CISPES). From 1981 through 1985 the FBI conducted an investigation on over one hundred individuals and groups opposed to the United States policy in El Salvador.   Fifty-two field divisions were involved. Informants were hired to infiltrate CISPES and other organizations that allegedly had contact with members of CISPES. FBI agents photographed CISPES rallies, recorded demonstrations, and wrote down license plate numbers of individuals attending demonstrations or visiting members of CISPES.   Agents also followed college students and monitored church workers.   The investigation never uncovered any criminal activity.

The CISPES investigation also covered such organizations as the National Council of Churches, the Maryknoll Sisters, the United Church of Christ, the United Automobile Workers, the National Education Association, and, of course, the Commission on Racial Justice and the Southern Christian Leadership Conference. The FBI contended that these organizations were not involved in criminal activity, but were part of a front organization that included communists and "unsuspecting" liberals.

I did not become aware of the intricacies of the CISPES investigation until after joining the FBI. Had I known beforehand, it would have confirmed my suppressed belief that the FBI had not changed. After all, the CISPES investigation took place during the eighties. Nate and Dwayne were right; the FBI was not out for justice. Despite the revelations about the handling of the Marion Barry case and about the CISPES fiasco, I still held a faint and fading belief in the potential fairness of such a well-organized and skilled agency as the FBI. Later, when I urged the FBI to investigate blatant civil rights violations, I became the subject of a CISPES-style investigation that expanded to include my family.

The FBI had always been able to find informants. There were always those who were willing to betray the trust of their partner, friend, organization, or even their husband or wife, for the right price. Price did not always mean money. It could be that the informer wanted revenge for some wrong that he believed had been committed against him. It could be that the informant was acting out of patriotism—identifying those who were committing crimes or were involved in activities that were detrimental to the United States of America. It could be that the informant legitimately believed that the actions of a particular person or group of people were wrong and felt that informing on that person or group was the right and just course of action to take. It could be that the informant just wanted to work with the FBI. No matter the reason, the FBI was a more than willing partner.

It was up to the individual Special Agent to identify what would influence the person who was the target of recruitment for the position of informant. It was up to the agent to find out what made the target tick. Offer him whatever he wanted, within reason, in order to get from him what was deemed necessary to bring the FBI on board. The FBI could not function without informants. No effective law enforcement or intelligence agency can.

The thought of informants gave rise to a feeling of contradiction. In reality, informants were traitors to someone. I had grown up despising traitors. I had grown up around people who believed that no death was too horrible for a snitch. I had witnessed the beating of snitches and felt no remorse for their sorry plight. In my youth I had viewed tattletales with utter disdain. I had been adamantly instructed to shun those who had been identified as stooges for the police. Now it would be my job to seek out these traitors and convince them to continue their treacherous activities. In fact, I would be required to give them advice on how to be more effective against their unsuspecting targets.

No doubt about it, "ignorance is bliss." My knowledge of FBI history was interfering with what should have been the robot-like carrying out of simple directives. I thought of the many Black informants, or Uncle Toms, as they were described in the African American community, who had infiltrated organizations like the NAACP, the Southern Christian Leadership Conference, the Nation of Islam, and the Black Panther Party during the fifties, sixties, and seventies. This was during a time that whites outwardly and blatantly abused Blacks. These were the years of numerous lynchings. This was the period which included the murders of Emmett Till, Medgar Evers, Malcolm X, Fred Hampton, Mark Clark, Dr. Martin Luther King Jr., and many other innocent African Americans. During these years, a bomb had been thrown into the Sixteenth Street Baptist Church in Birmingham, Alabama, killing four little innocent Black girls by the names of Denise McNair, Carole Robertson, Addie Mae Collins, and Cynthia Wesley. Yet, despite the obvious brutal treatment of Black people, there had been those informants/snitches/Uncle Toms/handkerchief heads/house negroes willing to infiltrate and bring down the very organizations and the very leaders that were seeking to uplift the race and thus the nation. There had always been those willing to make Faustian deals. Now I had to seek out these unscrupulous, to put it mildly, sell outs.

Although I would not be actively seeking out infiltrators for Black organizations, for a time this type of informant filled my narrow view of an FBI snitch. And it was my opinion that those who were willing to sell out their race had to be dealt with in a swift and brutal fashion. I agreed with Winnie Mandela. Winnie Mandela was a pragmatist and a realist. She was not a bleeding-heart liberal who didn't understand, or who didn't want Black folk to understand, that sometimes goals had to be achieved "by any means necessary." Sometimes it was necessary to fight fire with fire instead of with water. Some types of fires responded even more violently when water was thrown on them. As Malcolm X stated, sometimes it becomes necessary to speak the same language as your adversaries in order for them to fully understand.

Traitors did more damage than any Ku Klux Klansman ever could. The Klansman let you know right up front where he was coming from. He never tried to hide the fact that he was the natural enemy of Black people. He showed his true colors, though he covered his face. He was not unlike a predatory animal in that he never tried to be anything but what he was, and when he approached you it was obvious that his intention was to destroy you. If I saw the sheeted imbecile coming, I liked my chances.

The traitor was different. He befriended those whom he wanted to destroy. He joined his victims' organizations and sometimes climbed to very important positions. All the time, he plotted against those whom he had befriended. He plotted against those who looked like him and talked like him—destroying himself in the process and taking others with him. As Malcolm X said, this was the worst kind of negro, who, having caused Black people much hardship and harm, had to be destroyed, before any progress could be made. There was, and is, nothing worse than a traitor. Such thoughts of FBI traitors troubled my soul.

On the other hand, I didn't regard as traitors the people who provided information on drug dealers. I believed that drug dealers—whom I considered indiscriminate murderers—were traitors themselves. I understood that most Black drug dealers were brainwashed into destroying their race for the sake of material gain. America taught its youth from the very beginning that "the end justifies the means." That is the lesson of unbridled capitalism. But no matter the justification for their becoming traitors, they were traitors nonetheless. I had explained this to Nate. I told him that despite his lecturing to me on my role in helping inner-city youth, his drug dealing was nothing more than a betrayal of his people. Nate didn't enjoy being called a traitor. He didn't want to think about it. I believed the word *traitor* cut into him deeply. Deep within he knew I spoke the truth. But he couldn't accept it without committing suicide, and suicide would mean that he had been defeated by the powers that be.

My training continued. I excelled in the physical fitness part of the New Agents Training Program, thanks to Doris' urging me to physical preparedness. We were required to run two miles every day. The running freed me from the annoying and sometimes burdensome thoughts of my life's contradictions, but it also made me think of my family back in Baltimore. The trees I passed as I jogged along Hoover Road seemed to bear the faces of those I left on the white marble steps of The Blue Gardenia Bar and Lounge. The chirping of birds sounded like the playful laughter of the beautiful, brown neighborhood girls. The explosion of artillery fire boomed like the strong baritone voices of the muscular, shirtless men.

I called Doris and my mother every night to learn what was going on at home. They would tell me everything was fine and demanded that I not worry. They insisted that I concentrate on my studies. They wanted to know everything that was going on at the academy. The questions kept coming: How was I doing on my tests? How was I being treated? What were they feeding me? How was I sleeping? I tried to answer all their questions and then I questioned them: How were my daughter and son? How were Frank, Quincy, Nate, and Sugar? How was Grandma? How was Warren doing in his studies and on the football field at the University of Maryland? Had they heard from Dwayne? Did he say how Operation Drug-Out was coming along? What was going on in the news? The conversations were always the same. If there was trouble at home, Doris and Mom never told me. They didn't want me to worry. Now that I had made the decision to be a Special Agent with the Federal Bureau of Investigation, they wanted me to succeed.

Besides calling Doris and Mom and studying in the evening, I went to the library and read. The library was located within the academy and was pretty well stocked. I would find a secluded booth on the second floor and sit up late into the night reading books on what the so-called experts termed the criminal mind. I learned that most serial killers were white males who seldom had a background steeped in poverty, unlike Black male offenders. The serial murderers' crimes seemed to be motivated by psychological problems, which none of the experts could get a firm handle on. The researchers were sure there was some very understandable reason for white men's perpetrating such heinous, animalistic crimes. Only Blacks, who were regarded as somewhat primitive and barbaric, were considered "capable" of "unjustifiable" murders. The viciousness of the crimes committed by these Caucasian killers contradicted the widespread myth that Black males in particular, and Blacks in general, were a lower form of life, with cannibalistic qualities that could never be quite cured and had no equal. It contradicted the constitutional assumption that Africans were three-fifths of a man. It required the experts to contemplate the "preposterous" idea that criminal activity was not solely based on the color of one's skin. Maybe criminal activity had some *other* contributing factors that had not been honestly analyzed. Although these experts selected their terms carefully, Black males were easily diagnosed and described as poor, depraved, intellectually inferior barbarians and thus prone to commit crimes. For whites, criminal activity was considered a rare aberration with a concrete psychological explanation.

I read statistics which indicated that murderers who killed whites were ten times as likely to get the death penalty as those who murdered Blacks. From these facts I was able to glean that proportionally there were more Blacks in prison than whites, and Blacks were more likely to get the death penalty. I easily discerned that if the death penalty were fully implemented and made operational in every state, many more Blacks would be killed than whites. In order to mitigate the reaction of the critics, it could and would be made to appear that the death penalty was being evenly dispensed among "criminal" members of the human race. However, based on mere numbers and the unblind meting out of "justice" by the judicial system, the death penalty would ultimately result in white executioners killing Black men, women, and children at a disproportionate rate. Some things never change.

The more I read, the more I wanted to read. I became addicted to knowledge, intoxicated by its allure. I enjoyed tracking down the facts as if I were tracking fugitives. I began to understand the motives of the haborers of this coveted knowledge. Knowledge was gold and riches beyond belief. But knowledge was also dangerous to those who hoped to control the ignorant masses—dangerous to the status quo. An ignorant populace, passive and childlike, was easily managed and easily led. Give it toys and gadgets and trinkets; give it sports and entertainment; give it religion. Keep the natives preoccupied so that the talented tenth of the nation, of the world, can run things or ruin things as they see fit. Democracy isn't democracy when the citizens are ignorant. This was the lesson of Plato in his treatise, *The Republic*. Someone in America didn't really want democracy. America was truly a republic, but not one in which the citizens had much say. The elite "chosen" leaders were to be the sole arbiters of democracy. I now understood the compelling and powerful lesson of the Garden of Eden: never eat of the fruit of the tree of knowledge.

The study of history is extremely important. Never had this been clearer to me than when I sat in my Malcolm X-like cell of the FBI Academy's library. I read and stared out into the winter darkness, contemplating and analyzing what I was reading. I understood why the slavemaster would beat his slave almost to the point of death to keep him or her from reading. In the book *Bullwhip Days* Ellen Betts, a slave, stated, when interviewed, that her master did not allow any bright "niggers" around. If the master caught the slave with a piece of paper in his hand, the slave would get whipped. Ellen Betts stated that if a Black man even acted as if he was bright, the master would sell him quick.

There is a great deal of knowledge on the shelves of libraries. If the literature is read and honestly evaluated and analyzed, a crystal understanding of the situation in which Black people, and others, find themselves can be garnered. It was obvious to me that someone did not want this to happen, at least not en masse. As I began to understand the extraordinary methods historically employed in order to keep a segment of the population ignorant, the condition of inner-city schools no longer surprised me. The dilapidated housing and passive "war on drugs" made sense. One couldn't pay much attention to such matters as the electing and monitoring of "leaders," if one was busy trying to keep warm or fight off drug-addicted muggers. The milquetoast Black politicians with enormous campaign chests and financial backing were now predictable. My burden became heavier.

I began to request that Doris send me books from home. Needless to say, she was more than happy to oblige. My reclusive nocturnal reading sessions became more frequent. I read books on white supremacist groups throughout the United States. They are heavily armed and prepared for an all-out war against Blacks and Jews. The government keeps tabs on their movements and confronts them when their acts become obvious and too violent. (They couldn't be allowed to upset the status quo; it would wreak havoc on Wall Street.) Nonetheless, I didn't believe that African Americans should be putting their personal defense and the defense of their children in the hands of a sometimes hostile government. I thought it ludicrous for African American people to talk about gun control, with these violent, well-trained groups preparing to wipe us off the face of the earth. No other group of people would even consider such a notion when surrounded by its declared enemy.

Definitions sometimes had to be adjusted; words and subjects, redefined according to a group and its particular situation or circumstances. *Webster's Dictionary* isn't God; it isn't always right. Gun control for Blacks had to mean something different. It had to mean that Blacks controlled themselves when using such weapons, that they controlled when they used them and on whom they used them. Gun control, like the alleged war on drugs, needed to mean gun education and preparation for self-defense. We Blacks had to understand that true education would keep us from hating ourselves and thus from killing ourselves. Guns didn't make us hate the color of our skin. Guns didn't shackle our legs, arms, and minds and stop us from thinking wisely. Gun control was a trap. Mayor Coleman Young of Detroit was right when he refused to disarm his city of African American residents who were surrounded by hostile gun-toting suburbanites.

I understood all too well what was happening on the streets of urban America. I understood, and understand, the urgency of stopping another bloody episode in the history of African Americans. I have lived through shoot-outs and shoot-ups. I have seen brown flesh punctured with hot lead. I have seen the long and dreary funeral processions. I have heard almost every possible rendition of "Precious Lord." Yet, I am not willing to be duped into a position that could be far more bloody for Black folk. History has taught me what happens to an unarmed community of people. An analysis of the *unprecedented* African slave trade has helped me to understand what one group of people is capable of doing to another, defenseless group of people. The concentration camps of Germany and the internment of two hundred and forty thousand Japanese Americans in America during WWII have helped me to understand what one group of people is willing to do to its unarmed, undeclared "adversaries." The total destruction of the *civilian* population by the dropping of atomic bombs on the Japanese cities of Hiroshima and Nagasaki has helped me to understand why it is important to be in a position to retaliate against those who have no qualms about killing *innocent* men, women, and children. The result of what happens when a hostile government and an unarmed populace meet was made clear, once again, in 1989 at Tiananmen Square in China. The United States granted China "Most Favored Nation" status after China used tanks to crush its unarmed citizens' protest for democracy.

African Americans have to be careful about jumping on someone else's bandwagon too quickly. We have to realize that knives and bats and forks and ice picks could kill, too. It is our minds that we need to regain; it is alcohol, drugs, self-hatred, and ignorance that we need to give up. Having studied history, I was not one to help dupe Black folks into a defenseless position. When it came to self-defense, I was a staunch supporter. I was convinced that no one who did serious research could argue that African Americans should turn in their guns. No one who cared anything about the Black race and knew the history of this country and other countries, and their treatment of people of color could even suggest such a ludicrous proposal. I found it ironic that such organizations as the NAACP and the Southern Christian Leadership Conference acknowledged the fact that the African American male was at risk from a racist society and then in the same breath advised African Americans to disarm. It was, and continues to be, a conspicuous contradiction. People at risk from an identified enemy arm themselves and prepare for future battles. Preparation—making oneself ready—always includes the procuring of weapons to deter the aggressor. These weapons include education, but should not automatically exclude guns. If the Ku Klux Klan can have guns, why shouldn't Black folk? Are we really gullible enough to believe that the Klan will disarm? Will the Jewish Defense League disarm? Would anyone suggest that the United States of America disarm in the face of Soviet aggression? Such a suggestion would leave one labeled a spineless, idiotic *fool*.

The white supremacist groups had books and plans on how to strike against the government and Black people. No one with any sense could discount their infamous manifesto, the *Turner Diaries*. Blacks could not sit back and wait on the government or the "good Lord" for protection. As reported by Joseph Lelyveld in his Pulitzer Prize-winning book *Move Your Shadow*, G. McMurtrie Godley, U.S. Ambassador to South Africa, stated, in response to suggestions that the American government intervene in South Africa on behalf of Blacks, "The day has not come yet, when white men will fight white men in Africa for the sake of Black men." The same is true in America. And if Blacks needed more evidence, they need only allow their memories to revisit the fifties and sixties in the United States and note how much protection they received from "their" government. Prior to the fifties the government didn't even make the pretense of caring. Any race of people who are not prepared to defend themselves is doomed. Malcolm X was right when he stated that we, Black people, had to "be prepared to protect ourselves in case trouble comes our way. And no one can find fault with that."

The remarkable thing about these white supremacist groups is that they blatantly publish their goals and techniques. It is their assumption that the masses of African Americans will not read their publications. Dr. Ellis informed me that it is a must that the thoughts and actions of supremacist groups and their *many* sympathizers be known. To shun their publications can be likened to a general, in the midst of a war, throwing away the stolen battle plans of the opposing army. The *Turner Diaries* is an excellent example of a book that needs to be read by all Americans and African Americans in particular. It isn't hidden away. Groups like the Ku Klux Klan, the Aryan Nation, Posse Comitatus, and the brutal organization the Silent Brotherhood publish their intentions. These groups set up survivalist training camps like the Klan-run camp at Anahuac, Texas, and teach guerrilla "urban" warfare techniques. According to Kevin Flynn and Gary Gerhardt in their book *The Silent Brotherhood*, "a Christian survival school deep in the Arkansas Ozarks taught urban warfare in a silhouette city constructed Hollywood set-style in the forest." Also, according to Flynn and Gerhardt, "the leader of the Carolina Knights of the KKK, Frazier Glenn Miller, claimed a thousand men would answer his trumpet call at Angier, North Carolina, and that they'd be dressed not in white sheets but in combat fatigues, ready for race war."

Flynn and Gerhardt also revealed that there was a computer bulletin board called Liberty Net, initiated by the Aryan Nations, which could be dialed from anywhere in the country, provided the dialer had a computer modem. The bulletin board warned that whites will rise up against Blacks. The message stated, "And now, as we had warned, now come the Icemen! Out of the north, out of the frozen lands, once again the giants gather."

The only thing that we Blacks need to do to access and assess the threat against us is to pick up a book and read. It is not necessary to listen to a fiery leader. Most white hate groups subscribe to the African American folk saying, "If you want to keep something secret from Black folks, put it between the covers of a book." African Americans need to be aware of the historical and current threats, before Black-on-Black crime results in total disarmament. The subject of gun control and the motives of those espousing it need candid discussion and serious examination.

My reading convinced me that many African Americans did not fully understand that America, and the rest of the world, was principally based on "pure," cold economics. Humanitarianism was never a factor. No one gave a damn about the plight of Black people, unless there was some economic angle. African Americans had to build a solid independent economic foundation. As long as someone else controlled the purse strings to the African American community, we would always be subservient. We would always have to shuffle and smile to get some crumbs from the white man's pie. In the Black community, there were plenty of ingredients that would allow for the baking of our own pie. Blacks had to stop believing that some white bleeding-heart liberal really gave a damn about us. In the United States, the end justified the means. If that meant wiping out the Native American population, so be it. If it meant trampling over Black folk, so be it. *The end justifies the means.* In a rudimentary way, the young men and women of the urban streets were more aware of this European-concocted principle than the Black middle class.

It is essential that African Americans understand that relationships and alliances are built on the principle of "What's in it for me?" History tells us that almost every country and race of people, except Africans, have rooted their relationships with others in what they could get out of such a union. Understanding this connection allowed me to understand the unholy alliance between the Jews and the white Nazi government of South Africa. The joint nuclear tests and the sanction-defying trading between Israel and South Africa had previously been perplexing to me, but to Israel it made perfect sense. It was economics over religion, ethics, morals, and perceived alliances. Survival is based on economics and land, not friendship. Alliances between Jews and Black civil rights leaders were fine as long as they did not interfere with the economic goals of Israel and its people. In fact, the African American/Jewish alliance was a mirage. Jewish people benefited from this low maintenance affiliation. They yelled "never forget" in regard to the Jewish Holocaust—rightfully so—but expected African Americans to forget the Jewish role in the African slave trade. As I conducted further research I understood that Israel and South Africa had been unequivocal allies since the European creation of Israel in 1948. Israel, by association, had assisted in the brutal and unmerciful murder of thousands of Black people. Some alliance! Dr. John Henrik Clarke was right when he wrote in his book *African World Revolution*:

> We need to do what all people do, that is, ask the question: Who is loyal to this house? Too many people walk among us, live among us, but declare no loyalty to us. They eat our bread and sleep in our beds. No one asks whether they are loyal to the cause of our liberation. Africans throughout the world must begin to practice the essential selfishness of survival. Our open-mindedness and our hospitality to strangers have been turned against us.

History explained the present, and the understanding of history allowed for proper future alliances based on hard, cold, sometimes ugly facts.

The Christian religion—which had been given to enslaved African Americans, along with the hoe—acted as an opiate. It had been a sedative to relieve the pain caused by the red-hot sun and its simmering heat, which seared the scarred backs of tormented Black bodies. It had helped create and sustain a thin but effective smoke screen of deception which allowed relationships between Blacks and others to be one-sided. Jean-Jacques Rousseau stated in his book *The Social Contract*, published in 1762:

> Christianity preaches only servitude and submission. Its spirit is too favorable to tyranny for tyranny not to take advantage of it.

True Christians are made to be slaves. They know it, and they hardly care. This short life has too little value in their eyes.

This is not necessarily a criticism or indictment of the Christian religion per se, but more an indictment of how it has been used and abused to the detriment of people in general and the African race of people in particular.

African Americans need an economic base. As Gil Scott-Heron stated, "we deal in too many externals." We have to get away from the conspicuous consumption of other folks' products. That Nike gym shoes cost nine dollars to make but are purchased for one hundred and seventy dollars by our young ignorant brothers and sisters is pure exploitation and makes us the laughing stock of the world. I understand the real world now, so I understand that railing against exploitation is not going to solve anything. Exploitation is here to stay. We Blacks have to be able to recognize exploitation when it stares us in the face and sits its huge, heavy posterior down in our devastated neighborhoods. We have to be able to recognize grifters of every creed, color, and religion. Those conservative negroes who are always complaining about Black folk, for the edification of their white employers, need to come into the "hood" and instruct young men and women on how to start up and run their own businesses. Entrepreneurship—Black Capitalism—needs to be taught in every inner-city school. "It is time for more of us to be producers instead of just consumers. We have to produce jobs for our youth. We have to train them to be landlords. As stated in Toni Morrison's classic novel *Song of Solomon*:

> Stop picking around the edges of the world. Take advantage, and if you can't take advantage, take disadvantage. We live here. On this planet, in this nation...*No*where else! We got a home in this rock, don't you see!...Grab it. Grab this land! Take it, hold it, my brothers, make it, my brothers, shake it, squeeze it, turn it, twist it, beat it, kick it, kiss it, whip it, stomp it, dig it, plow it, seed it, reap it, rent it, buy it, sell it, own it, build it, multiply it, and pass it on—can you hear me? Pass it on!

I read books on the histories of the FBI, the CIA, the KGB, the MOSSAD, and other intelligence organizations around the world. It was a necessity that any country or group of people, who hoped to survive, have an intelligence agency or some sort of organized apparatus for studying the actions of other countries or groups. I began to understand that "Big Brother" really was watching and that, in reality, there was nothing that was really private. Intelligence agencies prided themselves on knowing everything about everyone. And they had the advanced technology to secretly and successfully invade the lives of their targets. It was becoming clear to me that the secret (or maybe it was not so secret) of success was to know everything about your enemies and your friends. If you could understand them, get inside them, discern their goals and objectives, and understand what motivated them or made them angry, then you could control them, or at least keep them from controlling you. You could know where they were headed and meet them at the crossroads. You could predict what they would do tomorrow, in ten years, or a hundred years into the future. The exceptional historian Dr. Carter G. Woodson was right when he wrote in his profound book *The Mis-Education of the Negro*:

> If you control a man's thinking you do not have to worry about his action. When you determine what a man shall think you do not concern yourself about what he will do. If you make a man feel that he is inferior, you do not have to compel him to accept an inferior status, for he will seek it himself. If you make a man think that he is justly an outcast, you do not have to order him to the back door. He will go without being told; and if there is no back door, his very nature will demand one.

Mind control. That's what it was. Controlling the thinking of targeted individuals and groups. Attacking what they thought were hidden vulnerabilities. This is what had been done to Black folk. Slavery demanded that it be done. There was no other way to keep a man or a group of people in bondage. The so-called rulers of the world knew this. Control a man's thinking—keep him from reading. Control a man's thinking—provide him with meaningless entertainment, amuse him. Control a man's thinking—provide him with alcohol and drugs. Control a man's thinking—put him at his brother's throat. Control a man's thinking—make him think he is loved when in fact he is hated. Control a man's thinking—make him think he is being helped and disarm him. *Control a man's thinking and you do not have to worry about his action.*

Intelligence organizations subscribe to the effective philosophy of secretly getting inside the mind of a declared enemy. The FBI, under J. Edgar Hoover, utilized phone taps and hidden microphones to gain access to their targets' most treasured secrets and intimate thoughts. Hoover didn't need tanks or missiles. He could accomplish with a cassette tape what others couldn't accomplish with guns. He could destroy a life with a small recording device. J. Edgar Hoover gathered the necessary information to whitemail his subjects. He understood what motivated them. He knew their fears by monitoring them when their guard was down. His slew of informants gave him insight into what his subjects intended to do. He then met them at their point of decision and guided their choices without their knowing it.

J. Edgar Hoover was willing to do anything to obtain empowering secrets. He thirsted for secrets, for hidden information. He used those secrets to dictate to the country what and who they should and should not like. He used his information to destroy people or to make them submit to him. And if the secrets he found were not good enough for his purposes, he manufactured some that were. He used these secrets and the power derived from them to vent his racism. Because he sneaked up from behind like a coward, Hoover was more of a menace to Black people than Adolf Hitler, who openly and directly confronted those he despised. He slipped into a closet and practiced his perverted voyeurism. Hoover's FBI men secretly slithered into Black organizations. These agent provocateurs moved through the bloodline of African American organizations, causing dissension and destruction like a cancerous cell in an outwardly healthy body. By the time the cancer was detected, the body was already in a state of decline.

Hoover was a tyrant who wanted to control everyone and everything. He opposed Dr. Martin Luther King's undaunted fight for equal rights and attempted to drive King to suicide by sending a letter:

KING
In view of your low grade...I will not dignify your name with either a Mr. or a Reverend or a Dr. And, your last name calls to mind only the type of King such as King Henry the VIII....

King, look into heart. You know you are a complete fraud and a great liability to all of us Negroes. White people in this country have enough frauds of their own but I am sure they don't have one at this time that is anywhere near your equal. You are no clergyman and you know it. I repeat you are a colossal fraud and an evil, vicious one at that. You could not believe in God....Clearly you don't believe in any personal moral principles.

King, like all frauds your end is approaching. You could have been our greatest leader. You, even at an early age have turned out to be not a leader but a dissolute, abnormal moral imbecile. We will now have to depend on our older leaders like Wilkins a man of character and thank God we have others like him. But you are done. Your 'honorary' degrees, your Nobel Prize (what a grim farce) and other awards will not save you. King, I repeat you are done.

No person can overcome facts, not even a fraud like yourself....I repeat—no person can argue successfully against facts. You are finished....And some of them to pretend to be ministers of the Gospel. Satan could not do more. What incredible evilness....King you are done.

The American public, the church organizations that have been helping—Protestant, Catholic and Jews will know you for what you are—an evil, abnormal beast. So will others who have backed you. You are done.

King, there is only one thing left for you to do. You know what it is. You have just 34 days in which to do (this exact number has been selected for a specific reason, it has definite practical significant [sic]). You are done. There is but one way out for you. You better take it before your filthy, abnormal fraudulent self is bared to the nation.

J. Edgar Hoover was the director of the number one law enforcement organization in the world, yet he was trying to get a man—whom the world, by awarding him the Nobel Peace Prize, recognized as the number one fighter for peace and justice—to kill himself. History had taught Hoover and his FBI robots that mind control worked wonders. As long as their thinking was controlled, a man, a country, a race of people would be kept in eternal servitude.

J. Edgar Hoover understood Carter G. Woodson's pronouncement, "Control a man's thinking...." He intended to do just that. The ultimate control of a man's mind is having the ability to convince a man to take his own life. That was the kind of power and control Hoover wanted and had. That's the kind of mind control that is engulfing and directing the minds of Black youth today.

J. Edgar Hoover desired more power than his commander in chief, the president. He was willing to be a lawbreaker to get what he wanted. Nate was right: Hoover was a criminal no better than the drug pusher. He was addicted to power. His thoughts would be the thoughts of the nation. His vision would be the vision of the nation, whether the nation wanted it or not. And his vision of America did not include people of color.

On many nights I left the library with my shoulders slumped and my head hung low. I was the character James Jones in W.E.B. DuBois' powerful classic, *The Souls of Black Folk*. I could feel my body going through a metamorphosis. The skin on my face felt like dried stretched cowhide. I ran my trembling fingers across the wrinkles that at some point had been carved into my previously smooth brown forehead. I didn't feel the same inside or out. I was aging. My back and knees ached from the heavy burden of unfiltered, unedited knowledge. I avoided the eyes of those I passed in the corridors. I didn't want them to look into my eyes. I figured that they would be able to tell that I was on a type of high. A knowledgeable Black man had a glow in his eyes. His eyes weren't sunken and glazed over like those of the purposely and successfully destroyed "ghetto zombies."

I didn't want my fellow agents to know yet. Corporal Zachary had taught me that it wasn't prudent to appear wise or to display my wisdom. It was like planning an escape from prison and walking around brandishing the weapon that would be utilized for the flight. I had to pretend that I was still a duped "negro." I knew that the gaining and exhibiting of unfettered knowledge could bring a sudden and abrupt end to my career and possibly my life. This theory would be proven as my career "progressed." Further, I didn't want anyone to peer into my agitated soul. On future nights I would sneak into the library as if I were entering a prohibited area. *Top Secret—Knowledge stored here—Authorized Personnel Only.* I was tasting the forbidden fruit. My soul had felt light and free when I was conducting my research in my library cell, but the more I read, the more my eyes became open and irritated. It was as if I had been in a dark room for a thousand years and suddenly walked out into the brightest light, the brightest sun. The truth was painful. Nonetheless, I swallowed it, as I had gulped down the castor oil Mom used to give us.

In the days and weeks that followed, I walked the halls of the FBI Academy realizing that I would be required to act upon my new-found knowledge. I knew now that I could no longer stand idly by as if I were brainwashed. I would be compelled to act. Compelled to stand up for right. Compelled to deliver the truth to others or, at least, to put them on the road to truth. In the coming days, much would be required of me.

Classes continued Monday through Friday. On the range we were taught how to shoot a variety of weapons, from the U.S. military's M-16 to the Chinese AK-47. We fired shotguns, assault rifles, and an assortment of handguns. We were instructed on how and when to employ tear gas. We were taught what to do in a weapons firefight. We learned how to conceal ourselves and how to find others who had concealed themselves. We learned surveillance techniques and were taught how to photograph our subjects of investigation or surveillance without being detected. We were taught how to surreptitiously obtain intricate information on our targets so that we could predict their future movements and actions. DEA instructors thoroughly provided us with information on the international drug trade. The training was well organized and comprehensive. We were taught in a professional manner by very professional people who believed in and were sure of what they were talking about. I was impressed with the meticulous attention to detail.

The FBI was a well-structured organization and, probably, had been so under the Hoover administration. Unfortunately, Hoover utilized his well-organized machine to achieve goals that were contrary to the United States Constitution as well as contrary to everything America was supposed to stand for. Despite his lawlessness he was honored. Now I understood why. I was no longer naive and blinded by thoughtless patriotism. As I sat through classes, I hoped that the new generation of exceptionally prepared agents would make the FBI the organization it should have been. I realized that there would always be those who would use the FBI as a personal tool to further their twisted philosophies. I hoped against hope that these people could be kept out of positions of power and influence. Maybe, for once, the good of the many would overcome the evil of the few. Unfortunately, or fortunately, the academic schedule at the academy left precious little time for such fanciful thoughts. There was always another test. Tests and more tests.

I passed every test, along with most of my classmates, keeping in mind what Corporal Zachary had told me. Those who happened to fail a test were permitted to retake the examination, as had been advised by Special Agent John Finnegan. I had been forewarned by a group of African American Special Agents of the racist atmosphere at the FBI Academy. They advised me not to allow the racism in the academy to defeat me. They told me to ignore it, or I would become a statistic—a Black agent who was allowed in but just couldn't make the cut. The FBI had perfected the art of deception. They created cultural events and promoted diversity training programs to appease those who demanded that the FBI change. Many of these events and maneuverings were pure window dressing. The FBI garnered statistics, to take before the public and Congress, indicating that African Americans had been "allowed" in the Bureau but had left of their own accord. There were no statistics to indicate exactly why these African Americans had left the Bureau. There were no statistics that accounted for those Blacks who had taken a stand against racism and were forced to resign. Many African Americans were afraid to reveal their true reasons for leaving the FBI, thinking that it would prevent them from securing employment elsewhere.

I heard my share of racist jokes and comments at the academy, but I *managed* to get along with almost everyone, including all of my class counselors. Edward Sulzbach enjoyed my humor. He thought it was great that I was able to keep up such drollery throughout sixteen weeks of rugged, stressful training. He noticed that I seemed unpressured by the barrage of difficult tests. James Carter and I had discussions about work in the field offices and about the FBI in general. He described his role as an undercover agent and the dangerous situations he had been in.

John Finnegan also enjoyed my sense of humor. He watched my test scores carefully and told me that with my intelligence, sense of humor, and ability to function undisturbed by the events going on around me, I would someday be at least a Special Agent in Charge of some FBI field division. On the day I received my orders indicating that my first field assignment would be the Cincinnati division of the FBI, John Finnegan called me to his office. He told me that my orders had actually been to Jackson, Mississippi and that he had pulled some strings in order to get me Cincinnati. Finnegan had previously been assigned to the Cincinnati division and was in the process of trying to get re-assigned there. He stated that Cincinnati would get me off to a good start in my career. He knew the Special Agent in Charge in Cincinnati, Terrance Dinan, and felt I would be treated fairly there and would be given a fair opportunity for advancement. He wasn't so sure what would happen to me in Jackson, Mississippi. Another African American male agent, Fred Ramson, received my orders to Jackson, Mississippi.

My roommate and I continued to get along fine. There were other agents with whom I did not have a very good relationship. One of the white male agents in the room next to mine had been a New Jersey State Trooper. He and I would have discussions on everything from politics to police work. In one of our discussions on history and the Civil Rights Movement, he told me that he did not like Dr. Martin Luther King Jr. and did not think that he was a good leader for African American people. I listened to him, though I cared nothing about his choice of leaders for African

Americans. He admitted that most of his views were a result of what he had been taught by his father, who had also been a policeman. He said that there was no doubt that his father had been a racist but was now beginning to change. He explained that his father would come home from work and tell them stories about his day at work and what he had done to some "nigger." He told me that his father referred to all Black people as "niggers." I could tell that he still agreed with his father on racial issues. I was a nigger to him and always would be. Nothing could change that, not even the fact that I was doing just as well or better than he on all my class work. I knew that he could not be trusted, and he probably felt that I was not to be trusted, either. His dad's philosophy would never allow him to trust a "nigger." While he had criticized Dr. Martin Luther King Jr., I never condemned any of his leaders or heroes. I had never spoken a word to him against white people, or any other group of people, for that matter. He told me that his father was a racist, who had brought his racist philosophy home to his children every day after work. I told him no stories about my dad. I told him nothing about my life at all. I listened to him and learned from him. Soon, this agent, with his views on "niggers," would be on the streets of America, representing the FBI and, most of all, representing his dad.

One evening after dinner, I returned to my room to go to sleep early. I had decided to forgo my nightly expedition to the library. I had stayed up late the night before reading, and my eyes were irritated. Upon returning to my dormitory room, I showered, brushed my teeth, and got in bed. I couldn't sleep, so I picked up the book by Edward Gibbon, *The Decline and Fall of the Roman Empire*, and began to read. Surely this book would quickly cure my insomnia. I read a chapter and then turned off the light to go to sleep. My roommate came in a short time later and went to bed. There were no locks on the doors to our rooms. After all, this was the FBI Academy. A short time after my roommate had gone to bed, the door to our room crept open. I sat up in bed and prepared to chastise the discourteous intruder. The light from the hallway momentarily blinded me and called to mind the lesson I learned that cautioned against reacting blindly to an unknown situation. The invader could have been one of my class counselors. He was not.

Three men entered the room, wearing white sheets as if they were Ku Klux Klansmen. They were laughing loudly and staggering as if they were drunk. I thought I recognized one of the voices but wasn't absolutely sure at the time. I tried to identify the men through the lenses of my still unfocused eyes. My eyes failed me and their sheets served them well. The voices were muffled by their drunkenness and my seemingly thunderous heartbeat. The drunken FBI Klansmen didn't put me in fear. I only feared that I would not be able to restrain the fire in my burning soul—in which case someone in that room was going to die that night. My roommate prevented that from happening. "Get the fuck out of here, you drunk stupid assholes." The troglodytes disappeared into the hallway.

The room was dark again. I sat still and silent for a moment, trying to think of the appropriate counteraction for such a bizarre and revealing incident. I slowly eased back into a prone position and stared up toward the ceiling. I contemplated this significant juncture in my FBI "career." I thought of packing up and walking out. I thought of going home to the comparatively not-so-mean streets of Baltimore City. The echo of Ralph Ellison's words, "keep the nigger running," prevented such a craven reaction.

In the darkness of my room, I visualized the beautiful and anguished faces of my mother, sister, and brothers. I saw the contorted face of my father. This is what had broken him. Years and years of harassment. Years and years of sparks and fires in his soul being ignited and then suddenly doused. He had served his country during the war; he had worn the uniform of patriotism. But then he came home to the "land of the free" and the "home of the brave" to be called a nigger by cowards wearing white sheets and three-piece suits. His family had to sit in the car and hear uniformed policemen call their daddy "boy" on one of the many "routine" traffic stops. It was enough to break a man. To drive him to alcohol and drugs. But it wasn't going to break me. Despite FBI instructions to the contrary.

I turned over on my side and thought deeply about the episode with the sheeted imbeciles. I suppose I should not have been surprised by their antics. The atmosphere at the FBI Academy had led these agents to believe that it was all right to be racist. This was an organization that employed only a little over four hundred Black agents out of a total agent population of about ten thousand five hundred. This was an organization that was founded in 1908, and in 1985 called the employment of four hundred African Americans progress. It was an organization that employed agents like the sheet wearers.

I had no fear of bigoted agents. My lessons at the Blue Gardenia had prepared me for this type of event or confrontation. I was not going to attack them. Should an assault occur, I knew that I would be the one quickly dismissed from the academy. I would be made the offender and they, the innocent white victims.

I thought about telling John Finnegan or James Carter, but I believed that nothing would be done and that I would be the one labeled the "troublemaker." I had no faith in the Equal Employment Opportunity Commission (EEOC). Later, my lack of faith in the EEOC would be justified by their actions. The EEOC was staffed by FBI employees who feared for their jobs should they rule against the FBI. Going to the EEOC was like sending the hen to complain to the fox about the brutal attacks of other foxes. The FBI was just a microcosm of the country under President Ronald Reagan, or any other president, for that matter. Reporting Equal Employment Opportunity violations would be a pathetic joke. I decided to do nothing for the moment. It was not something that a strong Black man in America could not handle now or had not handled, in some form, in the past.

I was not going to run to "the man" to solve a problem that I was sure he cared nothing about. It seemed that we African Americans were always running to someone else to be our savior. Somehow, despite what history had taught us, we truly believed that someone gave a damn. Malcolm X was right: many of us had lost our minds. James Oppenheim was also right when he wrote in his book *The Slave*,"free men set themselves free." I decided not to mention the Klan prank to Mom or Doris. They would just worry unnecessarily. Finally, before falling deep into an unusually peaceful sleep, I decided that if I were physically attacked, I would respond with maximum retaliation. I would wage total and absolute war, no matter what the consequences.

The incident with the FBI Klansmen was my first encounter with blatant racism in the FBI, but it wouldn't be my last. On another occasion, I had gone down the hall to the dormitory room of fellow agent Gregory Lockett. Greg was a Black agent who had played football at Ohio University prior to joining the FBI. He and I often discussed the fact that he had tried out for a fullback position with several of the National Football League teams. I told him about my brother Warren and the success he was having playing football at the University of Maryland.

Upon entering Greg's room on this particular day, I found him and his roommate engaged in a heated argument. Greg walked into the bathroom. His roommate, who was white, yelled after him, "You goddamn nigger. You fuckin' niggers are all alike." I stood there as he slowly turned toward me. He was red in the face. He stared at me in silence for a few seconds. I watched as his eyes moved down my body and inspected my fist which had subconsciously been rounded into a ball of tight brown flesh and rugged knuckles. Greg walked up behind the trembling agent and lowered his voice. "If you ever call me that again, I'll break your fuckin' neck." The trembling agent never turned toward Greg. His eyes found the floor. He moved around my statue-like body, opened the door, and faded into the hallway. I sat down at his desk, expecting Greg to explain to me what had happened. He never did.

I recall that one Friday evening the agent in the room next to mine—who I suspected had been involved in the Klan prank—asked me to drive him to Washington National Airport so that he could fly home to New Jersey for the weekend. I was driving home to Baltimore, and Washington National Airport was not too far out of my way, so I agreed. I left the academy parking lot and slowly drove north on Interstate 95 toward Washington National Airport. I put in a cassette tape which contained Dr. Martin Luther King's speech, "The Drum Major Instinct." I drove and used my peripheral vision to watch the reaction of my passenger. Halfway through the speech I reached forward and turned the cassette player off. My passenger spoke in a slow, low, deliberate tone. "Turn it back on. Please, turn it back on." I turned the cassette player back on and we listened in silence to the rest of the speech. When we arrived at the airport. He turned to me and said, "He was one powerful man." He then smiled and said, "Thanks." I will never know if he was thanking me for the ride or for playing the tape of Dr. Martin Luther King Jr.

March 20, 1986. I was glad to see graduation day come. I was proud that I had completed the training, as expected, without failing a test. I had learned a great deal. The agents and instructors at the academy had prepared me well. Enmeshed within my training were the lessons of Mom, Dad, Frank, Quincy, Sugar, Nate, Doris, Dr. Raymond Ellis, Dr. Elizabeth Gray, Dr. Richard Bright, Marcus Garvey, Malcolm X, Vernon Johns, Martin Luther King Jr., Harriet Tubman, Frederick Douglass, Carter G. Woodson, John Henrik Clarke, John Hope Franklin, Cheikh Anta Diop, Ivan Van Sertima, Patrice Lumumba, Jomo Kenyatta, Kwame Nkrumah, Toussaint L' Ouverture, Denmark Vesey, Nat Turner, Louis Lomax, John Jackson, Alex Haley, George Jackson, Toni Morrison, Ralph Ellison, Lorraine Hansberry, Zora Neale Hurston, Maya Angelou, Jesse Jackson, W.E.B. DuBois, Rev. Albert Cleage, Paul Robeson, John Quincy Adams, Thomas Jefferson, Theodore Roosevelt, Franklin D. Roosevelt, Dwight Eisenhower, Harry S. Truman, John F. Kennedy, Robert Kennedy, Richard Nixon, and many others. Ironically, I had turned J. Edgar Hoover's house into my own institute of higher learning.

Doris, her mother Shirley, and her Aunt Pearl came to the graduation. They sat with Mom, Betty Jean, Grandma and some close friends of the family, Mrs. Ruby Griffin and her daughters, Cheryl and Patricia. Secluded in a corner in the back of the auditorium, sat my father, Frank Powers, Sr. Father Time had prematurely cut down Dad's body. He was graying and he looked tired. Drooping wrinkled lids of skin rested heavily on his aching wet eyes that had seen so much pain. He had gained more weight since I had last seen him in September. He was moving farther away from the image of that strong and sturdy soldier who had confronted the redneck checker players at the dusty bus station in Wilson, North Carolina. I wanted to reach out and embrace him. I wanted to let him know that I still loved him and was happy to see him. I didn't want him to fade out of my life. I didn't want these people to look into my father's eyes and read his soul. He was none of their business. I wondered if at some point in my life I would be sitting in some dark corner of some room, fading away, rejected by my children for being broken into tiny irreparable pieces.

The agents seated around me smiled in anticipation of receiving their FBI credentials. We each awaited the calling of our names, when we could take the short trek up onto the stage and shake hands with the director of the FBI training division. It had been a long journey. As my name was called I walked up onto the stage with my head held high. I smiled at my family, shook hands with the director, and took hold of my FBI credentials. I was now a member of that "exclusive club" that James Thorton had spoken of.

24

Special Agent Tyrone Powers

He thinks too much; Such men are dangerous.
—Shakespeare, Julius Caesar, I, 2

Men who are in earnest are not afraid of
consequences.
—Marcus Garvey, The Philosophy and
Opinions of Marcus Garvey

Any Black man today who strives to be a man
among men is singled out and accused of
everything except what he is trying to do.
—Betty Shabazz, Malcolm X

"There it is!" Right there in southern Ohio. Prior to running my index finger slowly across the map, from east to west, I had no idea exactly where Cincinnati, Ohio was located. I knew it was in the Midwest, but hell, there were a lot of cities in the Midwest. I didn't like its German-sounding name, because I initially associated Cincinnati with Germany and everything German with World War II, Hitler, and his Nazi disciples, several of whom I'm sure I have worked with during my career in law enforcement. I had fallen prey to the brainwashing that was so much a part of my early education. (Of course, Black folk weren't the only people being brainwashed. A whole lot of white folk were being intentionally miseducated and brainwashed when it came to

303

understanding people of color.) Even after my enlightenment, there was a tendency to relapse into easy and comfortable ignorance. Once I caught myself falling into this dark dungeon, I quickly plunged into reading, contemplating, analyzing, and a little praying for forgiveness of my lapse.

Cincinnati was named after the oldest military organization in the United States, the Society of the Cincinnati. Actually, the name Cincinnati came from the Roman dictator, Lucius Quintius Cincinnatus. In a single day he defeated an invading army and then returned to his small farm. In other words, he didn't seek re-election. He didn't even finish his term. Once he completed his altruistic, patriotic duties he got the hell out of office. Once out of office he didn't travel the world, charging enormous speaking fees. More of our modern-day politicians need to read the history of Lucius Quintius Cincinnatus.

At any rate, Cincinnati was the place where I would start my career in the Federal Bureau of Investigation. It was the place where Doris, Tamara, and I would begin a new life of sorts. We would have to acquaint ourselves with supermarkets, cleaners, schools, churches, hospitals, roads, parks, furniture stores, hardware stores, malls, movie theaters, the Cincinnati Zoo, museums, libraries, and people. I would have to acquaint myself with being an FBI agent.

The most difficult part of our migration to the Midwest was leaving our families behind in Baltimore City. I have always been convinced that families, and especially African American families, need to be close together in times of crisis. The Black race is falling victim to all of the subtle, and not so subtle, traps of genocide. In fact, during the brutal reign of slavery, as practiced in the United States, Black families were intentionally separated to prevent unity and to help create blind obedience. I believe that the effects of these historical separations are deeply seated in the very psyche of Black folk and have strained family relations. Moreover, when the awful ingredients of miseducation, alcohol, drugs, and unbridled lust are dumped in the inner-city Black community, the consequence is Black-on-Black violence, disrespect for Black women, conspicuous consumption, middle-class flight, Uncle Toms, Aunt Tomasinas, Chicken Georges, child abandonment, crack babies, crack mothers, crack fathers, and hundreds of other resulting maladies.

On the other hand, if African Americans are going to take full advantage of what America has to offer, travel is a necessity. It is an integral part of the gaining of knowledge, which is a vital element of the attaining of self-sufficiency. Not only are people in countries around the globe different, but people in the separate regions of America possess their own uniqueness. If we African Americans are going to have relations with other Americans and with people around the world—and we must—there is a need for a deep understanding of what motivates different segments of the population. Of course, the understanding of others necessitates the study of history, but it also entails close observation and analysis. Travel would help in our crucial quest to learn about others, to become knowledgeable. As time passed I found that staying spiritually close to my family and traveling did not pose a dilemma, as I had initially anticipated. Nonetheless, I believe eventually we all should return home.

I suppose that deep within I still had not completely accepted the peculiar fact that I was an FBI Special Agent. I found my mind intermittently revisiting the streets of Baltimore City. I thought of Chas, Dwayne, Craig, Stanley, Sheldon, and, of course, Angel. I thought of the back porch with its sunshine, rain, laughter, joy, and pain. I thought of Baltimore Street, Carey Street, Old Frederick Road, Lexington Avenue, Eutaw Street, Edmonson Avenue, Cold Spring Lane, Pall Mall Road, Monroe Street, Pratt Street, Hilton Parkway, Park Heights Avenue, North Avenue, and the famous Pennsylvania Avenue. I thought of Congressman Parren J. Mitchell and Operation Drug-Out. I thought of Southwestern High School and Coppin State College.

Baltimore City was my home. I was determined to go back there as often as possible and sit with the remaining fellows and the new generation of ghetto scholars on the steps of The Blue Gardenia Bar and Lounge. I would visit the alley, I mean, stadium, where I initiated my little Negro League. I would sit on the steps of Dad's back porch and peer across the alley, awaiting a glimpse of the breathtaking beauty of Angel. I would visit Southwestern High School and Coppin State College. I would visit Dwayne's parents—my adopted mother and father—Mrs. Arlene Robinson and Mr. Samuel Robinson. And, of course, I would spend hours conversing with Mom, Frank, Quincy, Sugar, Nate, and Warren.

Despite my reservations, I settled easily into my new career as a Special Agent in the Cincinnati division of the FBI. I had studied hard at the academy and was sure that with experience I would become one of the most productive FBI agents in the history of the Bureau. I also desired to assure the African American community that the FBI could be fair. How I was going to accomplish this herculean task single-handedly never crossed my mind. I was confident of my abilities. So were others. An instructor at the FBI Academy, Supervisory Special Agent Ron Kirkland, wrote a memorandum to my personnel file and to the Special Agent in Charge of the Cincinnati division stating that I "exemplified the type of hard work, dedication and perseverance that had made the FBI the organization it currently is." He indicated that I was and would continue to be an asset to the FBI. Further, when I was in the academy, a representative from "CBS Evening News with Dan Rather," contacted the FBI and informed them that they would be airing a segment of my speech to students at Southwestern High School. The representative told Special Agent Edward Sulzbach that the FBI had made a very wise choice in accepting me into the academy.

I was to find out later that the memorandum that Supervisory Special Agent Ron Kirkland had written never made it to the Special Agent in Charge (SAC) in Cincinnati or into my personnel file. The only copy of the memorandum was the one that I had made and kept. After showing my copy to the SAC's secretary, she stated that she should have received the memorandum and it should have been presented to the Special Agent in Charge prior to my arrival, but somehow it never was. There was also no further mention of the comments by the representative from CBS Evening News. Later, during a campaign launched to "handle" me, there would be derogatory information that easily made its way into my personnel file. Spurious, disparaging comments made about me by white Special Agents would be circulated throughout several divisions of the FBI. I would report it all to division FBI supervisors and to FBI headquarters in Washington, D.C. No action would be taken.

Doris, Tamara, and I moved into a two-bedroom apartment in Anderson Township, an apartment complex on the east side of Cincinnati. A few other FBI agents lived in the same complex. I became good friends with Ken West and his wife Martha. Ken was a Black agent who was originally from Florida. He and I loved basketball and we engaged in several heated one-on-one basketball games, which he usually won. Well, he always won. He had been a high-school basketball all-star. There was nothing I could do to stop his quick moves to the basket and his deadly jump shot.

What I admired most about Special Agent Ken West was not his athletic prowess but his calm, quiet intelligence. Ken was older than I. He had been a Special Agent for approximately two years. I valued his advice and experience. He and I were the only African American FBI Special Agents assigned to the Cincinnati division. We discussed everything from politics to FBI investigative work. He never lectured me, but gave me solid advice on my career and finances. He told me that no job was ever secure for an African American; thus it was important to prepare myself financially to survive for a period without employment. If, for whatever reason, the FBI decided I was no longer an asset—and the decision did not have to be work-related—I had to be prepared to carry on.

I recall sitting down on a curb with Ken after one of our basketball battles. The hot sun beamed down on our sweat-covered bodies. We looked like the glistening shirtless men of Baltimore Street. I was proud of that. Ken gulped down a bottle of clear, cold water. I wiped my face with a towel and thought of the beads of perspiration that I had so often seen resting placidly on Nate's bald head on hot days like this one. I smiled to myself. Ken's discourse came from nowhere. I hadn't asked him a question. We hadn't been talking at all since his fifteen-foot jumper ended another exhausting game. "Being an FBI agent is an excellent career. You get to travel and you have a much better understanding of the country and the world. It pays well and the benefits are good. You get to do interesting work. And for once, we get to take a look from the inside out."

I watched Ken closely. A sorrowful veil dropped over the African features of his firm brown face. I had seen it before—the look, the veil, the deep and sometimes painful reach into the soul of a Black man. Ken continued, "There might come a time when you are asked to sacrifice your beliefs, your personal heartfelt beliefs and allegiances, for the Bureau. At that point you must make a decision. I know what mine will be. Think about it. You don't have to say a thing to anybody about what your decision will be. Just know within you what you will do and how you will respond should the situation arise."

Without Ken's expounding on what he had just mentioned, I understood him. Every *conscious* African American Special Agent of the FBI understood something about the history of the FBI and the African American community. We knew of the infiltrations and the divide-and-conquer and murder schemes. We knew of the Uncle Toms. What's more, we realized that one of the extra unstated employment requirements for Black agents was that we be *very* conservative and sever most of our meaningful ties with our communities and with our past. We also had to be willing to do whatever the Bureau thought was in its best interest. I heard echoes of the conversation with my FBI recruiter, James Thorton, in Ken's stern baritone voice.

I continued to observe Ken. He gazed up into the fiery sun and took a deep swig of God's soothing water. I believe Ken was trying to douse the fire that was burning deep within his soul. The sun didn't bother him. The sun had been there all day. It had been there through his Globetrotter-like basketball exhibition. Another type of heat was disturbing Ken. An internal, unconquered heat. Yet he wanted to maintain his composed, quiet way of expressing himself. So he stilled his rumbling soul with the cool liquid and calmly spoke. "Your long-term goal has got to be entrepreneurship. It's the only way. Every man who has to depend on someone else for his income is a slave of sorts, especially a Black man. Somehow you've got to obtain the ability to be independent and self-sufficient. A man who can't speak his mind suffers internally and indefinitely. If he says the wrong things, he's punished—even if what he says is true. The fear that keeps men from telling the truth is the worst type of slavery. We're in an organization in which that fear is omnipresent. The master who keeps this fear in his workers is powerful. Fear will keep us all quiet and will slowly destroy us."

Ken was right. Lloyd Douglas once stated, "If a man harbors any sort of fear, it percolates through all his thinking, damages his personality, makes him landlord to a ghost." I just didn't know why Ken was sharing these thoughts with me at this particular point in my young career. In hindsight, I believe he was trying to forewarn me of ominous things to come.

The Cincinnati division, like all other FBI field divisions, is divided into squads. Each particular squad is designated an assortment of federal violations to investigate. Ken worked on the White-Collar Crime Squad and I was assigned to work fugitive and drug cases on a Reactive Squad. The Reactive Squad was set up to handle investigations that required the immediate attention of the FBI. But in Cincinnati, the Reactive Squad covered narcotics, interstate theft of stolen property, fugitives, and a few other violations.

The supervisor of my squad was a frail man with glasses. In my opinion, he was determined to make it into the top echelon of the FBI, and he saw every other "not so special" agent as a rung on the golden ladder to the top. He pursued his goal with reckless abandon. I was not alone in my assessment of his selfish, unbridled ambitions. Some of the other agents on the squad secretly speculated that his personality was a result of his conspicuous frailness. I came to the conclusion that since he could not command much attention or respect on his looks, expertise, and competence, he made a feeble attempt to gain it through his brash actions. Most of the agents on the squad worked exceptionally hard and took pride in their efforts. They immediately informed me that nothing I did would ever be good enough for him, unless I became one of his pet agents. Needless to say, I immediately discerned that nothing I did would ever be good enough for him. My co-agents instructed me to do my work and to try to ignore the supervisor, if at all possible. I took their advice, for as long as it was possible.

Over my years in the Bureau I encountered many FBI managers who were on the same power-hungry high as my squad supervisor. It is my belief that some of them sacrificed the noble and patriotic goal of solving crime in order to "get ahead." Doing what one was sworn to do was not necessarily the most expedient road to promotion. At times the stated mission of the FBI coincided with the ambitions of these zealots; however, if they were required to make a choice between the two, the public suffered. One of these supervisors stated to me, "A lot of complicated cases equals a lot of complicated problems; no complicated cases equals no problems." For example, street-level drug investigations yielded high arrest statistics for vote-hunting politicians and a public looking for any sign of impact on the illusory war on drugs, but negligible real results.

These insecure power-hungry supervisors had unrealistic assessments of their power or the extent of their authority (which they seemed to believe was limitless). *Supervisor* does not automatically denote superiority. I came to the conclusion that my supervisor in Cincinnati had lost all sense of reality when he requested the presence of an agent who was on the phone speaking with an agent from another division of the FBI in regard to a case. When the agent told the supervisor that he would be there in a minute, the cantankerous supervisor walked over to the agent's desk, took the phone out of the agent's hand, and hung it up. A look of astonishment immediately dropped over the pale white face of the victim agent. I put my head down and said a little prayer thanking God that the obnoxious supervisor hadn't made the awful mistake of selecting me as the subject of his idiotic show of power, for I surely would have been unemployed and most probably criminally charged with assault and battery.

The obviously addle-brained agent who was subjected to this humiliation told me that the supervisor would never do to me what had been done to him because I was Black. Mind you, I was the only African American on the squad at the time, and the supervisor hadn't done his deed to any of the other agents. This agent—who would later have complaints filed against him for racial slurs, to no avail—was telling me that my race was of benefit in this situation. Or he was stating that the cowardly supervisor was afraid to confront Black folk and Black men in particular, a theory that would be disproved, by my confrontation with the frail defender of South Africa. I was to take as a compliment the supposed ability of my Blackness to strike fear in this frailest of white men. This agent had scanned the room, found me, and launched a deceptive attack on me instead of confronting his obvious antagonist. Later, the future supervisors and the co-workers of this agent, in an almost humorous attempt to paint me as a "racist," would accuse *me* of associating everything with race.

The "sacrosanct" history of the FBI creates an arrogance and false sense of power in many Special Agents, and it manifests itself most prominently in supervisors, many of whom have no true concept of what real power is, and never will. Therefore, whatever power they secure, they automatically abuse. Many of these supervisors are nothing more than low-level bureaucrats who actually control very little and make very few significant decisions. They are just cogs in a vast machine that most probably could run fairly well without their insignificant input. In fact, some of the more experienced street agents would make better supervisors than these designated "leaders."

Part of the problem that prevents the FBI from utilizing the best of its talent in supervisory positions is the mandatory quinquennial transfer of managers. Special Agents who are most qualified and most dedicated to the communities in which they serve are not willing to uproot their families every five years and move across the country to do essentially the same job they were doing before their move. It is my opinion that the agents who are willing to move are those who are financially capable of making such a move and those who desire power at all cost, even at the risk of destabilizing their very families. This system would be easier to accept and understand if supervisors were relocated based on a unique expertise that they possessed and that was needed in another area of the country. But that is not the case. Many supervisors sought only to exercise minimal power with maximum force.

It was this philosophy that motivated the frail supervisor to leave his den in search of easy prey on a cold autumn morning. I can still see him sauntering through the squad area, trying desperately, and failing miserably, to display an air of authority. I sat at my desk following my routine of reading the daily newspapers prior to going over my files and starting work on my cases. It was not unusual to find in the newspapers case-related matters of which the FBI was not aware. The often-stated myth that the FBI knows everything about everything and everyone is just that, a myth. The FBI certainly has the technology and the know-how, but there is just too much going on to know everything. The paranoia that this myth creates sometimes proves advantageous and is seldom dispelled by the Bureau.

The frail supervisor interrupted the rhythm of my routine. Standing there behind me, he broke my concentration. I prepared myself for a cowardly attack. Having glanced at the article on the sanctions against South Africa, he proceeded to make provocative statements about his acceptance of racism, the "righteousness" of racists, and the "inconveniences" that he and his wife "suffered" because of the sanctions. His contempt for the Black South Africans and their plight and his disregard of the South African government's heinous atrocities committed against the Black Africans were made obvious with each statement. His defense of the South African Holocaust appalled me. For him to reduce the suffering of the Black masses to whether or not he could purchase a diamond for his wife sent chills through my body. I realized that he was attempting to engage me in a battle of words in order to determine whether I was a "good negro" or a "trouble-making nigger." I stood up and spoke out.

After the confrontation with the frail FBI supervisor, I came to the conclusion that he was the victim of the mentally debilitating disease termed racism. As my career advanced, or regressed, I found out that he was only one of many agents infected with this tragic malady.

I reported the supervisor's comments to the Assistant Special Agent in Charge (ASAC) in the Cincinnati division. He informed me that he, too, had noted the insensitivity of the supervisor. He stated that the issue had also been brought to his attention by a female Special Agent. He stated that he had rated the supervisor low in this area on his performance appraisal. Within four years of this incident, the supervisor was promoted twice. Further, I was informed by a supervisor in Detroit that the ASAC in Cincinnati had labeled me a "racist" and a "troublemaker" and had passed these comments on to the ASAC in the Detroit division prior to my being transferred there. In the weeks, months, and years that followed, the supervisor, with the assistance of the Bureau, tried to "break" me and make me cry "Uncle." They tested my resilience and gradually increased the level and severity of their onslaught, eventually targeting and attacking what I cared about most—my family.

The new government vehicle that had been assigned to me was taken away and given to a white agent with less seniority, and apparently less loyalty, since he eventually quit to sell trophies! I was assigned a ragged vehicle that could barely start. The supervisor informed another African American Special Agent that he was trying to teach me a lesson. It wouldn't work. Material things were never that significant to me. Apparently someone had told this supervisor that everyone has a price and a Black man can be bought or "broken" for next to nothing.

The Assistant Special Agent in Charge (ASAC) in the Cincinnati division stated to other supervisors and to high-level administrators, in essence, that I was to be denied any further training at FBI expense. A document was placed in my personnel file with a circle around information indicating that I had received a master's degree from the University of Cincinnati. I suppose that the ASAC subscribed to the old European adage that an educated negro is a dangerous negro. His philosophy seemed to fall in line with the old slavemasters. In the powerful book *Bullwhip Days*, former slave William McWhorter stated, "Dey jus' beat 'em up bad when dey catched 'em studyin', readin', and writin', but folks did tell 'bout some of de owners dat cut off one finger every time dey catch a slave tryin' to get larnin'."

When I was later transferred to Detroit, my integrity and loyalty were questioned and information was furnished to top administrators indicating that I was to be denied access to a position on the Intelligence Squad in Detroit "until a work ethic is displayed to Detroit's satisfaction." What "ethic" they wanted me to "display" is unclear, but I'm sure it had something to do with the instructions given by the Detroit ASAC to "handle" me.

I was labeled an incompetent agent although my statistical accomplishments were higher than most other agents in the Cincinnati division. Supervisors in Detroit would later admit there was no indication of incompetency in my personnel file, although they were sent written comments by the Assistant Special Agent in Charge (ASAC) from Cincinnati stating that I had "yet to display my talents to the FBI as an accomplished investigator." These comments were made despite the fact that I had worked numerous cases that were successfully prosecuted by Cincinnati's Assistant United States Attorney, Patrick J. Hanley, in which hundreds of thousands of dollars of cash and property were forfeited to the United States Government. I had risked my life by working undercover in brutally violent drug organizations and had made substantial purchases of drugs from the ring leaders. I had convinced these ring leaders to work for the government and to give up their sources, thus allowing for the successful investigation and prosecution of the ring leaders' sources. I had written extensive Title III affidavits in order to obtain wiretaps. These affidavits were read, agreed upon, and signed by federal judges. I had prepared numerous complaints to obtain arrest warrants for violent fugitives and had then gone out and made the arrests. I had testified before several federal grand juries and trial juries, and a verdict of guilty was handed down in *all* of my cases. My method and mode of investigation were *never* questioned by the Assistant United States Attorney, the defense attorneys, the judges, or the juries, all of whom believed that I displayed exceptional investigative talents. What talent did the ASAC wish that I display? Was it the talent to do "Stepin Fetchit" routines?

These vicious rumors of my being an incompetent racist were not only circulated in Cincinnati but were forwarded to the Detroit division upon my transfer there. I managed to get a copy of these comments, which were recorded on a document that had been signed by the Assistant Special Agent in Charge (ASAC) in Cincinnati. I was told that the document was not meant for my eyes and that I never should have been able to get a copy of it. The Special Agent in Charge and the ASACs in Detroit attempted to get me to forget about the document, the comments, and the authors of those comments. One of the ASACs in Detroit told me that "if I just wanted to get a piece of someone's ass, I could file an Equal Employment Opportunity (EEO) complaint." He also told me that if I did not let the matter drop, it would come back to "haunt" me later in my career.

After I had filed a futile EEO complaint, the Special Agent in Charge of the Detroit division tried to talk me into dropping the whole matter by offering me a "hard to get into" training course. I suppose I could have taken it and been silent. But what would happen to the agents who came after me and who dared to speak out? Many good agents would be lost if those responsible for the internal injustices were not reprimanded. The FBI and the nation would suffer if good, patriotic, justice-seeking investigators were crushed by racist bureaucratic tyrants.

One of the two ASACs in Detroit told me that the ASAC in Cincinnati must have "got up on the wrong side of the bed" on the day he wrote the comments claiming that I was incompetent and requesting that I not be allowed any further training at Bureau expense. No one would address the comments that labeled me a "racist." No one ever denied that the comments had been made. In fact, when interviewed in regard to the disparaging comments, one of the two ASACs in Detroit stated that the ASAC in

Cincinnati had indicated that I was a "problem" employee who required "close" supervision. He stated that he didn't recall my being called a racist specifically but did recall the ASAC's saying I was an individual who was *very race conscious.*" The ASAC admitted that he and the other ASAC passed the "very race conscious" and "problem" comments on to my immediate supervisor in Detroit. The cancer spreads.

The other ASAC in the Detroit division of the FBI, when interviewed, stated that he had informed my immediate supervisor in Detroit that I was "arriving [from Cincinnati] with a 'questionable reputation'" and had inquired whether my supervisor was up to the potential *"challenge"* of being responsible for an employee who might be "troublesome." However, the supervisor, when interviewed under oath, stated that the ASAC specifically said, "Special Agent Powers could be a *racist or troublemaker."* As a result, the supervisor called the Cincinnati division and spoke with a white Special Agent, asking him if I were a "racist *and* troublemaker." The supervisor stated that the agent told him that I was "one of the nicest guys you ever want to meet and was not a racist and a troublemaker." Nonetheless, the seed was planted and would sprout into an overgrown thicket of falsehood and harassment that would culminate in an FBI raid on the house of my sister with a warrant for my *deceased* brother. This would occur in the midst of the investigation of my EEO complaint and after I gave a sworn deposition in the case of another African American agent who had been targeted.

As a result of my complaining about the documented comments and as a result of the "racist" label that had been attached to me, I would be watched as I entered and left other divisions of the FBI. My purpose for being in another division other than the one I was assigned to would be questioned. My leave status was monitored and questioned. Any and every mistake I made would be magnified and investigated beyond what was normal. One supervisor in Detroit specifically instructed me to be careful because someone within the Bureau was out to get me.

Friends of mine were surreptitiously questioned about what vehicle I used to travel between cities while on vacation. Whom I visited and where I stayed while out of town were thoroughly examined. Addresses and telephone numbers of my hosts were sought out. Even the type of clothing I wore out of town was noted. On one occasion I was told that I had been investigated because "[I was] wearing all black."

Friends and co-workers were questioned about my comings and goings. They were asked to furnish addresses and phone numbers of the people I visited. An administrative inquiry (internal investigation) was initiated to examine why I had repaired a pair of faulty brakes on my car in an FBI garage. A supervisor assigned to investigate this matter told me later that before his investigation was even completed, he had been told by one of the ASACs that I was to be recommended for a two-week suspension without pay. After it was determined that an investigation based on the repair of faulty brakes would be "too flimsy," the matter was dropped for one associated with leave status. This supervisor, an African American, informed me that he and others at FBI headquarters thought the whole investigation was "bullshit." I gave a sworn deposition in regard to my conversation with him. I signed a statement under the penalty of perjury indicating that he had made these statements to me. However, when he was interviewed by a white FBI employee from the Equal Employment Opportunity unit, he denied that he had made such statements to me. I agree with Robert Frost: "There's nothing I'm afraid of like scared people."

During an investigation of me based on the pretense that I had been absent without leave (AWOL), one of the investigators in Cincinnati approached me during one of my trips there and asked whether he needed to call back to Detroit and inquire about my leave status. He was telling me that despite all that had been done to me, I was still being watched. He was warning me that I had better not complain anymore. After a lengthy investigation which cost the FBI thousands of taxpayer dollars, the FBI informed me that it was obvious that I had only made a mistake and had not intentionally practiced deception on my leave sheet. Thus, I was instructed to be more careful. This investigation lasted several months and involved seven FBI supervisors and numerous interviews. Criminal cases, and certainly civil rights cases, had never received this much high-level attention. Nonetheless, the trap had failed. I would not be intimidated. I would not be broken.

On another occasion during my assignment to the Cincinnati division, the woman in charge of Housing Opportunities Made Equal (HOME) called to inquire what investigation, if any, was being conducted by the FBI on a discrimination and civil rights case in which an African American woman's home had been vandalized and racial epithets had been written on her walls. The woman lived in an all-white community. I took the woman's questions to the Assistant Special Agent in Charge since his squad handled civil rights matters. I provided him with the information and a contact number. He said that he would handle it.

Approximately one week later, the lady from HOME recontacted me because she had not been contacted by anyone else from the FBI. I returned to the ASAC's office and informed him of the second call. He closed the door to his office and told me to have a seat. He pulled a chair up close to me and stared into my eyes. I stared back. He spoke in a low tone, "You have to understand that the FBI is not interested in investigating civil rights cases. It's always been that way and things haven't changed because of the civil rights era. Civil rights cases don't produce high statistics. They don't give us numbers to take before Congress to increase our budget. Most congressmen don't care about civil rights. You are dreaming. Thinking about the way things should be. But you are part of the team now."

Damn "part of the team." From the streets of Baltimore to the FBI. Part of the team. From Southwestern High School to the FBI. Part of the team. From Coppin State College to the FBI. Part of the team. From the Maryland State Police to the FBI. Part of the team. What did that mean? Did it mean that right and wrong had different definitions now? Was I to develop an acute case of selective amnesia? I was no longer naive. I knew something of real power and how it is wielded. But this "part of the team" shit when it came to civil rights was a bit too much.

The ASAC continued to speak. It was as if he were pleading for my understanding. "Look here, if a civil rights case is high profile and covered widely by the media, the FBI will become involved. And nine times out of ten we'll get a conviction. But, other than that, nobody cares. I assign my least productive agents to such cases. Look where the Bureau has civil rights listed on the prioritization sheet." I said nothing. I stood up and left the room.

I reported the ASAC's comments to a supervisor from FBI headquarters, who had come to Cincinnati to conduct a biennial inspection. He said that what the ASAC had relayed to me was essentially true. He explained that the Bureau was not interested in investigating this type of violation especially when the civil rights violations were directed at police departments. He stated that the Bureau had to work with these police departments and officers every day. The Bureau spent a great deal of time and a lot of expense to foster its close relationship with state and local police departments. He asked me whether I was aware of the cost of the FBI National Academy classes.

The Bureau brought in police officers from across the country and the world to attend the National Academy at Quantico,

Virginia. At the academy the officers learned the latest law enforcement techniques and technologies. At the completion of the classes, after twelve to fourteen weeks, a graduation ceremony was held. The Director of the FBI presented the officers with a certificate. The importance of the Director's presence was not lost on the National Academy class members or on the FBI agent trainees. The Director did not attend the graduation of FBI agents. The National Academy was like a huge fraternity, with the FBI at the center. The relationship developed with each of the various police departments was seen as an enormous benefit to the Bureau. The downside of this relationship, according to what was being explained to me by the Bureau supervisor from headquarters, was that the Bureau refused to allow bona fide civil rights cases to interfere with this "vital alliance."

There were other incidents that revealed the philosophy of the FBI as an institution, not necessarily the philosophy of every individual agent. On one occasion a group of FBI and Drug Enforcement Administration agents along with police officers were to make an arrest on what was believed to be a street gang in Cincinnati, Ohio. The pre-arrest meeting was held at the FBI office. A sergeant from the Cincinnati Police Department brought a cassette player into the room where the meeting was taking place. He put in a tape of the rap group NWA (Niggaz With Attitude) and turned the player on. The song played was "Fuck The Police." In this song the group uses the word "nigger" on many occasions. During the playing of the song an FBI agent, who was not a part of the arrest team, walked into the squad area and yelled, "They use the word 'nigger' more times in that song than they do at the local Klan rally." It sounded as though he had been a frequent visitor to these Klan rallies. Other agents in the room began to laugh. The frail supervisor was present. He laughed with the rest of the white agents and officers.

After the sergeant turned the tape off he stated, "These are the attitudes of the people who you are going to arrest. So be prepared." I had assisted in the investigation of the so-called gang. First, there was nothing concrete in the investigation that indicated that the individuals targeted for arrest were gang members. They were low-level street dealers from which we had made several one-ounce, or smaller, purchases of cocaine. Secondly, we never noted a copy of the NWA tape in their possession or heard them mention anything about shooting or killing a police officer. Remember, we had worked with them in undercover roles; therefore, they could have made threatening comments without anticipating their being repeated in court at a later date. Finally, the law enforcement officers had been well trained and knew what to expect and be prepared for whenever they made an arrest. They did not need a "fight song" to heighten their wariness. Why was it necessary for an NWA tape to be played? It was as if it were mood music for the hunting of "niggers."

After the meeting was over, I approached the frail supervisor and complained about the incident. Much to my surprise, he agreed that the playing of the tape was unnecessary and insensitive to the African American agents involved in the arrest. He also stated that it could possibly cause some of the agents involved to overreact during the arrest, although he doubted it. He confessed that the sergeant had played the tape for him prior to the meeting and that he had given the sergeant the green light to play it during the meeting. He shrugged his shoulders and stated, "Your complaint is noted and the matter is closed. Good luck on the arrest." He returned to the shuffling of papers on his desk. Other African American Cincinnati police officers and DEA agents who were present at the meeting came to me and complained. "Man, this is the fucking FBI office and we have to sit down and listen to nigger, nigger, nigger. What the fuck does that have to do with arresting these punks? Do they got a song they play before you all go out to arrest white people? This is bullshit." I stood in the middle and accepted the barrage of comments from my co-workers. They were looking to one of the two African American agents assigned to the Cincinnati division to assure justice in the FBI. I explained to them that I had complained to the frail supervisor. They retorted, "Fuck him. Fuck the FBI."

The agent who had walked through the squad area and made the statement about the Klan rally was later elected to represent the Cincinnati division in meetings with the FBI Director as part of the Special Agent Advisory Committee (SAAC). He also became a prominent member of the Agents Association.

The Agents Association was an organization that was set up to speak for the agents of the FBI when dealing with FBI management and Congress. It was like a union in that it spoke up for raises and better working conditions for agents. For the most part it had been successful; however, it never spoke out against inequities when it came to the Bureau's relationship with its minority agents. In fact, the Agents Association denied that problems even existed despite volumes of statistical information to the contrary. The Association never cared to look at the information that had been provided to the court in the Hispanic agents' lawsuit against the FBI. But when the verdict came down against the Bureau, all the members of the Association with whom I spoke were incensed. Now they wanted to protect the managers and the good name of the FBI. They could not understand that the good name of the FBI could be best protected by assuring equal justice for all FBI agents. They did not understand that the agency, ostensibly responsible for the investigation of civil rights, should make sure that the civil rights of its employees are not violated.

The Agents Association's stance on issues involving minorities was abundantly clear: it was apparent that the Association wanted to represent only issues involving white agents. They turned a blind eye to issues of racism; they ignored the problem instead of trying to fix it. Dealing with racism and ethnicity-based inequities in the FBI would have given the Agents Association the legitimacy it craved. It could have been identified as an organization that was truly interested in fairness, an unbiased professional organization that wanted what was best for Special Agents in particular and the public in general. All it had to do was set up a research committee to look at the numbers, to look at the punishment meted out to African American agents and the punishment prescribed for white agents for the same offenses. The research committee could have looked at hiring and firing practices. It could have studied the promotional system and the transfer policy. It could have studied the award system. Perhaps the study could have been conducted by the head of the FBI's behavorial science unit, Roger L. Depue, a white agent who was considered a conservative. Afterwards, the research committee could have filed a scholarly report with its observations, analyses, and findings. If researching the status of minorities in the FBI were too time-consuming for an Agents Association committee, it could have hired an outside research agency. Many colleges and universities would have taken on such a project. It would have been much cheaper than what the Association paid their attorneys to fight the FBI agreement with African American Special Agents. Had they conducted the proper research and spoken with their African American and Hispanic colleagues, they would have come to the same conclusion as the FBI director and the courts, but at a lot less cost.

The Agents Association's adversarial relationship with African American and Hispanic Special Agents gave the perception that the Association did not consider non-white agents as real Special Agents. One prominent member of the Agents Association in the Detroit division wrote a memorandum to all Special Agents, including the Special Agent in Charge and his assistants, describing African American agents as a "sub-group." Most African American Special Agents with whom I spoke relinquished their membership in what they believed had become, or had always been, the "White Agents' Association." In hindsight, this was a mistake. It would have been easier to study the positions of the Association from within. I believe this FBI civil war—initiated by the Agents Association, with its battle to thwart the Bureau's rectifying age-old, widely recognized racial inequities—tarnished the image of the Agents Association held by its friends in Congress. It certainly had to sour its relationship with FBI management.

The FBI was, and is, a divided house; "two nations." African Americans are treated unfairly based on the color of their skin. The Agents Association can emotionally deny this fact, but they cannot back up their hollow denials with concrete information. Many African American Special Agents are afraid to take a stand against the veiled and the obvious inequities. They fear that they will be labeled, that the little upward mobility afforded them will be obstructed, and that they will lose their jobs. I empathize with them, for their fears are warranted. The FBI has a way of dressing the victim up and making him or her appear to be the violator or troublemaker.

When an African American Special Agent in the Detroit division of the FBI, Prince Earl Ross, complained about the racial inequities, he was told that he had a chip on his shoulder. He was denied promotions for which he was more than qualified. He had to retain the services of prominent Washington D.C. attorney James William Morrison to protect him from further harassment. Another African American agent complainant was told he was beginning to act like Malcolm X. An African American female Special Agent in the Chicago division, after identifying race-based inequities, was told she could not hold closed-door meetings with other African American Special Agents. I was accused by the ASAC in Cincinnati of polarizing the Cincinnati division of the FBI along racial lines. Strange, since there was a total of only two African American Special Agents (and after some time, three) initially assigned to the Cincinnati division.

•••••••••••••••••••

I had all but ended my chances for advancement or a successful career with the FBI, by standing up and speaking out. I would stand up for what was right over and over again and each time my career with the FBI crumbled. I was trying to make a difference, trying to make the FBI the agency that it professed to be. I was confronted at every turn, investigated and harassed. Many of my African American Special Agent friends admired my stances, which they considered brave and masochistic. However, they would not or could not stand with me. They had too much to lose. And in the end, the FBI was not going to change its wicked ways. As one African American Special Agent put it, "They will batter you until you fall and then they'll step right over you and keep going in the same direction. You wouldn't have changed their mode, method, or path. The crowd that cheered your bravery will go back and humble themselves before your conquerers. After a while, no one will remember that Special Agent Tyrone Powers ever existed."

Most of the cases that I was assigned during the time I was in Cincinnati were drug matters. I worked with Royce Winters, an African American Cincinnati police officer assigned to the Drug Task Force. Royce was an excellent law enforcement officer and a master of deception. He did a great deal of undercover work and made hundreds, possibly thousands, of arrests against drug dealers in Ohio. Royce despised drug pushers and the destruction they sowed in America. I stood with him many days and watched him as he watched the drug-addicted zombies on the ghetto streets of Cincinnati. I listened to his burdened soul as he spoke. "Look at our people. Look at what this man-made shit is doing to them. All fucked up. Walking around not knowing and not caring. Damn, Tye, we took a fall, didn't we? I mean, you've schooled me on our greatness. Damn, we took a hell of a fall. I want the son of a bitch that pushed us off our mountain. I want so badly to catch that motherfucker at the top that keeps sliding this shit down a well-greased chute into these streets."

Royce sincerely believed that he could make an impact, that he could slow down and eventually eradicate the menace of drugs in his little part of the world. He was not alone. Special Agent Stephen Barnett of the Cincinnati division worked day and night to rid the streets of drug dealers. He gave his heart and soul to the war. Special Agent Barnett is white. Yet, most of his efforts were concentrated in the African American community. I never saw Special Agent Barnett abuse a prisoner. In fact, it was his sincere demeanor that allowed him so much success. He could convince a dealer to give up his source. It was obvious to him that African Americans were suffering most from the unabated drug trade. He was an expert at breaking down drug organizations and relentlessly tracking them to their roots, usually in Florida or New

York. Of course, he realized that the roots extended beyond the shores of the United States. I admired his dedication. When he was later promoted to supervisor on a squad that did not handle drug investigations, I felt that the FBI and the nation suffered.

Royce was my teacher when it came to undercover work. He taught me what to say and when to say it. He taught me how to react to different statements, situations, and circumstances. He immediately noted my propensity toward truthfulness and candidness and informed me that I would have to suppress these usually noble attributes. He apprised me of the warning signs of imminent danger. He told me when to walk away and how to walk away. He instructed me on how best to get the "drop" on my adversary should he or she reach for a weapon.

Royce taught me how to check the weight of the drugs I purchased without a scale. He advised me never to taste or take any drugs that were offered to me. He told me "that tasting shit" was for movie actors. "Why the hell would you taste something handed to you by a low-life motherfucker whose only goal in life is to sell poison to his own people? A fuckin' Judas. Why the hell would you sniff something from a filthy motherfucker who would shoot you quicker than a Klansman? A blood-sucking traitor who cares nothing about you or your family. Hell, I don't even taste shit from the supermarket until I see white folks taste it—that shit could be poison, too. If he ain't willing to sell you the shit because you won't taste it or sniff it, fuck him. It's only a drug deal and I'll guarantee you, his dumb ass will eventually get popped anyway. They all do. It's just a matter of time."

I had witnessed hundreds of drug deals, growing up on the streets of Baltimore City, but this was different. Now I was "the man," and I had to pretend not to be. I had to be deceptive. My life depended on my ability to convince the drug-dealing traitors that I was something other than what I really was. I had to be an unscrupulous street politician. I had to stare into the cold eyes of the zombies and show no fear.

I wanted to do well. I wanted to master the powerful weapon of deception. I had witnessed its negative effects on African Americans. I had witnessed how it had convinced so many of our children that they could not compete against the rest of the world. I had witnessed its use by insincere white and Black politicians whose goal was to keep African Americans on the welfare rolls. I had witnessed deception in some "pro-life" activists who were only pro-life until the baby was out of the womb. These were pro-lifers who could easily yell to an African American child, "Not in my neighborhood." I witnessed it with the "pro-choice" (African) population-control advocates. Maybe, for once, I could utilize deception for something positive. If the zombies were arrested, maybe they could be rehabilitated in prison by an organization such as the Nation of Islam. The title of the organization didn't matter—these zombies had to be resuscitated or destroyed.

Learning can take place anywhere and anytime, as long as one is prepared and willing to learn. My absorption into undercover drug work taught me lessons for life in general. I learned that it was not always an advantage to be candid; there was a measurable benefit to the art of deception. I reread Sun Tzu's *The Art of War*. Wang Xi interpreted Sun Tzu as saying "[d]eception is for the purpose of seeking victory over an enemy; to command a group requires truthfulness." Mei Yaochen interpreted Sun Tzu as saying, "Without deception you cannot carry out strategy, without strategy you cannot control the opponent." Master Sun Tzu stated, "a military operation involves deception. Even though you are competent, appear to be incompetent. Though effective, appear to be ineffective." I was learning to discern when to be truthful and when to be deceptive. But I wondered whether I had done the right thing by confronting the frail supervisor. I wondered if I would have been better off had I deceived him into believing that my views were no different from his.

Royce Winters introduced me to Cincinnati police officer Edward Larkin Jr. Edward was a short, muscular African American with a strong, confident personality. He was extremely intelligent and had a natural distrust of most people. Before he befriended you, or before you could befriend him, he would look you over and try to evaluate your sincerity. Edward and I had many conversations as we lifted weights in police station District 4. Edward and I agreed that many African Americans did not intentionally betray their people. We believed some were infected with a virus called Uncle Tomism. The vaccination to prevent this pathogen from causing a full-blown case of betrayal was education, especially in the field of history. Once African Americans got a firm grip on historical events, they would seek out self-reliance. For they would know that the countries of the world were willing to destroy a group of people viewed as unproductive, dispensable, and weak. Our search for self-reliance would lead us to colleges, universities, and technological centers. We would understand that we had to learn economics, bricklaying, finance and architecture; sociology, engineering, political science and marine biology; psychology, mathematics, computer science, and aeronautics. We would have to attend war academies and peace conferences.

I worked several undercover projects with Royce, Edward, and later with Martha Dunbar, an African American female Special Agent who had been transferred to Cincinnati from Mississippi. She and I developed a strong friendship and depended on each other for support. Despite the frail supervisor's insistence that we weren't handling our cases right, we continued to get indictments and convictions. Royce did most of the undercover work while Edward, Martha, and I provided back-up. We did most of our work in the African American community and had our most success in the small city of Lincoln Heights, Ohio. We truly believed that we were doing those communities a favor by getting rid of some of the drug pushers. In fact, some people in the community complimented us on our sincere efforts. We knew that we could not completely eradicate the drug problem. The drugs were being forced into the Black community by those outside it who had intentions of destroying the people within the community. We hoped that our small efforts would lead us to the people who really controlled the drug trade. That was our expectation; that was our belief; that was our motivation.

When Royce and Edward were assigned to the Drug Enforcement Administration (DEA) Task Force in Cincinnati, Martha and I continued to work cases with them. The frail supervisor kept a watchful eye over our operations. He and a sergeant from the Cincinnati Police Department, assigned to the DEA, demanded that they be involved in the planning of all our cases. Whenever we proceeded to make an arrest, execute a search warrant, or conduct an undercover drug buy, they took over the operation. This was not the case with white agents. What was so remarkable about this childish treatment was that Royce was probably the best undercover drug agent in the state of Ohio. The frail supervisor and the overzealous sergeant were incapable of providing Royce with any meaningful, substantive advise. Special Agent Stephen Barnett was probably the only qualified expert advisor on drug matters, other than Royce, in the Cincinnati division. We had no problem with seeking advice from Barnett.

The number of cases Royce Winters made on a consistent basis was staggering. Instead of being watched he should have been consulted on his wealth of knowledge of the illegal drug industry. No one in *real* power wanted to hear what Royce had to say. Unfortunately, but understandably, we could only get funding for low-level drug buys. This was discouraging and enlightening. The drug war in the United States is an awful deception. I am convinced that every politician that is honest with himself knows this. The mayor of Baltimore City, Kurt Schmoke, knows this, and dared to suggest that the politicians stop playing games with the people of America. Kurt Schmoke, in his own way, was trying to unveil the deception. He was crucified for exposing the truth.

••••••••••••••••••••

Edward Larkin Jr. was promoted to the rank of Specialist within the Cincinnati Police Department. I overheard other officers, who were assigned to the DEA Task Force, state that he had been promoted only because he was Black. Edward's promotion was also discussed in the FBI office. Several agents were upset about the promotion and voiced their complaints amongst themselves. They felt that a white officer, who they personally knew and believed was more qualified than Edward, had been passed over for the sake of promoting Edward Larkin Jr. That they had very limited working experience with either officer and could not have known how much more qualified one was than the other was irrelevant to these agents. They did not have a copy of the test, so they could not determine the relevancy of it to the position that was competed for. They were not members of the police department board that selected Edward for promotion. Further, it was not a personal competition between Edward and the white officer, so why did the agents suggest that Edward Larkin Jr. had been promoted *instead* of the white officer? In fact, several white officers were promoted at the same time as Edward. Why didn't they compare the white officer with other white officers? Why did they make it a choice between white and Black? Without doing any research, they blamed the illusive affirmative action program.

I informed Edward Larkin Jr. of the discussion that had taken place amongst the agents. He did not get upset. He seemed to understand the reasons for the backbiting and disparaging accusations. He understood that no matter what he did or how well he did it, he would always be thought of as being inferior to white officers. But it no longer mattered what others thought of him—he was beyond that. He was sure of who he was and what he was capable of. He would not waste his time and energies arguing with those who spoke from ignorance. He would not allow his detractors to hinder his progress.

Once the agents in the discussion found out that I had provided the details of their conversation to Edward, they became incensed with me. They stated that they had not meant any harm.

I never said they did. They stated that they had not intended for Larkin to be provided with the contents of their discussion. If they hadn't meant any harm, why was their conversation to be kept confidential? Why didn't they just talk to Larkin? They stated that they did not want to be thought of as racists. Mind you, not once had Edward, I, or anyone else called them racists. This was another learning experience. For in the years to come, I noted that those with guilty consciences were the first to deny a connection with racism without ever having been identified as racists. Moreover, the individuals with a guilty conscience were the first to scream "reverse discrimination."

Martha Dunbar was a rarity in the FBI: an African American woman in an organization that sought to preserve the white male status quo and that had no real intention of allowing in African American men. She was a diligent worker, yet Martha was consistently rated lower than every other agent on the squad by the frail supervisor. She was criticized for being an FBI agent and a divorced mother of four children. Martha persevered. She had a Bachelor of Science degree in Finance and a Master of Science degree in Business Administration. (Her educational achievements may have been the root of her problems.) She worked undercover during the day and went home to care for her family at night. She attended PTA meetings, parent/teacher conferences, and Grand Jury hearings. She disciplined her children and arrested violent felons all within the span of twelve hours.

Martha acquiescently accepted the unjustly low ratings. I suggested that she let the frail supervisor know that she was dissatisfied. She said she was sure that he was keenly aware of her dissatisfaction. Despite the fact that undercover work was not mandatory in the FBI, whenever they asked Martha to take on dangerous and life-threatening undercover assignments, she agreed. She received little credit for her unselfish, patriotic deeds. Very few of the white male agents were willing to go undercover, yet all of them were rated higher than Special Agent Martha G. Dunbar.

I worried about Martha Dunbar. I worried about her four children. I was concerned that her undercover work would one day leave her children motherless. If Martha were killed in the line of duty, the FBI could and would easily forget about her young children. I tried to talk her out of working undercover. She was overexposed to danger and underappreciated by those she worked for. They obtained promotions based on her unselfish work. She received low ratings and criticism. They went home to the suburbs carefree. She lived in the city and had to be ever watchful for those whom she had arrested. On several occasions, Martha promised that she was going to stop. But as soon as the frail supervisor approached and asked her to work undercover, she capitulated. I tried to make sure I was assigned to the surveillance team when she went undercover. I wanted to be close by in the event that something went wrong.

As time went on I could tell that the undercover work and the low ratings were getting to Martha. She would come out of the supervisor's office after her performance appraisal, with her head down. It wasn't fair. All she wanted was a chance to continue in her chosen career. She desired no preferential treatment. She never asked to go home early, and she worked just as many hours as every other agent, perhaps more. She thought things would eventually change if she continued to work hard. She had faith in the fairness of human nature. "Hard work will be rewarded." Finally, she came to the conclusion that her low ratings had very little to do with her effort and productivity. Within three years, Special Agent Martha G. Dunbar resigned from the Federal Bureau of Investigation.

Later, the same lessons that Martha and I had learned would become clear to Royce. Royce was a hard worker who despised the use of drugs. Everyone knew this. However, his sergeant approached him one day and informed him that the DEA had received an anonymous call indicating that he, Royce, was using drugs. The call had come in a week earlier, and the sergeant and the DEA had spent some time investigating the allegations. They called Royce in and questioned him as if he were a common criminal. Royce couldn't understand how they could give any merit to the unfounded allegations of an anonymous caller.

The lessons became even clearer to Royce when he was suspended for three days without pay for not reporting an adulterous affair that another officer was having while on duty. He couldn't understand why he was suspended for so minor an infraction as not snitching on his partner. The lessons became clearer to him still when he was called in and told to avoid me and not to allow me to influence him because I was a "troublemaker." He was told this by an African American supervisor at the Drug Enforcement Administration who was later forced to leave Cincinnati by the very white police officers and agents he had so adamantly defended to Royce. Royce informed me that the supervisor had been told that I was a troublemaker, by my supervisors in the FBI.

In the end Royce came to me and thanked me for the lessons that we shared.   Royce Winters, the quintessential undercover agent, would leave the DEA task force and become a homicide detective and polygraph operator.   Edward Larkin Jr. would follow shortly thereafter to become an instructor in the Cincinnati Public Schools/Cincinnati Police Department Drug Awareness Reduction Education (DARE) program.   After I was transferred to the Detroit division of the FBI, Ken West was transferred to an east coast division.   Martha Dunbar resigned.   Thereafter there were no African American Special Agents assigned to the Cincinnati division of the FBI.

25

Soul Searching

For what is a man profited, if he shall gain the world and lose his soul?
                              –Matthew, XVI, 26

So you should take away the energy of their armies and take away the heart of their generals.
                              –*Master Sun Tzu,* The Art of War

The dense heat slowly drifted down from the heavens and smothered the inhabitants of Baltimore City. It was Nate's belief that Baltimore had received more than its allotted amount of heat for this summer day in July 1987. Whoever had been assigned the heavenly job of dispensing the sun's heat had fallen asleep. Or maybe he was intentionally scalding the citizens of Baltimore. Maybe they were being punished by one of the mythical Greek gods for a violation of some sacred law. He laughed to himself at the absurdity of his fanciful thoughts. Baltimoreans being punished for sins against the gods. He was beginning to think like the idiotic white racists who justified the enslavement of Black people by the quoting and misquoting of King James' Bible.

Leaning back in his chair, Nate stared up into the clear blue sky and toyed with the idea that heaven was hell and hell was heaven. He had never felt any heat from below. In fact, the waters below land were cool. Mom sent us *down* to the basement to seek refuge from the hot days of Baltimore summers. Wine was kept cool in wine *cellars*. All the fiery heat that preachers talked

329

about seemed to come from above or from the earth's surface. What could be hotter than the sun? What could be more intense than the pressure placed on a Black man in America, at ground level?

When things went wrong people didn't look down and say "That damned devil." They looked up and asked the curious and age-old question, "Why me, God?" The trouble, the problems, and the heat all seemed to emanate from an aboveground source, not *down* below in some deep mysterious chamber guarded by a fearsome, dreaded red man with sharp horns, a long pointed tail, and a pitchfork. Hell didn't produce anything—positive or negative. At least not the hell that Nate's Sunday school teachers taught him. It was all fucked-up. He had been lied to, misled. Nothing was as it was said to be. Everything seemed inverted and muddled. His life was a tangled and twisted ball of confusion and contradictions. That would all end soon, very soon.

Nate didn't realize that this thought-provoking day in July would be his last. There would be no more sitting and thinking and reflecting. Had he known, he would have spent his final moments on Earth daydreaming about more important things, more pleasant things. God doesn't give many warnings. And even if He did, I'm not sure that Nate would have heeded them. He didn't think much of God anymore. Life as a Black man on the streets of Baltimore made the notion of the existence of a munificent God a little hard to accept or even envision.

Nate squinted as he stared into the eye of the sun. No doubt, the blazing ball of hellfire burning in the heavens was causing him pain. But he refused to turn away from it. He would confront it and allow it to do whatever damage it thought he deserved. No more running. There was nowhere else to run to. "Come get me. Come deal with this Black man who has stared death in its gleeful eyes." The eyes of Death were bright with anticipation, not cold and somber as most people expected. The eyes of the dead were dull and sullen. And the eyes of the dead were not exclusively the eyes of people who were physically dead but also were the eyes of those who were dead spiritually.

Nate's mind was in high gear now. He was racing down a road full of dangerous and frightful memories. He lashed out at the ugly memories alongside the jagged, bloody road. He lashed out at the faces hidden within the memories, concealed in the jungles of his mind, camouflaged. They were the faces of those who were at least partially responsible for his downfall and the downfall of his people. Who had manipulated and brainwashed him. Who had turned him against himself and his people. Who had made lying, stealing, cheating, and killing respectable as long as they did it or organized it, but who labeled him a liar, a thief, a traitor, a killer.

It was all too much for him to handle. The vise was clamped tight against his skull, and he was crying out from the pain. He knew too much. It was as if he were undergoing an operation without being anesthetized. He wasn't a sleepwalker. He was conscious of what was being done to him and his people, but felt powerless to stop it. Knowledge and impotency were jabbing at him. If he were void of knowledge, he would not have understood that his people had once been powerful and then were stripped of their power by a violent, uncivilized horde of colonists. If he thought that he and his people had always been powerless, then he could have accepted his position as preordained by some divine being—some white, long-haired, blue-eyed, hippie-looking, sandal-wearing being. He could have settled down and partied on Friday nights, danced with Soul Train on Saturday nights, and listened to sell-out, hypocritical preachers on Sunday mornings. He could have drunk malt liquor and been fooled by the advertised "smooth taste," like the Native Americans. He could have thoughtlessly shot himself up with readily available drugs. He could have done all of this without once thinking about what he was doing, without once understanding that he was being controlled like a lifeless puppet. But knowledge had killed the opiate called ignorance. He knew. He was awake and watching the horror of his life. He was watching the African Holocaust as it took place and continued to take place...and continued...and continued. He could smell the invisible gas from white society's ovens as it seeped across Black America. In fact, urban America was becoming a gas chamber. He knew. Damn, he knew.

The burning pain caused by the sun was tormenting Nate. Like a powerful magnet, the sun was pulling memories from the deep recesses of his soul. He hated the devilish fireball for what it was doing. He was sweating profusely. The sun was boiling his blood. It was causing the volcano within him to rumble and erupt, to spill forth red-hot, liquid fire that melted away the calcified falsehoods and revealed the undeniable, painful truths.

Nate wanted to claim ignorance, if not to the world, then to himself. He couldn't face the fact that he had been duped and had stood idly by, watching himself being duped. He couldn't handle the thought of his being led and misled and laughed at. He wanted to get *it* over with. To confront it. To deal with it. He was sure that the horrible white heat emanating from the hell above was what he needed to confront. He was never afraid of death. But now he sought it out, chased it down, lassoed it.

Fuck death. Death is a challenge. It's the ultimate battle. The supreme confrontation. The gunfight at O.K. Corral. The battle at Gettysburg. The Mau Mau. That's why poor ghetto Black men go off to fight the wars of greedy, rich white men. They've tasted the salty, tantalizing flavor of blood and now they want to know how to do it right. How to do it legal. How to become a trained killer. A praised, proud, uniformed killer, but a fuckin' killer nonetheless. They will kill, then die. Die and be honored for their willingness to kill. Their willingness to be killed. To take on death. To stare it in its eyes and beg it to come get them.

Come on, death. Come get Nate. Come get Cornelius Elijah Powers. Ha-ha-ha, come on, you ugly white motherfucker you. You fuckin' invader of Africa. You provocateur. Ain't nothing else you can do to this Black man. You've stripped me of everything meaningful. You've got me killing my brother in America and in the land that Leo Africanus named. You got me shooting your dope and beating my African queen and running away from my Nubian children. I should've known that this dope was like the alcohol or firewater you gave the Native Americans. It destroyed them. Now it's us you're after. You're trying to slow-walk us down. To sucker-punch us. Well, come on—I ain't scared of you. Come on and deal with me, you motherfucker you. You no good, Martin-killing, Malcolm-killing, war-loving, deceitful, divisive motherfucker you!

A tear trickled down the side of Nate's face and tried to enter his mouth, finding tightly sealed angry lips; it continued its journey down around his perfectly rounded chin, picked up speed and followed the sweat down his neck, finally disappearing into nothingness. Another tear began its journey. Nate's clean white silk shirt lay open, revealing a small jungle of deep dark hair on his muscular chest. A pair of flawlessly pressed, lightly starched black jeans covered his lower body and accepted the tail of his shirt. His long thin fingers wrapped around the metal handle at the end of the arm of a frayed lawn chair. He sat still. Silent. Outwardly peaceful. Nothing about him gave an indication of the massive storm that was raging within his brown shell. Nonetheless, Mom knew her boy was not at peace.

Mom stood inside the doorway, looking out from behind the dark screen. Sprinkles of bleached white flour clung to the red and white apron that was tied around the waist of the strong and gentle woman we knew only as Mom. She had come to the door to get respite from the suffocating heat of her kitchen. The hot air from outside felt like a gentle warm and pleasant breeze. She stopped in her tracks and stared at her tormented son. She read his discomfort. She looked through his thin brown shell and watched the mighty storm raging within his agitated soul. Her eyes followed his charcoal-brown eyes upwards toward the mighty heavens, the home of her God. She prayed that Nate was praying.

Nate breathed deeply and painfully as if he were a mother-to-be in the final stages of a long and arduous labor. Mom watched him closely. Nate looked as if he were confused, yet at peace. He looked strong, yet vulnerable. He was a bundle of contradictory emotions. He was like one of Mom's prized cakes, comprised of so many mixed-up elements. But they weren't all coming together, as they always did in Mom's cakes. There had been a pinch too much of this or maybe a tad too little of that. The recipe had been bungled and the cake would never come out right. Her son—her baby boy—was heading everywhere and nowhere. He knew where he was going, yet he was lost. It was difficult to understand Nate. It was difficult for Nate to understand himself.

Mom stood there trying to understand her son—trying to unravel the mystery of the soul of a tormented, downtrodden Black man who at times seemed so invincible. She had been trying to understand Nate for quite some time. Nate wasn't like Dad. He had never pretended to be anything other than what he was. He had never denied the truth or disguised his hate in the uniform of the United States armed forces. He had never run from anything or anyone. But now he was sitting on her front porch, crying and trying to hide his tears within his sweat. Trying to hide from something, or maybe trying to hide from himself.

Mom wanted to be inside Nate—to walk through the corridors of his soul. She wanted to feel what he was feeling. To think his thoughts. Maybe then she would know why he was living so dangerously, playing Russian roulette with his life. Maybe then she could understand his actions and reactions. If she understood him, she would know exactly what to ask God and how God could help Nate. She could then pray that God lead him in a certain direction and away from certain death.

Nate was only a few feet away from Mom but it seemed as if he were miles away. He never noticed her watching him, as she had done so many nights when he was a child. She had stood there in the dark of our room, with her Bible pulled close to her bosom, praying and watching over the children God had given her. She was still watching and praying and waiting and watching.

Nate sat there in his own world, trying, once again, to figure out the meaning of his existence. *Damn*, if he could just figure out this unfair, unjust, perplexing riddle called a Black man's life. There had to be a reason for the distinct difference between the life of a Black man and the life of a white man. No matter what bullshit the religious fanatics offered about us all being human, there was a difference. We had to be realistic. Things were not as they should be in the world and probably never would be. So we had to play with the hand that was dealt us or we had to become so powerful that we could *demand* a *genuine* reshuffling of the deck.

"We've got to get on the offensive. We've got to stop bunkering down and waiting for another attack. Oh yeah, they will attack, but if we keep waiting we are doomed. We can't repel them forever. That's what I liked about General Lee during the Civil War. When he went to Gettysburg, he was taking the war to the enemy. Win, lose, or draw—his men would not succumb to the victim mentality. Hell, we all know that we are victims of European aggression. Now we have to turn the tables, or at least turn the table that has been pushed over on us upright. I don't necessarily mean in a physically violent kind of way—although I won't rule that out completely. I mean, we have got to be aggressive in owning our own businesses and taking care of our own neighborhoods and educating our own babies. We got to create our own diplomats to create bridges with our African brethren around the world. We can't worry about being disliked and being called anti-white and anti-Korean and anti-Semitic. We have to stop beginning our statements with 'I'm not anti this or anti that.' Do white folks or Jews or Koreans or Japanese ever preface their statements to us with 'I'm not anti-African.'? Fuck it—maybe it's time for us to be anti something. We've got to try a new line of aggressive thinking. We just need to march forward, brother. Win, lose, or draw. No more retreating."

It was at times like this that Nate was so baffling. He spoke so eloquently and intelligently on important historical lessons. He had knowledge of the slave trade, the Revolutionary War, the Civil War, World War I, World War II, the Korean War, the Viet Nam War, and the Mau Mau. He knew such important historical figures as Kwame Nkrumah, Jomo Kenyatta, Patrice Lumumba, Marcus Garvey, W.E.B. DuBois, Booker T. Washington, Paul Robeson, and many, many others. He analyzed the significance of these great men. He understood the clandestine forces that had surreptitiously brought about the demise of these notable leaders and that were busy mapping out the annihilation of their followers and benefactors. He could easily identify the freedom-professing hypocrites such as slaveowners George Washington and Thomas Jefferson. He understood the trap that had been set. He understood how African Americans had fallen into the trap. He understood the forces behind the Black-on-Black crime wave. He understood the inner-city drug proliferation program and the intentionally bad schools. He sat and spoke to Warren and me about avoiding the traps and identifying the enemy.

Yet, Nate spent his life in the streets of Baltimore City, entangled in the vices he very much understood and very much despised. There was a civil war occurring within Nate. A war that he felt he could not win. So, at times, he surrendered to the wrong side, the side of evil. And when he did, he could be as brutal as any other ghetto zombie or power-hungry politician. He could order an assassination or carry one out with all the coldness and precision of a "patriotic" member of the Special Forces, Navy Seals, CIA assassination team or the Mossad. Nate absorbed fully the schizophrenic personality of the United States of America, which he had read so much about in the distorted history books provided to him in the public schools.

Those who did not really know Nate would have thought his exegesis impossible. He was ignored, like all the other ghetto dwellers. He and those like him would never be canvassed for a solution to the problems of drug abuse and youth violence. Only those who had never lived in the ghetto or experienced the problems of ghetto life would be solicited. Only those with the title "Dr." would be allowed to write books and get them published—even if they knew little about the subject they addressed. They would write on the causes of Black-on-Black crime without ever understanding, in the words of W.E.B. DuBois, the souls of Black folk. Only *their* explanations and suggestions would be considered. Nate was right. Part of the problem of Black-on-Black crime and Black drug use and abuse was rooted in the battered and sometimes crumbled souls of Black folk. The souls had to be rebuilt and protected. That was the only way the problem would be solved. That was the only point on which Nate agreed with those whom he labeled "the cadillac-driving, female-chasing, money-hungry, blood-sucking preachers."

When the answers were clear to Nate, or at least when he thought they were clear to him, he would call me long distance. At these times, he seemed to have the intuition and wisdom of some great Egyptian prophet and philosopher. We would talk for hours. He would tell me that he was going to stop using cocaine and spite the white man. "You know that would do it. A strong...well, I guess I ain't strong right now...but a knowledgeable brother like me and you is dangerous to these tyrants. You see, we won't submit to their slavery. We don't respect their pseudo power. You know they only got power if we act powerless. There has got to be powerless people in order for the concept of powerful people to work. They derive their power from us. And this shit I'm on kinda makes me powerless. It also makes it easy for the world to hate me and those like me. Once the world believes we ain't worth a shit, they'll turn their backs on us. Even Black folk will turn their back. But if I get off this shit...then I–I'm a threat. You a threat, brother. You clean as they come. You ain't even drank a beer or puffed a joint. Your head is clear and you know your history—better yet, you know their history. You've never committed a crime or violated one of their laws. You haven't cursed your mother or your worthless father. You have yet to be termed a racist or anti-Semitic. They haven't dirtied your name yet. You've been on the inside as a defender of the Constitution of the United States of America. You've been stamped and approved; therefore, people will listen to you. People will consider you legit. See, that makes you a threat. You better be careful. You hear me, little brother? You watch those no-good cowboy motherfuckers."

As I listened to my big brother, tears formed in my eyes. He had so much unrealized potential. So much knowledge and no one but me, Chas, Quincy, Frank, Sugar, Gas, Michael, and Mom recognized it. Dad had beaten Nate to within inches of death, trying to punish him for not knowing his school lessons. Dad had never listened to his boy. He had despised him for not being as smart as the white children. He wanted Nate to challenge the white world, as he had challenged the redneck checker players. And when Nate didn't do well in school, Dad saw the checker players winning. He saw them overcoming him and throwing him to the dusty earth outside the bus station in Wilson, North Carolina. He saw them and heard them laughing at him and his offspring. The laughing bounced off the walls of his skull, and he beat Nate harder and harder and longer and harder each time his skull was hit by the blunt, irritating, hollow sounds of ignorant redneck laughter. If only Dad could have said "Fuck the worthless, shiftless checker players." Fuck the idiotic Ku Klux Klan and their silent comrades in the White House. If only he could have ignored them and not recognized their perceived power. If he had rendered them invisible—just as Blacks were— then he could have heard his son. He could have seen the potential in Nate.

Nate's telephone soliloquies would continue on for hours. I would listen and interject a comment every once in a while. "When you gonna come home, brother? We need you here. Mom needs you. We gotta get a business going. We can't work for the man forever. As soon as he finds out that you will stand up for what's right, they gonna come after you. And when you complain about them coming after you, they gonna call you paranoid. Can't you see, brother, they know what kind of niggers they want? They know how to find buck-and-grin, Stepin Fetchit Blacks. As soon as they find out that you ain't the one, you gonna catch hell. They gonna try to discipline you. They gonna try to break you and make you a 'responsible negro.' I know it ain't gonna happen. But believe me they gonna try. Why you want to put up with that bullshit, when you can come back here and be appreciated? Oh, it ain't easy back here. Our people have been fed poison and are reacting to its deadly effects. They are having convulsions. They are acting like a panicked swimmer who reaches out and pulls under his would-be rescuer. And when you come home, you will be one of the rescuers. Plus, you ain't gonna be making that good government green. But for you, brother, it's dirty money. It don't mean nothing. Unless, like most of our brothers, you have become a slave to things."

I sighed deeply. Taking in all that Nate was saying was exhausting. He paused to give me time to respond. "No matter what they do to me, Nate, I'm not running. This is an excellent investigatory organization. I have a lot to learn, but I can do this job and do it well. We can't run every time the heat is turned up. If we do, we are allowing ourselves to be broken. I'm not going to buck and grin. I don't participate in the ethnic jokes that I frequently hear. I think these people know where I stand. There will come a time when I will decide to make a move. But I alone will make that decision. It won't be based on how much money I'm making. I'm not a slave to material things. I have survived on and can survive with a lot less. I do understand the lack of job security for a knowledgeable, aware African American. But I won't be forced out; I won't run. When they come, I will stand strong like a deep-rooted tree, and if they don't come, all the better. And I'm not forgetting about my people. I'll help them from where I am. We have got to be everywhere and we can reach out from anywhere. I'm not a sellout. There are a lot of sellouts here, but I'm not one of them. Don't worry—I'm with it and with you."

During these conversations, Nate would ask me to send him some literature and books on subjects that I thought would enlighten him. He had started me down the road to consciousness, and now he was asking me to educate him. He was asking me to be his teacher and to teach others, a task for which I did not feel prepared at that time. Before I stood before young impressionable minds, I wanted to make sure I had the facts right. I didn't want to teach hate. I didn't care to use the smooth rhythm of poetry to say something that sounded good but meant very little to the eager young African Americans. We had enough fiery rhetoricians. We needed speakers and leaders that could turn the rhetoric into practical action. We needed to move, not stand and talk. Over the years I found that those working the hardest toward upliftment were the silent volunteers in community centers and neighborhood programs across America. They were the unsung heroes.

Nate pushed me onward toward the gaining of more knowledge. He agreed that I should be fully prepared before I started to teach, but he felt that I was too patient with my education. Everyday I needed to be reading and learning and analyzing; there could be no weekend breaks from the pursuit of knowledge. If I increased my pace, I would hasten my return to Baltimore. I could get back and become one of the much-needed rescuers. Nate wanted to be with me when I spoke to Black youth; he wanted to stand with me or watch me from his seat at the rear of a high-school auditorium. He wanted to attach himself to me, to be my co-pilot on the voyage of acquiring knowledge. He wanted us to study together. To discuss, critique, and analyze our lessons.

We had something to give to each other. Nate had done some reading on his own. He had experience. A great deal of his knowledge came from the brutally cold, hard streets of Baltimore's ghetto. Drugs, robbery, rape, and murder were part of his everyday life. He had been a victim of merciless assaults; he had also been the assaulter. Nate realized that I had done more reading than he. He knew that I had witnessed another form of the greed and brutal violence of America. Now he wanted us to combine our lessons, studies, and experiences to create a powerful force that would enable us to actively do something positive for our people.

Nate was smoothing the rough edges of his person. He began to write poetry about his life and times. He would call me at 2:00 a.m. and read his morose thoughts on this miserable, unjust, evil world. He wrote poems about the murders he witnessed and the ones he had committed. He vowed never to kill again unless in self-defense. I was having a hard time believing that this was the same Nate that I had grown up with; he was changing drastically.

It was as if Nate were trying to escape from the suffocating confines of his twisted and tormented soul, trying to vomit up the painful memories of his childhood, trying to cleanse himself of the evil deeds that "the devil made him do."

Nate began to talk more about God. "Maybe there is someone up there or out there looking over us. Wouldn't it be good having someone or something or some being that the white man couldn't buy with his dirty money or corrupt with his dirty drugs? If I just could believe in Mom's God, I would laugh at that white man 'cause I would know that someone was going to get even with his hateful ass one day. Wouldn't it be good knowing that a day of revenge is coming and that all the nuclear bombs in the world can't stop the avenger? The white man can't believe in God, 'cause if he did, he would know his silly ass is in big trouble. He would be praying and asking forgiveness for killing one hundred million Africans during the slave trade. He would be praying for forgiveness for cutting off Black men's penises and raping little Black girls and hanging their innocent brothers. Even the pope would be asking for forgiveness for sanctioning the slave trade under the name of God. I wouldn't want to be standing in front of God in the court of law if I was a white man."

Nate would pause and then ask me a question. "Tyrone, you...you believe in God? I mean, you never say much about nothing when it comes to God." My answer would be: "Yeah, Nate. Yeah, I believe in God. I don't always understand Him, but I believe in a God. I don't know His name and don't know what religion He would sanction or disavow, but I believe. I don't run around with religious pendants on my chest or Bibles and other holy books under my arm. I don't wake up people by knocking on their doors and pushing a magazine in their faces. I don't stand on the corner and sell newspapers. I don't sell roses or flowers. I damn sure ain't kissing a man's finger or hand or ring or any other part of him. I don't chant. But I believe. I believe like my ancient African brothers. It's all inside me. My church and sanctuary are all inside my soul. I get dressed up and walk through the aisles of my soul and bow down to my God and pray. I pray for knowledge and understanding. I pray for the strength to do what is right and necessary. I'm a stronger believer than many professors of faith."

****

On July 23, 1987, the night before Nate's last day on earth, he called me and told me about the inverse position of heaven and hell. He reminisced about our youth. He spoke of the good times we had had. It seemed as if he wanted to go back, to start over again, to try something different. He seemed to be pleading with God or to me or to anyone who he thought could help him gain a second chance. As he spoke, a cold chill raced up my spine and rested like an ice cube at the base of my brain. Mom said there were clear and evident signs when death was near. But I ignored the signs. I listened to Nate and begged him to get to his point. There was no going back. And what made him think that things would be better the second time around? What made him think that we would have a better dad who wouldn't rape our beautiful sister and put butcher knives at the throat of our mother? What made him think that we would have a better house? The icy sensation was making me irritable; yet I ignored its significance.

Nate continued in spite of my pleading that he stop his trek down memory alley. "Re–remember that back porch; remember the thunderstorms, the pouring rain? Remember that old broken radio and the Kool Aid and the dancing? Remember Mom standing in the doorway, smiling? Remember Angel and Chas and Old Man and Timmy and Cookieman and Gas and Sheldon and Michael and Stanley and Earl and Sammey and Van and Ronald and Clifton and Red Dog and Reds and Robert and Mr. Lightning? Remember that time when we were little and Dad was at work and we thought a burglar was in the house and Mom took her Bible and walked down the stairs into the darkness to protect us? She said she didn't need no weapon. She just needed God to go with her. I swear there was a burglar in the house that night, but when Mom walked down there with that Bible, he disappeared into thin air. I swear it."

Nate spoke of our playing tag and hide-and-go-seek. He spoke of our laughing as we sat in the last row at the back of the Christian Community Church of God. He spoke of Mom's Sunday breakfasts and dinners, the summer picnics at Gunpowder Falls State Park, the family trips to King's Dominion. He laughed about our trips to Wilson, North Carolina and laughed at our working in our uncle's rented tobacco fields. He mentioned our days at Bentalou Elementary School and our neighborhood brawls in Baltimore City. He remembered the house parties. He remembered the cold snow and the blinking lights at Christmas. He remembered the gifts lying under the tree, the smells emanating from the kitchen as Mom prepared Christmas dinners.

Nate was looking backwards. Looking back seemed so much easier than looking into the future or dealing with the present. I wanted Nate to look forward and to move forward. His reasons for looking back were not positive. He had taught me to keep going forward. He had so often said that what was done was done and that history should be reviewed only as a lesson of what ought not to be done in the future. But now not only was Nate thinking of the past, he actually wanted to go back. As if the past would somehow be different. As if the road that he had once traveled would not be the same. Traveling backwards would not change things any more than putting a car in reverse and driving backwards would change the scenery. It was the present and the future that we had the opportunity to change—that was the lesson of history. Nate had once understood this. He had explained it to me. Now he was talking and acting differently. It was as if he were degressing into a state of nonconsciousness, going back to a time when he had not been aware of the truth.

The calls from Nate came more frequently. It seemed the lantern that Nate had used to show me the way through the darkness was burning out. I could see the final flickering of the flame in his eyes. I could hear the crackling of a dying flame in his mournful voice. That little fragment of Nate's soul that had remained vital for so long was gasping its last painful breath. The only thing that Nate had to draw on was a few glimpses of past "good" times. The cancer that destroyed the souls of so many Black men had made its way deep into that part of Nate desirous of living, and was letting him know that it wanted all of him. For the first time in Nate's life he began to sound frantic. I could detect some residue of fear in my brother. He had taught me to be fearless. He had taught me to take on all of my enemies without ever running away. I remembered his words: "Never take the coward's way out."

I detected some weakness in Nate. Not much. But any measure of weakness in a Black man would be exploited. I wanted to cover Nate's weakness so no one else could see it. I wanted to cover it as I would an awful wound or some bleeding repulsive sore. I didn't want him to change. I knew that there was something deeper and more meaningful than all that this world had forced into him. I wanted him off the drugs. I wanted him to stop killing. But I didn't want him to become weak. I didn't want him to become broken as Dad had been. I needed him to hold on to that little piece of soul that still belonged to him, that little piece of his soul that also belonged to me. I wanted Nate to hold on, because if he didn't or couldn't, it could mean that sooner or later I wouldn't or couldn't remain strong. That I wouldn't be able to protect my soul. That sooner or later, I would start running.

Despite our differences—despite the fact that I had never killed another man, or used drugs, or even taken a sip of any alcoholic beverage—I saw myself in Nate's eyes. I had gained strength from his many lectures. I had gained courage, had conquered fear. And now my mentor seemed to be showing some cracks. I looked into the mirror of my soul and searched myself for those same cracks. I asked Doris if I were changing. Was she starting to detect weakness in her strong African man? Had I started to sell my soul? Doris assured me that I was not breaking down under the intense pressures. She would not allow it. She would watch my flanks. But the cracks in Nate's soul were evident. The dying out of the flame was apparent. I was not the only one who detected the demise of my brother's soul.

Mom continued to watch Nate. A tear rolled down her cheek. She wondered where she had gone wrong. What could she have done to make things better for him? What could she have done to make him turn out differently? Mom was battling with the thoughts that most mothers—especially mothers of ghetto children—fought with. She was blaming herself for things that she didn't completely understand. Mom had prayed for understanding. She had asked God to give her all the right answers. She had asked Him to lead Nate in the right direction. Mom had done her best; yet Nate was headed for disaster, and Mom knew it. She watched as sweat rolled over his clammy body. It was as if his body were shedding tears, crying out in pain.

Mom stared as Nate looked deeper into the heavens. She thought of his birth at Providence Hospital in Baltimore, Maryland in June 1958. She thought of how small and innocent he had been when he entered the world. She could hear his gentle cry and see his small arms and legs struggling to be free of all that had restrained him for nine months. Even after birth, Nate never found freedom. It was as if he were still in her womb, kicking to be free. Only God could free Nate from his yoke. Mom silently prayed that God would give Nate what he searched for. She prayed that God would free him before it was too late. *Never too late. It ain't ever too late for God.*

Nate broke off his stare from the hot round ball that he concluded was Satan's refuge in the heavens. He turned and blinked his eyes. He rubbed them and tried to make out the tall, strong figure standing in the doorway. He smiled at Mom. "What's up, Ma? Why you standing there like that?" Mom cleared her throat. "I'm just trying to catch a little breeze. It's hot in the kitchen." Nate responded, "Ain't no breeze out here, Mom. Ain't nothing but hot air and that burning hot sun." He shielded his eyes with his hand and looked back into the sun. "Don't worry, Mom. One day, I'm going to buy you a big house with an air conditioner and a white maid. You ain't gonna have to do no more cooking. Yeah, Mom, one day we are going to turn things around. You ain't gonna have to go down to that hospital and have those lazy white folks work you to death anymore. Me and my little brothers are gonna take care of you. Brothers are gonna work it out."

Mom smiled a gentle, fragile smile. She hoped that Nate wouldn't see the tears now streaming down her face like a miniature waterfall. She hoped that the sweat would disguise her tears. Her voice trembled as she spoke. "It ain't so bad, Nate. I'm happy to have a job. I'm happy that God has kept all of you healthy and living. I'm happy that ain't none of you hungry or homeless. I don't need a big house and you know I don't want a maid, be she white or Black. I can do for myself—never minded working hard down at the hospital or anywhere else. I've worked hard all my life and it ain't always been easy, but I know there's a God and I know that one day all of my hard work and praying is going to pay off. Not that it hasn't paid off already."

Mom didn't want to offend God. She didn't want Him to think that He hadn't done well by her. After all, she had managed to purchase the house at 4461 Old Frederick Road in Baltimore. She had managed to keep her children well fed and clothed. She had kept us going when it would have been so easy for us to quit and become one of the zombies of the ghetto. She was the reason for my earning a bachelor's degree in 1985. She was the reason that Warren was now at the University of Maryland earning his bachelor's degree. She would be the reason for Warren's being drafted to the Denver Broncos in the second round of the National Football League's draft in April 1989. Mom was the reason that both Quincy and Frank had good jobs. She was the reason they were taking care of their families. Mom was the reason that Sugar had been able to weather the rape by Dad and become an extraordinary wife and mother of two beautiful girls. Sugar borrowed her strength from Mom.

Nonetheless, Nate, like the rest of us, thought Mom deserved so much more. She had been pregnant with us for a total of fifty-four months. She had worked so hard for so long, always giving to us before giving to herself, always putting us first. Holding us together while trying to put Dad back together was no easy task. But Mom didn't quite see it that way. She had been taught what the slaves were told after the Emancipation Proclamation—that things could be worse. She had been told not to ask for too much, not to expect too much. God knew just how much she could bear; God knew what she needed. Mom didn't understand that it wasn't God who was telling her this. Someone else, trying to play God, was requesting that she not ask for too much or expect too much. Someone else was telling her that she was getting exactly what God wanted her to have.

Nate listened to Mom and slowly turned toward the door. He tried to focus his eyes on Mom. She appeared as a ghost, standing there and yet not standing there. It was as if he were watching her spirit. He wanted to get up and embrace her, yet he was afraid. Afraid that she would not be there. What would he do if Mom were gone? He needed her. And, for some unknown reason, he seemed to need her more today than ever. Mom would be there for him. She had always been there for him. He couldn't figure out what kept her going. He couldn't understand how she kept faith. He thought that if Mom ever woke up and found out that there was no God, she would go crazy. God was what kept her going. Her faith had kept her strong through her tumultuous marriage. It had kept her strong when she saw Nate handcuffed and carried off to prison for armed robbery. It had kept her strong when she saw Quincy carried off to prison. It had kept her strong as Sugar lay on the floor unconscious in a puddle of blood, hemorrhaging as a result of—unknown to Mom—one of Dad's sexual assaults. Nate was happy that Mom had God.

Nate got up and opened the screen door. Mom stood there, as she knew he would come to her. She tried to stand steady but Nate's spirit reached her before he did and caused her to sway in its eerie breeze. Nate hugged Mom. "Girl, I love you." Mom squeezed Nate. She didn't care about the sweat that was being pressed into her clothing. She was glad to hear him say that he loved her. That was all she wanted from her children. She just wanted to be loved and appreciated. She just wanted her children to love her enough to do the right thing.

Mom thought back to the night when Nate had denied her. High on cocaine, he had pushed her away as she had tried to talk to him. He had told her to get her hands off him. He told her that she was not his mother and stormed out the door. Mom cried. Warren and I sat on the steps, watching her tears. Nate ran out the door into the night.

Now Nate was embracing her, telling her that he loved her. Telling her that he was going to provide for her. He was admitting that he had put Mom through hell. He had not been a good son. He knew the pain and suffering that he had caused her. He reached into his pocket and pulled out two crinkled fifty dollar bills. He pressed them into her hand, kissed her on the cheek, turned quickly and walked out the door. Mom yelled after him, "Aren't you going to stay for dinner?" Nate kept going and yelled back without looking back, "No, Mom, I've got to get home to my baby girls." Mom smiled through her tears as Nate faded into the glare of the sun, faded into the streets of Baltimore. Mom would never see him smile or cry again. She would never see him walk or run or hug or kiss. Nate was going home.

26

By Way of Deception

We wear the mask that grins and lies.
–Paul Laurence Dunbar, "We Wear the Mask"

Attack when they are unprepared, make your move
when they do not expect it.
–Master Sun Tzu, The Art of War

My investigative assignments as a Special Agent in the Cincinnati division of the Federal Bureau of Investigation remained almost exclusively drug work. It was an area for which the FBI seemed to believe African Americans—civilians or agents—were best suited. I worked undercover assignments under the watchful guidance of Royce Winters and Stephen Barnett. Of course, the frail supervisor/overseer kept a close eye on my activities. He critiqued my undercover operations as if he were an expert DEA advisor—or a slave driver. In the beginning his critiques and evaluations were annoying; after a while they became comical. Here was this insecure, inept, ineffectual man telling me how to handle brutal drug-dealing capitalists. No doubt he thought that he understood the ways of Black folks—since most of the subjects of the Cincinnati division's narcotics cases were Black—and believed that he was in an advantageous position to advise me on how "these people" would act and react and how I should act and react toward them. He seemed not to have given any thought to the fact that I might have known a little bit more about street survival than he. Because the FBI had hired me, it was assumed that I was not like other Blacks and therefore would not understand them, or know their history, or live with them, or associate with them. There was the assumption that I was a "good," naive house negro. The frail supervisor understood "these people" better. He had made it a career to study them—but he was no expert.

On one of my excursions into the dangerous and brutal underworld of drugs, I was assigned to penetrate an infamous family of drug dealers who supposedly were responsible for a major portion of the drug trade throughout Cincinnati. As usual, I had conducted the required extensive background investigation on my subjects. I knew who their family members were, who their associates were, what time they got up in the morning, and what time they went to bed at night. I knew who they dated and learned all I could about their companions. I knew what restaurants they frequented and what kind of food they ordered. I knew more about their lives than they did. They unconsciously followed a set pattern, like many other unsuspecting people in America, without once giving any thought to how easily they could be targeted by would-be predators. In this case the FBI was the predator justifiably seeking a prey that was knowingly destroying his own kind.

The members of this drug-distribution family were ruthless—at least that was the information we had received from our well-placed informants. I was introduced to one of the male family members by another unsuspecting drug dealer, to whom I had been introduced by a convicted drug dealer who was trying to get the judge to be lenient with him when it came time for his sentencing. Loyalty is a rare, seldom-sought trait among drug dealers. I had arranged to purchase one ounce of cocaine from my subject. This small purchase was to be a confidence booster that would lead to purchases of more significant quantities of cocaine and eventually to identification of the supply line.

I was electronically wired with a body recorder and transmitter. This would allow me to record the conversation between the dealer and me. It would also allow my back-up agents to monitor the conversation and activities for any signs of trouble. The monitor is supposed to offer a small sense of security for the undercover agent. In reality it creates the added burden of making sure the subject or subjects do not perform a body search. There is no way to logically explain having a recorder and monitor attached to one's body. The undercover agent knows that if the electronic equipment is found, he or she will probably be dead before help arrives. It is the risk every undercover agent is willing to take. I have yet to meet an undercover agent or police officer who does not earnestly believe that he or she is having an impact on the war on drugs. The shame is that America is not serious about ending the drug trade. Thus, a great many law enforcement officers lose their lives in vain while politicians play public relations games.

I knew bad things could happen to me and those around me while I was "under." And *under* is the proper term. Being undercover is like being submerged in the depths of the ocean. One feels alone although one is surrounded by many other living things. One has to hold one's breath and pray that when it is time to emerge, one can successfully make it to the surface. No matter how much one knows about the territory, there is always the possibility of a surprise attack from one of its creatures. While growing up on the streets of Baltimore I had witnessed, up close, the results of a drug deal gone bad. I had witnessed hot lead cutting through brown skin as a result of a confrontation over white powder. I had witnessed brutal stabbings over as little as ten dollars of drug money.

I knew the powerful draw of drugs for the unsuspecting neophyte users. Once a man falls under the powerful hypnotic spell of drugs, he loses his ability to function as a human being. Nothing he does makes sense anymore. He can't be trusted. Every step he makes must be watched. Drug-addicted fathers and mothers sell their young, innocent, virgin daughters to sexual deviants for a quick high. Drug-addicted sons and daughters rob, beat, and kill their brothers, sisters, and parents for a ten-minute trip into fantasy land. Obtaining drugs becomes the only goal in the life of the addicted. They think of it in the morning when they wake up, and it is their last thought at night before they close their eyes for a restless sleep. They think about it while they are sitting behind their mahogany desks in their plushly carpeted corporate offices. They think about it as they walk through the halls of power in Washington D.C. They think about it while on the assembly lines of General Motors, Ford, Chrysler, and Toyota. They think about it as they stand before classrooms of students and as they treat sick patients. They think about it as they stand with their client before a judge. They think about it as they look down on a defendant and his lawyer, from their high bench. They think about it as they enforce the laws of the United States of America. They think about it as they stand in unemployment and welfare lines. Drugs become their god. The users become religiously dedicated drug fanatics who respond to nothing else but their mighty god. An unknown author wrote the following harsh, truthful words about the deadly drug cocaine:

My name is cocaine—call me coke for short.
I entered this country without a passport.
Ever since then I've made lots of scum rich.
Some have been murdered and found in a ditch.
I'm more valued than diamonds, more treasured than gold.
Use me just once and you too will be sold.
I'll make a school boy forget his books.
I'll make a beauty queen forget her looks.
I'll take a renowned speaker and make him a bore.
I'll take your mother and make her a whore.
I'll make a school teacher forget how to teach.
I'll make a preacher not want to preach.
I'll take all your rent money and you'll be evicted.
I'll murder your babies or they'll be born addicted.
I'll make you rob and steal and kill;
When you're under my power, you have no will.
Remember, my friend, my name is "Big C,"
If you try me one time you may never be free.
I've destroyed actors, politicians and many a hero.
I've decreased bank accounts from millions to zero.
I make shooting and stabbing a common affair.
Once I take charge, you won't have a prayer.
Now that you know me, what will you do?
You'll have to decide; it's all up to you.
The day you agree to sit in my saddle
The decision is one that no one can straddle.
Listen to me, and please listen well,
When you ride with cocaine you are headed for HELL.[1]

I'm convinced that if America responds to the drug problem just as it has responded to problems in Grenada, Libya, Panama, and Iraq, there will be no drug problem, or a very minute one at worst. Drugs have killed and are killing more Americans than all the United States' declared enemies combined. Why don't we just declare a *real* war on drugs and attack it at the source—the same way we expertly identify and attack nuclear weapons facilities and

---

[1]This poem was widely circulated in the African American community in Detroit, Michigan. I have always admired the poem for its truthfulness and frankness. I am disappointed that my search for its author has been futile. It appears to be a version of James Brown's song entitled "Heroin."

ammunition depots in *Third World countries*? Can't our multi-billion-dollar satellites that are capable of identifying minor troop movements detect coca fields in Bolivia and Peru? Are we afraid of a counterattack by Bolivia and Peru? Would it not be a worthwhile investment to provide financial assistance to these countries—just as we now generously provide billions of dollars in aid to Russia and Israel—rather than have them provide the United States with poison? Why doesn't the United Nations invoke stringent sanctions against any nation that facilitates and allows the unabated manufacture and distribution of the destructive chemical warfare substance termed illegal drugs?

Someone doesn't want the drug problem to go away. Someone is enjoying the enormous profits. Some leader or group of leaders is benefiting economically and politically from the illegal drug use of "we the people." These leaders are enjoying an easy deception—a deception that entails their publicly taking a stand against drugs without taking the obvious and readily available steps to eradicate the problem. Ask the undercover agents and the officers who are on the front line of the feigned "war on drugs" whether they feel the United States is earnestly using all the weapons it has at its disposal. You may be surprised at the answer you get—that is, if the anti-drug warriors feel assured that they will not be punished or lose their jobs for giving an honest, unedited answer.

The problem is that now this menace of illegal drug use is starting to increase its speed through the clean, quiet streets of suburban America. Drug abuse has always existed in suburban America, but it was kept hidden like a dirty secret. It was kept within closed doors on glass-top tables at social gatherings. It was kept within the rock star poster-filled bedroom walls of long-haired white teenagers. But now that drug use is boldly stepping out of the closet, it has to be covered up, not eradicated. For eradicating it might also release the ghetto dwellers from their drug-induced spell. Once the ghetto dwellers are no longer anesthetized and miseducated, they will recognize the route to actual freedom. They will understand that they are being duped and bamboozled. They will understand that they are being targeted for drugs and alcohol, cigarettes and pork, and heart attacks, strokes, and AIDS. Maybe they will pick up the book *Bad Blood* by James H. Jones and understand that the conspiracy theories implicating the government are not all that farfetched. Franklin D. Roosevelt was quoted as stating that "in politics, nothing happens by accident. If it happens, it was planned that way." Pulitzer Prize-winning author and crime researcher Ed Reid is quoted as saying, "There is no question but that the youth of this country are the victims of a conspiracy. The object is to get the kids on drugs and effectively destroy the next generation of adults."

I had no false perception of my value to the FBI or the "war on drugs." I realized that should I be killed on one of my patriotic undercover missions, it would mean very little to the FBI. In fact, there would be a mild celebration. Of course, I would be given the obligatory insincere ceremony. The Special Agent in Charge of whatever FBI division I was stationed in at the time of my demise would read the obligatory remarks from a laminated card prepared for just such an occasion. No tears would be shed, and the discussion amongst the few agents gathered around my grave site would be in regard to where they were going to meet for lunch. I realized that to the FBI I was expendable. In fact, my demise was desirable and the FBI would certainly try to hasten it. I did not have the traitorous value of a Clarence Thomas, a Walter Williams, or a Thomas Sowell. I realized that as an African American who had stood up and spoken out, my chances of advancement in the FBI were nil. Yet, at this point I had not anticipated my co-workers' future cowardly attack on the residence of my mother and sister.

As I prepared myself to go out and meet the subject from whom I was to purchase drugs, I noted the irony of my situation. I was a little apprehensive about trying to play the role of someone that I wasn't. I had never thought I was good at doing that—at least, not until James explained that I had been playing a role for years and had perfected the art. No matter how I tried to shove James's words from my mind, they haunted me. I had promised never to be an actor again. But then I realized the power inherent in the fine art of deception. Master Sun Tzu taught me that to be deceptive at times gave me a distinct advantage over my opponents. I perused the annals of history and found that deception was a necessary ingredient in the building of great nations. Deception was the tool used to subdue the great kings and queens of Africa. They had been tricked into believing their European invaders were friends truly interested in the equal trading of products and ideas for the benefit of all mankind. If I was to survive during my undercover assignments, I would have to become a master of deception.

The buy was to be surveilled by a group of FBI agents who would be well hidden at strategic locations around the meeting site. There was to be no arrest immediately after the buy. The plan was to gain the trust of the dealers, at least enough of their trust to afford me the ability to make future multi-kilogram purchases. This type of begrudging trust was called "street trust." It was not complete, nor was it intended to be. It was the minimum amount necessary to get the deal completed. All parties understood the extent of the trust. All parties understood that because of the fragility of the trust, it was necessary to be prepared for a bad deal or a rip-off. Those who were the victims of a rip-off deserved it. It was the price they paid for not knowing the rules of the game, for not being prepared. All is fair in the polluted trenches of the drug trade.

At any sign of trouble, the surveilling agents were to move in and protect me from my would-be assassin. It was a peculiar situation. I had never trusted anyone—except family—with my life, and I had no illusions about my being part of a grand FBI family. But now I was placing my safety in the hands of a group of agents. I did not feel, at the time, that any of the agents would allow me to get hurt if they could help it. A sense of duty and well-trained reflexes would cause them to react to a call of help from a fellow agent. As I prepared myself mentally to deal with the drug-pushing zombie, I questioned my reasons for putting myself in this precarious position.

Initially I had been motivated by childhood experiences to do something about the drug problem. At one point I sincerely and naively believed that the United States government was interested in the fight against drugs. I found that many of the African American agents were also motivated by what they saw in their neighborhoods and by what they had personally experienced. They developed a healthy hate for the drug pushers, and they wanted to personally lock them away in order to protect the fragile lives of African American youth. The youth were the impetus that made the agents more than willing to put their lives on the line. Later I would realize that going undercover to capture mostly street-level dealers, with the hope of having a positive impact was an exercise in futility. But in July 1987, at the young age of twenty-six, it was my time to put my life on the line for "the cause."

I engaged in a pep talk soliloquy in order to facilitate my submersion into the undercover role:

"Drug dealers are the enemies of every African American child who hopes to grow up to be somebody. They are the enemies of every African American mother who watches her child bleed to death from a gunshot wound delivered after a drug deal gone sour. They are the enemies of every

African American father whose daughter is forced into prostitution to feed her wicked addiction. Drug dealers are being manipulated and used against their people. Drug pushers are pawns in a game that they really don't understand. They are puppets on a string. They are guided missiles aimed at the African American community. They are selling their race deeper into slavery—just as some mis-guided African kings did many years ago. Black drug dealers have to be rehabilitated, educated, or permanently removed *by any means necessary.*"

I met with the drug dealer. His name was Lewis. He was a heavyset Black man with a gerri curl hair style. His eyes were watery, and thin red lines ran through them. His faded blue jeans hung low from his waist and revealed a pair of multicolored boxer-style underwear. His clothing was not an indication of how much money he made. He was trying not to draw attention from the police. My investigation of him had revealed the considerable extent of his wealth.

Upon meeting him at the pre-determined location, Lewis told me that plans had changed. He would have to go to another location and wait for the delivery of the dope. I would have to give him the money and await his return. I surmised that his brother, by far the smarter of the two, had advised him to test me. I was up to the test. If I had fallen for the idiotic request of fronting him the money, he would have surely known that I was ignorant of the rules of the game. He would have rightly assumed that I was a cop. On the other hand, I could tell that Lewis was high on his own supply. He had violated the rules. I also knew that he profited personally from any individual sales he made. I was a new customer in his pyramid scheme—I was his customer. I sensed how badly he wanted the deal completed. I looked deep into his hollow sockets and read his empty soul.

"My money ain't walking, man. You said to bring the money and you would have the dope. Things ain't changing 'cause you fucked up." He sighed deeply and tried to look hard. The cocaine betrayed him. I knew he was no threat in his condition. If he reached for a weapon, I would surely be able to grab and subdue him. My back-up would handle any guardians he had around. I was sure by now my colleagues had scanned the area for all possible threats.

He responded, "Fuck that. I don't trust you, motherfucker. This is the first time I'm meeting with you and you starting out like you 'the man.' But let me tell you this: I'll put a hole in your ass, no matter who you are. I hope you understand who you are trying to fuck with." His entire body swayed with the slightest movement of the warm summer breeze. He cleared his throat, sniffed up the thin mucus that had escaped, and continued, "How do I know that you won't try to rip me off? It ain't gonna happen, man. Fuck you and your money. I ain't doing time for nobody."

He was using the lines that I had scripted for myself. I was supposed to talk about getting ripped off. I paused, stared at him, turned and walked toward my car. I could hear the voice of the frail supervisor: "Why did you let him off the hook? You had him. You had the whole fuckin' family in the midst of your hand and you let them get away." I could see myself sitting before him, smiling at his best attempts to pretend that he was a man. I had a plan. The addict-dealer needed me. I had seen his type before: I had lived near addicts and dealers and had confronted them. I knew he needed to sell his cocaine to me. I did not pressure him; I played the game cool, calm, and collected. I remembered just how powerless he was: he was incapable of letting my dirty money walk away from him. It was right there in my pockets. Right there within several feet of him. I read him, read him well, read him completely, figured him out. He was not only addicted to the drugs he sold, he was also addicted to the selling of drugs. He was addicted to living on the edge and taking chances. The drugs had clouded his mind; his addiction had left him without common sense.

I felt him moving toward me. I saw his cold, pale hands reaching out to pull me back toward him. The dirty government bait money was summoning him to me. He was begging, pleading to the green devil that enticed him. He grabbed my arm with all the strength he had. The drugs and sickness of his soul had sapped him of his inner and physical strength. I could have grabbed him, shaken him, choked him, crushed him into the powder that controlled and ruined his once hope-filled life.

I spun around and raised my hands to crush him. He sensed the danger and immediately stepped back. Sweat rolled down his face. His shirt was drenched. His voice trembled. "All right, motherfucker, all right. You can go with me. But if you're the man, I'm gonna kill you." I was angry. Angry about all the lives he and his kind had ruined. I wanted him to identify me as a cop. I wanted him to try to kill this strong, drug-free African. It would have been no contest. I yelled back, "Fuck you. I ain't the man, but even if I was, a motherfucker like you wouldn't scare me. I don't want you to trust me. Fuck trust. All I want is the dope so I can make some money. You ain't the only motherfucker selling dope in this town. I'll go buy it from the white boys. That's where you're getting the shit from anyway. You ain't got nothing that they ain't gave you."

He didn't understand what I was saying. I knew he wouldn't. He turned and began to walk toward his car. "Come on." I followed behind him and looked around for my fellow FBI agents. I assumed that they would be moving into position to follow us. We got in his car. Lewis drove around the city for about an hour, trying to see if he was being followed. I sat calmly, contemplating the best way to terminate his meaningless life, should he try to end mine. He drove up one-way streets and ran red lights. It didn't matter. My mind was engulfed in thoughts of justified murder. At any rate, the agents who were covering me were well aware of all the counter-surveillance maneuvers that he was utilizing. We had learned them at the FBI Academy and we had been taught how to overcome them.

Lewis slowly pulled the old beat-up Buick onto a small, dirty side street. I prepared for an imminent physical confrontation. I scanned the area for other attackers. I looked around for the covering agents. They were doing a hell of a job at being unseen. Lewis broke the tense silence. "We gotta go in the bar here and wait for a phone call. Ain't nobody following us, so don't worry about that. I'm sorry for checking you out so hard, but it ain't easy for a drug dealer out here." He smiled. "You know, you got the fuckin' cops, politicians, and civil rights leaders trying to put a brother out of business." I turned and gazed out the side window. "Don't worry about it, Lewis; I understand how you feel. You never know when a motherfucker is planning to take you down and out." He smiled again, "Yeah, yeah, you right, man—now let's break."

We got out of the car and entered the bar. I again checked for my surveillance team. Once inside we ordered drinks. Lewis ordered a vodka. I took a dangerous chance at being unmasked by ordering a Coke. Lewis was no challenge for my deception skills; thus, I let my guard down. I really didn't care anymore if he found out. I wanted a fight. I was concentrating all of my anger on Lewis. In him, I saw the reflection of all the murderous drug pushers. I knew he wasn't the root cause of the drug problem, but I was blaming him for allowing himself to become a victim. Nate was absolutely right: we have to get away from the habit of becoming easy victims. We Black folk know we are standing in quicksand, with no one reaching out to help us, so we have to help ourselves. Standing still and pointing the finger will only lead to our stagnating, our sinking deeper and becoming mired. Those who are partially responsible for our position will stand idly by and laugh at our hollow rhetoric. Lewis should have put up a fight.

I sat at the bar waiting for one of the surveillance agents to come in and let me know that my team was with me. I expected it to be Special Agent Martha Dunbar, since she was the only other African American assigned to the squad and one of only three African American agents assigned to the entire Cincinnati division. The patrons in the bar were predominantly African American; Martha could mingle with them easily. She would not have been suspected by the patrons as being an FBI agent. The FBI hardly recognized Special Agent Dunbar as an FBI agent.

Lewis slowly stood up and said, "I got to use the pay phone." I nodded and watched him as he moved across the bar toward the pay phone booth. When I was out of his view, I reached down and rubbed the butt of my Smith and Wesson snub-nosed .38-caliber revolver. Since I had not seen any back-up, my gun was my only security. I had to make sure it was still with me.

Marvin Gaye's "Trouble Man" played on the juke box. I scanned the room and watched closely the movements of the patrons. Any one of them could be part of a life-threatening plan. I looked toward the phone booth. Lewis hung up the phone and began to walk back toward me. I blocked out the pleasant, mellow sounds of the troubled Marvin Gaye. I needed to concentrate completely on every subtle motion Lewis made. I watched to see whether he was giving some kind of signal to one of his criminal collaborators. I didn't know whom he had called. Maybe he had talked to someone who had identified me as an FBI agent. Maybe he was walking toward me to end my existence. I watched his hands closely and prepared for a gun battle that I was sure to lose. The snub-nosed revolver only afforded me five shots. Lewis and his cohorts would be carrying superior firepower. I had no assistance. Nonetheless, I would go down fighting and shooting.

Lewis walked to the bar, grabbed his drink, and swallowed it down. He motioned for me to follow him. I threw the money for the drinks on the counter and followed him out. I watched his every gesture and the movements of those around us. He had chosen this bar. This was his territory. He had the advantage. There had been no reconnaissance mission. In his book *The Art of War* Master Sun Tzu wrote, "The terrain is to be assessed in terms of distance, difficulty or ease of travel, dimension, and safety." The FBI had taught me that it was important to gather beforehand intelligence information on any location where I was going to conduct an operation. I should have identified all the entrances and exits. I should have known where every chair was located. I should have been familiar with every hiding place. But Lewis had caught me off guard. Getting caught off guard was a sure route to death.

As we stepped out of the dark, drab bar onto the warm summer street, I felt relieved. Lewis wouldn't take me on the street. I could maneuver easily, find cover, and fire back with precision. The other agents would move in quickly and foil any surprise attack with one of their own. The agents were better trained in the use of weapons. Training at the FBI Academy's excellent facilities in Quantico, Virginia had prepared them for just such an urban encounter. I knew the street-learned tactics of Lewis and his boys would be no match. The agents had been trained to make every shot count, to allow the adversary to fire aimlessly and endlessly with the hope of getting lucky. The agents would remain cool and calm and seek out the proper cover. They would breathe rhythmically and squeeze their triggers back slowly, taking deadly aim at the hearts of their targets. The shots would be true. Lewis and his street thugs would get a taste of the weapons of those in power. They would understand that all their streetwise tough talk is no match for well-trained, properly prepared, patriotic and loyal servants of the true power brokers.

Lewis scanned the area. I watched him and then peered up into the hot comforting sun and thanked God for its warm reassuring presence. We walked to Lewis' car. I looked up and down the street. Lewis looked at me and smiled. "Don't worry, motherfucker—ain't nobody following us. I'm too good to be caught by the dumb-ass cops. These Cincinnati cops ain't nothing but wannabees. Now, don't get your ass caught up in New York or L.A. Those motherfuckers are dangerous. Anybody out in L.A. could be a cop. One motherfucker I know was arrested by his mother." I laughed. "Man, that's bullshit." Lewis shook his head. "I ain't lying. Moms handcuffed that motherfucker while he was asleep in bed in her house. He started yelling, 'Mama, Mama, Mama.' She pulled out a badge on his ass and told him he was under arrest for distribution. Called the meat truck and had his ass hauled up out of there. Nigger got ten years. Mama got promoted." I continued to laugh. "You a lying motherfucker." He smiled and raised his right hand. "I ain't lying. I tell you what, take your ass out to L.A. to the Hollywood precinct and ask for Lieutenant Robinson. That's his mama."

Lewis opened his car door and got in. He reached across the seat and pulled up the lock to the passenger-side door. I scanned the area once more and then entered the ragged Buick. Lewis continued to talk—continued to allow his mouth to walk him deeper and deeper into the midst of the confining walls and filthy cells of the penitentiary. "I've been doing this shit a long time. I'm a pro at this shit. You came to the right person to get your shit from." I smiled deeply. Deception was a beautiful tool. I was proud of my ability to utilize it. I realized that this was a minor test. Nevertheless, I was witnessing the power of deception. It was about to take away a man's freedom. It was about to put another ghetto zombie in the judicial morgue.

Lewis reached down and turned on the radio; music blared out. He lay back against the seat and looked up into his rearview mirror as if he were waiting for someone. "What the fuck we waiting here for? Lewis smiled. "Be cool—I got to handle some business. You're gonna get your shit in a minute." I turned and looked out the back window. "Look, man, I got some business to handle, too. I ain't buying this shit to snort it. I've got customers waiting. You know how those fuckin' addicts are—they need their shit right away. Anyway, I done spent a half a day with your ass. If you can't supply me any quicker than this, I can go somewhere else to get an ounce." He smiled. "Aw, motherfucker, you know we got the best shit. You know we got the right connections and you know we can and will deliver. Things are just a little fucked-up today. Our supply was a little late coming in. Now we got to check it out and package it up so we can make sure we are doing you right. Those fuckin' baseheads will wait all night for this shit, especially when it's coming right."

Fully expecting a surprise attack now, I continued to look around. Several cars pulled up next to us. Lewis got out. I reached into my waistband and pulled out the .38. I placed my finger on the trigger and put the gun down between my legs. Lewis went into the trunk and handed the occupants of the other cars small packages of cocaine. He was given money in return. I thought that the other agents might move in. I thought that they might not allow the cocaine he was selling to reach the streets. I could do nothing by myself. But the easy flow of cocaine from the trunk of the beat-up Buick should have been stopped, otherwise it was sure to end up in the nostrils or veins of some neophyte to drugs or a zombie-addict. No one came.

Lewis got back in the car and opened up a small package of cocaine. I eased the gun back into my waistband without his noticing. He pulled a tiny spoon from under the seat, dug it into the package, and snorted the deadly white powder up one of his sweating nostrils. He put some more cocaine on the spoon and moved it toward my nose. I moved back. He pushed the spoon closer to me. "Take a snort, man. It will calm your hyper ass down. Anyway, I can't trust a motherfucker who won't take a snort." Lewis was sweating profusely. His hands were trembling. I ran my eyes over his flabby soft body and looked for a weapon on him. I didn't see one. At any rate, I was still sure that I could disarm him quite easily; I could hold him off until my coverage arrived.

I pushed the spoon full of mind-controlling white poison away from my face. "I don't use the shit, Lewis; I sell it. I'm a business man. You could make a hell of a lot more money too, if you would stop snorting the shit." He smiled. "I am going to stop snorting this shit. In fact, I bought me a whole box of needles yesterday." He laughed. I continued, "And I told you before, I don't give a fuck about your trust." He stopped laughing and tried to stare into my eyes. He was trying to read me, but it was impossible. My shield was up. He would only be able to read what I purposely showed him.

I didn't move. I was sure that the conversation was being monitored by the other agents. I hoped that my wire hadn't failed me. (It had.) I hoped that the recorder was picking up the entire conversation. (It wasn't.) Lewis pulled the spoon back to his nose. He took a deep snort and dropped the spoon to the seat. "I swear I'll kill you if you are the man." He started the car and drove off.

We rode around the city for another twenty minutes. Lewis constantly watched his rearview mirror. He drove down a small side street and parked. We sat there quietly for about ten minutes. I was getting worried that he had figured out who I was and was setting me up for an ambush. I had not seen any of the other agents for about two hours now. I spoke up. "Fuck it. Just take me back. An ounce, two ounces, or a kilo ain't worth this shit you're putting me through. Take me back to my ride or I'll get out and walk back. I'll tell you what, when the cops stop chasing you all around the city, you bring me my dope." Lewis ignored me and opened the door. "Wait here—I'll be back in about five minutes." He ran down the street and around the corner. I spoke into the wire. "He's out of the car. Will one of you drive by to let me know that someone is out here?" No one drove by.

I began to believe that I was on my own for sure now. I was in a part of the city that I didn't recognize, with a cocaine-addicted drug dealer. I had no cover and only a five-shot revolver. If I survived, it was to be the last time that I worked undercover. It wasn't worth it. What good would I be to my people if I died here on this street, in this car? Who would give a damn? I wanted to do my part, but I began to think deeply about what I was doing and what impact it was having. I began to think more about Lewis. What or who had driven him to the state of nothingness that he now was in? He was once somebody's baby, just as Mom had said. I thought of Nate. I could see Nate somewhere, with a spoon to his nose, snorting his life away. Lewis was no different from Nate. He had a mom who loved him and reared him. Now he was a shell of that once full-of-potential baby, that infant who had the world before him, the power to be somebody and to help somebody, and the ability to change things. But all that infant had done was to grow up into a zombie of a man. His hope-filled soul had been gutted and what remained was a dangerous, empty shell. The infant, the boy, the teenager, the adult was no longer in control; he was no longer a man. Cocaine was his autopilot; he wasn't even the co-pilot.

I looked out the front window. Lewis was running up the street toward the car. He had a desperate look on his face. I looked past him, fully expecting to see someone with bad intentions chasing him. I reached for the revolver. He reached the car quicker than I expected—in spite of his narcotized condition. Maybe I had underestimated him. He opened the door and jumped in. His seat made a horrible sound, as if it despised his return. Lewis was sweating and breathing heavily. He tossed two ounces of cocaine into my lap. The cocaine was packaged in two separate, clear sandwich bags. "I only asked for one." Lewis never looked at me. "You ain't my only customer. Some motherfuckers do front their money. But I agree with you: only a fool or a cop would front the money. I happen to know the motherfucker that other ounce is for. He ain't a cop. But he damn sure is a fool. I'll do him right because he's a good customer."

I looked the packages over and shoved them into my waistband. I took the government bait money out of my pocket and handed it to Lewis. "Count it." Lewis shook his head. "I ain't got to count it. I been reading you up and down ever since we hooked up. You're straight. Besides, you know if it's short, you're a dead motherfucker." I shook my head. "You don't get it, Lewis. A motherfucker like you don't contribute any fear to my life. The money is straight because this is business and I don't play games. It ain't because I'm afraid of you or your brothers. I think that you all bleed just like I do. The same type of bullet that can kill me, can kill you. We all can die. And what makes us different from the scared motherfuckers is that we are willing to kill and kill and kill again—that is, for the right cause." He smiled and said, "You should be working for us." I turned and looked out the passenger-side window.

Lewis scanned the area, started the car, and drove off. He went through his counter-surveillance maneuvers, constantly peering into the rearview mirror. It was automatic for him—a reflex reaction to the roar of the unstable engine and the rolling of the steel-belted radial tires. It was part of his training as a drug dealer and part of his routine during drug deals. We returned to the original meet-site using a different circuitous route. We never said a word to each other during the drive. Lewis kept looking up into his rearview mirror for police. I kept looking into my sideview mirror for my cover agents.

When we arrived back at the meet-site, I got out of the car with both ounces of cocaine in my possession. I just couldn't allow the second ounce to reach the streets. Lewis would find out later and would be upset. But it no longer mattered: I would never work undercover again, and he would not seek out an FBI agent to ask for his ounce of cocaine back. He leaned over toward me. "Try it out or let your people try it out and let me know how much you like it. Call me if you need more."

I looked deep into Lewis' eyes—and saw Nate's eyes. I heard Nate's voice. But Lewis seemed colder. He had progressed farther down the road of spiritual and mental death than Nate. He certainly didn't have the intelligence of Nate. Yet, he reminded me of where Nate was headed if I didn't make a drastic move to turn him around, to put him on the right road. Nate had helped me: he had made me conscious. Now it was my time to go home and help him. He wasn't too far gone; his vision was becoming clearer. I held the key. I was the antidote to the disease that was afflicting him. I couldn't allow Nate to become Lewis. Lewis was already dead. I closed the car door. The old Buick—or hearse—drove off.

I drove to the pre-arranged meet-site and met with the other FBI agents. Martha walked over to the car and asked me if I was all right. I told her that I was fine. Other agents came to the car and asked me if I had gotten the dope. I answered yes. They asked me how it had gone and if I had recorded the entire conversation between Lewis and me during the buy. I answered their questions. They wanted to know when and where he had given the dope to me. They asked if he had met with anyone else. I was sure now that they had not been with me. I was sure that they had not even monitored me. I had been alone.

I drove back to the Cincinnati office of the FBI, processed the evidence, and began to do my paperwork. Special Agent Martha

Dunbar came to my desk to help with all the required forms that needed to be filled out. I removed the body recorder and began to rewind the tape. We held some light conversation in which Martha told me that if I hadn't been working with an inebriated drug dealer, I would have been an uncovered agent. She teased me about how I walked and talked. We laughed. In the midst of our gleeful conversation Martha suddenly got quiet. Her low, soft, gentle voice broke into the impromptu silence. "You know, we lost you for about two hours. They're not going to tell you that." I looked up into her warm brown eyes and said, "I knew you all weren't there, but it doesn't matter. Everything went well anyway. I think I work better alone." Martha winked her eye at me and smiled. I didn't want to say anything else to her. I didn't want to tell her that I would never work undercover again. I didn't feel like going over the reasons. This wasn't the time for revealing thoughts and plans.

About one week after the undercover drug operation with Lewis, I received the paperwork from the other FBI agents who were part of the surveillance team. They all had falsified their reports to indicate that they had been with me the entire time I was with Lewis. They would have had to testify to their lies, had Lewis not pled guilty. Special Agent Martha G. Dunbar would have told the truth.

27

The Federal Bureau Of Investigation

The ones who are actually hurt cannot do any harm. All others remain untouched, which is a persuasion to keep quiet, yet they also become fearful of making a mistake and suffering like those who have already been despoiled.
—Niccolo Machiavelli, The Prince

You're not supposed to be so blind with patriotism that you can't face reality. Wrong is wrong no matter who does it or says it.
—Malcolm X, Malcolm X Speaks

As I sat at my desk in the Cincinnati division of the FBI, I reflected on my long and arduous journey from the streets of Baltimore City to the office of the Federal Bureau of Investigation. An improbable story. Some would say my journey was conceivable only in the mind of a great novelist with an extensive imagination and maybe a hidden social agenda. I had been born a ghetto child, and now I was a part of what was considered the number one law enforcement agency in the world. My mother had always emphasized that I could accomplish anything and everything if I would just believe in myself, have faith in God, never give up, and never be deterred by situations and circumstances. Mom told me to reach for and seize my goals and dreams. She said that there would no doubt be plenty of hurdles for me to jump over, but if I believed in myself, nothing—not even the highest hurdle—would or could keep me from breaking the victory tape at the end of the marathon race of life. If I believed, nothing could keep me from completing the 40-, 50-, and 100-yard dashes in between. Mom said that's what oppressed people do: "They don't lie down and let their oppressors roll over them. They fight back and they fight harder and they become tougher. They become educated and self-reliant. They become an essential spoke in the world's wheel, not just an unnecessary spare part."

It hadn't been easy. It never would be. There were those who were constantly betting against my success. There were those who were determined that I trip and fall as I attempted to leap over those intentional, well-placed hurdles. The race is not yet won. I am an African American man in the United States of America, where African Americans are yet to be recognized as full-fledged citizens. Thomas Jefferson's constitutional "three fifths of a man" assumption seems deeply ingrained in the American psyche. But it doesn't matter anymore. I can no longer afford to spend my time and energy trying to change the twisted points of view of those who despise me and consider me inferior because of the color of my skin, for they will never see an African American as anything else but a nigger. My experiences and education have allowed me to remove the heavy shackles of mental slavery. I'm no longer seeking anyone's approval.

From my vantage point in the FBI, the world has been made clearer. The deception and lies are more vivid and easily unveiled. I know the game now. Having interviewed individuals from around the globe, I know the images of African Americans, and Africans in general, that foreigners are fed by America and her extensive, far-reaching media apparatus. I know the power of the propaganda machine, which causes African Americans to be despised whenever and wherever we are encountered. One Chinese student told me that all he ever knew about African Americans had been taught to him by white Americans who believed African Americans were worthless. He stated that while in China he was given a packaged negative image of African Americans. To him and many other foreign students, visitors, and immigrants whom I interviewed, African Americans are brutal, gun-toting, drug-abusing, unemployed, welfare recipients.

African Americans are considered lazy, uneducated, uneducable, unmotivated, immoral, sex-starved, primitive thugs. This view is reinforced when foreigners arrive on the shores of the United States and are greeted by the news media with their characteristic affinity for covering only negative stories about African Americans or Blacks. These foreigners are not made to understand that the crimes that cost the United States citizens the most and that do the most damage to the frayed fabric of America—such as the Savings and Loan crisis and the BCCI scandal—are not committed by African Americans. Moreover, the crimes that cause the most damage to the greatest amount of people do not carry the penalty of death.

My world view made me understand that it was most important and necessary for African Americans to travel the world and network. I understood that not all African Americans had the resources to travel, but it was incumbent upon those who were able to travel to do so, and to bring back the messages that the world offered. It was also the duty of the African American travelers to deliver the truth about the African American image transmitted around the globe. The negative images had to be countered. Staying within the well-defined boundaries of the ghetto would only reinforce the Hollywood and Madison Avenue images of Africans.

An equally distressing image of African Americans (which the media tried to convince us was positive) was highlighted when the media's spotlight, including the Black media, was turned on the conspicuously consuming high-profile African American athletes and entertainers. The image of a single athlete in a forty-five-room mansion generated the opinion that as soon as African Americans gained financial wealth they spent it, purchasing items "to be seen," not necessarily to be used. Not all African American athletes and entertainers engaged in this conspicuous consumption, but many in the white and Black media were, and are, unwilling to cover an athlete or entertainer who is saving and building his or her wealth to pass on to the next generation or who is opening community-based businesses or in some way giving back to the community. There is no outcry from the Black media or from the highly paid, high-profile Black athletes, when a Craig Hodges is banned from the NBA—despite his superior skills—because of his willingness to give to the community and his suggestion that other high-profile athletes do the same.

I now understood that these negative images were part of a mean-spirited worldwide propaganda campaign directed against African Americans. The world would have no sympathy for the plight of such a seemingly "backward," "savage" people. Indeed, the world would despise such a wretched people. It was this international propaganda that led to the Japanese Prime Minister's likening African Americans to prostitutes. The negative images would have the effect of putting a muzzle on some "wild, uncivilized species" that no one would miss if eliminated from the face of the earth. Never again would the world or the United Nations (U.N.) come close to listening to the complaints of African Americans, as was the case when Malcolm X came dangerously close to getting an audience at the U.N.

My improbable journey to the FBI had not only toughened me but made me understand even more clearly that African Americans are a people who can too easily be pitted against each other. Lifelong brainwashing has had a devastating effect on us: we African Americans have been duped into infiltrating and destroying our own organizations of uplift. We make the best informants, because many of us are all too willing to sell our souls for short-term satisfaction. Stripped of self-confidence at an early age, we are constantly seeking the approval of white America. This seeking of approval has led to our selling out for white-collar jobs with blue-collar pay. The seeking of approval has led to our saying and doing anything that will elicit that sought-after pat on the back and that much-treasured statement, "He's not like the rest of them." The seeking of approval has caused us to soften our protest and to accept whatever crumbs are offered. This seeking of approval has led to our willingness to spy on and subvert perfectly legal African American entities. The approval of white America is not easily garnered unless, in the words of Maryland State Police Sergeant Stoney, we "act like a white man."

I had observed that the approval of white America made us sit up into the wee hours of the night waiting to see if our musical artists had garnered the needed votes of "approval" to win awards—awards that had no bearing on the upliftment of our race. Year after year, we watched as white actors and white actresses walked away with best actor and best actress awards. Still, we put our children to bed early and waited patiently, hoping that one day our artist would receive the coveted "approval" of the selection committee. Every once in a while they would give us our hard-earned award, and, like Whoopi Goldberg, we would kiss their feet, their trophy, or whatever else they put before us, to show our appreciation. The world could not and would not respect us for desperately seeking such trivial "approval." These awards had nothing to do with what we needed to do to secure our future, our survival. They were a side show that too easily diverted us from the *real* world.

I recall reading that one of the most extraordinary artists of all time, Marvin Gaye, had become severely depressed after not being nominated for a Grammy award for his classic song "What's Going On." This saddened me. We could not and would not be satisfied with self-approval. We could not be satisfied with the approval of our own race. Our success meant nothing unless others—who were intentionally distorting our image—assured us that it was worthy of praise. Neither award—not the Oscar or the Grammy—had been named after anyone who looked remotely like us.

●●●●●●●●●●●●●●●●●●

I had learned much on the long and lonely road that I had taken to escape the clutches of ignorance. Having watched, listened, and read, I was no longer that naive ghetto child. I understood the concept of power, for which all the countries of the world seemed to be fighting and dying; I understood why those without power were kept powerless. I understood the divide-and-conquer scheme with all its devastating effects and the reason that it worked over and over and over again. But it was one thing to identify the problem and another thing to actively, realistically, and intelligently plan for the eventual eradication of it. Both Marcus Garvey and Theodor Herzl understood what needed to be done. Never mind the motives or rationales for their actions. They created well-thought-out, intelligent, practical plans and decided to act—despite the odds and the nay-sayers. Marcus Garvey's task was made far more difficult—thanks to the intentional splintering of the enormously intelligent, yet depressingly naive, African American leadership. The divide-and-conquer scheme continues to work efficiently in the African American community.

History proves we have been targeted. In fact, the FBI had helped to thwart any movement forward by African Americans. The FBI had helped to weaken and unlink the unified chain of African Americans that was and is so necessary for progress and advancement. The COINTELPRO/Racial Matters communications and files revealed the extent to which the FBI had gone to sabotage legal, justice-seeking African American entities. These communications and documents indicated that there had been discussions about the need for Black FBI agents and Black police officers to infiltrate certain Black groups and organizations. Instructions concerning the "neutralization" of certain Black leaders had been forwarded from FBI headquarters to different field divisions of the FBI. Information on the most intimate aspects of the lives of targeted African Americans was disseminated by the FBI to such intelligence agencies as the Central Intelligence Agency (CIA), the United States Secret Service, the Office of Naval Intelligence, and others. The revelations concerning the COINTELPRO/Racial Matters investigations are available to the African American community. There is much to be learned from this recent episode in American history. The files should be the impetus for African Americans to move forward in spite of the barriers.

My access to inside information, my studies, and my personal FBI experiences made me less tolerant of those whom I believed to be traitors—the Walter Williamses, Thomas Sowells, Gerald Earlys, and Clarence Thomases of the world. In my opinion, they were sellouts who had been too cheaply bought off. They should have demanded much more for their souls than middle-class jobs, publication deals, and editorial columns. Nonetheless, thanks to the scholarly work of Dr. Carter G. Woodson, I understood that Williams, Sowell, and those like them were also victims. In his classic book, *The Mis-Education of the Negro*, Dr. Carter G. Woodson wrote:

> ...the Negro's mind has been all but perfectly enslaved in that he has been trained to think what is desired of him. The 'highly educated' Negroes do not like to hear anything uttered against this procedure because they make their living in this way, and they feel that they must defend the system. Few mis-educated Negroes ever act otherwise; and, if they so express themselves, they are easily crushed by the large majority to the contrary so that the procession may move on without interruption.

●●●●●●●●●●●●●●●●●●●

I often stayed late into the night at the FBI office in Cincinnati. I would sit at my cluttered desk, listening to the quiet and the intermittent hum of some machine that someone had failed to turn off in their haste to exit the secret world of the FBI. With my tie loosened from the unbuttoned collar of my starched white shirt, my elbows resting on the arms of the drab government chair, and my fingers intertwined and folded under my chin, I stared out into the deep dark blue sky. Occasionally, I would flip the switch on my portable cassette player and listen to the soothing voice of Marvin Gaye mournfully singing "What's Going On," and asking the perplexing questions, Can the world be saved? Is humanity destined to die? Are the children fated to suffer? Do we care enough to save ourselves?

On these solitary evenings that I shared only with Marvin Gaye, I thought of the streets of Baltimore. I no longer viewed them as depressing. There was much life and hope there. There was even a deeply hidden feeling of peacefulness and gaiety. I pictured the quietness at Christmas time. I pictured the silent snow and the flashing multicolored lights. I thought of the smiling faces of little chocolate-hued children running up and down the warm summer streets, playing tag and declaring themselves "safe" from their pursuers as they wrapped their innocent arms around tall green lamp poles. I constantly reminded myself that someday I would have to return there and reach out to the youth. It was essential that every "successful" and enlightened African American help untangle those children—our children—from the snares of ghetto life. Marvin and Nate kept me focused. Although I was learning many meaningful lessons in the FBI, I would not allow the process of acculturation to destroy my sense of duty. I wasn't going to be bought.

I continued to investigate the cases assigned to me, but kept my vow never to work undercover again. Some of the white FBI agents that I worked with told me that they needed me to go under and that I was copping out for not doing so. Some of the DEA agents in Cincinnati were also upset over my unwillingness to purchase drugs. They needed Black agents to buy from Black drug dealers. And, of course, the idea of hiring more African American agents was too far-fetched for them to consider. I was accused of being afraid. However, I never responded to their attempts to demean and coerce me into going under. Those methods of persuasion—taught at the FBI Academy—would never work on me again; I understood the art of deception all too well. I never gave them any reason for my choosing not to work undercover. My mind was made up and there was nothing they could do or say that would make a difference.

Nonetheless, their attempts to persuade me to go under continued. They persisted with their subtle psychological game of trying to make me feel that I was doing something wrong and unpatriotic by not working undercover. They had no success. I had seen and heard them use the same tactics when they tried to convince individuals to become informants, and again when they attempted to persuade these same individuals to put their lives on the line by buying drugs from dangerous dealers. In fact, I had utilized these methods. I have no idea why they thought these same deceptive tactics would work on me. I guess because they had worked so brilliantly on others who looked like me. At any rate, nothing could overcome my strong conviction that buying drugs undercover was an enormous waste of time and energy.

•••••••••••••••••••

After working undercover and conversing with callous drug dealers, I am more convinced than ever that education is the key to winning the fight against drug abuse and its catastrophic effects. My buying drugs undercover for the FBI while the government permits the import of drugs from South America makes no sense. I feel bad for all the agents and police officers who diligently and patriotically, but naively and senselessly, put their lives on the line, working undercover in a war that has never been declared or seriously fought. The United States government leaders are aware that several countries around the world are legalizing the use and possession of small amounts of marijuana and cocaine, yet they mount no protest. It is obvious that if drugs are made legal in other countries, many of which are allies of the United States, production will increase. An increase in production will mean an increase in distribution, with no regard for the invisible borders that divide the United States from the rest of the world. Why should agents and officers continue to purchase drugs in the dangerous and deadly back-alleys of America? America will have to wean itself off this disastrous weapon of destruction.

There are at least thirteen different federal agencies with the authority to participate in the war against drugs. These agencies have overlapping responsibilities. However, there is little or no coordination. FBI agents, in many cases, do not get along with DEA agents. One agency competes with and hides information from the other. FBI agents have bought fake drugs from undercover DEA agents and vice versa. DEA agents have worked sting operations against FBI agents. Each agency considers itself the sole authority on how the "war" on drugs should be fought. This lack of coordination and infighting have resulted in the complete disorganization of an already futile law enforcement battle against illegal drugs. The organized drug cartels continue to operate efficiently. The disorganized street-level dealer is arrested by the disorganized federal drug-fighting apparatus. These arrests have little effect on drug distribution. In order to kill a tree you have to destroy its roots. The pseudo "War on Drugs" is nothing more than a small-scale Viet Nam: all the firepower in the world but not enough guts or desire to utilize it. The United States government, with all its tough talk to street dealers, is unwilling to attack the root of the tree. Breaking branches off now and then serves little purpose.

The dire drug situation is unfortunate. A glance at history will clearly indicate that when it comes to mind-altering substances, America would rather use them than eliminate them. Remember prohibition? There appears to be too much money to be made by the government, and those who run it, for them to destroy the drug trade. The United States has made too many alliances with rulers who deal in drugs. (Our "leaders'" reply to this accusation is that the average American can't see the big picture.) And in the end (and at the major risk of my being considered paranoid) drugs assist in the destruction of Black folk—a destruction which the government has never been too eager to halt.

African Americans must seriously and diligently educate themselves about the devastating effects of drugs and about the death trap we are being led into. We African Americans must get it through our thick skulls that no one else gives a damn. History has taught us that we are on our own; yet our "leaders" still wait and beg and beg and wait for some government superman draped in an American flag to drop down from the heavens (or from a police helicopter) into our neighborhoods and "save" our children. Listen to me, as I speak from insider knowledge: *It ain't gonna happen.* African Americans have to come to the indisputable truth and obvious conclusion that the drug war will only begin when we initiate it. We will have to decide upon the strategy and the weapons to be utilized for the fight. The primary and most powerful anti-drug weapon is education—true, honest, undiluted education!

●●●●●●●●●●●●●●●●●●

As time passed I began to re-analyze my role in the FBI. I came to the conclusion that I had to work other violations besides the ones that the FBI tried to channel all African American agents into. I had to learn all that I could and disseminate the knowledge to the youth. I had to go out to the schools and the neighborhoods and speak with the youth, as I had promised Nate. I had to go onto the college campuses and talk to students. I had to help recruit more African Americans into the FBI. We had to be on the inside to see what was going on.

I noticed that the FBI's recruitment program did very little to target the areas, such as college campuses, where qualified African American candidates could be found. I could now appreciate what James Thorton had done for me on that quiet early morning in his small sunlit apartment in Reisterstown, Maryland. That apartment, that room, was now a significant place and point of reference in my life. I was learning that no place, no moment was insignificant. Everything had significance, and I had to make all my actions count. In my role as an FBI agent, I had a small impact on law enforcement in America. Even a minor impact was better than none at all. Maybe I could locate and recruit an African American who would take a civil rights investigation seriously. Maybe another African American agent would thoroughly investigate the actions of cowardly cops who gang-beat unarmed Black motorists.

If there were going to be more African American agents in the FBI, African American Special Agents already in the FBI would have to go out and recruit them. And I hoped that they would recruit African Americans who were not afraid to be good, strong men as well as excellent investigators. The FBI had stacked its ranks with milquetoast, malleable African Americans who seemed to be afraid of their own shadows and who were certainly afraid to stand up and fight for what was *just* and *right*. The path to promotion for an African American agent was passivity and submission. This is not to say that every African American who is promoted in the FBI is passive, but the vast majority of those whom I have met wouldn't stand up to a boy scout if he were white. These African American agents spent the majority of their time trying to persuade their white counterparts and "superiors" that they were of the non-African, western man, Eurocentric mindset. If an African American agent approached them with an Afrocentric mindset they immediately shunned him. I would never get promoted, despite the fact that I considered myself an excellent agent. The FBI's definition of African American excellence had little to do with job performance.

As I began to look deeper into the FBI's recruitment program, I heard numerous comments about affirmative action bringing in too many unqualified African American candidates. This thought was ludicrous. During most of J. Edgar Hoover's administration, a college degree wasn't required in order to be an FBI Special Agent. Even after Hoover made it a requirement, he still made exceptions whenever he felt like it. Now every agent entering the FBI had to have a four-year degree. This included the African Americans who some white agents complained were getting in under "lower" standards. How could the requirements or standards be lowered when more was required now than in the past? Moreover, the test for a position of FBI Special Agent was irrelevant to anything required on the job. Some white agents complained that African American applicants could get in with test scores that were lower than those of white agents. What they failed to mention in their gripes about the FBI's affirmative action program and about the test scores was that the threshold score necessary for passing to the next stage of the application process was lowered for lawyers, engineers, and accountants, most of whom were white. No one complained about that. Furthermore, the FBI test was racially biased and was finally identified as such and discontinued in 1992. The irrelevancy of the test reminded me of the test freedmen were required to take in the South in order to register to vote. The FBI entrance examination might as well have asked "How many bubbles are in a bar of soap?"

In regard to the claims of the unfairness of affirmative action, out of ten thousand FBI agents less than five hundred are African American. The FBI official count states there are five hundred twenty-six African Americans. I'm not wholly convinced of the numbers. Nonetheless, we know there are no more than five hundred twenty-six African American FBI agents throughout the world. If there was or is an affirmative action program in the FBI, it has failed miserably. Also, the FBI never discussed the 1,800 white agents who had been given copies of the entrance test weeks before they took it. This sounded more like "affirmative action" to me. An FBI agent who was a recruiter secretly informed me of this incident during my first year in the FBI. I asked other white agents for the particulars of the incident. They confirmed that it had occurred but refused to give specifics. They informed me that the FBI considered dismissing the agents who had cheated but decided against it. The FBI hushed the incident and did nothing to rectify the situation. Some of these agents are still working for the FBI today. They are now heard complaining about affirmative action.

Other white Special Agents told me that when they took the FBI entrance examination during the seventies, all that was required was a spelling test. They stated that the white Special Agent who was to administer the test would walk into the examination room, give them the spelling words on which they were to be tested, and then leave the room for approximately thirty minutes. Upon his return, he would administer the test. Needless to say, everyone passed the test. This procedure was not conducted for African American Special Agent applicants. Affirmative action?

Further, while assigned to the Detroit division, I became aware of a white agent who had purposely put false information into a report on an African American applicant in order to keep him from getting employed. Initially, it worked; the candidate's application was turned down. He persisted and his file was reassigned to an African American agent who went out and reinterviewed the same people who had been interviewed by the white agent. The African American agent found that the white agent had falsified reports in an attempt to disqualify the applicant. He was sure that it had been done because the applicant was Black. He wasn't sure of how many other Black applicants had been disqualified because of this kind of racism. This African American agent came to me and asked what I recommended. I told him to contact the Applicant Unit at FBI headquarters and advise them of the matter. He did. He came back to me and told me that the supervisor at headquarters told him to forget about the false report of the white agent and to just submit his own report. I told the African American agent that he should document what had occurred and what he had been instructed to do by the supervisor at FBI headquarters. He told me that he didn't want any trouble and that he was just going to forget about the false report. The white agent was reassigned to another squad and never disciplined. He, too, was one of those complaining about affirmative action. I wondered how many other qualified African American applicants had been—and were still being—disqualified by this type of blatant racism. How many other African American agents silently stood by, merely watching? I wrote a memorandum to the Director of the FBI concerning this matter. He never replied.

Another white agent, who was a representative for the Agents Association, stood up at an all-employee conference in Detroit, with the Special Agent in Charge (SAC) present, and indicated that the Bureau should be ninety-five percent white. (I suppose the other five percent could be composed of submissive negroes.) The SAC gave a speech at another all-employee conference and identified an agent who was heading a unit at headquarters as being "Black and intelligent too." When he realized the "mistake" he had made, he apologized. A Freudian slip?

A white male supervisor in the FBI Detroit division stated that a high percentage of the African American agents allowed into the Bureau had since been in trouble for violating Bureau rules. He had no evidence to back this statement up. The problem that some of the white agents had with African American agents was the color of the African American agents' skin. To these white agents, skin color was the disqualifying factor. Despite the negatives in the FBI, I was determined to do the best job I possibly could. In fact, the negativity of the FBI only made me more determined. Nonetheless, I was not the type of person to put on blinders and ignore all that was going on around me. I couldn't ignore how the FBI acted and reacted toward African American agents and applicants. I couldn't ignore the fact that some white agents were defending the actions taken by other white agents against Special Agent Donald Rochon.

Donald Rochon was a Black Special Agent who was subjected to pictures of apes pasted over the faces of framed pictures of his children that sat on his desk in an *FBI office*. White FBI agents allegedly threatened Rochon's very life by taking out a life insurance policy on him and forwarding it to his home as a scare tactic. They forged his name on the policy—a criminal act—and a copy of the policy ended up in the hands of his petrified wife. Some white Special Agents of the FBI took up a collection for the white agents who were suspended—not indicted—for their *unlawful* actions against Special Agent Donald Rochon.

I couldn't ignore how some white agents spoke so negatively about the Reverend Dr. Martin Luther King Jr. and so positively about J. Edgar Hoover. I couldn't ignore how they linked Malcolm X and Ho Chi Minh together because their birthdays were the same day, May 19th, and because they both, according to these agents, were enemies of the United States of America. I couldn't ignore the racist comments made to me and to other African Americans, by white agents. One white FBI agent came up to me and stated that he saw Nelson Mandela on television and was surprised that he was intelligent and articulate. I understood that most of what they did and said was out of ignorance and racial hatred. I could not and would not allow them to break me.

I was learning a lot as a sharp-eyed Special Agent in the FBI. It was a different world. A world that had been, and was supposed to be, concealed from all except those with special passes—those who had taken a solemn oath to keep the unholy secrets and to maintain the status quo. I was convinced now more than ever that America needed more African Americans in the FBI—not to disrupt the noble job of enforcing the law, gathering necessary intelligence, and preventing anarchy, but to learn and to participate in the cleansing of crime from the streets of America, especially urban America. African Americans understood the culture and mindset of urban dwellers. Some of us *truly* understand the history, the conditions, and the circumstances that have led to the present situation in our communities. The enlightened African Americans are an asset to—not a burden on—the FBI.

The FBI apparently did not share my opinion. In fact, it seemed that the FBI did everything within its power to make the agency uncomfortable for African Americans. One out of every four African American agents was under some type of internal investigation (or close observation) that was to lead to disciplinary action. Many of the African American Special Agents refused to stand up against the obvious injustices. They had been specially selected, and they knew their place. They were happy just to have a job and thought things would gradually get better if they just remained silent and kept "bucking and grinning." They were engulfed in fear, certain that speaking up could only cause problems and maybe even loss of employment. They did not want to be considered *malcontents*.

Some African American agents would acknowledge the injustices when they were away from their white counterparts but would not dare speak out in their presence. A veteran African American agent in Detroit stated to other Black agents that he didn't understand why the Detroit Public Corruption Squad only investigated Black public officials and the predominantly Black Detroit Police Department, when it was evident that white public officials and predominantly white police departments within the state of Michigan, which the FBI had jurisdiction over, were similarly suspect. When asked why he didn't bring this to the attention of the Special Agent in Charge, he stated that nothing would change and that he would become the target of a vicious elimination campaign.

An African American agent in a southern division of the FBI refused to speak up and speak out when he learned that his supervisor, who had spent the previous evening sitting with him in a car on a surveillance, complained about being stuck in the car with a "nigger" all evening.

In the Detroit division an African American agent declared that he would not make waves concerning a lower rating that he and two other African Americans received on their performance appraisals, despite the fact that every white male agent on the squad received exceptional ratings and performance certificates.

The FBI had selected the right people and then injected them with a strong dose of paralyzing fear. The negroes who were promoted were to act as overseers and keep the "field negroes" in line. For the most part they did an excellent job. An African American agent in Detroit who had been given a position that he had intensely desired informed me that the managers of his office stated that they expected him to put out the fires that flared up amongst other African American Special Agents. They sent him to me to douse my fire. He feared that if, in his role as "negro firefighter," he didn't garner the expected results, he would be transferred out of the coveted position and labeled. He said the managers were putting him in the awkward position of being considered an Uncle Tom. They were emasculating him and making him cry out "Toby." They were splitting him in two and further igniting the civil war that rages in the soul of a Black man who is trying to succeed in an organization that requires him to forget or deny his identity. They thought they had found his price, and were trying to extract the maximum amount from their investment.

To say that racist attitudes in the FBI were condoned is an understatement. On one occasion, while assigned to Detroit, I pointed out to a group of African American agents and other African American employees, that a white agent whose duty it was to investigate discriminatory actions taken against minorities had several newspaper articles which denigrated African Americans, on the bulletin board behind his desk. These articles were degrading Nelson Mandela and making disparaging statements about African Americans. He also had scribbled comments on his desk calendar indicating that the Equal Employment Opportunity Commission was only good for hiring the dumb, the lame, the handicapped and minorities. I made the managers in Detroit aware of the bulletin board and the scribbled comments, although I was sure they already knew. The bulletin board was large enough so that anyone who entered the area could see it. Yet, neither the squad supervisor, nor the ASACs, nor the SAC said anything about it. The agent even left the articles up when then FBI Director William Sessions came into the area where the board was displayed, during one of his visits to the Detroit office.

In the same squad area was a picture of Detroit Police Chief William Hart next to a black bulldog in an apparent effort to indicate a physical likeness. Chief Hart, a Black man, was being investigated by the FBI at that time. There was also an unconfirmed, but widely believed, rumor within the Detroit division of the FBI, that the FBI had leaked to the press derogatory, unconfirmed information on the mayor of Detroit, Coleman Young. This allowed the press to draw Mayor Young into a heated confrontation during a nationally televised interview on ABC's news program 20/20. Some of the white agents sat back and enjoyed the results of their handiwork.

The vigor with which the FBI pursued Mayor Coleman Young was unbelievable. Mayor Coleman Young had spoken out against the white political establishment in the state of Michigan. Some white agents in the Detroit division talked about how badly they wanted to get criminal charges against Mayor Young. In the end they concluded that Mayor Young was just too smart to be caught. They would not concede that he was not doing anything illegal. In my opinion Mayor Coleman Young was a marked man. He was on the FBI's "most wanted" list.

Many Blacks in Detroit were angry with Mayor Coleman Young for allowing a city that was eighty-five percent African American to deteriorate so badly. They were angry about the abject poverty, the dilapidated houses, the lack of hope, the horrible murder rate, and the unrestrained drug abuse. Much of this anger may have been justified; however, the white FBI agents who were pursuing Coleman Young seemed to care nothing about these issues. One of those agents indicated his lack of concern for the citizens of Detroit by stating he "felt safe in the city of Detroit," because "fortunately" most of the murders were "Black on Black."

In my opinion, the FBI agents with whom I spoke hated Mayor Coleman Young because he was an African American who defied white people and said as much. He refused to beg them for their patronage. He refused to cry "uncle." He believed that he was their equal. Moreover, he was the mayor of Detroit, and historically politics dictated that the mayor had power. He would not be treated as if he were a common beggar. Most of the whites with whom I spoke believed that the statue of the fist of boxer Joe Louis, which had been erected on Jefferson Street in downtown Detroit, was an intolerable symbol of "Black Power." Coleman Young was too Black and too bold. He didn't understand his place in the white power structure and there had to be a legal means of bringing him down. The legal system has always been used to silence strong Black leaders. Marcus Mosiah Garvey was among its many victims.

Mayor Coleman Young refused to disarm the African American population of Detroit as long as Detroit remained surrounded by well-armed, hostile white suburbanites. Mayor Coleman Young subscribed to the philosophy and wisdom of poet and musician Gil Scott-Heron in his poem/song "Gun." In this song Gil Scott-Heron states, in regard to the gun, "The philosophy seems to be, at least as near as I can see, when other folks give up theirs, I'll give up mine."

The hatred for Mayor Coleman Young was so great that a white Special Agent severed his relationship with an African American Special Agent who stated that it was obvious that Coleman Young was clean and that the FBI needed to leave him alone. The white agent stated that he thought the African American agent was intelligent until he defended Coleman Young. The African American agent refused to back down from his assessment. The white agent went around the office describing the African American agent's statement to other agents. The African American agent would be permanently tainted; he would now be considered a malcontent.

Detroit wasn't the only office of the FBI that experienced racial problems in regard to public officials. During the time I was assigned to the Cincinnati division of the FBI, Chicago Mayor Harold Washington died of a heart attack. When his death was announced on the radio and on television, a white FBI agent leaped to his feet in a fit of joy and exclaimed, "Good, I'm glad he's dead; I'm glad the bastard is dead. He deserved to die. He was a fuckin' racist. Who's got the power now?" This white agent was immediately confronted by me and another African American Special Agent. He was surprised that we confronted him. We were supposed to agree with him or at least smile and bow our heads. He settled back in his chair and lowered his head. This was an FBI agent. A man assigned to uphold the laws of the United States of America. He was celebrating the death of a *democratically* elected African American.

There were some strong African American agents in the Detroit division of the FBI who spoke out against these injustices and discriminatory practices. Special Agent Prince Earl Ross was one of them. He had been out on an investigation one day and returned to the office to find a small white statue of a Ku Klux Klansman on his desk, with an official membership card bearing his name. Prince kept the statue and the card at the front of his desk for years, as a reminder of the racism inherent in the FBI. Prince is still in the Detroit division of the FBI, and the statue is still on his desk.

On another occasion, Special Agent Ross and another African American agent had effected the arrest of an individual on the FBI's Ten Most Wanted fugitive list. It was a policy of the FBI to give incentive awards to the arresting agents of a Most Wanted fugitive. Prince and the other agent received what had to be one of the lowest amounts ever for this type of award. I recall Prince telling me that it was as if they were less than agents. He said that it was as if their lives and their families didn't mean as much.

Prince complained about the award. He was called in and lectured by the ASAC on having "a chip on his shoulder."

In the years to come, Special Agent Prince Ross was denied promotions. Supervisory positions that he applied for were given to less qualified white agents. One of the white agents in the Detroit division of the FBI, who was given a supervisory position over Special Agent Ross, admitted to me that he did not earn the position based on what he knew about the job. He also stated that he had been told by the administrators of the Detroit division to put his name in for the position. Special Agent Prince Ross finally had to file an Equal Employment Opportunity (EEO) complaint in order to be considered for a supervisory position.

Like many other African American Special Agents who utilized the EEO process, Prince Ross would find out that it was all a joke. The FBI ran its own EEO office. Needless to say, the investigators in the EEO office were not inclined to find fault with what was essentially an extension of themselves. Who do you think the FBI selected to fill the positions within the EEO unit? Whenever I spoke to a supervisor in the EEO unit, he or she tried to talk me out of filing a complaint. Having the FBI man its own EEO unit was like telling a young child to investigate his own unruly actions and, if he is guilty, to discipline himself. *It ain't gonna happen.* The EEO investigations should be conducted outside the FBI, by people whose promotions are not on the line. One FBI supervisor who was investigating an EEO complaint that I filed told me that he had no incentive to find in my favor, no matter what the evidence indicated. He stated that it was more likely that he would have to work for one of the people whom I had accused than he would have to work for me. He stated that quite frankly, my best bet was to solve the complaint quietly and informally or to file in federal court.

Another African American Special Agent in Detroit was promoted to supervisor and then was forced to step down because of the pressures put on him as one of the few African American supervisors in the FBI. He stated that unethical demands, which he could not go along with, were placed on him. After being transferred to another division, the agent applied for thirteen different positions for which he was highly qualified. Each time, the position was given to a white agent. In many of the cases, the white agents were less qualified. None of the white agents selected were more qualified. The agent later became a part of a class action lawsuit against the FBI.

Special Agent Johnnie Mae Gibson, an African American woman who was the subject of a movie on her life as the first

African American female FBI Special Agent, also spoke out against the FBI's treatment of African Americans. Special Agent Gibson had been the only African American female field supervisor in the FBI. The FBI made her the supervisor of an Applicant/Civil Rights Squad. She was only allowed to be in charge of supervising agents who were conducting background investigations on new employees and presidential appointees. The FBI did very little investigation on civil rights matters. Prior to her taking over the squad, the agents on the squad had been responsible for fugitive and bank robbery investigations. These types of investigations improved the status of the supervisor and usually led to promotions. When Special Agent Gibson became supervisor, these violations were moved to a newly created squad. Supervisory Special Agent Johnnie Mae Gibson later filed an Equal Employment Opportunity complaint and hired prominent Washington, D.C. attorney James William Morrison to initiate legal proceedings against the FBI for its discrimination.

An African American male supervisor in the Detroit division of the FBI, who spoke out against the dearth of African American supervisors and the pressures put on African American supervisors, was told by the SAC of the Detroit division that he was surprised that he, the African American supervisor, concerned himself with those "Black issues."

In other divisions of the FBI, similar injustices were occurring. In Chicago an African American female Special Agent who had been discussing a case in an office with two African American male agents was told she was not allowed to meet in private with the two African American agents.

When Bill Clinton was elected as President of the United States of America, some of the white agents in Detroit feared that he might "give a damn" about civil rights. They unprofessionally and boldly expressed those fears. They complained that President Clinton was going to give minorities too many "undeserved" rights. (I suppose they thought he might even give us forty acres and a mule.) I watched as a white Special Agent carefully put pictures of Bill Clinton and Al Gore in plastic covers and placed the plastic-covered pictures in the men's room urinals in the office of the FBI. Grown men—Special Agents of the world's most elite law enforcement agency—came into the restroom, laughed, and urinated on the photographs of their Commander in Chief and the Vice President. (Yet African Americans are considered unpatriotic parasites.) These same white agents would be required to investigate the death of the President if he should meet the bullet of an assassin. These types of attitudes and expressions of disrespect should make the country appreciate the conspiratorial theories held and the investigations conducted by such authors and researchers as Mark Lane, Dick Gregory, and even Oliver Stone. When two white Detroit police officers, Walter Budzyn and Larry Nevers, were charged with beating to death a Black citizen, Malice Green, the Detroit division of the FBI opened a civil rights case and then hung on the office walls flyers advertising a fund raiser to offset the attorney fees for the defense and the eventual appeals of the officers. Needless to say, nothing came of the civil rights investigation.

Speaking out against racial injustices in the FBI could be dangerous. Upon my arrival in the Detroit division of the FBI in 1990, I was assigned a truck to be utilized as my official FBI vehicle. I went out and conducted FBI interviews in the old, ragged pickup truck. On one cold winter morning in November 1990, the truck mysteriously caught fire while I was in it. The electric locks would not open and I watched, from inside, as the truck became engulfed in flames. I continued to pry at the locks and door handles until I finally managed to get the door open and escape. A motorist assisted me as I rolled around on a dirt embankment, coughing and trying to catch my breath. The motorist had a car phone in his vehicle and I utilized it to call the fire department and the FBI office for assistance. The FBI office was only a quarter of a mile away. An FBI supervisor later admitted that he saw the flames from his office window. The fire department arrived in approximately two to three minutes.

The firemen put out the fire. I informed them that other FBI agents and a tow truck were in route to assist me. The firemen waited approximately fifteen minutes and then left the area. I stood in the cold, in smoke-saturated clothing, for another fifteen to thirty minutes awaiting my assistance from the FBI office. The FBI office was less than five minutes away. Finally, Special Agent Prince Ross arrived. He stated that he had just arrived at the office and was instructed by one of the FBI supervisors to go and get me. The truck was towed to the FBI garage. I was instructed, by an FBI supervisor, not to do a report on the incident.

Approximately one week later, I went to the FBI garage and asked the mechanic what had caused the fire and the jamming of the door locks. The mechanic told me that he had inspected the truck and was not sure about what had caused the fire or the jamming of the doors. He told me that the truck had been totaled and would not be inspected again.

I didn't want to seem paranoid, so I kept my suspicions to myself. Nonetheless, I described this incident to several other

Black agents. They quietly told me to be careful. Understandably, none of them were willing to speak out with me and complain. As time passed and FBI actions against me accumulated, more agents agreed that I was a marked man. A white FBI supervisor told me that someone had it in for me. Another white Special Agent disclosed to me that a rumor had been circulating that I was to be fired for stealing government funds. This vicious, disparaging rumor spread through three divisions of the FBI, and agents began to call to get the details of my rumored firing. Another rumor was put forth that I had been refused a position on the FBI Special Weapons and Techniques Team (SWAT) because none of the other agents trusted me. Never mind the fact that I had never applied for a position on the SWAT team, nor was it one of my career aspirations. I was certainly being set up as the target of a fall or as the victim of an "accident." The Special Agent in Charge of the Detroit division told me that the negative actions were tragic but unconnected, unfortunate coincidences. In the end, the FBI attacked my family at gun point. At that point, many agents, both Black and white, agreed that I was under siege. When I finally resigned from the FBI in August 1994, the new SAC of the Detroit division, Joseph P. Martinolich (who came to Detroit from Denver with a reputation of not tolerating racism), informed me that after looking over my personnel file and reviewing the incidents that had occurred, it was obvious to him that I had been wronged by the FBI.

The actions of some racist white FBI agents should not tarnish the image of all white FBI agents. I worked with some extraordinary FBI agents, both African American and white. Agents who put their lives on the line every day to uphold the Constitution of the United States of America and to protect the United States against all invaders both foreign and domestic. There were agents who worked long hours to solve cases because they believed firmly in what they were doing. I was amazed at the multitude of talents that the FBI had amassed to form the most effective and efficient law enforcement, investigatory, intelligence-gathering agency in the world by far.

I also worked with other FBI employees who symbolized what the FBI should have been or could be. The FBI could not only be the number one law enforcement agency in the world, but could also be the number one organization in the world. It could exemplify the phrase "and justice for all." Unfortunately, racism has engulfed the body of the FBI like a malignant case of cancer. Despite the good agents, the FBI remains an organization that practices institutional racism. It is an organization that still has the desire to be lily-white again. Nonetheless, in spite of my experiences, I am convinced that it would be a fatal mistake for African Americans to shy away from employment with the FBI. We have to be on the inside in order to watch the keeper of the secrets and to do our best to make sure the laws are equally enforced.

28

The Shadow
of Death

Account ye no man happy till he dies.
> *–Euripides,* Daughters of Troy

Ghetto Pedagogy:
"Dad?"
"Yes?"
"Why do Black men always kill each other?"
(long pause)
"Practicing."
> *–Walter Mosley,* Black Betty

July 23, 1987. The air was hot and still. The temperature continued to rise to unbearable levels as a great heat wave rolled into Baltimore. The giant fireball in the heavens came to a halt in the midst of the city and tortured the captive inhabitants. Groups of shirtless, glistening young men stood around basketball courts staring up into the deadly sun. One or two of them held basketballs against the tight, wet skin of their African bodies. The courts remained silent. It was too hot for games. Other shirtless men walked the streets with sweating water bottles in their hands. They wore shorts with sneakers and no socks. A few of them carried radios that blared out the euphonious sounds of Prince, Run DMC, Public Enemy and other popular artists. Everyone searched for some form of relief from the hellfire.

Clear, cold water gushed from bright orange, yellow, and red fire hydrants onto the little brown bodies that danced in front of them. Beautiful young Black women sat on white marble steps within rectangular doorways, holding plastic bags full of melting ice against their tender foreheads. The humming of small window air conditioners could be heard in between the intermittent sounds of agitated traffic. Those fortunate enough to be able to afford the air conditioners gathered in front of them and closed their doors to the world outside. Now and then a mother's distinctive voice could be heard as she summoned her children in from the heat or out of the sometimes dangerous streets of Baltimore City.

A group of old men with beaded sweat on their wrinkled foreheads gathered outside The Two Spot Bar and Lounge and discussed the politics of the city. They pointed to the boarded-up houses and the burnt-out corner stores. The neighborhood elders spoke of putting some money together and opening up the stores themselves. An investment by the elders would be a popular draw to a group of people who had been, and were being, exploited by outsiders with little interest in the well-being of Black inner-city dwellers.

One of the wise old men walked to the curb and spat. He squinted his eyes and looked up into the clear blue sky. He turned back toward the other men. "You know we got to buy up these stores before those goddamn Koreans come in here and buy them all up. You know how they always jack the prices up 'cause they know that they got us by the balls. We ain't driving out to the malls. Hell, I don't think we should drive out there and give those arrogant, stuffy white folks our hard-earned dollars. Seems like we always chasing behind their rear ends, always trying to eat with them or sleep with them, or go to school with them. I tell you, we got to put an end to this foolishness."

One of the other old men spoke up. "John, where we gonna get the money? Those damn Koreans get their money from that Reverend Moon. Moon ain't gonna give us no loan. He just give his people a loan and then they come down here and buy us out. We don't have no choice but to sell because if we don't, they'll buy the store down the street or on the next corner, offer lower prices, and put us right out of business. You know those banks ain't gonna lend no Black folks no money. They just as soon have us keep being dependent on other folks. That way they know they own us. They'll give us a loan to buy a car, but they sure don't want to see Black folk buying up land. Sure don't."

John shook his head. "All we got to do is buy from our own people even if it cost a little more. 'Cause you can bet as soon as the Koreans own all the stores in our neighborhoods, we gonna pay a lot more. So it's pay a little more now or a lot more later. It's what you call long-term planning. If we don't, we ain't gonna have a fuckin' thing to give our children—not a fuckin' thing. We got to do it. We gotta stop those Koreans, Jews, and any other invaders of our neighborhoods from stripping us down and raping us. They come in here just like they did in the motherland. And once again we standing around and allowing it to happen. History ain't taught us a damn thing. It's been too damn long. It's been happening too damn long."

John was trembling. His skin tightened around hard overworked knuckles as he balled his hand into a perfect fist. He used the long fingers of his other hand to reach up and wipe tears from his tired eyes. The other old man, who had been conversing with John, saw that he was hurting. "Let's go inside, John, and feel some of this cool air conditioner. You need to cool down or you gonna have a stroke right where you standing. I'll buy you a drink. A drink of water, that is." The elders laughed and moved inside the lounge.

In the basement of one of the city's numerous row houses a group of conscious young men found refuge from the heat by reading books and by discussing their plight. One of the men spoke up. "Man, I just didn't know how much of our history had been left out of those school textbooks. I mean Garret Morgan, a Black man, invented the traffic lights; Madame C. J. Walker invented numerous hair care products; George Washington Carver was an agricultural genius, who discovered over three hundred different uses for the peanut plant. We built the pyramids, which are still a mystery to modern architects. We were the first mathematicians and the first scientists."

The young man leaned back and shook his head. "So much of our greatness has been kept from us. We don't have any idea as to what we are capable of. We've been stripped naked and presented to the world as primitive heathens. Our minds have been invaded and ransacked. We are just so busy giving credit and praise to everyone else, when we should be carrying on what others like us have started. We could make ourselves indispensable to the human race if we just continued to add to what our ancestors have started for us. The white man's public school system has failed us so miserably. It doesn't matter if we are integrated if all we are going to be taught is of the greatness of the ancestors of the little white kid sitting next to us. It doesn't matter what deceptive book they make available to us if it is full of falsehoods and lies that constantly belittle the brown people of the world. All they teach us is about our history of slavery. They teach us only about how much we have accomplished when we worked for the white man or under the white man. We've got to wake up. Damn, we need to control our schools. We need good conscious teachers who really care about and understand the importance of their role in the lives of our young people. No wonder so many brothers and sisters are dropping out. Look at what they're dropping out from. The public school system is at the bottom. How can you drop out from something that is sitting on the bottom?"

The other young men stared at the brother who was speaking. At the age of sixteen, he was the oldest member of the group, but they all had done extensive reading. They had been directed by one of the older brothers in the neighborhood to books and all the knowledge they held. He had told them to read all they could, to read at every opportunity. He told them to continue in school and to learn their lessons well but to supplement what they learned in school with some independent reading and thinking. With the help of others in the neighborhood, he started a library in the basement of one of the houses. Each week, a different member of the neighborhood was required to supplement the library with a new book. Teachers who lived in the neighborhood were required to give a lecture one night a week. The program did not reach all the youth, but for many of them it was their savior and they reached out to bring in others. (When I spoke to the African American who started the program, in my effort to understand what Baltimore was like on my brother's last day, he requested that I keep the program confidential for fear that the media would distort his goals. He was not trying to become a short-lived celebrity. He was and is interested in the uplift of young people.)

The boys in the basement on this day cared nothing about the heat outside. They were reading and learning and burning for more knowledge. They were not looking for relief from the heat inside their souls. In fact, they wanted the temperature to rise. This knowledge, which had escaped them for so long, was addictive. The more they learned, the more they wanted to learn. It was all coming together.

As the temperature outside reached 110 degrees, the sound of ambulance sirens could be heard throughout the city. It was the hottest July in years in Baltimore and the hospital emergency rooms were full of people suffering from heat-related ailments. The shelters were full of people searching for the relief of an air conditioner. Those who could not find cool air inside tried to find shaded areas and sipped cold water. Television and radio announcers instructed everyone to go to a cool place and limit their indoor and outdoor activities. It was only eleven o'clock in the morning and there was no relief from the heat, as predicted in the area weather forecasts.

Nate slowly opened his eyes and focused in on the red digital numbers on the wood-stained alarm clock. Eleven o'clock. He rolled over onto his back and rested his head in the middle of his hands, which were connected by his long intertwined fingers. He wondered whether his daughters, Alice and Rosalyn, had gotten up yet. Their mother, Carrol, had gone to work. She had become the love of Nate's life. She had stood by him in his worst times, while trying to convince him to stop using cocaine. She was trying to put Nate back together again. He was her Black man. Her warrior. And she would not easily give up on him. He appreciated her help; he appreciated her not running out on him. And he was trying to be the best mate and father that he could be.

Nate had taken classes in carpentry at a local vocational school and had obtained a good job at a construction company. Unfortunately, he had fallen and injured his ankle. The company had admitted responsibility and was paying for his doctor visits and rehabilitation. He was determined to work hard and take care of his family. He wanted to rear his children right. He didn't want them to grow up as ghetto dwellers. He didn't want them to walk in his shoes and fall into the same deceptive, painful traps that had captured him. He and Carrol rented a spacious apartment in Baltimore County. Now, if he could only get off the "white hallucinogenic shit."

Carrol worried about Nate. She hated to see him high on drugs. He would become a different person. He would become paranoid and curl up in bed in a cold sweat. She would rub his head and tell him it was going to be all right. She would turn the radio on and listen to some soothing blues music. Tears rolled down her dark face. Her strong warrior lay before her like a helpless fetus prematurely released from the womb. She would close the door to the bedroom and turn out all the lights. She wanted to hide him from the world. He was so strong when he was sober, but when he was high, he seemed so vulnerable. So unaware of the ominous dangers that surrounded him like a heavy fog.

Carrol was convinced that when Nate was high, he was easy prey. He was a John F. Kennedy in a convertible limousine. He was a Dr. Martin Luther King Jr. on the balcony of the Lorraine Motel. It was up to her to defend Nate when his guard was down. She would not fail at her duties, as others had obviously and intentionally done.

Carrol was convinced that drugs in the African American community had no other purpose than to break and destroy strong Black men and to encourage them to leave their women and children defenseless. She believed that what forced African American women to be so strong is that their shield had been taken away from them. They were fighting naked with no back-up, so they had to be strong. The brothers who were not on drugs were in jail or, worst of all, were sleepwalkers.

Nate was not a sleepwalker. He understood what was happening to the community. He understood what had happened to him. His downfall was that he could not muster up enough strength to overcome the power of the forces aligned against him. He was more like his father than he realized or was willing to admit. Nate explained to Carrol that not all brothers were using drugs or committing crimes. He explained that not all brothers were sleepwalkers. He told her not to succumb to the stereotypes and the propaganda put out by those who wanted to besmirch the image of a whole race of people. Carrol was not yet convinced.

Nate pushed the top sheet back and rolled to the side of the bed. He sat up and rubbed his eyes. He thought about what he would do with his day until his four o'clock doctor's appointment. He got up and grabbed his robe, put it on, and walked into the hallway. After checking the setting on the thermostat to make sure that the air conditioner was working properly, he peered down the hall and noticed Alice sitting on the living room floor in front of the television set. He smiled and checked the reading on the thermostat again. He knew that it had been very hot outside the day before and figured the weather had not changed much. He wanted Alice and Rosalyn to be comfortable.

Nate thought of the heat that had engulfed him when he ran from Mom's doorway after pressing the money into her gentle yet strong hands. He smiled to himself. No doubt, he had done a good deed for a deserving mother. A mother who had willingly sacrificed her life in order to tend to the lives of her children. Damn, she is a beautiful strong woman. They just don't come any better. He had listened to her voice yelling—painfully yelling—good-bye as he disappeared into the wide streets of Baltimore City. Yes, he had heard her. How could he not hear her? It was as if she were always with him, always calling him away from danger, always standing in front of him, wrapping herself around him and accepting his pain. He wanted that moment back. He wanted to return to the porch and the worn chair. He wanted to return to the strong hug of the church woman's arms.

Nate checked the thermostat one last time. Although the reading indicated that the apartment was cooler than normal, Nate felt hot. He couldn't understand it. Maybe the thoughts of yesterday, when he had peered up into the devilish sun, were causing him discomfort. He reached up to his forehead to wipe away beads of sweat. There were none there. He walked back into the bedroom and sat on the side of the bed. His insides began to tremble. He could see the sun hovering before him. Maybe it had followed him home from Mom's house. Maybe it was punishing him for calling it the work of the devil, for espousing the theory of an inverted hell and heaven. But hadn't he been right? Didn't violent lightning and hurricanes and tornadoes and floods come from above the ground? Nate shook his head. He was being silly. He would call Sugar and laugh about his foolish thoughts.

He picked up the phone and dialed Sugar's number. She answered in an agitated voice. Nate began to explain his silly thoughts and feelings. Sugar was hot. Her apartment had no air conditioner. Maybe on any other day she would have been blessed with patience. Maybe she would have been willing to give him her undivided attention and to thoroughly analyze his thoughts and feelings. She probably would have offered him some logical, or illogical, solution to his trivial, gut-felt, puzzling musings. She would have told him that there was nothing that was silly or senseless between a brother and a sister. She would tell him that most of the things that had happened to her made no sense on the face of them. What sense could she make of her father violating her when she was a virgin? What sense did it make for her own dad to take from her what her mother had told her to hold on to until marriage? Why did her first husband burn holes in her back with lit cigarettes? Why? Only God had the answers to these questions. But there was nothing at all wrong with asking them. Sugar was still asking, and waiting for the answers.

But today Sugar was hot and she had made an appointment to get her hair done. She just didn't have time to explain away the volcanic trembling of Nate's restless soul. "I don't know why you are having those thoughts, Nate. Just cool out and enjoy your babies. Those heated thoughts will go away. I can't talk no more now. I've got to get up out of here and see my hair lady. I'll call you later, baby." Nate sighed deeply. There was a quiver in his voice that Sugar will never forget. "Okay, Sis. Than–thanks anyway. I love you."

Nate slowly hung up the phone. It was nothing. It was just hot outside. That's all. Or maybe he was coming down with one of those dreaded summer colds. Maybe the air conditioner just wasn't working right. Yeah, that's it. He continued to search for answers. The ones he was coming up with would never do. He had never been easily appeased by superficial solutions; today would be no exception. There had to be a deeper reason for his internal discomfort. Just hearing Sugar's voice was of some comfort to him, but he needed more. He and the girls would visit Sugar when she returned from the hairdresser. He needed to see her face. Anyway, being in the heat would be good for him. It would disguise the boiling inside him. It would give him a plausible reason for being so hot.

Nate picked up the receiver and dialed Quincy's and Frank's numbers. No answer. He called Mom. She had gone to work. He tried to reach Warren in his dorm at the University of Maryland. The phone just rang. Nate hung up the phone and stared straight ahead, trying to think of someone to call. He needed to talk with someone, to hear another voice besides his own. He needed a pound of reassurance. He needed to hear someone say that it was all right.

Alice sauntered down the short, narrow hallway and brought her wide smile to the bedroom door. She knocked. "Daddy, can I please come in?" Nate returned her smile with a bigger and brighter one. "Sure, baby, come on in." Alice entered quickly, ran and jumped up on Nate's lap. Nate peered down the hallway, fully expecting Rosalyn to follow the lead of her rambunctious big sister. "She's in her room playing with her toys, Daddy." Alice gave Nate a big hug and kissed his cheek. "I love you, Daddy." Nate smiled bigger and brighter. The troublesome thoughts of the unbearable heat dissipated into the cool beige walls. "I love you too, baby." Alice grabbed his ear and whispered, "Daddy, I'm gonna ask you something but it's got to be a secret and you got to give me a secret answer and it's got to be yes." Nate laughed. "What is it, baby girl?" Alice pulled Nate's ear and spoke into it in a low, hushed tone. "Daddy, can we go over Aunt Sugar's house?" Nate smiled again. "Of course, baby; I was thinking the same thing. We'll go later." Alice shook her head. "I want to go now, Daddy; I want to go right now."

Nate was happy. He had a family. This was how it was supposed to be. A close-knit family, with the father leading, guiding, and protecting. With the children looking up to, respecting, and loving their parents. He had it all now. This is how it was in Africa before the invaders came and things fell apart. Besides, he had found someone to talk to. Someone who truly made him feel that things were all right. A voice that soothed his fiery soul.

Nate looked deep into Alice's bright eyes. He saw hope and faith. She had faith in him—faith that he would take care of her and provide for her. Faith that he would protect her from all those who might try to harm her. He was proud that he was finally able to give someone a feeling of security. He was happy that he was beginning to be able to make people feel good. First Mom, then Carrol, now Alice and Rosalyn. For the first time he felt appreciated and needed. He felt wanted and loved. He had his family. He no longer needed cocaine to help him escape. There was no longer anything to escape from.

Alice's sweet voice broke into Nate's pleasant thoughts. "Daddy, what you thinking about?" Nate pulled her close. "I'm just thinking about you, baby." Alice smiled. She kissed Nate's cheek again. "Daddy, I love you. Please don't ever leave us. Please don't go away."

Nate looked down at her. He was puzzled. He hadn't mentioned anything about going anywhere. He didn't understand why Alice was saying this. Maybe it was because so often in the African American community, African American men deserted their Nubian wives and children. Maybe Alice had noticed that a lot of her friends had mommies but no daddies. Their daddies had run away or were somewhere getting high on drugs and alcohol or were incarcerated or dead. That's what it looked like through the eyes of a young girl who didn't have the answers, who didn't understand.

Nate gently moved his rugged hand over Alice's smooth face. "Daddy isn't going anywhere, baby. Daddy is going to be right here to watch you grow up. Daddy is going to protect and take care of you, Mommy, and Rosalyn. Don't you worry about that." Alice smiled again. She jumped down off Nate's lap and ran down the hallway toward her bedroom. She called to Rosalyn and then disappeared into the doorway that led to their room. Nate smiled and sighed deeply. He fully took in the pleasant scene of his baby girl running happily down the carpeted hall. He slowly got up and took some underwear out of the dresser drawer. He grabbed a towel out of the hall closet and went into the bathroom to shower.

Nate turned on the radio that sat on the bathroom counter. He put a cassette tape in, pushed play, and got into the shower. The warm water flowed freely over his muscular body. He leaned his clean-shaven head back against the green tiled wall and closed his heavy eyelids. He began to sing in a low tone along with the music from the tape:

Little child, running wild, watch awhile,
you'll see he never smiles...
Broken home, father gone, mother tired, so
he's all alone...
Kind of sad, kind of mad, Ghetto Child,
thinking he's been had...
And I didn't have to be here, you didn't have
to love me, when I was just a nothing child,
why couldn't they just let me be, let me be...
let me be, let me be...

Nate loved all of Curtis Mayfield's songs, but "Little Child Runnin' Wild" was his favorite. Nate called it "Ghetto Child." The song reminded him of himself. It conjured up pleasant and unpleasant thoughts of growing up in Baltimore. It made him think deeply and ask perplexing questions for which, he determined, there were no answers, at least not in this world. But he asked them anyway: "Why did Mom and Dad lay down to have me? Why couldn't they have just let me be? Why couldn't they have just left me in my state of nothingness where my existence was known only to God? What's so great about life? What's so great about being a ghetto child?" Nate and Curtis continued to ask questions. Water continued to roll over Nate's body. His soul continued to rumble. Faces and events continued to flicker on the inside of his closed eyelids. Nate watched the movie of his life.

Nate finished his shower. He stood still for a moment as beads of water trickled down from his chest. He sighed, pulled the shower curtain back, and stepped out onto the black rug. He faced the mirror and stood staring at himself. His chest moved slowly up and down, in and out. Curtis Mayfield hadn't stopped singing. Nate had. He stared at the reflection of the man in the mirror as if it were someone new to him, something that he had never seen before. He grabbed a towel off the rack and began to dry himself.

Nate turned the radio down and began to dress. He froze when he heard the low murmur of deep male voices out in the hallway. He turned toward the door. "Alice." No answer. "Rosalyn." Still no answer. He moved toward the door and pressed his ear against it. He could hear nothing but the hum of the air conditioner. He called out, "Alice." Still no answer. He slowly locked the door and continued to dress. He began to feel warm, and sweat took the place of the clear, clean water that had covered his body.

Nate sensed danger. It was a feeling that he had experienced over and over again throughout the twenty-nine years of his tumultuous life. He was a Black man in America and that alone meant danger surrounded him. But besides that, he lived amongst a people who had been made to feel that they were worth nothing or that could do nothing. A people who had been made to think that the most they should look forward to was a welfare check each month. A people who had been trained to rely on everyone but themselves. And once people feel they are worth nothing, they have no problem killing others who look like them. You can't hurt what is worthless.

Nate thought of Alice and Rosalyn out in the hallway with whoever had come to do him harm. He would not allow his children to be hurt, no matter what the consequences to him. No doubt he wanted to live, but his life would be meaningless if someone harmed his daughters. Now he knew how Mom felt when she went to confront the burglars with the good book in her hand. Nate had promised Alice that he would be there for her. But he would easily sacrifice his life for her safety. He was not as brave in the face of death as he had been at one time, but Nate still did not fear it. It would be him against death.

Nate thought of his gun in the bedroom closet. That was a mistake. He had listened to Quincy tell him that he should have his weapon in whatever room he was in. Of course, he should keep it up high, away from the kids, but he had too many enemies to be that far away from his gun. Nate had thought that things had changed. He was not out in the streets harming people, as he had once been. He was trying to do the right thing and rear his daughters in the right way. He was trying to be there for Carrol. He was finally putting all that he had learned into practice. Now, if he could only get off the drugs, things would be fine.

Quincy had told Nate that once a man made enemies, he had to always be prepared. "A man's enemies never dissipate. They don't go away. They don't forgive and forget. They wait. They might even befriend you, while all the time in the back of their minds they are planning revenge. They are planning to cut your throat and watch the warm blood of vengeance flow over their shoes." Quincy told Nate to remember the lesson that was given in the epic movie *The Godfather.* "Your enemies never forget and if you don't deal with them now, you will surely have to deal with them later." Quincy explained that when one country defeats another country in war, it demands that the defeated country destroy all of its major weapons and dismantle its army. "Hitler was able to bring Germany back as a military power by causing the people to remember the humiliation they had suffered in World War I. Jews still hunt down Nazis. Americans will never forget the Alamo or Pearl Harbor. The Union army never forgot their defeat at Fredericksburg, which made the victory at Gettysburg all the more pleasing. The fire for revenge never completely burns out. There is no statute of limitations on revenge. Remember the words of Shaka Zulu: "Strike an enemy once and for all. Let him cease to exist as a tribe or he will live to fly at your throat again. If there must be war, let it be *impi ebomvu*—total war."

Hatred and anger eased their way into Nate's blood stream. They joined hands and traveled throughout his body, pumping him up. His soul's rumbling increased. Lava-like sweat ran easily over his stoney face. He balled the rock-hard bones in his hands into tight fists and moved closer to the door. Involving his kids in this war violated all the rules. Whoever was on the other side of the door wanted him badly. No doubt they had come to end his existence. Fools, Nate thought. His attacker or attackers would pay for using his baby girls. They should have been men and confronted him. They should have had the nerve to stare him in the eyes and state their grievance. Fuckin' sissy-ass drive-by shooters. Punk-ass, spineless Klansmen covered with long white dresses to hide their lack of manhood. That's all they are. Any man can have heart when he's driving at sixty miles per hour or covering himself with a white veil. I got to get to my gun. They gonna pay.

Nate opened one of his fists into a flat pancake and slid it across the door. For the first time he paused to consider who his attackers might be. He thought of Chas. It had been years since he had last seen him. In fact, he had not sought revenge against Chas for the baseball bat incident at The Blue Gardenia Bar and Lounge. They both had lived through the attack and counterattack of that civil war. They had come to a Korean War-like truce, with no clear winner and no formal surrender. Chas would not launch another attack—despite the law of revenge. No, it can't be Chas.

Nate returned his thoughts to the immediate danger lurking outside the bathroom door. It really didn't matter who was out there. They would have to be dealt with. His warm, sweaty hand carefully turned the brass knob. He opened the door slightly and peered out into the hallway in both directions. He saw no one. He opened the door wide enough for him to turn his body sideways and slip into the shadow of death.

The short hall seemed to be a long, dark tunnel. Nate started toward his bedroom—the safe haven that Carrol closed off to the world when the cocaine-induced danger surrounded and moved in on Nate like an advancing army. As he got closer to the bedroom door he turned and looked back down the tunnel. Nothing seemed as it had been earlier when Alice had given him that smile which had rejuvenated him, the smile that had soothed his soul.

Nate saw a figure in the dark. It was the same figure that he had discussed with me on many occasions. Someone or something that looked like him. It was the shadow that stalked him as he walked the concrete streets and dark alleys of Baltimore City. The twin that lay down with him for another restless sleep. The thing that haunted him when he did wrong, that threatened to attack him when he snorted the deadly white powder, that choked off his breathing when he disobeyed or sassed his kind, loving mother. It never seemed to be real. But this time the figure stood and stared and then moved down the hallway toward him. It had always stared, but it had never moved at him.

Nate noticed the figure's shaved head with beaded sweat on it. He noticed that the figure was naked except for a watch on its left wrist. The shadowy figure looked down at its watch and then looked up toward Nate. It suddenly dissipated into the eerie darkness, just as it always did when danger was near. Nate told me that when the shadow looked at its watch, it would be his time. It did. It was. *Yea though I walk through the valley of the shadow of death I shall fear no evil.*

Nate wiped sweat from his heavy eyelids. He wiped tears from his glassy eyes. He slowly entered the bedroom. As he turned toward the closet, he was knocked against the wall by a powerful blow of what felt like a bat. A bright flash of light blurred his vision, before his world went completely black. A cool liquid raced down the side of his face. He fell to the floor and rolled onto his back. He tried to clear his vision. Eric stood above, pointing a .9-mm at him. "Don't move, motherfucker, or I'll do you." Nate still could barely see. His teeth seemed to be floating in his mouth. Eric continued, "Don't say a fuckin' thing."

Nate squinted his eyes and tried to bring Eric into focus. "You and your boy Kevin sold me and my boy some bad shit. It fuck my boy all up. Now we gonna give you a little bit of what he got. How about that, motherfucker?"

Nate's vision began to clear. He didn't understand what Eric was talking about. He hadn't sold any cocaine to anybody in a long time. He and Kevin had got high with Eric and Carl but he

hadn't sold them anything. He certainly hadn't dealt in any bad
dope. "Your boy Kevin got it last week; now it's your time."

Kevin had been shot in the head outside Nate's apartment.
Nate thought it had been a simple robbery and murder. Just
another of the many fatalities that happened every night
throughout America's ghettos. Kevin had been a casualty of a
"war" that no one was trying to end, or so it seemed.

Nate looked up and gazed around the room, or maybe the
room was spinning around him. Everything was moving. He
wanted to reach out and grab on to something. He wanted a few
minutes to gain control of his mind. Then he could talk some
sense into the zombie that was standing above him. He thought of
his baby girls. "Where's my little girls? What have you done
with my babies?" Eric responded, "Ain't nobody hurt those girls.
We just put them in the bedroom so they don't have to see their
father die." Nate tried to ease himself up off the floor. A foot to
the forehead stopped him. "Motherfucker, I said don't move."
Nate yelled back, "Fuck you, if you gonna do me, go ahead. I
ain't sold you or nobody else no bad dope. But I ain't gonna sit
down here and beg you for my life either. Fuck you and fuck your
boy."

Eric stepped back. "Naw, Nate, it ain't gonna be that easy.
You see, motherfucker, I'm gonna make you suffer just like my
boy did off that bad shit you sold him. If a motherfucker don't
suffer, what good is revenge. Plain, boring death is too easy. A
sorry, lowlife motherfucker like you would probably enjoy leaving
this here white man's world. You gonna leave it, but you gonna
beg me for mercy first. I'm gonna be your white man as you
depart." Eric pulled a syringe out of his pocket. "Here you go,
Nate. Slow death."

Nate was wet with perspiration now. "I ain't gonna take that
shit. Bitch, you are just going to have to take me out like a man. I
ain't dying squirming around on the floor like some fuckin' punk."
Eric smiled. "Oh you will, Nate. You're gonna squirm. Either
you gonna take this shit or those baby girls of yours are gonna take
this shit after we shoot you. We ain't leaving out of here before
somebody stick this little bit of evil in their blood."

Nate began to shiver. He thought of Alice's smile. He
thought of his promise to her that he was never going to leave her
and Rosalyn. But he had no choice. He knew Eric would do it.
He knew Eric would kill him and then poison his babies. He knew
how cold brothers like Eric could be. He figured that he could get
to the hospital right after he took it. He had a chance of surviving
it. His daughters would surely die.

Eric kicked Nate in the face. Blood oozed from his lip. "All right, motherfucker, get up and go to the living room." Nate held onto the wall and stood up. Eric moved back. Nate stumbled down the hallway. As he reached the living room, he looked around for Alice and Rosalyn. "Where the fuck are my girls?" Eric kicked Nate in the back. He fell onto the sofa and jumped back to his feet. Eric pushed the gun against his face. "Go ahead, Nate, be a fool."

Tom opened the bedroom door and walked out with Alice and Rosalyn. Alice was crying, "Daddy, make these men go away." Nate reached out to her. "It's gonna be all right, baby." Eric pushed Nate onto the sofa. "Give me your arm." Nate looked at Alice and Rosalyn. He didn't know what Eric was about to shoot into him. He didn't know how long he would last afterwards. He didn't know if he would ever see Alice's and Rosalyn's faces again. He held his arm out. Alice began to cry aloud, "No, Daddy. No, Daddy, don't let them, Daddy. You big and strong, Daddy. Don't let them. Beat them up, Daddy. Call Uncle Quincy and Uncle Warren. Call Uncle Frank." Tears rolled down Rosalyn's cheeks.

Eric and Tom ignored the pleas of the innocent girls. They ignored the tears. Tom grabbed Nate's arm and tied a torn piece of sheet around it. He pulled it tight. Eric handed Tom his gun. Tom backed up. Eric grabbed Nate's arm, found the vein, and pushed the needle deep into it. Nate's arm absorbed the thin silver needle. A bead of blood popped above the skin. Eric forced the fluid into Nate. Nate stared at Alice. Tears rolled down his face. Alice ran down the hallway to the bedroom. Tom started to follow. Eric yelled out, "Fuck her. Let her go. He's done." Tom looked down the hallway. "Fuck, she's on the phone with the cops." He ran down the hallway and snatched the phone out of Alice's hand and hung it up." Eric yelled to him, "Fuck her, Tom—let's get the fuck out of here." Tom ran back down the hallway. Eric was by the window. "Let's go out here. Too many people will see us if we go out the door." They climbed out the window and up onto the roof.

Nate got off the sofa and eased down onto the floor. The poison joined his blood and flowed through his veins. His body began to shiver. He no longer had control of it. It belonged to that shadow now. Nate rocked back and forth. Sweat ran freely over the African features of his face and through the jungle of hair on his chest. His eyes were wide open and he stared straight ahead. He began to mumble,

Little child...runnin' wild...and I didn't have to be here, you didn't have to love me, when I was just a nothing child, why couldn't they just let me be...let me be...

Rosalyn walked over to Nate. "Daddy, Daddy, what you saying?" Alice walked over and hugged Rosalyn. "I called the police, Daddy. I called 911." Nate didn't respond. He continued to stare straight ahead into the cool beige wall. The trembling increased. Alice began to rub Nate's wet bald head. "It's all right, Daddy. You said it's gonna be all right. You said you ain't going nowhere and you ain't gonna let anyone hurt us. Well, we ain't gonna let no one hurt you either, Daddy. The police are coming Daddy." Tears moved freely from Nate's eyes now. He had never cried like this before. Never. He no longer looked at the wall or at Alice or Rosalyn. He just watched the shadow as it sat before him.

"Yea as I...fear no evil...I love you, Mom...
Yeah as...I walk through the valley...I...I...
Quincy and Frank and Warren and Sugar and
Tyrone...little child...I didn't have to be
here...shadow of death...running wild...."

It didn't make any sense. But nothing had made much sense to Nate in a long time. It was all too confusing. But it was clear. It was too difficult to figure out. Answers that had been right before him now seemed distant. But he had reached for them and held them and dissected them and explained them. Maybe the answers were never there. Maybe this was all a bad dream. But bad dreams weren't real. And this torture had gone on too long for it not to be real. Hadn't it?

Nate felt as if he had been spanked by God forever. No matter how he pleaded for God to stop, the spanking went on. But was there really a God? Did it matter? Was the devil spanking him? Was he spanking himself? Didn't he deserve this for all the wrong he had done? Does anyone get what he deserves? What about Mom? She was being spanked too and she had never hurt anyone—didn't know how to. It didn't matter. Or did it? What mattered and why?

Outside two Baltimore County police cars pulled up. The officers got out and shielded their eyes from the sun with their hats. The temperature had risen to 115 degrees. They got together in a small circle and discussed the call that had come in from a little girl indicating that she needed help. They looked around for any sign of trouble in the area. A few children mingled around and played tag. A small group of people stopped and stared at the policemen. The officers slowly walked to the building and up the steps to Nate and Carrol's apartment. One of the officers put his ear against the door. He heard Alice crying. He knocked on the door.

The knock startled Alice and Rosalyn. They both began to cry a little louder. The officer yelled out, "It's the police—open the door. Alice grabbed Rosalyn's hand and slowly moved toward the door. Nate continued to stare straight ahead into the cold eyes of the shadow of death. Alice opened the door. The four uniformed officers walked in. They noticed Nate. Two of the officers checked the rest of the apartment while the other two stood with Alice and Rosalyn. Alice explained to the officers what had happened. She told them about the two men who had hurt her daddy. She pointed to the window and showed the officers the escape route the men had taken.

The officers moved close to Nate. They began to talk to him. "Hey buddy, you all right?" Nate didn't move. The officer spoke again. "Hey buddy, we got to get you to a hospital." Nate sat still. The officers who had been checking the apartment returned to the front room. "All's clear."

The voice of the officer seemed to awaken Nate. "All is clear." No, nothing is clear. He looked up at the officers. He couldn't make out their faces. The poison had blurred his vision. The room was moving around him. Sweat continued to pour out of his body like tears. He didn't know where he was. It was all like some bad dream—that he was trapped in. Some nightmare where nothing was clear. Anyone who thought "all was clear" about anything in this fuckin' world had to be an idiot or an enemy.

Nate felt as if the room was closing in on him. The floor was gone. He looked at the officers and saw Chas and Eric. He looked around the room and saw the distorted faces of Timmy and Sheldon. He saw Stanley and Gas and Mom and Dad and Quincy and Frank. Everyone was moving in circles. He heard nothing. Then he heard Alice and Rosalyn crying. He was hot and cold.

The officer nudged Nate again. Nate grabbed his legs and yelled out, "Leave me alone. Leave me alone, you motherfuckers." The officer fell backwards onto the floor. The other officers jumped on Nate. Alice and Rosalyn cried out as the officers and Nate rolled around on the floor. Nate fought to get away. The officers fought to subdue him. One of the officers pushed Nate's face against the floor. Another officer pulled his arm around and handcuffed him while the other officers held him down. Nate cried out, "You motherfuckers...you fuckin' punk-ass motherfuckers. Ain't nothing you can do to this Black man..." Tears continued to run down his cheeks. The officers stood up. They were out of breath. Alice tried to run to Nate. A female officer held her back. Another officer grabbed his radio and spoke into it. "Send me a paddy wagon."

Rosalyn and Alice stood holding on to each other as one officer tried to get information from them about Nate. Alice cried, "Le...leave my daddy alone. Just take him to the hospital. He ain't bad. He's just sick." Other officers came up the stairs and into the apartment. They tied Nate's feet together, then four of them lifted him up and carried him out into the hot stuffy air. Nate gasped for his breath. The officers carried him down the stairs and tossed him into the rear of the paddy wagon. They closed the door.

The temperature outside was 115 degrees. Inside the paddy wagon the temperature reached 125 degrees. Nate lay on the floor in this dark hot box. His arms and legs were locked behind his back. Poison ran through his veins. His blood bubbled and boiled. He no longer had control of his body. He urinated on himself. He quivered. Pain, pain, more pain. A headache, a heartache, sore arms, sore legs, sore wrists. Sweat, tears, blood. Swollen lips and swollen ankles.

This is how the slaves felt in the belly of those horrible ships. Bound and forced to drink their own blood and urine. Lying in their own or someone else's waste for hours, days, weeks, months. Locked up or locked down for no reason. Asking God questions for which He gave no answers. Free men and women and children seized and shackled, raped, tortured, toyed with, tossed overboard. Whipped and whacked. Nate beat his head against the metal floor.

The officers stood outside and talked. They waited for their supervisor. They wondered whether Nate had AIDS. They seemed to have forgotten that Nate's daughter had called and reported that Nate was a victim. They forgot that she had told them about some bad guys climbing out of the window and onto the roof. They forgot that they were supposed to be putting the men who had injected Nate with poison in the paddy wagon.

The driver of the paddy wagon got in and drove to the Baltimore County Police station in Towson, Maryland. He got out and walked into the station. Nate was still in the rear of the paddy wagon. The temperature in the wagon continued to rise. Nate shook. He tried to move his arms and legs. The cuffs tightened. He thought of Quincy. Quincy was the brother he admired most.

He wanted Quincy to come to his rescue. Quincy, come get these motherfuckers. Don't let them do this to me. He rolled from side to side. His heart raced. He could feel it thumping against his chest. He thought of his beautiful brown sister. He thought of Frank and Warren and Carrol and Alice and Rosalyn and his other daughter Tia. He thought of me. Of our conversations. Of how we had planned to work together in the future. How we had planned to make a positive impact. No more "bullshit" and rhetoric.

For the first time in his life, Nate felt completely powerless. He didn't have the power to free himself from the bowels of the modern-day slave ship. He didn't have the power to end his suffering. He didn't have the power to stop the descendants of the white men who had controlled so many Black people from controlling him. But he couldn't give up. He had to mount a revolt even if it was only psychological. Was he any less of a man than Gabriel Prosser or Denmark Vesey or Nat Turner? He had to overcome this, just as so many of his ancestors had done. He had to be strong like them. They had survived the slave ships. Many of them had survived slavery and gone on to do great things for their people. He had to survive it. He had promised Alice.

Blood began to seep from Nate's broad nose. He stared into the deep darkness. Death might not be so bad. I can handle it. I can handle anything. I'm a Ghetto Child.

The officer left the station and opened the rear door to the paddy wagon. He looked at Nate. He saw that Nate's eyes had sunk back into his head. He saw the blood and a white foam-like substance coming from Nate's mouth. He closed the door and drove him to the Greater Baltimore Medical Center Hospital. When the officers opened the door, Nate's eyes were closed. His body was limp. The officers and hospital emergency room personnel removed Nate from the wagon and put him on a dull black stretcher covered with a dingy white sheet. Nate's tears had dried. He wasn't sweating or struggling. For the first time in twenty-nine years, he seemed peaceful. He would not cry and plead or beg for his life. He would not ask anyone for anything. He no longer cared about the spanking God had been giving him. He lay there, tied up like some wild animal that finally had been tamed or broken. But Nate wasn't broken. He never would be. The officers and emergency room personnel slowly pushed the stretcher toward the emergency room doors. The sun looked down on Nate. They pushed him out of the heat.

29

Going Home

Home is the place where, when you have to go there, they have to take you in.
Robert Frost, The Death of the Hired Man

Charles Fowler and I sat at my desk in the Cincinnati division of the Federal Bureau of Investigation. A hot summer sun peeped through the large tinted plate-glass window. Other employees moved busily about, taking care of FBI business. Charles and I had decided to forgo a midday meal in order to spend our lunch break discussing an issue that he said was important to him. He had called as soon as I arrived at work and said he had an important proposition to make to me. "An offer you can't refuse."

Charles had already begun to speak before I was able to take my eyes off the haunting sun and focus in on him. He was describing an organization that he had joined called the Black Male Coalition. They were doing a lot in the Cincinnati area to give young African American men the support and guidance they needed to make it in a hostile world that never had been and never would be kind to people of color, African American men in particular.

Charles leaned back in his chair. Worry lines cut through his dark brown forehead. He folded his hands before him as if in prayer. "Everyone is aware of the problems that Black folk face. Anyone with any sense at all knows that no one wants or expects us to succeed. That's why when one of us does something that they—and you know who *they* are—view as significant, they publicize it as if to say 'see, there are some good ones out there.' We are doing positive things all the time, but they get to decide

404

which items the world will hear about. Now, when it comes to the 'niggers' who are destroying themselves, as well as the rest of the African American community, the media exercises no such discretion. They publicize everything these zombies do and try to make it a reflection of an entire race of people. They get help from a few well-placed, well-paid Uncle Tom negroes. But even those Blacks and whites who outwardly deny the existence of the obstacles placed before people of color know the truth."

Charles sighed deeply. "The Black Male Coalition, hopefully, will can the rhetoric and get active. That's why I joined them. I'm ready to get out in the community and communicate with our young people. I'm ready to give them alternatives and walk with them. I'm ready to do some tangible, practical things that will advance us. I'm ready to educate and operate. I think the Coalition has a lot of brothers who are of the same mindset. We've got to do something about the senseless Black-on-Black killings that are secretly and silently applauded by many others who profess to be appalled."

Charles said that he had to become more involved because it had become difficult for him to sleep at night. He constantly visualized a young African American brother or sister falling backwards into a puddle of dark-red blood. The blood would splash upwards and before it could settle, another African American child fell backwards into it. Up in the dark sky, above the pool of blood, were the faces of Marcus Garvey and W.E.B. DuBois; Paul Robeson and Booker T. Washington; Elijah Muhammad, Malcolm X, and Martin Luther King Jr.; Harriet Tubman, Sojourner Truth, Mary McLeod Bethune, Coretta Scott King, and Betty Shabazz. The faces seemed to be yelling and screaming at the falling brothers and sisters. They seemed to be saying, "No...not like this." Years later, while assigned to the Detroit division of the FBI, I was to have similar nightmares. I began to have them more vividly after the death of a young man by the name of Demetrius Francis. Demetrius' mother, Hattie Francis, was an FBI employee and a very close friend of mine. She was a single parent. I admired her strength as I watched her rear Demetrius. She taught him to be honest and to work hard. She emphasized education. Demetrius paid close attention to his mother's words of wisdom. He meticulously followed her lessons. He studied diligently and remained out of trouble. He planned for college. He never utilized drugs or alcohol. But all that Hattie and Demetrius hoped for was taken away by the self-hate that has engulfed the African American community and has left no family untouched.

On a cold and snowy Christmas Eve, while Hattie was in Washington, D.C. visiting relatives, Demetrius Francis was stabbed to death by his first cousin. Hattie's nephew murdered her son. High on crack-cocaine, his cousin decided to rob the trusting, unsuspecting Demetrius. He reportedly brought two of his zombie friends with him. Demetrius allowed his cousin and friends into the well-kept alarmed house, out of the bitter cold of a Michigan winter. His cousin, determined to find some money to feed his habit, turned on Demetrius. Demetrius begged for his life as his cousin dug a butcher's knife into his chest. As his cousin and his friends began to rob the house Demetrius cried out in a low and weakening voice, "How can you do this to me? I'm your cousin. I'm your blood."

While the zombies were preoccupied with searching for booty, Demetrius managed to crawl out the door into the cold white snow. When the cousin noticed that Demetrius was gone, he ran outside and dragged the weakened Demetrius through the snow back into the house. He then threw him down a flight of stairs which led to the basement. The cousin then went to the bottom of the stairs and stabbed Demetrius through the heart. Demetrius' last words to his cousin were, "I love you."

This is where a fragment of Black America has drifted. This is the result of over four hundred years of being taught to hate ourselves. This is how low we have been driven. We have been driven to depths where the strongest of bonds, the strongest love cannot overcome the power of self-hate. This hate that hate made led my father to rape my sister. This hate has Blacks killing other Blacks at alarming rates while many in the white population stand idly by. It is nothing less than a war. Casualties are high. The young are being killed off by the young. Almost everyone else seems to be shedding tears at funerals and then moving on with life and death. As a close friend and co-worker at the Detroit Police Department, Daryl Martin, told me, "Everyone is just putting up yellow crime scene tape around brown bodies and staying away."

Now, this worst of all hate, self-hate, had overcome the whisperings of love by Demetrius Francis when he begged his own flesh and blood for his life. Self-hate had suffocated and lynched Hattie's little boy. Self-hate is as deadly as any slavemaster. It shackles its victims and bull whips them into mental illness. It is the root of educational problems, unemployment, and exploitation. It has destroyed the drive and the motivation of nearly an entire generation. Self-hate is a deadly, dangerous, poisonous weapon. I knew what had killed

Demetrius Francis. I knew why Demetrius Francis was killed. And I knew I had to be part of the solution to stop the disease of self-hate from spreading and swallowing up more Demetrius Francises. I bled with Demetrius Francis. I felt the point of the knife. Every African American man in the world bled a little as Demetrius Francis was cut down by the self-hate of another.

Charles leaned forward in his chair and moved closer to me. He lowered his voice as others moved in and out of the area. He realized that some of the agents with whom we worked viewed any discussion of the plight of Africans as dangerous, subversive talk. Any magazine or book about African American issues was viewed as radical, unless it was authored by those who had received the stamp of approval. Charles stated that at one point, right here in America, we had to carry registration papers at all times to show we were in good standing with the "leaders." In South Africa we needed to carry identification badges. Now, if we did not care to be labeled, we had to watch what we said and where we said it. We had to be careful about what we read and where we read it. Speaking out and speaking up as an African American in the FBI almost always led to persecution. I was, and am, living proof of that. I had been denied the stamp of approval. My "registration papers," my personnel file, had been sullied.

I recall having an *Emerge* magazine on my desk which featured an article about Malcolm X. A white female Special Agent came by and looked at the magazine. She told me that the magazines I read scared her. I didn't respond. I understood what she meant. There were only a few magazines that featured African American people and issues. There were thousands that featured Europeans. Should I have been scared by these Eurocentric magazines? One African American magazine could cause this type of unjustified hysteria. The magazine automatically connoted something ominous and threatening about its reader. This, too, is a result of long-term, concentrated brainwashing.

Charles's body tightened. The worry wrinkles on his forehead changed their pattern. "I can't believe that every Black person in America is not out in the streets or in the schools trying to put an end to this genocide. Can't we understand that we are close to being eliminated from the face of the earth? Usually, when a man is about to be killed, his survival instincts take over and he fights with all his might to eliminate the force that has come against him. Even animals are equipped with God-given defense mechanisms to defend their very life. All we have to do is use our minds. The direction in which we need to go is clear. But our minds and the

minds of our youth have been targeted for destruction by
television and dance halls and the Soul Train gang and video
games. We have no concept of what is important anymore. We
seem not to understand that in order for one to truly enjoy leisure
one must first have worked hard and be deserving of it. Otherwise
it's not leisure time—it's sleepwalking. But many of us just go
along like nothing is happening. Damn, why don't we just take a
microscopic look at our infant mortality rate?   Look at this
biological or chemical warfare being waged against us which they
call AIDS and we call Africans In Deep Shit (AIDS). Look at our
dropout rate—and even staying in these bullshit schools doesn't
guarantee an education."

Charles sighed and put his head in his hands. "You see, we all
have to do something.   We have to do something active and
positive. Many of us know what the problem is but as Booker T.
Washington said, the world cares very little about what a man or
woman knows; it is what the man or woman does that is
important." Charles held his head up and looked me straight in the
eyes.   "It is unthinkable that in nineteen eighty-seven we still
accept this madness and continue on like all the world is fine. Our
neighborhoods have been relegated to war zones."

Charles and I both agreed that if the drug dealing and murders
in our neighborhoods continued, there would be those who would
beg the police and the national guard to come in and end it. But,
once the militia was in, our neighborhoods would become like the
occupied territories in Palestine. We would be in concentration
camps and, unlike those in the Palestinian territories, we would
have asked to be locked in, guarded, and watched. After having
been out of physical slavery for over one hundred years, we would
now be calling for the master, his overseers and slavedrivers to
come back and keep us in line. That is where we are headed; that
was what we had to avoid.

I was glad that Charles and I had become close friends. It was
good to have someone with whom I could carry on a conversation.
Someone who understood but was more than willing to voice his
disagreement should he have one. Someone who had not been
bought off and who was not even willing to consider an offer.
Someone who cared to the point that nightmares replaced his
dreams, books replaced his television, and action replaced his
rhetoric. Someone who understood that we, as individuals, did not
and do not have the power to change the world but we have the
ability and duty to have some type of impact on it. Otherwise our
existence is meaningless. If we could not and would not be a part

of the solution, we were just parasites who had no right to share the oxygen God had put at our disposal.

I had also befriended other African Americans outside the FBI. This was not an easy task. There was a natural and justified distrust of any brother who was willing to work for the FBI. The Black infiltrators and provocateurs of African American organizations had caused a healthy paranoia in the African American community. Most African Americans did not have fond memories of the Bureau. African Americans still recalled COINTELPRO, the FBI-aided murder of the young and energetic Fred Hampton, the besmirching of Dr. Martin Luther King's good name, the lack of a serious investigation into the bombing of the Sixteenth Street Baptist Church in Birmingham, Alabama, and many other infamous crimes and offenses. Nonetheless, I had managed to make friends. I was able to convince them that African Americans had to be involved in all facets of America, and could be involved without losing their identity. Most of the brothers that I befriended were able to discern the sincerity within me. They were able to read my troubled soul and eliminate the possibility that I was a veiled traitor.

In the process of gaining their friendship, I had to answer the questions that are so often put to African American Special Agents by truly concerned and interested individuals. The same questions are asked over and over again: How can you be conscious and be a part of the organization that participated in the assassinations of the Reverend Dr. Martin Luther King Jr. and Malcolm X? What do you think about the deception the FBI utilized to bring about the untimely demise of the Black Panther Party? What about the FBI-instigated murders of several of the members of the Black Panther Party? Do you believe that the FBI and other federal law enforcement agencies single out Black politicians and public officials for investigation while allowing white politicians and public officials to operate corruptly?

I had questioned myself many times. I think that many African American agents had gone through the same self-examination process. It was a double-edged sword. My friends on the outside questioned my loyalty to African people. I fought to get respect for African American agents in the FBI. The FBI suffocated me with their indiscreet surveillances of me and their background investigations of my associates. (I suppose it had something to do with my reading "subversive," i.e. Black, magazines and my engaging in intolerable discussions of the Black-on-Black crime problem.) The FBI seemed to disregard the fact that I had already been through a more than thorough background investigation. I had successfully completed the application process and training. I had no legitimate allegations against me for any violations of the subjectively enforced rules.

Further, as an African American I had to endure the conversations of some white agents in which African people were made fun of. I had to endure talk about our intellectual inferiority and our inability to correctly speak the King's English. I had to endure jokes about Black "sexual prowess." One white agent told me that Black men didn't have to go to the gym and work out because we naturally had, what he called, "ghetto muscles." Prior to going out on an arrest with a white female FBI agent, who had befriended me and my family, I heard her state to a white male agent that we were going out to arrest "two Black males, a Black bitch, and a white female." The African American woman was automatically described as a "bitch," by this agent. I often felt as if I were in a vise. I was not the only brother experiencing this feeling.

Many of the conscious African American brothers whom I had befriended outside the FBI were experiencing some form of harassment as a result of standing up for what they believed in. On Mondays, Wednesdays, and Fridays, at the Cincinnati Central YMCA, I played basketball with basketball great Oscar Robertson and several of the Cincinnati Bengal football players, including Kevin Walker, Tim McGee, James Brooks, David Grant, Craig Taylor, John Holifield, and others. Occasionally they discussed the problems they were having in the National Football League. John Holifield played a prominent role in the discussions. The group respected his incisive wit. He never engaged in trifling rhetoric or bombastic claptrap. He was cool, calm, and collected. He was well read.

John was intimately involved in the problems facing African Americans, and he tried to get some of the well-paid African American athletes with whom he played to share his concerns. There seemed to be a paralyzing fear amongst African American athletes, causing them to remain silent. They undervalued their importance to the capitalistic owners of professional sports teams. The players were only pawns—but they were money-making pawns. They could speak up and speak out as a group without being denied their income, but they didn't seem to believe this. Every once in a while a Craig Hodges or a John Holifield was sacrificed to increase the psychological hold that the owners had on the players.

John Holifield was an exceptional running back with the Cincinnati Bengals. He was also a conscious brother. His problem was he was not willing to "buck and grin." He didn't laugh at jokes that weren't funny. He didn't shuffle about. He didn't go out and drink with the boys after the games. He wore tee shirts that indicated that he was aware of his heritage. It was my belief that because of all this John Holifield's career came to an abrupt, unexplainable end. I spoke with other members of the Cincinnati Bengals football team whom I had befriended. They were shocked when John was cut from the team. Many of them agreed that it had little to do with his talent, or improbable lack thereof. John was just one of many who were paying the price for being proud of who they were. They understood the statement by W.E.B. DuBois, "Freedom entails danger."

Eric Walker was a fireman with the Cincinnati Fire Department. He spent his spare time at the firehouse reading books by African American writers and historians. He didn't fritter away his hours watching the inane images on the idiot box. He would read the Nation of Islam newspaper, *The Final Call*, as well as *The Cincinnati Enquirer* and *The New York Times*. Some of the other firemen noticed Eric's activities. They noticed that he fed his mind and watched closely what he fed his body. Eric became a Sunni Muslim and decided to change his name to Mosi Haki Adisa Zuberi. He understood that Walker was the name of the slavemaster who owned his ancestors and probably raped his female ancestors. He also realized that no other race of people in the history of the world had taken on the name of their oppressors and wore it like a badge of honor. "We proudly carry the names of people who tortured, raped, branded, lynched, castrated, and murdered our great-grandparents. It is pure ignorance, disrespect, and lack of appreciation for what our ancestors had to endure that causes us to so casually and callously accept the brand of the tormentors of our people. Can you imagine a Jew named Hitler or Goering?"

Haki said keeping the name Walker was rewarding the brutal slavemasters for their inhuman deeds. It made no sense at all. He was familiar with the philosophy "To name it is to own it." It was the philosophy that the slaveowners employed. It was the philosophy that Israel employed whenever they discussed Judea and Samaria, which the rest of the world was calling the West Bank, the Gaza Strip, or the occupied territories. Israel *named* the territories. It was the philosophy that the Europeans had used when they took this land from the so-called Indians and *named* it America and then *named* the Native Americans. After changing his name, Haki came under intense pressure from his co-workers. It seemed they were afraid that he was becoming too independent.

He was removing the brand that was supposed to remain burned deep into his soul for as long as he lived. It was obvious that he was serious about his freedom. Changing his name was a major step, and those around him apparently recognized it. *Freedom always entails danger.*

Charles leaned back in his chair and locked his fingers behind his head. "So what about it, brother? Are you going to join the Coalition?" I smiled and said, "Of course I am. You didn't think I was afraid, did you? I know that the FBI will not smile upon my being involved in something to help African American youth, but I believe in the words of Mary McLeod Bethune: 'There is something infinitely better than making a living—it is making a noble life.'" Charles smiled.

Charles went on to explain that he had purposely chosen to work with the Black Male Coalition instead of the Black Church. He, like me, was concerned about what appeared to be a lack of effort by many Black churches to get intimately involved in the upliftment of our deteriorating communities. We agreed that the churches should adopt orphaned African American children, furnish college money to willing and qualified students, and provide economic and entrepreneurial guidance to those who were interested. We did not see how these types of programs would interfere with the churches' main goal of saving lost souls. In fact, we believed that participating in all facets of African American life could only enhance the churches' ability to bring the wandering souls into the fold. It would be similar to putting honey down to draw bees. Once inside the confines of the church sanctuary, the young souls could be deprogrammed and made to believe in themselves and in the power of God—a God who helps those who help themselves.

As it stood now, many churches were distant and misunderstood strangers in the African American community. Many of the members were not from the immediate area where the church was located. The church buildings were usually large and expensive, and they operated on improvised banker's hours. Our people were suffering twenty-four hours a day, three hundred and sixty-five days a year. Why was the church not open around the clock? It is difficult to have an impact on the lives of young African Americans while working strictly banker's hours, with special ceremonies on Sunday mornings.

During his sermon "A Knock at Midnight," Dr. Martin Luther King Jr. warned Black churches of the danger of not fulfilling their heavenly duties. He warned the church about leaving the people hungry. Dr. King indicated that a church that did not feed the people, could have its members sing their beautiful songs and pray their powerful prayers, but God would not hear them. God was not much interested in well-organized, exquisitely robed singers. He was not much interested in eloquent prayers or eloquent preachers who demanded enormous fees to spread the word. Many churches had lost their way, and the people refused to follow church "leaders" and compact disc-producing gospel singers who were more interested in the bottom line than in shortening the bread line or the line to hell.

Many Black churches refused to acknowledge this speech. Instead, when they spoke of Dr. King, they only mentioned the "I Have a Dream" speech and simply called him a dreamer. Dr. Martin Luther King Jr. was not a dreamer. According to the *Webster's Dictionary* a dreamer is "one who lives in a world of fancy and imagination; one who has ideas or conceives projects regarded as impractical." Dr. King was a doer. In order to dream, you have to be asleep or at least in a state in which you lack full consciousness. Dr. King was not asleep. His eyes were wide open. He saw America for what it was—and is. It is a shame that Dr. King's legacy has been reduced to one speech, reduced to a dream.

Many Black churches could not face the scolding Dr. King gave Black and white churches both, in "A Knock at Midnight." Many Black churches and pastors could not stand up to, and chose to ignore, the words of Dr. Carter G. Woodson in his book *The Mis-Education of The Negro*:

> We must feel equally discouraged when we see a minister driving up to his church on Sunday morning in a Cadillac. He does not come to feed the multitude spiritually. He comes to fleece the flock. The appeal he makes is usually emotional. While the people are feeling happy the expensive machine is granted, and the prolonged vacation to use it is easily financed. Thus the thoughtless drift backward toward slavery.

Charles suggested that once I became involved with the Black Male Coalition, I could expand it by recruiting African American men from the University of Cincinnati, where I was pursuing my Master's degree. Charles tracked every pursuit that afforded us with an opportunity to help our people. Charles was not the only one interested in my attending the University of Cincinnati.

My pursuit of a Master's degree became a point of contention with FBI administrators. I was attending the University of Cincinnati in the evening after work, on my own time. I was paying for the majority of the classes with my own hard-earned money. (Money earned under duress, thanks to the FBI.) Nonetheless, a form was placed in my personnel file, with information indicating that I was pursuing my Master's degree. A notation was made that I was not to be allowed any more training at Bureau expense. *An educated Negro is a dangerous Negro.* Especially if you can't buy, control, or break him. No matter what the FBI did to me, I refused to sell my soul. So many others had already been bought. I agreed with Dr. Carter G. Woodson:

> Denied participation in the higher things of life, the 'educated' Negro himself joins, too, with ill-designing persons to handicap his people by systematized exploitation. Feeling the case of the Negro is hopeless, the 'educated' Negro decides upon the course of personally profiting by whatever he can do in using these people as a means to an end. He grins in their faces while 'extracting money' from them, but his heart shows no fond attachment to their despised case. With a little larger income than they receive he can make himself somewhat comfortable in the ghetto.

Dr. Martin Luther King Jr. stated that the fight for freedom and righteousness would not be easy. He stated that it would entail sacrifice. My soul was not for sale at any price. I was willing to make the sacrifice. It had been a long journey. A tiresome journey. It had been a learning experience. But I would never forget whence I came. In the words of Robert Frost, "I have promises to keep, and miles to go before I sleep." I would be a part of the solution.

The ring of the telephone interrupted the conversation between Charles and me. It was Doris. She needed me to come home immediately. She didn't want to discuss the reason on the phone. I hung up. Charles's facial expression indicated that he already knew something had gone drastically wrong. I put my suit jacket on and left without saying anything. As I drove home I wondered what could be wrong. Doris hadn't sounded ill. I had not received any calls from Baltimore indicating that there was a problem. Yet, I realized that Doris would not call me home if it were not very important. I didn't panic. At worst, someone might have been ill.

I pulled in the driveway and looked up at the house. Everything seemed peaceful. *Nothing bad could happen on a day like this.* I looked up into the angry hot July sun and walked up the cement steps to the door. I could feel someone following me, but no one—who I could see—was there. For a moment, I felt empty. I turned back toward the door. I was in no hurry to go in, though I should have been. Doris could have needed me badly. But I felt there was no rush.

I pushed open the door. Doris ran down the hallway. "I've made plane reservations for you and packed a suitcase. You have to go to Baltimore. Your family needs you. Nate needs you. The shadow that he talked about has come to get him. Tyrone, Nate is in the hospital. He's not going to make it."

There was no other way to say it. Doris knew that I wanted it straight; she knew that she had to make it plain. I had never been a fan of the soap opera-type pronouncements of bad news. After living for twenty-seven years as an African in America, I had learned to hear bad news and then to identify a way to overcome it. Never give up or give in to it. Never let bad things, bad news, or bad people change or stop you. That was my philosophy.

I felt an internal warmness. It had nothing to do with the angry sun that was waiting for me outside. Doris hugged me. A tear rolled down my cheek. She looked up at me. "Not now, Black man. There will be a time for that, but not now." She wiped the tear away. "You must go to him. Go to your mother and your brothers. Go to Sugar." She held me tight. "I'll take care of Tamara. I'll be with you in spirit." I turned to her. I watched her closely. She looked so beautiful in her pregnancy. We were bringing someone into this wicked world. God was taking someone out. Both were of extreme importance to me. I couldn't figure out which one was better off. Doris put her fingers over my lips and said, "I'll take care of everything. You just go." I picked up my suitcase and walked down the steps. Tamara walked to the door. "Love you, Daddy...love you." I got in the car and started toward the airport. I was finally going home.

30

A Time To Cry

If you have tears, prepare to shed them now.
                    –Shakespeare, Julius Caesar

These are the times that try men's souls.
                    –Thomas Paine, The American Crisis

I should have known that it was going to be a restless night. I should have listened closely to the rumbling of my disturbed soul. It had saved my life many times while working undercover for the FBI. It had acted as my surveillance team. It had been my back-up that was up front and out in front. As soon as I headed toward danger my soul would talk to me. Shake me. Turn me around. Now I was trying to ignore its compelling voice.

How could I expect a peaceful sleep in the house where Nate and I had had so many tumultuous conversations? He was gone, but his spirit was with me. He was in this house. He had promised that he would always be watching me. Walking behind me like a friendly shadow. All I had to do was look over my shoulder and I would be staring deep into his warm eyes. Now I knew he had told the truth. Tonight, I felt his presence. He surrounded me like a comforter on a cold winter night. He sat on the front steps with me and watched the passing cars. He stood with me in the kitchen over Mom's cold stove. He sat with Warren and me on the back porch and peered up into the starry heavens. He stood with me outside Mom's closed bedroom door and listened to her weep and ask God why He had taken her boy.

He helped me wipe the warm wetness from Sugar's beautiful brown face. He helped me hold on to her limp hands. He leaned against the doorway with me and looked into the empty eyes of Frank and Quincy. He descended the basement steps with me and stood in the room where the young men had gathered to discuss my future. And as I lay down on the sofa, I felt his weight and then fell into a deep, fitful sleep.

It all seemed so real. Perhaps because I had seen autopsies conducted before. I knew exactly what would be done to my brother's shell. As the coroner slowly pulled the bright, sharp scalpel down Nate's deflated chest, tears rolled down from my sore, red eyes. I wanted to be brave. I knew Nate would have demanded that of me. I didn't want to shed a tear. Not now. Not ever again.

I felt like a coward, standing there watching this man in a white sheet-like gown slice my brother's chest wide open. Exposing his soul. The soul that he didn't want exposed. I wanted to stop this man, to crush him into tiny irreconcilable bits of flesh. To let him know that I would no longer tolerate the world's cutting my brother open and bleeding away all the good in him. He was supposed to be free now. Death was God's emancipation proclamation to him. Yet, this man clad in white would not let him rest in peace. And if Nate was not at peace, I was not at peace.

Just as I started to move toward the villain in white, I came to my senses. It was too late to save Nate. He was gone. Nate knew that he had been walking down the crooked path that led into the valley of the shadow of death. He had accepted the fact that he would not grow old. He knew that he would not see his children grow up. And he knew that his eyes would never witness the smiles of his grandchildren. So Nate spent all his time trying to keep me from making a premature entrance into the valley of death. He spent his time trying to get me to help others stay out of the valley for as long as they could. For the valley, fraught with young and old zombies trying to take a last bite out of anyone who had any life in him, had no outlet. Nate was screaming to me, begging that I not join him.

For some time now Nate was destined to be on this table, in this room, on this date, at this time, with this scalpel being pulled down his chest. I was destined to be here watching it all.

I wiped my tears away and focused in on my dead brother. I felt a sudden warmness inside. I was feeling his soul inside my shell. Nate was reaching out to me, joining with me, becoming a part of me. He was going to live through me. He was going to guide me. His eyes would be mine. Our eyes would recognize danger that my eyes alone had not seen before. I would understand things that had previously left me confused and perplexed. I would always be able to hear his voice exhorting me to help those like him. Through me Nate would make his contribution to the African race.

The coroner opened the flaps of skin on Nate's broad chest. The chest that had concealed his soul for twenty-nine years. Beneath the flaps were the white bars that were his ribs. When the ribs were cut open his soul would be free to escape. Free of its dark shell, his soul would no longer be judged, or held back, or persecuted because of the color of its covering. The freedom would be refreshing. In a way, it was what Nate had been seeking all his life.

I stared at my brother's carved body. I surveyed him. His toes pointed straight downward. His long brown fingers lay beside his cold, stiff cadaver. His closed eyelids covered his darkened eyes. I looked closer. The face no longer resembled Nate. But looks no longer mattered. It was only a lifeless shell. It could have been any shell, any body. It was the contents, the guts that mattered. The ribs lay open. His spirit had gone. It had escaped. Part of it was in me. I wasn't sure where the rest of it had ventured. I wasn't sure if there was a heaven or a hell for it to go to. At that moment, it didn't matter. I just knew that the cold, dead shell no longer held the warm spirit that once was my brother.

I turned away from the dissected corpse and examined the eerie, dark room. It wasn't a still darkness: it closed in on me and pushed me toward the metal tray. A large spotlight hung over what had been Nate like a full moon and provided the only brightness. I fought the draw of the magnetic darkness and the mechanical light to inspect the rest of the mausoleum. The walls were a shiny olive-green tile that appeared to have been smeared during washing. The floor was also tiled and dull black in color. Despite the smeared walls the room seemed clean. My eyes roamed until they locked in on a small puddle of blood on the floor beneath the autopsy table. The blood had dripped down from the cold metal tray that held my brother.

The darkness of the room made me feel, even deeper, the death of my brother. The black floor seemed to symbolize the land of the dead. I could hear Nate laughing at my twisted thoughts. He would often tell me that the brainwashing of Black people had been so complete that even we feared blackness. He said that it was ironic that dark people could fear darkness. How could we love ourselves if we feared our color? How could we go forward if we continuously backed up from that which was like us? Nate often said that we even helped in the denigration of our color, of our race, by using such negative cliches as "He has a dark cloud over his head" or "He is the black sheep of the family." He reminded me that even in law enforcement terminology terms such as *blackmail* and *black market* were used. We laughed at the fact that there was actually a law prohibiting "white slavery" on the books. Nate said he supposed that this indicated that Black slavery was okay. He said that we wore black to funerals and white to weddings without ever once questioning why. Nate said that now we couldn't think of doing it any other way. Angel cake was white, devil's food cake was dark brown. Why? The brainwashing started early on. A white Santa Claus, a white baby in the manger, white dolls for African children. The cartoon heroes, such as Masters of the Universe, were white. A white, blue-eyed, blond-haired Jesus.

I turned my attention back to the dark puddle of blood. I heard the dull splash as more blood dripped slowly and steadily into the widening puddle below. I thought of Charles Fowler and his distressing nightmare of dying children and bloody puddles. I thought of the puddle of blood that Nate had left on the steps of the Blue Gardenia Bar. I thought of Timmy's blood outside Club 2300. I thought of Cookieman lying face down in a puddle of blood. I thought of Craig lying in an alley, in a rivulet of blood. I thought of the blood that lay on Nate's sheet in the dying room at Greater Baltimore Medical Center. I thought of the puddle of blood that Sugar had lain in after hemorrhaging as a result of one of Dad's sexual assaults. I wondered if the spilled, puddled blood would continue widening until it engulfed me. Until it was my blood. The thought scared me. I slowly stepped backwards into the comfortable darkness.

The coroner slit the skin below Nate's neck. He reached down and pulled it up over Nate's face. More blood from Nate, more tears from me, more silence. I stood there hoping and praying that the silence would end. Praying that I could wake up from this nightmare. Hoping to hear the voices of my brothers or my sister or my mother. Hoping that my wife Doris would come and put her arms around me. Hoping that she would tell me that everything was going to be all right. That Nate had gone to a better place. That he was no longer a ghetto child.

I turned and walked toward the door of the morgue. I looked over my shoulder at what had once been Nate. The coroner turned from his work to look at me. He seemed to be smiling. Nate belonged to him now. He could cut and slice and twist and pull him, and I could do nothing about it. This shell was no longer my brother. It was no longer Mom's little baby boy or his wife's man. In fact, it would never be held and kissed again by Mom or anyone else. *Damn*—it was over.

I walked out the door into the hallway, leaving Nate's shell with the coroner. Thoughts of Nate followed me as I walked down the hall and into a bright, empty room. Nate was gone...

I fell to my knees. My body trembled. For a moment, I longed for death; I despised life. I wanted to take Nate's place on that autopsy table. I wanted to be cut open and emptied out. I no longer wanted to face life without Nate. I no longer wanted to go on without hearing his lessons. Seeing his smile. I wanted to go back to the basement at 4461 Old Frederick Road. This time I would listen. I would not leave. The hell with the Maryland State Police! To hell with the FBI! To hell with all those who hated Nate and who despised his beautiful brown skin. To hell with those who would label his life worthless. To hell with those who would label Nate a murderer. The whole world was full of murderers. The United States of America was a country made by war, killing, and murder. Nate was a product of self-hate spawned by white America's hatred of Black people. I loved him.

Tears rolled down my face. I thought of Doris. This must have been the time that she had said was all right for me to cry. I felt her comforting presence. She urged me to listen to myself. To listen to the silence. To get it all out. I talked to myself. I wanted Nate to come back. I wanted to go back down that road with him and see the smiling faces of Frank, Quincy, Sugar, and Warren. I wanted to sit down with him and eat some of Mom's good cooking. I even wanted us to sit down with Dad and listen to his old war stories. *Get it all out.*

I wanted Nate, Chas, Craig, Bay-Bay, and me to play baseball on the sandlot again. I wanted us to play basketball. I wanted Timmy, Stanley, Tank, Gas, and Michael to sit again with us on the steps of the Blue Gardenia. I clasped my fingers together behind my warm head and rocked back and forth. I prayed to God. But something told me that all the praying and hoping was simply too late. I don't know if it mattered at any point. Mom had been praying for us all our lives. She had said special prayers for Nate. Yet Nate was lying there on that cold metal tray, with blood dripping down from his soulless body.

I woke up drenched in sweat. The basement was dark and quiet. The weight of Nate had been lifted from me. I knew for sure, now, that he was gone forever.

31

Laid To Rest

Why is it that we rejoice at a birth and grieve at a funeral? Is it because we are not the person concerned?
–Mark Twain, Pudd'nhead Wilson's Calenda

The warm summer breeze slowly moved over us as we stood in complete silence around Nate's coffin at the Cedar Hills Cemetery located on Ritche Highway in Baltimore County, Maryland. The sun was out, but not bright and tormenting as it had been on Nate's final days. In fact, gray clouds settled in around us. It was as if they were heavenly spectators to this quiet and solemn cemetery scene.

Warren stood next to me with his arm around Jada, his soon-to-be wife. He towered over the rest of us even with his head held low. Warren was getting bigger and stronger. He was now six feet five inches and weighed two hundred seventy pounds. We were sure, now, that someday soon Warren would play in the National Football League. He never had any doubt. He had learned so much from Nate, and Nate had listened to and learned from him. Nate had told Warren things that were kept secret from the rest of us, and Warren held Nate's secrets close to him. Now Warren was delegated the keeper of Nate's secrets forevermore. He would do a good job of it.

Quincy stood on one side of Mom and Frank stood on the other. They held her warm hands. Every part of Mom's body seemed to be shedding tears. Mom prayed in a hushed tone. Quincy and Frank joined in intermittently.

"Our Father, who art in Heaven....and forgive his trespasses, Lord, as we forgive those who have trespassed against him, as we forgive those who have caused him to be here....Please, Lord, take him home with You and give him peace for once in his life. Take

421

him away from the ghetto and lay him next to You. For thine is the power...forever and ever and ever..."

There was nothing left for Quincy to say. He understood what had led Nate to an early retirement in a pine box. Quincy had been with Nate on the unforgiving and perilous streets of Baltimore City. He knew what it was like out there. He understood the frames of mind of the dangerous zombies. It could have easily been Quincy lying inside that dark, silent box. It could have been any ghetto child.

Frank felt a churning deep inside him. He was Mom's eldest son. He should have protected Nate. He, too, knew what danger lay in the streets and alleys of Baltimore. Somehow, in some way, he should have taken control and led Nate away from danger. Dad was a broken man, unable to assume his responsibility to Nate. For a while, Dad had been the shield of the family. But after Dad had been destroyed, Frank felt he should have taken over and protected his confused little brother. It was too late now. Nate was gone. Gone to heaven or to hell. In fact, to Frank, nothing mattered after Nate's death. It didn't matter to him if Nate's soul was lost to some so-called devil. It didn't matter if God took Nate to heaven to give him a second chance. What mattered was that Nate was not here. He would not be sitting and laughing with Frank anymore. He would not be telling jokes. He would not be looking forward to the time when his children were grown-ups. Nate was dead! He had died on Frank's watch—that's what mattered. That's all that mattered. That was all that he could think of. Frank promised himself that no one else would die on his watch.

Betty Jean Wilson held on to Sugar. Betty Jean had been at the bus station in Wilson, North Carolina when Mom met the man who produced Nate. She had become Nate's godmother. Betty Jean had always been there for Mom. And Mom had been there for her. Betty Jean had also married a strong Black man who had been broken by the white man's system. But all of that didn't matter today. Today was the day that we were laying Nate away.

Betty Jean was the only thing that kept Sugar from falling over into Nate's grave. All Sugar could think of was that telephone call from Nate. He just wanted to talk. He wanted some answers. He wanted an explanation for the rumbling of his uneasy soul. But Sugar didn't have time for him. She had to go and he was holding her up. Now Sugar would never see Nate again. She would never hear his voice. There would be no more phone calls from Nate. From now on, a ringing phone would have another meaning for Sugar. A ringing phone would be a constant reminder of her brother. Her brother who was trying to change. Her brother who was trying to keep from being completely broken into little pieces like his father. Her brother who was trying to get off drugs. Her brother who, in his last hours, fought so hard against death. Sugar just kept shaking her head and mumbling, "Nate just wanted to talk."

Carrol held her babies, Alice and Rosalyn, close to her. She realized that they didn't understand what was happening. They didn't realize that their dad would not be sitting with them and reading to them any longer. Alice turned to Carrol. "Mom, where is Daddy? Why didn't he come here with us?" Carrol tried to explain it all to Alice once again. "Dad...Daddy has gone, baby. He won't be coming back here anymore. He's in that box, baby. Daddy is in that box."

Alice looked out toward the coffin. Tears came to her soft, gentle eyes. "No, Mommy. Daddy ain't in that box. They put dead people in those boxes. Daddy ain't dead. He promised me that he wasn't gonna leave us. He promised that he was gonna be right here next to me. Those policemen just took my daddy to the hospital so he could get well. Daddy ain't in that box, Mommy." Carrol pulled Alice closer. She pointed to Alice's chest. "Daddy will be right here with you, baby. He'll always be right here with you."

The week leading up to Nate's funeral had been difficult. Somehow I had managed to keep my sanity and prepare to put my brother away. I took care of all the arrangements, while Frank, Quincy, Sugar, and Mom notified other family members of Nate's death. I also filed a civil rights complaint alleging that the police waited too long to get Nate medical attention. The Baltimore County Police Department violated Nate's civil rights by denying him adequate medical assistance because he was African American. There had been no need to force him to lie in the rear of a paddy wagon in one hundred and twenty-five degree heat with his feet and hands shackled. After all, Nate was the victim of a crime. I, like every other conscious African American person in America, knew that had Nate been white, he would have been placed in an ambulance, given immediate medical assistance, and taken directly to the nearest hospital. To some white police officers there is no such thing as a Black victim.

The FBI conducted the civil rights investigation and, needless to say, found no wrongdoing on the part of the Baltimore County Police Department. Just another dead nigger. In fact, an FBI supervisor would later explain to me that the FBI and the local police departments had to work together. It was counterproductive for the FBI to aggressively pursue unlawful activity by police departments—especially, those departments which cooperated one hundred percent with the FBI. Quid pro quo. Years later, the Rodney King case would add validity to the supervisor's frank comments.

There was no need for the FBI to await the outcome of the local trial of the four white police officers charged with beating Rodney King, before a civil rights investigation was launched and federal charges pursued. The local laws and the federal laws are separate. There could be no claim of double jeopardy. The charges were different. In my opinion, the FBI waited and hoped that they would not have to conduct an investigation into a local police department. It wasn't worth it. Not for some "nigger." If the locals charged the violator, whether a conviction was garnered or not, the FBI was off the hook. The outcry after the Rodney King verdict forced the FBI's hand. Otherwise, the FBI and the Department of Justice would have done nothing. Review the case of the death of Malice Green.

Nate's funeral was held on July 29, 1987 at March's Funeral Home, at the time located at 4400 Wabash Avenue in Baltimore City. As was his life, the planning for Nate's funeral was complex. March's Funeral Home quoted us a price and then raised it twice. It was as if they knew we were in no condition to protest. They notified us of the price increase while we all stood around Nate's coffin in one of the viewing rooms. The negro notifying us of the cost increase spoke in a loud and obnoxious voice while Mom, Sugar, Betty Jean, Warren, and Jada shed tears for Nate. I complained to the manager of this Black-owned funeral home. She apologized but, as far as I could tell, said nothing to the offensive employee.

The manager at March's Funeral Home explained that Nate was taller with his toes stretched out; therefore, he would need a longer coffin. She also stated that one of the white police officers said that Nate might have had AIDS. My brother's body would have to be draped in a plastic bag within his coffin. I asked whether she had seen any needle tracks on Nate's body when they had examined it. She said no. I asked whether the report from the hospital identified Nate as an intravenous drug user. She stated no. I asked whether she was aware of any cases where dead people had given living people AIDS as they walked by a coffin in a funeral home. She stated no. I asked her whether March's Funeral Home investigated the medical histories of everyone that they buried. She stated no.

All she had was the white police officer's word. I checked Nate's hospital records and I found nothing that indicated that he was a possible carrier of the AIDS virus. This incident demonstrated the power white people had over the minds of negroes. All that the white police officer—not the doctor or the medical examiner—had to do was say it and it was so. Carter G. Woodson had been correct when he stated that "the Negro has failed to recover from his slavish habit of berating his own and worshipping others as perfect beings." Negroes have been hoodwinked. I was willing to have Nate's body moved to another funeral home. Mom just wanted to get it over with.

Nate's funeral was held in one of the chapels at March's Funeral Home. The chapel was full. Many of the nurses from Maryland General Hospital attended. I believed that most of them were sincere in their grief. Many of Nate's friends from Baltimore Street were present. I noticed a great many of the people from the Christian Community Church of God. The line of people slowly moved down the aisle and paused at Nate's coffin. Some cried. Others just stared. Mom, Frank, his wife Peaches, Quincy, his wife Sheila, Sugar, her husband Charles (Bay-Bay), Warren, Jada, and I sat in the front row of the chapel. They all were crying. I did not shed a tear. Not because I was not hurting—I was. I just knew that Nate would be proud of me if I didn't cry. I could hear him saying, "Be strong, brother. Be strong." Even in death, I wanted to please him.

As the line of faceless people moved by us and arms reached out to embrace our bodies, my mind wandered. I knew that the only people who really loved Nate were in this room. The world didn't care about the death of some ghetto child. Outside, on the streets of Baltimore, people were moving about without any inkling of Nate's death. I wanted the world to stop for a moment to pay homage to my fallen brother. They did it for crooked presidents. But I knew better.

Death is a part of life. There are large research institutes dedicated to finding cures for certain diseases and illnesses. Universities put their best minds to work to unravel the cause of cancer. At the same time, billions of dollars are being spent to create and test new weapons of mass destruction. New ways to bring about death. New ways to prevent death. The government was funding both. It made no sense.

Nate epitomized this contradiction. He wanted to live, yet he constantly walked through the valley of the shadow of death. He wanted to keep African people from being killed off, yet he committed the murder of Black men. America had no moral right to criticize Nate, because America was so much like Nate. In fact, Nate was an American creation. He lived what he saw in America. He lived the contradiction of construction and destruction.

My thoughts were pierced by the low, calm voice of a beautiful African American woman. She stood at the podium reading a letter I had written for Nate's funeral entitled "He's Not Heavy":

I cannot, for the life of me, understand why we are here. Now my brother is gone. He was with us for only twenty-nine years. As quickly as he was brought into this world, he has been taken away. He never found the right path, he never knew the right path. This sometimes cruel world was his captor and he, its victim.

He lived a fast life, as if he knew that he would not be here for long. Something deep inside him told him that his life would not be long. That his destiny would not be happiness and that this world would never be kind to him. He reached for God, but, for some unknown reason, he never found Him. So he turned to the mean streets, and he found no answers there. However, the rules of survival on the streets were easier to comprehend. The enemies could easily be identified. The streets were the only place he felt he fitted in. The streets made him feel intelligent. He was streetwise and capable.

There was always a civil war going on inside him. It was the historic battle between good and evil. The good in him was armed with a strong, God-loving mother, four close and loving brothers, and a sweet, loving sister. The bad or evil was assisted by a school system which failed to educate him, a world which failed to motivate him, and the streets which finally destroyed him. I'm glad that the war is over; the battle for peace is won; and now the world has to release its victim.

He is my brother, he was never heavy. I will miss him. I will carry him with me in all I do. Even in death he's not heavy.

Dedicated to the tumultuous life and peaceful death of my brother.

On July 30, 1987 the black hearse slowly led the funeral procession through the streets of Baltimore City in route to the cemetery. I looked out the window of the limousine that had been provided for Nate's immediate family. I noticed the boarded-up houses. I noticed the billboards that advertised alcohol and cigarettes. I knew that another generation of ghetto children was being prepared to take the ride in the hearse that held Nate's coffin. They, too, would take the ride at a very young age, unless something was done to stop the awful plot.

At the cemetery Dad stood off to the side by himself. I saw him reach up and wipe tears away from his eyes. He was well dressed in a dark suit, but it seemed as if he were ragged and worn. His son Nate was gone. He knew that he had not spent much time with Nate. He thought of all the times that he had called Nate stupid and had told him that he wouldn't amount to anything. He remembered how he had beaten Nate. He remembered the tears pouring down Nate's face as Nate begged him to stop spanking him. To stop punishing him for things he did not do or could not do. Dad could see Nate's sad eyes as he hesitated, then handed him the report card, and awaited the painful blows that would surely follow. He knew that he was partly the reason that Nate was in that box. He had done nothing to keep Nate from going astray.

Dad had so much knowledge. He had been in the war. He had come home to a country that was full of racial hatred. He could have and should have pointed the way for Nate. Dad should have directed Nate around the hurdles that he knew Nate was bound to encounter. Instead, he did nothing but criticize Nate, beat him down, bludgeon him. He did nothing but watch his own blood stagger down a path that could lead to nothing but swift and absolute destruction. As he stood there watching the box containing his son about to be placed in the ground, he knew that he had not been a father to Nate or to any of us.

We stood around Nate. Dad stood away from us, as he had always done. He watched his creations. He watched the beautiful daughter whom he had raped. He watched Frank whom he had beaten with his fist on numerous occasions. He watched Quincy and Warren and me. He realized that he had lost not only Nate but his whole family. He realized that in losing us and his place within the family, he himself was lost.

Dad looked at Mom—the woman he was supposed to love and cherish. The woman who had always tried to take care of him. The woman who had always prepared his meals. The woman who had never cheated on him. He knew that he had been no better than the slavemasters who raped and beat African women at will. He turned away from us and looked out across the cemetery. He was amongst the dead, and he felt as if he were one of them.

Nate's tombstone would be his tombstone. He would feel the weight of it. He would feel the grains of dirt on his body for the rest of his life. And nothing or no one would ever be able to make him clean again.

I looked at my family standing all together. All of us thinking about what could have been done to save Nate. Funerals bring families together. Funerals teach lessons that should have been learned a long time ago. They are like schools with a silent instructor. The instructor is usually the person lying in the casket. Nate was our teacher on this day. And although he said nothing, we heard him loud and clear. He didn't have a blackboard or a piece of chalk or a pointer, but we understood his lesson. We took notes and we all realized that we had homework assignments.

Nate had told me to listen to the silent lessons of so many dead Africans. "Read their souls as you breathe the air that blows across America from the motherland. Listen to the screams from the belly of wretched slave ships. Listen to the cries from the slave plantations. Listen to the rebellious warriors who settled for nothing less than freedom, or death. Listen to the exhortations of Black nationalists and the words of civil rights leaders and human rights advocates. Listen to those who have been silenced by the importation of drugs and alcohol and by government-sponsored assassinations. There are volumes of lessons in the wind. Feel them, breathe them in, and apply them. Listen to the silence."

As the long black limousine pulled away from the grave site, Warren slowly raised his hand to say good-bye to his brother. Tears trickled down his face. Mom and Sugar cried. Frank and Quincy sat with their heads in their hands. I could tell that both of them were also crying. I turned and looked out the back window at the box that held my brave, intelligent brother. I felt as if we were leaving him too early. Leaving him alone in a dark box while we all drove away. Nate would be lonely. The hot summer heat and the cold winter air would be his to bear alone. No more laughter. No more smiles. No more lessons. I guess Nate was at peace. As the coffin disappeared, I raised my hand. "Good-bye, my brother. Good-bye, Nate." And out of the silence came a quiet "Be strong."

•••••••••••••••••••

After Nate had been laid to rest, the family was taken back to Mom's house on Old Frederick Road. I got in Quincy's car and drove to the 2200 block of West Baltimore Street. Still dressed in my black suit, I walked up the alley behind the house where we had spent so much time. I looked over what had been my little Negro League playing field. I could hear the voices of Craig, Ronald, Chas, and Nate. They were laughing.

I looked up at the porch. I could see Angel smiling down at me. She appeared to be motioning for me to come up on the porch. I could see Sugar and Bay-Bay dancing. I saw Chas and Nate pulling on Mom's arm. Mom was laughing. A cold pitcher of Kool-Aid sat on the table against the wall. Frank and Quincy walked over to the table and poured some Kool-Aid into a couple of glasses. They drank it down and smiled at me. Music blared from a radio. And then came the silence. Everyone was gone. I turned and walked back down the alley.

I walked over to the steps of The Blue Gardenia Bar and Lounge. The steps were empty. I sat down. Suddenly I was surrounded by Cookieman, Sheldon, Stanley, Gas, and Timmy. They were laughing. A Baltimore Mass Transit Administration bus #20 pulled to the curb. Nate got off. He was wearing a pair of well-pressed black jeans and a white shirt. He slowly ran his hand over his bald head. "What's up, boy?" I couldn't answer him. I couldn't move. He sat down next to me. Everyone else disappeared. Nate stared into my eyes and smiled. "It ain't so bad. But you gotta come home, Tyrone. I ain't here no more to call you and beg you. I don't think I need to be. It's time to come home. It's time to come home, brother."

I reached down to touch him. To run my hand over his sweating head. Nate disappeared. I touched the steps. I ran my trembling hands over the sacred blue walls of The Blue Gardenia Bar and Lounge. This was my wailing wall. I could feel the names of Cookieman, Craig, Timmy, and Nate engraved in the wall. This was Baltimore Street's Viet Nam memorial. A long difficult war was being waged, with no immediate end in sight. In fact, it was escalating. Who would call for a cease-fire? When would the peace conference be held? Who would be left when this war was over?

32

A Conversation Between Brothers

If we must die—let it not be like hogs hunted and penned in an inglorious spot.
—Claude McKay, "If We Must Die"

The bright morning sun shone into the dark bathroom through the small window. It was July 31, 1987. Warm water ran over my aching body. I was feeling the aftereffects of the indescribable anguish of the emotionally draining events of the previous day. The laying away of Nate had wreaked both physical and mental havoc on me. I closed my eyes and prayed for the pain to subside. It was as if it had all come down on me at once. It had waited for the dropping of my guard and then attacked with maximum force. I was no longer immune to the poignant memories of a living brother. I could no longer fight off the image of him squeezed into that decorated box. Shackled like a slave, thrown into a metal oven, pushed into a cold morgue, attached to a lifeless machine, wrapped in a plastic bag and then fitted into a coffin that had no more room for movement than the hold of a slave ship. The traditional ceremonies were over and now, instead of relief, I was steeped in more pain. I had hoped that once Nate was at peace, I could have peace. It was not to be. God was not yet ready to grant me a reprieve. I leaned back against the wall of the shower and let the water coat my listless body.

Finally, I managed to get my body parts to move. I stepped from the shower and grabbed a towel from the closet. I slowly dried myself as I stared into the mirror. I was hoping that I could wipe the pain away. Hoping that I could watch the pain slide off my body like the water, or like the sweat from Nate's bald head. I knew that most of the pain I was feeling was internal. The pain was confined within the walls of my aching soul. There was no way to reach in and just wipe it away. It would take time for the pain to ease, or maybe it would take some action on my part to alleviate the ache in my soul, or maybe the pain would never go away. Maybe I shouldn't want to wipe it away. Maybe wiping it away would mean trying to erase my memories of Nate.

I slowly dressed. Every movement hurt. Every pulling on of some piece of clothing reminded me of some unrelated thing about Nate. Something he had said or done, or wanted to do. Something that he had succeeded in or failed at. Some lesson that he had taught me that I had not heeded. I smiled and frowned. I laughed a little, then cried a little. Just getting dressed proved to be such a difficult task.

I opened the door to the bathroom. The light from the hallway entered the room. For the first time I noticed how dark the bathroom had been. I had gotten dressed in the dark, with a little assistance from a single bright ray of sunlight. I had never given it a thought. I walked into the hallway and down the stairs to the basement where Warren and I had slept the previous evening. The basement was also dark except for the ray of light that entered through the small basement window. Every room I entered seemed to greet me with darkness. I walked over to my suitcase and began to pack for my journey back to Cincinnati. Cincinnati seemed so far away. It seemed as if I were planning a trip across the world. It seemed as if I were leaving everything and everybody and traveling alone to some unknown destination.

I looked over at Warren. He was sleeping so peacefully. Only hours earlier, he had been sitting on the side of the bed, rocking back and forth. I had watched his tall, strong figure in the dark. I wanted to reach out to him or say something to him. But I didn't know what to do or say. Nothing I could say would ease the void in our lives. Nate was gone and he couldn't be replaced.

I finished packing. I walked over to Warren and gently shook him. He awakened easily. He slowly opened his eyes and looked up at me. "What's up, brother?" I responded in a hushed tone, "I'm out of here." He pulled himself up in bed. "What time does your flight leave?" "About 1 o'clock." Warren rubbed his eyes and looked across the room at the clock. "Well, if your flight

leaves at 1 o'clock, what the hell are you up at 6 o'clock for?"
"I've got a stop to make on the way to the airport."

Warren got up and slid his pants up his long legs. He stared
across the room into the darkness, "So, where do we go from here,
brother? Do we just go on with our lives and act as if Nate was
never here?" I shook my head. I don't think Warren saw me. He
never looked my way. He continued, "You know that's what the
rest of the world will do. Nate and others like him don't mean
shit. Nobody cares about another dead ghetto child. And what do
we do? You go back to Cincinnati and protect the white man's
property. I go back to the University of Maryland and entertain
the white man and his children. When we die, ain't nobody going
to give a fuck. Just like they don't give a fuck about Cornelius
Elijah 'Nate' Powers.

"You ever notice how we don't even know the full names of
the brothers we grew up with? I mean we only know them as Gas,
Stanley, Timmy, Cookieman, Oldman, Mookie, Nard, Earl, Gi-Gi,
and other bullshit names. Hell, if we read about the death of one
of them in the newspaper, under their slave names, we wouldn't
even know who they were. I know we rebel against the slave
names assigned to us, but at least the slave names give us a start in
identifying our roots. I mean, we don't even know the parents of
many of our friends. How can there be unity of the Black
community, when we can't even identify the Nubian women from
whom we came? From whom our friends came? This is part of
the divisiveness that has become a part of our daily lives. And this
divisiveness is rooted in our willingness to trivialize the important.
It is rooted in our refusal to really know who we really are. So, we
kill each other without ever realizing who we are killing. Without
realizing that we are committing genocide."

I listened as Warren spoke. I was proud of him. But this was
not the time to compliment him on his wisdom. I didn't have to
look at Warren. I could feel the tears running down his face. I
could feel his strong body trembling. "I don't know what we do
now, Warren. I don't have the answers this time. Maybe I never
did and maybe I never will. Maybe no one has the answers but the
God that Mom keeps talking about and praying to. I'm not going
to just forget about Nate and I don't really give a fuck if the rest of
the world remembers him. They didn't give a fuck about him
while he was here, so I'm not surprised that they won't miss him."

I sat down on the bed. Warren just stood there, staring. "I
don't want to go back to Cincinnati. But what can I do? I wish I
could just pack my little family up and bring them back home.
But I can't see it now. There's a time and a season for everything.

I know that I've got to make a move, and trust me Warren, it won't be long." Warren sat down on his bed and turned toward me. "How long is not long? Will you come back home when they put another one of us in a pine box? Will you come back home when Mom just can't stand it anymore and goes off somewhere and kills herself? Or, will the only way you'll come back home will be in a casket, with Tamara laying a rose on top of you? Didn't Nate teach you that time waits for no one?"

I didn't respond. I couldn't respond. I sighed deeply, grabbed my suitcase, and walked up the stairs. Warren followed. I quietly spoke to him without turning to look in his eyes. "I don't want to wake Mom. Tell her I'm gone. I told her last night that I would be leaving early." I walked to the front door and onto the porch. The warm morning sun dried the tears that I had concealed from Warren by briskly ascending the stairs from the basement conference room. Warren stepped onto the porch with me and said, "Now, you be cool, brother. Don't go back to Cincinnati trying to be a hero." I smiled. "You know I'm not going to do anything brave. You and Nate always said I was too soft for law enforcement." Warren's voice quivered. "I know what Nate and I said. Nate and I said a lot of things." His deep, raspy voice began to fade. "Nate and I said that we were going to visit each other when we grew old. Things change, brother...things change."

33

Crossroads

*God offers to every mind its choice between truth
and repose. Take which you please—you can
never have both.*
                    —Emerson, Essays: Intellect

*You have seen how a man was made a slave; you
shall see how a slave was made a man.*
          —Frederick Douglass, The Life and Times of
                                Frederick Douglass

*There is in this world no such force as the force of
a man determined to rise. The human soul cannot
be permanently chained.*
          —W.E.B. DuBois, The Souls of Black Folk

Dr. Raymond Ellis had been expecting me. I felt a little
uneasy about being late. He hated when anyone was late for
anything. He had informed our Introduction to Criminal Justice
class at Coppin State College that he could not, and would not,
tolerate lateness. I slowly opened the door and walked into his
office. He sat behind his desk, writing in silence. He didn't
acknowledge my presence—an indication that he was not going to
lecture me on the downfall of people who were late for
appointments. The silence was a relief. Maybe the death of my
brother was a justifiable excuse.
    Dr. Ellis' office was dark except for the concentrated bright
light which came from a small banker's lamp that sat on the corner
of his desk. The light's beam was aimed at the piece of paper on

which Dr. Ellis was writing. The walls of the room were lined from top to bottom with perfectly placed hardcover books. A computer sat on a table behind him. Next to it sat a printer, and beneath the table were stacks of packaged Printer's Choice copier paper. On a small wood stand to the left of his desk were two evenly stacked groups of research papers, one marked *graded* and the other marked *ungraded.*

I sat down in the black plush leather chair in front of his desk and looked down toward the tiled floor. I rested my arms on my thighs and clasped my fingers together. Dr. Ellis sat before me, but my thoughts were with Nate. I was thinking of his life, his death, his funeral, and his children. I could still hear his voice. I could hear his lectures and his warnings. I could see his face. I could see him frowning as he rolled in pain on the floor of that police paddy wagon. I could see him struggling to get away from the police officers as they tied him in a knot and prepared him for his last hours on God's earth. Nate spent his last hours in this world bound and gagged.

Dr. Ellis leaned forward and rested his arms on his desk. His distinctive thin voice pierced the calm, memory-filled silence. "Pick your head up. Your brother is dead and there is nothing that you can do to bring him back. Everyone who is living will eventually die. There are no exceptions to this sacred rule handed down by some omnipotent force that goes by a hundred different names. The poor die sooner than the rich. The weak die sooner than the strong. The meek die sooner than the brash. The righteous die sooner than the wicked, or so it seems. But in the end, we all die. Dr. Martin Luther King Jr. called death 'life's final common denominator.' Unfortunately, or fortunately in some cases, man has not found a way to circumvent death. In fact, man has only manufactured new ways to bring about death. Nate has served his time within this country, which has all too often been made into a Black man's prison. His sentence has been permanently commuted.

"If you are to make your brother's death meaningful, your grieving period must be very short. You will miss him—I understand. However, there is much to be done. Booker T. Washington said the circumstances that surround a man's life are not important. How that man responds to those circumstances is important. His response is the ultimate determining factor between success and failure."

I slowly raised my head. Dr. Ellis sounded so callous. He was talking about my brother. He made it sound as if Nate didn't matter. He continued. "At any rate, it's not our death that is significant. It is not our funeral that we want people to remember. It is our life that is important. It is how we live and what we do while we are here that is of significance.

"Remember your brother's life. It doesn't matter if he made mistakes. Within each of his errors, there is a lesson. If he made mistakes, you learn from them and take a different path. It no longer matters that he did wrong. There is nothing he can do now to right those wrongs. It is up to you to turn those wrongs into something positive by your actions. You have always said that you believed that somehow you and your brother were one. Siamese twins attached at the souls is how you put it. If you spend all of your time concentrating on his death, then your soul will die. You will become another one of those faceless morally numb zombies that you have avoided becoming for so long. You must live. You must make your life significant, and in making your life significant you will be making your brother's life even more significant. That's what you can do for your brother. Holding your head down does nothing. Praying and asking God why He took your brother accomplishes nothing. And, I assure you, God will not answer anyway. God doesn't appreciate a person or a people that waits on Him to do everything. Infants wait for their mothers and fathers to feed them and to clean them up. Not grown folks. Not men! Your brother is gone. Let him alone. Let him rest in peace, or you might as well be dead, too. Don't bury yourself with him. Leave your God to tend to him while you handle business in the land of the half-living."

Dr. Ellis had often told me that there was an advantage to being an atheist. He said that an atheist depended on no God. An atheist believed that he had complete control of his life and destiny. An atheist believed that no one—no entity—of this world, or any other world, was going to guide him to success. Nothing but hard work would overcome obstacles. An atheist blamed no one for his failures. To an atheist, anything of significance that was to be achieved had to be achieved within this lifetime. There is no afterlife. Therefore, there are definite deadlines for the attainment of accomplishments. There are deadlines for the achievement of goals. There is a sense of urgency to life. Dr. Ellis explained to me that he was not an atheist—he believed in a God. But he hated what some of the different religions had done to his people: the waiting and wishing and begging and singing. The self-reliance aspect of atheism appealed to him.

Dr. Ellis stood up and took off his navy blue double-breasted jacket. He placed it on a wood hanger and hung it on a well-polished brass coat rack that stood in the corner behind and to the right of him. I noticed his perfectly pressed white shirt. His dark burgundy and blue tie hung down in a straight line from his neck and was the perfect length. His belt buckle was perfectly centered. Dr. Ellis was impressive. He always made sure that he was properly dressed. He always had his lessons properly prepared. If he said he was going to give an exam on a certain day and at a certain time, he gave it without fail. Every moment of every day was important. He didn't want to waste a minute of time doing things that he thought were unproductive. He watched very little television, and for vacation he would travel to different countries on the continent of Africa and live in the community, getting to know the people and gathering information to share with his students when he returned. His goal was to build a bridge between the people of Africa and African Americans. He wanted his students to communicate with students in Africa. He was determined to do his part to link Coppin State College with the African continent.

Dr. Ellis believed that the divisions among the people of color in the world were an intentional travesty. He visualized a link between Africans and African Americans. He sincerely believed that this bridge was necessary for the survival of African people. He often spoke of Marcus Garvey's Black Star Line. He spoke of the connection that Malcolm X had made with the leaders of African countries. He spoke of Pan-Africanist Edward W. Blyden.

The connection had to be made despite the assassination of every sincere African American leader who earnestly and honestly tried to make the link. The college campus was an ideal place to plant this seed of unity. It was the ideal place to start building this bridge. Coppin State College, which sat in the midst of Baltimore City, could be the center of a unity drive. Dr. Ellis constantly reminded me of the former Prime Minister of Ghana Kwame Nkrumah's goal of a United States of Africa. Coppin and its students could help bring it about.

Dr. Ellis traveled to Ethiopia, Egypt, Nigeria, Senegal, the Ivory Coast, Ghana, Kenya, and other countries in Africa. He took slide photographs and showed them to his classes. He showed us that these countries were not in complete anarchy. They had a system of justice. In fact, Africa had a constitution before the framers of the United States Constitution were born. Africa was not a lawless land. African American criminal justice students at a predominantly African American college needed to know something of the origin of justice—*true justice!*

Dr. Ellis wanted to make sure that we understood that Africa was not the backward continent that the western media portrayed it as. It was Dr. Ellis' belief that the images of Africa and African people, presented by the press, are what compelled us to deny our African roots. Sure, Africa—like every other continent—had its problems. There were dictators and tyrants. There were zombies. There were murderers and thieves. As Chinua Achebe wrote, things had fallen apart since the invasion of Europeans. But the presentation of Africa by the western media was intentionally one-sided and negative. The western media saw no good in Africa or its people—except in the white folks of South Africa. This biased, negative coverage made unconscious African Americans hate the continent of Africa and its people. Malcolm X once said, "You can't hate the roots without hating the tree." The western press manufactured hatred and caused us to hate ourselves.

Dr. Ellis walked over to the large window. His office was on the eighth floor of a tall building that overlooked the campus. He opened the blinds and looked down at the students moving about. "There is so much raw power right here on this campus. If we could just channel it, refine it, and then utilize it. Our students have to understand how the world really works. But they have been miseducated and therefore they are lost. They have been brainwashed and programmed. This virus which was planted into their brains at a young age, and has remained there since, must be removed before it destroys them completely. That's what happened to your brother and those young men from the Blue Gardenia of which you often speak. The virus went undetected for so long until it found its way into their souls and shut their systems down."

The mere mention of the Blue Gardenia by Dr. Ellis made me shiver. Dr. Ellis continued. "I've been there, you know? I've been down to the Blue Gardenia and I've witnessed the gathering of the young men there. By the way, I was also at your brother's funeral. I watched your family. I watched your father. In fact, I visited your brother's grave site after you all had left. He is in lot number 194B, site number 4, plot number 5829. Cornelius Elijah Powers is in part *KKK* of the Cedar Hills Cemetery. How ironic."

My eyes widened and I stared at Dr. Ellis' back. Why had he gone to my brother's funeral? Why was he watching me and my family? I wanted him to turn around and explain himself to me. But he never did. "Let your brother go. Visit him there from time to time if you must. But, trust me, he will never hear what you say to him. It is time that you reach out to the living. It is time that you share some of that knowledge that you have acquired on your trek out of the so-called ghetto."

Dr. Ellis had explained to me that the term *ghetto* had originally been defined as a place where Jews were quartered. The definition was later expanded to include the location where less-privileged minorities resided. It was just another negative label for Black people to live down. If the area where Blacks lived was regarded as a negative place, it would be difficult for Blacks to ever see it as anything else. Therefore, it was all right to destroy and deface the ghetto because that was how it was supposed to be. "The naming or the defining of something or some group of people is a powerful weapon."

Dr. Ellis explained that the term *nigger* had once denoted ignorance and stupidity and had identified no specific race of people. But now the definition, according to *Webster's New Collegiate Dictionary*, is "Negro, black; a member of any dark-skinned race." Therefore, we—all Black people—are officially called niggers by the *Webster Dictionary,* the *Random House Dictionary,* the *American Heritage Dictionary,* and many others. It mattered not if an African was a doctor, lawyer, teacher, nurse, inventor, engineer, prime minister, congressman, senator, priest, pastor, bishop or whatever. We all are "niggers" because we are members of a dark-skinned race. Our children and grandchildren are "niggers." Our mothers, fathers, sisters, brothers, and grandparents are "niggers." This is the definition that students around the world read. This is how they will label us and define us. This is why they will never care if the world destroys us. This is the definition that our children will read. And they will accept it, just as we accept it—and every other definition in the dictionary. We must accept it, because we go out and purchase these dictionaries and put them in the hands of our people. We say that if you want to know what that word or this word means, look it up in the dictionary. Webster had called us all niggers, and we never said a word about it. We accepted it along with the term *ghetto.*

Dr. Ellis continued, "Our people need young brothers like you." He turned and stared down at me. "You know the truth, if there is such a thing. You have learned how to differentiate between indoctrination and education. You have learned how to uncover facts. You know the difference between his-story and history. You know how to motivate youth. How to give them a reason for living. How to help them set goals and overcome obstacles without selling out. You have learned how to control your anger. How to channel it into something active, not something futile and self-destructive. You are past the stage of 'knowledge exuberance.' That's the stage where knowledge is so new and enlightening that it makes you want to change the world overnight. You have learned many of your lessons here at Coppin State College from Dr. Bright, Dr. Gray, Dr. Carrol, Dr. Avery, and others. I've been watching you. I've paid more attention to you than you think. I know that you have learned a great deal on your own. You've learned from your brothers. You have learned much from your reading. And you've certainly obtained up-close, firsthand knowledge by being a part of the Maryland State Police and the FBI. Truth is the antidote that can destroy this virus that has affected our people. Truth is the vaccine that can prevent this sickness from entering the brains of our young people."

A chill crept over my body. I shivered. In an instant, the coolness was gone and I began to sweat internally. Dr. Ellis moved away from the window. He picked up a pitcher of water that had been on a small table against the wall. He slowly and meticulously watered the plants that sat on the file cabinets behind his desk. He spoke without turning toward me. "Plato said those having torches will pass them on to others. Maybe in his death, your brother has passed a torch on to you. What are you going to do with it?"

I looked around the room and then turned back toward Dr. Ellis. "What do I have to pass on? What torch do I hold?" Dr. Ellis smiled and asked, "You have read *The Souls of Black Folk* by W.E.B. DuBois?" I answered quizzically, "Yes, I have." Dr. Ellis set the pitcher of water down and asked, "Do you remember the story of James Jones?" "Yes, I do." "Do you remember how he walked slouched over like a burdened old man after he had gone away and obtained knowledge?" "Yes." "Do you remember his sister asking him if it made everyone unhappy when they studied and learned lots of things?" Before I could answer Dr. Ellis continued, "James Jones's reply was 'It does.' Then she asked him if he was glad he studied and he replied, 'Yes.' And his sister said, 'I wish I was unhappy, too.'"

Dr. Ellis stood silent for a moment and then remarked, "You have that tired, burdened, unhappy look in your eyes. You are not unlike James Jones." I hesitated to speak, but the words fell from my mouth. "Dr. Ellis, if I remember correctly, James Jones was killed by a group of Klansmen." "You remember correctly. Are you afraid of dying? Because if you are, you can't live." I slowly shook my head and said, "I'm not afraid of dying. But neither am I afraid of living. Therefore, it is not my desire to run blindly toward death." Dr. Ellis smiled and replied, "I don't think you have done anything blindly for a long time. You are aware of the consequences of your actions."

Dr. Ellis moved around his desk toward me and said, "Your torch is knowledge and the willingness to put that knowledge to use—to make it more than mere rhetoric. Knowledge is the key to it all. You question things. You do not accept the white man's indoctrination as truth. That in itself is a rarity. I've watched you and I've taught you. You question everything that I say and then you go and research it thoroughly. I know where your research leads. It is a path that I have led you down. I've tested you with bait. I test all of my students and I watch how they respond. I look in their eyes for that James Jones look. They don't know I'm looking because I use the art of deception. I make them think that I am something that I am not. I play the devil's advocate with them and disagree with their points of view. Whatever theory they put forward, I oppose and put forward the extreme opposite theory. If the fire is there, they will dare to prove me wrong. If the fire is not there, I know they are easy prey for the world and for the white man's inferiority theory. They will accept the white man's perception of them as truth. Therefore, they will not believe in themselves. I can't turn them around because it would cause me to drop my veil, and then I would be ineffective. I don't have time to turn them around because I am out tracking down brothers like you. It is your job to turn them around. To educate them. To unshackle them from the brainwashing machine. To make them believe in themselves and in their kind. To put James Jones in their souls.

"You can't do it alone. I'm here to make sure you don't have to. I'm here trying to find help for you and those who came before you. All you have to do is be willing, really willing, to stand up and speak out despite the accusations, laughs, and smirks. Unless I'm getting old and have read you wrong, you don't care what people say. You follow your soul or your God, as you say. You are undeterred. You will fight for what you believe is right despite the odds. Those who oppose you must be prepared to fight. Even if they win, they will have to look over their shoulders because you will never completely give up. Justice will be served. That's the torch you have to offer. That's the torch you must pass on to young, eager, waiting hands. Pass it on, Tyrone. In God's name, *pass it on!*"

Dr. Ellis sat down and pulled a blank white pad from his desk drawer. He sighed deeply and picked up a pen. He spoke in a quiet, calm, soothing voice. "For example, what do you know about the Federal Emergency Management Agency?" It was another one of Dr. Ellis' pop quizzes. But this time I didn't mind. Maybe he would come to the conclusion that I was not the student he was looking for. "I know that it started off as the Federal Emergency Preparedness Agency and its purpose was to develop plans to take control of American financial institutions in the case of a national emergency." Dr. Ellis smiled and said, "That's correct. It was also mandated to take control of energy resources in the case of a so-called 'emergency,' and Congress would not be allowed to review the actions of this agency for up to six months after they took place. It's all in Presidential Executive Order 11921."

I continued, "In 1977 it became the Federal Emergency Management Agency (FEMA). Under Ronald Reagan a man by the name of Louis Giuffrida was appointed to handle the anticipated emergencies. Earlier in his career, Giuffrida indicated that martial law should be imposed in case of an uprising by militant Negroes. He also indicated that at the time of this uprising, all Negroes should be rounded up and placed in camps." Dr. Ellis looked pleased and said, "That's right. How many of our young people know this? How many middle-class Blacks or whites understand that FEMA does so horribly in responding to natural disasters like hurricanes, tornadoes, and earthquakes because that is not the purpose for which it was created. FEMA was forced to change gears and respond to these disasters in order to keep up its false pretense, its deception. Master Sun Tzu stated, 'A military operation involves deception. Even though you are competent, appear to be incompetent. Though effective, appear to be ineffective.'"

I sat up in my chair and stared at Dr. Ellis. His eyes seemed bright. He looked like the proud father of a newborn child. He continued, "Explain to me the theory of future money." I sighed. "In the future there will be no paper money. There will be bank cards and debit cards. Welfare recipients will use cards to purchase their goods. This way the government has complete control of all transactions. Direct deposit is the start of it. Soon no transaction will be made without the government knowing about it. It will all go through one giant Federal Reserve computer. And we all should know that the Federal Reserve, which determines who can and cannot afford property by its manipulation of the interest rates, is not even controlled by 'we the people'! At any rate, the government will eventually control the whole bartering system. Research indicates that eventually there won't even be a need for plastic cards. They will just stamp your number on your skin or in your skin like they do at amusement parks. A bar code waved under a laser light. The same way packages are waved over the light in supermarkets! You won't be able to eat or buy or ride a bus without this mark. The Bible would call such a stamp the mark of the devil. This theory might seem paranoid and farfetched—but just watch what is happening to money and computers. Man will continue to progress. We will continue to become more technological and automated. Where are we heading? Chart the course and tell me where it leads. Listen to what is not being said. Listen to the silence!"

Dr. Ellis smiled. "This is part of that torch. We cannot act or react unless we understand what's happening around us. Long-term planning cannot be accomplished without the ability to look ahead as well as behind. We sit by and watch those joint military training exercises in our cities. We need to know for what and for whom they are training. It should be obvious that urban training exercises are conducted to deal with urban dwellers. And correct me if I'm wrong, but is it not true that people of color occupy most of the inner cities?"

Dr. Ellis swiveled his black leather chair around and faced the window. "You know about these exercises. You know that the FBI, CIA, Army, Marines and the Secret Service all participate in these maneuvers. This is vital information to a group of people who have already been brutalized by this country for years and who still can't understand that we are on the verge of being annihilated. We can't afford to ignore anything the government does. A race who has lost over two hundred and fifty million people to violence, from the slave trade on up to the present, should be paranoid of the descendants of the people who did this to them. Especially, when the descendants are still in power and have the same basic points of view with regard to us as did their ancestors. It makes good sense to be paranoid when some group of people has tried, and are continuing to try, to remove you from the face of the earth. But as a race, we are not paranoid. We are not even awake or alert. We are asleep. And the only explanation that I have for our anesthetized state of being is that we are just not aware of the truth. It is difficult for us to comprehend the harsh brutality of this world.

"We applaud when this country invents some new sophisticated weapon. But if *we* come up with some type of device or utilize some weapon invented by others that would help in our defense against racists, we are labeled as having devious minds. We marvel at an explosion caused by a two-megaton bomb dropped from a plane bearing the United States flag. But if *we* own and utilize a rifle in our own defense, it is considered part of our 'barbaric' nature. We stand with the rest of America and cheer soldiers when they come home from murdering thousands, sometimes millions of people, yet we call ourselves a Christian nation or a Christian people. We pray and ask God that our children come home safely from these wars as if God will watch over them while they murder the children of other God-created human beings. We applaud the murder, death, and destruction conducted by this country against other countries whose citizens look like us. This is how screwed up and confused we are.

"We talk about the brutal attacks in the streets of our cities. We talk about the senseless murders. We speak of the twisted minds of serial murderers, yet we drop bombs that kill innocent women and children and then sing victory songs before they are even buried. No serial murderer in the history of the world has killed more people than we have in one bombing raid. 'God bless America.' I attribute this insensitivity on our part and our inability to realize the gross brutality of this world to a lack of knowledge.

"Once we realize that this is how others deal with their enemies—and are dealing with us; once we realize that most of these modern wars and most of this military training is being directed against people of color, then we will be able to deal with others the way they deal with us. We will be able to prepare for what is coming and what is already here. We won't look at these training exercises around our cities as just the military preparing for some urban war in another country. We will begin to wake up."

Dr. Ellis didn't seem to be upset. He spoke in a calm voice. He had analyzed and thought through these facts. The emotions, at least on the surface, were gone. I spoke up. "I agree with your assessment of our state. I know about the McCarran Act. I know that despite what others say, the McCarran Act is a living document just like the constitution which declared us three-fifths of a man. It is a brutal world. And I realize that we have to deal with others in the same manner in which they are dealing with us. As you stated Dr. Ellis, we must first and foremost understand how the world is dealing with us. Then we must reveal what we know to those of us who are ignorant of the facts. I'm just not sure that I can contribute to this awakening."

Dr. Ellis responded, "You already have. I received your paper on how to deal with Klan rallies. I thought it brilliant in its simplicity." I had sent Dr. Ellis a paper, at his request, which proposed a method which African Americans should utilize in dealing with Klan rallies. I indicated to him that first and foremost it was important to understand that the Ku Klux Klan was mainly made up of ignorant "white trash." In the whole scheme of things, the Klan was not a real threat. They had little power and were simply a diversion, a smoke screen at which to vent our anger, while others with real power and with the capability to do the most harm to us remained silent. It was the silence that we had to pay attention to.

No doubt, the Klan, with their cowardly sporadic violence, could inflict injury. In those cases, we had to match power for power. If they murdered one of our sons or daughters, then our reaction should be to seek out the individuals responsible and destroy their sons or daughters. It was a brutal response to a brutal act, but it was necessary. It was the only language that they understood. Seeking revenge against the perpetrator would not satisfy our goal. Our goal would be to say to them that whatever you do to us, we will do to you. If it is my son or daughter that you have harmed, then I will harm your son or daughter. It was the same message that Moses had delivered for God to the Pharaoh in Egypt when the Pharaoh ordered that the first-born male of every Hebrew family be killed. God *killed* the Pharaoh's son, not the Pharaoh. *Whatever a man soweth, that shall he also reap.*

I also suggested that when the Klan held rallies or marches, we send a group of well-dressed, well-groomed brothers with cameras to photograph the participants. We should also find the starting and ending points of the march and write down the vehicle license tag numbers. Some Klan members didn't want to be recognized as such. It was a tactic that I had learned while I was a member of the Maryland State Police and the FBI. It was my belief that at some point in their lives, some of the younger members of the Klan might seek a political office or a position of power. We had to make sure that we identified them so that we could utilize their participation in Klan rallies or marches against them. We had to keep a list of our enemies.

There was no need for us to go to these Klan marches and rallies and yell and scream. There was no need to hurl rocks or bottles or insults at the participants. We needed only to remain silent, watch, and photograph. *Listen to the silence.*

I leaned all the way back in my chair and closed my eyes. I thought of the conversation that Dr. Ellis had had with our Criminal Justice class. I could see the classroom so clearly. Dr. Ellis had been lecturing on urban crime. He digressed from his subject matter when one of the students complained about middle-class Blacks moving out of the inner city. Dr. Ellis stated that strategically it was a bad move for African Americans to be concentrated in any one area. Sun Tzu stated in his book, *The Art of War*, "...forces are to be structured strategically, based on what is advantageous."

Adolf Hitler was successful in his war against the Jews because they—like modern-day Blacks—were concentrated in one area. Jews said "Never again." They spread out. They integrated the lands without destroying their culture. They also interposed a fence between themselves and what they secretly believed were their white enemies. Their fence is known as urban Blacks.

Dr. Ellis stated that the fact that some cities were seventy to eighty percent Black meant that should the government decide to enact the McCarran Act, they would not have to do much of a round-up job. He said that any military strategist would tell you not to concentrate all your troops in one area. The spreading out of Blacks into the suburbs could work to our advantage in the end. We had to remember that by the truest definition of the word, we were at war. And there would be an end. The class sat stunned. This was one of the rare occasions that Dr. Ellis decided to let down his veil. I hadn't understood it at the time, but now it was all coming together.

One of the students in the class raised his hand in response to Dr. Ellis' statement. Dr. Ellis turned to him. The student hesitated. "Dr. Ellis, is it just the extremists who believe that one day there will be a major uprising in this country?" Dr. Ellis smiled and said, "A long, long time ago a white man by the name of Alexis de Tocqueville stated that white Americans could countenance slavery only by persuading themselves that human beings of African origin were inherently inferior to the other races of mankind and hence suited for bondage. He stated that this view was so firmly entrenched that it would persist after emancipation. No one can deny that Tocqueville was right."

The room was silent now, except for the sound of Dr. Ellis' shoes as they moved across the tiled floor. Everyone waited for some clarification of his point. Dr. Ellis stopped and looked toward the student who had asked the question. Every student felt as if Dr. Ellis had turned toward and was staring at him. Dr. Ellis had a way of doing this. He continued, "Tocqueville also stated that the abolition of slavery would increase the repugnance of the white population for Blacks. He stated that with liberty, Blacks would acquire a degree of instruction that enabled them to appreciate their misfortunes and to discern a remedy for themselves. At this point, if Blacks were not raised to the level of free men, they would soon revolt at being deprived of almost all their civil rights. And, as they cannot become the equals of the whites, they will speedily show themselves as enemies."

Dr. Ellis flashed a quick unhappy smile and then his face turned solid. "Tocqueville stated that this danger of a conflict between white and Black inhabitants perpetually haunts the imagination of the Americans, like a painful dream. Another white man by the name of John Brown, an abolitionist, stated that he was quite certain that the crimes of this guilty land will never be purged away but with blood."

Dr. Ellis must have sensed that I was deep in my thoughts, because he had remained silent during my mental absence. When I opened my eyes he smiled. "Are you through with your mental trek?" "I'm sorry, Dr. Ellis. I was..." He put his hand up and said, "No need for an apology. I realize that you were probably examining all that I have put before you today. I understand your analytical mind." "Dr. Ellis, will our efforts to awaken our sleeping brothers be worth it? I mean, we have so much against us. Besides dealing with those whites who will try to crush any legitimate attempt we make at providing our youth with the truth, we have to deal with those Blacks who are willing to sell their own mother into slavery for a favorable position in the white man's world."

Dr. Ellis placed his pen on top of the pad on which he had scribbled some notes. "There will always be those types of Blacks. Walter Williams, Thomas Sowell, and others like them have always existed and always will. They just want money and peace. But Malcolm X said it best when he stated that 'you cannot separate peace from freedom, because no one can be at peace unless he has freedom.' You should not waste your time thinking about these types of Blacks. They will only drain energy that you may better use in other efforts. Don't get involved in discussions with them or about them. They will only make it seem as if brother is against brother. They will cause others to believe that we are disunited. That is their role and they have learned to play it well. They will try to put you on the defense, while their benefactors enjoy the handiwork of their well-paid robots. They are nothing but articulate smoke screens, diversions. They are insignificant in the whole scheme of things. They do not have an allegiance to anything or anybody. This is not the time to deal with them—ignore them.

"As for the other forces that are arrayed against us, I suggest you remember the words of William Edward DuBois, 'There is in this world no such force as the force of a man determined to rise.

The human soul cannot be permanently chained.' Our efforts are not futile."

I rubbed my eyes and focused in on Dr. Ellis. I slowly began to speak. "It is not that I'm afraid of the task set before me. And I certainly realize that I am not alone in this fight. There are a lot of other sincere conscious brothers engaging the enemy of ignorance and deception every day. I know that we are in for a long battle. Not only do we have to deal with miseducation and indoctrination, but now we have to deal with this AIDS virus, which is nothing less than biological warfare."

Dr. Ellis swiveled his chair around to face his file cabinet. He opened a drawer and pulled out a copy of the *London Times* newspaper dated May 11, 1987. He put the newspaper on his desk, facing me. On the front page was an article by Pearce Wright entitled "Smallpox Vaccine Triggered AIDS Virus." The article stated that the World Health Organization had triggered the AIDS epidemic in Africa through the use of its smallpox immunization program. Dr. Ellis waited patiently for me to finish reading the article and then stated, "The literature on AIDS goes back to at least 1969. In a survey of chemical and biological warfare by Cookson and Nottingham, it was indicated that biological and chemical research by the United States, Canada, Britain, and Germany was taking place. The experimentation and research were conducted on a virus that would attack the immune system of people. We should have been dealing with this a long time ago. But so few people knew of the research and those who did remained silent. Sometimes silence can be deadly."

Dr. Ellis tore the top sheet of paper off the pad. He picked up his pen and began to write on the next sheet. "I want you to get your Master's degree and your Doctorate. I want you to make your thesis and your dissertation significant to our cause. No thesis or dissertation whose only purpose is to allow you to obtain a degree is worth your time. Do thorough research that can be utilized for the good of your people. In the end your education will indicate to you that not all white people are our enemies. There are some John Browns out there that will assist you with your task if they know that you are sincere. Your goal is not to change the world or to overthrow the government. Your goal is simply to uplift your people. You must not allow emotionalism and unbridled anger to overcome you and guide your actions. Think things through. Make sure that your efforts are active. Identifying the problem is an important first step, but you must be part of the solution. I'm proud of you for your efforts in the FBI. I can tell that it has been an education. But when you have completed your research and are prepared, it will be time for you to move on."

Dr. Ellis put his pen down and continued, "But don't be naive: when you start telling the truth, there is always a risk—and that holds especially true for our race. We don't take good care of our leaders. If you will remember, Marcus Garvey dedicated his life to his people and he died poor and in exile. Go back and study the financial situations of Harriet Tubman, Booker T. Washington, and Mary McLeod Bethune. Examine the life of Paul Robeson and how he died in financial distress, living with his sister. At the peak of Paul Robeson's career he earned over one hundred thousand dollars a year. Once he began to speak out against racial injustice, his salary dropped to less than three thousand dollars a year. Malcolm X was assassinated by the government. Dr. Martin Luther King Jr. was persecuted and assassinated by the very organization for which you work. Fred Hampton was murdered in his sleep. Louis Lomax died in a mysterious car accident while filming a movie on the life of Malcolm X. The CIA overthrew Premier Kwame Nkrumah and assassinated Patrice Lumumba.

"Remember that you will be betrayed by many. They will challenge every truth you reveal. False and vicious rumors about you will be circulated. Derogatory statements will be made about your personal life. Your friends will deny you. Those who appear to be with you will be found out to be traitors and infiltrators. But I'm sure you know that by your working for the FBI.

"We should take care of our strong men and women who are willing to stand up for those of us who lack courage. How could we allow men to walk in and shoot down Malcolm X? How could we allow Martin Luther King Jr. to stand on a motel balcony unprotected? How could we allow the government to harass Paul Robeson? We are asleep on the watch and everyone is taking advantage of us."

I took a deep breath and asked, "Dr. Ellis, will your role always be behind the stage curtain? I mean, are you saying you will never be out front like a Jesse Jackson or Minister Louis Farrakhan? Will you never voice your strong, well-founded thoughts and ideas to your students? To many of the students and other professors, you appear aloof. You appear to be in agreement with those who oppress us." Dr. Ellis smiled and said, "Deception. Isn't it wonderful? It is not my role to be a Jesse Jackson or a Louis Farrakhan. Jesse Jackson has been giving the same speeches for years, but I can't see where he has made much progress. We are closer to destruction now than at any other time. 'Keep hope alive' is not going to free us. Louis Farrakhan is legitimate. If I had a son, I would send him to the Nation of Islam for an education. They are teaching self-reliance; they are teaching our young people how to stand up and not back down. Farrakhan is wise. Watch him closely. There are many lessons within that man. Malcolm X taught him a great deal and his loyalty to Elijah Muhammad taught him even more. I read somewhere once that the reality of the other person is not in what he reveals to you; therefore, if you would understand him, listen not to what he says but rather to what he does not say. Listen deeply to Farrakhan. He's no saint, but I don't suppose we need heavenly saints right now.

Dr. Ellis stood up and put on his jacket. "I have defined my role quite clearly for you. I have even defined your role and prepared you for it. And looking into the eyes to your soul, I think I've been doing a pretty good job, or at least I hope so. Training and preparation are important." Dr. Ellis stared out the window and said, "You know, it's strange. We will prepare our children to be football players and basketball players but we refuse to prepare them for life. We have to prepare this young generation for the fight. We have to equip them with the truth. It is hard to fight a battle, when everything you think you see, is not there; when everything that you have been told is true, is really false. It is difficult, when you sink deeper into the quicksand of deception every day. In the midst of this entanglement of deception, you strike out against everything and everybody because it doesn't matter. Black is white and white is black. All you want to do is hurt something or someone. You just want to free yourself from the sticky web of lies and falsehoods that are constraining you. Ye shall know the truth, and the truth shall make you free."

Dr. Ellis removed a brush from his desk and brushed off his jacket. "You see, Tyrone, we have to release the youth from this tangled web that they are in. We can do it. All is not lost. True knowledge will slowly dissolve the web of lies.

"Our youth have been trained to do exactly what they are doing. We are trained to party every weekend. We are trained to get drunk. We are trained to drop out and quit. We are trained to kill our own. We are trained to abuse our women and our children. We are trained to destroy our neighborhoods. We are trained to be ghetto children all of our lives. 'Train up a child in the way that he should go; and when he is old, he will not depart from it.'"

Dr. Ellis moved toward the door. He turned the brass knob and opened the door slowly. "I must go now. I have a very important meeting to attend. There is a need to keep the veil in place. At any rate, you must go back home. It is up to you to determine where *home* is."

As I left Dr. Ellis' office, I felt lighter. I hadn't forgotten Nate. I still missed him. But Dr. Ellis had given my life a little more meaning. He had made me believe that I had an important role to play. I had to prepare myself and then get on the playing field. I didn't have to go out and save the world. All that was required of me was to do my part. To be significant. "A part of the solution." Anything short of that and I would be forsaking my people and wasting my life.

The FBI did not break me, though they tried very hard in the weeks, months, and years to come. No matter how hard they tried, I would not allow them to destroy me. I would stand up for right, no matter what the consequences. I was determined to do something positive for my people. I had no more doubts about my ability to be effective. Shakespeare had written that our doubts are traitors, and make us lose the good we might often win, by fearing to attempt. Dr. Martin Luther King Jr. stated that freedom is the right to fight for right. If I am not willing to stand up and fight for what is right for my people, then I am not really free. And if I am not free, life matters not.

I drove through the streets of Baltimore City on my way to the airport. I smiled when I saw the beautiful brown faces of little boys and girls. Their laughter echoed throughout my body. I could feel it bouncing off the walls of my joyful soul. The sun shone down on the brown sweat-coated bodies of basketball players. In front of a group of young Black men an older man stood with a book. I kept smiling. All was not lost. I looked to my right and saw Nate seated next to me. He smiled and stared into the eyes to my soul. I thought, "I'm coming home, Baltimore. I must be a part of the solution." The words of Adam Clayton Powell resonated throughout my soul: "Mix a conviction with a man and something happens." The world was about to witness the strength of a so-called GHETTO CHILD.

Epilogue

It has been a long journey for me. I no longer think it improbable. I know what every individual is capable of if he or she is properly educated and prepared. It is my belief that there are those who try to ensure that the masses of Americans, especially African Americans, remain ignorant. There is an advantage to having an ignorant population, an ignorant world. There is an advantage to initiating and engaging in war. There is an advantage to having a people who are always at each other's throat because of the color of their skin. Those who have discovered the advantage to fostering and maintaining racial intolerance and hatred continue to build upon and profit from it. Thus, they make sure the people will concentrate on hating and destroying each other and will never be able to analyze the root cause of the division.

Unfortunately, too many of us buy stock in the commodity of division. We accept the superiority/inferiority scenario and buy into it, sell it, trade in it, run with it, live with it, argue it, justify it, fight for it and die for it. We live with a calcified ceiling of division under which African Americans, and Africans the world over, have suffered most. We have been the victims of the invasion of Africa, the enslavement of millions of our people, and the brutal killing of over one hundred million of our people during the slave trade. Under the system of slavery our women were brutalized and raped at will. Our young female children were raped and sodomized. Our men were bought and sold, beaten, whipped, and lynched. We were prohibited from reading and learning and analyzing. We were denied the knowledge of our ancestral greatness. The world doesn't want to remember all of this. The world wants to deny that these things ever occurred. This explains the lack of funding for movies about the unprecedented holocaust suffered by Africans and the seemingly bottomless pit of money provided for movies on the sufferings of other non-dark-skinned people.

Many of us have been conditioned not to read, study, and analyze. We are channeled onto the path of endless leisure. I know. For a while I, too, had taken the road *most* traveled. Robert Frost was right: taking the right road can make all the difference. In order that this country and this world drill through this calcified ceiling of ignorance and hatred, we will have to study, analyze, and critique. Those above the ceiling have no intention of brushing the tartar away. They have no plans for a deep cleaning. We must rot away their plan. We must destroy their deceptively pretty smile. It will not be easy.

●●●●●●●●●●●●●●●●●●●

After the death of my brother Cornelius Elijah Powers, in July 1987 the FBI mounted a more vicious campaign against me. They initiated investigations and surveillances of me. They accused me of violating Bureau rules and regulations, and then failed to prove that I had. It is my belief that it was the Bureau's goal to heap unbearable stress upon me, to pressure me into acting violently and irrationally. One experienced African American Unit Chief told me that the Bureau wanted me to "act like a nigger." Finally, in September 1991, my co-workers at the Federal Bureau of Investigation attacked my family by raiding the residence of my sister, with an arrest warrant for my brother whom they knew to be deceased. (They sent flowers to his funeral.) They surrounded the house and accosted neighbors. (This was the same residence where I had once lived. The FBI knew this.) They forced their way in past my sister, who was still in her night gown and who was due to have surgery the next day. They compelled her to present identification, as if she could possibly have been a deceased Black man. They made her call my mother, who was disabled due to having suffered two strokes. My co-workers insisted that my mother produce a death certificate. My mother became so upset that she stated if they still wanted to harass her boy, she would give them directions to his graveyard plot and they could go and dig him up. She consequently suffered a state of depression and severe dizziness. The agents left, in my opinion, satisfied that they had sent the right message to me.

When confronted by me and required to investigate the incident, the FBI emphasized that the agent who initiated the raid was Black. (Of course he, a Black agent, wouldn't purposely attack the family of another African American agent.) The FBI investigation concluded that it was just an awful mistake. They offered me their apologies and asked whether I wanted them to *visit* and apologize to my mother. My family was not up to another "visit" from FBI agents, even if one of them was Black.

•••••••••••••••••••

In February 1994 the Detroit chapter of the Agents Association and the Special Agent Advisory Committee held a joint meeting. Because of the division created by the Agents Association, no African American Special Agents attended this session. Several white Special Agents came to me after the meeting and stated they were hurt and embarrassed by the comments made at the meeting about me. They stated that for two hours the leaders of the meeting "murdered me." The agents informed me that the meeting took on a lynch-mob mentality. Jokes were made about Rodney King and some of the agents suggested that what was justifiably done to him should be done to me. I reported the atmosphere and mentality of this meeting to the Assistant Special Agent in Charge of the Detroit division in a memorandum. Nothing was done or said about it.

•••••••••••••••••••

In January 1995—despite the Agents Association's repeated attempts to intervene—the FBI and B.A.D.G.E. (Black Agents Don't Get Equity) signed an agreement to rectify past and present inequities at the Federal Bureau of Investigation. The shame is that many of the African American agents who will immediately benefit from this agreement are those who failed to stand up. In my opinion this is the type of agent that is paraded around by the Bureau to give speeches to the public. On the other hand, despite a barrage of evidence that indicated a pattern of discrimination against Special Agent Prince Earl Ross, his complaint against the Bureau was closed with no action taken. It should be noted that Special Agent Ross was one of the brave souls who allowed his name to be printed in the public court document charging the FBI with discriminatory actions. Many African American Agents had refused. I was another one of those brave souls, and here I stand. Neither Prince Ross nor I have any regrets.

●●●●●●●●●●●●●●●●●●

In August 1994 I resigned from the FBI. Not from any pressure they brought to bear upon me. I never allowed them to force me to flee, although they never stopped trying. I understand the game. I left because it was time. It was time for me to further my education. It was time for me to go home to my family and to my community. It was time for me to work with the youth. To help make an impact on the problems facing them. It was time to grab my drill and do my small part to chip away at that calcified ceiling.

I'm a realist. I have no vision of changing the entire world by myself. But I have obtained enough knowledge to realize that as long as we feel that the problem is too big to be fixed, no one will work on it. There are those who are banking on our having this attitude. I must be *A PART OF THE SOLUTION.*

●●●●●●●●●●●●●●●●●●

On October 16, 1995, Nation of Islam leader Minister Louis Farrakhan led the greatest march in the history of this nation. Over one million Black men responded to his call for unity, atonement, and change. The forgotten Black men from inner-city Baltimore were there; the new crew from the Blue Gardenia showed up; Nate was there in spirit and he smiled when he saw me. As I noted in the final chapter of this book, all is not lost.

There's a move to bring about the needed change for Black people. The energy from the Million Man March has engulfed the bodies and troubled souls of Black America. Now more than ever, Blacks recognize the need for education, not indoctrination, and entrepreneurship and self-help. We understand the philosophy behind drugs in our neighborhoods, and new plans are being developed to remove them. We understand that self-defense is a very important aspect of self-help. We will no longer be the victims of anyone in any form. We will no longer run and hide.

We understand that there will be detractors. There are those who do not wish that we succeed. We heard them and saw them as they were paraded before us, before the Million Man March. Their goal was simple and simple-minded: "Stop the Million Man

March. Put an end to the concepts of self-help and self-love." We were introduced to people whom we hadn't heard from in years and probably won't hear from again until the addicting microphone of disunity is shoved to their lips. Their strong and confident critical voices were conspicuous by their silence when it was reported that 17 Black churches had been burned down in the South in the last 2 years. Why have these detractors not been given a microphone to rail against the racist arsonists? Why have they not even asked for that microphone? History tells us that these individuals are not unique. My background tells me that they have made the ignoble list of "reliable sources."

We cannot discount all our detractors as insignificant. As a million-plus Black men descended on Washington for a day of atonement and peace, the FBI SWAT team reportedly assembled on the 6th floor of the Washington metropolitan field office with no peaceful intentions. They were dressed in black, fully locked and loaded. Their weapons of peace consisted of MP-5's, Swiss-made Sigsuaer .9 millimeters, Remington 12-gauge shotguns, and an assortment of knives and other peacemaking gadgets. They watched a big screen television and waited for this peaceful gathering to turn riotous. The Fruit of Islam, they surely thought, would meet their match. Much to the surprise and chagrin of the men dressed in black, nothing went "right."

I am not sad about my life experiences. In fact I am glad. My journey has been an education and will continue be. Fate has put me in a position to tell a story. And tell the story I will.

Appendix

Some of the following documents were acquired through the Freedom of Information Act and relate to my service with the FBI.

January 4, 1984

Md. State Police
Lt. N.F. Bechtel
1001 W. Patrick St.
Frederick, Md.   21701

Dear Lt. Bechtel:

Early last month my wife and I experienced problems in
our neighborhood which warrented action from the State
Police. Trooper Powers responded to this call and I
would like to inform you about the superior way in which
he handled the case. His efficient, intelligent and professional manner helped us immediately with our problem.
Trooper Powers even came on his own time when problems
started flaring up again. Because of his outstanding
diplomatic skills he quickly diffused an issue which had
potential for being a time bomb. By speaking to quite a few
of the neighbors and listening to them he opened up the
lines of communication.

The State of Maryland should take this as an example of
outstanding police work as demonstrated by Trooper Powers.
We should all consider ourselves very fortunate to have a
man of this excellence who exhibits such dedication on
the force.

Sincerely,

cc: Senator John Derr
    Trooper Powers

FD-204 (Rev. 3-3-59)

UNITED STATES DEPARTMENT OF JUSTICE
FEDERAL BUREAU OF INVESTIGATION

Copy to:

Report of: SA [REDACTED]   Office: BALTIMORE
Date: JULY 5, 1985

Field Office File #: [REDACTED]   Bureau File #:

Title: TYRONE (NMN) POWERS

Character: BUREAU APPLICANT - SPECIAL AGENT

Synopsis: [REDACTED]

–RUC–

DETAILS:

BIRTH

On June 6, 1985, IA [REDACTED] caused a search of the
BUREAU OF VITAL STATISTICS, Baltimore, Maryland, which verified the
applicant's date of birth as April 22, 1961, at Baltimore, Maryland,
according to certificate number 61-11170 which was filed April 25, 1961.

NEIGHBORHOOD

On June 7, 1985, [REDACTED] Old Frederick Road,
Baltimore, Maryland, verified the applicant's residence at 4461 Old
Frederick Road, for approximately five years. She stated the applicant
caused no problems in the neighborhood and she knew of nothing derogatory
regarding the applicant's character, associates, reputation or loyalty.
SUITE stated she knew of no illegal drug use or alcohol abuse on the part
of the applicant and recommended the applicant for a position of trust with
the FBI.   1

U.S.GPO:1975-0-575-861

On June 7, 1985, ███████████████████ Old Frederick Road,
Baltimore, Maryland, verified the applicant's residence at 4461 Old Frederick
Road from February 1976 to July of 1981. She advised the applicant was a good
neighbor who caused no problems in the neighborhood. She advised she knew of
no derogatory information regarding the applicant's character, associates,
reputation or loyalty and knew of no illegal drug use or alcohol abuse on the
part of the applicant. She highly recommended the applicant for a position
of trust with the FBI.

On June 7, 1985, ██████████████████ Old Frederick Road,
Baltimore, Maryland, verified the applicant's residence at 4461 Old Frederick
Road from February 1976 to July of 1981. He stated the applicant was a fine
neighbor, caused no problems in the neighborhood and was respected by his
neighbors. He advised he knew of no derogatory information regarding the
applicant's character, associates, reputation or loyalty and knew of no
illegal drug use or alcohol abuse on the part of the applicant. He highly
recommended the appliant for a position of trust with the FBI.

On June 11, 1985, ██████████████ 12000 Tarragon Road,
Baltimore, Maryland, advised that he has known the applicant as a neighbor
for a year and a half. ████████ knew of nothing derogatory regarding
the applicant's character, associates, reputation or loyalty and knew of
no illegal drug use or alcohol abuse on the part of the applicant. He
advised the applicant is a friendly and level headed individual and he
highly recommended the applicant for a position of trust with the FBI.

On June 27, 1985, ████████████████████████
Baltimore, Maryland, advised that he has only known the applicant for
only one month. He stated he knew the applicant to be a Maryland State
Trooper. ████████ described the applicant as a nice and polite individual
and advised he knew of no derogatory information concerning the applicant's
character, associates, reputation or loyalty. ████████ could not give a
recommendation regarding the applicant because of his limited contacted
with him.

On June 27, 1985, MR. ████████████████, Manager, TIFFANY SQUARE
APARTMENTS, 11907 Tarragon Road, Baltimore, Maryland, advised that the
applicant has been a tenant for approximately 3½ years. He described the
applicant as a very nice person, calm and even tempered. He avised the
applicant has always paid his rent on time and has never created any problems
for the management of the complex. He is not aware of any illegal drug
use or alcohol abuse by the applicant. He had no reason to question the
applicant's loyalty to the United States and highly recommended him for
a position of trust with the FBI.

2

Memorandum

To : Finnegan   Date 1/14/86

From : R. M. Kirkland

Subject : STANDARDS OF PERFORMANCE
NEW AGENTS TRAINING PROGRAM
NAC 8601 - EOD: 12/2/85

      This memorandum is written to recognize the Superior performance of members of NAC 8601. It is my privilege to inform you that the following trainees in NAC 8601 achieved Superior ratings for the first six weeks of training in the Physical Fitness portion of the FBI Academys Program. They are to be applauded for their efforts:

      1. SA Trainee Tyrone Powers who had an entry score of 21 and achieved 36 at six weeks making an improvement of 15 points.

      It is noted the above listed trainees arrived at the Academy and met all standards of physical testing. They then took it upon themselves to set extremely high goals in the truest sense of a Special Agent of the FBI. It is with this kind of effort that we will maintain our status as the number one law enforcement agency in the world.

August 4, 1987

Mr. Tyrone Powers
6605 Knotty Pine Drive
Cincinnati, Ohio 45230

Dear Mr. Powers:

    I want to convey my sincere sympathy to you and your
family on the passing of your brother.

    The thoughts of your many friends in the Bureau are
with you, and it is hoped that you will find some consolation in
this sharing of your sorrow.

Sincerely,

/S/

John E. Otto
Acting Director

1 - SAC, Cincinnati (Personal Attention)

67-860211
MEK:sk (3)

Exec AD Adm. ____
Exec AD Inv. ____
Exec AD LES ____
Asst. Dir.:
  Adm. Servs. ____
  Crim. Inv. ____
  Ident. ____
  Insp. ____
  Intell. ____
  Lab. ____
  Legal Coun. ____
  Off. Cong. &
    Public Affs. ____
  Rec. Mgmt. ____
  Tech. Servs. ____
  Training ____
  Telephone Rm. ____
Director's Sec'y ____ MAIL ROOM ____

PROMOTION
INFO. REQ.

A Disgrace to the FBI

THE FBI under J. Edgar Hoover was not a part of the federal government where blacks were welcome. There were a few token agents and undoubtedly some clerical personnel, but by and large job applicants and entry-level workers who were not white suffered discrimination. Statistics over the past 10 or 15 years show considerable improvement—there are now 400 black agents in the bureau. But the case of Donald Rochon, which was detailed in Monday's New York Times, is so egregious as to raise questions about real conditions for blacks inside the FBI.

Mr. Rochon's story sounds like one of the horror stories of the 1950s. He joined the bureau in 1981 and was first assigned to the field office in Omaha. There, according to reports filed by the Equal Employment Opportunity Commission and the Justice Department, he was subjected to continual harassment and humiliation by his co-workers. The face of an ape was pasted over a picture of his son in a family photograph on his desk. The message "Don't come" was scrawled on invitations to office parties. A photograph of a black man who had been beaten was placed in his mail slot. His supervisor considered these incidents "pranks" and said they were "healthy" and a sign of "esprit de corps" in the office.

More serious torments awaited him in Chicago when he was transferred there in 1984. His family began to get late-night obscene phone calls. He received unsigned, typewritten letters threatening him with death and mutilation; a photograph of a black man who had suffered this fate was attached. He received two letters from insurance companies requesting payment for death, dismemberment and burial insurance that he had not purchased. An FBI agent in the Chicago office, after an administrative inquiry, was found to have forged these documents, but he was simply suspended for 14 days, and his colleagues chipped in to pay his salary.

Can you imagine any large employer in the country—public or private—putting up with this behavior by employees, let alone calling it a "prank"? Yes, the investigation is continuing—criminal charges may be brought—and Mr. Rochon has filed a civil suit. But if the FBI knows who was behind this disgusting campaign—and more than one person was involved—why haven't they been fired? If agents are this cruel to colleagues, how can the public have any confidence in the way they treat criminal suspects? Weed them out. There is no room in the federal work force for such racism, and no excuse for countenancing it:

Washington Post, 1988

U.S. Department of Justice

JPT:LKD:aww
DJ 144-35-1056

Washington, D.C. 20530

July 03, 1989

Mr. Tyrone Powers
Federal Bureau of Investigation
Cincinnati Division
550 Main Street
Cincinnati, Ohio 45202

Dear Mr. Powers:

The Civil Rights Division recently completed its review of
the investigative report submitted by the Federal Bureau of
Investigation concerning allegations that Cornelius Elizah Powers
was the victim of a criminal violation of the federal civil
rights statutes.

After a careful review of that report, we concluded that
this matter lacks prosecutive merit, and we closed our file.
Accordingly, we intend to take no further action at this time.

Thank you for bringing this matter to our attention. This
Division is dedicated to the enforcement of federal criminal
civil rights statutes. We appreciate your cooperation in our
effort to achieve that goal.

Sincerely,

James P. Turner
Acting Assistant Attorney General
Civil Rights Division

By: *Linda K. Davis*

Linda K. Davis
Chief
Criminal Section

Memorandum

To : SAC, DETROIT   Date 8/6/90

From : SA TYRONE POWERS

Subject : PERSONNEL MATTER

Subsequent to approval under provisions of the Freedom of Information (FOI) Act, on August 1, 1990, I was allowed to review my personnel file. As a result, I noted various comments made by my former Assistant Special Agent in Charge (ASAC) ████████ Cincinnati Division. ████████ made references to my talent as an investigator and my work ethic; that I should be placed on a reactive squad under close supervision and counseling; and that until my work ethic improves, I should not be allowed any additional training at the Bureau's expense.

In response to the above allegations, I am bringing attention to facts that my personnel file contains several performance appraisals, of which none indicate a need of close supervision or counseling; my investigative skills were graded from fully successful to superior, allowing me to enter and become a part of the Career Development Program; and my statistical accomplishments while assigned to the Cincinnati Division show that I am more than an adequate investigator and a productive asset to the FBI.

It should be noted, I was prompted to review my personnel file, after having learned of information alleging me to be a racist and that this information eminated from the Cincinnati Division. I have since determined that this allegation is totally baseless and that ████████ comments are not based on facts. I therefore can only assume his comments were made as a result of false information he received or a false perception he has of me.

I have notified my immediate supervisors at Detroit and they have confirmed having prior knowledge of the above. They further advised me that I was assigned to my current squad based upon ████ comments.

It is evident to me that my career within the FBI has been affected by ████████ comments and notations. I am currently in consultation with my immediate family and close associates; at the conclusion of which I will make a determination as to a course of action to protect my interest.

Memorandum

To   :   SAC, DETROIT   Date   8/19/90

From :   SA TYRONE POWERS

Subject: PERSONNEL MATTER

      Subsequent to approval under provisions of the Freedom
of information Act (FOIA), on August 1, 1990, I was allowed to
review my personnel file. As a result I noted comments on a form
designed to indicate my desires in terms of squad assignment.
These comments were written by my former ASAC in the Cincinnati
Division.████████████ I found the comments to be inaccurate,
baseless and a possible detriment to my carrer within the FBI.

      Due to the fact that the insertion of this form is not
in accordance with the procedure for placing items into a
personnel file, I request that the above described form be
removed.

TP/tp
(2)

*I concur
w/ SA Powers
request.*

D-725 (Rev. 10-13-87)

Federal Bureau of Investigation
Performance Management System – Special Agent
Performance Appraisal Report – Cover Page

[SEE INSTRUCTIONS ON REVERSE]

1. Payroll Name of Employee POWERS TYRONE	2. Social Security Number ▇▇▇▇
3. Position Title, Grade and Number SPECIAL AGENT ▇▇▇▇	4. Office of Assignment 3220 DETROIT

5. General Nature of Assignment
VIOLENT CRIME MAJOR OFFENDERS PROGRAM;
FUGITIVE SUBPROGRAM

6. Summary Rating   SUPERIOR

7. _SSA Jean R Lopez_ _____   _4-11-91_
Signature of Rating Official   Date

I have reviewed and approved this appraisal. ( ) See my comments attached.

8. _____   _____
Signature of Reviewing Official   Date

I am aware that a rating of less than Fully Successful on any critical element may preclude me from consideration for promotion and/or office of preference transfer. In addition, I am aware that my summary rating, if below the Fully Successful level, may preclude my consideration for a within-grade increase (WIGI) and that a summary rating of Unacceptable may be the basis for my reassignment, reduction in grade, or removal. My signature only indicates that I have reviewed this appraisal, not that I am necessarily in agreement with the information herein or that I am relinquishing my right to request reconsideration of it.

9. _____   _4/11/91_
Signature of Employee   Date

10. Basis/Reason for Issuance

				PRAU USE ONLY
A	☒	End of Annual Period		Logged _____
T	☐	Position Change	Date ____	Reviewed _____
O	☐	Change in Rating Official	Date ____	Entered _____
M	☐	Current Appraisal	Date ____	Verified _____
Q	☐	Requested by FBIHQ	Date ____	Printout _____
D	☐	Conclusion of Detail	Date ____	
W	☐	Unacceptable – Warning	Date ____	
F	☐	Warning Resolution	Date ____	

FD-728b (3-30-87)

Federal Bureau of Investigation
Performance Management System – Special Agent
Performance Appraisal Report – Narrative Page

[SEE INSTRUCTIONS ON REVERSE]

1. Payroll Name of Employee	2. Social Security Number
POWERS TYRONE	

3. Critical Element # __2__ . (Include specific examples of positive/negative performance.)

REPORT INFORMATION:

SA POWERS consistently prepared written communications which were clear, concise, and grammatically correct. Documentation relating to criminal investigations reveal a clear understanding of the elements to be proved in such matters. The quality of all written work prepared by SA POWERS requires only general review by his Supervisor and is always submitted on a timely basis.

On occasion, SA POWERS has been called upon to make oral presentations to FBI personnel and outside agencies. These presentations have consistently reflected thorough preparation, and concepts are clearly understood by the recipients.

SA POWER's performance in this element is considered Superior.

4. Initials of Employee _____ Date _____

D-725b (3-30-87)

Federal Bureau of Investigation
Performance Management System – Special Agent
Performance Appraisal Report – Narrative Page

[SEE INSTRUCTIONS ON REVERSE]

Payroll Name of Employee	2. Social Security Number
POWERS TYRONE	

Critical Element # __1__ . (Include specific examples of positive/negative performance.)

CONDUCT INVESTIGATIONS:

During the rating period, SA POWERS handled a substantial number of complex investigations which subsequently resulted in 16 complaints and 7 arrests. During the course of these assignments, SA POWERS displayed efficient and effective use of sophisticated investigative techniques, the results of which were consistently collected within established time frames. All investigation was aggressively conducted and reflected a thorough understanding of the elements associated with applicable Federal statutes. SA POWERS demonstrated a self-motivated investigative style which required Supervisory input only when higher authority was required to proceed.

Case load management reflected attention to detail and superior organizational ability. SA POWERS frequently accepted additional assignments to assist other Agents, thus contributing to the overall accomplishment of the squad. Investigations handled by SA POWERS are consistently conducted in accordance with FBI rules, regulations, and guidelines and routine file reviews reflect the Agent's full compliance.

4. Initials of Employee   Date

Benefit For Fired Officers

WALTER BUDZYN
&
LARRY NEVERS

on
THURSDAY
SEPTEMBER 16, 1993
at
ROSIE'S ANTEROOM TOO
14234 GRATIOT AVENUE
1 Block South of 7 Mile

6:00 P.M.   Until ???

BEER   HOT DOGS   CHIPS   SNACKS

DONATION: CASH AT DOOR

50/50 RAFFLE & DOOR PRIZES

White Detroit FBI agents raise funds
for white policemen subsequently
convicted of second degree murder in the
death of Black motorist, Malice Green.

SEMMES, BOWEN & SEMMES

ATTORNEYS AT LAW

A PARTNERSHIP OF PROFESSIONAL CORPORATIONS

401 Washington Avenue Towson, Maryland 21204	SUITE 500 1025 CONNECTICUT AVENUE, N.W. WASHINGTON, DC 20036	250 West Pratt Street Baltimore, Maryland 21201
1220 North Market Street Wilmington, Delaware 19801	TELEPHONE 202-778-2901	339 E. Antietam Street Hagerstown, Maryland 21740
Labor and Employment Law *Direct Dial:* *David J. Shaffer* *202-778-8686*	FACSIMILE 202-463-4971	PLEASE REPLY TO WASHINGTON, D.C. OFFICE

September 21, 1993

Tyrone Powers
28415 East Larkmoor Drive
Southfield, MI 48076

Re: *Johnson, et al. v. Reno*

Dear Mr. Powers:

As you know, the Federal Bureau of Investigation Agents Association was granted intervention in this case on May 25, 1993. As a result, we and the FBI filed Motions for Summary Judgment and to Dismiss them from the case. They, in turn, filed a Cross-Motion for Summary Judgment, essentially asking that our case be dismissed, allegedly on the grounds that we had provided insufficient evidence of discrimination at the FBI.

Last Friday, September 17, 1993, these motions were heard in front of Judge Hogan in U.S. District Court for the District of Columbia. After a lengthy oral argument, Judge Hogan granted the Motions for Summary Judgment of the FBI and us and denied the Motion of the FBIAA. Thus, the FBIAA is now dismissed from this case.

Judge Hogan further made several findings regarding our case which now clears the way for his approval of the settlement agreement. Specifically, Judge Hogan found that there was a manifest imbalance in the way black agents have historically been treated in their employment with the FBI. Also, he found that the Justice Department's decision to enter into this settlement agreement was reasonable based upon the evidence presented, and that the relief was narrowly tailored to the discrimination that exists.

The next important date in this case is Friday, October 8, 1993. On that date, at 10:00 a.m., Judge Hogan will hold a hearing concerning the fairness of the Settlement

Tyrone Powers
September 21, 1993
Page Two

Agreement. Although individual agents will have the opportunity to present any objections that they may have to the settlement agreement, we believe that the Judge will likely approve the agreement, at that time.

Again, this past Friday was a big victory for B.A.D.G.E. We are very proud of the results that we have achieved. Should you have any questions, please feel free to contact me.

Very truly yours,

DAVID J. SHAFFER, P.C.

By _____

DJS/ge

FD-700 (Rev. 1-19-88)

Federal Bureau of Investigation
Performance Management and Recognition System
Progress Review Sheet

[SEE INSTRUCTIONS ON REVERSE]

1. Payroll Name of Employee	2. Social Security Number
SA TYRONE POWERS	▬▬▬▬▬
3. Payroll Name of Rating Official	4. Date of Progress Review Session
SSA WILLIAM J. KOWALSKI	

5. Comments:

CONDUCT INVESTIGATIONS: FULLY SUCCESSFUL

REPORT INFORMATION: SUPERIOR

INFORMANT DEVELOPMENT: FULLY SUCCESSFUL

OVERALL: FULLY SUCCESSFUL

Suggested Reading List

"Of all our studies, history is best qualified to reward our research."
          –The Hon. Elijah Muhammad

Achebe, Chinua. *Things Fall Apart*. New York: Fawcett Crest, 1969.

Agnew, Spiro T. *Go Quietly...or else*. New York: William Morrow & Company, 1980.

Akbar, Na'im. *Visions for Black Men*. Nashville, Tennessee: Winston-Derek, 1991.

Al-Mansour, Khalid Abdullah Tariq. *Betrayal By Any Other Name*. San Francisco: The First African Arabian Press, 1993.

Ali, Muhammad and Richard Durham. *The Greatest: My Own Story*. New York: Random House, 1975.

Ambrose, Stephen E. *Nixon: The Education of a Politician 1913-1962*. New York: Simon & Schuster, 1987.

Baldwin, James. *The Evidence of Things Not Seen*. New York: Henry Holt & Company, 1985.

Barashango, Ishakamusa. *Afrikan People and European Holidays: A Mental Genocide. Book I*. Silver Spring, Maryland: IVth Dynasty Publishing, 1980.

_____. *African People and European Holidays: A Mental Genocide. Book II*. Silver Spring, Maryland: IVth Dynasty Publishing, 1983.

Bell, Derrick. *And We Are Not Saved*. New York: Basic Books, Inc., 1987.

ben-Jochannan, Yosef and John Henrik Clarke. *New Dimensions in African History*. Trenton, New Jersey: Africa World Press, 1991.

Bennett, Lerone, Jr. *Before the Mayflower*. New York: Penguin Books, 1984.

The Holy Bible. King James Version.

Bloom, Allan. *The Closing of the American Mind*. New York: Simon & Schuster, 1987.

Bonner, Raymond. *Waltzing with a Dictator*. New York: Time Books, 1987.

Bowser, Charles W. *Let the Bunker Burn*. Philadelphia: Camino Books, 1989.

Breitman, George, Herman Porter, and Baxter Smith. *The Assassination of Malcolm X*. New York: Pathfinder, 1976.

Brown, Claude. *Manchild in the Promised Land*. New York: The New American Library, 1965.

Caro, Robert A. *The Path to Power*. New York: Vintage Books, 1983.

_____. *The Power Broker*. New York: Vintage Books, 1975.

Carter, Jimmy. *The Blood of Abraham*. Boston: Houghton Mifflin, 1985.

Clark, Eric. *The Want Makers*. New York: Viking Press, 1988.

Clarke, John Henrik. *African World Revolution*. Trenton, New Jersey: Africa World Press, Inc., 1991.

_____. *Malcolm X: The Man and His Times.* Trenton, New Jersey: Africa World Press, Inc., 1990.

Cleage, Albert B., Jr. *Black Christian Nationalism.* Detroit: Luxor Publishers, 1972.

_____. *The Black Messiah.* Trenton, New Jersey: Africa World Press, 1989.

Cleaver, Eldridge. *Soul on Ice.* New York: McGraw-Hill Book Company, 1968.

Cooper, William. *Behold a Pale Horse.* Sedona, Arizona: Mission Possible Commercial Printing, 1991.

Crouch, Stanley. *Notes of a Hanging Judge.* New York: Oxford University Press, 1990.

Cruse, Harold. *The Crisis of the Negro Intellectual.* New York: Quill, 1984.

Dean, John. *Blind Ambition.* New York: Simon & Schuster, 1976.

Diop, Cheikh Anta. *Great African Thinkers.* New Brunswick, New Jersey: The Journal of African Civilizations, 1986.

Dorsett, Tony and Harvey Frommer. *Running Tough.* New York: Doubleday, 1989.

DuBois, W.E.B. *The Autobiography of W.E.B. DuBois.* New York: International Publishers Co., Inc., 1968.

_____. *The Souls of Black Folk,* New York: New American Library, 1969.

Ellison, Ralph. *Invisible Man.* New York: New American Library, 1947.

Fanon, Frantz. *Toward the African Revolution.* New York: Grove Press, 1967.

Farrakhan, Louis. *Back Where We Belong.* Philadelphia: PC International Press, 1989.

Flynn, Kevin and Gary Gerhardt. *The Silent Brotherhood.* New York: The Free Press, 1989.

Ford, Henry, Sr. *The International Jew.* Dearborn, Michigan, 1921.

Garrow, David J. *Bearing the Cross.* New York: William Morrow & Company, 1986.

_____. *The FBI and Martin Luther King, Jr.* New York: Penguin Books, 1983.

Garvey, Amy Jacques, Ed. *The Philosophy & Opinions of Marcus Garvey.* Dover, Massachusetts: The Majority Press, 1986. First published 1923 and 1925.

Greenlee, Sam. *The Spook Who Sat by the Door.* London: Allison & Busby, 1969.

Gregory, Dick. *Nigger.* New York: Washington Square Press, 1964.

Greider, William. *Secrets of the Temple.* New York: Simon & Schuster, 1989.

Hacker, Andrew. *Two Nations: Black and White, Separate, Hostile, Unequal.* New York: Charles Scribner's Sons, 1992.

Haley, Alex. *The Autobiography of Malcolm X.* New York: Ballantine Books, 1964.

Hampton, Henry and Steve Fayer. *Voices of Freedom.* New York: Bantam Books, 1990.

Hastings, Max. *The Korean War.* New York: Simon & Schuster, 1987.

Henderson, Thomas and Peter Knobler. *Out of Control.* New York: G.P. Putnam's Sons, 1987.

Hersh, Seymour M. *The Price of Power: Kissinger in the Nixon White House.* New York: Summit Books, 1983.

Hislop, Alexander. *The Two Babylons.* Neptune, New Jersey: Loizeaux Brothers, Inc., 1943.

Hurst, Jack. *Nathan Bedford Forrest.* New York: Alfred A. Knopf, 1993.

Jackson, John G. *Man, God, and Civilization.* Secaucus, New Jersey: Citadel Press, 1972.

Jackson, Terrance. *Putting It All Together.* New York: Akasa Press, 1991.

James, C.L.R. *The Black Jacobins.* New York: Vintage Books, 1963.

James, George G. M. *Stolen Legacy.* San Francisco: Julian Richardson Associates, 1988.

Johnson, James Weldon. *The Autobiography of an Ex-Coloured Man.* New York: Vintage Books, 1989.

Jones, Del. *Culture Bandits: Volume 1.* Philadelphia: Hikeka Press, 1990.

_____. *Culture Bandits: Volume 2.* Philadelphia: Hikeka Press, 1993.

Jones, James H. *Bad Blood.* New York: The Free Press, 1981.

Kennedy, Paul. *Preparing for the Twenty-First Century.* New York: Random House, 1993.

_____. *The Rise and Fall of the Great Powers.* New York: Random House, 1987.

Kimche, Jon. *There Could Have Been Peace.* New York: Dial Press, 1973.

King, Martin Luther, Jr. *Where Do We Go From Here: Chaos or Community?* Boston: Beacon Press, 1967.

_____. *Why We Can't Wait.* New York: New American Library, 1963.

Koestler, Arthur. *The Thirteenth Tribe.* New York: Random House, 1976.

Kozol, Jonathan. *Savage Inequalities.* New York: Crown Publishers, Inc., 1991.

Lane, Mark. *Plausible Denial.* New York: Thunder's Mouth Press, 1991.

_____. *The Strongest Poison.* New York: Hawthorn Books, 1980.

Lane, Mark and Dick Gregory. *Code Name "Zorro".* New Jersey: Prentice-Hall, 1977.

Larrabee, Eric. *Commander in Chief: Franklin Delano Roosevelt, His Lieutenants & Their War.* New York: Harper & Row, 1987.

Lederer, William J. *A Nation of Sheep.* New York: Fawcett Publications, 1961.

Lomax, Louis E. *To Kill a Black Man.* Los Angeles: Holloway House, 1968.

Madhubuti, Haki R. *Black Men: Obsolete, Single, Dangerous?* Chicago: Third World Press, 1990.

Marcuse, Herbert. *Counter-Revolution and Revolt.* Boston: Beacon Press, 1972.

Martin, Tony. *Race First: The Ideological and Organizational Struggles of Marcus Garvey and the UNIA.* Dover, Massachusetts: The Majority Press, 1976.

McPherson, James M. *Battle Cry of Freedom: The Civil War Era.* New York: Oxford University Press, 1988.

Morris, Donald R. *The Washing of the Spears.* New York: Simon & Schuster, 1965.

Muhammad, Elijah. *Message to the Blackman.* Hampton, Virginia: United Brothers Communications Systems, 1965.

Nalty, Bernard C. *Strength for the Fight: A History of Black Americans in the Military.* New York: The Free Press, 1986.

The Nation of Islam. *The Secret Relationship Between Blacks and Jews.* Boston: Historical Research Department, 1991.

Niebuhr, Reinhold. *Moral Man and Immoral Society.* New York: Charles Scribner's Sons, 1932.

O'Reilly, Kenneth. *"Racial Matters".* New York: The Free Press, 1989.

Ostrovsky, Victor and Claire Hoy. *By Way of Deception.* New York: St. Martin's Press, 1990.

The Holy Quran.

Robeson, Paul. *Here I Stand.* Boston: Beacon Press, 1958.

Shakur, Assata. *Assata.* Chicago: Lawrence Hill Books, 1987.

Speer, Albert. *Inside the Third Reich.* New York: The Macmillan Company, 1970.

Stockwell, John. *The Praetorian Guard: The U.S. Role in the New World Order.* Boston: South End Press, 1991.

Szulc, Tad. *Fidel: A Critical Portrait.* New York: William Morrow & Company, 1986.

Taylor, Jared. *Paved With Good Intentions.* New York: Carroll & Graf Publishers Inc., 1992.

Terry, Wallace. *Bloods.* New York: Random House, 1984.

Thomas, Gordon. *Journey Into Madness.* New York: Bantam Books, 1989.

T'Shaka, Oba. *The Art of Leadership.* Richmond, California: Pan Afrikan Publications, 1990.

_____. *The Art of Leadership: Volume 2.* Richmond, California: Pan Afrikan Publications, 1991.

Van Sertima, Ivan. *They Came Before Columbus.* New York: Random House, 1976.

Wade, Brent. *Company Man.* Chapel Hill, North Carolina: Algonquin Books, 1992.

Welsing, Frances Cress. *The Isis Papers.* Chicago: Third World Press, 1991.

Wilkins, Ivor and Hans Strydom. *The Broederbond.* New York: Paddington Press Ltd., 1978.

Wise, David and Thomas B. Ross. *The Invisible Government.* New York: Bantam Books, 1964.

Woodson, Carter G. *The Mis-Education of the Negro.* Philadelphia: Hakim's Publications, 1933.

Woodward, Bob. *Veil: The Secret Wars of the CIA 1981-1987.* New York: Simon & Schuster, 1987.

Wyden, Peter. *Bay of Pigs.* New York: Simon & Schuster, 1980.

X, Malcolm. *Malcolm X: By Any Means Necessary.* New York: Pathfinder Press, 1970.

_____. *Malcolm X Speaks.* New York: Grove Press, 1965.

Yergin, Daniel. *The Prize.* New York: Simon & Schuster, 1991.

Yette, Samuel F. *The Choice.* Silver Spring, Maryland: Cottage Books, 1971.

Index

Books from the Majority Press

THE NEW MARCUS GARVEY LIBRARY

Literary Garveyism: Garvey, Black Arts and the Harlem Renaissance.
Tony Martin. $19.95 (cloth), $9.95 (paper).

The Poetical Works of Marcus Garvey. Tony Martin, Ed. $17.95 (cloth),
$9.95 (paper).

Marcus Garvey, Hero: A First Biography. Tony Martin. $19.95 (cloth),
$8.95 (paper).

The Pan-African Connection. Tony Martin. $22.95 (cloth), $10.95 (paper).

Message to the People: The Course of African Philosophy. Marcus Garvey.
Ed. by Tony Martin. $22.95 (cloth), $9.95 (paper).

**Race First: The Ideological and Organizational Struggles of Marcus Garvey
and the Universal Negro Improvement Association.** Tony Martin. $12.95
(paper).

The Philosophy and Opinions of Marcus Garvey. Amy Jacques Garvey, Ed.
$14.95 (paper).

Amy Ashwood Garvey: Pan-Africanist, Feminist and Wife No. 1. Tony
Martin. Forthcoming.

**African Fundamentalism: A Literary and Cultural Anthology of Garvey's
Harlem Renaissance.** Tony Martin, Ed. $14.95 (paper).

THE BLACK WORLD

Brazil: Mixture or Massacre? Essays in the Genocide of a Black People.
Abdias do Nascimento. $12.95 (paper).

**Studies in the African Diaspora: A Memorial to James R. Hooker (1929-
1976).** John P. Henderson and Harry A. Reed, Eds. $39.95 (cloth).

**In Nobody's Backyard: The Grenada Revolution in its Own Words. Vol. I,
the Revolution at Home.** Tony Martin, Ed. $22.95 (cloth). **Vol. II, Facing
the World.** Tony Martin, Ed. $22.95 (cloth).

Guinea's Other Suns: The African Dynamic in Trinidad Culture. Maureen
Warner-Lewis. $9.95 (paper).

Carlos Cooks: And Black Nationalism from Garvey to Malcolm. Robert,
Nyota and Grandassa Harris, Eds. $9.95 (paper).

From Kingston to Kenya: The Making of a Pan-Africanist Lawyer. Dudley
Thompson, with Margaret Cezair Thompson. $10.95 (paper).

The Jewish Onslaught: Despatches from the Wellesley Battlefront. Tony
Martin. $9.95 (paper).

The Afro-Trinidadian: Endangered Species/Oh, What a Nation! Tony
Martin. Forthcoming.

Marcus Garvey/Makis Gave. Florie-N. $9.95 (paper). In Haitian Creole.

Eyes to My Soul: The Rise or Decline of a Black FBI Agent. Tyrone Powers.
$14.95 (paper).

*Order from The Majority Press, P.O. Box 538, Dover, MA 02030, U.S.A.
Mass. residents add 5% sales tax.*